Lecture Notes in Computer Science 15836

The series Lecture Notes in Computer Science (LNCS), including its subseries Lecture Notes in Artificial Intelligence (LNAI) and Lecture Notes in Bioinformatics (LNBI), has established itself as a medium for the publication of new developments in computer science and information technology research, teaching, and education.

LNCS enjoys close cooperation with the computer science R & D community, the series counts many renowned academics among its volume editors and paper authors, and collaborates with prestigious societies. Its mission is to serve this international community by providing an invaluable service, mainly focused on the publication of conference and workshop proceedings and postproceedings. LNCS commenced publication in 1973.

Ryutaro Ichise
Editor

Natural Language Processing and Information Systems

30th International Conference on Applications of Natural Language to Information Systems, NLDB 2025
Kanazawa, Japan, July 4–6, 2025
Proceedings, Part I

Springer

Editor
Ryutaro Ichise
Institute of Science Tokyo
Tokyo, Japan

ISSN 0302-9743 ISSN 1611-3349 (electronic)
Lecture Notes in Computer Science
ISBN 978-3-031-97140-2 ISBN 978-3-031-97141-9 (eBook)
https://doi.org/10.1007/978-3-031-97141-9

This Springer imprint is published by the registered company Springer Nature Switzerland AG
The registered company address is: Gewerbestrasse 11, 6330 Cham, Switzerland

Preface

We are delighted to present the proceedings of the 30th International Conference on Natural Language and Information Systems (NLDB 2025), held in Kanazawa, Japan, from July 4 to July 6, 2025.

As a well-established forum at the intersection of natural language processing and information systems, NLDB has brought together researchers, practitioners, and industry professionals for three decades to share advances, explore challenges, and foster interdisciplinary collaboration. The 30th edition continued this tradition, providing a venue for both foundational research and innovative applications across a range of domains.

This year, NLDB 2025 received 120 submissions. Following a rigorous single-blind peer-review process in which submissions received on average 2.1 reviews each, 33 full papers, 19 short papers, and 2 demo papers were accepted. Among the short papers, 4 were selected for the Industry Track, reflecting the conference's commitment to bridging academic research and real-world applications. Due to the exceptionally high quality of submissions this year, the selection process was particularly competitive. Papers with an average review score of approximately 1.0 or higher were generally accepted as long papers, while those scoring around 0.5 or higher were considered for short paper presentation.

We sincerely thank all authors for their contributions and the reviewers and Program Committee members for their thoughtful evaluations and dedication to maintaining the high standard of the conference. We also acknowledge the invited speakers, whose keynotes enriched the program by highlighting emerging trends and open challenges in the field.

Finally, we extend our deepest appreciation to the Organizing Committee, Local Chairs, volunteers, and sponsors whose support made NLDB 2025 possible. We hope that these proceedings will serve as a valuable resource and inspiration for future research in natural language and information systems.

May 2025 Ryutaro Ichise

Organization

General Chairs

Akiko Aizawa	National Institute of Informatics, Japan
Farid Meziane	University of Derby, UK
Kiyoaki Shirai	Japan Advanced Institute of Science and Technology, Japan
Vijayan Sugumaran	Oakland University, USA

Program Committee Chair

Ryutaro Ichise	Institute of Science Tokyo, Japan

Local Chair

Natthawut Kertkeidkachorn	Japan Advanced Institute of Science and Technology, Japan

Web and Publicity Chairs

Rungsiman Nararatwong	OUTSCALE, Dassault Systèmes, France
Patipon Wiangnak	Japan Advanced Institute of Science and Technology, Japan

Local Committee

Miura Takuto	Japan Advanced Institute of Science and Technology, Japan
Oda Kohei	Japan Advanced Institute of Science and Technology, Japan

Program Committee

Luigi Lomasto	Università degli studi di Salerno, Italy
Cédric Lopez	Emvista, France
Natalia Loukachevitch	Moscow State University, Russia
Vladimiro Lovera Rulfi	Alma Mater Studiorum - Università Di Bologna, Italy
Paloma Martínez Fernández	Universidad Carlos III de Madrid, Spain
Farid Meziane	University of Derby, UK
Alessio Miaschi	Institute for Computational Linguistics "A. Zampolli" (CNR-ILC), Italy
Luisa Mich	University of Trento, Italy
Nada Mimouni	Conservatoire National des Arts et Métiers Paris, France
Jelena Mitrović	University of Passau, Germany
Soto Montalvo	Universidad Rey Juan Carlos, Spain
Manuel Montes-y-Gómez	Instituto Nacional de Astrofísica, Óptica y Electrónica, Mexico
Dror Mughaz	Lev Academic Center, Israel
Benedetta Muscato	University of Pisa, Italy
Rafael Muñoz	University of Alicante, Spain
Roberto Nai	University of Torino, Italy
Rungsiman Nararatwong	National Institute of Advanced Industrial Science and Technology, Japan
Thanapon Noraset	Mahidol University, Thailand
Manjula Perkinian	VIT.chennai, India
Davide Picca	University of Lausanne, Switzerland
Stephan Reiff-Marganiec	University of Derby, UK
Mathieu Roche	Cirad, TETIS, France
Muhammad Yasir Shabir	University of Turin, Italy
Kiyoaki Shirai	Japan Advanced Institute of Science and Technology, Japan
Lucia Siciliani	University of Bari Aldo Moro, Italy
Krung Sinapiromsaran	Chulalongkorn University, Thailand
Irene Siragusa	Università degli Studi di Palermo, Italy
Giancarlo Sperlì	University of Naples Federico II, Italy
Vijayan Sugumaran	Oakland University, USA
Emilio Sulis	University of Turin, Italy
Maguelonne Teisseire	Irstea - UMR Tetis, France
Krishnaprasad Thirunarayan	Wright State University, USA
Federico Torrielli	University of Torino, Italy
Areerat Trongratsameethong	Chiang Mai University, Thailand
Dan Tufis	Institutul de Cercetări pentru Inteligență Artificială, Academia Română, Romania
L. Alfonso Ureña-López	University of Jaén, Spain

Tiberio Uricchio	University of Pisa, Italy
Sunil Vadera	University of Salford, UK
Peerapon Vateekul	Chulalongkorn University, Thailand
Gennaro Vessio	University of Bari, Italy
Sabrina Villata	Università degli Studi di Torino, Italy
Esau Villatoro-Tello	Idiap, Switzerland
Dittaya Wanvarie	Chulalongkorn University, Thailand
Konlakorn Wongpatikaseree	Mahidol University, Thailand
Ziwei Xu	Institute of Science Tokyo, Japan
Sumeth Yuenyong	Mahidol University, Thailand

Additional Reviewers

Rathachai Chawuthai	King Mongkut's Institute of Technology Ladkrabang, Thailand
Greta Damo	Université Côte d'Azur, France
Francesca Grasso	University of Turin, Italy
Rajalida Lipikorn	Chulalongkorn University, Thailand
Yun Liu	Kyoto Institute of Technology, Japan
Lankeshwara Munasinghe	Robert Gordon University, UK
Minh-Phuong Nguyen	Japan Advanced Institute of Science and Technology, Japan
Naruemon Pratanwanich	Chulalongkorn University, Thailand
Mohammad Golam Sohrab	National Institute of Advanced Industrial Science and Technology, Japan
Kamonphop Srisopha	Chiang Mai University, Thailand
Ekaterina Sviridova	Université Côte d'Azur, CNRS, Inria, I3S, France
Xiaoou Wang	Inria, CNRS, Université Côte d'Azur, France
Ratsameetip Wita	Chiang Mai University, Thailand
Nicola Zeni	University of Trento, University of Bergamo, Italy

Contents – Part I

Contents – Part II

Demo Papers

Full Papers

Multi-scale Convolutional Fusion with Contrastive Feature Alignment for Imbalanced Data Classification

Keito Inoshita[1(✉)], Takato Ueno[2], and Xiaokang Zhou[1,3]

[1] Kansai University, Osaka, Japan
k845578@kansai-u.ac.jp
[2] Shiga University, Hikone, Japan
[3] RIKEN Center, Tokyo, Japan

Abstract. In recent years, with the explosive growth of user-generated content in online spaces such as social media and review platforms, automated text analysis has become crucial for corporate marketing and understanding societal trends. Sarcasm poses a significant challenge for sentiment analysis and opinion mining, as its surface meaning often contradicts its true intent, substantially impairing accuracy. To address this issue, we propose the Multi-Scale Convolutional Fusion with Contrastive Feature Alignment (MSCF-CFA), a model designed to capture semantic discrepancies while effectively handling imbalanced data classification. The model integrates Multi-Scale Convolutional Fusion (MSCF) to capture dependencies at various scales, Contrastive Feature Alignment (CFA) to enhance class-specific feature representation using contrastive learning, and adjustments to the loss function, aiming to effectively detect the complex patterns unique to sarcasm while addressing data imbalance. Experiments using a sarcasm detection dataset demonstrated that MSCF-CFA outperformed existing methods and models designed to handle imbalanced data across all evaluation metrics. Furthermore, feature visualizations and ablation studies confirmed that the MSCF, CFA, and loss function adjustments significantly enhance class separation, making them critical components of the model's effectiveness. This study highlights the efficacy of multi-layered feature extraction and contrastive learning for advanced language understanding tasks, including sarcasm detection, and opens new possibilities for further applications.

Keywords: Convolutional Neural Network · Feature Alignment · Contrastive Learning · Class Imbalance · Sarcasm Detection

1 Introduction

In the modern field of Natural Language Processing (NLP), text classification plays a crucial role in a wide range of applications. Text classification refers to the technology that automatically categorizes and organizes vast amounts of textual data, finding its applications in diverse tasks such as information retrieval, spam filtering, and sentiment

R. Ichise (Ed.): NLDB 2025, LNCS 15836, pp. 3–18, 2026.
https://doi.org/10.1007/978-3-031-97141-9_1

analysis [1]. These technologies have been widely utilized across various domains, such as formulating corporate marketing strategies and enhancing customer support, thereby supporting the efficient processing and utilization of information in daily life [2]. Particularly, with the proliferation of social media and online platforms, the amount of user-generated content has increased exponentially. Platforms like Twitter and review websites, where users openly express their opinions, generate an overwhelming number of posts and comments daily. Leveraging such data effectively holds immense value for businesses and researchers. Automated analysis of user-generated content is crucial as it aids in real-time understanding of market trends, consumer needs, and societal trends, offering a competitive advantage in marketing and interactive approaches with users [3]. Among such analyses, sarcasm detection is a highly significant task in sentiment analysis and opinion mining. Sarcasm typically conveys intentions opposite to the literal meaning, making it particularly challenging to interpret accurately. For instance, the statement "What a wonderful weather!" could be expressing dissatisfaction with bad weather, which conventional text classification methods struggle to interpret accurately. Such misclassifications could lead to misleading analysis outcomes and fail to reflect the users' true intentions.

Previous research on sarcasm detection has proposed approaches centered around models such as CNN and LSTM [4]. CNN-based models, in particular, have demonstrated higher accuracy compared to RNN-based models due to their superior ability to extract local representations [5]. Multi-Filter CNN (MF-CNN), which employs convolutional filters of varying sizes to effectively capture n-gram features, has shown notable performance. However, traditional MF-CNN faces several limitations. First, they struggle to capture multi-scale dependencies effectively, as they typically rely on a limited number of kernel sizes. This dependency on a constrained set of kernels hampers their ability to extract features across long-range dependencies and varying scales, making it challenging to detect complex patterns or context-dependent sarcasm expressions. Second, there is a lack of discriminative power in feature embeddings. Insufficient similarity within samples of the same class and unclear separation between different classes may result in reduced classification accuracy and increased risk of misclassifications. Lastly, traditional approaches lack adequate handling of class imbalance. Sarcasm detection tasks often involve a relatively small proportion of sarcastic expressions, which prevents models from effectively learning minority classes [6]. In cases of class imbalance, models tend to favor the majority class, resulting in reduced accuracy for minority classes. Addressing these challenges necessitates more advanced model structures and effective training methods.

To tackle these challenges, this study proposes Multi-Scale Convolutional Fusion with Contrastive Feature Alignment (MSCF-CFA), a model designed for imbalanced data classification. The proposed framework incorporates a Multi-Scale Convolutional Fusion (MSCF), which employs convolutional layers with varying dilation rates to capture dependencies at multiple scales, and a Contrastive Feature Alignment (CFA), which enhances class separability through contrastive learning by refining feature representation across multiple feature spaces. While leveraging the strengths of MF-CNN, the integration of MSCF and CFA provides a more structured and discriminative feature representation. These components enable the extraction of richer and more discriminative features from textual data, thereby improving the accuracy of sarcasm detection. Additionally, the model incorporates an adjusted loss function that considers minority classes to facilitate balanced learning. Specifically, MSCF-CFA achieves its objectives by integrating the following structural features: i) An MSCF effectively captures dependencies at varying scales, enhancing the diversity of feature representations to accommodate the variability of sarcasm expressions. ii) A CFA enhances intra-class similarity and inter-class separability for extended features, improving classification performance. Iii) a Weighted Cross Entropy (WCE) addresses class imbalance, improving the accuracy for minority classes while enhancing overall classification performance. By integrating these components, MSCF-CFA surpasses traditional models in its ability to extract balanced feature representation from textual data, thereby significantly improving sarcasm detection accuracy. It also presents an effective approach for tasks involving class imbalance.

The contributions of this study are summarized as follows:

i) An MSCF is devised to leverage convolutional layers with varying dilation rates, enabling the effective capture of multi-scale dependencies and ensuring precise recognition of long-range dependencies and sarcasm expressions across diverse scales, thereby significantly enhancing the model's adaptability to complex patterns.
ii) A CFA module is devised to integrate feature expansion with contrastive learning, enhancing class separability within refined feature spaces by strengthening intra-class similarity and increasing inter-class dissimilarity, thereby improving classification performance for sarcasm detection.
iii) A WCE mechanism is designed to address class imbalance by assigning higher weights to minority classes, ensuring balanced learning and improving accuracy for minority classes while maintaining robust overall classification performance.

The rest of this paper is structured as follows. Section 2 reviews related work on CNN, contrastive learning, and approaches to address class imbalance in text classification. Section 3 describes the overall framework and mechanisms of the proposed model. Section 4 presents evaluations and discussions based on experiment results. Finally, Sect. 5 provides conclusions and future directions.

2 Related Works

2.1 CNN for Text Classification

N recent years, CNNs have been widely adopted for text classification tasks due to their strong capability in extracting local features, with numerous advancements reported. Chen et al. [7] demonstrated improved classification accuracy for handwritten text using a model based on LeNet-5. This study validated its effectiveness on the EMNIST dataset, reaffirming the foundational applicability of CNNs. Similarly, Du et al. [8] developed a CNN-based classification method that integrates NLP technologies tailored to the requirements and application scenarios of text classification, achieving high accuracy compared to traditional methods. Prabhakar et al. [9] proposed a novel architecture named "ECCNN," which considers adjacent data to provide a deeper understanding of data properties. Furthermore, Wang et al. [10] introduced a new 3D CNN model,

Text3D, which leverages BERT's hierarchical features to efficiently extract both global and local text representations. This method has demonstrated competitive results in sentiment analysis and topic classification tasks. Additionally, Peng and Huo [11] proposed a hybrid approach combining CNN and Support Vector Machine, enhancing feature extraction capabilities while reducing computational overhead. Efforts to automate CNN architecture design have also been made. Londt et al. [12] employed genetic programming to evolve CNN architectures, enabling high-precision model designs. This method is regarded as a significant milestone in automated CNN design. Similarly, Andersen et al. [13] successfully utilized genetic algorithms for automatic design and validated its effectiveness on the IMDB dataset. While these studies provide a solid foundation for applying CNNs to text classification tasks, they are insufficient for realizing multi-scale feature extraction capable of effectively capturing dependencies at varying scales.

2.2 Contrastive Learning for Discriminative Feature Representation

Contrastive learning has garnered significant attention as a critical method for learning highly discriminative feature representation in text classification. Numerous studies have made significant advancements in this area. Chen et al. [14] proposed DualCL, which leverages label information to perform contrastive learning within the same feature space of input samples and model parameters, achieving high classification accuracy even in low-resource environments. Additionally, Chen et al. [15] introduced contrastive learning to augment data from minority classes, improving classification performance on imbalanced datasets. Li et al. [16] proposed the SharpReCL model, which mitigates data imbalance by utilizing class prototypes to strengthen relationships among samples through contrastive learning, thereby enhancing classification accuracy. He et al. [17] proposed a new model integrating contrastive learning with adversarial learning, improving the robustness of text classification models. Dou et al. [18] introduced Virtual Contrastive Learning (VACL), a method to enhance classification model robustness by learning relationships among samples using label information, achieving high accuracy on multiple benchmark datasets. Xu et al. [19] conducted a comprehensive review of contrastive learning applied to sentence representation learning, categorizing diverse approaches to improve sentence representation quality. Their study demonstrated applicability beyond text classification, extending to a wide range of NLP tasks. Wang et al. [20] incorporated gradient penalties into contrastive learning, enhancing feature representation in text classification models. This method proved effective even for variable-length text and multilingual data. Despite existing research advancing feature representation through contrastive learning, studies that combine contrastive learning with multi-scale feature extraction remain limited.

2.3 Techniques for Addressing Class Imbalance

Class imbalance is a critical challenge in text classification, especially for improving the performance of minority class identification. Numerous methods have been proposed to address this issue. Yang et al. [21] introduced a hybrid classifier framework combining density-based undersampling with cost-sensitive techniques to reduce data bias and improve minority class classification performance. Wang and Sun [22] improved the traditional AdaBoost algorithm by introducing new weighted voting parameters, achieving higher F1 scores and effective classification on imbalanced datasets.

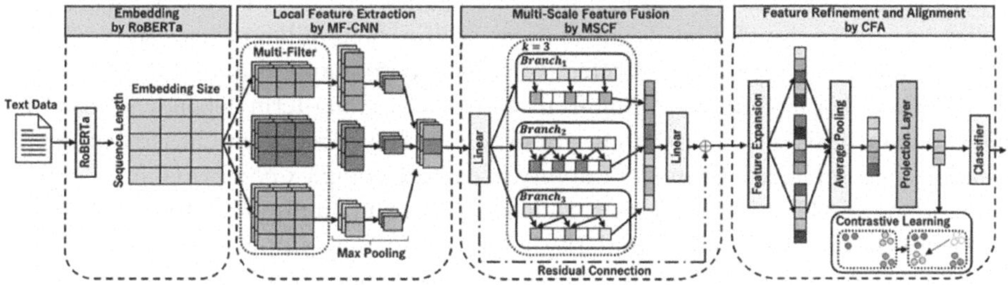

Fig. 1. Framework Overview of MSCF-CFA.

Shaikh et al. [23] proposed a text generation algorithm utilizing GPT-2 and LSTM to complement imbalanced data, increasing classification accuracy by up to 17%. Rashid et al. [24] focused on Bengali datasets, employing synthetic data generation and data augmentation techniques, achieving over 90% improvement in F1 scores for minority classes. This study contributed significantly to addressing imbalanced data issues in low-resource languages. Ponce et al. [25] proposed a two-stage undersampling algorithm combining noise removal and graph-based methods, effectively improving classification performance while mitigating dataset imbalance. Ahmadi et al. [26] developed a novel method using semantic search to optimally select annotation texts, improving classification accuracy for minority classes. Badiei et al. [27] proposed an imbalanced text classification method combining Graph Neural Networks (GNNs) with adversarial weight balancing, dynamically assigning weights to minority class samples, resulting in substantial improvements in classification accuracy and F1 scores. While these studies represent significant progress in mitigating class imbalance, approaches that integrate multi-scale feature extraction through varying dilation rates remain insufficiently explored.

3 Modeling of MSCF-CFA

3.1 Framework Overview

This section provides a detailed explanation of the architecture and training methodology of the proposed MSCF-CFA for text classification tasks. The overall framework of MSCF-CFA is illustrated in Fig. 1. The proposed model builds on the foundation of MF-CNN and integrates an MSCF for multi-scale convolutional fusion, along with a CFA that combines feature expansion with contrastive learning. Together, these components enable the model to extract, enhance, and aggregate features from textual data effectively and discriminatively. Additionally, WCE is introduced to adjust the loss function, ensuring the model can address class imbalance effectively. First, the MF-CNN plays a pivotal role in extracting initial features from text by employing convolutional filters of varying sizes. Specifically, by using multiple filter sizes capable of capturing patterns such as bigrams and trigrams, MF-CNN allows the model to simultaneously capture diverse features within text data. This diversity forms a robust foundation for classification tasks. Next, the MSCF receives features extracted by the MF-CNN and applies one-dimensional dilated convolutions with varying dilation rates in parallel to capture multi-scale dependencies effectively. By incorporating different dilation rates, the MSCF can learn patterns ranging from short-term to long-term dependencies within text, simultaneously accommodating various scales. This process enriches feature representations and enhances the model's ability to capture complex contextual information. Furthermore, the CFA aggregates expanded features and employs contrastive learning to increase intra-class feature similarity while enhancing inter-class separability. By extending the feature space, the CFA integrates information from multiple perspectives, aligning feature representations to generate robust and highly discriminative embeddings. This improvement significantly enhances class separability and is expected to improve classification performance. Finally, the aggregated features are passed to the classifier for class prediction. The classifier uses a fully connected layer combined with an activation function to output accurate classification results based on discriminative features. To address class imbalance, WCE is employed to emphasize the losses associated with minority classes, thereby maintaining balance across the dataset and achieving high classification accuracy.

3.2 MF-CNN for Local Feature Extraction

The MF-CNN component is responsible for extracting initial features from text embeddings using convolutional filters of varying sizes. For input data $x \in \mathbb{R}^{B\times1\times128\times768}$ (batch size B, , channels 1, sequence length 128, embedding dimension 768), the following convolutional operations are performed. First, two-dimensional convolutional layers with different filter sizes $k \in K$ (e.g., 2, 3, 4) are applied to capture n-gram features. The convolution operation for each filter size k is defined as follows:

$$Conv_k(x) = \sigma(W_k * x + b_k) \tag{1}$$

where σ is the activation function ReLU, $W_k \in \mathbb{R}^{C_{out}\times C_{in}\times H_k\times W_k}$ is the weight matrix for filter size k, and $b_k \in \mathbb{R}^{C_{out}}$ represents the bias term. Here, C_{in} and C_{out} denote the input and output channel dimensions, while H_k and W_k correspond to the height and width of the filter. This convolution operation generates feature maps corresponding to each filter size. Next, one-dimensional max pooling is applied to the outputs of each convolution, extracting the most salient features:

$$Pool_k(x) = \max(Conv_k(x)) \tag{2}$$

The outputs $Pool_k(x)$ are then concatenated and transformed through a linear function:

$$h_{cnn} = Linear(Concat(Pool_k(x)|k \in K) \tag{3}$$

resulting in $h_{cnn} \in \mathbb{R}^{B \times C_{out}}$. In this study, two-dimensional convolutional layers were applied in the MF-CNN to capture n-gram features from text data. Two-dimensional convolutions are particularly advantageous for spatial feature extraction and are well-suited for data with a two-dimensional structure, such as text represented by sequence length and embedding dimension. By employing filters of varying sizes, the model can parallelly extract diverse n-gram features, achieving rich feature representations.

3.3 MSCF for Multi-scale Feature Fusion

The MSCF captures complex dependencies in text by combining dilated convolutions with varying dilation rates. Its detailed architecture is shown in Fig. 2.

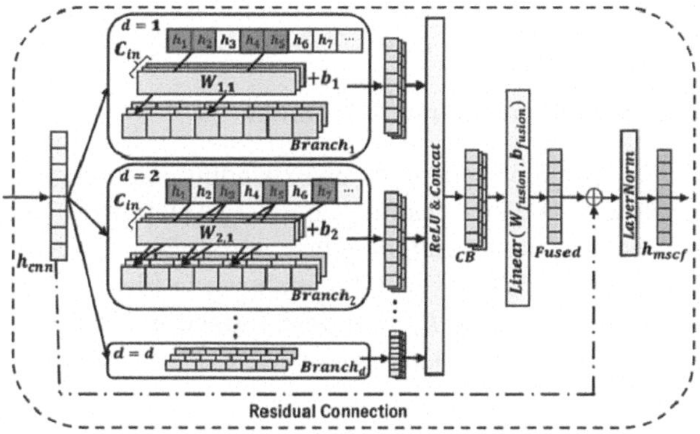

Fig. 2. Mechanism of MSCF.

The MSCF applies one-dimensional dilated convolutions in parallel with different dilation rates $d \in D$ (e.g., 1, 2, 4), generating multi-scale feature representations. For h_{cnn}, appropriate padding is applied based on each dilation rate d, followed by one-dimensional dilated convolutions. Each dilated convolution branch operates as follows:

$$Branch_d(h_{cnn}) = \sigma\left(\sum_{n=1}^{C_{in}} \sum_{m=1}^{k} W_{d,n,m} \cdot h_{cnn,n} + b_d\right) \tag{4}$$

where σ is the activation function ReLU, $W_d \in \mathbb{R}^{C_{out} \times C_{in}}$ is the weight matrix for the one-dimensional dilated convolution with rate d, and $b_d \in \mathbb{R}^{C_{out}}$ is the bias term. The diverse dilation rates allow the MSCF to capture dependencies at multiple scales effectively. The outputs from each branch are concatenated and passed through a linear transformation to produce the final fused features:

$$CB = Concat(Branch_d(h_{cnn}) | d \in D) \tag{5}$$

$$Fused = W_{fusion} \cdot CB + b_{fusion} \tag{6}$$

where $W_{fusion} \in \mathbb{R}^{C_{out}}$ is the weight matrix, and $b_{fusion} \in \mathbb{R}^{C_{out}}$ is the bias term. To stabilize learning and mitigate vanishing gradients, residual connections and Layer Normalization are applied, producing the output of the MSCF $h_{mscf} \in \mathbb{R}^{B \times C_{out}}$:

$$h_{mscf} = LayerNorm(Fused + h_{cnn}) \tag{7}$$

In the actual proposed model, the number of the MSCFs (U) are connected in series, and $h_{mscf,u}(u = 1,2\ldots, U)$ becomes the input of the next MSCF. The MSCF employs one-dimensional convolutions, which are particularly suitable for capturing temporal dependencies in sequential data. By varying the dilation rates, the MSCF efficiently extracts information at multiple scales, capturing long-range dependencies in text data. Combined with the two-dimensional convolutions in the MF-CNN, this approach enables the model to extract features across different scales, significantly improving classification performance.

3.4 CFA for Feature Refinement and Alignment

The CFA enhances feature representations by expanding features, mapping them into lower-dimensional spaces, and incorporating contrastive learning to increase intra-class similarity and inter-class separation, aligning feature representations for improved class distinction. The detailed structure of the CFA is shown in Fig. 3. The CFA consists of three components. First, the output h_{msdf} is transformed into multiple feature spaces using the $FeatureExpansion(FE)$ function, defined as:

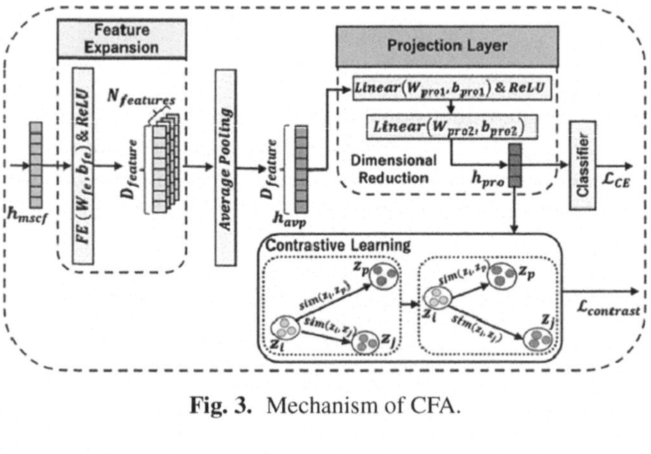

Fig. 3. Mechanism of CFA.

$$h_{fe} = FE(h_{mscf}) = \tanh(W_{fe} \cdot h_{mscf} + b_{fe}) \tag{8}$$

where $W_{fe} \in \mathbb{R}^{N_{features} \times C_{out} \times D_{feature}}$ and represents the weight matrix, and $b_{fe} \in \mathbb{R}^{N_{features} \times D_{feature}}$ represents the bias term. $N_{features}$ and $D_{feature}$ denote the number and dimensionality of feature spaces. Next, the expanded features $h_{fe} \in \mathbb{R}^{B \times N_{features} \times D_{feature}}$ are aggregated into unified representations via average pooling:

$$h_{avp} = AveragePool\left(h_{fe}\right) = \frac{1}{N_{features}} \sum_{i=1}^{N_{features}} h_{fe,i} \tag{9}$$

The aggregated features $h_{avp} \in \mathbb{R}^{B \times D_{feature}}$ are then mapped to a lower-dimensional feature space $h_{pro} \in \mathbb{R}^{B \times D_{pro}}$ using a projection layer:

$$h_{pro} = W_{pro2} \cdot \sigma\left(W_{pro1} \cdot h_{avp} + b_{pro1}\right) + b_{pro2} \tag{10}$$

where $W_{pro1} \in \mathbb{R}^{D_{hidden} \times D_{feature}}$, $W_{pro2} \in \mathbb{R}^{D_{pro} \times D_{hidden}}$, $b_{pro1} \in \mathbb{R}^{D_{hidden}}$, and $b_{pro2} \in \mathbb{R}^{D_{pro}}$ are the parameters, and σ is the ReLU activation function. Finally, contrastive loss is defined to maximize intra-class similarity and minimize inter-class similarity:

$$\mathcal{L}_{contrast} = -\frac{1}{B} \sum_{i=1}^{B} \frac{1}{|P(i)|} \sum_{p \in P(i)} \log\left(\frac{exp\left(\frac{sim\left(z_i, z_p\right)}{\tau}\right)}{\sum_{j=1}^{2B} [j \neq i] exp\left(\frac{sim\left(z_i, z_j\right)}{\tau}\right)}\right) \tag{11}$$

where z_i represents the normalized h_{pro}, $P(i)$ denotes the set of positive pairs for sample i, z_p and z_j correspond to the normalized h_{pro} of the positive and negative pairs for sample i, respectively. τ is the temperature parameter, and $sim(\cdot, \cdot)$ indicates the cosine similarity function. These mechanisms improve class separability in the feature space, leading to enhanced classification performance. By utilizing the CFA, the similarity among samples within the same class is increased, and the separation between different classes is strengthened by aligning feature representations, thereby improving the classification performance of the model.

3.5 Optimization in MSCF-CFA

The MSCF-CFA is a comprehensive architecture built upon MF-CNN, integrating an MSCF, a CFA, and the final classifier. The model workflow proceeds as follows. First, the input data x is processed through the MF-CNN to generate the feature representation h_{cnn}. Next, h_{cnn} is passed into MSCF, where multi-scale dilated convolutions are applied to produce enhanced features h_{mscf}. These enhanced features are then aligned by the CFA, resulting in the final feature representation h_{pro} and the contrastive loss $\mathcal{L}_{contrast}$. The final feature representation h_{pro} is fed into the classifier, which outputs $logit \in \mathbb{R}^{B \times num\_classes}$ corresponding to the number of classes. To address class imbalance, the proposed model incorporates WCE to adjust the loss function. WCE assigns different weights w_c to each class, increasing the loss contribution of minority classes to prevent the model from neglecting them. Specifically, the weight for each class is set as the inverse of its frequency, and the cross-entropy loss is defined as follows:

$$\mathcal{L}_{CE} = -\sum_{c=1}^{C} w_c y_c \log(p_c) \tag{12}$$

where C denotes the total number of classes, y_c represents the true label, and p_c indicates the predicted probability. The objective of the proposed method is to minimize the $\mathcal{L}_{total}$:

$$\mathcal{L}_{total} = \mathcal{L}_{CE} + \alpha \cdot \mathcal{L}_{contrast} \tag{13}$$

where α is the weighting parameter that balances the contributions of the classification loss and contrastive loss. By adjusting the loss functions in this manner, the proposed method effectively addresses the class imbalance problem, enhancing accuracy for minority classes while maintaining robust overall classification performance.

4 Experiment and Analysis

4.1 Dataset and Experiment Design

This study utilizes a sarcasm detection dataset [28], which consists of 3,834 text samples specifically designed for sarcasm detection tasks, with each sample labeled as either "sarcasm" or "non-sarcasm." The dataset is divided into a training set (80%) and a test set (20%). Each text sample is tokenized, and the tokens are converted into embedding vectors using pre-trained RoBERTa [29]. To evaluate the performance of the proposed MSCF-CFA, the following models were adopted as baselines for comparison:

- MF-CNN: A simple Multi-Filter CNN architecture was included to assess its effectiveness in extracting features for text classification.
- BiLSTM: A basic bidirectional LSTM was employed to evaluate the baseline performance of recurrent models in sarcasm detection tasks.
- Transformer: A basic Transformer encoder was used to evaluate the effectiveness of self-attention in capturing contextual features for sarcasm detection.

Table 1. Hyperparameter Settings.

Component	Parameter	Value
MF-CNN	Embedding dim	768
	Filter size (K)	[2, 3, 4]
	Num filters	100
	$C_{out}(h_{cnn})$	256
MSCF	Dilations (D)	[1, 2, 4]
	Num blocks	2
	$C_{out}(h_{mscf})$	256
CFA	$N_{features}$	4
	$D_{pro}(h_{pro})$	64

(continued)

Table 1. *(continued)*

Component	Parameter	Value
	Temperature (τ)	0.7
Training	Batch size	64
	Num epochs	100
	Learning rate	1e–4
	$\alpha(L_{total})$	0.1

- DualCL: This model employs contrastive learning in a shared feature space between input samples and model parameters. It leverages label information to expand samples and improve both classification accuracy and discriminative feature representation learning. It performs particularly well in low-resource environments.
- BERT + DBLoss [30]: To address long-tail distributions and label co-occurrence issues, this approach combines the BERT model with a custom "Distribution-Balanced Loss" function. It utilizes label-frequency-based weighting and negative-resistant regularization, enhancing the performance of minority classes.
- MHA-BiLSTM [31]: This model integrates Multi-Head Attention (MHA) with BiLSTM to capture contextual information effectively and combine it with auxiliary features, improving sarcasm detection accuracy.

These baseline models allow for a comprehensive evaluation of how MSCF-CFA performs compared to existing reserches, demonstrating the value of the proposed approach. Additionally, Principal Component Analysis (PCA) and ablation studies were conducted to validate the effectiveness of each mechanism within MSCF-CFA, clarifying the contribution of its structural components. The hyperparameters used in the experiments are detailed in Table 1. These evaluations were specifically designed to support the development of a model capable of improving performance in sarcasm detection tasks.

4.2 Evaluation on Model Performance

To assess the effectiveness of the proposed MSCF-CFA, its performance was compared with several baseline models, including MF-CNN, BiLSTM, Transformer, DualCL, RoBERTa + DBLoss, and MHA-BiLSTM. The evaluation metrics included Accuracy, Precision, Recall, and F1-Score. The performance results of each model are summarized in Table 2. The proposed MSCF-CFA achieved the highest scores across all evaluation metrics, with an Accuracy of 79.40%, Precision of 79.58%, Recall of 79.42%, and F1-Score of 79.37%. This represents a significant improvement over the best baseline model, RoBERTa + DBLoss, which achieved an Accuracy of 75.23%. The basic model MF-CNN also performed well, with an Accuracy of 74.84%, surpassing both BiLSTM (71.58%) and Transformer (74.45%).

Table 2. Evaluation of MSCF-CFA Compared with Other Models for Sarcasm Detection.

Model	Accuracy	Precision	Recall	F1
MF-CNN	74.84	75.88	74.88	74.60
BiLSTM	71.58	71.82	71.60	71.51
Transformer	74.45	75.10	74.41	74.26
DualCL	69.49	69.61	69.51	69.45
RoBERTa + DBLoss	75.23	75.53	75.21	75.14
MHA-BiLSTM	73.66	73.98	73.69	73.59
MSCF-CFA	**79.40**	**79.58**	**79.42**	**79.37**

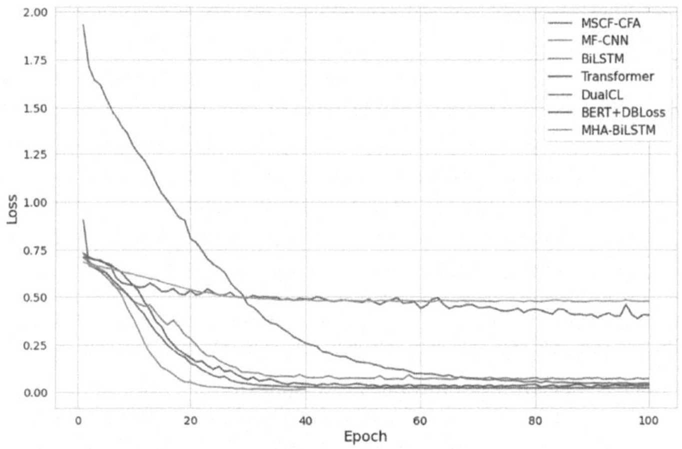

Fig. 4. Evaluation of Loss Curves across Models.

4.3 Evaluation on Learning Performance

A detailed evaluation of the loss curves, as shown in Fig. 4, indicates that MF-CNN exhibits the fastest reduction in loss during training, likely due to its relatively simple architecture, which allows for efficient learning. However, while more complex models, such as MSCF-CFA, demonstrated slower initial convergence, they ultimately achieved lower final loss values, fully converging around 40 epochs. Among all models, MSCF-CFA exhibited relatively rapid convergence and consistently achieved lower loss values than other models, emphasizing its high learning efficiency and superior representational power. These findings highlight that, despite its structural complexity, MSCF-CFA maintains an optimal balance between learning efficiency and classification performance, outperforming existing baseline models.

To further evaluate how different components of MSCF-CFA contribute to feature representation, PCA was applied to features extracted at different processing stages—after MF-CNN, MSCF, and the CFA. The results, presented in Fig. 5, visually illustrate the progressive improvement in class separability across these stages. As depicted in

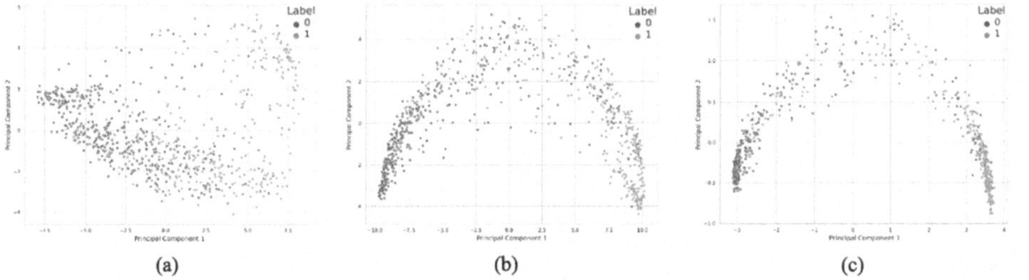

Fig. 5. Evaluation of Feature Representations for Each Module. (a) represents the feature representations h_{cnn} after the MF-CNN, (b) represents the feature representations h_{mscf} after the MSCF, and (c) represents the feature representations h_{pro} after the CFA.

Fig. 5(a), the feature representations obtained after MF-CNN exhibit limited class separability between sarcasm and non-sarcasm labels. While Label 1 (sarcasm) points tend to cluster towards the right, there remains significant overlap with Label 0 (non-sarcasm), indicating that MF-CNN alone struggles to clearly distinguish between these classes within the feature space. Figure 5(b) shows that applying the MSCF leads to noticeable improvements in class separability. Label 1 points shift further to the right, while Label 0 points shift towards the left, reducing overlap and enhancing class distinction. However, some ambiguous data points remain near the center. Finally, Fig. 5(c) presents the feature representations after the CFA, where the separation between Label 1 and Label 0 becomes significantly more pronounced. The two classes occupy opposite ends of the feature space, with a notable reduction in ambiguous data points near the center. This suggests that the CFA enhances class separability by expanding the feature space and leveraging contrastive learning to emphasize inter-class differences.

Overall, these results demonstrate the progressive refinement of feature representations through the MF-CNN, MSCF, and CFA, as well as the efficient learning process of MSCF-CFA. The loss curve analysis further supports this, showing that while MSCF-CFA exhibits a slightly slower initial convergence compared to simpler models, it ultimately achieves lower final loss values, indicating superior learning efficiency and generalization ability. The CFA plays a pivotal role in effectively capturing complex data patterns and reinforcing class distinction, contributing to the overall superior classification performance of MSCF-CFA.

4.4 Ablation Study

To evaluate the contribution of each component in the proposed MSCF-CFA, an ablation study was conducted. Specifically, models were created by removing the MSCF,

CFA, and WCE loss adjustment, and their performances were compared. The results are summarized in Table 3. As shown in Table 3, removing the MSCF or the CFA resulted in decreases in performance metrics, with Accuracy around 78.75%, Precision 78.84%, Recall 78.76%, and F1-Score 78.74%, which is approximately 0.7% lower than the original MSCF-CFA. Furthermore, removing WCE caused a more significant drop, with Accuracy at 77.71%, Precision 77.91%, Recall 77.69%, and F1-Score 77.66%, marking a decrease of approximately 1.69%. These results highlight the significant role of the

Table 3. Ablation Study Evaluation of MSCF-CFA.

Model	Accuracy	Precision	Recall	F1
MSCF-CFA	**79.40**	**79.58**	**79.42**	**79.37**
w/o MSCF	78.75	78.83	78.76	78.74
w/o CFA	78.75	78.84	78.74	78.73
w/o WCE	77.71	77.91	77.69	77.66

MSCF and CFA in improving model performance, with WCE having the most substantial impact on classification accuracy and balance. Thus, each of these components plays a crucial role in facilitating effective learning and enhancing the representational power of MSCF-CFA.

4.5 Discussion

The proposed MSCF-CFA demonstrated superior classification performance compared to existing baseline models, contrastive learning approaches, and prior studies addressing class imbalance. It achieved the best results in key metrics. The results of the ablation study revealed that the MSCF is critical for capturing diverse dependencies through multi-scale dilated convolutions, while the CFA significantly enhances class separability in the feature representation by expanding the feature space and applying contrastive learning. The evaluation of feature representations further corroborated these findings. These results underscore the effectiveness of the stepwise, multi-faceted feature extraction and enhancement processes for capturing the nuanced linguistic patterns inherent in sarcasm detection.

Nevertheless, as indicated by the PCA results after applying the CFA, some ambiguous data points remain unresolved, requiring deeper textual understanding or supplemental input. The scarcity of labeled data for sarcasm detection also poses challenges due to annotation inconsistencies. Future research should explore weakly and self-supervised learning for data augmentation and robust multi-label learning techniques. Additionally, MSCF-CFA's use of multi-scale dilated convolutions and expanded feature spaces increases parameter complexity, limiting deployment in resource-constrained environments. Techniques such as model distillation, quantization, and pruning should be considered. Further improvements in multi-filter design and feature fusion could enhance performance, enabling MSCF-CFA to evolve into a robust and interpretable sarcasm detection model applicable across diverse settings.

5 Conclusion

With the increasing prevalence of user-generated content online, sarcasm detection has become increasingly important in tasks such as sentiment analysis and opinion mining. This study proposed MSCF-CFA, a more advanced architecture built upon MF-CNN by integrating the MSCF for multi-scale convolutional fusion and the CFA for contrastive feature alignment. Experimental results demonstrated that MSCF-CFA outperformed baseline models across all evaluation metrics. Notably, the ablation study confirmed that the introduction of the MSCF and CFA played a pivotal role in improving class separability and classification accuracy.

Future work should focus on complementing input text, expanding sarcasm detection datasets, and refining MSCF and CFA for greater accuracy. Optimizing inference efficiency for practical use is also crucial. These improvements will help MSCF-CFA evolve into a highly accurate and reliable sarcasm detection model.

References

1. Yu, F., Zhang, H., Tiwari, P., Wang, B.: Natural language reasoning: a survey. ACM Comput. Surv. **2**(5), 1–39 (2024)
2. Iyelolu, T.V., Agu, E.E., Idemudia, C., Ijomah, T.I.: Leveraging artificial intelligence for personalized marketing campaigns to improve conversion rates. Int. J. Eng. Res. Dev. **20**(8), 253–270 (2024)
3. El Mendili, F., Fattah, M., Berros, N., Filaly, Y., El Bouzekri El Idrissi, Y.: Enhancing detection of malicious profiles and spam tweets with an automated honeypot framework powered by deep learning. Int. J. Inf. Secur. **23**(2), 1359–1388 (2024)
4. Boutsikaris, L., Polykalas, S.: A comparative review of deep learning techniques on the classification of irony and sarcasm in text. IEEE Trans. Artif. Intell., 1–15 (2024)
5. Razali, M.S., Halin, A.A., Ye, L., Doraisamy, S., Norowi, N.M.: Sarcasm detection using deep learning with contextual features. IEEE Access **9**, 68609–68618 (2021)
6. An, T., Yan, P., Zuo, J., Jin, X., Liu, M., Wang, J.: Enhancing cross-lingual sarcasm detection by a prompt learning framework with data augmentation and contrastive learning. Electronics **13**(11), 2163–2176 (2024)
7. Chen, A.: Handwritten text classification based on convolutional neural network. Highlights Sci. Eng. Technol. **34**, 39–44 (2023)
8. Du, Z., Qin, H., Han, Z., Lu, K., Li, H., Li, Z.: Research on text classification based on convolutional neural networks. In: IEEE 7th Information Technology and Mechatronics Engineering Conference, Chongqing, China, vol. 7, pp. 733–737 (2023)
9. Prabhakar, S.K., Rajaguru, H., So, K., Won, D.-O.: A framework for text classification using Evolutionary Contiguous Convolutional Neural Network and swarm-based Deep Neural Network. Front. Comput. Neurosci. **16**, 1–17 (2022)
10. Wang, J., Li, J., Zhang, Y.: Text 3D: 3D convolutional Neural Networks for text classification. Electronics **12**(14), 3087–3096 (2023)
11. Peng, J., Huo, S.: Application of an improved convolutional neural network algorithm in text classification. J. Web Eng. **23**, 315–340 (2024)
12. Londt, T., Gao, X., Xue, B., Andreae, P. M.: Evolving Character-level Convolutional Neural Networks for Text Classification. ArXiv (2020)
13. Andersen, H., Gao, X., Xue, B., Zhang, M.: Evolving network structures for text classification using genetic algorithms. In: Genetic and Evolutionary Computation Conference Companion, Cancún, Mexico, pp. 109–110 (2020)
14. Chen, Q., Zhang, R., Zheng, Y., Mao, Y.: Dual Contrastive Learning: Text Classification via Label-Aware Data Augmentation. ArXiv (2022)
15. Chen, X., Zhang, W., Pan, S., Chen, J.: Solving data imbalance in text classification with constructing contrastive samples. IEEE Access **11**, 90554–90562 (2023)
16. Li, M., Liu, Y., Giunchiglia, F., Feng, X., Guan, R.: Simple-sampling and hard-mixup with prototypes to rebalance contrastive learning for text classification. ArXiv (2024)

17. He, J.-L., Zhang, X.-L., Wang, Y.-P., Zhang, H.-X., Gao, L., Xu, E.-H.: Contrastive adversarial learning in text classification tasks. J. Intell. Fuzzy Syst. **45**(2), 3473–3484 (2023)
18. Dou, X., Zhao, J., Li, M.: VDCL: A supervised text classification method based on virtual adversarial and contrast learning. In: International Joint Conference on Neural Networks, Gold Coast, Australia, pp. 1–8 (2023)
19. Xu, L., Xie, H., Li, Z., Wang, F.L., Wang, W., Li, Q.: Contrastive learning models for sentence representations. ACM Trans. Intell. Syst. Technol. **14**(4), 1–34 (2023)
20. Wang, D., Cheng, L., Wang, Z.: Augmenting feature representation with gradient penalty for robust text categorization. Int. J. Intell. Syst. **2023**, 1–19 (2023)
21. Yang, K., et al.: Hybrid classifier ensemble for imbalanced data. IEEE Trans. Neural Netw. Learn. Syst. **31**(4), 1387–1400 (2020)
22. Wang, W., Sun, D.: The improved AdaBoost algorithms for imbalanced data classification. Inf. Sci. **563**, 358–374 (2021)
23. Shaikh, S., Daudpota, S.M., Imran, A.S., Kastrati, Z.: Towards improved classification accuracy on highly imbalanced text dataset using deep neural language models. Appl. Sci. **11**(2), 869–888 (2021)
24. Rafi-Ur-Rashid, M., Mahbub, M., Adnan, M. A.: Breaking the curse of class imbalance: Bangla text classification. ACM Trans. Asian Low-Res. Lang. Inf. Process. **21**(5), 1–21 (2022)
25. Guzmán-Ponce, A., Sánchez, J.S., Valdovinos, R.M., Marcial-Romero, J.R.: DBIG-US: a two-stage under-sampling algorithm to face the class imbalance problem. Expert Syst. Appl. **168**, 114301 (2021)
26. Ahmadi, S., Shah, A., Fox, E.: Retrieval-based text selection for addressing class-imbalanced data in classification. ArXiv (2023)
27. Badiei, F., Kananian, M., Ghahramani, S. A. G.: Text classification on imbalanced data using graph neural networks and adversarial weight balancer. In: IEEE Asia-Pacific Conference on Computer Science and Data Engineering, Nadi, Fiji, pp. 1–6 (2023)
28. Rohanian, O.: datasets/train/SemEval2018-T3-train-taskA.txt. In: omidrohanian/irony_detection, Github. Accessed Apr 2025
29. Liu, Y., et al.: RoBERTa: a robustly optimized BERT pretraining approach. ArXiv (2019)
30. Huang, Y., Giledereli, B., Köksal, A., Özgür, A., Ozkirimli, E.: Balancing methods for multi-label text classification with long-tailed class distribution. In: Empirical Methods in Natural Language Processing, Online and Punta Cana, Dominican Republic, pp. 8153–8161 (2021)
31. Kumar, A., Narapareddy, V.T., Srikanth, V.A., Malapati, A., Neti, L.B.M.: Sarcasm detection using multi-head attention based bidirectional LSTM. IEEE Access **8**, 6388–6397 (2020)

Memory Efficient LM Compression Using Fisher Information from Low-Rank Representations

Daniil Moskovskiy[1,3](✉), Sergey Pletenev[1,3], Sergey Zagoruyko[2,3], and Alexander Panchenko[1,3]

[1] AIRI, Moscow, Russia
[2] MTS AI, Moscow, Russia
[3] Skolkovo Institute of Science and Technology, Moscow, Russia
{Daniil.Moskovskiy,S.Pletenev,A.Panchenko}@skol.tech

Abstract. Although modern language models (LMs) demonstrate excellent performance in diverse text processing tasks, the substantial GPU memory required to load and infer these models can be prohibitive to users. To compress and accelerate LMs, various techniques, such as quantization, distillation, pruning, and low-rank factorization, are used. In this work, we focus on improving a method from the latter category, namely, a recent technique Fisher-Weighted Singular Value Decomposition (FWSVD). Despite its efficiency, FWSVD requires fine-tuning of the whole model on a downstream task. We introduce a simple, yet powerful, modification of FWSVD that enables compression of models previously unavailable with the original approach. By combining LoRA with FWSVD we demonstrate that low-rank-based compression can be achieved without storing the full gradients, sometimes even outperforming the original full fine-tuning. We evaluate our proposed approach on various NLP tasks, including NLU, NER, text summarization, and QA, showing its effectiveness compared to strong baselines.

Keywords: Compression · LoRA · SVD · Fisher information

1 Introduction

The recent emergence of transformers and large language models (LLMs) has revolutionized the field of natural language processing. However, the growing size of these models poses significant challenges: the high performance of NLP models comes with enormous size. They require enormous amounts of computational

D. Moskovskiy and S. Pletenev—Contributed equally to this work.

Supplementary Information The online version contains supplementary material available at https://doi.org/10.1007/978-3-031-97141-9_2.

R. Ichise (Ed.): NLDB 2025, LNCS 15836, pp. 19–33, 2026.
https://doi.org/10.1007/978-3-031-97141-9_2

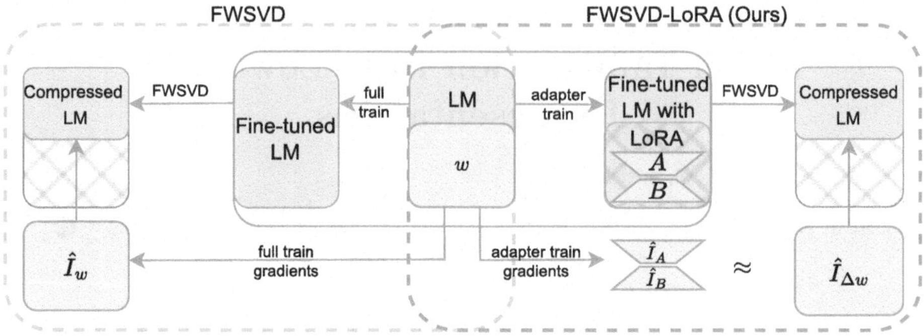

Fig. 1. Workflows of the original FWSVD-based LM compression and the proposed approach FWSVD+LoRA which saves peak GPU RAM during the compression by approximating full model gradients using LoRA.

resources to train and run, making it difficult to fit them on consumer-grade GPUs. Most-of-the-art LLMs have at least 7 billion parameters [12]. Therefore, there is an urgent need to reduce the size of language models or make their fine-tuning computationally affordable.

We focus on the recent method for low-rank factorization compression: the Fisher-Weighted Singular Value Decomposition (FWSVD) [9]. While theoretically grounded and yielding strong results among factorization-based methods, the method requires several cycles of training the full-size model to gather the empirical Fisher information. In the case of large models, these cycles can be resource-intensive, as the training loop requires the increased amounts of GPU memory.

At the same time, parameter-efficient fine-tuning (PEFT) methods, e.g. [10] allow training only several thousand out of billions of model parameters and yet provide performance comparable to full fine-tuning, but such PEFT methods were never applied to FWSVD as examined on several commonly used models in Table 1. We propose FWSVD-LoRA: a technique to effectively reduce model size without the need to perform full-scale fine-tuning and gradient calculation FWSVD and ours meth are illustrated in Fig. 1. First, we combine the FWSVD low-rank compression with parameter-efficient fine-tuning by training only low-rank representations of the fully connected part of the model and collecting gradients for FWSVD only for these layers. We achieve compression quality almost similar to that of the original FWSVD approach. By training only low-rank representations of the fully connected part of the model and collecting gradients for FWSVD only for these layers, we achieve significant compression without sacrificing performance.

The contributions of this work are two-fold:

1. We propose FWSVD-LoRA: a novel technique for both parameter and memory-efficient low-rank approximation based on Fisher information collected from low-rank representations.

2. We conduct a comprehensive experiments[1] of the proposed approach, demonstrating its effectiveness across 12 NLP datasets for NLU, QA, NER, and summarization tasks.

Our results show applicability of the proposed technique to various model architectures: encoder-only, encoder-decoder, and decoder-only LMs, suggesting that the proposed approximation of empirical Fisher information using low-rank representations is either on par or better than the original FWSVD compression method in almost every considered setup. Based on the results of our exhaustive experiments we can conclude that is almost always preferable to use our FWSVD-LoRA instead of the original FWSVD compression technique.

2 Related Work

Research addressing challenges posed by the enormous size of the current state-of-the-art LLMs attracted substantial attention recently of both academia and industry. For model compression, various methods were proposed, most notably, quantization [4] and pruning [36], are used for inference and fine-tuning of LMs in a limited computational budget. Other SOTA approaches for model compression include methods based on Fisher information (FWSVD) [9,11], Layer-Wise Relevance Propagation [6], or Saliency Score [15].

In our work, we focus on improvement of factorization methods for compression: an alternative and complementary method to the conceptually simpler ones such as pruning and quantization. Singular Value Decomposition (SVD) is one of the simplest low-rank decomposition methods and has been widely used to prune word embeddings [13,16] and transformer models [20]. While there are other decompositions, surprisingly, SVD-based methods often provide better results. There are works applying Tensor-Train (TT) decomposition [23]: for embedding layers these yield good results [8], but for FFN layers TT obtain lower quality than SVD [24]. Tucker decomposition [31] is also applied to model compression, but similar to TT, the results have not been shown to be better than those of SVD [33]. LoRAPrune [35] is a recent approach for LLM compression that utilizes the importance weights obtained by PEFT which is similar to our method. Yet its scope was limited to pruning methods. Our study demonstrates the efficacy of LoRA approach for factorization techniques.

For computing gradients, offloading techniques such as DeepSpeed's ZeRO-2 [28] offer a potential solution. By offloading optimizer states to CPU memory during training, ZeRO-2 reduces VRAM usage, as shown in Table 1. This method significantly slows down training, while not *shrinking* but *shifting* memory allocation from VRAM to RAM, which is a major limiting factor. We emphasize that offloading is not a substitute for our proposed approach, but rather a complementary technique which may be applied in addition to it.

[1] We release our code: https://github.com/s-nlp/lora/_fwsvd.

Table 1. Peak VRAM usage (in GB and %) and Samples Per Second (SPS) during training for various PEFT methods across different models.

FT method	`roberta-base`				`t5-large`				`Mistral 7B`			
	#Params	GB	%	SPS	#Params	GB	%	SPS	#Params	GB	%	SPS
full	124.00	3.80	100	218	737.00	22.00	100	22.6	7241.00	119.69	100	2.30
ZeRO-2	124.00	2.10	55	22.1	737.00	12.50	57	2.27	7241.00	27.47	23	0.61
$\texttt{LoRA}_{r=1/8/16}$	0.68	2.92	77	287	3.93	16.84	77	30.0	28.31	20.05	16	4.74
$\texttt{LoRA}_{r=8/32/64}$	1.32	2.93	77	282	15.72	16.95	77	29.3	113.20	20.93	16	4.69
$\texttt{QLoRA}_{r=1/8/16}$	0.68	1.14	30	194	3.93	3.12	14	20.3	28.31	7.71	6	3.03
$\texttt{QLoRA}_{r=8/32/64}$	1.32	1.15	30	190	15.72	3.22	15	19.9	113.20	8.79	7	3.00

3 Background

3.1 SVD: Singular Value Decomposition

Consider a weight matrix of an LM model $w_{m\times n} \in \mathbb{R}$. An SVD of this matrix is $w = U_{m\times m}\Sigma_{m\times n}V^{\mathrm{T}}_{n\times n}$. A truncation by rank r: $U_r = U[:, : r]$ of shape (m, r), $\Sigma_r = \Sigma\,[: r, : r]$ of shape (r, r), $V_r = V[:, : r]$ of shape (n, r), and split w into two low-rank matrices $w_1 = \sqrt{\Sigma_r}V_r^{\mathrm{T}}$ and $w_2 = U_r\sqrt{\Sigma_r}$ is done to perform a compression. Below by SVD_r we denote a decomposition and truncation of the original matrix w to the low-rank matrix $\hat{w}$. Hence, $w \approx w_2w_1$. If w was of shape (m, n) and had $m \times n$ parameters, then after SVD, the number of parameters becomes $r \times (m + n + r)$. As the number of parameters goes down, the forward pass time for the models reduces as well, which improves kernel efficiency by reducing the memory footprint and computation time. It is beneficial for dense matrix multiplications, as the two resulting low-rank matrices (w_1 and w_2) are smaller and involve fewer FLOPs. We demonstrate this in Fig. 2 for the `t5-large` model. Furthermore, SVD does not necessitate the use of complex software and can be readily incorporated into existing pipelines or combined with alternative acceleration techniques. However, the extent of kernel efficiency enhancement is dependent on the underlying hardware architecture, as not all accelerators optimize low-rank operations in an equivalent manner. Sadly, SVD-based compression *alone* frequently yields suboptimal performance at various ranks, with the exception of those closely aligned with the original matrix rank.

3.2 Fisher Information

Fisher information, denoted I_w^{def}, is a measure that quantifies the amount of information a data set $\mathcal{D}$ provides about a weight matrix w in a model:

$$I_w^{\mathrm{def}} = \mathbb{E}\left[\left(\frac{\partial}{\partial w}\log p(\mathcal{D}|w)\right)^2\right]. \tag{1}$$

In this equation, the likelihood function $p(\mathcal{D}|w)$ is the probability of observing the data $\mathcal{D}$ given the model parameters w. The partial derivative $\frac{\partial}{\partial w}\log p(\mathcal{D}|w)$

represents the rate of change of the log-likelihood function with respect to the model parameters w. The expectation is taken over the data distribution, which means that we are averaging over all possible realizations of the data.

Its computation is challenging due to the need for taking the expectation over the entire data distribution [21]. Therefore, various approximation methods have been proposed in the literature, such as the use of score function estimators [2], or the use of natural gradient descent which implicitly approximates the Fisher information matrix [1]. The latter, while not giving any theoretical guarantees [14], works well in practice.

3.3 FWSVD: Fisher-Weighted SVD

Despite all its advantages, SVD-based model compression typically results in poor performance at various ranks, except for those closest to the original matrix rank. To address the limitations of SVD, Hsu et al. [9] proposed FWSVD, an enhanced compression approach that integrates empirical Fisher information into the SVD decomposition and improves compression performance.

A direct estimation of Fisher information is intractable. Therefore, following previous work [1,9], we estimate the empirical Fisher information. Let I_w be the empirical Fisher information matrix for weight matrix w:

$$I_w^{\text{def}} \approx I_w = \frac{1}{|\mathcal{D}|} \sum_{i=1}^{|\mathcal{D}|} \left(\frac{\partial}{\partial w} \mathcal{L}\left(d_i; w\right) \right)^2 \tag{2}$$

where $\mathcal{L}\left(d_i; w\right)$ is the cross-entropy loss function. Given that $\hat{w} = \text{SVD}_r(w)$ and $\text{rank}(\hat{w}) = r$, SVD-based low-rank approximation problem transforms into:

$$\min_{\hat{w}} \| \sqrt{I_w}(w - \hat{w}) \|_2^2 \tag{3}$$

Problem 3 does not have a closed-form solution [30]. To avoid this issue, [9] suggest solving the low-rank approximation problem using row-wise weighting: $\hat{I}_w = \text{diag}\left(I_w \cdot \mathbf{1}\right)$ As a result, we get weighted SVD components:

$$\text{FWSVD}(w) = (\hat{I}_w)^{-1} U \Sigma V = \hat{U} \hat{\Sigma} \hat{V}, \tag{4}$$

$$\text{FWSVD}_r(w) = \hat{U}_r \hat{\Sigma}_r \hat{V}_r. \tag{5}$$

The advantage of this approach is that in most cases there is no need for separate gradient calculation and collection, as all the needed gradients are collected during model fine-tuning.

3.4 LoRA: Low Rank Adaptation

LoRA [10] restricts the fine-tuning of a weight matrix $w \in \mathbb{R}^{n \times m}$ to the tuning of its low-rank decomposition $w + \Delta w = w + BA$, where $A \in \mathbb{R}^{n \times r}$, $\text{B} \in \mathbb{R}^{r \times m}$, and $r \in \mathbb{R} : r \ll \min(n, m)$. Only Δw is updated during the fine-tuning. The forward pass for input x is simple: $h = wx + \Delta wx = wx + BAx$.

The trained parameters Δw are then added to the model weights without the need to store additional weights for inference. With the advent of large language models (e.g., Mistral [12]), LoRA became a standard technique for tuning LLMs for a downstream task. A common pipeline is the following: LLM is quantized to half-precision (fp16) or even more (int4), and the LoRA adapter is trained on a given downstream task.

Recent works show that training only low-rank representations of fully connected layers provides performance comparable to full fine-tuning for different types of models [10,19] and tasks [34] and enable LLM with a new factual knowledge [25]

4 FWSVD-LoRA: A Memory Efficient Compression Method

4.1 Approximating the Empirical Fisher Information Matrix

We assume that empirical Fisher information can be effectively obtained based solely on low-rank representations, enabling FWSVD to perform comparably to its original implementation. This eliminates the need for extensive gradient computation and storage, resulting in a more efficient and scalable compression. Given a LLM, its compression with FWSVD will require storing gradients for the whole model, which often doubles the amount of required GPU memory, while our approach does not require this extra memory to perform the compression.

So, instead of calculating $\hat{I}_w$ for each weight matrix w we will compress, we will calculate $\hat{I}_w \approx \hat{I}_B \hat{I}_A$.

After we fine-tune the model with LoRA, we merge the weight matrix approximated by LoRA, $\Delta w = BA$, back into the original weight matrix w and compress it using the approximated Fisher information matrix:

$$\begin{aligned} \text{FWSVD}\,(w) &= \text{SVD}((\hat{I}_w)^{-1} w) && (6)\\ &\approx \text{SVD}((\hat{I}_B \hat{I}_A)^{-1}(w + BA)) && (7)\\ &= \text{SVD}((\hat{I}_B \hat{I}_A)^{-1} w') && (8)\\ &\approx \text{FWSVD}\,(BAw)\,. && (9) \end{aligned}$$

In this way, we only need to train less than 0.01% of model parameters instead of full model training with FWSVD. Moreover, our approach can be combined with quantization techniques like QLoRA [5], even further optimizing the VRAM overhead. Similarly, one can use other approaches like kernel optimization [3] to further decrease VRAM usage. We leave such experimentation for future work.

In this study, similarly to the original FWSVD work, we consider the "fine-tune → compress" pipeline. Through comprehensive experimentation, we prove the comparable to the original FWSVD performance across wide range of tasks and NLP models.

5 Experimental Setup

We begin by introducing the datasets and benchmarks used for evaluating our proposed approach and baselines. Next, we detail the models employed in our evaluation, along with links to their corresponding checkpoints. Additionally, we specify the layers compressed in each model.

5.1 Datasets

We evaluate the performance of our proposed method compared to standard SVD, FWSVD, and standard LoRA approaches. For the experiments, we use the RoBERTa model [17] and test its performance on GLUE [32], CoNLL-2003 [29] and SQuAD 2.0 [27] datasets. We also conduct summarization experiments on dataset XSUM [22] with T5 [26] and evaluate Mistral v2 7B [12] on the MMLU benchmark [7] using 5-shot evaluation.

5.2 Models

In our classification experiments, we use `roberta-base` model[2] from the HuggingFace model hub. We set the batch size to 32 and 128 during training and evaluation. In each task, we fine-tune the model for 3 epochs using AdamW optimizer [18] with a learning rate equal to $3 \cdot 10^{-5}$. For LoRA we set rank r to 1 and 8, and scale s to 2 and 16 respectively, other parameters we leave as default.

In summarization experiments, we use `t5-large` model[3], for LoRA we set r to $8, 32$ and s to $16, 64$, respectively.

For MMLU evaluation, we use `neural-chat-7b-v3-1`, a checkpoint[4] of Mistral 7B that was calibrated on DCLM dataset. The gradients for the model were collected with additional fine-tuning. This DCLM dataset consists of 5.72 millions rows, which is a time-consuming task to calculate gradients. So, we take only first 150,000 rows for calibration.

5.3 Layers for Compression

Since for the majority of the Transformer-based models, the heaviest parts of the model are always the fully-connected layers [24], we apply LoRA and compress only these parts of the model. For `roberta-base`, we choose the same fully-connected layers: `intermediate` and `output`. For the `t5-large` we compress `wi` and `wo`. Finally, for the `mistral-7b` model we use `gate_proj`, `up_proj` and `down_proj`.

---

[2] huggingface.co/roberta-base.
[3] huggingface.co/t5-large.
[4] huggingface.co/neural-chat-7b-v3-1.

6 Results

In this section, we compare the performance of our approach to simple baselines across various NLP tasks. The fraction of trainable parameters and peak VRAM utilization for is available in Table 1.

6.1 GLUE: Natural Language Understanding

We provide results of our experiments on the GLUE benchmark in Table 3 and Fig. 3a. At high compression ranks, neither Fisher Weighted SVD (FWSVD) nor our proposed methods approach the performance of fully fine-tuned models. The difference between FWSVD and our FWSVD+LoRA (QLoRA) approach is minimal, with a mere 4% difference in performance between FWSVD and FWSVD+LoRA$_{r=8}$ at a compression rank of 540. As compression rank decreases, the performance gap between FWSVD and FWSVD+LoRA becomes negligible. However, non-weighted SVD yields significantly inferior performance, comparable to random evaluation. The reported metric represents the average performance across all GLUE tasks. Examination of non-weighted SVD performance reveals that only two subtasks, SST2 and QQP, exhibit quality a little better than random answer, and only under conditions of minimal compression rank 540, compared to FWSVD which shows a superior quality to random answer for most of the subtasks at ranks above 220.

6.2 CoNLL: Named Entity Recognition

We present experimental results on the CoNLL-2003 NER benchmark in Table 3 and Fig. 3b. For the case of CoNLL-2003, we observe a significant difference in compression quality between the standard FWSVD and our proposed FWSVD+LoRA$_{r=8}$ and FWSVD+QLoRA$_{r=8}$ on almost any rank with both FWSVD+LoRA$_{r=8}$ and FWSVD+QLoRA$_{r=8}$ drastically outperforming both FWSVD and SVD by a large margin.

We also note the surprising performance drop for both SVD and FWSVD and analyze it. We suppose that the substantial drop in performance for these approaches between neighbouring ranks (e.g., from 0.8 F_1 at rank 480 to 0.10 F_1 at rank 340 for FWSVD) suggests that the model either ceases functionality due to accumulated error or loses its training knowledge on the CoNLL-2003 dataset.

6.3 SQuAD: Question Answering

We present our experimental results in Table 3 and Fig. 3c.

In contrast with GLUE and CoNLL-2003 benchmarks, for SQuAD 2.0 we observe that for most of the ranks both our proposed FWSVD+LoRA$_{r=8}$ and FWSVD+QLoRA$_{r=8}$ demonstrate superior performance to both FWSVD and SVD across an overwhelming majority of the ranks (see Fig. 3c).

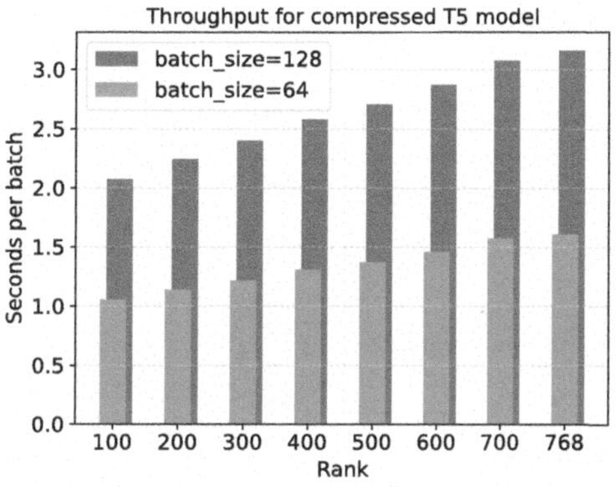

Fig. 2. Speed-up of batch processing for the compressed `t5-large` model. The last bar is the speed for the uncompressed model.

As it can be seen at Fig. 3, FWSVD+LoRA provide significantly better results than full-ranked SVD for both CoNLL-2003 and SQuAD 2.0. Our hypothesis for such low performance comes from the compressed model itself, which learns patterns so quickly (with full-rank models) that it is overfitting in 1 epoch. With low-rank learning, such as LoRA, the model does not have enough features (or memory) to overfit so quickly. The assumption about overfitting is only a hypothesis, which we indicate as a possibility for future research. The observed performance drops are not repeated in other tasks, which may be due to several reasons that are worthy of a separate analysis that goes beyond this work.

6.4 XSUM: Text Summarization

We experiment on XSUM with `t5-large` and discuss the results below.

Experimental results for are presented in Table 2 and Fig. 3d. The summarization quality of the full-sized fine-tuned model is not significantly higher than for those that were fine-tuned with LoRA or QLoRA. Gradually, the quality of all models approximates, but the full-size models remain slightly better. However, as we show in Fig. 3d, the difference in ROUGE-L is marginal: from 0.2 to 0.5 across all compression ranks, but we save a lot of VRAM by using our proposed FWSVD+LoRA approach (see Table 1).

We also experimented with a setup based on a low GPU budget, or as we called it, a VRAM-limited setup.

6.5 MMLU: Few-Shot Language Understanding

In this section, we apply our approach to the decoder-only `Mistral-7B`. Namely, we provide results of the experiments on the MMLU benchmark with 5-shot evaluation on Fig. 4 and Table 4. We have no information about VRAM usage from the creators of `neutral-chat-7b-v3-1` and, thus, leave the memory consumption for full model fine-tuning in Fig. 4 blank.

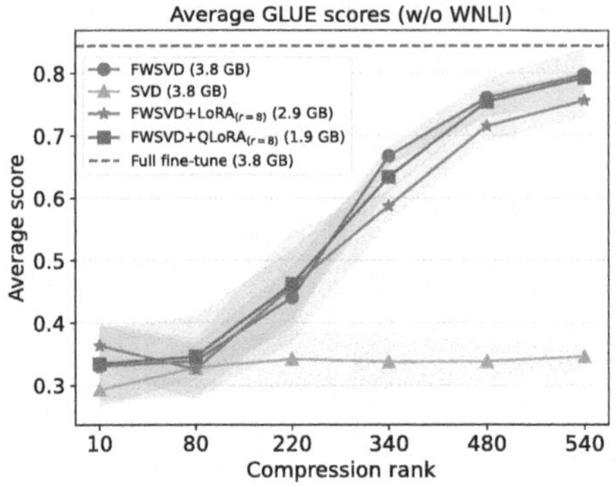

(a) Average GLUE benchmark scores for different compression ranks of the **roberta-base** model.

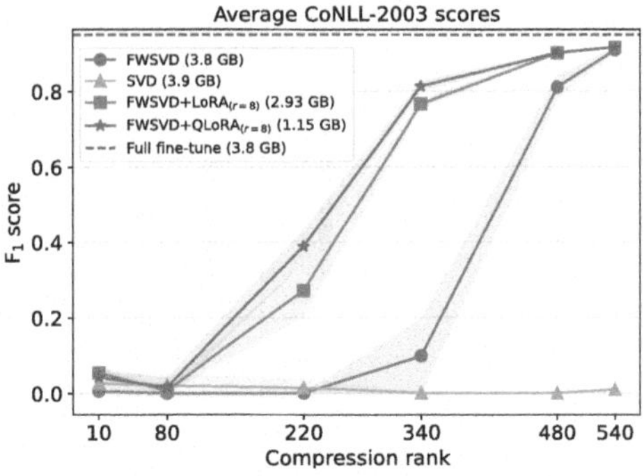

(b) Average F_1 scores on the CoNLL-2003 dataset for different compression ranks of the **roberta-base** model.

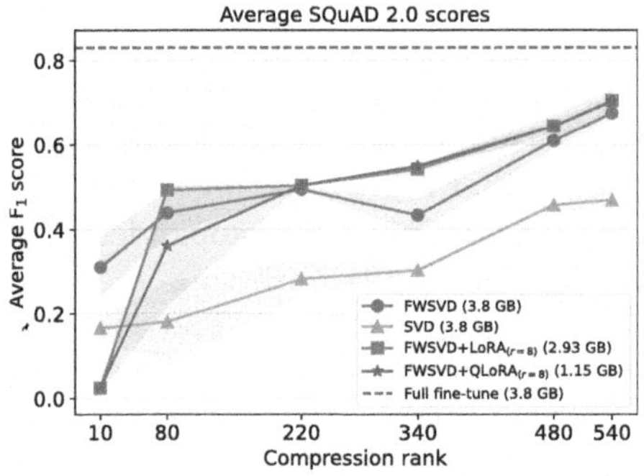

(c) Average F_1 scores on the SQUAD 2.0 dataset for different compression ranks of **roberta-base**.

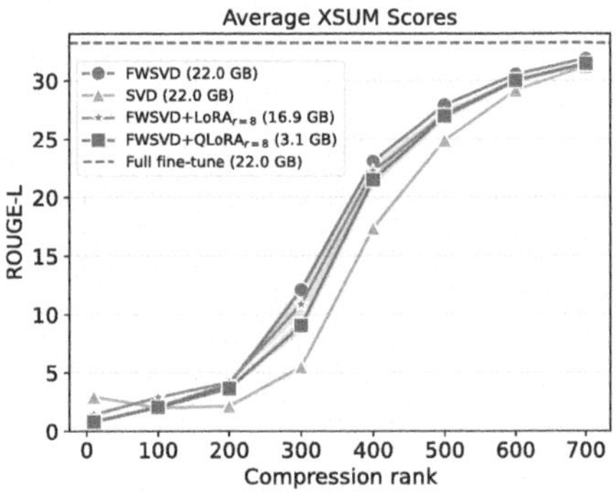

(d) Average ROUGE-L scores on the XSUM summarization dataset for **t5-large** model.

Fig. 3. Performance comparison of different compression ranks.

Table 2. ROUGE-L-sum on XSUM for **t5-large** model. Row *model size* represents the fraction of the uncompressed model size left after compression. Full rank is 768.

Model size	72%	79%	85%	92%
VRAM, GB	3.099	3.290	3.468	3.649
Rank	400	500	600	700
SVD	16.3$_{\pm 0.02}$	24.7$_{\pm 0.03}$	29.3$_{\pm 0.01}$	31.4$_{\pm 0.02}$
FWSVD	**22.9**$_{\pm 0.01}$	**27.8**$_{\pm 0.01}$	**30.4**$_{\pm 0.01}$	**31.8**$_{\pm 0.01}$
FWSVD+LoRA$_{r=8}$	22.4$_{\pm 0.01}$	27.2$_{\pm 0.01}$	30.0$_{\pm 0.01}$	31.4$_{\pm 0.01}$
FWSVD+QLoRA$_{r=8}$	21.5$_{\pm 0.01}$	27.0$_{\pm 0.01}$	30.0$_{\pm 0.01}$	31.4$_{\pm 0.01}$

Table 3. Average GLUE, CoNLL-2003 and SQuAD 2.0 results for several compression ranks. The best results for each rank are in **bold**.

Benchmark	GLUE Average scores			CoNLL F_1 scores			SQuAD 2.0 F_1 scores		
Model Size	80%	90%	95%	80%	90%	95%	80%	90%	95%
Rank	340	480	540	340	480	540	340	480	540
VRAM, GB	0.799	0.848	0.867	0.799	0.848	0.867	0.799	0.848	0.867
SVD	$0.34_{\pm 0.04}$	$0.34_{\pm 0.03}$	$0.35_{\pm 0.02}$	$0.00_{\pm 0.00}$	$0.03_{\pm 0.02}$	$0.02_{\pm 0.02}$	$0.30_{\pm 0.00}$	$0.46_{\pm 0.01}$	$0.47_{\pm 0.02}$
FWSVD	$\mathbf{0.67}_{\pm 0.02}$	$\mathbf{0.76}_{\pm 0.03}$	$\mathbf{0.80}_{\pm 0.04}$	$0.10_{\pm 0.08}$	$0.81_{\pm 0.03}$	$0.91_{\pm 0.00}$	$0.48_{\pm 0.03}$	$0.57_{\pm 0.02}$	$0.64_{\pm 0.01}$
FWSVD+LoRA$_{r=8}$	$0.59_{\pm 0.03}$	$0.71_{\pm 0.03}$	$0.76_{\pm 0.03}$	$\mathbf{0.83}_{\pm 0.01}$	$\mathbf{0.92}_{\pm 0.00}$	$\mathbf{0.93}_{\pm 0.00}$	$0.53_{\pm 0.01}$	$0.59_{\pm 0.01}$	$0.64_{\pm 0.01}$
FWSVD+QLoRA$_{r=8}$	$0.63_{\pm 0.02}$	$0.75_{\pm 0.01}$	$0.79_{\pm 0.01}$	$0.81_{\pm 0.01}$	$0.90_{\pm 0.00}$	$0.92_{\pm 0.00}$	$\mathbf{0.55}_{\pm 0.00}$	$\mathbf{0.64}_{\pm 0.03}$	$\mathbf{0.70}_{\pm 0.03}$

Table 4. Average accuracy scores for MMLU benchmark after 5-shot evaluation. The best results for each rank are in **bold**.

Model Size	60%	69%	79%	90%
Method/Rank	1550	1950	2350	2800
VRAM, GB	18.59	21.29	23.99	26.69
SVD	$0.26_{\pm 0.05}$	$0.27_{\pm 0.06}$	$0.24_{\pm 0.04}$	$0.24_{\pm 0.04}$
FWSVD+QLoRA$_{r=16}$	$\mathbf{0.26}_{\pm 0.05}$	$\mathbf{0.34}_{\pm 0.06}$	$\mathbf{0.46}_{\pm 0.11}$	$\mathbf{0.54}_{\pm 0.12}$
FWSVD+QLoRA$_{r=64}$	$\mathbf{0.26}_{\pm 0.05}$	$\mathbf{0.34}_{\pm 0.07}$	$\mathbf{0.46}_{\pm 0.11}$	$\mathbf{0.54}_{\pm 0.13}$

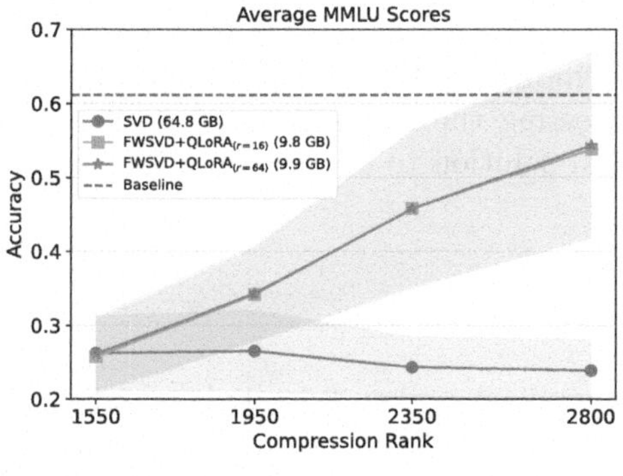

Fig. 4. Results for Mistral 7B on MMLU benchmark with 5-shot evaluation. Numerical results are in Table 4.

Since the computation and collection of the gradients for the whole 7 billion parameters model using the original FWSVD in fp16 requires approximately 120 Gb of VRAM, the application of the FWSVD is simply intractable. On the contrary, using ours FWSVD+LoRA approach, one *actually can calculate* the empirical Fisher information and perform low-rank compression using either LoRA or QLoRA depending on the exact hardware limits.

Despite a slight decrease in performance compared to the baseline quality of the uncompressed model, our proposed FWSVD+QLoRA approach provides almost identical performance at both ranks 16 and 64. For our proposed approach, we need only 9.8 Gb of the VRAM compared to 64.82 Gb of VRAM for SVD: we save 85% of the VRAM. Compression with SVD, however, completely lowers the performance of the model even with the compression to from rank 4096 to 2800.

7 Conclusion

In this work, we introduce FWSVD-LoRA, a novel method that combines the FWSVD model compression technique with LoRA parameter-efficient fine-tuning (PEFT). We show that collecting empirical Fisher information across the entire model, as required by FWSVD, is unnecessary and resource-intensive. Instead, gathering Fisher information solely from LoRA-trained layers significantly simplifies the process. Tested across multiple architectures and 12 NLP tasks, our approach achieves *on par* or *better* compression performance compared to FWSVD, with up to 20% model size reduction while preserving downstream task accuracy. This efficiency stems from using only low-rank representations and minimizing gradient storage demands, requiring little additional VRAM.

FWSVD-LoRA performs best in resource-constrained settings, such as deploying large language models (LLMs) on low-end GPUs with limited VRAM. While our method underperforms at extreme compression rates, similar to baseline methods, it often delivers superior stability and quality in scenarios where compressed models typically degrade rapidly. Comprehensive experiments across diverse NLP tasks, including NLU, QA, NER, and summarization, validate its effectiveness. By addressing the computational challenges of LLMs, FWSVD-LoRA offers a practical solution to optimize model compression without sacrificing performance.

References

1. Amari, S.: Natural gradient works efficiently in learning. Neural Comput. **10**(2), 251–276 (1998)
2. Casella, G.C.: Theory of Point Estimation. Springer, Heidelberg (2001)
3. Dao, T.: Flashattention-2: faster attention with better parallelism and work partitioning. In: The Twelfth International Conference on Learning Representations, ICLR 2024, Vienna, Austria, 7–11 May 2024. OpenReview.net (2024)
4. Dettmers, T., Lewis, M., Belkada, Y., Zettlemoyer, L.: Gpt3.int8(): 8-bit matrix multiplication for transformers at scale. In: Koyejo, S., Mohamed, S., Agarwal, A., Belgrave, D., Cho, K., Oh, A. (eds.) Advances in Neural Information Processing Systems 35: Annual Conference on Neural Information Processing Systems 2022, NeurIPS 2022, New Orleans, LA, USA, 28 November–9 December 2022 (2022)
5. Dettmers, T., Pagnoni, A., Holtzman, A., Zettlemoyer, L.: Qlora: efficient finetuning of quantized llms. In: Oh, A., Naumann, T., Globerson, A., Saenko, K., Hardt, M., Levine, S. (eds.) Advances in Neural Information Processing Systems 36: Annual Conference on Neural Information Processing Systems 2023, NeurIPS 2023, New Orleans, LA, USA, 10–16 December 2023 (2023)

6. Fan, C., et al.: Layer-wise model pruning based on mutual information. In: Moens, M., Huang, X., Specia, L., Yih, S.W. (eds.) Proceedings of the 2021 Conference on Empirical Methods in Natural Language Processing, EMNLP 2021, Virtual Event/Punta Cana, Dominican Republic, 7–11 November, 2021, pp. 3079–3090. Association for Computational Linguistics (2021)
7. Hendrycks, D., et al.: Measuring massive multitask language understanding. In: 9th International Conference on Learning Representations, ICLR 2021, Virtual Event, Austria, 3–7 May 2021. OpenReview.net (2021)
8. Hrinchuk, O., Khrulkov, V., Mirvakhabova, L., Orlova, E., Oseledets, I.V.: Tensorized embedding layers. In: Cohn, T., He, Y., Liu, Y. (eds.) Findings of the Association for Computational Linguistics: EMNLP 2020, Online Event, 16–20 November 2020. Findings of ACL, vol. EMNLP 2020, pp. 4847–4860. Association for Computational Linguistics (2020)
9. Hsu, Y., Hua, T., Chang, S., Lou, Q., Shen, Y., Jin, H.: Language model compression with weighted low-rank factorization (2022)
10. Hu, E.J., et al.: Lora: Low-rank adaptation of large language models. In: The Tenth International Conference on Learning Representations, ICLR 2022, Virtual Event, 25–29 April 2022. OpenReview.net (2022)
11. Hua, T., Hsu, Y., Wang, F., Lou, Q., Shen, Y., Jin, H.: Numerical optimizations for weighted low-rank estimation on language models. In: Goldberg, Y., Kozareva, Z., Zhang, Y. (eds.) Proceedings of the 2022 Conference on Empirical Methods in Natural Language Processing, EMNLP 2022, Abu Dhabi, United Arab Emirates, 7–11 December 2022, pp. 1404–1416. Association for Computational Linguistics (2022)
12. Jiang, A.Q., et al.: Mistral 7b. CoRR arxiv:2310.06825 (2023)
13. Konovalov, V., Tumunbayarova, Z.: Learning word embeddings for low resourse languages: the case of buryat. In: Komp'juternaja Lingvistika i Intellektual'nye Tehnologiithis, pp. 331–341 (2018). http://www.dialog-21.ru/media/4528/konovalovvp_tumunbayarovazb.pdf
14. Kunstner, F., Hennig, P., Balles, L.: Limitations of the empirical fisher approximation for natural gradient descent. In: Wallach, H.M., Larochelle, H., Beygelzimer, A., d'Alché-Buc, F., Fox, E.B., Garnett, R. (eds.) Advances in Neural Information Processing Systems 32: Annual Conference on Neural Information Processing Systems 2019, NeurIPS 2019, Vancouver, BC, Canada, 8–14 December 2019, pp. 4158–4169 (2019)
15. Kurtic, E., Frantar, E., Alistarh, D.: Ziplm: Inference-aware structured pruning of language models. In: Oh, A., Naumann, T., Globerson, A., Saenko, K., Hardt, M., Levine, S. (eds.) Advances in Neural Information Processing Systems 36: Annual Conference on Neural Information Processing Systems 2023, NeurIPS 2023, New Orleans, LA, USA, 10–16 December 2023 (2023)
16. Lan, Z., Chen, M., Goodman, S., Gimpel, K., Sharma, P., Soricut, R.: ALBERT: a lite BERT for self-supervised learning of language representations. In: 8th International Conference on Learning Representations, ICLR 2020, Addis Ababa, Ethiopia, 26–30 April 2020. OpenReview.net (2020)
17. Liu, Y., et al.: Roberta: a robustly optimized BERT pretraining approach. CoRR arxiv:1907.11692 (2019)
18. Loshchilov, I., Hutter, F.: Decoupled weight decay regularization. In: 7th International Conference on Learning Representations, ICLR 2019, New Orleans, LA, USA, 6–9 May 2019. OpenReview.net (2019)
19. Mao, Y., et al.: A survey on lora of large language models. Front. Comput. Sci. **19**(7), 197605 (2024)

20. Michel, P., Levy, O., Neubig, G.: Are sixteen heads really better than one? In: Wallach, H.M., Larochelle, H., Beygelzimer, A., d'Alché-Buc, F., Fox, E.B., Garnett, R. (eds.) Advances in Neural Information Processing Systems 32: Annual Conference on Neural Information Processing Systems 2019, NeurIPS 2019, Vancouver, BC, Canada, 8–14 December 2019, pp. 14014–14024 (2019)
21. Murphy, K.P.: Machine learning - a probabilistic perspective. Adaptive computation and machine learning series, MIT Press, Cambridge (2012)
22. Narayan, S., Cohen, S.B., Lapata, M.: Don't give me the details, just the summary! topic-aware convolutional neural networks for extreme summarization. In: Riloff, E., Chiang, D., Hockenmaier, J., Tsujii, J. (eds.) Proceedings of the 2018 Conference on Empirical Methods in Natural Language Processing, Brussels, Belgium, 31 October–4 November 2018, pp. 1797–1807. Association for Computational Linguistics (2018)
23. Oseledets, I.: Tensor-train decomposition. SIAM J. Sci. Comput. **33**, 2295–2317 (2011)
24. Pletenev, S., Chekalina, V., Moskovskiy, D., Seleznev, M., Zagoruyko, S., Panchenko, A.: A computational study of matrix decomposition methods for compression of pre-trained transformers. In: Huang, C.R., et al. (eds.) Proceedings of the 37th Pacific Asia Conference on Language, Information and Computation, pp. 723–742. Association for Computational Linguistics, Hong Kong (2023)
25. Pletenev, S., et al.: How much knowledge can you pack into a LoRA adapter without harming LLM? In: Chiruzzo, L., Ritter, A., Wang, L. (eds.) Findings of the Association for Computational Linguistics: NAACL 2025, pp. 4309–4322. Association for Computational Linguistics, Albuquerque (2025). https://aclanthology.org/2025.findings-naacl.243/
26. Raffel, C., et al.: Exploring the limits of transfer learning with a unified text-to-text transformer. J. Mach. Learn. Res. **21**, 140:1–140:67 (2020)
27. Rajpurkar, P., Jia, R., Liang, P.: Know what you don't know: unanswerable questions for SQuAD. In: Gurevych, I., Miyao, Y. (eds.) Proceedings of the 56th Annual Meeting of the Association for Computational Linguistics, vol. 2: Short Papers, pp. 784–789. Association for Computational Linguistics, Melbourne (2018)
28. Ren, J., et al.: Zero-offload: democratizing billion-scale model training. In: Calciu, I., Kuenning, G. (eds.) Proceedings of the 2021 USENIX Annual Technical Conference, USENIX ATC 2021, 14–16 July 2021, pp. 551–564. USENIX Association (2021)
29. Sang, E.F.T.K., Meulder, F.D.: Introduction to the conll-2003 shared task: language-independent named entity recognition. In: Daelemans, W., Osborne, M. (eds.) Proceedings of the Seventh Conference on Natural Language Learning, CoNLL 2003, Held in cooperation with HLT-NAACL 2003, Edmonton, Canada, 31 May–1 June 2003, pp. 142–147. ACL (2003)
30. Srebro, N., Jaakkola, T.S.: Weighted low-rank approximations. In: Fawcett, T., Mishra, N. (eds.) Machine Learning, Proceedings of the Twentieth International Conference (ICML 2003), Washington, DC, USA, 21–24 August 2003, pp. 720–727. AAAI Press (2003)
31. Tucker, P.A.: On the reduction of induced indecomposable representations. Am. J. Math. **87**(4), 798–806 (1965)
32. Wang, A., Singh, A., Michael, J., Hill, F., Levy, O., Bowman, S.R.: GLUE: a multi-task benchmark and analysis platform for natural language understanding. In: 7th International Conference on Learning Representations, ICLR 2019, New Orleans, LA, USA, 6–9 May 2019. OpenReview.net (2019)

33. Wang, B., Ren, Y., Shang, L., Jiang, X., Liu, Q.: Exploring extreme parameter compression for pre-trained language models. In: The Tenth International Conference on Learning Representations, ICLR 2022, Virtual Event, 25–29 April 2022. OpenReview.net (2022)
34. Zanella, M., Ayed, I.B.: Low-rank few-shot adaptation of vision-language models. In: IEEE/CVF Conference on Computer Vision and Pattern Recognition, CVPR 2024 - Workshops, Seattle, WA, USA, 17–18 June 2024, pp. 1593–1603. IEEE (2024)
35. Zhang, M., et al.: Loraprune: structured pruning meets low-rank parameter-efficient fine-tuning. In: Ku, L., Martins, A., Srikumar, V. (eds.) Findings of the Association for Computational Linguistics, ACL 2024, Bangkok, Thailand and Virtual Meeting, 11–16 August 2024, pp. 3013–3026. Association for Computational Linguistics (2024)
36. Zhu, X., Li, J., Liu, Y., Ma, C., Wang, W.: A survey on model compression for large language models. Trans. Assoc. Comput. Linguist. **12**, 1556–1577 (2024)

Accelerating End-to-End PDF to Markdown Conversion Through Assisted Generation

Changxu Duan(✉)

Technische Universität Darmstadt, Darmstadt, Germany
duan@linglit.tu-darmstadt.de

Abstract. Converting data from machine-unreadable formats like PDFs into Markdown has the potential to enhance the accessibility of scientific research. Existing end-to-end decoder transformer models can transform screenshots of PDFs into Markdown, offering more flexibility than pipeline-based methods. Yet, decoding text token by token from scratch is inefficient, especially when dense text can be directly copied from the PDF. To address this challenge, this paper modifies Prompt Lookup Decoding (PLD) to extract candidate sequences directly from PDF files, leveraging the high n-gram overlap between PDFs and their Markdown equivalents. A new method, Copy Lookup Decoding (CLD), is introduced here to enhance PLD's candidate generation mechanism. Experiments demonstrate that CLD can accelerate the conversion process by up to 1.70 × at original quality. The codebase for this paper is open-source on GitHub (https://github.com/Fireblossom/CopyLookup).

Keywords: PDF-to-Markdown Conversion · Assisted Generation · Document Layout Analysis

1 Introduction

Scientific research is almost exclusively published in PDF, which is an unstructured text format whose content is not readily machine-readable. PDF formatted scientific documents contain complex elements like mathematical formulas, figures, headers, and tables, as well as densely laid-out text. Vision-Language Models (VLM) can understand documents in the form of document screenshots, but their comprehension is not yet reliable enough [9].

Markdown is an ideal format in terms of machine-readability due to its simple syntax and structured format which preserves context and enhances comprehensibility. Its support for rich text elements such as boldface, italics, and hyperlinks enriches the data, providing a more detailed context for models to generate accurate outputs. Furthermore, the Markdown community has extended the syntax so that it can support tables as well as advanced mathematical and chemical formulas [23]. Therefore, converting PDF files to Markdown is worth the effort.

R. Ichise (Ed.): NLDB 2025, LNCS 15836, pp. 34–48, 2026.
https://doi.org/10.1007/978-3-031-97141-9_3

A widely used method for converting PDFs to Markdown utilizes a pipeline-based approach, as demonstrated by Marker [37]. This process begins with a document layout analysis that segments each PDF page into various blocks and identifies the type of each block. Marker then determines the reading order of these blocks. Based on their types, different modules are called to convert specific elements, such as formulas and tables, into Markdown. The process concludes with a cleanup phase to correct errors. However, pipeline-based approaches can struggle with documents that have complex layouts, as errors made in one step can propagate and accumulate through subsequent steps, impacting overall performance, as shown in Fig. 1.

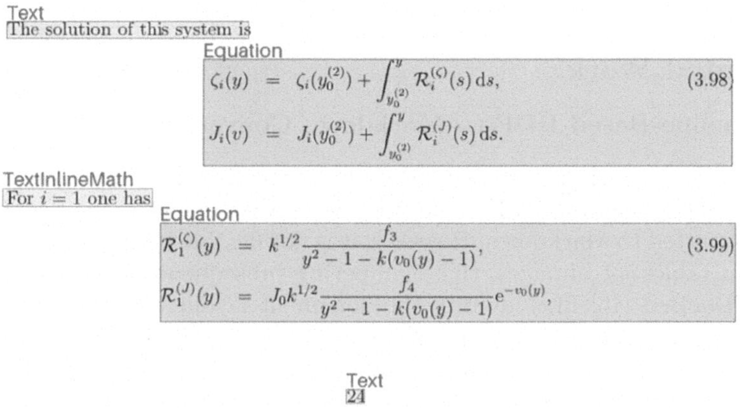

Fig. 1. Example of Marker's layout analysis on a scientific document with a complex layout. Marker detects math equations and plain text lines correctly. However, the inline math expression and the plain text line near it were incorrectly merged; the page number was also recognized as plain text. Error results from the document layout analysis accumulate and are propagated to the next steps in the pipeline.

An alternative to pipeline-based methods is end-to-end decoder transformer models, such as Nougat [4]. The model is a tiny VLM that reads a screenshot of a PDF page and directly extracts the content into Markdown, automatically preserving the correct reading order and converting mathematical formulas into LaTeX code. However, Nougat faces limitations in processing speed as it generates text token-by-token from scratch, which can significantly slow down the document conversion process.

Assisted Generation [14,16] can accelerate transformer decoder models without degrading generation quality because all candidates are validated by the transformer model. Prompt Lookup Decoding (PLD) [31] proves particularly advantageous when there is a substantial overlap of n-grams between the input (prompt) and the output of LLM. This method is up to 2.4× faster in tasks such as summarization and contextual question answering. Given that PDFs frequently contain dense text suitable for direct copying, implementing PLD could streamline the conversion process and decrease computational expenses.

The contributions of this paper include:

1. Modifying original PLD (mPLD) to enable the extraction of candidate sequences from PDF files. mPLD is plug-and-play, requires no fine-tuning, and is compatible with any end-to-end PDF-to-Markdown conversion models.
2. Proposing Copy Lookup Decoding (CLD) to enhance candidate generation in mPLD.
3. Releasing the dataset-making scripts and the arXiv IDs of the documents used in the experiments to enhance reproducibility and observe copyright.

2 Related Work

2.1 Pipeline-Based PDF-to-Markdown Conversion

GROBID [1] is a machine learning library for extracting, parsing, and restructuring documents, including PDFs, into structured XML encoded documents, which can be converted to Markdown. However, it is not flexible because it converts formulas and tables into images, thus hampering subsequent accessibility. DocTR [25] and DocBed [46] first identify the document layout and then extract text content. Marker, MinerU [6] and Docling [36] realize PDF-to-Markdown conversion through text layout analysis, reading order detection, formula or table extraction, and finally combine them into Markdown. Some close-sourced online services such as LlamaParse[1] and Mistral OCR[2] also provide PDF-to-Markdown conversion, using a process similar to Marker as described in their documentation.

2.2 End-to-End PDF-to-Markdown Conversion

End-to-end PDF-to-Markdown conversion models build on top of Vision-Language Models (VLM) and Document Understanding (DU) transformer models. Donut [15] is a DU model consisting of a visual encoder and a language model decoder without obtaining texts directly from the document. Donut's pre-training objective is to retell the text from a document screenshot. Nougat [4] follows Donut in implementing a screenshot-to-Markdown conversion of academic documents with an arXiv-sourced dataset. μgat [30] extends Nougat's input to handle elements that cross the single-page limit. LOCR [35] solves the problem of Nougat's hallucination and repetition using an additional location prompt. Kosmos-2.5 [22] implements a generalized screenshot-to-Markdown conversion with a larger model size. The approaches described in this paper attempt to speed up Nougat and Kosmos-2.5.

[1] https://cloud.llamaindex.ai/parse.
[2] https://mistral.ai/news/mistral-ocr.

General-purpose VLMs are also used to achieve screenshot-to-Markdown conversions. LlamaOCR [24], Zerox OCR [2] and Parallex [34] all feed screenshots of PDFs to open- and closed-source VLMs and direct the models to return the desired output by passing in the appropriate prompts. In this paper we replicate their methodology and conduct experiments on acceleration with two off-shelf open-source models Llama3.2 [3] and Qwen2-VL [38] as backbones.

2.3 Document Layout Analysis

Recent Document Layout Analysis (DLA) models have become increasingly powerful thanks to the availability of large-scale document layout datasets [13,18,28,45]. Computer vision models have been able to extract layouts in screenshots of documents [17,39,42]. Language models have also been applied to recognize layouts. LayoutLM [41] and its variant VILA [32] are transformer encoder models that analyze document layouts from the texts and their 2D coordinates. LayoutLMv2 and v3 [12,40] additionally attach visual features to the transformer encoder.

In this work, our Copyable Text Identification module for CLD is fine-tuned from ERNIE Layout [27].

2.4 Assisted Generation

To mitigate the high inference latency stemming from autoregressive decoding in Large Language Models (LLMs), Assisted Generation [16] has emerged as a novel decoding paradigm for LLM inference. In each decoding step, this method first uses a smaller LLM drafts several future tokens efficiently, and then verifies them in parallel. PLD [31] and LLMA [43] matches the last few tokens against an earlier position in the input prompt and selects the text span as a candidate. LookaheadDecoding [10] introduces multiple special tokens at the end of the input prompt to enable parallel drafting and convert the draft into an n-gram candidate. Lookahead [44] implements a multi-branch drafting strategy. Due to the low time overhead of the drafting phase, these methods can consistently improve the inference speed of the target LLM.

Some recent studies [5,19,20] have used the hidden states of the LLM as inputs to their draft models. However, these methods require additional parameters and need to be trained for each backbone model. In this work, we modified PLD to demonstrate the effectiveness of our approach as PLD is the simplest to implement and has already been integrated into the huggingface library.

3 Methodology

Initially, PLD checks for a matching n-gram to the current prediction in the input (prompt) of the transformer model, copying several tokens directly from the prompt as candidates. Subsequently, the LLM would verify all the candidate tokens simultaneously, determining whether each is a plausible next token in sequence from left to right, until encountering the first implausible candidate. The transformer model would then accept the last sequence that was deemed reasonable. Modified PLD (mPLD) involves a straightforward change: shifting the source of the candidate sequences from the prompt to all the text on the PDF page.

However, this modification introduces two significant issues. First, not all text in a PDF is readily copyable, which can limit the effectiveness of the extraction. Second, by default, mPLD extracts the candidate sequence from the first matching n-gram position on the page, posing the risk that candidates located later in the document may not be correctly matched.

To solve these problems, we designed Copy Lookup Decoding (CLD), which both filters out possible PDF noise and matches candidates to the back of the page through Copyable Text Identification and Candidate Generation.

3.1 Copyable Text Identification

Inspired by DLA-related works, we assert that whether the text is copyable or not is correlated with its layout information. Specifically, we suggest that:

1. Plain text found in paragraphs should be copyable.
2. Page elements such as mathematical formulas, tables, and figures should **not** be copyable.
3. Elements that do not convey relevant content, including headers, footers, and page numbers, should **not** be copyable.

Following VILA [32] , we assume that text copyability is homogeneous at the span level. We use PyMuPDF [29] to extract span-level text and bounding boxes from the PDF. PyMuPDF generally preserves the correct reading order, except in cases of floating elements such as footnotes and captions. We fine-tune the ERNIE Layout model for token classification using LoRA [11] and an unofficial implementation [26] that supports an extended input length of 1024 tokens through RoPE [33], addressing the issue of PDF pages often exceeding 512 tokens. The classification head of ERNIE Layout was modified to classify tokens as either `KEEP` or `DELETE`, simplifying the target from the broader range of layout categories typically used in DLA models (e.g., up to 10 categories in VILA) to just two.

As we have fine-tuned ERNIE Layout for token classification, and each span may contain more than one token, a voting classifier [7] is applied to decide the prediction of the spans. We demonstrate an example of Copyable Text Identification in Fig. 2.

3.2 Candidates Generation

After identifying which spans of text in the PDF are copyable, we merge adjacent copyable spans while keeping non-adjacent copyable spans separate. All merged spans are stored in a list for subsequent processing.

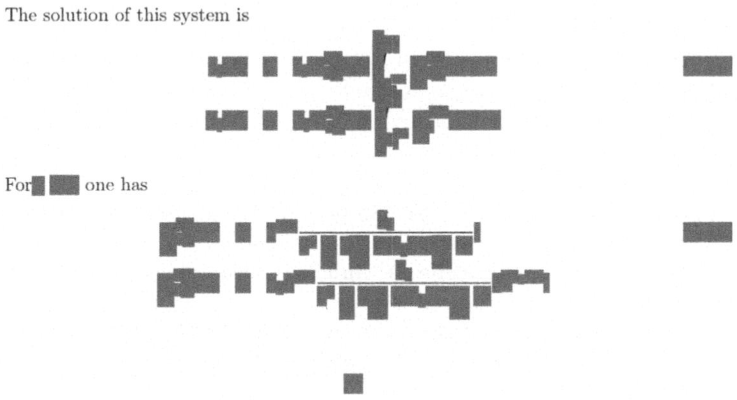

Fig. 2. Example of Copyable Text Identification. In this example, our model detects the same scientific document as in Fig. 1. The `DELETE` parts, including in-line and standalone mathematical formulas, and page numbers are identified and masked out. The `KEEP` parts including copyable texts are returned by the CLD's candidate generator.

During candidate generation, CLD checks each span in the list, starting from the first, to find a matching n-gram. If no match is found in the first span, the search continues through subsequent spans until a match is found or all the spans are exhausted. When a matching n-gram is detected in any span, the following tokens from that span are taken as candidates.

To align with the PDF-to-Markdown conversion's adherence to reading order, we implemented a topping mechanism. Once candidates are extracted, the PDF-to-Markdown conversion model evaluates whether these candidates are acceptable tokens in sequence. If a candidate is accepted, it indicates that the model is progressing within the span containing that candidate. At this juncture, we reassemble the span list by moving the currently active span and all subsequent spans to the front of the list while relocating all preceding spans to the end. This approach allows CLD to dynamically generate candidates that are synchronized with the ongoing progress of the PDF-to-Markdown conversion, enhancing both candidate accuracy and efficiency.

4 Experiments

4.1 PDF-to-Markdown Models

We test the conversion times and quality differences for scratch generation, mPLD, and CLD using two publicly available PDF-to-Markdown conversion specialized models, plus two general-purpose and open-sourced VLMs across the three test datasets described in Sect. 4.2. All tests were conducted on a machine with 1×A100 GPU.

- **Task specialized models:** Nougat[3] and Kosmos-2.5[4]
- **General-purpose VLMs:** Llama-3.2-11B-Vision-Instruct[5] and Qwen2-VL-72B-Instruct-AWQ[6]. Qwen2-VL is labeled as a 12.6B parameter in the model card because of the quantization technique [21]. We use Prompt in Prompt 1 for these models.

~~~
Convert the following PDF page to Markdown. Return only the Markdown with no explanation text.
Leave out any page numbers and redundant headers or footers.
Do not include any code blocks (e.g. "```markdown" or "```") in the response. If unable to parse, return an empty string.
~~~

Prompt 1: Prompt that instructs Llama and Qwen2-VL to complete PDF-to-Markdown conversion task.

4.2 Dataset Building

As there is no existing dataset released as PDFs at this time, we downloaded the LaTeX source code bundles for the July and August 2023 papers from arXiv. Then we used LaTeX-Rainbow [8], which compiles LaTeX to PDF and annotates semantic labels, reading order, and LaTeX code

corresponding to mathematical formulas and tables for each element on a page. A total of 14,320 papers were annotated.

Spans are extracted from these pages and are labeled as either `KEEP` or `DELETE` based on the results of the annotation from the previous step. Pages that are challenging to read, such as those containing full-page images, long tables, or bibliographies, are excluded from the dataset. Finally, a dataset was assembled consisting of 180,146 pages, each annotated with span-level text copyable labels and their corresponding bounding boxes. We randomly split the training set to 162,127 pages and the test set to 18,019 pages. The vast majority of the pages in this dataset are in English.

Our method extracts text spans from PDFs, which requires access to the full text of academic papers. As arXiv does not grant permission to repost the full text[7], we publish the scripts for creating the datasets along with the arXiv numbers of the documents to provide reproducibility.

For the PDF-to-Markdown conversion speed test, we randomly selected 128 pages from the test set. In addition, we also randomly selected 128 pages each from papers categorized in Economics and Quantum Physics respectively to test the performance of mPLD and CLD in different domain documents.

---

3 https://huggingface.co/facebook/nougat-base.
4 https://huggingface.co/microsoft/kosmos-2.5.
5 https://huggingface.co/meta-llama/Llama-3.2-11B-Vision.
6 https://huggingface.co/Qwen/Qwen2-VL-72B-Instruct-AWQ.
7 https://info.arxiv.org/help/license/reuse.html#full_text.

5 Results

5.1 Copyable Text Identification

We use F1 scores as the metric, without averaging because our model is a binary classifier. We tested token-level scores and span-level scores separately, and the prediction of spans was implemented by voting, as shown in Sect. 3.1.

The F1 score for token-level is **0.985**, while the F1 score for span-level is **0.988**. The average inference time per page for the classifier is **0.03** s.

5.2 PDF-To-Markdown Conversion Speed

Table 1. The speed of PDF-to-Markdown conversion models and Assisted Generation methods was evaluated across three test datasets, with $t(s)$ representing the average generation time per page in seconds. The extra 0.03 s required for CLD is due to the overhead of Copyable Text Identification.

		Test Dataset					
		arXiv		Economics		Quantum Physics	
Backbone Model	Assisted Generation	$t(s)$	Speed Up	$t(s)$	Speed Up	$t(s)$	Speed Up
Nougat-base	-	6.48	-	5.73	-	6.80	-
(349M)	mPLD	5.92	1.09×	5.05	1.13×	6.13	1.11×
	CLD	5.85 (+0.03)	**1.10**×	4.60 (+0.03)	**1.24**×	5.56 (+0.03)	**1.22**×
Kosmos-2.5	-	12.21	-	11.09	-	12.77	-
(1.37B)	mPLD	9.42	1.30×	8.04	1.38×	9.23	1.38×
	CLD	8.37 (+0.03)	**1.45**×	7.60 (+0.03)	**1.45**×	7.85 (+0.03)	**1.62**×
Llama-3.2-Vision	-	33.83	-	30.53	-	35.03	-
(10.6B)	mPLD	29.20	1.16×	23.28	1.31×	32.08	1.09×
	CLD	26.02 (+0.03)	**1.30**×	21.83 (+0.03)	**1.40**×	27.61 (+0.03)	**1.27**×
Qwen2-VL	-	138.85	-	119.42	-	156.06	-
(12.6B)	mPLD	97.65	1.32×	75.21	1.59×	100.00	1.56×
	CLD	91.53 (+0.03)	**1.41**×	72.88 (+0.03)	**1.64**×	91.88 (+0.03)	**1.70**×

The conversion speed test results are shown in Table 1. In our experiments, both mPLD and CLD speed up PDF-to-Markdown conversion. Larger models benefits more from mPLD and CLD in terms of conversion speed. The inference time of Copyable Text Identification module in CLD is included in the average conversion time per page. In Fig. 3 we show an example of how CLD can accelerate Kosmos-2.5.

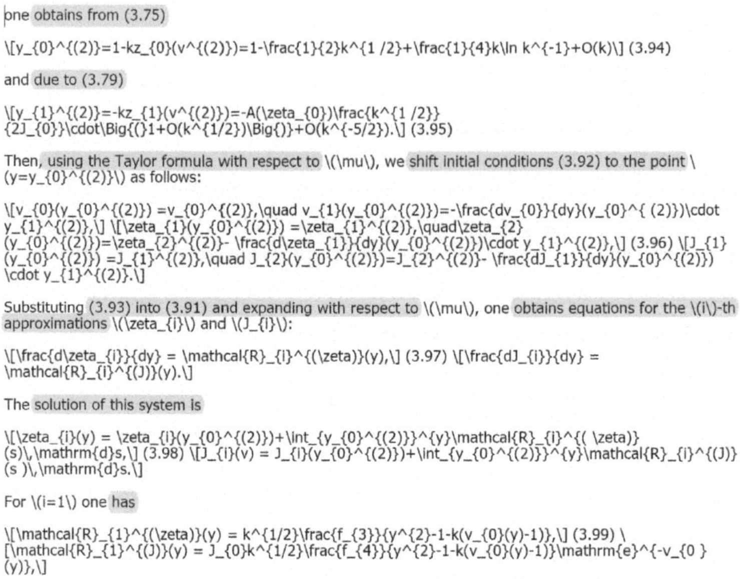

```
one obtains from (3.75)

\[y_{0}^{(2)}=1-kz_{0}(v^{(2)})=1-\frac{1}{2}k^{1 /2}+\frac{1}{4}k\ln k^{-1}+O(k)\] (3.94)

and due to (3.79)

\[y_{1}^{(2)}=-kz_{1}(v^{(2)})=-A(\zeta_{0})\frac{k^{1 /2}}
{2J_{0}}\cdot\Big{(}1+O(k^{1/2})\Big{)}+O(k^{-5/2}).\] (3.95)

Then, using the Taylor formula with respect to \(\mu\), we shift initial conditions (3.92) to the point \
(y=y_{0}^{(2)}\) as follows:

\[v_{0}(y_{0}^{(2)}) =v_{0}^{(2)},\quad v_{1}(y_{0}^{(2)})=-\frac{dv_{0}}{dy}(y_{0}^{ (2)})\cdot
y_{1}^{(2)},\] \[\zeta_{1}(y_{0}^{(2)}) =\zeta_{1}^{(2)},\quad\zeta_{2}
(y_{0}^{(2)})=\zeta_{2}^{(2)}- \frac{d\zeta_{1}}{dy}(y_{0}^{(2)})\cdot y_{1}^{(2)},\] (3.96) \[J_{1}
(y_{0}^{(2)}) =J_{1}^{(2)},\quad J_{2}(y_{0}^{(2)})=J_{2}^{(2)}- \frac{dJ_{1}}{dy}(y_{0}^{(2)})
\cdot y_{1}^{(2)}.\]

Substituting (3.93) into (3.91) and expanding with respect to \(\mu\), one obtains equations for the \(i\)-th
approximations \(\zeta_{i}\) and \(J_{i}\):

\[\frac{d\zeta_{i}}{dy} = \mathcal{R}_{i}^{(\zeta)}(y),\] (3.97) \[\frac{dJ_{i}}{dy} =
\mathcal{R}_{i}^{(J)}(y).\]

The solution of this system is

\[\zeta_{i}(y) = \zeta_{i}(y_{0}^{(2)})+\int_{y_{0}^{(2)}}^{y}\mathcal{R}_{i}^{( \zeta)}
(s)\,\mathrm{d}s,\] (3.98) \[J_{i}(v) = J_{i}(y_{0}^{(2)})+\int_{y_{0}^{(2)}}^{y}\mathcal{R}_{i}^{(J)}
(s )\,\mathrm{d}s.\]

For \(i=1\) one has

\[\mathcal{R}_{1}^{(\zeta)}(y) = k^{1/2}\frac{f_{3}}{y^{2}-1-k(v_{0}(y)-1)},\] (3.99) \
[\mathcal{R}_{1}^{(J)}(y) = J_{0}k^{1/2}\frac{f_{4}}{y^{2}-1-k(v_{0}(y)-1)}\mathrm{e}^{-v_{0 }
(y)},\]
```

Fig. 3. Example of PDF-to-Markdown conversion done by Kosmos-2.5 with the assistance of CLD. In this example, the highlighted parts are the tokens proposed by CLD and accepted by Kosmos-2.5's validation steps.

Table 2. Ablation study results showing the impact of Copyable Text Identification (CTI) and Candidate Generation (CG) on inference time (t in seconds). Both modules contribute to reducing inference time, with their combination achieving the highest speed-up. CLD degrades to the original mPLD method when CTI and CG are removed.

	Backbone Model							
	Nougat-base		Kosmos-2.5		Llama-3.2-Vision		Qwen2-VL	
Modules	$t(s)$	Speed Up	$t(s)$	Speed Up	$t(s)$	Speed Up	$t(s)$	Speed Up
base (mPLD)	6.13	-	9.23	–	32.08	-	100.00	–
base + CTI	5.80 (+0.03)	1.05×	8.66 (+0.03)	1.06×	27.83 (+0.03)	1.15×	92.83 (+0.03)	1.07×
base + CG	5.78	1.06×	8.68	1.06×	29.30	1.09×	96.99	1.03×
base + CTI + CG	**5.60 (+0.03)**	**1.10×**	**7.85 (+0.03)**	**1.17×**	**27.61 (+0.03)**	**1.16×**	**91.88 (+0.03)**	**1.08×**

Table 3. Assisted Generation methods losslessly preserve the original output.

Assisted Generation Quality Loss		
Model	mPLD	CLD
Nougat-base	0%	0%
Kosmos-2.5	0%	0%
Llama3.2-Vision	0%	0%
Qwen2-VL	0%	0%

5.3 Ablation Study

Table 2 demonstrates the impact of different module combinations on inference time and relative speed-up for Nougat-base and Kosmos-2.5 backbone models. Additionally, ablation studies on Llama and Qwen2-VL show the same trend. These findings emphasize the practical relevance of our methods.

5.4 PDF-to-Markdown Conversion Quality

In addition to the conversion speed, we also discuss the conversion quality of the models. In this work, comparing the accuracy of individual models is highly unfeasible, mainly due to the following reasons:

- Assisted Generation is a lossless method and it doesn't change the original output. Therefore, we may quote its accuracy in the model's original papers.
- Neither Nougat nor Kosmos-2.5 have publicly released their test datasets, which may be due to copyright reasons described in Sect. 4.2. It is difficult for us to reproduce their results fairly.
- The output style of the PDF-to-Markdown conversion task is flexible. Specifically, the reading order of floating elements in a page, including tables and figures, is not fixed; Nougat tends to add floating elements at the end of a page, while Kosmos-2.5 tends to add floating elements at the beginning of a page.
- The formatting of tables and formulas is also flexible. Specifically, Nougat uses the LaTeX format for tables, while Kosmos-2.5 uses the Markdown format. Formulas can start and end with either a dollar sign or a backslash with parentheses.

For these reasons, we can only provide a very unfair comparison of conversion quality. Unquestionably, Assisted Generation does not degrade the quality of model generation, as shown in Table 3. We adopted the evaluation metric from the Nougat [4]. Our evaluation of the four models on our test datasets, as shown in Table 4. However, lower scores do not necessarily indicate poorer readability on a manual inspection basis, making this evaluation an imperfect quality assessment.

Table 4. PDF-to-Markdown Conversion Quality of Different Models. This is not a fair comparison, we are simply presenting the results.

Models	Edit Dist↓	BLEU↑	F1 ↑
Nougat-base	0.38	0.54	0.73
Kosmos-2.5	0.43	0.51	0.68
Llama-3.2-Vision	0.53	0.42	0.61
Qwen2-VL	0.46	0.47	0.64
Marker (Pipeline-based)	0.45	0.44	0.62

A case-by-case analysis revealed that Llama and Qwen2-VL struggled to follow instructions precisely. Llama frequently generates incorrect LaTeX code in formulas, often rendering them invalid in Markdown. Additionally, it tends to reconstruct PDF content as LaTeX rather than converting it to Markdown. Both Qwen2-VL and Llama misplace footnotes, placing them at the end of the document instead of their cited positions, increasing their error rates. We plan to refine our evaluation metrics in future work.

6 Conclusion

In this paper, we introduced mPLD and CLD, which are lightweight Assisted Generation methods for end-to-end PDF-to-Markdown conversion using decoder transformer models. mPLD does not add any parameters that require training, and it can be seamlessly added to an existing transformer decoder model. CLD is based on the off-the-shelf ERNIE Layout model. Minimal fine-tuning was performed, and the weights file size is kept at 27 MB.

The ever-increasing number of PDF publications appearing year after year shows no signs of slowing down. While pipeline-based approaches can help to get the flood of scientific information and new knowledge under control, the development of such technologies is very complex in practice and hinders the creation of infrastructures and systems to track research and assist the scientific community with applications such as dedicated scientific search engines and recommender systems.

Through our efforts, we hope to make end-to-end PDF-to-Markdown conversions with simpler structures that better drive accessibility and structured extraction of scientific information.

7 Limitations

In the work, we observed that CLD improves over mPLD mainly by extracting candidates more accurately through a filtering mechanism and a topping mechanism that better recognizes the current PDF-to-Markdown conversion progress.

However, CLD does not yet explicitly detect the position of the conversion progress of the decoder transformer on the page. The contemporaneous work, LOCR, which predicts the position of the next token on the PDF page using a miniature Prompt Module attached to Nougat, might enhance candidate generation. We plan to incorporate LOCR with CLD in the next step.

Kosmos-2.5, Nougat, Llama, and Qwen2-VL discard figures from pages, as they can only generate text. ERNIE Layout is capable of identifying them. Our goal is to explore additional ways to properly integrate figures into Markdown output. For example, Mistral OCR encodes images with base64 strings.

Acknowledgments. This work was conducted within the research project InsightsNet (insightsnet.org), which is funded by the Federal Ministry of Education and

Research (BMBF) under grant no. 01UG2130A. We gratefully acknowledge support from Dr. Wolfgang Stille and the hessian.AI Service Center (funded by the Federal Ministry of Education and Research, BMBF, grant no. 01IS22091) and the hessian.AI Innovation Lab (funded by the Hessian Ministry for Digital Strategy and Innovation, grant no. S-DIW04/0013/003). We want to thank Dr. Sabine Bartsch for supervising this research. We also thank the anonymous reviewers for their insightful comments and suggestions, which greatly improved the manuscript.

References

1. Grobid (2008–2024). https://github.com/kermitt2/grobid
2. getomni ai: zerox (2024). https://github.com/getomni-ai/zerox. gitHub repository
3. AI, M.: The llama 3 herd of models (2024). https://arxiv.org/abs/2407.21783
4. Blecher, L., Cucurull, G., Scialom, T., Stojnic, R.: Nougat: neural optical understanding for academic documents (2024). https://openreview.net/forum?id=fUtxNAKpdV
5. Cai, T., et al.: Medusa: simple LLM inference acceleration framework with multiple decoding heads. In: Salakhutdinov, R., et al. (eds.) Proceedings of the 41st International Conference on Machine Learning. Proceedings of Machine Learning Research, vol. 235, pp. 5209–5235. PMLR (2024). https://proceedings.mlr.press/v235/cai24b.html
6. Contributors, M.: Mineru: A one-stop, open-source, high-quality data extraction tool (2024). https://github.com/opendatalab/MinerU
7. Diem, M., Kleber, F., Sablatnig, R.: Text classification and document layout analysis of paper fragments. In: 2011 International Conference on Document Analysis and Recognition, pp. 854–858 (2011). https://doi.org/10.1109/ICDAR.2011.175
8. Duan, C., Tan, Z., Bartsch, S.: LaTeX rainbow: universal LaTeX to PDF document semantic & layout annotation framework. In: Ghosal, T., Grezes, F., Allen, T., Lockhart, K., Accomazzi, A., Blanco-Cuaresma, S. (eds.) Proceedings of the Second Workshop on Information Extraction from Scientific Publications, pp. 56–67. Association for Computational Linguistics, Bali (2023). https://doi.org/10.18653/v1/2023.wiesp-1.8. https://aclanthology.org/2023.wiesp-1.8/
9. Fu, D., et al.: Isobench: benchmarking multimodal foundation models on isomorphic representations. In: First Conference on Language Modeling (2024). https://openreview.net/forum?id=KZd1EErRJ1
10. Fu, Y., Bailis, P., Stoica, I., Zhang, H.: Break the sequential dependency of LLM inference using lookahead decoding. In: Salakhutdinov, R., Kolter, Z., Heller, K., Weller, A., Oliver, N., Scarlett, J., Berkenkamp, F. (eds.) Proceedings of the 41st International Conference on Machine Learning. Proceedings of Machine Learning Research, vol. 235, pp. 14060–14079. PMLR (2024). https://proceedings.mlr.press/v235/fu24a.html
11. Hu, E.J., et al.: LoRA: low-rank adaptation of large language models. In: International Conference on Learning Representations (2022). https://openreview.net/forum?id=nZeVKeeFYf9
12. Huang, Y., Lv, T., Cui, L., Lu, Y., Wei, F.: Layoutlmv3: pre-training for document AI with unified text and image masking. In: Proceedings of the 30th ACM International Conference on Multimedia, MM '22, pp. 4083–4091. Association for Computing Machinery, New York (2022). https://doi.org/10.1145/3503161.3548112

13. Jaume, G., Kemal Ekenel, H., Thiran, J.P.: Funsd: a dataset for form understanding in noisy scanned documents. In: 2019 International Conference on Document Analysis and Recognition Workshops (ICDARW), vol. 2, pp. 1–6 (2019). https://doi.org/10.1109/ICDARW.2019.10029
14. Gante, J.: Assisted generation: a new direction toward low-latency text generation (2023). https://doi.org/10.57967/hf/0638. https://huggingface.co/blog/assisted-generation
15. Kim, G., et al.: Ocr-free document understanding transformer. In: European Conference on Computer Vision (ECCV) (2022)
16. Leviathan, Y., Kalman, M., Matias, Y.: Fast inference from transformers via speculative decoding. In: Proceedings of the 40th International Conference on Machine Learning. ICML'23. JMLR.org (2023)
17. Li, K., et al.: Cross-domain document object detection: benchmark suite and method. In: 2020 IEEE/CVF Conference on Computer Vision and Pattern Recognition (CVPR), pp. 12912–12921 (2020). https://doi.org/10.1109/CVPR42600.2020.01293
18. Li, M., et al.: DocBank: a benchmark dataset for document layout analysis. In: Scott, D., Bel, N., Zong, C. (eds.) Proceedings of the 28th International Conference on Computational Linguistics, pp. 949–960. International Committee on Computational Linguistics, Barcelona (2020). https://doi.org/10.18653/v1/2020.coling-main.82
19. Li, Y., Wei, F., Zhang, C., Zhang, H.: EAGLE-2: faster inference of language models with dynamic draft trees. In: Al-Onaizan, Y., Bansal, M., Chen, Y.N. (eds.) Proceedings of the 2024 Conference on Empirical Methods in Natural Language Processing, pp. 7421–7432. Association for Computational Linguistics, Miami (2024). https://doi.org/10.18653/v1/2024.emnlp-main.422. https://aclanthology.org/2024.emnlp-main.422
20. Li, Y., Wei, F., Zhang, C., Zhang, H.: EAGLE: speculative sampling requires rethinking feature uncertainty. In: Salakhutdinov, R., et al. (eds.) Proceedings of the 41st International Conference on Machine Learning. Proceedings of Machine Learning Research, vol. 235, pp. 28935–28948. PMLR (2024). https://proceedings.mlr.press/v235/li24bt.html
21. Lin, J., et al.: Awq: activation-aware weight quantization for llm compression and acceleration. In: MLSys (2024)
22. Lv, T., et al.: Kosmos-2.5: a multimodal literate model. arXiv preprint arXiv:2309.11419 (2023)
23. Mathpix: mathpix-markdown-it (2024). https://github.com/Mathpix/mathpix-markdown-it. gitHub repository
24. Mghari, H.E.: llama-ocr (2024). https://github.com/Nutlope/llama-ocr. gitHub repository
25. Mindee: doctr: Document text recognition (2021). https://github.com/mindee/doctr
26. NormXU: Ernie-layout-pytorch (2023). https://github.com/NormXU/ERNIE-Layout-Pytorch. gitHub repository
27. Peng, Q., et al.: ERNIE-layout: layout knowledge enhanced pre-training for visually-rich document understanding. In: Goldberg, Y., Kozareva, Z., Zhang, Y. (eds.) Findings of the Association for Computational Linguistics: EMNLP 2022, pp. 3744–3756. Association for Computational Linguistics, Abu Dhabi (2022). https://doi.org/10.18653/v1/2022.findings-emnlp.274. https://aclanthology.org/2022.findings-emnlp.274/

28. Pfitzmann, B., Auer, C., Dolfi, M., Nassar, A.S., Staar, P.: Doclaynet: a large human-annotated dataset for document-layout segmentation. In: Proceedings of the 28th ACM SIGKDD Conference on Knowledge Discovery and Data Mining, KDD '22, pp. 3743–3751. Association for Computing Machinery, New York (2022). https://doi.org/10.1145/3534678.3539043
29. pymupdf: Pymupdf (2024). https://github.com/pymupdf/PyMuPDF. gitHub repository
30. Quattrini, F., Zaccagnino, C., Cascianelli, S., Righi, L., Cucchiara, R.: mugat: improving single-page document parsing by providing multi-page context (2024)
31. Saxena, A.: Prompt lookup decoding (2023). https://github.com/apoorvumang/prompt-lookup-decoding/
32. Shen, Z., Lo, K., Wang, L.L., Kuehl, B., Weld, D.S., Downey, D.: VILA: improving structured content extraction from scientific PDFs using visual layout groups. Trans. Assoc. Comput. Linguist. **10**, 376–392 (2022). https://doi.org/10.1162/tacl_a_00466. https://aclanthology.org/2022.tacl-1.22/
33. Su, J., Lu, Y., Pan, S., Murtadha, A., Wen, B., Liu, Y.: Roformer: enhanced transformer with rotary position embedding (2023). https://arxiv.org/abs/2104.09864
34. Summed-AI: parallex (2024). https://github.com/Summed-AI/parallex. gitHub repository
35. Sun, Y., Zhou, D., Lin, C., He, C., Ouyang, W., Zhong, H.S.: LOCR: location-guided transformer for optical character recognition. In: Al-Onaizan, Y., Bansal, M., Chen, Y.N. (eds.) Findings of the Association for Computational Linguistics: EMNLP 2024, pp. 5480–5497. Association for Computational Linguistics, Miami (2024). https://doi.org/10.18653/v1/2024.findings-emnlp.314. https://aclanthology.org/2024.findings-emnlp.314
36. Team, D.S.: Docling technical report. Technical report (2024). https://doi.org/10.48550/arXiv.2408.09869
37. VikParuchuri: marker (2025). https://github.com/VikParuchuri/marker. gitHub repository
38. Wang, P., et al.: Qwen2-vl: enhancing vision-language model's perception of the world at any resolution (2024). https://arxiv.org/abs/2409.12191
39. Wu, X., Hu, Z., Du, X., Yang, J., He, L.: Document layout analysis via dynamic residual feature fusion. In: 2021 IEEE International Conference on Multimedia and Expo (ICME), pp. 1–6 (2021). https://doi.org/10.1109/ICME51207.2021.9428465
40. Xu, Y., et al.: LayoutLMv2: multi-modal pre-training for visually-rich document understanding. In: Zong, C., Xia, F., Li, W., Navigli, R. (eds.) Proceedings of the 59th Annual Meeting of the Association for Computational Linguistics and the 11th International Joint Conference on Natural Language Processing, vol. 1: Long Papers, pp. 2579–2591. Association for Computational Linguistics (2021). https://doi.org/10.18653/v1/2021.acl-long.201. https://aclanthology.org/2021.acl-long.201/
41. Xu, Y., Li, M., Cui, L., Huang, S., Wei, F., Zhou, M.: Layoutlm: pre-training of text and layout for document image understanding. In: Proceedings of the 26th ACM SIGKDD International Conference on Knowledge Discovery & Data Mining, KDD '20, pp. 1192–1200. Association for Computing Machinery, New York (2020). https://doi.org/10.1145/3394486.3403172
42. Yang, H., Hsu, W.H.: Vision-based layout detection from scientific literature using recurrent convolutional neural networks. In: 2020 25th International Conference on Pattern Recognition (ICPR), pp. 6455–6462 (2021). https://doi.org/10.1109/ICPR48806.2021.9412557

43. Yang, N., et al.: Inference with reference: lossless acceleration of large language models (2023). https://arxiv.org/abs/2304.04487
44. Zhao, Y., Xie, Z., Liang, C., Zhuang, C., Gu, J.: Lookahead: an inference acceleration framework for large language model with lossless generation accuracy. In: Proceedings of the 30th ACM SIGKDD Conference on Knowledge Discovery and Data Mining, KDD '24, pp. 6344–6355. Association for Computing Machinery, New York (2024). https://doi.org/10.1145/3637528.3671614
45. Zhong, X., Tang, J., Jimeno Yepes, A.: Publaynet: largest dataset ever for document layout analysis. In: 2019 International Conference on Document Analysis and Recognition (ICDAR), pp. 1015–1022 (2019). https://doi.org/10.1109/ICDAR.2019.00166
46. Zhu, W., Sokhandan, N., Yang, G., Martin, S., Sathyanarayana, S.: Docbed: a multi-stage ocr solution for documents with complex layouts. In: Proceedings of the AAAI Conference on Artificial Intelligence, vol. 36, no. 11, pp. 12643–12649 (2022). https://doi.org/10.1609/aaai.v36i11.21539. https://ojs.aaai.org/index.php/AAAI/article/view/21539

Comparison of Pipelines, Seq2seq Models, and LLMs for Rare Disease Information Extraction

Shashank Gupta, Xuguang Ai, Yuhang Jiang, and Ramakanth Kavuluru(✉)

University of Kentucky, Lexington, KY, USA
ramakanth.kavuluru@uky.edu

Abstract. End-to-end relation extraction (E2ERE) is an important application of natural language processing (NLP) in biomedicine. The extracted relations populate knowledge graphs and drive more high level applications in knowledge discovery and information retrieval. E2ERE is frequently handled at the sentence level involving continuous entities. A more complex setting is document level E2ERE with discontinuous and overlapping/nested entities. We identified a recently introduced RE dataset for rare diseases (`RareDis`) that has these complex traits. Among current E2ERE methods, we see three well-known paradigms: (1) pipeline based approaches where a named entity recognition (NER) model's output is input to a relation classification (RC) model; (2) joint sequence-to-sequence style models where the raw input text is directly transformed into relations through linearization schemas; and (3) generative large language models (LLMs), where prompts, fine-tuning, and in-context learning are being leveraged for RE. While LLMs are becoming popular because of tools such as ChatGPT, the biomedical NLP community needs to carefully evaluate which paradigm is more suitable for E2ERE. In this effort, using the `RareDis` dataset as a complex use-case, we evaluate the best representative models from each of the three paradigms for E2ERE. Our findings reveal that pipeline models are still the best, while sequence-to-sequence models are not far behind. We verify these findings on a second E2ERE dataset for chemical-protein interactions. Although LLMs are more suitable for zero-shot settings, our results show that it is better to work with more conventional models trained and tailored for E2ERE when training data is available. Our contribution is also the first to conduct E2ERE for the `RareDis` dataset.

Keywords: biomedical relation extraction · end-to-end models · large language models · encoder-decoder models · information extraction

1 Introduction

Named entities and relations among them are basic units of information in many disciplines. A relation is typically expressed as a triple that has a subject entity and an object entity connected via a predicate (or relation type) as in the example (`subject`: atorvastatin, `predicate`: treats, `object`: hyperlipidemia). Disease

R. Ichise (Ed.): NLDB 2025, LNCS 15836, pp. 49–63, 2026.
https://doi.org/10.1007/978-3-031-97141-9_4

and treatment mechanisms are often driven at the biological level by protein-protein and chemical-protein interactions while clinical relations such as drug-disease treatment relations and disease-symptom causative relations are helpful in providing care. Most new relational information is first discussed in textual narratives (e.g., scientific literature, clinical notes, or social media posts), and extracting and storing it as triples enables effective search systems [5], high-level reasoning, hypothesis generation, and knowledge discovery applications [11]. As such, named entity recognition (NER) and relation extraction (RE) have become standard tasks in biomedical natural language processing (BioNLP) [14].

Many RE efforts in the past assume that the entity spans are already provided as part of the input and hence addressed an easier problem of relation classification (RC) [13,34]. However, a more realistic setting is the ability to extract both entity spans and associated relations from the raw text where entities are not provided. RE in this setting is generally called end-to-end relation extraction (E2ERE). With the recent deluge of deep neural networks (or deep learning methods), the NLP community has been focusing more on E2ERE efforts [19,26,31]. Efforts have also been expanded from single sentence E2ERE to a more complex setting of extractions at the document level, involving cross-sentence relations, where entities expressed in different sentences are to be linked [23,29]. Additional intricacies arise when named entities are discontinuous or when their spans overlap [16]. For example, consider the string "*accumulation of* fats (lipids) called *GM 2 gangliosides*," where entity span "accumulation of GM 2 gangliosides" is discontinuous with a gap involving outside words. In the example phrase "central pain syndrome," both the full three-word string and the middle word "pain" can constitute two different entities, where the latter entity is fully nested in the longer 3-word entity. Thus far, we have not seen efforts handling these complex document-level E2ERE settings involving discontinuous and overlapping/nested entities. In this paper, we address this using the recently introduced RE dataset called `RareDis` [18], which focuses on information extraction for rare diseases and has the complex traits indicated earlier. Although there is another dataset that focuses on rare diseases at the sentence level [7], we use `RareDis` since it operates at the document level.

Over the past decade, neural methods especially those involving dense word embeddings have supplanted conventional NLP methods that relied on n-gram statistics. For E2ERE, joint learning neural methods that simultaneously optimized for NER and RE objectives [6,27] have gained popularity over pipeline-based methods that build two separate models for NER and RE, where the NER model's output is fed to the RE model. However, the recent Princeton University Relation Extraction (PURE) framework [33] proposed an intuitive pipeline method that takes advantage of the so-called typed "entity markers" to encapsulate entity spans provided as input to contextualized language models (LMs). The PURE method reignited the relevance of cleverly designed pipeline methods when compared with joint learning methods. Simultaneously, sequence-to-sequence (seq2seq) models that became popular for machine translation have been repurposed [21] effectively for E2ERE where the encoder-decoder architecture is used to transform raw text to directly output relations encoded through so-called "linearization schemas" and "copy mechanism" [30]. The state-of-the-art (SoTA) for this paradigm of models is the Seq2Rel architecture [9] that inherently allows for E2ERE. Another latest seq2seq architecture called T5 (Text-To-Text Transfer Transformer) [25] and its variant Flan-T5 (Instruction finetuned version of T5) [4] have shown promising results in many NLP tasks needing language understanding. Finally, generative pre-trained transformers (GPTs) have gained traction and publicity (thanks to ChatGPT), especially for zero-shot and few-shot settings [3]. In biomedicine, BioGPT [17] and BioMedLM [2] have been shown to work well for relation extraction and question answering, among generative decoder-only language models (LMs), simply called LLMs[1], producing SoTA scores on a few datasets. Thus we identify (a) PURE for pipelines, (b) Seq2Rel, T5, and its variant Flan-T5 for seq2seq models, and (c) BioMedLM[2] for generative (autoregressive) LMs as representative models for prevailing competing paradigms for RE. Now the central question is, which of these approaches works well for the complex document level E2ERE task involving discontinuous and overlapping entities manifesting in the `RareDis` dataset? Toward answering this, we make the following contributions in this paper.

- We explore and provide descriptive statistics of the `RareDis` dataset and fix certain formatting/annotation errors in the original dataset (acknowledged by its creators) to ensure availability for the community.
- We adapt the PURE pipeline approach to the `RareDis` dataset since the original method does not handle discontinuous and nested entities.
- We design linearization schemas for the Seq2Rel method and appropriate supervised prompting strategies for T5 and BioMedLM in the context of E2ERE for the `RareDis` dataset.
- We provide quantitative evaluations of the four models (and associated variants) and conduct qualitative evaluations through manual error analyses.
- We also include zero-shot results with frontier LLMs, specifically Open AI GPT-4 and GPT-o1, to assess out-of-the-box performance of recent advances.

Currently, our effort is the first to address E2ERE for the `RareDis` dataset and also to compare SoTA approaches arising from three different competing paradigms for RE. We make publicly available the modified `RareDis` dataset and code for all our experiments: https://github.com/bionlproc/Raredis/.

---

[1] We realize that some definitions of LLMs also include encoder-models or encoder-decoder models. However, the general consensus and the default use of the term refers to decoder-only models these days.

[2] Though we experimented with BioGPT models, they are smaller than BioMedLM and were quite inferior (more later), and as such our focus in this manuscript is more on BioMedLM, a 2.7B model exclusively trained on biomedical literature. While there are much bigger biomedical LLMs ($\geq$ 7B parameters), BioMedLM is already **eight times** the size of our top pipeline model and considering the major performance gap (13 F1 points), for this paper we deemed it may not be judicious to try even bigger models, given cloud GPU costs.

2 The RareDis Dataset

The National Institutes of Health (NIH) estimates that around 7,000 rare diseases impact between 25 and 30 million Americans, which translates to approximately 1 out of every 10 Americans [20]. Around 95% of the known rare diseases currently lack any treatment options [20]. Because these diseases are so rare, they can be challenging to diagnose and treat—nearly 95% of rare diseases have no known cure, and the number of drugs available for treating these conditions is limited to 100 [15]. The average diagnostic delay is around seven years [10]. Many rare diseases are genetic in nature and are caused by mutations in a single gene. However, because there are thousands of rare diseases, each with unique symptoms and genetic causes, developing effective treatments can be a significant challenge. Developing a structured compendium of information about rare diseases has the potential to help expedite search, discovery, and hypothesis generation for these conditions. This necessitates developing NLP models for RE in this setting and toward this goal, Maritinez-deMiguel et al. [18] created an annotated corpus for rare disease-related information extraction. This resource is based on the database of articles about rare diseases maintained by the National Organization for Rare Disorders (https://rarediseases.org/rare-diseases/). The dataset contains six entity types and six relation types and the annotation process is described in detail by the authors [18].

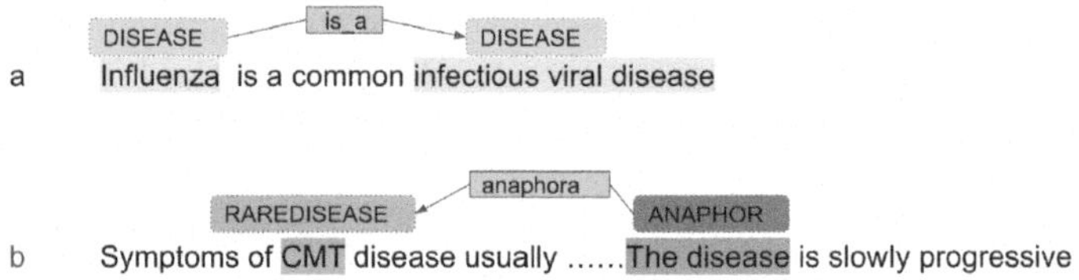

Fig. 1. Examples of **is_a** and **anaphora** relations in the RareDis dataset.

2.1 Entity and Relations Types

The six entity types in RareDis are: **disease**, **rare disease**, **symptom**, **sign**, **anaphor**, and **rare skin disease** with frequencies shown in the first six rows of Table 1. There are six relation types (with counts shown in the last six rows of Table 1): **produces** (relation between any disease entity and a sign/symptom produced by that entity), **increase_risk_of** (relation between a disease entity and another disease entity where the subject disease increases the likelihood of suffering from the object disease), **is_a** (relation between a given disease and its classification as a more general disease), **is_acron** (relation between an acronym and its full or expanded form), **is_synon** (relation between two different names designating the same disease) and **anaphora** (relation of an anaphor entity with its antecedent entity).

Here an anaphor entity refers to pronouns or pronominal constructs (e.g., 'it" or "this disease") that point to a named entity that is already mentioned in the preceding context (the "antecedent" of the **anaphora** relation). An example is shown in Fig. 1. The dataset contains discontinuous and overlapping/nested entities as discussed with examples in Sect. 1; Table 2 throws light on the relative frequency of these situations where "flat" corresponds to continuous entities. While in both tables in this section we show training, development, and test set counts, the original dataset consisted of only training and development datasets where the authors claim to withhold the test set for a future shared task, which has not happened yet. We split up their training dataset into training and development for our experiments and their development split became our test split.

Table 1. Statistics of entity types (first six rows) and relation types (last six rows) in RareDis.

Type	Training	Dev	Test
sign	2945	798	528
rare disease	2533	624	480
disease	1369	278	230
anaphor	913	195	151
skin rare disease	393	58	45
symptom	275	44	24
produces	3256	850	556
anaphora	918	195	151
is_a	544	149	88
increase_risk_of	161	8	22
is_acron	142	44	34
is_synon	66	14	16

Table 2. Counts of entity types in the corpus.

Dataset	Training	Dev	Test
Flat	7103	1666	1212
Discontinuous	528	136	103
Overlapped	720	166	112
Nested	77	29	31
Total	8428	1997	1458

2.2 Modifications to the Original Dataset

While exploring the dataset, we observed some annotation issues that we confirmed with the creators of the `RareDis` dataset through email communication. Next, we describe what they are and how we fixed them at a high level in this section. We created a custom train, validate, test split of the full dataset after fixing the following errors. This modified dataset is available on our GitHub repo indicated at the end of Sect. 1.

- *Relation argument error:* Fig. 2 shows an example of how the annotations are provided for each instance. For this example, we see the entities (T1, ..., T9) listed first along with types, character based offsets, and lexical spans. Next, relations between entities are listed (R1, ..., R5) along with the relation type and the arguments (subject and object). Although there are only nine entities, we see for anaphora relation R5, the second argument is T90 with a trailing 0 after 9. This happened several times—arguments in relations referring to entity IDs that are not present in the preceding entity list. This almost always

T1	RAREDISEASE 0 28	Vitamin-D deficiency rickets
T2	SIGN 109 154	insufficient amounts of vitamin D in the body
T3	DISEASE 160 178	vitamin deficiency
T4	RAREDISEASE 571 599	vitamin D deficiency rickets
T5	DISEASE 608 620	bone disease
T6	SIGN 608 620	bone disease
T7	SIGN 622 634	restlessness
T8	SIGN 640 651	slow growth
T9	ANAPHOR 653 666	This disorder
R1	Produces Arg1:T1 Arg2:T2	
R2	Produces Arg1:T4 Arg2:T6	
R3	Produces Arg1:T4 Arg2:T7	
R4	Produces Arg1:T4 Arg2:T8	
R5	Anaphora Arg1:T4 Arg2:T90	

Fig. 2. An example of the argument error due to an extra trailing zero in entity IDs. Here, T90 ought to be just T9.

happened with a trailing extra zero. We safely removed that zero and it fixed all these errors, which accounted for 9% of the total number of relations. In Fig. 2, the anaphora relation R5 was referring to the bigram "This disorder".

- *Span mismatch error:* There were a few occasions (< 1% of the full dataset) where the character offsets for entities captured an extra character than needed or missed the last character of a word. We used simple rules to remove the extra character or add the missing character. For example, in the sentence "Balantidiasis is a rare **infectious disease** caused by the single celled (protozoan) parasite Balantidium coli," the bold phrase was annotated as [T24, DISEASE,1272 1289, infectious **diseas**] with a missing trailing character 'e'.
- *Offset order error:* For some discontinuous entities where more than one span is part of the full entity, the order used for the spans was not left to right and we simply reordered them as such.

3 Methods

As outlined earlier (Sect. 1), we experiment with three different SoTA approaches each representing a competing paradigm for E2ERE. Each of these is highly involved and hence we focus on high level explanations of how they work.

3.1 Pipeline: The PURE Approach

PURE by Zhong and Chen [33] is a span-based model that has two different models for NER and RE parts of the E2ERE system. It improved upon prior joint modeling approaches even though it separately trains NER and RE models. The main argument by Zhong and Chen, the authors of PURE, is that NER and RE need different representations of tokens because they need different types of signals to make the predictions; and combining the signals can hurt the performance of both.

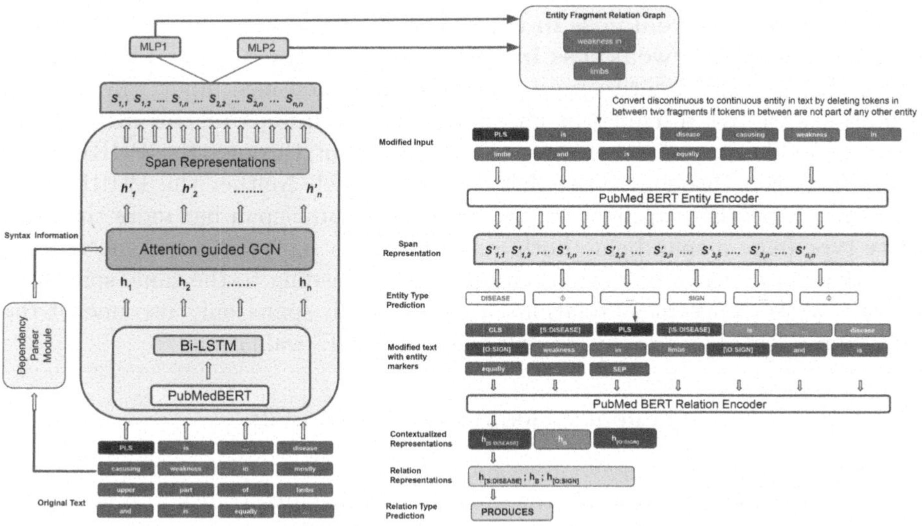

Fig. 3. Pipeline approach using SODNER and PURE models for E2ERE.

One weakness of PURE is that it does not handle discontinuous entities in its NER component while it easily handles flat and nested entities. So we needed to adapt the PURE approach to the `RareDis` setting. Since PURE is pipeline based, we could simply use a different NER model for identifying discontinuous entities and retain the PURE model to spot flat and nested entities. Hence, we use a specialized model that was exclusively developed for handling discontinuous entities called SODNER [16], which is also a span-based NER model that models discontinuous NER task as a classification problem to predict whether entity fragments with gaps ought to be linked to form a new entity. To do this, SODNER uses dependency parses of the input document to guide a graph convolutional neural (GCN) network that obtains enhanced contextual embeddings to link disparate fragments and form discontinuous entities. Figure 3 shows the schematic of the pipeline we use. It starts on the left with the SODNER model identifying discontinuous entities.

Even if SODNER successfully identifies discontinuous entities, PURE's relation extraction model cannot handle them. The PURE relation model puts exactly one start and one end entity marker token around each candidate subject (or object) entity span. This modified input is passed through the contextual language model (such as PubMedBERT) and the marker token embeddings are used to predict the relation type. This is reflected by the purple [S:Disease] and [\S:Disease] tokens on the right side of Fig. 3. But SODNER outputs multiple fragments for discontinuous entities. Rather than change the PURE relation model architecture, we use the discontinuous entity fragments and straightforward rules to convert the input sentence to a modified one where the discontinuous entities are rendered in a continuous format. For instance, consider the input, "weakness in the muscles of the arms and legs," which contains two entities: one flat entity, "**weakness in the muscles of the arms** and legs" and one discontinuous entity, "**weakness in the muscles of the** arms and **legs**." Both entities have the gold entity type **Sign**. Our modified new input will read as: "**weakness in the muscles of the arms** and **weakness in the muscles of the legs**". This transformed sentence is now input through the PURE NER model and then through the PURE relation model. Neither the PURE NER model nor SODNER can handle cases where the same span has more than one entity type (e.g., a span being both a disease and a sign). This is a special case of overlapped entities where the overlap is exact, leading to the same span having two types. Since most relations involving such spans only use one of the entity types, this has not caused major issues in RE evaluation.

3.2 Sequence-to-Sequence: Seq2Rel & T5 Models

The Seq2Rel model [9] model uses an encoder-decoder framework to process the input document and output relations akin to machine translation where the source language sentence is ingested into the encoder and the target language sentence is output by the decoder one token at a time. Here the target sequence is essentially a list of relations. Unlike the machine translation setting where the target is a natural language sequence where an order is inherent, relations do not have any order amongst them. Hence, during training an order is imposed on the relations in a document. Special tokens are also used to represent entity types. For example, the relation R2 in Fig. 2 indicates: (**Rare disease** "Vitamin D Deficiency Rickets", produces, **sign** "bone disease"), where the entity types are in bold. This will be linearized in Seq2Rel as: Vitamin D Deficiency Rickets `@RareDisease@` bone disease `@Sign@` `@PRODUCES@`, where `@ENTITY-TYPE@` and `@RELATION-TYPE@` are special tokens indicating entity and relation types, respectively. The `@ENTITY-TYPE@` tokens are preceded by the actual entity spans in the input. If an input does not contain any relations, a special `@NOREL@` is coded as the output. The order imposed during training is simply the order in which the entities occur in the document. This is reflected in Fig. 2 where relations involving entities that occur earlier in the document are annotated before relations that involve entities that occur later. This left-to-right order is followed until all relations are output followed by a special end of sequence token `@END@` signaling that all relations have been output. Besides this linearization schema, a "copy mechanism" [30] is applied to the decoder, restricting it to generate tokens only from the observed input sequence, unlike the full vocabulary of the target language in machine translation. This mechanism enables the decoder to output spans of the input text that correspond to entities, as well as special tokens representing relation labels that connect these entities. The Seq2Rel model [9] uses a PubMedBERT model as the encoder and a long short-term memory (LSTM) network as the decoder.

T5, developed by Google Research, challenges the conventional task-specific architectures by converting every NLP problem into a text-to-text input-output format. A key aspect of T5 is its baseline pre-training objective. For this, a large free text dataset known as the "Colossal Clean Crawled Corpus" was created and random spans of text are masked with the model tasked to predict these spans. Unlike masked language modeling in BERT models, each masked spans is replaced with only one sentinel token given a unique ID. This approach helps the model learn a broad understanding of language and context. This baseline model is further trained on a suite a suite of NLP tasks (e.g., sentiment analysis, word sense disambiguation, and sentence similarity) in the text-to-text format. Another significant feature of T5 is its scalability, with versions ranging from small (60 million) to extremely large (11 billion), allowing it to be tailored to specific computational constraints and performance requirements.

Table 3. Templates used to encode **RareDis** relations as BioMedLM outputs.

Relation type	**Natural language output template** (An example for the template)
produces	ent_1Span is a ent_1Type that **produces** ent_2Span, as a ent_2Type (Asherman's syndrome is a rare disease that produces abdominal pain, as a symptom)
anaphora	The term ent_2Span is an **anaphor** that refers back to the entity of the ent_1Type ent_1Span (The term "it" is an anaphor that refers back to the entity of the disease encephalitis)
is_synon	The ent_1Type ent_1Span and the ent_2Type ent_2Span are **synonyms** (The disease diastrophic dysplasia and the rare disease disastrophic dwarfism are synonyms)
is_acron	The **acronym** ent_1Span stands for ent_2Span, a ent_2Type (The acronym LQTS stands for long QT syndrome, a rare disease)
increases_risk_of	The presence of the ent_1Type ent_1Span **increases the risk of** developing the ent_2Type of ent_2Span (The presence of the disease neutropenia increases the risk of developing the disease infections)
is_a	The ent_1Type ent_1Span **is a** type of ent_2Span, a ent_2Type (The rare skin disease Bowen disease is a type of skin disorder, a disease)

Flan-T5 is an extension of T5 that is *instruction fine-tuned* on 1800 tasks. During this phase, the model is fine-tuned on a diverse range of tasks but with instructions provided in natural language. This training method enables Flan-T5 to understand and execute tasks based on straightforward instructions, making it more flexible and applicable to a wide range of real-world scenarios without requiring extensive task-specific data. It is fine-tuned both with and without exemplars (i.e., zero-shot and few-shot) and with and without *chain-of-thought* [28], enabling generalization across a range of evaluation scenarios. Please note that unlike Seq2Rel architecture, the outputs for T5 models variants are expected to following natural sentence structures, which are discussed in the next section as they are common to both T5 and GPT models.

3.3 GPT Models: BioMedLM, GPT-4, and GPT-O1

Generative pre-trained transformers (GPTs), also called LLMs, have captured the fascination of the general public and researchers alike, especially since the introduction of ChatGPT in December 2022. However, the in-context learning and few-shot capabilities have already surfaced in June 2020, when Open AI released GPT-3 [3]. Building on the decoder component of the transformer architecture with the main objective of autoregressive left to right next token prediction task, they have excelled at text generation tasks (e.g., summarization). However, there is a growing interest in assessing their capabilities for language understanding tasks including relation extraction. BioGPT [17] and BioMedLM [2] have been pre-trained from scratch on biomedical abstracts from PubMed and full text articles from PubMed Central (from the corresponding subset from Pile [8]) based on the GPT-2 model [24]. In this effort, we focus on BioMedLM, a 2.7B parameter model, comprised of 32 layers, a hidden size of 2560, and 20 attention heads. BioMedLM is an order of magnitude larger than BioGPT and nearly twice as large as BioGPT$_{large}$. It has been shown to be superior to BioGPT models (including in our experiments for this paper where BioGPT underperforms by 10-15% in F-score). Hence, we only show BioMedLM results in this manuscript for the sake of clarify and simplicity. Unlike Seq2Rel whose sequence generation capabilities are highly constrained to terms observed in the input, BioMedLM and BioGPT are purely generative, and supervised fine-tuning involves using appropriate prompts and output templates. Technically, we could simply use the linearization schemas introduced for Seq2Rel. However, these generative models generate natural language statements and are not quite adept at following unnatural-looking templates—our initial experiments using a Seq2Rel style output schemas have failed. So, we considered two types of schemas here:

- `rel-is` template: This output template is the same as that used by the original BioGPT paper for E2ERE: "The relation between **subject-span** and **object-span** is **relationType.noun**," where **relationType.noun** is the noun form of the predicate. With this template, as an example, the output for the gold relation (Wilm's tumor, is_a, kidney cancer) is: "The relationship between Wilm's tumor and kidney cancer is hyponym". We can see here that we converted "is a" predicate to a noun representation "hyponym" in the template and a similar strategy was followed for all predicates.
- `natural-lang`: We came up with different natural language templates tailored to each relation type in `RareDis`. They are fully specified in Table 3, each with a representative example.

In addition to supervised experiments, we also use a customized JSON output template (available in project's GitHub repo) to generate zero-shot results from Open AI API calls to GPT-4 and GPT-o1 models, the latter being a reasoning model with test time "chain of thought" approach [22].

3.4 Training Objectives and Evaluation Metrics

For the SODNER+PURE pipeline model, the training objective is the well-known cross entropy function for both NER and RE components. Seq2Rel and BioMedLM, however, produce sequences (based on the schemas and templates selected) that need to be interpreted back into the triple format (which we accomplish using regular expressions). Since their outputs are sequences, the training objective is the well-known auto-regressive language model objective based on predicting the next token given previously predicted tokens. The loss function is the average cross-entropy per target word (more details in Chapter 9.7 of Jurafsky and Martin [12]).

For evaluation, we note that `RareDis` annotations are at the span level and hence the same exact relation connecting the same entities can occur multiple times if it is discussed several times in the document. However, Seq2Rel and BioMedLM do not keep track of the number of times a relation occurs as they are generative and do not operate on spans; but the pipeline models output all connections as they operate at the span level. To ensure fair evaluation, if the same relation occurs multiple times within an instance, it is collapsed into a single occurrence. This is natural and harmless because there is no loss of information if duplicate relations are ignored. Since Seq2Rel and BioMedLM produce sequences, we use regular expressions on top of the output templates and schemas to produce the triples we need. The evaluation metrics are precision, recall, and F1-score, which are standard in RE. For a relation to be counted as correctly predicted, the subject and object entity types, their spans, and the relation type all need to exactly match the ground truth relation.

4 Experiments and Results

For all experiments, learning rates, batch sizes, and numbers of epochs were determined based on experiments on the validation dataset and are discussed in the **supplementary_info** file at the GitHub link from the introduction.

We needed some post-processing tricks to handle the idiosyncrasies of the three different models. As we discussed earlier in Sect. 3.1, for the pipeline models, since discontinuous entities are not handled natively by the PURE relation model, we had to transform the inputs to render the discontinuous entities in a flat fashion before passing them on to the PURE model. For the Seq2Rel model, due to the WordPiece tokenization in BERT models, the output sometimes contains extra spaces around hyphens and brackets. To align such output strings with the input text, as a post-processing step, we removed these additional spaces, specifically around hyphens, curved brackets, and forward slashes. For the rel-is template, T5 and its variant were predicting the synonym relation with the string **"synonyms"**; so as a part of the post-processing, we replaced with "synonym."

The main results of the comparison using different models are presented in Table 4. For BioMedLM and T5 models, the 'copyInstruct' column in the table indicates the additional input prompt discussed earlier in this section where models are directed to only generate tokens observed in the input. We observe that the SODNER+PURE pipeline (with PubMedBERT$_{base}$ encoder) produces the best F1-score of 52.2, which is 5 points more than the best-performing Seq2Rel model with the PubMedBERT$_{large}$ encoder (47.15 F1), 5.2 points better than the best-performing model from T5 family (Flan-T5-large), and 13 points more than best performing BioMedLM model (38.9 F1). The pipeline's performance does not increase when using the PubMedBERT$_{large}$ model. For Seq2Rel, using PubMedBERT$_{large}$ outperforms a model with PubMedBERT$_{base}$ (44.53 F1) by 2.5 points, with an increase in both precision and recall. Potentially, the increased model capacity of PubMedBERT$_{large}$ enables it to capture more complex and subtle relationships between medical terms and concepts. However, it is not clear why similar gains were not observed with PubMedBERT$_{large}$ in the pipeline.

Table 4. Performances of different models on the `RareDis` dataset.

Method	Configuration	copyInstruct	Score		
			P	R	F
SODNER + PURE	PubMedBERT$_{base}$	NA	55.99	**48.89**	**52.20**
SODNER + PURE	PubMedBERT$_{large}$	NA	**56.20**	48.52	52.08
Seq2Rel	PubMedBERT$_{base}$	NA	47.60	40.90	44.53
	PubMedBERT$_{large}$	NA	51.46	43.51	47.15
Flan-T5-Large	`rel-is`	yes	46.52	46.58	46.55
	`rel-is`	no	48.63	45.54	47.04
	`natural-lang`	yes	43.83	42.82	43.32
	`natural-lang`	no	40.07	40.17	40.12
T5-3B	`rel-is`	yes	41.13	39.36	40.22
	`rel-is`	no	45.72	41.50	43.51
	`natural-lang`	yes	44.25	40.71	42.40
	`natural-lang`	no	37.80	41.21	39.43
Flan-T5-XL	`rel-is`	yes	45.00	40.82	42.82
	`rel-is`	no	44.16	38.10	40.91
	`natural-lang`	yes	44.68	42.87	43.76
	`natural-lang`	no	42.05	40.87	41.45
BioMedLM	`rel-is`	yes	40.19	29.68	34.14
	`rel-is`	no	42.14	36.10	38.89
	`natural-lang`	yes	38.64	32.81	35.49
	`natural-lang`	no	44.22	33.76	38.29
GPT-4 (zero-shot)	JSON template	NA	12.27	09.11	10.46
GPT-o1 (zero-shot)	JSON template	NA	26.42	16.63	20.41

The best performance for BioMedLM is an F1 score of 38.89 using the `rel-is` template for prompting the model when copy instructions were not provided. When copy instructions are not provided, `rel-is` does slightly better (<1% F1) and when copy instructions are not provided, `natural-lang` does better job (1.35 of points gain) So looks like there is no advantage to using copy instructions. (However, when using the smaller **BioGPT** models, the natural language prompting seemed to perform slightly better than the `rel-is` template.) Note that, BioMedLM's best performance is still $\approx$ 6 points lower than then Seq2Rel's best score and 11 points lower than the pipeline score. Note that BioMedLM is over eight times larger than our best-performing pipeline model (considering it has three encoders based on the encoder PubMedBERT$_{base}$, which has

110M parameters). However, its low performance compared to the pipeline is not surprising because LLMs are autoregressive and do not benefit from language understanding arising from the bidirectional masked language modeling objective used in BERT models. Although the original BioMedLM [2] effort did not perform RE, it reports SOTA scores on biomedical Q&A tasks. The smaller BioGPT models were shown to do better than BERT models for E2ERE too. Hence we repurposed them for this RE task and found that BioMedLM outperformed BioGPT models [17] by 10–15% in F1 score. Hence, we do not see these as worthy of reporting in this manuscript.

The best-performing model from the T5 family is Flan-T5-large with an F1 score of 47 using the `rel-is` template for prompting the model when copy instructions were not provided, which is the same configuration that worked best for BioMedLM. It is surprising to see that even though Flan-T5-Large (780M) is much smaller than T5-3B and Flan-T5-XL (3B), it outperforms the other two in every setting, except Flan-T5-XL with the `natural-lang` template. On comparing the same size T5 models (T5-3B and Flan-T5-XL), Flan-T5-XL performs better in most settings. Thus, the overall performance pattern observed for the `RareDis` dataset is Pipeline > Seq2Rel > Flan-T5-Large > Flan-T5-XL > T5-3B > BioMedLM. To verify this with at least one other dataset, we repeated our E2ERE experiments using the BioCreative Shared Task VI dataset on chemical-protein interaction extraction [1,32]. The results showed the same performance pattern with pipeline leading to a 69 F1 score, followed by Seq2Rel with 49, and BioMedLM with 37 points. Due to space constraints, we do not provide more elaborate details here. Coming to zero-shot results, for `RareDis`, GPT-o1 model was six times as expensive and took twice as long per instance compared with GPT-4. The results are in the final two rows of Table 4 where the o1 model still only scored 20% F-score, but doubling the score from GPT-4.

5 Conclusion

In this paper, we explored four representative models for E2ERE from three competing paradigms: pipelines (SODNER + PURE), sequence-to-sequence models (Seq2Rel, T5), and LLMs (BioMedLM). Our evaluations used a complex dataset (`RareDis`) involving discontinuous, nested, and overlapping entities. Even with the advances in Seq2Seq models and LLMs, a custom-built pipeline still seems to be the best option based on our experiments in this paper. The performance gap between Seq2Rel and the pipeline is not as high as that between BioMedLM and pipeline. So, there could be other datasets where Seq2Rel matches the pipeline methods especially for simpler scenarios without discontinuous entities. We still would not want readers to conclude that more advanced models are not suitable for this task and not to take away from the few-shot abilities of LLMs; however, zero shot results from GPT-4 and GPT-o1 appear inferior to simpler low cost supervised pipelines as of now. Also, the generative aspects of LLMs may not be suitable for the type of strict evaluation imposed here where an exact match with gold spans is required. More innovative methods are needed to marry the best of the both worlds from smaller encoder-decoder pipelines and the larger GPT models to improve E2ERE. Due to space constraints, we included analyses of different types of errors and predicate-specific performance variations in our project's GitHub repo (https://github.com/bionlproc/Raredis/) in the **supplementary_info** file.

References

1. Ai, X., Kavuluru, R.: End-to-end models for chemical–protein interaction extraction: better tokenization and span-based pipeline strategies. In: 11th International Conference on Healthcare Informatics (ICHI), pp. 610–618. IEEE (2023)
2. Bolton, E., et al.: BiomedLM: a 2.7B parameter language model trained on biomedical text. arXiv preprint arXiv:2403.18421 (2024)
3. Brown, T., et al.: Language models are few-shot learners. Adv. Neural. Inf. Process. Syst. **33**, 1877–1901 (2020)
4. Chung, H.W., et al.: Scaling instruction-finetuned language models. arXiv preprint arXiv:2210.11416 (2022)
5. Dietze, H., Schroeder, M.: Goweb: a semantic search engine for the life science web. BMC Bioinf. **10**, 1–13 (2009)
6. Eberts, M., Ulges, A.: Span-based joint entity and relation extraction with transformer pre-training. In: ECAI 2020, pp. 2006–2013. IOS Press (2020)
7. Fabregat, H., Araujo, L., Martinez-Romo, J.: Deep neural models for extracting entities and relationships in the new RDD corpus relating disabilities and rare diseases. Comput. Methods Programs Biomed. **164**, 121–129 (2018)
8. Gao, L., et al.: The pile: an 800 gb dataset of diverse text for language modeling. arXiv preprint arXiv:2101.00027 (2020)
9. Giorgi, J., Bader, G., Wang, B.: A sequence-to-sequence approach for document-level relation extraction. In: Proceedings of BioNLP, pp. 10–25. ACL (2022)
10. Global Genes: Facts. https://globalgenes.org/learn/rare-disease-facts/
11. Henry, S., McInnes, B.T.: Literature based discovery: models, methods, and trends. J. Biomed. Inf. **74**, 20–32 (2017)
12. Jurafsky, D., Martin, J.H.: Speech and Language Processing, 3rd edn. (2023). https://web.stanford.edu/~jurafsky/slp3/
13. Kavuluru, R., Rios, A., Tran, T.: Extracting drug-drug interactions with word and character-level recurrent neural networks. In: IEEE International Conference on Healthcare Informatics (ICHI), pp. 5–12. IEEE (2017)
14. Kilicoglu, H., Rosemblat, G., Fiszman, M., Shin, D.: Broad-coverage biomedical relation extraction with semrep. BMC Bioinf. **21**, 1–28 (2020)
15. Klimova, B., Storek, M., Valis, M., Kuca, K.: Global view on rare diseases: a mini review. Curr. Med. Chem. **24**(29), 3153–3158 (2017)
16. Li, F., Lin, Z., Zhang, M., Ji, D.: A span-based model for joint overlapped and discontinuous named entity recognition. In: Proceedings of the 59th Annual Meeting of the ACL and the 11th International Joint Conference on Natural Language Processing, vol. 1: Long Papers, pp. 4814–4828 (2021)
17. Luo, R., et al.: Biogpt: generative pre-trained transformer for biomedical text generation and mining. Brief. Bioinf. **23**(6) (2022)
18. Martínez-deMiguel, C., Segura-Bedmar, I., Chacón-Solano, E., Guerrero-Aspizua, S.: The raredis corpus: a corpus annotated with rare diseases, their signs and symptoms. J. Biomed. Inf. **125**, 103961 (2022)

19. Miwa, M., Bansal, M.: End-to-end relation extraction using lstms on sequences and tree structures. In: Proceedings of the 54th Annual Meeting of the ACL, vol. 1: Long Papers, pp. 1105–1116 (2016)
20. National Organization for Rare Disorders (NORD): Rare Disease Database Frequently Asked Questions. https://rarediseases.org/wp-content/uploads/2019/01/RDD-FAQ-2019.pdf (2019)
21. Nayak, T., Ng, H.T.: Effective modeling of encoder-decoder architecture for joint entity and relation extraction. In: Proceedings of the AAAI Conference on Artificial Intelligence, vol. 34, pp. 8528–8535 (2020)
22. Open AI: Learning to reason with LLMs (2024). https://openai.com/index/learning-to-reason-with-llms/
23. Peng, N., Poon, H., Quirk, C., Toutanova, K., Yih, W.T.: Cross-sentence n-ary relation extraction with graph lstms. Trans. ACL **5**, 101–115 (2017)
24. Radford, A., Wu, J., Child, R., Luan, D., Amodei, D., Sutskever, I.: Language models are unsupervised multitask learners (2019). https://insightcivic.s3.us-east-1.amazonaws.com/language-models.pdf
25. Raffel, C., et al.: Exploring the limits of transfer learning with a unified text-to-text transformer. J. Mach. Learn. Res. **21**(1), 5485–5551 (2020)
26. Tran, T., Kavuluru, R.: An end-to-end deep learning architecture for extracting protein–protein interactions affected by genetic mutations. In: Database, pp. 1–13 (2018)
27. Tran, T., Kavuluru, R.: Neural metric learning for fast end-to-end relation extraction. arXiv preprint arXiv:1905.07458 (2019)
28. Wei, J., et al.: Chain-of-thought prompting elicits reasoning in large language models. Adv. Neural. Inf. Process. Syst. **35**, 24824–24837 (2022)
29. Yao, Y., et al.: DocRED: a large-scale document-level relation extraction dataset. In: Proceedings of the 57th Annual Meeting of the ACL, pp. 764–777 (2019)
30. Zeng, X., Zeng, D., He, S., Liu, K., Zhao, J.: Extracting relational facts by an end-to-end neural model with copy mechanism. In: Proceedings of the 56th Annual Meeting of the ACL, vol. 1: Long Papers, pp. 506–514 (2018)
31. Zhang, M., Zhang, Y., Fu, G.: End-to-end neural relation extraction with global optimization. In: Proceedings of EMNLP, pp. 1730–1740 (2017)
32. Zhang, Y., Lin, H., Yang, Z., Wang, J., Sun, Y.: Chemical–protein interaction extraction via contextualized word representations and multihead attention. Database **2019**, baz054 (2019)
33. Zhong, Z., Chen, D.: A frustratingly easy approach for entity and relation extraction. In: Proceedings of NAACL:HLT, pp. 50–61 (2021)
34. Zhou, P., et al.: Attention-based bidirectional long short-term memory networks for relation classification. In: Proceedings of the 54th Annual Meeting of the ACL, pp. 207–212 (2016)

A Multiple Graphical Convolution Networks Approach for Aspect-Based Sentiment Classification

Diana Kazakova, Flavius Frasincar(✉), and Jasmijn Klinkhamer

Erasmus University Rotterdam, PO Box 1738, 3000 DR Rotterdam, The Netherlands
kazakovadiana432@gmail.com, frasincar@ese.eur.nl, 584059jk@eur.nl

Abstract. Aspect-Based Sentiment Classification (ABSC) has attracted a lot of attention in recent years. Some of the best performing models for ABSC are the hybrid ones and the ones based on deep learning. This work presents a model for ABSC dubbed HAABSA4GCN, as an extension to the state-of-the-art hybrid model HAABSA++. The HAABSA4GCN model combines a domain ontology from HAABSA++ with a novel backup model based on the Graph Convolution Neural (GCN) network, dubbed 4GCN. This backup model uses four graphs: syntactic, semantic, lexical, and ontological. For the evaluation, the SemEval 2015 and SemEval 2016 datasets are used. The evaluation results show that HAABSA4GCN outperforms HAABSA++, suggesting that the combination of different graphs within the model increases the prediction accuracy. In addition, 4GCN performs better than HAABSA4GCN, implying that 4GCN is better in dealing with cases that the domain ontology can decide upon.

Keyword: Aspect-based sentiment classification · Graph convolution neural network · Domain ontology

1 Introduction

In the information age, individuals freely express their opinions about various topics, including products, media, and people. Approximately 47% of consumers actively share their thoughts and experiences through reviews on websites like Google, Yelp, Facebook, and TripAdvisor, enriching the digital landscape with user-generated content [9]. This surge in online feedback provides businesses with valuable insights into customer opinions, aiding in informed decision-making for product development, leading to better product quality, and market competitiveness. By monitoring brand positioning and managing customer satisfaction, businesses can better understand market perceptions and make necessary adjustments to enhance overall customer satisfaction.

To gain insights from textual data, the most valuable field is sentiment analysis. This involves a natural language processing task to categorise text with a sentiment score that reflects the author's opinion, emotion, or attitude, typically

R. Ichise (Ed.): NLDB 2025, LNCS 15836, pp. 64–79, 2026.
https://doi.org/10.1007/978-3-031-97141-9_5

as positive, neutral, or negative. Sentiment can be computed at three levels: document, sentence, or aspect. Document level analysis assigns a single sentiment to the entire text, sentence level evaluates each sentence separately, and Aspect-Based Sentiment Analysis (ABSA) assesses sentiment towards specific entities or aspects within the text [20].

ABSA encompasses two main phases: Aspect Detection (AD), which identifies aspects, and Aspect-Based Sentiment Classification (ABSC), which determines the sentiment related to these aspects [20]. The primary goal of ABSC is to associate aspects with their corresponding opinions, a challenging task requiring contextual understanding. Recent efforts [7] use attention mechanisms to prioritise crucial text sections for sentiment analysis, capturing subtle word relationships. However, these mechanisms do not inherently distinguish between aspects. Hierarchical attention mechanisms have been introduced to address this [11]. [23] proposed the HAABSA++ model that significantly enhanced sentiment prediction. Despite this, the complexity of language can still pose challenges for accurate ABSC.

Graph Neural Networks (GNNs) are proven to effectively handle the complexity of assigning opinions to specific targets, considering the challenges presented by language [28]. However, GNNs have limitations, such as ignoring dependency types and varying encoding techniques that can affect model stability [30]. To address these issues, different graphs are used in GNNs: syntactic (Syn), semantic (Sem), lexical (Lex), and knowledge (Kno) graphs.

Recent studies have developed several models that make use of GNNs for ABSA. The Relational Graph Attention Network (R-GAT) model uses a syntactic graph [26]. The Dual Graph Convolutional Network (DualGCN) leverages syntactic and semantic graphs [12]. The dependency connections and the usage of dependency types are combined in the T-GCN model [22]. Lexical and semantic graphs are covered in the Bi-level interactive Graph Convolution Network (BiGCN) [29]. Last, an ontological graph is used in [13] where the relationship between an opinion/aspect word and words from the domain ontology is analysed and exploited for ABSA.

This study aims to enhance the effectiveness of the HAABSA++ model in addressing ABSC by combining the syntactic, semantic, lexical, and ontological graphs in a GCN model. We replace the LCR-Rot-hop++ backup model of the HAABSA++ model with 4GCN, a novel graph-based neural model using the four GCN modules operating in parallel, resulting in the new hybrid model HAABSA4GCN. The Python source code and data are available on GitHub at https://github.com/DianaKazakova/HAABSA4GCN.

The rest of the paper is organised as follows. Section 2 discusses existing related research. Then, Sect. 3 presents the used data. Section 4 explains the methods used in this work, including our newly proposed method. The evaluation is presented in Sect. 5. Last, Sect. 6 provides the conclusion with suggestions for future research.

2 Related Works

ABSC is a subtask of ABSA addressing the determination of the sentiment polarity of an aspect target word in a given sentence. [2] classifies the present ABSC models into knowledge-based, machine learning, and hybrid. Hybrid models combine the knowledge-based approach with machine learning methods. HAABSA++ [23] is such a model and has achieved state-of-the-art results in the class of hybrid models. First, we present graph neural networks, as a special class of machine learning methods that have been recently successfully used for ABSA. Then, we describe hybrid models.

2.1 Graph Neural Networks

Neural networks designed to process graph structures, and pioneered by [19], were described as a variant of RNNs. [27] divides the GNNs into four distinct types: recurrent GNNs, convolutional GNNs, graph autoencoders, and spatial-temporal GNNs. Among these diverse categories, two particular types are popular and effective: GCNs and GATs.

GCN, introduced by [10], builds on spectral graph convolutional neural networks [5]. [10] addresses the lack of self-loops and the use of unnormalised adjacency matrices, by modifying the adjacency matrix to include self-loops and applying normalisation to the adjacency matrix to preserve feature vectors scales. However, GCN approaches depend on the graph structure, hence a trained model can not be directly applied to another graph. [24] introduced GATs, which incorporates an attention mechanism to give different importance levels to neighbouring features, improving feature aggregation [8]. In ABSC tasks, the attention mechanism is also used for the GCN models [4]. However, ABSC tasks employing GCN or GAT models, often face limitations like, a lack of utilisation of semantic relationships and sentiment knowledge among words or phrases. These limitations can be handled with the help of graph modules.

Several works have used a text classification model based on GCN, which constructs the word relationship graph using word co-occurrence and word-text relationships [14]. BiGCN [29] combines syntactic and lexical graph modules to group lexical word pairs based on their co-occurrence frequency. [14] constructs a text graph tensor describing semantics, grammar, context, and other information. [31] used a semantic module in the GCN model to capture the semantic dependence between multiple aspects and used an attention mechanism to encode aspects and context.

[26] presents R-GAT to handle sentences containing multiple aspects, acknowledging the significance of the dependency relation type for the preservation of syntactical information. Similarly a Type-Aware Graph Convolution Network (T-GCN) addresses the oversight of dependency types, targeting a more comprehensive integration of dependency structures [22]. Moreover, the Dual-GCN model addresses parsing inaccuracies and informal expressions using a syntactic module and identifies semantic relationships using a semantic module [12]. In addition, BiCGN leverages lexical and semantic information [29].

However, most models based on graph networks overlook the incorporation of domain ontology information during graph construction [3]. External affective commonsense knowledge can enrich sentiment feature representations in sentiment analysis tasks [17]. An ontological graph is used in [13] where the relationships between an opinion/aspect words and words from the domain ontology are analysed.

2.2 Hybrid Models

Hybrid approaches for ABSC aim to combine the strengths of knowledge-based and machine-learning algorithms. [21] creates a specialised ontology for the restaurant sector, utilising it to compute the sentiment, with an SVM as a backup model. In more recent studies, neural networks have been utilised as a backup model. Recently, the domain-specific ontology of [21] was used with an attention-based model using hierarchical attention and deep contextualised word embeddings (BERT). This combination led to the development of HAABSA++, which includes the LCR-Rot-Hop++ neural network as the backup model [23].

HAABSA++ has achieved state-of-the-art results for the sentiment classification task. The process unfolds in distinct phases. Firstly, it uses the ontology from [21] to identify aspect-related sentiment. If the ontology provides inconclusive results due to neutral sentiments (not modelled in the ontology), conflicting sentiments, or lack of coverage, the LCR-Rot-hop++ neural network is activated. Combining the neural network with the ontology improves accuracy over using the neural network alone and enhances the interpretability of the results. HAABSA++ represents a significant advancement in the field of ABSC, skillfully detecting nuanced expressions of sentiment through semantic information and structural dependencies.

3 Data

For our research, the datasets SemEval 2015, Task 12, Subtask 2 [16] and SemEval 2016, Task 5, Subtask 1 [15] are used. Previous ABSA works have chosen SemEval datasets, indicating their reliability and relevance, and facilitating meaningful comparisons to our research. Besides, we use the same evaluation measures proposed by SemEval to maintain a fair comparison with the existing models. The datasets consist of reviews from various domains. Since our approach relies on an ontology designed for the restaurant domain, we focus only on the restaurant datasets. These consist of online reviews in English, annotated by human linguists, and formatted in an XML structure.

Each review comprises multiple sentences that each may contain aspects. In cases where a word in the sentence does not explicitly identify the aspect category, the target is marked as NULL.

As in this work we are doing a sentiment classification task, we consider only sentiment polarity datasets, where each observation consists of a sentence, the target aspect within the sentence, and its corresponding polarity—negative (-1), neutral (0), or positive (1). The opinions with implicit targets were excluded for this dataset.

Table 1 summarises the distribution of sentiment polarities in our datasets, highlighting the prevalence of positive sentiment and the rarity of neutral sentiment. Furthermore, both training sets show class imbalance. The SemEval 2016 dataset exhibits a slightly more similar distribution between training and test data than the SemEval 2015 dataset. However, the 2016 test set displays more imbalance than the 2015 test set, featuring fewer negative examples but more positive examples. Also, we can note that the 2016 dataset is larger than the 2015 dataset.

Table 1. The number of observations and the distribution of polarity (for the SemEval 2015 and SemEval 2016 datasets).

	Positive		Neutral		Negative		Total
	Frequency	%	Frequency	%	Frequency	%	Frequency
SemEval 2015 train	962	75.3	36	2.8	280	21.9	1278
SemEval 2015 test	353	59.1	37	6.2	207	34.7	597
Total (Av. for %)	**1315**	**67.2**	**73**	**4.5**	**487**	**28.3**	**1875**
SemEval 2016 train	1319	70.2	72	3.8	489	26.0	1880
SemEval 2016 test	483	74.3	32	4.9	135	20.8	650
Total (Av. for %)	**1802**	**72.25**	**104**	**4.35**	**624**	**23.4**	**2530**

4 Methodology

In this section, our methodology is presented. First, we introduce the reference HAABSA++ model. Then, we present our novel 4GCN model.

4.1 HAABSA++

The HAABSA++ model, developed by [23], first uses a rule-based method based on a domain sentiment ontology [21] to determine the sentiment of a given aspect. Then, the LCR-Rot-hop++ neural network model is employed for handling sentences for which the ontology is inconclusive.

The domain sentiment ontology predicts sentiment using predefined classes, class relations, and axioms. It has three main classes: SentimentValue, AspectMention, and SentimentMention [21]. SentimentValue assigns Positive and Negative subclasses to words or phrases expressing sentiments, excluding Neutral due to its intrinsic ambiguity. AspectMention represents mentions of specific features or attributes. SentimentMention categorises sentiment expressions into three types: Type-1 for general positive or negative sentiment, Type-2 for a particular category of aspect mentions, and Type-3 for aspect category dependent mentions. Furthermore, the classifier checks for negation and inverts the sentiment polarity if a certain concept is negated.

Nevertheless, the ontology encounters inconclusiveness in three scenarios: prediction of conflicting sentiments (both positive and negative) for a target, instances with no hits due to the limited coverage of the ontology, or the sentiment is neutral. To address these limitations, the LCR-Rot-hop++ model is used as a backup model.

The LCR-Rot-hop++ model was enhanced by [25] with multiple iterations of rotatory attention to better distinguish sentiment words. [23] further improved it using hierarchical attention and contextual word embeddings (BERT), leading to the refined LCR-Rot-hop++ model.

4.2 4GCN

4GCN is a GNN-based model using four GCN graphs: SynGCN, SemGCN, LexGCN, and KnoGCN. These graphs are used in parallel, each taking a BERT-encoded sentence as input and applying graph convolutions to produce updated hidden representations, incorporating syntactic, semantic, lexical, and domain-specific ontology information. The results of every graph, the modules' last hidden representations of the aspect terms, are then concatenated to obtain the final output representation. The resulting vector is reduced to three dimensions through a fully connected layer. Last, a softmax function is applied to compute the probabilities associated with each sentiment class. The class with the highest probability is selected as the final label.

Encoding. The initial phase of the neural network classifier involves transforming each sentence s to understand its hidden contextual meaning. This transformation is achieved by leveraging a pre-trained BERT model to generate encodings of sentences, as BERT has been proven to excel in these kinds of tasks [12,23]. BERT uses the [CLS] and [SEP] tokens to derive aspect-aware hidden sentence representations. Each sentence is first tokenised into words or subwords. Then, BERT combines these tokens with two unique tokens: [CLS] at the beginning and [SEP] at the end of the sentence. Another [SEP] token is used to construct a sentence-aspect pair (s, t) as an input for our model. This process allows BERT to distinguish between the aspect of a sentence and the context where the polarity is expressed. The optimal encoding is shown in Eq. (1).

$$\text{[CLS] sentence [SEP] aspect [SEP]} \quad (1)$$

For instance, given the sentence "The selection of desserts was small", we input it into BERT-large to generate aspect-aware hidden representations $h_i^{(0)}$ of 1024 dimensions for each word i in sentence s (word embeddings are averages of token embeddings initially produced by BERT). The encoded input format is "[CLS] The *selection* of desserts is small [SEP] *selection* [SEP]", where the word *selection* was encoded as an aspect of the sentence. Moreover, sentences are extended with padding to achieve a uniform length of 100 tokens, ensuring consistent dimensions across all inputs.

Graph Convolutional Network. The fundamental structure of each network layer is expressed in Eq. (2). Each element A_{ij} in matrix A signifies the connection between the i-th and j-th nodes (nodes denote words). Specifically, A_{ij} equals 1 if the i-th node is linked to the j-th node, and 0 otherwise. Moreover, the adjacency matrix A, consisting of binary values (0 s and 1 s), can be the discrete output from a dependency parser. For the i-th node at the l-th layer, its hidden state representation, formally denoted as h_i^l, undergoes an update according to the following equation:

$$h_i^{(l)} = \sigma\left(\sum_{j=1}^{n} A_{ij} W^{(l)} h_j^{(l-1)} + b^{(l)}\right) \tag{2}$$

where n is the number of words in a sentence, $W^{(l)}$ is the weight matrix, $b^{(l)}$ is the bias term, and σ is an activation function.

This research employs the *ReLU* activation function for the graph convolution layers. Each module creates a graph over s using a distinct approach: SynGraph for syntactic information, SemGraph for semantic relations, LexGraph for lexical dependencies, and KnoGraph for ontology relations. The associated adjacency matrices A are utilised to perform graph convolutions, following Eq. (2), for multiple layers.

SynGCN Module. To exploit syntactic relations in a sentence and construct the graph for the SynGCN module, the dependency parser is first used to obtain the dependency tree of every sentence [22]. In a dependency tree, each word is represented as a node, and the edges between nodes signify the syntactic dependencies. The root of the dependency tree, often an artificial symbol, represents the main governing element in the sentence.

The general results of a dependency tree can be represented by three elements $(x_i, x_j, r_{i,j})$, where $r_{i,j}$ is a dependency type between x_i word and x_j word. Moreover, the adjacency matrix $A = \{a_{ij}\}_{n \times n}$ is utilised to record the existence of an edge between x_i word and x_j word and n is the number of words in a sentence. Consequently, A is a 0–1 matrix where a_{ij} equals 1 if there is an edge between x_i word and x_j word and a_{ij} equals 0, otherwise. Additionally, the relation type matrix $R = {r_{ij}}_{n \times n}$ is created to obtain the dependency type between x_i and x_j words if there is an edge between them. Given the set of dependency relations R, the corresponding type embeddings e_{ij}^r are generated.

In evaluating the importance of an edge for sentiment polarity within a sentence, the weighting of edges by their contribution is proposed. In detail, for every edge connecting words x_i and x_j, the l-th GCN layer leverages the hidden vectors $h_i^{(l-1)}$ and $h_j^{(l-1)}$ derived from the (l-1)-th GCN layer for x_i and x_j words. The initial hidden vectors, $h_i^{(0)}$ and $h_j^{(0)}$, are obtained from the BERT encoder. Subsequently, hidden vectors are combined with the corresponding type embeddings e^r_{ij}. Equations (3) and (4) represent the concatenation process for the words x_i and x_j:

$$s_i^{(l)} = h_i^{(l-1)} \oplus e^r_{ij} \tag{3}$$

and

$$s_j^{(l)} = h_j^{(l-1)} \oplus e^r_{ij} \tag{4}$$

where $\oplus$ denotes the concatenation operator.

Next, a weight $p_{i,j}^{(l)}$ (contribution) of an edge for the sentiment polarity is computed with the following formula:

$$p_{ij}^{(l)} = \frac{a_{ij} \cdot exp\left(s_i^{(l)} \cdot s_j^{(l)}\right)}{\sum_{j=1}^{n} a_{ij} \cdot exp\left(s_i^{(l)} \cdot s_j^{(l)}\right)} \tag{5}$$

To transform the dimension of e^r_{ij} to $h_i^{(l-1)}$ we used trainable matrix $W_{\mathcal{R}}^{(l)}$ of the l-th GCN layer. Therefore, the type embeddings are transformed into the hidden representations by the following equation:

$$h_i^{(l-1)'} = h_i^{(l-1)} + W_{\mathcal{R}}^{(l)} \cdot e^r_{ij} \tag{6}$$

Lastly, the output of x_i at the l-th layer from the SynGCN module is computed by applying $p_{ij}^{(l)}$ to Eq. (2):

$$h_i^{(l)(sym)} = \sigma\left(\sum_{j=1}^{n} p_{ij}^{(l)} W^{(l)} h_j^{(l-1)'} + b^{(l)}\right) \tag{7}$$

where $W^{(l)}$ and $b^{(l)}$ denote the trainable parameters in the l-th GCN layer, and σ refers to the *ReLU* activation function.

SemGCN Module. The SemGCN module is constructed via a self-attention mechanism to analyse semantic associations. Self-attention can capture semantically related terms of each word in a sentence [12]. Computing the attention score of each pair of elements in parallel, the attention score matrix $A^{(l)(sem)} \in R^{n \times n}$ is constructed as follows:

$$A^{(l)(sem)} = softmax\left(\frac{Q^{(l)}W^Q \times \left(K^{(l)}W^K\right)^T}{\sqrt{d}}\right) \tag{8}$$

where $Q^{(l)}$ and $K^{(l)}$ are both equal to the hidden representation of the previous layer $H^{(l-1)}$. W^Q and W^K are learnable weight matrices, and d is the number of features for each node (word).

The semantic graph representation $H^{(l)(sem)}$ is obtained from the SemGCN module using Eq. (2), where $h_i^{(l)(sem)} \in R^d$ is a hidden representation of the ith node at the l-th layer.

$$h_i^{(l)(sem)} = \sigma\left(\sum_{j=1}^{n} a_{ij}^{(l)(sem)} W^{(l)} h_j^{(l-1)} + b^{(l)}\right) \tag{9}$$

where $W^{(l)}$ and $b^{(l)}$ denote the trainable parameters in the l-th GCN layer, and σ refers to the $ReLU$ activation function.

LexGCN Module. To employ a LexGraph to ABSC and represent the relationships between words quantitatively, a global co-occurrence matrix A^{gc} is constructed [29]. This global co-occurrence matrix A^{gc} is generated using a corpus combining the SemEval training sets with the WebText corpus. The WebText corpus, containing informal language texts, is sourced from NLTK [1] and is intentionally employed to augment the information in the SemEval training corpus. Equation (10) presents the global co-occurrence matrix:

$$A^{gc} = \{a_{ij}^{gc}\}_{N\times N} \tag{10}$$

where i and j denote indexes for x_i and x_j words in the corpus, respectively, and a_{ij}^{gc} denotes the co-occurrence frequency between x_i and x_j words in the corpus whose vocabulary size is N. The weights of a_{ij}^{gc} are scaled by the frequency of i and j in the training corpus. The scaling provides a more balanced representation of co-occurrence relationships, considering the importance of each word in the context of the entire training corpus.

The local co-occurrence matrix A^{lc} for each sentence s is constructed to delve into sentence-level analysis [29]. To reduce overemphasising specific sentence structures and avoid redundancy, up to one co-occurrence per x_i word is tallied within each sentence when constructing the local co-occurrence matrix. This matrix, acting as the adjacency matrix for the LexGCN module, is formulated using Eq. (11),

$$A_s^{lc} = \{a_{ij}^{lc}\}_{N\times N} \tag{11}$$

where i and j denote indexes for x_i and x_j words in the sentence, respectively, and a_{ij}^{lc} denotes the co-occurrence frequency between x_i and x_j words in the sentence.

To integrate global word distribution information from A^{gc} into the local lexical co-occurrence matrix A_s^{lc}, the co-occurrence weights of existing words in A^{gc} are maintained. Specifically, if the sentence co-occurring word x_i and word x_j are present in the training corpus of A^{gc}, a_{ij}^{lc} is set equal to scaled co-occurrence of word x_i with word x_j in the global co-occurrence matrix A^{gc}, otherwise, a_{ij}^{lc} $= 0$.

The output of the LexGraph module for x_i at the l-th layer is then obtained using Eq. (2). The lexical graph representation is presented as $H^{(l)(lex)}$, where

$h_i^{(l)(lex)} \in R^d$ is a hidden representation of the ith node at the l-th layer.

$$h_i^{(l)(lex)} = \sigma \left(\sum_{j=1}^{n} a_{ij}^{lc} W^{(l)} h_j^{(l-1)} + b^{(l)} \right) \tag{12}$$

where $W^{(l)}$ and $b^{(l)}$ denote the trainable parameters in the l-th GCN layer, and σ refers to the *ReLU* activation function.

KnoGCN Module. In this work, the domain ontology of [25] serves as structured representations of knowledge, capturing relationships and dependencies regarding the restaurant domain. This ontology is employed to form the KnoGCN graph. Developing this graph involves the creation of a domain knowledge vocabulary $V = \{v_1, v_2, ..., v_s\}$, where s is the vocabulary size.

The process begins with identifying words recognised by the ontology, which are then utilised to construct a KnoGCN graph within the 4GCN model. Steps analogous to those outlined for the SynGCN module have been followed to construct the KnoGCN graph. These steps involve creating an adjacency matrix to represent semantic relations between words recognised by the ontology. Once the KnoGCN graph is built, we apply a similar approach to weigh the importance of edges for sentiment polarity. The weighting involves computing importance $p_{ij}^{(l)}$ of each edge, where l represents the GCN layer. The computation of $p_{ij}^{(l)}$ involves utilising the hidden vectors derived from the GCN layers, as well as the type embeddings associated with each edge within the KnoGCN graph.

Lastly, the output of each word at the l-th layer from the KnoGCN graph is computed using an adapted version of Eq. (6) utilised in the SynGCN graph. This output encapsulates the enhanced representation of each word, incorporating a domain-specific ontology to enrich sentiment analysis capabilities.

Decoding. A final output vector **o** is created by concatenating the last hidden layer of every graph constructed within the 4GCN model for aspect term a.

$$o_a = \underset{1024\times 1}{h_a^{(L)(SynGCN)}} \oplus \underset{1024\times 1}{h_a^{(L)(SemGCN)}} \oplus \underset{1024\times 1}{h_a^{(L)}(LexGCN)} \oplus \underset{1024\times 1}{h_a^{(L)(KnoGCN)}} \tag{13}$$

where L represents the last layer for the graph g, and g stands for SynGCN, SemGCN, LexGCN, or KnoGCN. $h_a^{(L)(g)}$ is a layer output with dimension 1024. a is the aspect term used within a sentence.

To decode the results and obtain a C-dimensional output, the vector **o** undergoes processing through a fully connected layer, yielding a three-component vector.

$$\underset{|C|\times 1}{u_a} = \underset{|C|\times 4096}{W} \cdot \underset{4096\times 1}{o_a} + \underset{|C|\times 1}{b} \tag{14}$$

where $C = 3$ for (positive, negative, neutral), a is the aspect term, W and b are the trainable matrix and the bias, respectively.

To make a sentiment polarity prediction for aspect term a, a softmax function to $\mathbf{u_a}$ is applied. It maps the $\mathbf{u_a}$ for each dimension to a probability.

$$\underset{|C|\times 1}{u'_a} = softmax(\underset{|C|\times 1}{u_a}) \tag{15}$$

Then, a sentiment prediction $\hat{y_a}$ is made as follows:

$$\underset{1\times 1}{\hat{y_a}} = \arg\max \underset{|C|\times 1}{u'_a} \tag{16}$$

To update model weights through backpropagation, the standard cross-entropy loss function is used:

$$\underset{1\times 1}{L} = -\sum_a \underset{|C|\times 1}{y_a} \times \log(\underset{|C|\times 1}{u'_a}) + \lambda||\Theta||^2 \tag{17}$$

where y_a represents a vector containing the true sentiment value for the a-th aspect, u'_a denotes a softmax probability comprising the predicted sentiment for the a-th aspect, λ corresponds to the weight assigned to the L_2-regularization term, and Θ represents all trainable parameters.

5 Results

This section presents the obtained results for the proposed HAABSA4GCN hybrid model and existing models. First, we present a hyperparameter tuning process applied to all the models. Second, we consider the results obtained from HAABSA++ and LCR-Rot-hop++ and compare them with HAABSA4GCN and 4GCN results, respectively. In addition, we compare the results obtained from DualGCN, R-GAT, BiGCN, and T-GCN models with 4GCN model.

5.1 Implementation Details

The Stanza toolkit, as described by [18], implements the dependency parser of [6]. This work uses this dependency parser due to its rapid processing and high accuracy.

We randomly sample 20% of the training data to create a validation set. The validation set is used to select the model hyperparameters using a Tree-structured Parzen Estimator (TPE). The highest accuracy on the validation set highlights the best hyperparameters and relates to the final model.

The word embeddings are initialised using a pre-trained BERT-large uncased model with 1024 dimensions. To address overfitting, dropout rates of 0.2286 are applied to each graph g and the concatenated output o. Each graph is configured with two layers. The Adam optimiser has a learning rate of 0.000011 and a weight decay of 0.027. The 4GCN model undergoes 15 epochs with a batch size of 4.

5.2 Evaluation

The novel model has been evaluated using the test sets from the SemEval 2015 and SemEval 2016 restaurant datasets. In Table 2 the following comparisons are made. The HAABSA4GCN model was compared against the HAABSA++ model [23]. Furthermore, the backup models, 4GCN (HAABSA4GCN) and LCR-Rot-hop++ (HAABSA++), were compared against each other. Accuracy results for HAABSA++ and LCR-Rot-hop++ were reported from [23].

Table 2. Comparison of HAABSA4GCN and HAABSA++ and their respective backup models using classification accuracy.

	SemEval 2015	SemEval 2016
HAABSA++	81.7%	87.0%
HAABSA4GCN	**83.1%**	**87.7%**
LCR-Rot-hop++	81.1%	86.7%
4GCN	**83.4%**	**89.1%**

Interestingly, 4GCN achieves an even higher accuracy when used on the entire testing sample, outperforming HAABSA4GCN by 0.3 and 1.4% points for 2015 and 2016, respectively. The ability of the 4GCN model to capture underlying relationships and predict sentiment surpasses that of LCR-Rot-hop++. This superiority is attributed to the unique combination of various modules within 4GCN, which enables it to capture a broader spectrum of relationships within the dataset. While 4GCN achieves a higher classification accuracy, the interpretability of the hybrid model's results remains valuable.

The novel hybrid model and proposed neural network model outperform previous results of HAABSA++ and LCR-Rot-hop++, respectively. HAABSA-4GCN outperforms HAABSA++ by 1.4% points for the SemEval 2015 dataset and 0.7% points for the SemEval 2016 dataset. 4GCN outperforms LCR-Rot-hop++ by 2.3% points for the SemEval 2015 dataset and 2.4% points for the SemEval 2016 dataset. The better classification accuracy of 4GCN compared to HAABSA4GCN indicates that the GCN model based on four different graphs is more effective at predicting examples classified by the ontology across the entire testing sample.

In addition to the analysis provided in Table 2, Table 3 presents a comparison of the prediction accuracy of the 4GCN model with the DualGCN, R-GAT, BiGCN, and T-GCN models from the literature (all GCN models).

In the SemEval 2015 dataset, 4GCN shows strong performance with an accuracy of 83.4%, proving that the introduced extensions have boosted the result. T-GCN follows closely with marginally lower accuracy of 83.0%, illustrating its strong ability to handle complex relationships within sentiment analysis using dependency relations. The DualGCN, R-GAT, and BiGCN models also perform

Table 3. Comparison of 4GCN and DualGCN, R-GAT, BiGCN, and T-GCN models using classification accuracy.

	SemEval 2015	SemEval 2016
4GCN	**83.4%**	89.1%
DualGCN	81.6%	86.9%
R-GAT	81.2%	85.7%
BiGCN	81.1%	88.9%
T-GCN	83.0%	**90.3%**

well, achieving accuracy of 81.6%, 81.2%, and 81.1%, respectively. Although the HAABSA4GCN is better than HAABSA++, the 4GCN model outperforms HAABSA4GCN on the SemEval 2015 dataset.

Moving to the SemEval 2016 dataset, 4GCN reaches an accuracy of 89.1%. Except for the T-GCN model, this performance is significantly higher than its peers. The leading performance of 4GCN and T-GCN in this dataset is connected to the usage of the SynGCN graph. This graph presents the dependency relations in the adjacency matrix for prediction purposes. BiGCN, DualGCN, and R-GAT have lower accuracy, i.e., 88.9%, 86.9%, and 85.7%, respectively. The reasons for the higher accuracy of DualGCN and BiGCN are based on using two graphs for the prediction. DualGCN uses syntactic and semantic information, BiGCN uses syntactic and lexical information, and R-GAT uses only syntactic information.

Interestingly, every model achieves significantly higher accuracy for the SemEval 2016 dataset than the SemEval 2015 dataset. This disparity can be attributed to the more data available in the training set of the SemEval 2016 dataset, i.e., almost 1.5 times larger (Table 1). This consequently offers more robust data for model training purposes. In addition, it is notable that even though HAABSA4GCN is more accurate than HAABSA++ on the SemEval 2016 dataset, the 4GCN model surpasses HAABSA4GCN.

6 Conclusion

This research proposes two models for ABSC: HAABSA4GCN and 4GCN. The first is a hybrid, two-stage model with a domain-specific ontological classifier and a backup model, 4GCN, a novel approach based on GNN, employing four different graphs, specifically, a syntactic graph, a semantic graph, a lexical graph, and an ontological graph. Additionally, DualGCN, R-GAT, BiGCN, and T-GCN, four core GCN models, are used for evaluation purposes.

We compare HAABSA4GCN with HAABSA++ [23] to assess whether a GNN-based backup model could enhance performance over the LCR-Rot-hop++ model. Our findings indicate that the 4GCN and HAABSA4GCN models outperform the LCR-Rot-hop++ and HAABSA++ models, respectively. The prediction accuracy of HAABSA4GCN on the SemEval 2015 and SemEval 2016 datasets are 83.1% and 87.7%, respectively. In addition, 4GCN is better than HAABSA4GCN, with prediction accuracy of 83.4% and 89.1%, respectively. 4GCN also beats DualGCN, R-GAT, BiGCN, and T-GCN on the SemEval 2015 dataset and DualGCN, R-GAT, and BiGCN on the SemEval 2016 dataset.

As future work we suggest experimenting with alternative dependency parsers for the SynGCN module, as only the Stanza parser was used in this study. Still, others might provide better results. Additionally, constructing a global co-occurrence matrix from a large corpus of restaurant reviews could improve the reliability of the LexGCN module's adjacency matrix.

References

1. Bird, S., Klein, E., Loper, E.: Natural Language Processing with Python: Analyzing Text with the Natural Language Toolkit. O'Reilly Media, Newton (2009)
2. Brauwers, G., Frasincar, F.: A survey on aspect-based sentiment classification. Comput. Surv. **55**(4), 1–37 (2023)
3. Cambria, E., Hussain, A., Havasi, C., Eckl, C.: Common sense computing: from the society of mind to digital intuition and beyond. In: Fierrez, J., Ortega-Garcia, J., Esposito, A., Drygajlo, A., Faundez-Zanuy, M. (eds.) BioID 2009. LNCS, vol. 5707, pp. 252–259. Springer, Heidelberg (2009). https://doi.org/10.1007/978-3-642-04391-8_33
4. Chen, J., Hou, H., Ji, Y., Gao, J.: Graph convolutional networks with structural attention model for aspect based sentiment analysis. In: 2019 International Joint Conference on Neural Networks (IJCNN 2019), pp. 1–7. IEEE (2019)
5. Defferrard, M., Bresson, X., Vandergheynst, P.: Convolutional neural networks on graphs with fast localized spectral filtering. In: 30th International Conference on Neural Information Processing Systems, pp. 3844–3852. Curran Associates (2016)
6. Dozat, T., Manning, C.D.: Deep biaffine attention for neural dependency parsing. In: 5th International Conference on Learning Representations (ICLR 2017). OpenReview.net (2017)
7. Fan, F., Feng, Y., Zhao, D.: Multi-grained attention network for aspect-level sentiment classification. In: 2018 Conference on Empirical Methods in Natural Language Processing (EMNLP 2018), pp. 3433–3442 (2018)
8. Gehring, J., Auli, M., Grangier, D., Dauphin, Y.: A convolutional encoder model for neural machine translation. In: 55th Annual Meeting of the Association for Computational Linguistics (ACL 2017), pp. 123–135. ACL (2017)
9. Global Web Index: What percent of customers write online reviews? (2019). https://www.gwi.com/reports/product-reviews
10. Kipf, T.N., Welling, M.: Semi-supervised classification with graph convolutional networks. In: 5th International Conference on Learning Representations (ICLR 2017). OpneReview.net (2017)
11. Li, L., Liu, Y., Zhou, A.: Hierarchical attention based position-aware network for aspect-level sentiment analysis. In: 22nd Conference on Computational Natural Language Learning (CoNLL 2018), pp. 181–189. ACL (2018)
12. Li, R., Chen, H., Feng, F., Ma, Z., Wang, X., Hovy, E.H.: Dual graph convolutional networks for aspect-based sentiment analysis. In: 59th Annual Meeting of the Association for Computational Linguistics and the 11th International Joint Conference on Natural Language Processing (ACL-IJCNLP 2021), pp. 6319–6329. ACL (2021)

13. Liang, B., Su, H., Gui, L., Cambria, E., Xu, R.: Aspect-based sentiment analysis via affective knowledge enhanced graph convolutional networks. Knowl.-Based Syst. **235**, 107643 (2022)
14. Liu, X., You, X., Zhang, X., Wu, J., Lv, P.: Tensor graph convolutional networks for text classification. In: 34th AAAI Conference on Artificial Intelligence (AAAI 2020), pp. 8409–8416. AAAI Press (2020)
15. Pontiki, M., et al.: SemEval-2016 task 5: aspect based sentiment analysis. In: 10th International Workshop on Semantic Evaluation (SemEval 2016), pp. 19–30. ACL (2016)
16. Pontiki, M., Galanis, D., Papageorgiou, H., Manandhar, S., Androutsopoulos, I.: SemEval-2015 task 12: aspect based sentiment analysis. In: 9th International Workshop on Semantic Evaluation (SemEval 2015), pp. 486–495. ACL (2015)
17. Poria, S., Chaturvedi, I., Cambria, E., Bisio, F.: Sentic LDA: improving on LDA with semantic similarity for aspect-based sentiment analysis. In: 2016 International Joint Conference on Neural Networks (IJCNN 2016), pp. 4465–4473. IEEE (2016)
18. Qi, P., Zhang, Y., Zhang, Y., Bolton, J., Manning, C.D.: Stanza: a python natural language processing toolkit for many human languages. In: 58th Annual Meeting of the Association for Computational Linguistics: System Demonstrations (ACL 2020), pp. 101–108. ACL (2020)
19. Scarselli, F., Gori, M., Tsoi, A.C., Hagenbuchner, M., Monfardini, G.: The graph neural network model. IEEE Trans. Neural Netw. **20**, 61–80 (2008)
20. Schouten, K., Frasincar, F.: Survey on aspect-level sentiment analysis. IEEE Trans. Knowl. Data Eng. **28**(3), 813–830 (2016)
21. Schouten, K., Frasincar, F.: Ontology-driven sentiment analysis of product and service aspects. In: Gangemi, A., et al. (eds.) ESWC 2018. LNCS, vol. 10843, pp. 608–623. Springer, Cham (2018). https://doi.org/10.1007/978-3-319-93417-4_39
22. Tian, Y., Chen, G., Song, Y.: Aspect-based sentiment analysis with type-aware graph convolutional networks and layer ensemble. In: 2021 Conference of the North American Chapter of the Association for Computational Linguistics: Human Language Technologies (NAACL-HLT 2021), 2021, pp. 2910–2922. ACL (2021)
23. Trușcă, M.M., Wassenberg, D., Frasincar, F., Dekker, R.: A hybrid approach for aspect-based sentiment analysis using deep contextual word embeddings and hierarchical attention. In: Bielikova, M., Mikkonen, T., Pautasso, C. (eds.) ICWE 2020. LNCS, vol. 12128, pp. 365–380. Springer, Cham (2020). https://doi.org/10.1007/978-3-030-50578-3_25
24. Velickovic, P., Cucurull, G., Casanova, A., Romero, A., Liò, P., Bengio, Y.: Graph attention networks. In: 6th International Conference on Learning Representations (ICLR 2018). OpenReview.net (2018)
25. Wallaart, O., Frasincar, F.: A hybrid approach for aspect-based sentiment analysis using a lexicalized domain ontology and attentional neural models. In: Hitzler, P., et al. (eds.) ESWC 2019. LNCS, vol. 11503, pp. 363–378. Springer, Cham (2019). https://doi.org/10.1007/978-3-030-21348-0_24
26. Wang, K., Shen, W., Yang, Y., Quan, X., Wang, R.: Relational graph attention network for aspect-based sentiment analysis. In: 58th Annual Meeting of the Association for Computational Linguistics (ACL 2020), pp. 3229–3238. ACL (2020)
27. Wu, Z., Pan, S., Chen, F., Long, G., Zhang, C., Yu, P.S.: A comprehensive survey on graph neural networks. IEEE Trans. Neural Netw. Learn. Syst. **32**, 4–24 (2019)
28. Zhang, C., Li, Q., Song, D.: Aspect-based sentiment classification with aspect-specific graph convolutional networks. In: 2019 Conference on Empirical Methods in Natural Language Processing and the 9th International Joint Conference on Natural Language Processing (EMNLP-IJCNLP 2019), pp. 4567–4577. ACL (2019)

29. Zhang, M., Qian, T.: Convolution over hierarchical syntactic and lexical graphs for aspect level sentiment analysis. In: 2020 Conference on Empirical Methods in Natural Language Processing (EMNLP 2020), pp. 3540–3549. ACL (2020)
30. Zhang, Y., Qi, P., Manning, C.D.: Graph convolution over pruned dependency trees improves relation extraction. In: 2018 Conference on Empirical Methods in Natural Language Processing (EMNLP 2018), pp. 2205–2215. ACL (2018)
31. Zhao, P., Hou, L., Wu, O.: Modeling sentiment dependencies with graph convolutional networks for aspect-level sentiment classification. Knowl.-Based Syst. **193**, 105443 (2020)

How Important is Domain-Specific Language Model Pretraining and Instruction Finetuning for Biomedical Relation Extraction?

Aviv Brokman[1] and Ramakanth Kavuluru[2(✉)]

[1] Department of Statistics, University of Kentucky, Lexington, USA
[2] Division of Biomedical Informatics, University of Kentucky, Lexington, USA
ramakanth.kavuluru@uky.edu

Abstract. Major technical advances in the general NLP domain are often subsequently applied to the high-value, data-rich biomedical domain. The past few years have seen generative language models (LMs), instruction finetuning, and few-shot learning become foci of NLP research. As such, generative LMs pretrained on biomedical corpora have proliferated and biomedical instruction finetuning has been attempted as well, all with the hope that domain specificity improves performance on downstream tasks. Given the nontrivial effort in training such models, we investigate what, if any, benefits they have in the key biomedical NLP task of relation extraction. Specifically, we address two questions: (1) Do LMs trained on biomedical corpora outperform those trained on general domain corpora? (2) Do models instruction finetuned on biomedical datasets outperform those finetuned on assorted datasets or those simply pretrained? We tackle these questions using existing LMs, testing across four datasets. In a surprising result, general-domain models typically outperformed biomedical-domain models. However, biomedical instruction finetuning improved performance to a similar degree as general instruction finetuning, despite having orders of magnitude fewer instructions. Our findings suggest it may be more fruitful to focus research effort on larger-scale biomedical instruction finetuning of general LMs over building domain-specific biomedical LMs.

Keywords: language models · biomedical information extraction · instruction finetuning · pretraining

1 Introduction

Biomedical entities and relations among them are at the forefront of biomedical knowledge discovery. Novel relational information among biomedical entities is often conveyed through text in scientific literature or clinical notes. For instance, protein-protein interactions (to understand disease etiology and progression),

R. Ichise (Ed.): NLDB 2025, LNCS 15836, pp. 80–94, 2026.
https://doi.org/10.1007/978-3-031-97141-9_6

gene-disease associations (to identify potential drug targets), drug-disease treatment relations (to spot off-label usage or assess potential for repositioning), and drug-gene interactions (to design targeted therapies) are often discussed in literature. The extracted relations are often used to build knowledge graphs to facilitate knowledge discovery and knowledge-based search systems [2,26]. Adverse event relations (linking medications and adverse effects) are often reported in clinical text and their extraction facilitates more effective post-market pharmacovigilance [5,30]. As such, biomedical relation extraction (RE) is a frequently pursued task in the BioNLP community, featuring in many shared task series (e.g., BioCreative, i2b2, n2c2). Our current contribution is about high-level questions regarding the value of biomedical domain specific language models (LMs) and instruction finetuning for biomedical RE. In the rest of this section, we overview the recent RE relevant methods landscape and frame our contributions in that context.

The last few years have seen a proliferation of transformer-based generative (encoder-decoder and decoder-only) LMs. In part, these have become popular because tasks such as summarization, paraphrasing, and code generation are fundamentally generative. But generative models have advantages over encoder-only LMs even in some tasks that were previously addressed with the latter. Encoder models were largely designed for classification problems, where a classifier is trained on top of the final layer embedding of the [CLS] token. They have been used in myriad other ways—notably in named entity recognition (NER) and RE where embeddings of spans are fed to classifiers [12,56]. These methods finetune weights from scratch and therefore require ample data. But few- and zero-shot learning have become focal areas of NLP research; their maturation promises improved scalability of NLP, as manual creation of large datasets is time consuming. Few-/zero-shot learning in encoder models is often achieved by aligning the NLP task objective function with the pretraining objective function. Prompting with templates containing [MASK] tokens to be predicted has been the few-/zero-shot method for encoder-only models [42,49]. Using such a strategy largely rests on whether the desired NLP task is a classification task or can be formulated as one. In summation, encoder-only LMs are well-suited to *full finetuning* (as opposed to the few-shot setting) for a variety of non-generative tasks. The additional layering and customization required on top of encoder models for RE can be obviated in generative models, by contrast, given their relatively flexible approach of formulating RE with straightforward natural language templates. This particularly comes in handy in few- and zero-shot learning.

In the past few years, instruction finetuning (IFT) in the general domain has become a major research theme for generative LMs [35,41,52]. In its basic form, IFT converts examples of a wide variety of labeled datasets into pairs of natural language instructions (along with input text) and responses (containing the correct output), and then trains a generative LM on them. This typically improves few-shot performance by aligning the model towards the goals that humans have. Then, for a new task, the corresponding instructions are generally more in-distribution than they would have been sans IFT.

Most advances in NLP are originally developed for the general domain, and only later adapted to the biomedical domain. Recently, this has manifested in the development of biomedical versions of popular general-domain LMs. Intuitively, it is sensible to do so because the distribution of text in biomedical NLP tasks is more similar to biomedical text than to general-domain text, and because biomedical-specific tokenizers can more parsimoniously represent biomedical entities. Likewise, inspired by the striking success of IFT, Parmar et al. [36] instruction finetuned BART-Base [27] on a biomedical meta-dataset they assembled (called BoX) to create In-BoXBART.

Biomedical generative LMs are quickly being trained, and we can safely assume that larger biomedical models will be trained in the near-future. Given the high labor, monetary, and effort costs of creating biomedical-specific LMs, it is prudent to ask if they are worthwhile. To some degree, this has already been tested in biomedical versions of T5 [38,40] and BART [27,53] in the context of full-finetuning, yielding underwhelming improvements in scores. However, the tasks tested largely require extremely short, simple generations. Plausibly, these models would differentiate themselves from their general-domain counterparts on more complex tasks, especially in the few-shot context. We investigate whether this is the case in the high-value task of RE[1]. Specifically we ask:

- Do generative models pretrained on PubMed-based scientific text outperform those trained on general-domain text?
- How do biomedical and general-domain instruction finetuned models perform compared to their base models?
- Are the answers to these questions different in the fully finetuned and few-shot settings?

We test these questions across four biomedical RE datasets using a variety of open biomedical and general domain LMs. We make our code and prompting templates available at https://github.com/bionlproc/DS-PT-IFT.

2 Related Work

2.1 Generative Relation Extraction

RE has traditionally been conducted via a pipeline in two steps—NER followed by relation classification (RC) between pairs of entities from NER. However, this pipeline approach was joined by end-to-end approaches that employ a joint loss function for both NER and RC phases beginning with [34]. Among them, Zeng et al. [55] used a copy mechanism to tackle generative RE without an intermediate NER step; several extensions followed suit [14,18,54]. One advantage of their strategy is that generation can naturally handle discontinuous entities (e.g., *hand pain* in the phrase *hand and arm pain*). Discontinuous entities pose such a

[1] Here we are explicitly dealing with end-to-end RE, where entities must be extracted by the RE system and are not provided *a priori*.

challenge to NER that there is an entire line of research dedicated to solving it [11,51]. But these copy-based models require training neural network components from scratch, and are therefore not well-suited to few-shot learning.

Cabot et al. [20] use BART to directly generate relation triples using special tokens to demarcate roles in the triple; this still requires training randomly initialized special tokens. Luo et al. [33] finetune BioGPT on natural language templates, aligning the current NLP task's output form most closely with the pretraining strategy. At test time, relations are extracted from generated text using regular expressions. We adopt this general strategy of Luo et al. [33] in the present study. Wadhwa et al. [48] finetune Flan-T5 [52] using templates that convert relations into a target sequence of structured data, rather than natural language. We note that in preliminary experiments, our performance was much lower with templates of this form.

2.2 Biomedical Language Models

Early transformer-based biomedical LMs had encoder-only architectures, usually based on BERT [10], and were trained on some combination of PubMed abstracts, PubMed Central full-text articles (PMC), and MIMIC III [22] clinical notes. BioBERT [25] was initialized using weights from BERT and continually pretrained on PubMed and PMC. Alsentzer et al. [1] continued pretraining BioBERT on MIMIC-III, yielding ClinicalBERT. Likewise, Gururangan et al. [16] continually pretrained RoBERTa [31] on additional full-text biomedical articles from S2ORC [32], obtaining BioMed-RoBERTa. Models that trained from scratch on biomedical text generally perform better than their continually trained counterparts. The BERT-based BlueBERT [37] and PubMedBERT [15], and the RoBERTa-based Bio-LM [28] are a few such models. Shin et al. [43] trained versions of BioMegatron, both from scratch and through continued pretraining from Megatron [44]. BioELECTRA [23], a biomedical version of the high-performing ELECTRA [9], was trained from scratch on PubMed and PMC.

As generative models (with encoder-decoder and decoder-only architectures) have risen in popularity, PubMed-based generative models have been trained from scratch as well. Biomedical versions of T5 [40] (SciFive [38]) and GPT (BioGPT [33] and BioMedLM [4]) have all been trained from scratch on PubMed and/or PMC corpora. BioBART [53] is a continually pretrained BART [27] model with PubMed text. SciFive and BioBART showed negligible improvement on most biomedical tasks, and modest improvements in a small number of tasks, over their general-domain counterparts. However, we believe the generative capabilities of SciFive and BioBART are under-explored by [38] and [53] because either the tasks tackled require modest generation (e.g., multiple choice answer) or are evaluated by ROUGE scores, which only provide rough estimates of generation quality compared to human evals. Luo et al. [33] tested BioGPT on three end-to-end RE datasets, where it substantially outperformed the comparably-sized GPT-2 Medium [39]. We are unable to find any performance scores for BioGPT-Large on end-to-end RE. BioMedLM [4] scored much higher than the comparably-sized GPT-Neo 2.7B model on three QA tasks. In summary, there is evidence that on very short generation tasks, in a fully finetuned setup, biomedical encoder-decoder LMs outperform general-domain counterparts. But there is a dearth of information about the efficacy of decoder-only model performance in more complex generation tasks, and even more so for encoder-decoder models. Few-shot performance patterns of performance are especially unknown.

2.3 Instruction Finetuning

Wei et al. [52] explore the effect of IFT on zero-shot performance by instruction finetuning on 60 tasks, constructing 10 templates per task, finding consistent improvements in performance. Sanh et al. [41] conduct similar experiments on a different set of datasets, yielding the T0 model. Chung et al. [8] build on these previous attempts, ramping up the scale of finetuning up to 1600 tasks and consequently release the Flan-T5 series of instruction finetuned models. InstructGPT [35] is trained using reinforcement learning with human feedback (RLHF) [7,45] on instructions to align GPT-3 [6] to human preferences. Wang et al. [50] create synthetic instruction data for IFT using GPT-3, attaining competitive performance with the more expensively trained InstructGPT. In-BoXBART [36], the only attempt at biomedical instruction finetuning (to our knowledge), is an IFT version of BART-Base trained on 32 biomedical tasks, with one template per task, making its scale of IFT considerably smaller than that of other IFT models.

3 Task Setup

Training: RE instances consist of a source text and a set of semi-structured relations that are asserted in it. To finetune generative LMs on a relation extraction dataset, we convert its training examples into sequences of natural language before finetuning the models in the usual manner. In essence, the natural language sequences contain the source text along with an instruction to extract relations followed by the relations expressed in natural language form. Figure 1 illustrates our approach for the drug combination extraction (DCE) task of extracting combination drug therapies from scientific text [46] as we formalize below.

Let (x, y) be a training example, where x is the input text and y denotes the relations present in it. To finetune LMs, we construct a single prompting template $T = (T_s, T_t)$ for each dataset. A template consists of a source transformation function T_s and a target transformation function T_t, which return source sequence x^T, containing the source text x along with an instruction to guide generation, and target sequence y^T, conveying the relations y in the form of natural language:

$$T_s(x) = x^T$$
$$T_t(y) = y^T$$

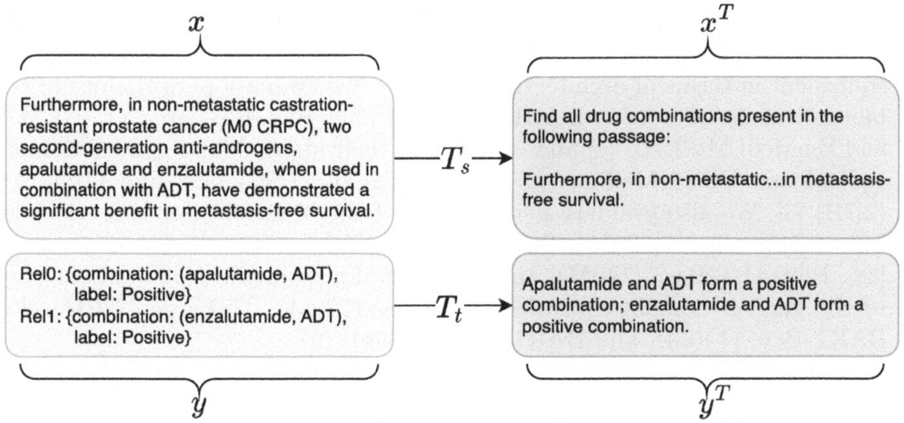

Fig. 1. Conversion of a training example of the DCE dataset into natural language sequences.

For encoder-decoder models, x^T and y^T respectively are supplied to the encoder and decoder modules. For decoder models, the sequences x^T and y^T are joined into one sequence with a function J, which then serves as a single input to the model. We take J to be

$$J\left(x^T, y^T\right) = x^T \| \backslash\mathrm{n}\backslash\mathrm{n} \| y^T$$

where $\|$ represents concatenation. Our formulation of J separates the source and target sequences with two line breaks, though other formulations can be used.

Evaluation: For validation and test examples, we only have source sequences, and our aim is to generate the target sequences. For encoder-decoder models, x^T again serves as input to the encoder. For decoder models, the input sequence is

$$J\left(x^T, \cdot\right) = x^T \| \backslash\mathrm{n}\backslash\mathrm{n}.$$

The generated output sequence of the model $\hat{y}^T$ must be transformed into a structured format so that predicted relations can be compared to annotated relations to calculate performance metrics. We design an information extractor for each template using regular expressions.

4 Experimental Setup

4.1 Main Experiments

We conduct two experiments to investigate the effect of domain-specificity: (1) We compare biomedical- and general-domain pretrained models and (2) we compare biomedical instruction fine-tuned, general-domain instruction fine-tuned, and base model performances. All experiments are repeated in fully fine-tuned and few-shot settings.

- *Biomedical vs general-domain pretraining*: In our first experiment, we compare the efficacy of biomedical LMs and their closest general-domain language equivalent in terms of architecture and size. We evaluate performance of the biomedical decoder LMs BioGPT (350M) [33], BioGPT-Large (1.5B) [33], and BioMedLM (2.7B) [4] and compare to their approximate general domain equivalents, GPT2-Medium (350M), GPT2-XL (1.5B) [39], and GPT-Neo (2.7B) [3]. We also evaluate performance of the biomedical encoder-decoder LMs SciFive-Base (220M), SciFive-Large (770M) (both PubMed versions) [38], BioBART-Base (140M), and BioBART-Large (400M) [53] and compare to the general domain equivalents T5-Base (220M), T5-Large (770M) [40], BART-Base (140M), and BART-Large (400M) [27].
- *Instruction finetuning vs base models*: In our second experiment, we compare the efficacy of IFT models and their base models. No biomedical models have been instruction finetuned in our literature review. General-domain models have been instruction finetuned with general-domain datasets and separately with biomedical datasets. For general-domain instructions, we compare the Flan-T5 [52] series of models to the base T5 models [40] they were trained from. For biomedical domain instructions, we compare In-BoXBART [36] to the base BART [27], from which it was trained.
- *Few-shot setting*: We repeat the experiments from above two scenarios, but in the few-shot setting. We emphasize that we finetune the models, rather than perform in-context learning. We experiment with 16-shot and 64-shot learning. Few-shot performance values are averaged over five runs with different random seeds for selecting training examples. Barring a single exception, fully finetuned decoder-only model performances were quite inferior (F1 $<$ 30) compared to encoder-decoder models; so we did not perform few-shot experiments on decoder-only models.

4.2 Datasets

We use four public biomedical RE datasets for our experiments. For datasets without an established train/validation split, we select 20% of the training dataset to serve as a validation set.

1. CDR [29] is a BioCreative V dataset consisting of PubMed abstracts for which all mentions of chemicals and diseases are annotated, as well as all relations between them describing chemical-induced diseases. Relations all belong to a single class and are annotated at the entity level. 1500 abstracts are split into train, validation, and test sets of equal size.
2. ChemProt [24] is a BioCreative VI dataset consisting of PubMed abstracts for which all mentions of chemical compounds/drugs and genes/proteins are annotated, as well as all intra-sentence relations between the two entity types belonging to a set of relation types of interest. Relations belong to the classes *agonist*, *antagonist*, *upregulate*, *downregulate*, and *substrate*, and are annotated at the mention level. Since relations are annotated at the mention level,

an example may contain multiple annotated relations that are conceptually identical but have different mentions. The dataset is split into 1,020 training, 612 validation, and 800 test examples.

3. The drug combinations extraction (DCE) [46] dataset consists of sentences selected from PubMed abstracts containing multiple drugs, annotated for drugs given in combination. Sets of drugs are annotated as consisting of a drug combination with a positive effect, a drug combination with an effect not clarified by the text, or not a drug combination. Though some studies combine the latter two relation types, [21,46] we model them as-is. The dataset is split into 1362 training and 272 test instances.
4. The DDI [17] dataset consists of texts from DrugBank and Medline annotated for drugs/chemicals and relations holding for pairs of co-occurring drugs. Mentions of drugs are classified as generic drug name, brand-name drug, drug group, or non-drug active substance. Relations holding for drug pairs are *pharmacokinetic mechanism*, *combination effect*, *advice regarding interaction*, or *interaction in the absence of supporting information*. Relations are annotated at the mention level. The dataset consists of 784 DrugBank documents and 233 Medline abstracts, split up into 714 train and 303 test examples.

We calculate precision, recall, and F1 for all tasks. Evaluation is done in a strict setting: relations are only considered correct if the entities are all correct and relation type, if applicable, is correct. A correct entity consists of an exact string match. For CDR, the predicted entity must match one of the mentions corresponding to the MeSH ID of the gold entity.

5 Results

All results are displayed in Table 1, primarily grouped into model series (e.g., T5) with an in-group ordering by model size. Before moving into the main results, we note two high level trends among the datasets and model series: (1) Performance was higher in general for CDR and DCE than in ChemProt and DDI, perhaps owing to the higher number of relation types in the latter datasets. (Henceforth, we refer to CDR and DCE as high-performing and ChemProt and DDI as low-performing as we explain other results). (2) Encoder-decoder models performed much better than decoder-only models, with the exception of BioGPT for CDR. In fact, decoder-only models performed so poorly that we largely limit our further discussion to encoder-decoder models. Potentially, this is because decoder models may be more amendable to generative outputs such as summaries and not as suitable for RE.

Biomedical vs General-Domain Pretraining: Overall, general-domain pretraining was superior to biomedical-domain pretraining in full and few-shot finetuning experiments (Figs. 2 and 3). In full finetuning, this pattern held for T5 models across all datasets and for BART models in low-performing datasets. Notable exceptions are the BART models in high-performing datasets,

Table 1. Comparison of model F1-scores across a range of model types and sizes for four biomedical RE datasets. Few-shot values are averages across five different random seeds for selecting training examples. Models marked with "b" are biomedically pretrained. Models marked with * are instruction finetuned with general-domain instructions, and those marked by † are instruction finetuned with biomedical instructions. It is important to note that the scores in this table are not necessarily the current state-of-the-art for each dataset, because our goal is to compare biomedical pretraining and IFT to corresponding general models, in the generative LM landscape for end-to-end RE.

		CDR			DCE			ChemProt	DDI
Model	# Param.	16-shot	64-shot	Full	16-shot	64-shot	Full	Full	Full
GPT-2-Medium	350M	–	–	16.3	–	–	0.2	14.7	14.2
BioGPT[b]	350M	–	–	44.1	–	–	0.7	9.7	17.1
GPT-2-XL	1.5B	–	–	16.1	–	–	0	14.9	24.3
BioGPT-Large[b]	1.5B	–	–	15.6	–	–	1.2	11.1	21.4
GPT-Neo-2.7B	2.7B	–	–	10.0	–	–	1.5	11.7	24.0
BioMedLM[b]	2.7B	–	–	7.9	–	–	11.9	17.1	19.1
BART-Base	110M	17.6	27.4	36.1	8.9	30.6	38.5	11.3	12.4
BioBART-Base[b]	110M	29.0	33.1	38.0	8.9	24.1	41.8	9.6	9.5
In-BoXBART[†]	110M	21.4	28.9	36.4	10.4	26.7	45.1	10.5	13.4
BART-Large	400M	26.4	32.5	40.1	9.6	30.4	41.7	15.7	17.0
BioBART-Large[b]	400M	30.7	33.0	40.1	8.7	29.2	43.3	13.2	13.7
T5-Small	60M	18.3	20.3	29.4	22.5	18.5	32.3	0.3	2.9
Flan-T5-Small*	60M	18.9	22.2	37.1	10.7	21.2	33.6	1.3	2.9
T5-Base	220M	30.3	29.8	42.8	30.0	39.3	50.3	15.6	15.4
SciFive-Base[b]	220M	28.8	10.1	41.5	0	21.6	47.6	12.4	11.9
Flan-T5-Base*	220M	30.5	33.1	45.0	30.0	33.8	44.1	16.2	15.2
T5-Large	770M	33.9	37.7	50.8	25.7	42.4	47.6	27.3	27.5
SciFive-Large[b]	770M	22.7	5.9	46.3	3.1	3.7	46.1	22.3	20.6
Flan-T5-Large*	770M	35.9	38.4	50.4	27.4	45.1	48.9	26.9	32.0

where biomedical models outperformed, or performed similarly to, corresponding general-domain models, and BioGPT which substantially outperformed its GPT2-Medium counterpart. However, BioGPT performed poorly in all other circumstances. In few-shot finetuning, biomedical T5 models performed much worse than general-domain models (Fig. 3). Biomedical pretraining had inconsistent effects in BART models, improving performance for CDR while generally lowering performance for DCE.

Effect of Instruction Finetuning: In full finetuning, IFT versions of models generally performed similarly or slightly better than their base versions (Fig. 4). The small benefits of IFT mostly manifested in high-performing datasets. In few-

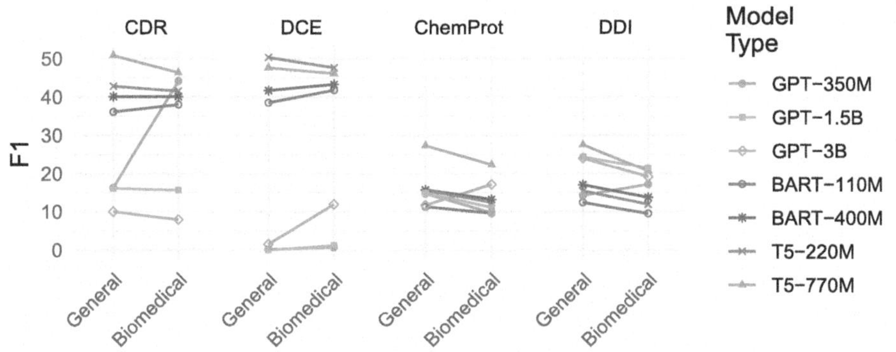

Fig. 2. Comparison of fully finetuned LMs pretrained on general-domain and biomedical text.

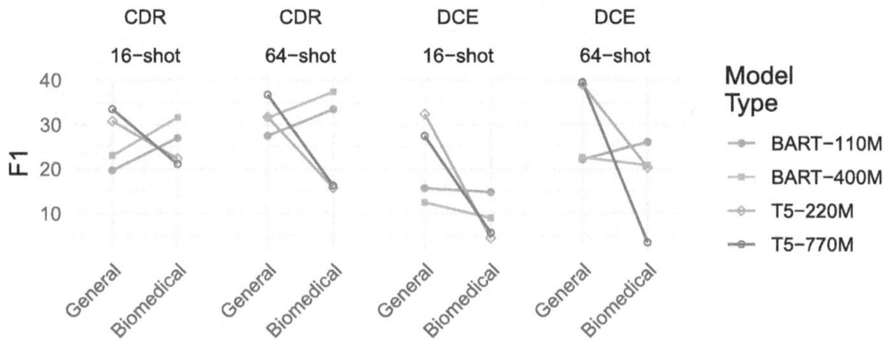

Fig. 3. Comparison of few-shot finetuned LMs pretrained on general-domain and biomedical text.

shot finetuning, both general-domain instructions and biomedical instructions consistently improved performance and to a similar degree (Fig. 5), even though there were orders of magnitude fewer biomedical instruction datasets.

6 Discussion

We were surprised that decoder-only models performed so poorly and so much worse than encoder-decoder models. Luo et al. [33] found BioGPT to attain state-of-the-art (SOTA) performance on CDR, DDI, and KD-DTI [19]. While we differed from their effort in some preprocessing of the dataset (e.g., we did not remove examples containing no relations, how many epochs we trained for, and how we determined if predicted entities matched gold entities), our performance on DDI was drastically lower than theirs, and our results on two additional datasets, DCE and ChemProt are far below SOTA. An unusual finding is that only for CDR, BioGPT performance is better than BioGPT-Large and BioMedLM (2.7B models). Preliminary experiments with Llama2-7b [47] were

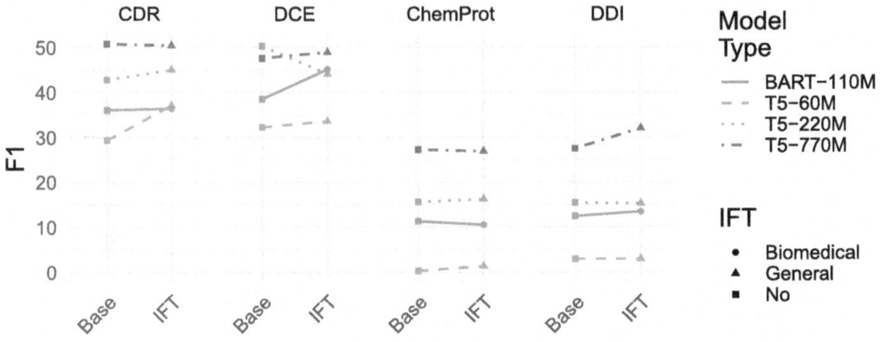

Fig. 4. Comparison of fully finetuned base and instruction-finetuned LMs.

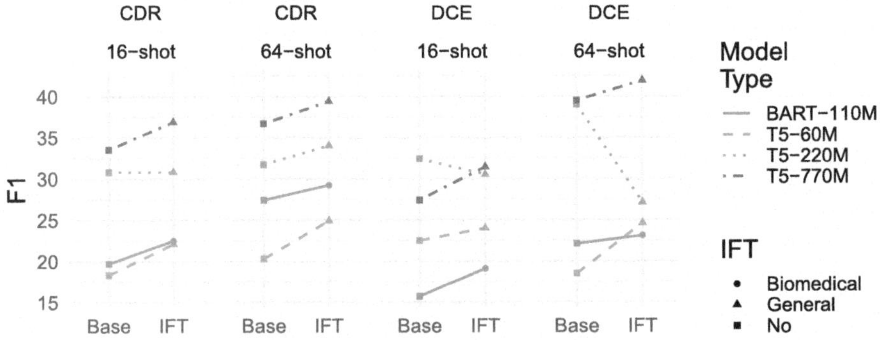

Fig. 5. Few-shot comparison of base and instruction finetuned LMs on high-performing datasets.

similarly fruitless and hence we do not report any scores given disappointing initial experiments. As encoder-decoder models performed so much better, future practical generative RE efforts may be more fruitful with encoder-decoder architectures; and if additional models are to be pretrained on biomedical corpora (PubMed), encoder-decoder models may be a safer bet.

However, training additional generative LMs (even encoder-decoder types) on PubMed generally yielded inferior models, at least as far as RE is concerned. This result held in both full and few-shot finetuning contexts. We found this pattern counterintuitive, since most of the datasets we experimented with consist of annotated texts from PubMed—one might expect that models trained on PubMed itself would be particularly well suited for these tasks, as they fall squarely inside of the pretraining corpus distribution. We hypothesize that (1) the sheer quantity of tokens available for training on general-domain text outweighs the benefits of domain-specificity, and/or (2) that biomedical-domain models may learn inferior linguistic representations as biomedical models are trained on a comparatively narrow subset of the distribution of the English language, and RE requires linguistic sophistication. Thus, even for encoder-decoder models, training biomedical LMs from scratch may not be judicious.

As for the IFT experiments, our results do not suggest that domain-specific training is altogether pointless. In the full finetuning case, IFT models achieved roughly the same performance as their base models, though they converged in far fewer epochs during training. In the few-shot setting, we found that small-scale biomedical IFT produced performance gains comparable to large-scale general-domain IFT. In-BoXBART was finetuned on 32 biomedical tasks with one template per task. By contrast, Flan-T5 models were finetuned on 1,836 tasks with multiple templates per task, and Wei et al. [52] found that performance continued to climb until $\approx$ 300 tasks. This suggests that IFT with additional biomedical datasets could yield strong benefits. While there are far fewer annotated biomedical datasets than general-domain datasets, the biomedical metadataset BigBIO [13], containing over 100 datasets currently, would be a valuable resource for biomedical IFT. Alternatively, synthetic biomedical instruction examples could also be generated *à la* Wang et al. [50]. Some nuance is required when interpreting the few-shot performance of In-BoxBART on the CDR dataset. Among the tasks that In-BoxBART was instruction finetuned on is the NER task for CDR. It is possible that some of In-BoxBART's capabilities on RE for CDR come from this sort of leakage. In addition to our previous suggestions for further research, our conclusions are limited to RE, a particularly high-value application of LMs. Other biomedical tasks should be evaluated as well.

To conclude, the fast evolving landscape of public LMs and their use in many fields naturally leads to domain specific models and IFT. In this paper, we took the first step toward rigorous assessment of the need for domain specificity in these models for biomedical RE. It would be interesting to see if our findings apply to other tasks (e.g., biomedical summarization) and domains (e.g., legal). Additionally, more detailed experiments are needed to tease out different types of errors caused by pretrained domain-specific LMs in comparison with general LMs, to see if there is a way to combine them for improved performance.

References

1. Alsentzer, E., Murphy, J., Boag, W., Weng, W.H., Jindi, D., Naumann, T., McDermott, M.: Publicly available clinical BERT embeddings. In: Proceedings of the 2nd Clinical Natural Language Processing Workshop, pp. 72–78 (2019)
2. Bakal, G., Talari, P., Kakani, E.V., Kavuluru, R.: Exploiting semantic patterns over biomedical knowledge graphs for predicting treatment and causative relations. J. Biomed. Inf. **82**, 189–199 (2018)
3. Black, S., Gao, L., Wang, P., Leahy, C., Biderman, S.: GPT-neo: large scale autoregressive language modeling with mesh-tensorflow (2021). https://doi.org/10.5281/zenodo.5297715
4. Bolton, E., et al.: BioMedLM: a 2.7 b parameter language model trained on biomedical text. arXiv preprint arXiv:2403.18421 (2024)
5. Botsis, T., Buttolph, T., Nguyen, M.D., Winiecki, S., Woo, E.J., Ball, R.: Vaccine adverse event text mining system for extracting features from vaccine safety reports. J. Am. Med. Inf. Assoc. **19**(6), 1011–1018 (2012)

6. Brown, T., et al.: Language models are few-shot learners. In: Advances in Neural Information Processing Systems, vol. 33, pp. 1877–1901 (2020)
7. Christiano, P.F., Leike, J., Brown, T., Martic, M., Legg, S., Amodei, D.: Deep reinforcement learning from human preferences. In: Advances in Neural Information Processing Systems, vol. 30 (2017)
8. Chung, H.W., et al.: Scaling instruction-finetuned language models. arXiv preprint arXiv:2210.11416 (2022)
9. Clark, K., Luong, M., Le, Q.V., Manning, C.D.: ELECTRA: pre-training text encoders as discriminators rather than generators. In: 8th International Conference on Learning Representations (2020)
10. Devlin, J., Chang, M.W., Lee, K., Toutanova, K.: BERT: pre-training of deep bidirectional transformers for language understanding. In: Proceedings of NAACL:HLT, pp. 4171–4186 (2019)
11. Dirkson, A., Verberne, S., Kraaij, W.: FuzzyBIO: a proposal for fuzzy representation of discontinuous entities. In: Proceedings of the 12th Workshop on Health Text Mining and Information Analysis, pp. 77–82 (2021)
12. Eberts, M., Ulges, A.: Span-based joint entity and relation extraction with transformer pre-training. In: Proceedings of the EACL, pp. 2006–2013 (2020)
13. Fries, J.A., et al.: BigBIO: a framework for data-centric biomedical natural language processing. arXiv preprint arXiv:2206.15076 (2022)
14. Giorgi, J., Bader, G., Wang, B.: A sequence-to-sequence approach for document-level relation extraction. In: Proceedings of the 21st Workshop on Biomedical Language Processing, pp. 10–25 (2022)
15. Gu, Y., et al.: Domain-specific language model pretraining for biomedical natural language processing (2020)
16. Gururangan, S., Marasović, A., Swayamdipta, S., Lo, K., Beltagy, I., Downey, D., Smith, N.A.: Don't stop pretraining: adapt language models to domains and tasks. In: Proceedings of the ACL, pp. 8342–8360 (2020)
17. Herrero-Zazo, M., Segura-Bedmar, I., Martínez, P., Declerck, T.: The ddi corpus: an annotated corpus with pharmacological substances and drug-drug interactions. J. Biomed. Inf. **46**(5), 914–920 (2013)
18. Hou, Y., et al.: Discovering drug-target interaction knowledge from biomedical literature (2021)
19. Hou, Y., et al.: Discovering drug–target interaction knowledge from biomedical literature. Bioinformatics **38**(22), 5100–5107 (2022)
20. Huguet Cabot, P.L., Navigli, R.: REBEL: relation extraction by end-to-end language generation. In: Findings of the ACL: EMNLP 2021, pp. 2370–2381 (2021)
21. Jiang, Y., Kavuluru, R.: End-to-end n-ary relation extraction for combination drug therapies. In: IEEE 11th International Conference on Healthcare Informatics, pp. 72–80 (2023)
22. Johnson, A.E., et al.: Mimic-iii, a freely accessible critical care database. Sci. Data **3**(1), 1–9 (2016)
23. Kanakarajan, K.r., Kundumani, B., Sankarasubbu, M.: BioELECTRA: pretrained biomedical text encoder using discriminators. In: Proceedings of the 20th Workshop on BioNLP, pp. 143–154 (2021)
24. Krallinger, M., et al.: Overview of the biocreative vi chemical-protein interaction track. In: Proceedings of the Sixth BioCreative Challenge Evaluation Workshop, vol. 1, pp. 141–146 (2017)
25. Lee, J., et al.: BioBERT: a pre-trained biomedical language representation model for biomedical text mining. Bioinformatics **36**(4), 1234–1240 (2019)

26. Lever, J., et al.: A collaborative filtering-based approach to biomedical knowledge discovery. Bioinformatics **34**(4), 652–659 (2018)
27. Lewis, M., et al.: BART: denoising sequence-to-sequence pre-training for natural language generation, translation, and comprehension. In: Proceedings of the ACL, pp. 7871–7880 (2020)
28. Lewis, P., Ott, M., Du, J., Stoyanov, V.: Pretrained language models for biomedical and clinical tasks: understanding and extending the state-of-the-art. In: Proceedings of the 3rd Clinical Natural Language Processing Workshop, pp. 146–157 (2020)
29. Li, J., et al.: Biocreative V CDR task corpus: a resource for chemical disease relation extraction. Database J. Biol. Databases Curat. (2016)
30. Liu, F., Jagannatha, A., Yu, H.: Towards drug safety surveillance and pharmacovigilance: current progress in detecting medication and adverse drug events from electronic health records. Drug Saf. **42**(1), 95–97 (2019)
31. Liu, Y., Ott, M., Goyal, N., Du, J., Joshi, M., Stoyanov, V.: Roberta: a robustly optimized bert pretraining approach. arXiv preprint arXiv:1907.11692 (2019)
32. Lo, K., Wang, L.L., Neumann, M., Kinney, R., Weld, D.: S2ORC: the semantic scholar open research corpus. In: Proceedings of the ACL, pp. 4969–4983 (2020)
33. Luo, R., et al.: BioGPT: generative pre-trained transformer for biomedical text generation and mining. Brief. Bioinf. **23**(6) (2022)
34. Miwa, M., Sasaki, Y.: Modeling joint entity and relation extraction with table representation. In: Proceedings of EMNLP, pp. 1858–1869 (2014)
35. Ouyang, L., et al.: Training language models to follow instructions with human feedback. Adv. Neural. Inf. Process. Syst. **35**, 27730–27744 (2022)
36. Parmar, M., Mishra, S., Purohit, M., Luo, M., Mohammad, M., Baral, C.: In-BoXBART: get instructions into biomedical multi-task learning. In: Findings of the ACL: NAACL 2022, pp. 112–128 (2022)
37. Peng, Y., Yan, S., Lu, Z.: Transfer learning in biomedical natural language processing: an evaluation of bert and elmo on ten benchmarking datasets. In: Proceedings of the Workshop on BioNLP, pp. 58–65 (2019)
38. Phan, L.N., et al.: Scifive: a text-to-text transformer model for biomedical literature. arXiv preprint arXiv:2106.03598 (2021)
39. Radford, A., Wu, J., Child, R., Luan, D., Amodei, D., Sutskever, I., et al.: Language models are unsupervised multitask learners. OpenAI blog **1**(8), 9 (2019)
40. Raffel, C., et al.: Exploring the limits of transfer learning with a unified text-to-text transformer. J. Mach. Learn. Res. **21**(1), 5485–5551 (2020)
41. Sanh, V., Webson, A., Raffel, C., Bach, S.H., Sutawika, L., Alyafeai, Z.: Multitask prompted training enables zero-shot task generalization. In: International Conference on Learning Representations (2022)
42. Schick, T., Schütze, H.: Exploiting cloze-questions for few-shot text classification and natural language inference. In: Proceedings of the 16th EACL, pp. 255–269 (2021)
43. Shin, H.C., et al.: BioMegatron: larger biomedical domain language model. In: Proceedings of EMNLP, pp. 4700–4706 (2020)
44. Shoeybi, M., Patwary, M., Puri, R., LeGresley, P., Casper, J., Catanzaro, B.: Megatron-lm: training multi-billion parameter language models using model parallelism. arXiv preprint arXiv:1909.08053 (2019)
45. Stiennon, N., et al.: Learning to summarize with human feedback. In: Larochelle, H., Ranzato, M., Hadsell, R., Balcan, M., Lin, H. (eds.) Advances in Neural Information Processing Systems, vol. 33, pp. 3008–3021 (2020)

46. Tiktinsky, A., et al.: a dataset for n-ary relation extraction of drug combinations. In: Proceedings of NAACL: HLT, pp. 3190–3203 (2022)
47. Touvron, H., Martin, L., Stone, K., Albert, P., Almahairi, A., Scialom, T.: Llama 2: open foundation and fine-tuned chat models (2023)
48. Wadhwa, S., Amir, S., Wallace, B.C.: Revisiting relation extraction in the era of large language models. In: Proceedings of the ACL (2023)
49. Wang, H., Xu, C., McAuley, J.: Automatic multi-label prompting: Simple and interpretable few-shot classification. In: Proceedings of NAACL: HLT, pp. 5483–5492 (2022)
50. Wang, Y., et al.: Self-instruct: aligning language models with self-generated instructions. In: Proceedings of the ACL, pp. 13484–13508 (2023)
51. Wang, Y., Yu, B., Zhu, H., Liu, T., Yu, N., Sun, L.: Discontinuous named entity recognition as maximal clique discovery. In: Proceedings of the ACL, pp. 764–774 (2021)
52. Wei, J., et al.: Finetuned language models are zero-shot learners. In: International Conference on Learning Representations (2022)
53. Yuan, H., Yuan, Z., Gan, R., Zhang, J., Xie, Y., Yu, S.: BioBART: pretraining and evaluation of a biomedical generative language model. In: Proceedings of the 21st Workshop on Biomedical Language Processing, pp. 97–109 (2022)
54. Zeng, D., Zhang, H., Liu, Q.: Copymtl: copy mechanism for joint extraction of entities and relations with multi-task learning. In: Proceedings of the AAAI Conference on Artificial Intelligence, vol. 34, pp. 9507–9514 (2020)
55. Zeng, X., Zeng, D., He, S., Liu, K., Zhao, J.: Extracting relational facts by an end-to-end neural model with copy mechanism. In: Proceedings of the ACL, pp. 506–514 (2018)
56. Zhong, Z., Chen, D.: A frustratingly easy approach for entity and relation extraction. In: Proceedings of NAACL: HLT, pp. 50–61 (2021)

ShortPathQA: A Dataset for Controllable Fusion of Large Language Models with Knowledge Graphs

Mikhail Salnikov[1,2(✉)], Andrey Sakhovskiy[1,3], Irina Nikishina[4], Aida Usmanova[5], Angelie Kraft[4], Cedric Möller[4], Debayan Banerjee[4], Junbo Huang[4], Longquan Jiang[4], Rana Abdullah[4], Xi Yan[4], Elena Tutubalina[2,3], Ricardo Usbeck[4,5], and Alexander Panchenko[1,2]

[1] Skolkovo Institute of Science and Technology, Moscow, Russia
{mikhail.salnikov,andrei.sakhovskii}@skol.tech
[2] Artificial Intelligence Research Institute, Moscow, Russia
[3] Sber AI, Moscow, Russia
[4] Universität Hamburg, Hamburg, Germany
[5] Leuphana University Lüneburg, Lüneburg, Germany

Abstract. In this work, we release the **Short**est **Path** subgraph **Q**uestion **A**nswering (ShortPathQA) dataset, the first dataset that provides textual questions with pre-computed relevant subgraphs retrieved from the Wikidata Knowledge Graph (KG), standardizing the evaluation framework for Knowledge Graph Question Answering (KGQA). For this purpose, we utilize the Mintaka dataset for both training and testing and additionally create a manual question-answering subset for testing. Our baseline experiments with both supervised approaches and unsupervised Large Language Model (LLM) inference indicate that even a simplified KGQA formulation with given KG subgraphs and candidate answers remains challenging. Our analysis has shown that LLMs are unable to correctly process and utilize graph data structures without detailed prompt engineering or model tuning. This limitation highlights the need for the creation of this dataset as a training ground for the development of methods that enable LLMs to work more effectively with graph data.

Keywords: Knowledge graphs · Question answering · KGQA · NLP

1 Introduction

Knowledge Graph Question Answering (KGQA) has emerged as a key research area, leveraging large-scale Knowledge Graphs (KGs) like Wikidata[1], DBpedia[2], and Freebase[3] to provide factually grounded answers to questions. KGs contain millions of entities and their relationships, providing a structured representation of real-world knowledge.

[1] www.wikidata.org.
[2] www.dbpedia.org.
[3] www.freebase.com.

M. Salnikov and A. Sakhovskiy—Equal contribution.

R. Ichise (Ed.): NLDB 2025, LNCS 15836, pp. 95–110, 2026.
https://doi.org/10.1007/978-3-031-97141-9_7

Common approaches to addressing the KGQA task involve the use of subgraphs, which are smaller, relevant portions of a KG that contain the necessary information for answering a question. Some studies utilize one or two hops of entities mentioned in questions to generate subgraphs [1,3,27], whereas others utilize the semantics of relationships and paths to construct subgraphs [7,11]. By concentrating on subgraphs, KGQA systems aim at enhancing answer retrieval effectiveness.

However, the use of subgraphs in KGQA systems presents several challenges. For example, selecting relevant subgraphs requires accurate Entity Linking and pathfinding algorithms. Variations in subgraph extraction lead to differences in extracted subgraphs, making it challenging to directly compare subgraph processing methods for KGQA tasks. To address these limitations, we propose **Short**est **Path** subgraph **Q**uestion **A**nswering (ShortPathQA)—a new dataset designed specifically for KGQA using subgraphs inspired by [23]. The core idea behind our dataset construction approach is to provide the community with already calculated ground-truth subgraphs, allowing them to focus on methods for processing these subgraphs rather than spending time on time-consuming KG subgraph retrieval.

Building on the idea, our **ShortPathQA** dataset includes a diverse set of questions sourced from the English Mintaka dataset [24], as well as new manually annotated questions. Each question is provided with answer candidates generated by an LLM further linked to Wikidata KG, and their corresponding Wikidata subgraphs computed as shortest paths between the question entities and an answer entity, as shown in Fig. 1.

By providing pre-extracted, unified subgraphs, **ShortPathQA** encourages and simplifies research on KG-LLM fusion, avoiding the computational complexity of entity linking and subgraph construction in large-scale knowledge graphs. Our dataset offers a standard framework with fixed subgraphs and answer candidates, enabling consistent comparison of different methods for selecting the correct answer.

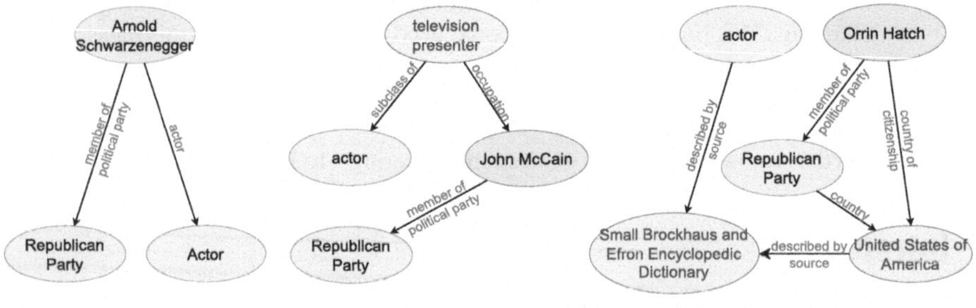

Fig. 1. Subgraph visualizations for question "*Who was formerly an actor and now a Republican senator?*" and three answer candidates: (i) Arnold Schwarzenegger, (ii) John McCain, and (iii) Orin Hatch. Entities mentioned in the question are blue, and intermediate nodes on the path from question entities to candidates are grey. Correct and incorrect answer candidates are green and red. (Color figure online)

The main contributions are as follows:

- By introducing the ShortPathQA dataset for the Knowledge Graph Question Answering task, we propose a unified format of questions, each accompanied by subgraph extracted by shortest path algorithm from Wikidata.

- We present an additional test set, manually annotated by experts, comprising more challenging samples that did not leak to any LLMs.
- We present a methodology for constructing a QA dataset aligned with knowledge graphs that can be adapted for use with any knowledge graph in any domain.
- We perform a thorough error analysis to show that LLMs struggle with graph data. Our approaches require careful prompt engineering or fine-tuning, which also highlights the need for specific methods for graph data.

We release both code and data online for further usage under the Apache License.[4]

Table 1. Comparison of the existing KGQA datasets with the newly proposed *ShortPathQA* dataset.

Dataset	# Questions	Reference KG	Natural Data	Multi-hop	Precomputed Graphs
GrailQA [10]	64.3K	Freebase	×	✓	×
WebQuestionSP [36]	4.7K	Freebase	✓	✓	×
Mintaka [24]	20K	Wikidata	✓	✓	×
SimpleQuestionsWikidata [5]	49K	Wikidata	✓	×	×
Natural Questions [15]	323K	Wikipedia(Wikidata)	✓	×	×
LC-QuAD 2.0 [9]	30K	DBPedia/Wikidata	✓	✓	×
PopQA [20]	14K	Wikidata	×	×	×
MuSiQue [29]	25K	Wikidata	×	✓	×
ShortPathQA (ours)	12,526	Wikidata	✓	✓	✓

2 Related Work

Subgraph Representations. Subgraph-based techniques have been extensively investigated in the context of KGQA. Prior works integrated a BERT-based [4] encoder with a relevant subgraph retrieved from a KG encoded with a separate graph encoder [11, 17, 27, 34, 35]. Pipenet [27] proposed a KGQA pipeline that incorporates grounding, pruning, and reasoning steps. QA-GNN [35] and DRAGON [34] extract relevant ConceptNet KG [26] subgraphs based on entities mentioned in an input question and perform joint LM-KG reasoning. However, they discard textual node and edge features names to capture only structural information with a graph encoder. Recent studies have explored integrating KG context with LLMs. In particular, [23] present a method of KG subgraph extraction and linearization to improve LLM interpretability.

LLMs for KGQA. Recent success of decoder-based generative LLMs leads to superior QA performance over KG-augmented BERT encoder-based methods [12, 16, 22, 32, 33]. However, existing LLMs suffer from hallucinations hindering their reliability [13, 28]. To overcome the issue, [1] retrieves relevant facts from a KG based on semantic similarity and concatenates them with an input question, which is then fed into an LM without

[4] https://github.com/s-nlp/ShortPathQA/.

additional training. Logic Query of Thoughts (LGOT) [18] framework explored dynamically constructing relevant subgraphs using large language models. KG-based Retrieval Augmented Generation (RAG) approaches aim to provide an LLM with additional context retrieved from a KG in the form of textual prompt [12, 16]. When multiple context sources are available (such as DBpedia and Wikipedia), Uncertainty Estimation (UE) scores were suggested to determine the most reliable source [2].

KGQA Datasets. Numerous datasets have been proposed to advance the KGQA research, each contributing unique characteristics and challenges. For instance, *LC-QuAD 2.0* [9], *WebQuestionSP* [36], and *SimpleQuestionsWikidata* [5] support a provided answer with a logical-form expression, e.g., with a SPARQL query. *PopQA* [20] focuses on simple questions related to rare entities from Wikipedia's long-tail distribution. In contrast, *MuSiQue* [29] and *GrailQA* [10] provide complex questions that require multiple reasoning steps over a reference KG (i.e. multi-hop questions). *Natural Questions* [15] draws queries to the Google search engine as questions to better align with real-world user needs. Each question-answer pair is supported with a Wikipedia which in turn is associated with a Wikidata KG. Alternatively, complex questions can be synthesized from simpler one-hop questions [29] or inferred from KG subgraphs [9, 10]. Table 1 summarizes the key features *ShortPathQA* in comparison with the existing KGQA datasets. In contrast to the approaches, *ShortPathQA* offers precomputed subgraphs generated by a deterministic algorithm for each question-answer pair, encouraging the research community to focus on developing methods to utilize and understand these subgraphs rather than extracting them.

3 ShortPathQA Dataset

ShortPathQA is the first QA dataset that combines textual questions paired with precomputed Wikidata KG subgraphs applying a unified yet simple subgraph construction approach. The overview of our dataset creation methodology is presented in Fig. 2. Overall, three key steps should be highlighted: (i) answer candidate generation using an LM; (ii) entity linking for both entities mentioned in a question as well as answer candidates from step (i); (iii) KG subgraph retrieval with a unified shortest path methodology applied to all questions within a given questions collection.

3.1 KGQA Methodology Overview

Question-Candidate KG Subgraphs. Let $\mathcal{G} = (\mathcal{V}, \mathcal{E}, \mathcal{R})$ denote a Knowledge Graph (KG) with entities set $\mathcal{V}$, labeled edges $\mathcal{E} \subset \mathcal{V} \times \mathcal{R} \times \mathcal{V}$, permissible relation types $\mathcal{R}$. The goal of KGQA task is to answer a natural language question q using a relevant KG subgraph $\mathcal{G}_q \subset \mathcal{G}$. To develop unified approach towards KG subgraph retrieval, we introduce a few key constraints on q and $\mathcal{G}_q$. First, each question q in our dataset mentions a non-empty KG entity subset $\mathcal{E}_q \subset \mathcal{V}$. Second, all correct answers $\mathcal{A}_q$ for q are KG entities: $\mathcal{A}_q \subset \mathcal{V}$ and any candidate answer is also a KG entity: $c \in \mathcal{V}$. Finally, for each answer candidate $c \in V$, KG subgraph is obtained as a union of shortest paths between mentioned nodes $e \in \mathcal{E}_q$ and a candidate answer node c: $\mathcal{G}_q = \mathcal{G}(q, c)$.

Table 2. Original Mintaka questions and answers that were used as a template for manually created new questions and answers linked to Wikidata.

Original Question	Original Answer	New Question	New Answer
What state is the author Misery from?	Sebago Lake (Q1781818)	What country is the author of Steppenwolf from?	German Empire (Q43287)
Which Netflix series has been watched more, Tiger King or The Queen's Gambit?	Tiger King: Murder, Mayhem and Madness (Q88306935)	Which netflix film has been watched more, Red Notice or the Irishman?	Red Notice (Q58815001)
How old is the actor who played Senator Palpatine?	77	Who was Marlon Brando's youngest son in The Godfather?	Al Pacino (Q41163)

Table 3. Detailed statistics of the ShortPathQA dataset, including the number of questions, answers, candidates, Wikidata entities mentioned in questions and answer candidates, as well as shortest path graph sizes. **Test (A)** and **Test (M)** stand for automatic and manual test sets, respectively.

Question & candidate statistics					Candidate graphs statistics				
Statistics	Train	Test (A)	Test (M)	Total	Statistics	Train	Test (A)	Test (M)	Total
Questions	9,750	2,430	350	12,526	**Nodes**	371,372	46,757	17,058	435,187
Candidates	123,666	15,577	3,818	143,061	**Unique nodes**	25,457	9,867	4,895	32,226
Unique names	19,956	7,789	2,979	24,773	**Avg. # nodes**	3	3	4.47	3.04
Covered Wikidata nodes					**Edges**	423,552	53,461	21,557	498,570
Mentioned	4,456	1,679	497	5,401	**Edge types**	593	450	318	635
Candidate	20,856	8,025	3,278	26,169	**Avg. # edges**	3.42	3.43	5.65	3.49

Task Formulation. To focus exclusively on LLM-KG interaction, we stick to the simplified binary classification formulation of the KGQA task: given a question q and a candidate entity $c \in \mathcal{V}$ paired with a retrieved KG subgraph $\mathcal{G}(q, c)$, the goal is to predict whether c is a correct answer for question q (i.e., whether $c \in \mathcal{A}_q$). Negative candidates $\mathcal{N}_q$ are generated with a sequence-to-sequence model followed by an entity linking to Wikidata KG: $\mathcal{N}_q \subset \mathcal{V}$. Thus, each sample in our dataset is a triple $(q, c, \mathcal{G}(q, c))$, where $c \in \mathcal{A}_q \cup \mathcal{N}_q$.

3.2 Collection of Questions

ShortPathQA dataset consists of 2 main parts: (i) A large collection of questions adopted from Mintaka corpus [24] and (ii) Manual test set - small collection of new manually curated questions for detailed testing and analysis.

ShortPathQA dataset in build on the Mintaka [24] question format, where each question is annotated with Wikidata entities mentioned in it. While Mintaka does not guarantee a correct answer to be a Wikidata entities, we a sample a subset of questions whose

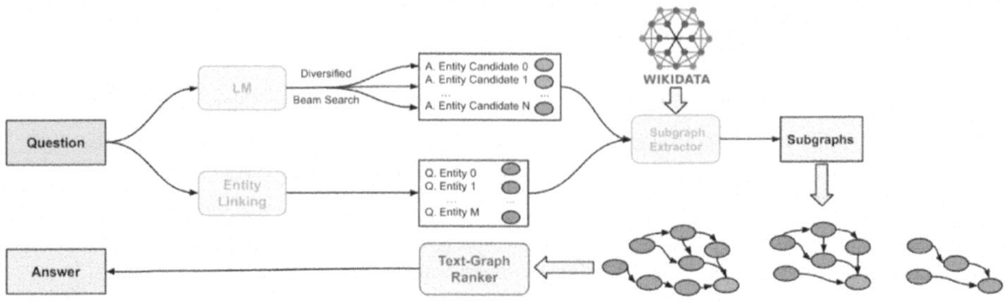

Fig. 2. Subgraphs dataset construction and QA pipeline for ShortPathQA dataset. We take a collection of questions (Sect. 3.2) and generate possible answer candidates with a language model further linked to Wikidata KG (Sect. 3.3). For each candidate, a shortest path between entities mentioned in a question and a candidate node is retrieved from the KG. Finally, a reranking network can be applied to distinguish between correct and incorrect answers based on both question and KG subgraph (Sect. 4).

Table 4. Statistics on train-test intersection in terms of Wikidata KG nodes and edge types for both Automatic and Manual parts of ShortPathQA dataset.

Statistics	Test Set	
	Automatic	Manual
# **Candidate Nodes**	8,025	3,278
Seen as candidates	4,992 (62%)	946 (29%)
Seen in graphs	5,151 (64%)	1,046 (32%)
# **Subgraph Nodes**	9,867	4,895
Seen in graphs	6,196 (63%)	1704 (35%)
# **Edge Types**	450	318
Seen in graphs	427 (95%)	298 (94%)

correct answers are the Wikidata entities. Specifically, we remove all *count* questions based on question types provided in the dataset. For questions inherited from Mintaka, we preserve the original train/test split (9,750 and 2,430 questions respectively). We will refer to these subsets as *train set* and *automatic test set*, respectively.

In addition to questions adopted from Mintaka, we release *ShortPathQA Manual test set*, a collection of 350 new questions. For consistency with first part of dataset, each question is formulated based on a reference template question from the original Mintaka. For instance, given a question *"Who is older, The Weeknd or Drake?"* with answer *Drake (Q33240)*, we construct a novel question *"Who was born earlier, Nikolai Ushin or Yossi Abulafia?"* whose answer is *"Nikolai Ushin (Q20203178)"*. For each new question, we ensure that (i) it mentions at least one entity with a valid Wikidata identifier; (ii) one or more correct answers to the new question are Wikidata entities. Both types of entities are linked to Wikidata manually. New questions examples as well as original Mintaka template questions are presented in Table 2.

Annotation Quality Assessment. For *ShortPathQA Manual test set*, we manually assess the quality of each new created question by ranking it on a scale from 1 to 5, where 1 is "the given answer is completely irrelevant for the question", 5—"the given answer is comprehensive for the given question". Moreover, we label each question to the question type according to Mintaka classes. Each question was assigned with two annotators. The Kohen's kappa which represents the annotation agreement is 0.81 for question type and 0.51 for question quality, the average quality of the questions is 4.81.

3.3 Candidate Subgraph Construction

For each answer candidate $c \in \mathcal{A}_q \cup \mathcal{N}_q$, either correct or incorrect, we present the shortest path Wikidata subgraph $\mathcal{G}(q, c)$ describing the shortest path from each entity from $\mathcal{E}_q$ (mentioned in a question) to candidate entity c. A visual representation of this process is provided in Fig. 2. Candidates generated by language model and linked to entities by Wikimedia provided search API[5]. In the following paragraphs, we describe two steps in detail.

Answer Candidate Generation. To generate a set of answer candidates, we utilize the T5-XL LM [21], which was trained on the Mintaka dataset by 8 epochs with AdamW [19] optimizer and 10^{-3} learning rate. The motivation for selecting the T5-XL model for generating candidates was based on the work that proposed a method for extracting subgraphs using the shortest path [23]. This method was tested with the T5 models. Furthermore, encoder-decoder models can be more effective than decoder-only models for QA problems due to their superior attention mechanisms and convergence properties [6]. Additionally, as demonstrated in our baseline experiments, the candidates provided a challenging task for modern models, making the T5-XL a suitable choice for this task. In order to increase the diversity of the answers candidates generated, we apply Diverse Beam Search [31], which is a framework that produces a collection of diverse sequences. We apply the algorithm with 200 beams, 20 beam groups, and a 0.1 diversity penalty and filter out duplicate candidates.

Subgraph Construction. For each question, we calculate the shortest path from all entities $\mathcal{E}_q$, to the answer candidate c. In case there are several ($|\mathcal{E}_q| > 1$) input entities in a question, we combine all shortest paths into one final subgraph $\mathcal{G}(q, c)$. Let $\mathcal{V}_{q,c}$ and $\mathcal{E}_{q,c}$ denote nodes and edges of graph $\mathcal{G}(q, c)$, respectively. As the union of multiple shortest paths combined into one subgraph might miss some edges between the intermediate nodes, we explicitly restore these missed edges. Specifically, if $u, v \in \mathcal{V}_{q,c}$ and $(u, r, v) \in \mathcal{E}$, we add edge (u, r, v) to $\mathcal{E}_{q,c}$. The example of three subgraphs created for different answer candidates can be seen in Fig. 1.

3.4 Dataset Statistics

Candidate and Node Statistics. Detailed statistics of the proposed ShortPathQA dataset is summarized in Table 3. As seen from the table, our dataset provides over 143K

[5] www.mediawiki.org/wiki/Wikibase/API.

question-candidate pairs with relevant KG subgraphs covering over 32K unique concepts from the Wikidata KG. Notably, the number of Wikidata nodes being answer candidates (26.1K) is higher then the unique candidate name count (24.7K). This implies that some answer candidates can be indistinguishable between each other from their textual names only and relevant KG subgraphs might help overcome the ambiguity.

Train-Test Intersection. Table 4 summarizes the intersection between the train set and two test sets: automatic and manual in terms of covered Wikidata nodes and edge types. Our released manual test set has half as many train-test intersections in terms of seen KG nodes as the one derived from Mintaka. Thus, the released test set leaves less space for simple train set memorization during supervised evaluation.

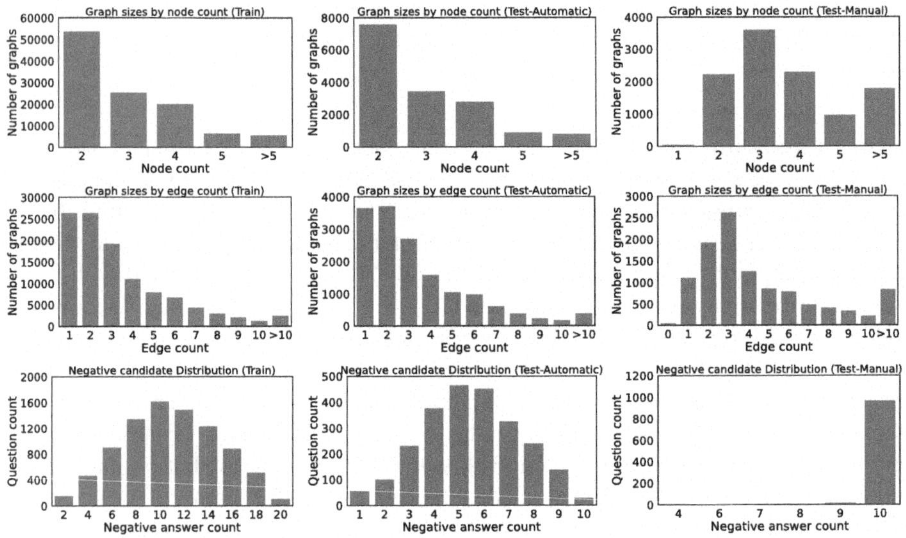

Fig. 3. Question-candidate graph sizes for ShortPathQA dataset in terms of node count (**1st row**) and edge count (**2nd row**). Negative candidate count for a given question (**3rd row**). **1st**, **2nd**, **3rd** columns correspond to **train**, **automatic test set**, and **manual test set**, respectively.

Graph Size Distribution. Graph Sizes for both *Automatic* and *Manual* subsets of *ShortPathQA* are summarized in Fig. 3. A few key features of the *ShortPathQA Manual test set* should be highlighted. First, it has larger graphs in terms of node and edge counts on average: while the original Mintaka questions included into *ShortPathQA* mostly involves 1-hop reasoning, newly annotated questions produce richer KG context under the proposed subgraph retrieval methodology. Second, new questions are provided with more negative samples.

4 Baselines

We adopt the following approaches as our baselines: (i) zero-shot LLM prediction; (ii) supervised finetuning of LLMs, both an encoder-only Transformer [30] and modern LLM decoder-only model LLaMA3-8b-Instruct [8]; (iii) positive/negative class constant; (iv) random baseline. For the first approach, we employ GPT4o, GPT4o mini, and LLaMA3-8b-Instruct models and experiment with adding graph information to the prompt. For the second approach, we adopt the graph linearization approach of [23] to create a textual representation of an input graph with candidate answers highlighted by special separator tokens. We present both of them in the subsections below.

4.1 Supervised Approaches

As supervised fine-tuning, we adopt MPNet[6][25] and LLaMA3-8B-Instruct [8] to encode both questions and linearized subgraphs. The task is formulated as a binary classification: given a question q, answer candidate c, and KG subgraph $\mathcal{G}(q, c)$, a model has to identify c is a correct answer for q. We experiment with two input types: (i) **No Graph**: a model is passed with textual information only: $q\,[SEP]\,c$; (ii) **With Graph**: a model can reason over graph $\mathcal{L}(q, c)$ to answer observed question: $q\,[SEP]\mathcal{L}(q, c)$. The linearization $\mathcal{L}(q, c)$ of graph $\mathcal{G}(q, c)$ is obtained iteratively by traversing and linearizing individual edges while moving from the mentioned entities $\mathcal{E}_q$ to the answer candidate c. Each edge (h, r, t) is linearized as "h, r, t". If either $h = c$ or $t = c$, they are additionally emphasized with separator tokens "[SEP]" for the MPNet model: e.g., "$[SEP]\,h\,[SEP]$, r, t" if $h = c$.

For supervised baselines, we use 10% random questions as validation set for tuning hyper-parameters. We train each supervised for 10 epochs with a batch size of 32 and learning rate of 1e-5 using Adam optimizer [14]. For prediction, we load the model weights from the best epoch in terms of validation F1-score.

The LLaMA3-8B-Instruct model was fine-tuned in a chat format that accepts system messages with short instructions and user messages with questions, answers, and, for the version that accepts subgraphs, a graph in linearized format without tokens. It was trained on 1 epoch of the training dataset.

4.2 Zero-Shot Evaluation

For zero-shot LLM-based baselines, we ask a model to select correct answers for a question q from the given candidate list C_q. If multiple candidates have a matching textual name, we append edge types leading to each candidate c in graph $\mathcal{G}(q, c)$. For example, for the question "*Which film directed by James Cameron became the highest-grossing movie of all time?*" with two candidates answers named "Titanic": (i) *1997 film by James Cameron* and (ii) *1953 film by Jean Negulesco* the candidates are (i) *Titanic (director)* and (ii) *Titanic (original language of performance work)*, respectively.

Prompt template for all models presented in Table 5. For **No KG** version, we did not used Graph part of user prompt, system prompt was simple instuction: *You are a helpful*

[6] https://huggingface.co/sentence-transformers/all-mpnet-base-v2.

Table 5. LLM prompt to LLaMA3-8b-Instruct, o3-mini, GPT-4o and GPT-4o-mini when given additional subgraph information.

System
You are an AI assistant tasked with evaluating the correctness of answers to questions based on provided graph information. The graph consists of triplets in the format (subject, property, object) that demonstrate the shortest path between the question entity and the answer entity
Your role is to:
1. Analyze the question and the provided answer carefully
2. Examine the graph triplets to find connections between the question entity and the answer entity
3. Evaluate if the shortest path in the graph supports the given answer
4. Consider that some paths may appear unrelated to the question at first glance but could still lead to the correct answer
5. Conclude whether the answer is correct, partially correct, or incorrect based on the graph information
6. If the answer is incorrect or partially correct, suggest the correct answer based on the graph data
7. Provide a short answer
Remember to be thorough in your analysis and clearly communicate your thought process. Your goal is to provide an accurate assessment of the answer's correctness while considering all relevant information from the graph
User
f"Question: {q}
Graph: {linearize_graph(g, a, sep_token='')}
Answer: {a} Is this answer correct? Respond with Yes or No:"

assistant that verifies answers to questions.. We employ the OpenAI LLMs[7] (versions *o3-mini*, *GPT-4o* and *GPT-4o mini*) and LLaMA3-8B-Instruct[8].

5 Experimental Results

Evaluation results in terms of positive class precision, recall and F1-score are presented in Table 6. Based on our experiments, GPT-4o is the best model for QA without using subgraphs.

Supervision Improves KG Reasoning. The improvement in tuning the LLaMA model has shown that even simple subgraphs can be beneficial for enhancing an LLM's reasoning abilities. The improvement of F1-score on manual test set is notably higher (4.9%) than on automatic test set (1.1%). Given a higher graph sizes in the manual part, we assume that relevant KG subgraphs are more crucial for reasoning on complex questions requiring multi-hop reasoning rather than 1-hop reasoning. Compared to zero-shot set-up, LLaMA-3b demonstrates a 14.2% F1 improvement with graph-aware

[7] chat.openai.com.

[8] huggingface:meta-llama/Meta-Llama-3-8B-Instruct.

Table 6. Evaluation results on ShortPathQA test set. Precision, recall, and F1-score are calculated for positive class. o3-mini used with low reasoning effort. The best set-up for each backbone LM is highlighted with **bold**. The best overall F1-score for each test set is underlined.

Model setup	Automatic Test Set			Manual Test Set		
	Precision	Recall	F1-score	Precision	Recall	F1-score
Negative class constant	0.0	0.0	0.0	0.0	0.0	0.0
Positive class constant	0.148	1.0	0.257	0.094	1.00	0.172
Random baseline	0.148	0.5	0.228	0.094	0.5	0.158
Supervised evaluation						
MPNet (no KG)	0.503	**0.639**	0.563	0.167	0.507	0.251
MPNet (with KG)	**0.609**	0.631	**0.620**	**0.275**	**0.515**	**0.359**
LLaMA3-8b-Instruct **FT** (no KG)	0.689	0.751	0.719	0.507	0.713	0.593
LLaMA3-8b-Instruct **FT** (with KG)	**0.707**	**0.755**	**0.730**	**0.561**	**0.749**	**0.642**
Zero-shot evaluation						
LLaMA3-8b-Instruct (no KG)	0.432	**0.649**	**0.519**	**0.376**	0.749	**0.500**
LLaMA3-8b-Instruct (with KG)	**0.460**	0.341	0.392	0.352	**0.783**	0.486
GPT4o mini (no KG)	**0.727**	**0.671**	**0.698**	**0.574**	**0.752**	**0.652**
GPT4o mini (with KG)	0.653	0.544	0.594	0.561	0.705	0.625
o3-mini (no KG)	**0.605**	**0.805**	**0.691**	**0.639**	0.830	**0.723**
o3-mini (with KG)	0.493	0.804	0.612	0.520	**0.872**	0.651
GPT4o (no KG)	**0.771**	**0.769**	**0.770**	**0.678**	**0.856**	**0.757**
GPT4o (with KG)	0.759	0.662	0.707	0.652	0.830	0.730

supervision. While LLMs have bigger capacity to memorize simple factual knowledge, the improvement when for small MPNet encoder when provided a graph is even more substantial: 5.7% and 10.8%, on automatic and manual test sets, respectively. Similarly to results observed on LLaMA, the observed F1-score improvement is more significant on more challenging manual test set.

LLMs Fail in Zero-shot KG Reasoning. While supervised evaluation results prove that KG subgraphs provide essential factual information that can boost question answering performance, all three LLMs show degraded performance when given the subgraphs. For some reason, the provided subgraphs-aware prompts turned out to be misleading with an F1 decreases of 2.7%, 2.7%, and 1.4% for GPT4o, GPT4o mini, and LLaMA3-8b on the manual test set, respectively. It follows that LLMs are unable to handle additional factual data and hypothesize that more thorough prompt engineering is required.

Analysis. To gain a deeper understanding of how subgraph information influences the accuracy of responses to given questions, we conducted a detailed analysis on *ShortPathQA Manual test set*. It is noteworthy that the mean subgraphs associated with correct and incorrect question-answer pairs exhibit distinct characteristics. Typically, subgraphs corresponding to correct answers are more concise. Detailed statistical information regarding these subgraphs is presented in Table 7.

To analyze the reasons for errors in different LLMs, we manually analyze predictions for all experiments. The models exhibit certain error patterns. One common pattern is domain confusion, where entities from related domains or with similar names are confused. This occurs frequently in geography, literature, and mythology. For example, the question "*Among the Final Fantasy games, which installment achieved the highest worldwide sales?*" includes the entity "*Final Fantasy*" *(Q99416119)*, but the correct answer is expected to be "*Final Fantasy VII*" *(Q214232)*. However, the model cannot distinguish between it, leading to incorrect results, where entities from related domains or with similar names are confused.

The presence of graphs can help provide context for complex queries, reducing the risk of misinterpretation. As we can see in Fig. 4, the density and content of a subgraph seem to be important features in distinguishing between correct and incorrect answers to a given question.

Table 7. Comparative analysis of subgraph characteristics associated with *Correct* and *Incorrect* question-answer pairs for manual test set. *All* subgraphs statistics calculated on balanced subset.

	All	Correct	Incorrect
Num. Nodes	3.925	3.295	4.589
Num. Edges	4.823	3.741	5.844
Density	0.497	0.582	0.405
Degree	2.223	2.073	2.337
Average Path Length	1.401	1.280	1.536

Subgraphs can be one of the most important feature that help the model understand the difference between entities with the same label, as shown in Fig. 5

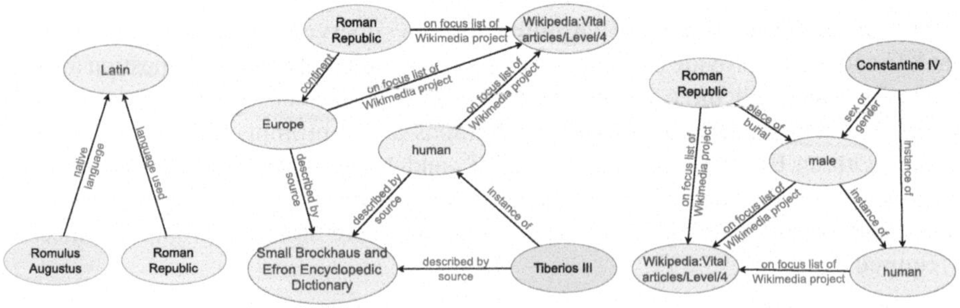

Fig. 4. Question-candidate graph visualizations for question "*Who was the last Roman Emperor?*" and three answer candidates: (i) Romulus Augustus (true answer), (ii) JTiberios III, and (iii) Constantine IV. Correct and incorrect answer candidates are green and red, respectively. (Color figure online)

However, despite tuning the LLaMA3-8b model or attempting to teach GPT-4o or o3-mini models to correctly understand subgraphs, in some cases, it is not an easy task, and on large subgraphs, models tend to misinterpret the subgraph and make incorrect predictions. For example, for the question "*Who is the main antagonist in the Star Wars Episode VII: The Force Awakens movie?*", all models using subgraph information are unable to understand that "*Kylo Ren*" is the correct answer, while models without a subgraph are able to. Similar results can be seen for at least 17 other questions, and in all these cases, there are at least 5 nodes in the subgraphs that motivate us to say that the correct answer is usually provided with smaller subgraphs.

In summary, our experiments and analysis of the results show that current large language models, such as LLaMA and GPT-4o, are not able to effectively work with graph data without careful prompt engineering or fine-tuning on graph structure data. This suggests that there is a need to develop specific methods for working with graph data, while the ShortPathQA dataset could be used as a benchmark dataset to measure the models' performance.

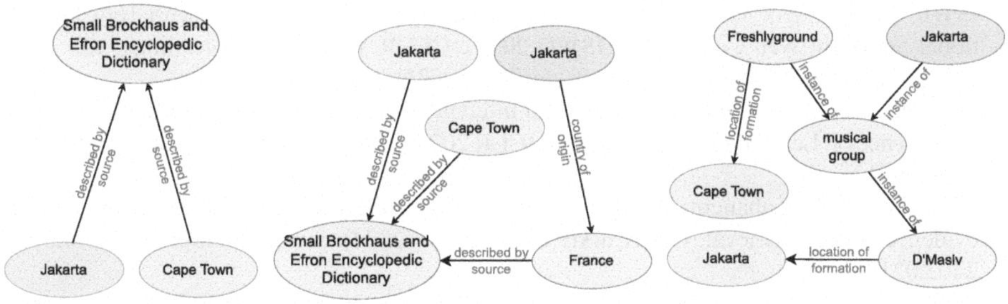

Fig. 5. Question-candidate graph visualizations for question "*Which city has larger population, Jakarta or Cape Town?*" and three answer candidates: (i) Jakarta (Q3630) - capital city and smallest province of Indonesia (true answer), (ii) Jakarta (Q4177898) - French electronic music project, and (iii) Jakarta (Q11716285) - Serbian and former Yugoslav rock band. Correct and incorrect answer candidates are green and red, respectively. (Color figure online)

6 Conclusion

We introduce ShortPathQA, a novel dataset for knowledge graph question answering based on a collection of novel manually curated questions and questions extracted from Mintaka [24]. Compared to existing datasets, ShortPathQA pairs textual questions with subgraphs from Wikidata based on shortest paths. Each subgraph represents relations between entities mentioned in a question, and a candidate answer entity from the KG. As the proposed dataset eliminates the errors in entity retrieval and variability of subgraph construction methods, we expect it to help speed up the future research on injecting factual knowledge from KGs to LLMs. The proposed dataset construction pipeline can be adopted and extended to an arbitrary knowledge graph in any domain. Our experiments show that including KG information to LLMs yields substantial improvements, yet is not trivial which suggest the need for further research of data fusion methods.

References

1. Baek, J., Aji, A.F., Saffari, A.: Knowledge-augmented language model prompting for zero-shot knowledge graph question answering. CoRR arxiv:2306.04136 (2023). https://doi.org/10.48550/arXiv.2306.04136
2. Belikova, J., Beliakin, E., Konovalov, V.: JellyBell at TextGraphs-17 shared task: Fusing large language models with external knowledge for enhanced question answering. In: Ustalov, D., et al. (eds.) Proceedings of TextGraphs-17: Graph-based Methods for Natural Language Processing, pp. 154–160. Association for Computational Linguistics, Bangkok (2024). https://aclanthology.org/2024.textgraphs-1.15/
3. Chen, Z., Zhao, X., Liao, J., Li, X., Kanoulas, E.: Temporal knowledge graph question answering via subgraph reasoning. Knowl. Based Syst. **251**, 109134 (2022). https://doi.org/10.1016/J.KNOSYS.2022.109134
4. Devlin, J., et al.: BERT: pre-training of deep bidirectional transformers for language understanding. In: Proceedings of the 2019 Conference of the North American Chapter of the Association for Computational Linguistics: Human Language Technologies, NAACL-HLT 2019, pp. 4171–4186 (2019). https://doi.org/10.18653/V1/N19-1423
5. Diefenbach, D., et al.: Question answering benchmarks for wikidata. In: Proceedings of the ISWC 2017 Posters & Demonstrations and Industry Tracks co-located with 16th International Semantic Web Conference (ISWC 2017). CEUR Workshop Proceedings, vol. 1963. CEUR-WS.org (2017). https://ceur-ws.org/Vol-1963/paper555.pdf
6. Ding, N., et al.: Causallm is not optimal for in-context learning. In: The Twelfth International Conference on Learning Representations, ICLR 2024 (2024). https://doi.org/10.48550/arXiv.2308.06912
7. Ding, W., et al.: Enhancing complex question answering over knowledge graphs through evidence pattern retrieval. CoRR arxiv:2402.02175 (2024). https://doi.org/10.48550/arXiv.2402.02175
8. Dubey, A., et al.: The llama 3 herd of models. CoRR arxiv:2407.21783 (2024). https://doi.org/10.48550/arXiv.2407.21783
9. Dubey, M., Banerjee, D., Abdelkawi, A., Lehmann, J.: LC-QuAD 2.0: a large dataset for complex question answering over Wikidata and DBpedia. In: Ghidini, C., et al. (eds.) ISWC 2019. LNCS, vol. 11779, pp. 69–78. Springer, Cham (2019). https://doi.org/10.1007/978-3-030-30796-7_5
10. Gu, Y., et al.: Beyond I.I.D.: three levels of generalization for question answering on knowledge bases. In: WWW '21: The Web Conference 2021, pp. 3477–348 (2021). https://doi.org/10.1145/3442381.3449992
11. Hao, J., Cheng, B.: A subgraph retrieval method for complex questions based on hybrid semantics and path representation. ITM Web Conf. **60**, 00017 (2024). https://doi.org/10.1051/itmconf/20246000017
12. He, X., et al.: G-retriever: retrieval-augmented generation for textual graph understanding and question answering. In: Advances in Neural Information Processing Systems 38: Annual Conference on Neural Information Processing Systems 2024, NeurIPS (2024). https://doi.org/10.48550/arXiv.2402.07630
13. Ji, Z., et al.: Survey of hallucination in natural language generation. ACM Comput. Surv. **55**(12), 248:1–248:38 (2023). https://doi.org/10.1145/3571730
14. Kingma, D.P., Ba, J.: Adam: a method for stochastic optimization. In: 3rd International Conference on Learning Representations, ICLR 2015 (2015). http://arxiv.org/abs/1412.6980
15. Kwiatkowski, T., et al.: Natural questions: a benchmark for question answering research. Trans. Assoc. Comput. Linguist. **7**, 452–466 (2019). https://doi.org/10.1162/TACL_A_00276

16. Li, M., Miao, S., Li, P.: Simple is effective: the roles of graphs and large language models in knowledge-graph-based retrieval-augmented generation. CoRR arxiv:2410.20724 (2024). https://doi.org/10.48550/arXiv.2410.20724
17. Lin, B.Y., Chen, X., Chen, J., Ren, X.: Kagnet: knowledge-aware graph networks for commonsense reasoning. In: Proceedings of the 2019 Conference on Empirical Methods in Natural Language Processing and the 9th International Joint Conference on Natural Language Processing, EMNLP-IJCNLP 2019, pp. 2829–283 (2019). https://doi.org/10.18653/V1/D19-1282
18. Liu, L., et al.: Logic query of thoughts: guiding large language models to answer complex logic queries with knowledge graphs. CoRR arxiv:2404.04264 (2024). https://doi.org/10.48550/arXiv.2404.04264
19. Loshchilov, I., Hutter, F.: Decoupled weight decay regularization. In: 7th International Conference on Learning Representations, ICLR 2019 (2019). https://doi.org/10.48550/arXiv.1711.05101
20. Mallen, A., et al.: When not to trust language models: investigating effectiveness of parametric and non-parametric memories. In: Proceedings of the 61st Annual Meeting of the Association for Computational Linguistics, pp. 9802–9822. Association for Computational Linguistics (2023).https://doi.org/10.18653/v1/2023.acl-long.546
21. Raffel, C., et al.: Exploring the limits of transfer learning with a unified text-to-text transformer. J. Mach. Learn. Res. **21**, 140:1–140:67 (2020). http://jmlr.org/papers/v21/20-074.html
22. Sakhovskiy, A., et al.: TextGraphs 2024 shared task on text-graph representations for knowledge graph question answering. In: Proceedings of TextGraphs-17: Graph-based Methods for Natural Language Processing, pp. 116–125. Association for Computational Linguistics (2024). https://aclanthology.org/2024.textgraphs-1.9/
23. Salnikov, M., et al.: Large language models meet knowledge graphs to answer factoid questions. In: Proceedings of the 37th Pacific Asia Conference on Language, Information and Computation, pp. 635–644. Association for Computational Linguistics (2023). https://aclanthology.org/2023.paclic-1.63/
24. Sen, P., et al.: Mintaka: a complex, natural, and multilingual dataset for end-to-end question answering. In: Proceedings of the 29th International Conference on Computational Linguistics, pp. 1604–1619 (2022). https://aclanthology.org/2022.coling-1.138/
25. Song, K., et al.: Mpnet: masked and permuted pre-training for language understanding. In: Advances in Neural Information Processing Systems 33: Annual Conference on Neural Information Processing Systems 2020, NeurIPS (2020). https://doi.org/10.48550/arXiv.2004.09297
26. Speer, R., Chin, J., Havasi, C.: Conceptnet 5.5: an open multilingual graph of general knowledge. In: Proceedings of the Thirty-First AAAI Conference on Artificial Intelligence, pp. 4444–4451. AAAI Press (2017). https://doi.org/10.1609/AAAI.V31I1.11164
27. Su, Y., Zhang, J., Song, Y., Zhang, T.: Pipenet: question answering with semantic pruning over knowledge graphs. CoRR arxiv:2401.17536 (2024).https://doi.org/10.48550/arXiv.2401.17536
28. Tonmoy, S.M.T.I., et al.: A comprehensive survey of hallucination mitigation techniques in large language models. CoRR arxiv:2401.01313 (2024). https://doi.org/10.48550/arXiv.2401.01313
29. Trivedi, H., et al.: MuSiQue: multihop questions via single-hop question composition. Trans. Assoc. Comput. Linguist. **10** (2022). https://doi.org/10.1162/tacl_a_00475
30. Vaswani, A., et al.: Attention is all you need. In: Advances in Neural Information Processing Systems 30: Annual Conference on Neural Information Processing Systems 2017, pp. 5998–6 (2017). https://doi.org/10.48550/arXiv.1706.03762

31. Vijayakumar, A.K., et al.: Diverse beam search: decoding diverse solutions from neural sequence models. CoRR arxiv:1610.02424 (2016). http://arxiv.org/abs/1610.02424
32. Wang, S., Qin, B.: No need for large-scale search: exploring large language models in complex knowledge base question answering. In: Proceedings of the 2024 Joint International Conference on Computational Linguistics, Language Resources and Evaluation (LREC-COLING 2024), pp. 12288–12299. ELRA and ICCL (2024). https://aclanthology.org/2024.lrec-main.1074/
33. Xiong, G., Bao, J., Zhao, W.: Interactive-KBQA: multi-turn interactions for knowledge base question answering with large language models. In: Proceedings of the 62nd Annual Meeting of the Association for Computational Linguistics, pp. 10561–10582. Association for Computational Linguistics (2024). https://doi.org/10.18653/v1/2024.acl-long.569
34. Yasunaga, M., et al.: Deep bidirectional language-knowledge graph pretraining. In: Advances in Neural Information Processing Systems 35: Annual Conference on Neural Information Processing Systems 2022, NeurIPS (2022). https://doi.org/10.48550/arXiv.2210.09338
35. Yasunaga, M., et al.: QA-GNN: reasoning with language models and knowledge graphs for question answering. In: Proceedings of the 2021 Conference of the North American Chapter of the Association for Computational Linguistics: Human Language Technologies, pp. 535–546. Association for Computational Linguistic (2021). https://doi.org/10.18653/v1/2021.naacl-main.45
36. Yih, W.t., et al.: The value of semantic parse labeling for knowledge base question answering. In: Proceedings of the 54th Annual Meeting of the Association for Computational Linguistics. Association for Computational Linguistics (2016). https://doi.org/10.18653/v1/P16-2033

Explaining Bias in Internal Representations of Large Language Models via Concept Activation Vectors

Jasper Kyle Catapang[1,2(✉)]

[1] Tokyo University of Foreign Studies, Fuchu, Tokyo, Japan
catapang.jasper.kyle.y0@tufs.ac.jp
[2] Money Forward, Inc., Minato, Tokyo, Japan

Abstract. Large language models (LLMs) often encode subtle biases that reflect historical disparities in their training data. While many studies evaluate bias solely based on model outputs, the internal mechanisms that give rise to such biases remain underexplored. In this work, the framework *Bias-CAVs* is proposed, an innovative framework that extends the concept activation vector methodology to probe and explain internal LLM representations for bias. This approach conducts a layer-wise analysis to quantify bias projections, revealing where bias is introduced, amplified, or mitigated within the network. In a two-stage process, activations are first extracted from key layers of diverse LLM architectures (e.g., LLaMA-3, Mistral, Phi, and Gemma) and then a linear classifier (via logistic regression) is trained on standardized activations to create Bias-CAVs that distinguish between biased and neutral representations. The findings across gender, race, profession, and political domains contribute to both the understanding of LLM internal bias propagation and the development of more explainable debiasing interventions.

Keywords: social bias · bias detection · AI fairness · large language models · concept activation vectors

1 Introduction

Recent advances in large language models have demonstrated unprecedented capabilities in natural language understanding and generation. However, these models also inherit and amplify subtle societal biases present in their training data. While prior research has predominantly focused on evaluating bias at the output level [5,8], relatively little attention has been paid to examining the internal representations that give rise to these biases.

Inspired by Xu et al.'s work on uncovering safety risks in LLMs through concept activation vectors [16], the underlying idea is extended to bias detection. In the proposed framework, *Bias-CAVs* leverages the linear interpretability assumption in deep models to project internal activations onto a bias-sensitive subspace. By performing a layer-wise analysis, the methodology quantitatively

R. Ichise (Ed.): NLDB 2025, LNCS 15836, pp. 111–125, 2026.
https://doi.org/10.1007/978-3-031-97141-9_8

tracks the propagation and transformation of bias as information flows through the network layers. Such an investigation not only provides an explanation for the model's output behavior but also uncovers potential intervention points for bias mitigation.

Several recent studies have emphasized the need to understand model bias beyond surface-level outputs. For example, Dong et al. [5,6] explored gender bias in LLMs by probing explicit and implicit signals in generated text, while Kumar et al. [9] proposed scalable bias detection using language model judges. However, these methods largely overlook the internal activation dynamics that shape model behavior. The Bias-CAV framework builds on Xu et al. [16] by directly probing internal representations to identify where bias is most pronounced.

This work makes three key contributions:

- Proposes Bias-CAVs, an interpretable diagnostic method for detecting bias within LLM activations.
- Conducts a layer-wise analysis across multiple LLM architectures to trace how bias is introduced, amplified, or attenuated.
- Discusses the implications for fairness evaluation and debiasing strategies.

By analyzing internal bias propagation, the gap is bridged between output-based detection and proactive model debugging. The rest of the paper outlines related work, methodology, experimental results, and broader implications.

2 Background

Large language models have transformed natural language processing while raising concerns about bias and fairness. Early studies primarily targeted model outputs: Dong et al. [5] revealed gender bias in conditional generation, while a follow-up [6] proposed mitigation strategies. Kotek et al. [8] evaluated gender stereotypes via keyword metrics and human annotation, and Kumar et al. [9] introduced scalable bias evaluation using model-judging techniques.

However, output-based methods often miss the internal mechanisms driving biased behavior, prompting growing interest in probing model representations. A prominent approach is Concept Activation Vectors (CAVs), which map high-dimensional activations into interpretable directions. Originally developed for vision models, CAVs were extended by Xu et al. [16] into Safety CAVs (SCAVs) for uncovering latent risks in LLMs, leveraging the assumption that concepts like bias are linearly separable in activation space–a premise supported across multiple domains.

Activation probing offers two key benefits. First, it enables layer-wise diagnostics: prior studies [10,17] have shown that early layers encode general linguistic structure, while intermediate layers capture socio-cultural cues that often correlate with bias. Later layers tend to refine or suppress these patterns. Second, by isolating biased subspaces, such methods enable precise interventions without degrading model performance–unlike coarse, output-level corrections.

Traditional debiasing strategies such as re-ranking, post-hoc filtering, and fine-tuning on curated datasets [12,13] can reduce bias but lack the interpretability and specificity offered by internal diagnostics. Bias-CAVs bridge this gap by pinpointing and potentially correcting biased representations within specific layers.

However, challenges remain. The assumption of linear separability may not hold across all bias types or model families. Understanding the relationship between internal bias representations and downstream behavior is also an open question. Future work must address these issues to enable more principled, transparent bias mitigation.

In summary, bias research has evolved from output-based evaluation [5,6,8,9] to methods that interrogate model internals [16]. Bias-CAV builds on this shift, offering a scalable, interpretable tool for diagnosing and addressing bias within the representational layers of LLMs.

3 Methodology

3.1 Social Bias

In this study, the focus is on four major types of social bias: gender, race, profession, and political orientation. Each bias type captures a different dimension of societal inequality, reflected in large language model representations.

- **Gender Bias:** This bias involves the association of certain roles, behaviors, or traits with specific genders [14]. For example, a model might more frequently associate "household" with women and "hardworking" with men.
- **Racial Bias:** Racial bias manifests as the differential association of racial groups with particular attributes or stereotypes [2]. For instance, a model might preferentially link African-American names with negative sentiment adjectives, such as "criminal" or "dangerous".
- **Profession Bias:** Profession bias refers to occupational stereotypes encoded in model representations. For example, associating the profession "software developer" more strongly with male-related contexts than female ones [3].
- **Political Bias:** Political bias surfaces when a model preferentially generates or supports ideologies aligned with a particular political leaning. For instance, consistently framing liberal statements more positively than conservative ones (or vice versa) [1].

These biases are not only measurable through quantitative metrics but also observable in practical examples. Consider a prompt asking for a brief character description: if the model describes a "teacher" as "a caring woman who loves helping children" but a "CEO" as "a confident man who drives results," it reflects both gender and profession bias operating simultaneously. Such intersectional examples highlight the subtle, compounded nature of social biases in large language models, emphasizing the need for careful internal probing and mitigation.

3.2 Data: The MD-Gender-Bias Dataset

The Multi-Dimensional Gender Bias (MDGenderBias) dataset is used in this research–a rich corpus capturing gender bias from pragmatic and semantic perspectives [4]. It decomposes bias along three axes: the subject (ABOUT), the speaker (AS), and the addressee (TO), and combines large-scale corpora with both automatic annotations and crowdsourced evaluations.

Dataset Summary and Supported Tasks. The dataset includes seven automatically annotated corpora (excluding Wikipedia from the HuggingFace version), a benchmark for gender rewrites, and lists of gendered names and words. It supports the `text-classification-other-gender-bias` task, where models predict gender-related labels. Prior transformer-based models report an average accuracy of around 67% on binary classification across the ABOUT, TO, and AS axes [4].

Dataset Structure and Configurations. There are five configurations:

- **convai2_inferred:** Persona-based dialogues with classifier-inferred ABOUT labels.
- **light_inferred:** Similar to convai2, also with inferred annotations.
- **opensubtitles_inferred:** Movie subtitles annotated using name lists and statistical measures.
- **yelp_inferred:** Yelp reviews where speaker gender is predicted and ABOUT labels are imputed.
- **image_chat:** Dialogues describing images, annotated with Boolean male/female fields.

Data Fields and Examples. Key fields include:

- **new_data:** Reformulated text, original text, gender labels (e.g., ABOUT: male), and annotator metadata.
- **funpedia/wizard:** Gendered text with persona or title context.
- **image_chat:** Image captions plus gender flags.
- **_inferred sets:** Text with `binary_label`, `binary_score`, and sometimes `ternary_label`.
- **Word/Name Lists:** Masculine/feminine word pairs and labeled name entries.

Example from `convai2_inferred`: `{'binary_label': 1, 'binary_score': 0.6522, 'text': ''hi, how are you doing? ...''}`

Example from `image_chat`: `{'caption': ''a young girl is holding a pink umbrella'', 'female': True, 'male': False}`

Splits and Annotation Process. Each configuration has its own partitioning:

- **Image Chat:** 39K male, 15K female, 154K unannotated entries.
- **Funpedia/Wizard:** Thousands of entries with ABOUT labels.
- **ConvAI2, LIGHT, Yelp, Subtitles:** Tens of thousands to millions of examples with AS/TO labels and inferred ABOUT annotations.

Most annotations were crowd-sourced via platforms like Mechanical Turk. Where gold-standard labels were unavailable, pretrained classifiers on curated data provided inferred labels. Annotator confidence was also recorded to assess label reliability.

Dataset Curation Rationale. MDGenderBias was designed to overcome limitations of earlier corpora that focused on narrow dimensions. By spanning conversations, reviews, and multimodal dialogue, the dataset captures both overt and implicit gender cues. Its multi-source structure supports diverse forms of bias detection and lays the foundation for effective debiasing strategies.

Experimental Usage. The author utilizes five configurations: `convai2_inferred`, `light_inferred`, `opensubtitles_inferred`, `yelp_inferred`, and `image_chat`. These span a wide range of linguistic and contextual scenarios, supporting the layer-wise analysis of bias propagation across LLMs.

Additional Bias Domains: Stereoset and Political Bias. To extend the analysis beyond gender, two additional datasets are incorporated:

- **Stereoset** [15]: A benchmark designed to evaluate social biases in LLMs, particularly across race and profession. The researcher uses the 'intersentence' split, which presents a context sentence and evaluates model preference between stereotypical, anti-stereotypical, and unrelated continuations. The data is formatted as a binary classification task between stereotypical and anti-stereotypical continuations.
- **Political Bias Dataset** [7]: A crowd-annotated corpus labeling political leaning of statements (liberal vs conservative). For this study,non-neutral labels are grouped into a single class and retain neutral statements as the control group, enabling binary classification.

From each dataset, 500 instances are sampled and applied the same train/validation split and layer-wise activation extraction procedure as in the MDGenderBias configurations.

3.3 Explaining Bias

This subsection details the mathematical foundation underlying the Bias-CAV framework. Inspired by the Safety Concept Activation Vector (SCAV) approach introduced by Xu et al. [16], this method leverages the linear interpretability assumption to both diagnose and mitigate bias in large language models. The subsection formalizes the bias detection process, then derives the optimal perturbation to shift biased embeddings into a safe subspace, and finally discusses the geometric interpretation of the formulation. The derivations closely align with the experimental code, where layer activations are standardized and a logistic regression classifier is trained to estimate bias.

Mathematical Formulation of Bias Detection. Let $e \in \mathbb{R}^d$ denote the embedding extracted from a given layer of an LLM. The bias (or "maliciousness") of e via a linear classifier is modeled by:

$$P_m(e) = \sigma(w^\top e + b), \tag{1}$$

where $\sigma(z) = \frac{1}{1+e^{-z}}$ is the sigmoid function, $w \in \mathbb{R}^d$ is the weight vector, and $b \in \mathbb{R}$ is the bias term. The probability $P_m(e)$ quantifies the degree to which the embedding is considered biased. The parameters w and b are learned by minimizing the cross-entropy loss over a labeled dataset D:

$$\min_{w,b} -\frac{1}{|D|} \sum_{(e,y)\in D} \Big[y \log P_m(e) + (1-y)\log\big(1 - P_m(e)\big)\Big], \tag{2}$$

where $y = 1$ indicates a biased (malicious) instruction and $y = 0$ indicates a safe (neutral) instruction.

Optimal Perturbation for Embedding-Level Bias Correction. To mitigate bias, a biased embedding e is minimally perturbed so that it moves into a safe region. The perturbed embedding is defined as:

$$e' = e + \epsilon v, \tag{3}$$

where $\epsilon \in \mathbb{R}$ is the perturbation magnitude and $v \in \mathbb{R}^d$ is the perturbation direction with $\|v\| = 1$.

The objective is to find the smallest ϵ such that the perturbed embedding satisfies:

$$P_m(e + \epsilon v) \leq P_0, \tag{4}$$

where P_0 is a predefined safety threshold (e.g., 0.01). Assuming that $P_m(e) > P_0$, the constraint in (4) is equivalent to:

$$w^\top(e + \epsilon v) + b \leq \sigma^{-1}(P_0), \tag{5}$$

with $\sigma^{-1}(P_0)$ denoting the logit of P_0. Solving for ϵ yields:

$$\epsilon \geq \frac{w^\top e + b - \sigma^{-1}(P_0)}{w^\top v}. \tag{6}$$

Since the maximum value of $w^\top v$ is achieved when v aligns with w (i.e. $v = \frac{w}{\|w\|}$), the minimal perturbation is obtained as:

$$\epsilon^* = I(P_m(e) > P_0) \cdot \frac{\sigma^{-1}(P_0) - b - w^\top e}{\|w\|}, \tag{7}$$

$$v^* = \frac{w}{\|w\|}, \tag{8}$$

where $I(\cdot)$ is the indicator function that ensures the perturbation is applied only if $P_m(e) > P_0$.

Geometric Interpretation and Experimental Alignment. Geometrically, the weight vector w defines the hyperplane that separates biased embeddings from safe ones. Perturbing an embedding e in the direction of w moves it perpendicularly to the decision boundary, ensuring the shortest path into the safe subspace. The magnitude ϵ^* (Eq. (7)) quantifies the distance e must be moved to fall below the safety threshold.

This mathematical framework directly informs the experimental pipeline. Layer activations are extracted and standardized before training a logistic regression classifier (see `train_bias_cav_with_cv`). The classifier computes the bias probability $P_m(e)$ and, if necessary, applies the minimal perturbation determined by Eqs. (7) and (8). This layer-wise approach pinpoints where bias is introduced and enables targeted corrections.

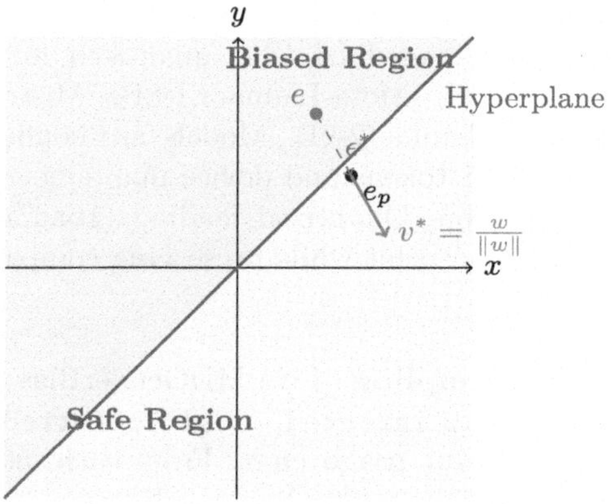

Fig. 1. Geometric interpretation of Bias-CAV. The hyperplane (blue line) separates biased (red region) and safe (green region) embeddings. A biased embedding e is minimally perturbed (ϵ^*) into the safe region along v^*. (Color figure online)

Figure 1 shows an illustrative diagram that visualizes this geometric interpretation.

The Bias-CAV framework leverages a linear classifier to both detect bias in LLM embeddings and compute an optimal, minimal perturbation to move these embeddings into a safe region. This principled geometric approach aligns directly with the experimental setup, enabling detailed, layer-wise analysis and targeted bias mitigation.

3.4 Experimental Setup

Experiments are conducted on Google Colab Pro, leveraging an NVIDIA A100-SXM4-40GB GPU (with approximately 39.557 GB of usable memory) on a Linux environment. All runs were performed in Python 3.10 using PyTorch 2.6.0+cu124, CUDA 12.4, and *Unsloth* v0.0.29.post3 for efficient low-bit quantization and rapid fine-tuning. Reproducibility code, including all scripts and supplementary materials, is available at https://github.com/jcatapang/bias-cavs.

Libraries and Configuration. The experimental pipeline leverages several core Python libraries: PyTorch for GPU-accelerated operations, NumPy and `random` for array manipulation and sampling, and scikit-learn (specifically `LogisticRegression`, `StandardScaler`, and `KFold`) for model training and cross-validation. The experiments use the Hugging Face `datasets` library to load MDGenderBias, Unsloth for efficient low-bit quantization and memory optimization, and the `transformers` library for tokenization, model configuration, and forward passes.

Model Variants and Configurations. Four representative large language models are evaluated, each loaded in 4-bit quantized form via the Unsloth `FastLanguageModel` interface: Meta-Llama-3.1-8B, Mistral-7B-instruct-v0.3, Phi-3.5-mini-instruct, and Gemma-2-9B. Models are configured with a maximum sequence length of 2048 tokens and device mapping set to `auto`, allowing efficient multi-GPU utilization. Quantized loading (`load_in_4bit=True`) substantially reduces memory footprint while preserving comparable model performance.

Dataset Selection and Sampling. Five MDGenderBias configurations from Sect. 3.2 are used: `convai2_inferred`, `light_inferred`, `opensubtitles_inferred`, `yelp_inferred`, and `image_chat`. From each, 500 records are sampled, splitting them into training (80%) and validation (20%). Preprocessing standardizes data into {`text`, `bias_label`} pairs across configurations.

Layer-Wise Analysis and Activation Probing. Following the Bias-CAV methodology, activations are probed at select model layers (e.g., early, middle, final). Forward hooks capture hidden states, which are aggregated and used to train logistic regression classifiers (`LogisticRegression`) that learn a linear separation between biased and neutral embeddings. Five-fold cross-validation is applied per layer and report validation scores on held-out samples.

4 Results and Discussion

In this section, a comprehensive analysis of the Bias-CAV framework across multiple dataset configurations and model variants, is presented. The layer-wise bias detection trends is first discussed, then the performance across different dataset configurations and models next. Finally, the detailed classifier performance metrics–including accuracy, precision, recall, and F1 score are presented–to validate the reliability of the logistic regression-based Bias-CAV.

4.1 Layer-Wise Bias Analysis

The experiments evaluate bias detection by computing a test score that reflects the average bias probability $P_m(e)$ across validation samples. For each model, activations are extracted from four key layers (early, intermediate, later, and final, corresponding to indices 0, 8, 16, and –1, respectively) and a logistic regression classifier is trained on these activations using five-fold cross-validation. The resulting CV metrics are consistently robust across layers, confirming that the Bias-CAV reliably distinguishes biased from safe embeddings even in the presence of training data variability.

For example, in the `convai2_inferred` configuration using unsloth/Meta-Llama-3.1-8B-bnb-4bit, the average bias test scores across layers were:

- Layer 0: 0.619
- Layer 8: 0.632
- Layer 16: 0.623
- Final Layer (−1): 0.590

These results suggest that bias signals are slightly amplified in the intermediate layers before partially diminishing in the final layer. Similar trends were observed across other configurations and model variants.

4.2 Comparison Across Dataset Configurations

The framework is evaluated on five configurations of the MDGenderBias dataset:

- **convai2_inferred** and **light_inferred**: Derived from persona-based conversations, these configurations yield moderate bias scores (roughly between 0.55 and 0.67).
- **opensubtitles_inferred**: Exhibits higher bias scores (0.81–0.87), indicating that movie subtitles tend to contain more pronounced bias cues.
- **yelp_inferred**: Yields bias scores in the mid-70% range, suggesting a consistent but slightly lower bias detection compared to subtitles.
- **image_chat**: Displays very low bias scores (approximately 0.20), likely reflecting the descriptive nature of image captions or a lower sensitivity of the classifier to non-textual modalities.

Table 1 summarizes the average test scores P_m for selected configurations and models at representative layers (0, 8, and final).

Table 1. Summary of Average Bias Test Scores (P_m) for Selected Configurations and Models

Configuration	Layer 0	Layer 8	Final Layer
`convai2_inferred` (Meta-Llama-3.1)	0.619	0.632	0.590
`convai2_inferred` (Mistral-7B)	0.645	0.597	0.571
`convai2_inferred` (Phi-3.5-mini)	0.647	0.669	0.564
`convai2_inferred` (Gemma-2-9B)	0.632	0.634	0.613
`opensubtitles_inferred` (Meta-Llama-3.1)	0.816	0.870	0.866
`yelp_inferred` (Meta-Llama-3.1)	0.738	0.790	0.797
`image_chat` (Meta-Llama-3.1)	0.202	0.203	0.204

4.3 Classifier Performance Metrics

To further validate the approach, the detailed cross-validation metrics–accuracy, precision, recall, and F1 score–are reported for each model variant across different dataset configurations. Table 2 summarizes these metrics.

Table 2. Cross-Validation Metrics (Averages) Across Dataset Configurations

Dataset	Model	Accuracy	Precision	Recall	F1 Score
`convai2_inferred` and `light_inferred`	Meta-Llama-3.1	0.71	0.74	0.77	0.75
	Mistral-7B	0.71	0.74	0.78	0.76
	Phi-3.5-mini	0.70	0.73	0.77	0.75
	Gemma-2-9B	0.72	0.75	0.77	0.76
`opensubtitles_inferred`	Meta-Llama-3.1	0.80	0.84	0.92	0.88
	Mistral-7B	0.81	0.84	0.94	0.89
	Phi-3.5-mini	0.78	0.83	0.91	0.87
	Gemma-2-9B	0.82	0.85	0.94	0.89
`yelp_inferred`	Meta-Llama-3.1	0.70	0.75	0.83	0.79
	Mistral-7B	0.70	0.75	0.84	0.79
	Phi-3.5-mini	0.70	0.75	0.82	0.78
	Gemma-2-9B	0.70	0.75	0.85	0.79
`image_chat`	Meta-Llama-3.1	0.99	0.97	0.95	0.96
	Mistral-7B	0.98	0.97	0.95	0.96
	Phi-3.5-mini	0.99	0.97	0.95	0.96
	Gemma-2-9B	0.99	0.98	0.95	0.96

4.4 Bias in Race, Profession, and Political Domains

In addition to gender, the Bias-CAV framework was evaluated on racial and professional stereotypes via the `stereoset` dataset, and on political bias via the `cajcodes/political-bias` dataset.

- **Stereoset (race, profession):** Results show weak to moderate signal separability, with average validation scores across all layers peaking around 0.46 (race) and 0.45 (profession). Bias detectability was most prominent in intermediate layers, with Gemma and Phi achieving slightly higher detection accuracy than other models.

- **Political Bias:** Models performed substantially better on this domain, with validation scores consistently above 0.72 across all layers and models. This suggests political leanings are more linearly separable in activation space–possibly due to the dataset's more topical and opinion-rich language.

Table 3 summarizes the bias detection scores for these extended domains.

Table 3. Bias Detection Scores Across Stereoset and Political Bias Domains

Dataset	Model	Layer 0	Layer 8	Final Layer
`stereoset` (Race/Profession)	Meta-Llama-3.1 (race)	0.499	0.478	0.443
	Mistral-7B (profession)	0.440	0.468	0.440
	Gemma-2-9B (race)	0.530	0.476	0.420
	Phi-3.5-mini (profession)	0.432	0.450	0.465
`political-bias`	Meta-Llama-3.1	0.738	0.723	0.719
	Mistral-7B	0.741	0.730	0.734
	Gemma-2-9B	0.736	0.731	0.714
	Phi-3.5-mini	0.738	0.741	0.730

These results demonstrate the versatility of the Bias-CAV framework in diagnosing bias across different sociolinguistic dimensions, not just gender. The stronger political scores suggest that some biases–especially those aligned with polarizing or opinionated content–are more robustly encoded in LLM representations.

4.5 Qualitative Analysis

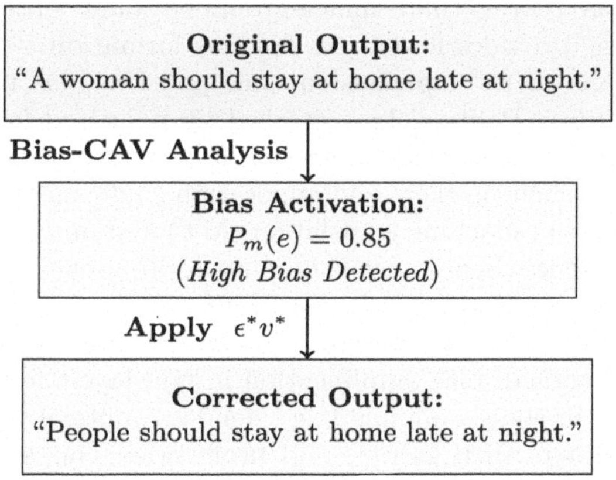

Fig. 2. A qualitative illustration of Bias-CAV. The original output (top) exhibits a biased phrase. Bias-CAV detects a high bias probability in the intermediate layers (middle). After applying the corrective perturbation $\epsilon^* v^*$, the model output is modified to a less biased version (bottom).

To further illustrate the impact of the Bias-CAV framework, Fig. 2 shows a representative example of gender bias in a language model output. In this example, the LLM initially produces a response that reinforces a gender stereotype. The Bias-CAV analysis reveals that the activations at the intermediate layers yield a high bias probability, which is then partially mitigated in the final layers. The diagram illustrates the original biased output, the intermediate bias activation state, and the corrected output after applying the Bias-CAV perturbation.

The original output of the diagram is problematic because it reinforces a gender stereotype associating domestic roles and behavioral expectations exclusively with women. Such statements implicitly suggest that women, more than men, are responsible for staying home late at night, perpetuating outdated notions of gendered responsibility and autonomy. Beyond being socially regressive, these stereotypes can influence how models respond in practical scenarios (e.g., content moderation, hiring), underscoring the importance of diagnosing and mitigating internalized biases.

This qualitative insight not only validates the quantitative results but also demonstrates the practical utility of the framework in diagnosing and addressing internal biases in LLMs.

4.6 Discussion and Implications

The results highlight how bias is internally encoded and propagated in LLMs. First, bias is unevenly distributed: intermediate layers tend to amplify bias signals–likely due to contextual interactions–while final layers reduce them, suggesting these mid-layers play a central role in shaping bias.

Second, the data domain and modality affect bias detectability. Text-based configurations (`convai2_inferred`, `opensubtitles_inferred`, `yelp_inferred`) yielded higher bias scores than image-grounded data (`image_chat`), where descriptive language provides fewer cues for bias formation.

Third, extensions to race, profession, and political bias revealed clear differences in separability. Political bias–marked by polarized language–was most detectable, followed by gender. Race and profession bias proved harder to isolate, likely due to implicit markers and annotation challenges. This phenomenon parallels observations in machine translation (MT) systems, where models automatically assign gender when translating neutral pronouns (e.g., Filipino *siya*), reflecting statistical associations between professions and genders learned from biased training data (e.g., male pronouns for male-dominated fields, etc.).

Fourth, while trends of bias amplification in mid-layers followed by attenuation are observable in some domains (e.g., gender, political bias), they are less consistent across others such as race and profession. This suggests that while hierarchical information processing influences bias propagation, the strength and clarity of amplification effects depend on the domain and the subtlety of the bias type.

While Bias-CAVs perform well in many settings, they assume bias is linearly separable in activation space. This holds for overt biases like gender and political alignment but may be limiting for subtler, context-dependent biases. The author hypothesizes that intermediate layers, tasked with integrating semantic, social, and pragmatic cues, naturally reinforce biases present in the training data, as they prioritize high-salience features for downstream predictive accuracy. In contrast, final layers, optimized for surface fluency or safety alignment objectives, may suppress such features. Thus, the architecture's hierarchical information processing inherently risks magnifying social biases unless explicitly corrected. Exploring nonlinear variants–e.g., kernel methods or neural probes–could improve coverage without sacrificing interpretability.

Finally, while this approach is efficient relative to full-model fine-tuning, training classifiers across layers and domains adds some overhead. The use of 4-bit quantized models keeps this manageable, but future scaling may require further optimization.

4.7 Proposed Debiasing Strategies

Based on the insights gained from the Bias-CAV framework and its mathematical formulation, two complementary strategies are proposed for debiasing large language models.

First, the proposal of a direct corrective approach applied during inference. Given an embedding e that exhibits a high bias probability $P_m(e)$, the Bias-CAV framework computes an optimal perturbation. Specifically, using the closed-form solution,

$$\epsilon^* = \frac{\sigma^{-1}(P_0) - b - w^\top e}{\|w\|} \quad \text{and} \quad v^* = \frac{w}{\|w\|},$$

the embedding can be transformed via

$$e' = e + \epsilon^* v^*,$$

so that the modified embedding e' ideally satisfies $P_m(e') \leq P_0$. This correction effectively shifts the biased representation into the safe subspace defined by the classifier's hyperplane. The key advantage of this approach is that it offers a principled, closed-form solution–eliminating the need for extensive grid searches to determine optimal perturbation magnitudes.

A second, complementary strategy is to incorporate debiasing directly into the model's training objective. In this approach, the primary task loss $\mathcal{L}_{\text{task}}$ is augmented with a bias regularization term that penalizes high bias probabilities. The modified loss function can be expressed as:

$$\mathcal{L} = \mathcal{L}_{\text{task}} + \lambda \cdot \max(0, P_m(e) - P_0),$$

where λ is a hyperparameter that controls the strength of the debiasing penalty. This term encourages the model to adjust its internal representations during fine-tuning, pushing them towards a region where the bias probability is reduced below the threshold P_0.

Both strategies build on the strengths of previous debiasing efforts in the literature [11,18] while leveraging the mathematical clarity provided by the Bias-CAV framework. The direct perturbation approach provides an immediate, layer-wise correction mechanism during inference, whereas the regularization strategy aims to produce inherently less biased representations through fine-tuning.

5 Conclusion

In this paper, Bias-CAVs is presented, a novel framework that extends the concept activation vector methodology to explain internal bias in large language models. Through a detailed, layer-wise analysis across multiple domains–namely gender, race, profession, and political–the author demonstrates that bias is not uniformly encoded throughout the network. Intermediate layers consistently exhibit stronger bias signals, which are then partially reduced in the final layers. Experimental results further reveal that the separability of bias signals varies by domain: political and gender biases are more easily detected, likely due to their association with overt linguistic markers, while race and profession biases prove more challenging to isolate, reflecting their subtler, context-dependent nature. These findings underscore the need for more nuanced representations and diagnostic tools to uncover implicit forms of bias.

To address these challenges, the author proposes two debiasing strategies grounded in the mathematical framework: (1) a direct inference-time perturbation that projects embeddings into a safer subspace, and (2) a loss-augmented training objective that penalizes biased internal activations. While still theoretical, these approaches provide a principled path toward more interpretable and effective bias mitigation. Bias-CAVs thus offer a scalable, interpretable, and architecture-agnostic method for probing and understanding internal bias propagation in LLMs.

Future work will focus on validating the proposed debiasing methods, integrating causal and contextual bias attribution techniques, and extending the framework to additional bias dimensions, including disability, religion, age, and intersectional identities. This research aims to contribute to the development of fairer, safer, and more transparent language technologies.

Acknowledgements. The author appreciates the invaluable guidance and support of colleagues at Money Forward Japan and the Tokyo University of Foreign Studies. Special thanks to Kenichiro Kurusu and Nathaniel Oco for providing the parallelism on MT systems and the suggestion of adding the discussion on social bias.

References

1. Baly, R., San Martino, G.D., Glass, J., Nakov, P.: We can detect your bias: predicting the political ideology of news articles. In: Proceedings of the 2020 Conference on Empirical Methods in Natural Language Processing (EMNLP), pp. 4982–4991 (2020)

2. Bertrand, M., Mullainathan, S.: Are emily and greg more employable than lakisha and jamal? A field experiment on labor market discrimination. Am. Econ. Rev. **94**(4), 991–1013 (2004)
3. Bolukbasi, T., Chang, K.W., Zou, J.Y., Saligrama, V., Kalai, A.T.: Man is to computer programmer as woman is to homemaker? Debiasing word embeddings. Adv. Neural Inf. Process. Syst. **29** (2016)
4. Dinan, E., Fan, A., Wu, L., Weston, J., Kiela, D., Williams, A.: Multi-dimensional gender bias classification. In: Proceedings of EMNLP 2020, pp. 314–331 (2020)
5. Dong, X., Wang, Y., Yu, P.S., Caverlee, J.: Probing explicit and implicit gender bias through llm conditional text generation. arXiv preprint arXiv:2311.00306 (2023)
6. Dong, X., Wang, Y., Yu, P.S., Caverlee, J.: Disclosure and mitigation of gender bias in llms. arXiv preprint arXiv:2402.11190 (2024)
7. Jones, C.: Political bias dataset: a synthetic dataset for bias detection and reduction (2024). https://huggingface.co/datasets/cajcodes/political-bias
8. Kotek, H., Dockum, R., Sun, D.: Gender bias and stereotypes in large language models. In: Proceedings of the ACM Collective Intelligence Conference, pp. 12–24 (2023)
9. Kumar, S.H., et al.: Decoding biases: automated methods and llm judges for gender bias detection in language models. arXiv preprint arXiv:2408.03907 (2024)
10. Li, B., Wisniewski, G.: Are neural networks extracting linguistic properties or memorizing training data? An observation with a multilingual probe for predicting tense. In: Merlo, P., Tiedemann, J., Tsarfaty, R. (eds.) Proceedings of the 16th Conference of the European Chapter of the Association for Computational Linguistics: Main Volume, pp. 3080–3089. Association for Computational Linguistics (2021). https://doi.org/10.18653/v1/2021.eacl-main.269. https://aclanthology.org/2021.eacl-main.269/
11. Li, T., et al.: Rethinking jailbreaking through the lens of representation engineering. arXiv preprint arXiv:2401.06824 (2024)
12. Masoudian, S., Frohmann, M., Rekabsaz, N., Schedl, M.: Unlabeled debiasing in downstream tasks via class-wise low variance regularization. arXiv preprint arXiv:2409.19541 (2024)
13. Mendelson, M., Belinkov, Y.: Debiasing methods in natural language understanding make bias more accessible. In: Moens, M.F., Huang, X., Specia, L., Yih, S.W.t. (eds.) Proceedings of the 2021 Conference on Empirical Methods in Natural Language Processing, pp. 1545–1557. Association for Computational Linguistics, Online and Punta Cana (2021). https://doi.org/10.18653/v1/2021.emnlp-main.116. https://aclanthology.org/2021.emnlp-main.116/
14. Moss-Racusin, C.A., Dovidio, J.F., Brescoll, V.L., Graham, M.J., Handelsman, J.: Science faculty's subtle gender biases favor male students. Proc. Natl. Acad. Sci. **109**(41), 16474–16479 (2012)
15. Nadeem, M., Bethke, A., Reddy, S.: Stereoset: measuring stereotypical bias in pretrained language models. In: Proceedings of the 59th Annual Meeting of the Association for Computational Linguistics (ACL), pp. 5356–5371. Association for Computational Linguistics (2021). https://aclanthology.org/2021.acl-long.416
16. Xu, Z., Huang, R., Chen, C., Wang, X.: Uncovering safety risks of large language models through concept activation vector. Adv. Neural. Inf. Process. Syst. **37**, 116743–116782 (2025)
17. Zheng, X., Jiang, J.: An empirical study of memorization in nlp. arXiv preprint arXiv:2203.12171 (2022)
18. Zou, A., Wang, L., et al.: Universal and transferable adversarial attacks on aligned language models. arXiv preprint arXiv:2307.15043 (2023)

Duplicate Bug Report Retrieval for New Bug Reports

Miao Hu(✉), Zhiwei Lin, and Adele H. Marshall

School of Mathematics and Physics, Queen's University Belfast, Belfast, UK
{mhu05,z.lin,a.h.marshall}@qub.ac.uk

Abstract. Issue tracking systems are used to manage and track software requirements and bug reports. In an issue tracking system, two bug reports created by two persons may be duplicate as they may refer to the same bug in a software system. Previous research shows that an estimated 35.8% to 41.6% of bug reports are duplicate, and this causes significant inefficiencies in software development and maintenance as developers have to waste time to identify if a bug report has duplicate reports prior to fixing the bug. Therefore, retrieving duplicate bug reports is important to improve productivity in software development. This paper proposes to use pre-trained language models (e.g., BERT and RoBERTa) to embed bug reports and to compute probability scores for retrieving duplicate bug reports. The proposed approach is evaluated with four common real datasets (i.e., Eclipse, Mozilla, NetBeans and Open Office) for the duplicate bug report retrieval task. The experimental results show that the proposed models are very effective for new duplicate bug report retrieval.

Keywords: Issue Tracking Systems · New Bug Reports · Duplicate Bug Report Retrieval · Pre-trained Language Model

1 Introduction

Issue Tracking Systems [6,17], such as JIRA[1] and Bugzilla[2], have been heavily used in software development to record and track software requirements and bugs. Once a software bug is reported, it is assigned to software developers for resolution. The bug remains as 'open' status until it is resolved, which typically includes code changes and a subsequent code review by peer developers.

Each bug report contains structured information, including fields, such as bug id, title, description, component, created time, *etc.*. A bug issue also has a field to show if this bug has duplicates. For example, in the issue tracking system for Mozilla project, the field of 'Tracking' shows that if a bug has duplicates, as shown in Fig. 1 (bug 'Mozilla-192993' from Mozilla project[3] has a relation of 'duplicate' with 'Mozilla-110718').

[1] https://www.atlassian.com/software/jira.
[2] https://www.bugzilla.org/.
[3] https://bugzilla.mozilla.org/show_bug.cgi?id=192993.

R. Ichise (Ed.): NLDB 2025, LNCS 15836, pp. 126–141, 2026.
https://doi.org/10.1007/978-3-031-97141-9_9

Bug 192993
Control-N doesn't work when page is loading.

▾ **Categories**
Product: Core ▾
Component: DOM: UI Events
Platform: x86 Windows 2000

Type: defect
Priority: *Not set* Severity: major
Created time : 2003-02-12 11:47 PST

▾ **Tracking**
Status: VERIFIED DUPLICATE of bug 110718

▾ **People**
Assignee: **aaronlev** ▾ Reporter: **jlim** ▾
QA Contact: **bugzilla** ▾ Triage Owner: **mccr8** ▾

Jing Lim ▾Reporter
Description

```
User-Agent:       Mozilla/4.0 (compatible; MSIE 5.5; Windows NT)
Build Identifier: Mozilla/5.0 (Windows; U; Windows NT 5.0; en-US; rv:1.2.1)
SOmetimes when I open a url, and the page takes a while to load (maybe network is slow), I press control-N to open
another browser window, but that doesn't work. The browser only responds to my control-N AFTER that page has loaded.
This is annoying because I don't want to wait for the page to load before I open another url. Reproducible: Always
Steps to Reproduce: 1. open a url (that is slow to resolve dns or slow to transfer or load) 2. hit control-N key
```

Fig. 1. A example of bug issue 'Mozilla-192993'. The field of 'Tracking' shows 'Mozilla-192993' has a duplicate bug issue (i.e., 'Mozilla-110718'). This bug issue also contains a title and a description, along with other information.

Duplicate bug reports, referring to an identical bug problem, are raised when users or testers submit a software problem at different times. On average, 35.8%–41.6% of bug reports have duplicate reports in an issue tracking system [8]. The existing issue tracking system cannot automatically determine whether a new submission is a duplicate bug report. Instead, duplicate bug reports are manually identified and labelled as 'duplicate' of each other, which is a labour-intensive process. Locating duplicate bug reports for each reported issue helps developers or users determine whether the referred software problem has already been resolved, saving developers' time by avoiding the need to resolve duplicate bugs and thus improving the productivity of software development.

This paper is focused on enhancing the performance of the duplicate bug report retrieval (DBR) task, where a new bug report (when it is created) is regarded as a query and it is used to search for its duplicate bug reports that were created before this bug report. Recent work in DBR [2–4,8,19,20] focuses on using word embedding models (such as Word2Vector [12] and Glove [14]) to initialize the representation for bug reports. The representations are integrated into cosine function or deep learning models (e.g., CNN and LSTM) to compute the similarity between a query bug report and a set of candidate bug reports for ranking purposes. However, the existing works do not consider the time series nature of the bug reports (each report has a timestamp to denote when it was created), and they split the data into training and test sets by random according to 8:2 ratio. An approach, named SABD [16], considered the time series nature of bug reports and proposed to use a cut-off point for splitting data, where a set of data before a cut-off point is used as training, with the remaining (after the cut-off point) as testing. However, existing deep learning-based models (e.g., CNN and LSTM) use a shallow model to embed bug reports. Such a shallow model exhibits limited capability in handling textual information [11].

To enhance the performance of duplicate bug retrieval, this paper introduces an approach to retrieving duplicate bug reports for new bug reports, using pre-trained language models, such as BERT [5] and RoBERTa [10]. The task of duplicate bug report retrieval for new bug reports will need to address: (1) computing scores for duplicate pairs to filter out irrelevant candidate bug reports, and (2) ranking the candidate reports to locate the duplicate reports. The contributions of this paper include:

1. a new representation method for duplicate bug pairs is introduced by converting them into a single, extended word sequence.
2. the pre-trained language models, such as BERT and RoBERTa, are used as encoders to embed duplicate bug pairs and to compute probability scores for evaluating each pair.
3. a filter strategy is proposed to filter irrelevant candidate bug reports, taking into consideration the bug component constraint.
4. four real-world datasets (i.e., Eclipse, Mozilla, NetBeans and Open Office) are used to evaluate the duplicate bug report retrieval task. The results indicate that the proposed models are highly effective for retrieving duplicate bug reports.

This paper is organized as follows: Sect. 2 reviews related works in the area of duplicate bug analysis. Section 3 introduces the embedding methods used for the duplicate bug report retrieval task. Experimental results for this task are presented in Sect. 4. Finally, the paper concludes with Sect. 5.

2 Related Work

This section presents the related work in this area.

2.1 Duplicate Bug Report Detection

The task of duplicate bug report detection is designed to automatically determine if two bugs in a pair are duplicate [8,13,18]. For instance, given a bug pair (s, o), the goal is to determine if the bug report s is a 'duplicate' of bug report o, which is a classification task and distinct from the duplicate bug retrieval process. A software-literature context method [1] proposed to extract the subject-specific contextual material, such as non-functional requirements and architecture keywords for representation, and the similarity of two reports is computed by a cosine function. DC-CNN [7] used a Dual-Channel Convolutional Neural Network for duplicate bug report detection. A pair of bug reports is represented with a dual-channel matrix fed to a CNN model to capture the correlated semantic dependencies between bug reports. Previous works based on neural networks have generated representations for individual bug reports without considering another report in the duplicate pair. Such independent representations fail to capture the dependencies between bugs within a duplicate pair. To address this, BERT-MLP was proposed in [11] using a pre-trained language model, i.e., BERT, as an encoder to combine embedding two bug reports within a pair for duplicate detection. This approach used the title and description as textual information to help embed. A recent work [8] studies if textual dissimilarity has an impact on duplicate bug report detection by using a pre-trained word embedding model, i.e., Glove, to initialize textual information of bug reports and CNN to compute the similarity between duplicate bug within a pair.

2.2 Duplicate Bug Report Retrieval

When a software bug emerges, it may be reported by two or more users or testers. Therefore, it is quite common that duplicate bug reports referring to an identical bug are created in an issue tracking system [20]. The task of duplicate bug report retrieval is distinct from duplicate bug detection. While duplicate bug report retrieval aims to locate a set of relevant duplicate bug reports for a query bug report based on similarity computation, and duplicate bug detection is to tell if two bug reports refer to the same bug, without the need to locate the bug reports.

The textual content and categorical information (e.g., priority and product version) of bug reports were first utilized for duplicate bug report retrieval in [19]. This approach employed the Term Frequency - Inverse Document Frequency (TF-IDF) method to represent bug reports and used the cosine function to compute similarities between the query bug report and each candidate bug report in the candidate set. The bug reports were then ranked in descending order based on their similarity scores. The Recall-Rate@k is used to evaluate the performance of approaches, which indicates the rate of duplicate bug reports ranked at the top k positions. Siamese Convolutional Neural Network (CNN) and Long Short Term Memory (LSTM) were used in the task of duplicate bug report retrieval [4]. Word embedding models, e.g., Word2Vector [12] and Glove [14], were used to initialise bug reports. The models, e.g., CNN and LSTM, are used to embed query and candidate bug reports to get representation vectors. Then, the cosine function is used to compute the similarity between the query and candidate bug reports. The datasets introduced from [9] are randomly split into the training and test set with 80% to 20%. The retrieval candidates are only from the test set, which is not a reasonable setting because the correct candidate may occur in the training set. DWEN [2] proposed averaging word embedding to represent bug reports. The embedding vectors of two bug reports within a bug pair are concatenated into a feature vector, which is fed into a fully connected network to compute scores. SABD [16] proposed using LSTM to embed bug reports composed of the categorical feature (e.g., system and version) and textual feature (e.g., summary and description). In the experiment, the datasets are split into the training set and test set according to the timeline to ensure the bug reports in the test set are unknown for the training set. Although this model achieved the best performance so far, the limitations of LSTM for dealing with long text are not ignored.

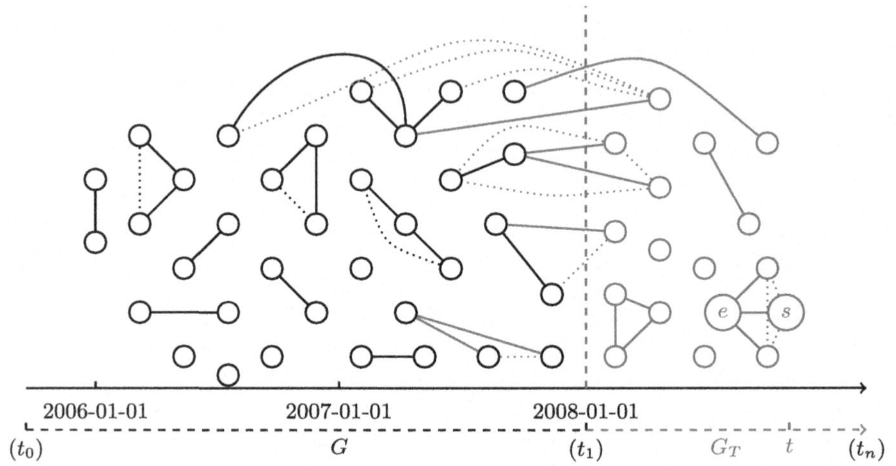

Fig. 2. A graph for bug reports with the 'duplicate' relation sampled from Eclipse project. Cut-off point t_1 ('1st Jan 2008') is used to split the data into training set of issues G and testing set of issues G_T ($G \cap G_T = \emptyset$). The edges (including the dashed edge) show that two issues (nodes) are duplicate. The dashed edges indicates that such duplicate relation is missing in the data.

2.3 Remarks

Figure 2 presents a sub-graph from Eclipse, using timestamp '1st Jan 2008' as the cut-off point. The bug reports created after this point are called new bug reports, where a new bug report created at time t may have duplicate bug reports that are created before t, in which those duplicate bug reports could be new bug reports that are created after the cut-off point. For example, issue s was created at t and it has a duplicate issue e, which was a new bug issue (also created after 1st Jan 2008, according to Fig. 2).

This paper aims to retrieve duplicate bug reports for newly emerged issues. To enhance the performance of duplicate report retrieval, we use textual information to create a long description for bugs and employ pre-trained language models, e.g., BERT and RoBERTa, as encoders to efficiently compute scores to identify 'duplicate' reports.

3 Duplicate Bug Report Retrieval for New Bug Report

This section introduces the duplicate bug report retrieval task for new bug reports as well as our embedding methods.

3.1 Research Definitions

Due to the characteristics of time series in bug reports of an issue tracking system, these reports are divided into two parts according to timeline: the training set G, comprising bug reports created before a timestamp t_1, and the test set G_T, which includes bug reports created after t_1, as illustrated in Fig. 2. When a new bug report $s \in G_T$ is created at timestamp t, duplicate bug report retrieval aims to locate the relevant duplicate bug reports created before time t. These duplicate bug reports are denoted by the set O_t. For the new bug issue s, a 'duplicate' label is established between s and each of its duplicate bug reports o ($o \in O_t$), thereby forming pairs of duplicates. It is important to note that the set O_t contains bug reports both from G and G_T, and the timestamp of bug reports in O_t is less than t. A new duplicate pair is represented as (s, o), where issue s is known as the query bug report and issue o is denoted as the candidate bug report.

3.2 Duplicate Pair Representation

The graph in Fig. 2 shows the bug reports with 'duplicate' relations from Eclipse project. It is observed that numerous bugs have only one or two edges connecting them, resulting in disconnected sub-graphs. This results in sparsity in the overall graph. As each bug report has textual information to explain the bug, it is important to use the rich textual information for DBR. For example, as shown in Fig. 1, a bug report includes textual details, such as the bug title and description, to describe the bug. Each title, typically a phrase or short sentence, offers a concise overview of the bug. The description, provided by users or testers, usually contains several sentences and provide a more detailed explanation. The 'component' field indicates the module to which the bug belongs. In this study, the 'component' field is also utilized as part of the textual information for embedding, aiming to increase the semantic information for bug report embeddings.

In this work, textual information, such as the component name, title, and description, is utilized to generate a long word sequence, serving as a semantic representation for the bug reports. Consequently, to represent a duplicate pair, the word sequences of the query bug report and the candidate bug report are concatenated, forming a single, extended word sequence. For instance, given a duplicate pair (s, o), the concatenated long word sequence that represents this pair is known as:

$$D_{(s,o)} = (X_s, X_o), \tag{1}$$

where X_s and X_o represent the word sequence of query bug report s and candidate bug report o, which is known as:

$$X_s = (w_{s_\mathrm{C}}, w_{s_\mathrm{T}}, w_{s_\mathrm{D}}) = (x_{s_1}, x_{s_2}, x_{s_3}, ..., x_{s_m}) \tag{2}$$

$$X_o = (w_{o_\mathrm{C}}, w_{o_\mathrm{T}}, w_{o_\mathrm{D}}) = (x_{o_1}, x_{o_2}, x_{o_3}, ..., x_{o_k}) \tag{3}$$

where $w_{s_\mathrm{C}}, w_{s_\mathrm{T}}, w_{s_\mathrm{D}}$ represent the word sequences for the component name, title, and description of query bug report s, respectively. These three items are concatenated to form a single word sequence, denoted as $(x_{s_1}, x_{s_2}, x_{s_3}, \ldots, x_{s_m})$, where each x_{s_i} for $1 \leq i \leq m$ denotes a word token in the representation X_s of the query bug report. Similarly, the candidate bug report o is represented in the same manner.

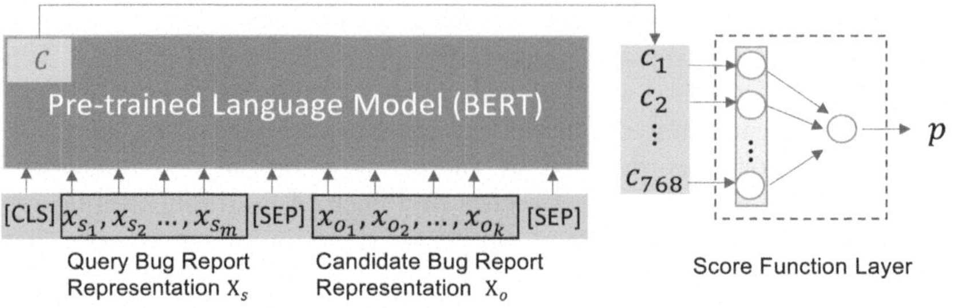

Fig. 3. An example of BERT model training. The representation of a duplicate pair, $D_{(s,o)} = (X_s, X_o)$, is inputted into BERT by packaging it into a single long sequence, separated by special tokens, e.g., `[CLS]`. In this sequence, each x_{s_i} for $1 \leq i \leq m$ represents a word in the query bug report representation X_s, etc. The first token is a special classification token and its final hidden vector, denoted as $C = [c_1, c_2, \ldots, c_{768}]$, is fed into a score function layer, (i.e., a fully connected layer) to compute the probabilities p for evaluating the input duplicate pair (s, o).

3.3 Embedding Models

BERT (RoBERTa) Model for Duplicate Pair Embedding. The deep learning models, such as CNN and LSTM, have been used in the task of duplicate bug report retrieval [4,16]. However, these models exhibit certain drawbacks, particularly when it is used to embed long texts. The CNN, primarily designed for pattern recognition in images, can struggle with the sequential and contextual nature of text. It depends on the kernel size used in capturing the contextual dependencies in embedding text data and might miss the broader context or long-range dependencies in text data [11]. The LSTM, though better at handling sequences and long-term dependencies, processes data sequentially and is limited in capturing bidirectional context dependencies, which is often crucial for understanding the full scope of a sentence or document [15].

BERT, a pre-trained language model [5], addresses long text data challenges with its bidirectional processing capability. The self-attention mechanism [21] is used to capture relevant dependencies of the context for each word regardless of the distance between words in long texts. The nature of pre-trained BERT allows for quick fine-tuning with less data, enhancing the performance of the model for specific tasks. RoBERTa [10], an advanced version of BERT, was trained on a larger dataset and incorporates a dynamic masking mechanism in its training, further refining BERT for improved performance.

In this work, BERT and RoBERTa are used to embed duplicate pairs to compute probability scores for retrieving duplicate bug reports for newly submitted bug reports. The new approaches are named DBR(BERT) and DBR(RoBERTa). Each duplicate pair representation $D_{(s,o)}$ is packed into a long sequence with special tokens (i.e., `[CLS]` and `[SEP]`) as input to BERT/RoBERTa. Then, the probability scores are computed by the score function layer to evaluate the possibility of input duplicate pairs.

Figure 3 shows an example of the fine-tuning process using BERT. For a duplicate pair (s, o), its representation $D_{(s,o)}$ is concatenated into a word sequence with special tokens (i.e., `[CLS]` and `[SEP]`), which is represented as (`[CLS]`, X_s, `[SEP]`, X_o, `[SEP]`), i.e.,

$$(\texttt{[CLS]}, x_{s_1}, x_{s_2}, ..., x_{s_m}, \texttt{[SEP]}, x_{o_1}, x_{o_2}, ..., x_{o_k}, \texttt{[SEP]}). \tag{4}$$

Each x_{s_i} for $1 \leq i \leq m$ denotes a token in the query bug report representation X_s and x_{o_i} for $1 \leq i \leq k$ denotes a token in the candidate bug report representation X_o. N is the number of tokens in the sequence, $N = |X_s| + |X_o| + 3$, where $|X_s|$ and $|X_o|$ denote the number of tokens in each component.

The long word sequence, i.e., Eq. (4), is fed into the BERT. The first token, i.e., `[CLS]`, serves as a special classification token. Its hidden state vector, produced by the final layer, is denoted as $C \in \mathbb{R}^H$, where H is the hidden state size in BERT, such as $H = 768$ in BERT-base (as well as RoBERTa-base). Finally, C is fed into a score function layer to compute the probability scores, which are computed with C and W (i.e., Eq. (6)), for evaluating the possibility of input duplicate pairs. The only new parameters introduced during training are score function layer weights $W \in \mathbb{R}^H$.

Loss Function. The model is trained by optimizing a cross-entropy loss function:

$$L = \sum_{G^+ \cup G^-} (y \log(p) + (1 - y) \log(1 - p)), \tag{5}$$

where

$$p = \text{softmax}(CW^T), \tag{6}$$

$p = [p_1, p_2]$, which has two probability scores indicating if the input is valid. The $y \in \{0, 1\}$ indicates either a valid or an invalid label. $G^+ = \{(s, o)\}$ is a set of valid duplicate pairs in the training set G of bug reports, and G^- is a set of invalid duplicate pairs [16].

3.4 The Process of Duplicate Bug Report Retrieval for New Issues

---

Algorithm 1. Compute Score for a Candidate Duplicate Pair (s_i, o_{i_j})

Input: Candidate Duplicate Pair $(s_i, o_{i_j}) \in \mathcal{H}$
Output: Probability Score $\lambda_{(i,i_j)}$

1. Represent the candidate duplicate pair (s_i, o_{i_j}) as $(X_{s_i}, X_{o_{i_j}})$ according to Eq. (1).
2. Apply the embedding model with Eq. (4) to compute the contextual embedding vector C.
3. Calculate the score $\lambda_{(i,i_j)}$ for the pair (s_i, o_{i_j}) using C as defined in Eq. (6). In this function, p_1 is determined to be $\lambda_{(i,i_j)}$.

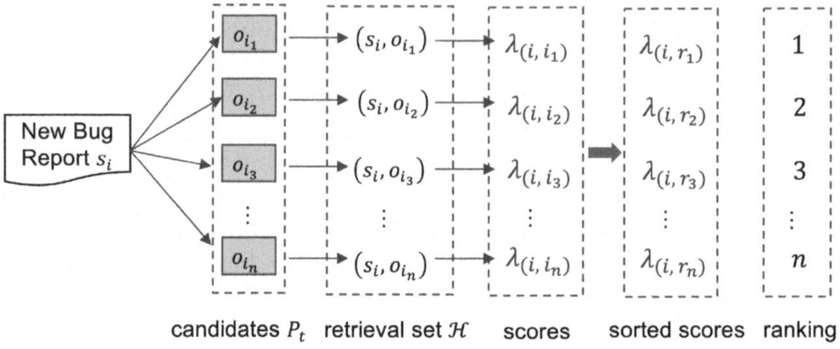

Fig. 4. The overall workflow of duplicate bug report retrieval for new bug reports. When i-th new bug report s_i emerges with timestamp t, a retrieval set (denoted as $\mathcal{H}$) is constructed by linking this new bug report s_i to the candidates, which are created before t and P_t denotes these candidates. Then, the scores for each candidate pair in $\mathcal{H}$ are computed according to Algorithm 1. Finally, these scores will be sorted in descending order, and the duplicate bug reports are retrieved among the top-k positions for this new bug report s_i.

Figure 4 shows the workflow for duplicate bug report retrieval for new bug reports. When a new bug report s_i is created at time t, let P_t denote the set of all bug reports that existed before that time. The trained model then targets retrieving a set O_t of relevant duplicate bug reports from P_t, where each bug report o in O_t is a duplicate of s_i. This will result in a set $\mathcal{H}$ for all candidate duplicate pairs, known as $\mathcal{H} = \{(s_i, o_{i_j}) | o_{i_j} \in P_t, 1 \leq j \leq n\}$, where n is the number of bug reports that were created before time t. To determine O_t, the scores will be computed for each candidate duplicate pair $(s_i, o_{i_j}) \in \mathcal{H}$ according to Algorithm 1. Next, the list of scores for all candidate pairs will be sorted in descending order. The duplicate bug reports are retrieved within the top k positions. Details on optimizing $\mathcal{H}$ will be provided in Sect. 4.2.

4 Experiments

In this section, we evaluate the proposed methods for the duplicate bug report retrieval task on four real datasets.

4.1 Datasets

The four real-world datasets, Open Office, NetBeans, Eclipse, and Mozilla, for duplicate bug report analysis were proposed by [9]. The summary of the bug reports and duplicate pairs is shown in Table 1. By taking into account the time-series nature of the bug reports, the datasets are split into the training set and test set according to the timeline [16], in which the cut-off points are '1st Jan 2008' for Open Office, NetBeans, and Eclipse, and '1st Jan 2010' for Mozilla. The bug reports that emerge before the cut-off point are the training set, the subset of the remaining set 10% is used for the validation set, and the rest becomes the test set.

Table 1. Statistics of four datasets.

Datasets	Data-split	#Duplicate Pairs	#bug Reports	Timeline
Open Office	Training	56751	84895	2000-10-16∼2007-12-31
	Validation	466	31333	2008-01-01∼ 2008-12-31
	Test	4198		
NetBeans	Training	46001	121900	1998-08-21∼2007-12-31
	Validation	501	31666	2008-01-01∼2008-12-31
	Test	4508		
Eclipse	Training	64781	212987	2001-10-10∼2007-12-31
	Validation	438	45783	2008-01-01∼2008-12-31
	Test	3942		
Mozilla	Training	997149	482820	1998-08-21–2009-12-31
	Validation	970	65940	2010-01-01–2010-12-31
	Test	8731		

Table 2. An example from the Eclipse Bugzilla system demonstrates that different components of a query bug report, such as 'General UI' and 'Chart', correspond with the component of candidate bug report under the 'duplicate' relation. By analogy, the corresponding candidate components can be obtained for each query component under a 'duplicate' link from the issue tracking system.

Component of Query Bug Report	Component of Candidate Bug Report
'General UI'	'General UI', 'PHP Search', 'Core', 'Problems view', 'Editor', 'PHP Modelling', 'Debugger'
'Chart'	'Chart', 'Report', 'Data', 'Core', 'Report Designer', 'Report Viewer', 'Report Engine'

4.2 Optimising Retrieval Set $\mathcal{H}$

To reduce the retrieval space, it is necessary to reduce the number of candidate pairs in $\mathcal{H}$. As proposed in [16], a time window (denoted as t_{gap}) is utilized, which indicates a period before the creation time of a new bug report. For instance, setting $t_{gap} = 365$ (days) implies that issue reports emerging within this 365-day period are considered as candidates for retrieving relevant bug report.

In the issue tracking system, the 'component' field in a bug report specifies its associated module. For instance, as shown in Fig. 1, the component for 'Mozilla-192993' is 'UI Event'. For each bug report s, the component of its relevant bug report o is constrained with respect to a 'duplicate' relation. An example, as shown in Table 2 from the Eclipse Bugzilla system, demonstrates how different components of a query bug report, such as 'General UI' and 'Chart', correspond to the components of duplicate candidates under the 'duplicate' relation. If the component of query bug report s is 'Chart', the possible component for duplicate candidate bug report o is bounded to be one of {'Chart', 'Report', 'Data', 'Core', 'Report Designer', 'Report Viewer', 'Report Engine'}. Therefore, in addition to the time window constraint (t_{gap}), the bug report component is considered a constraint aiming to filter out irrelevant candidates via aligning bug report components.

Let T_s be the set of components that candidate bug report o may have a relation of 'duplicate' with the query bug report s, and let y_o represent the component of o. Then, for a new query bug report s, $\mathcal{H}$ can be optimised according to

$$\mathcal{H} = \{(s, o) | o \in P_t, t_s - t_o \leq t_{gap}, y_o \in T_s\} \tag{7}$$

to reduce the number of possible pairs, where t_s and t_o are the timestamps for s and o.

4.3 Hyper-parameter Settings and Evaluation Metrics

The pre-trained language models, i.e., BERT-base and RoBERTa-base, are trained for the duplicate bug report retrieval. We set the following hyper-parameters in our model for training: the batch size is set as 16; the learning rate is set as 5e–5; the number of tokens N in the input sequence is set as 400; the number of epochs is set as among $\{1, 2, 3\}$; $t_{gap} = 365$ (days) according to [16]. The ranking strategy from [16] is used to evaluate proposed models. The evaluation metrics, Recall-Rate@k (Rr@k for short) and Mean Average Precision (MAP), are introduced from [19], which is defined as follows:

Rr@k: Rr@k denotes the ratio of test samples whose relevant duplicate bugs are ranked in the top k in the score-sorted list. The higher values of Rr@k indicate better performance.

$$Rr@k = \frac{N_{detected}}{N_{total}}, \tag{8}$$

where $N_{detected}$ denotes the number of test samples for which the relevant duplicate bug has been successfully detected in the top k position and N_{total} denotes the number of total test samples.

MAP: MAP can be defined as:

$$MAP = \frac{1}{N_{total}} \sum_{i=1}^{N_{total}} \frac{1}{\lambda_i}, \tag{9}$$

where λ_i is the position of the relevant duplicate bug in the ranked-score list. A higher MAP indicates that the retrieval methods are more effective, consistently placing the relevant duplicate bug for each bug report at a higher position within the ranked score list.

4.4 The Results of Duplicate Bug Report Retrieval

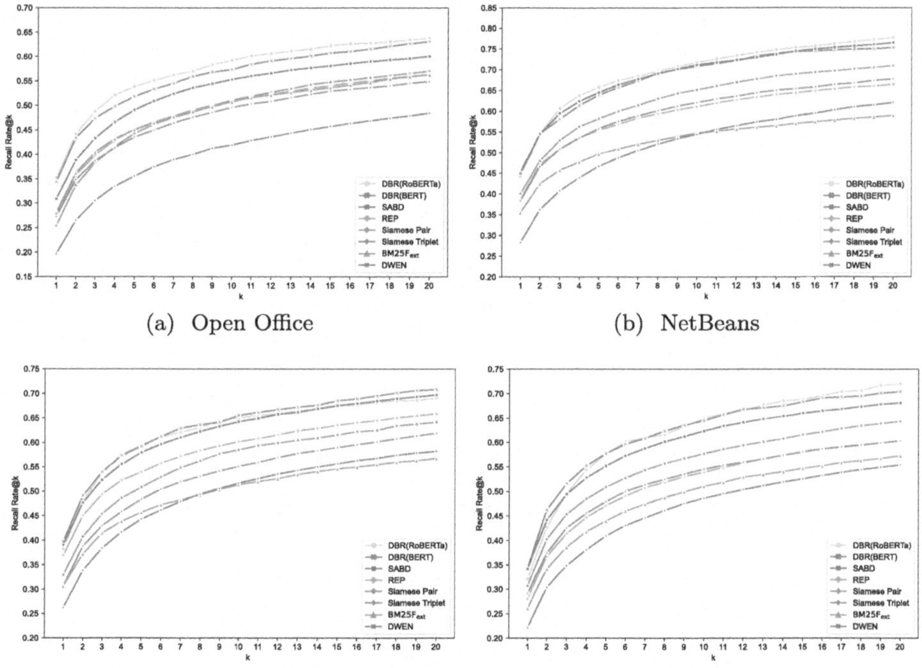

(a) Open Office (b) NetBeans

(c) Eclipse (d) Mozilla

Fig. 5. The result of Recall Rate@k on the test sets of Open Office, NetBeans, Eclipse, and Mozilla.

In this section, we evaluate the performance of two trained models, i.e., DBR(BERT) and DBR(RoBERTa), on four datasets using the Rr@k and k is for $1 \leq k \leq 20$ according to [19]. It is important to note that in instances where the relevant duplicate candidate for a query bug report is not retrieved within the predefined time window, this query is considered a miss for Rr@k computation, and its corresponding term $\frac{1}{\lambda}$ in the MAP expression (Eq. (9)) is assigned as zero [16].

We utilize six approaches as baseline methodologies for comparative analysis with our models. The methods $BM25F_{ext}$ and REP, which utilize TF-IDF for embedding bug reports, are introduced in [19]. Additionally, we compare against deep learning-based models, namely Siamese Triple and Siamese Pair (both from [4]), DWEN [2], and SABD [16]. The experimental results of basslines are from the work [16].

Figure 5 shows the result of Rr@k on four datasets. In all four datasets, our DBR(BERT) and DBR(RoBERTa) models achieve better Rr@k than other methods. For Open Office, DBR(RoBERTa) achieves the best performance. It outperforms DBR(BERT) by 1%∼3% after Rr@3 and outperforms the performance of SABD by 3%∼5%. In NetBeans, DBR(RoBERTa) achieves the best result; DBR(BERT) and SABD achieve comparable results, which are slightly lower than DBR(RoBERTa). DBR(RoBERTa) outperforms Siamese Pair by approximately 6%. In the case of Eclipse, DBR(BERT) and DBR(RoBERTa) show comparable performance, both slightly outperforming SABD. They are also higher than REP, with a margin of approximately 3% to 6%. For Mozilla, DBR(BERT) and DBR(RoBERTa) achieve the same performance before Rr@12, and after that, DBR(RoBERTa) is slightly higher than DBR(BERT). After Rr@4, DBR(BERT) and DBR(RoBERTa) outperform SABD by 3%∼5%.

DWEN method achieves the lowest performance in four datasets (specifically in Open Office and Mozilla), which may be because averaging the word embedding for representing bug reports would lose semantic information. In addition, the fully connected network used as an encoder may not effectively capture the dependencies between words in long text.

Table 3. The result of MAP on four datasets.

Method	Open Office	NetBeans	Eclipse	Mozilla
DWEN	0.276	0.365	0.353	0.305
$BM25F_{ext}$	0.315	0.417	0.402	0.338
Siamese Triple	0.356	0.466	0.401	0.376
Siamese Pair	0.346	0.482	0.425	0.401
REP	0.361	0.472	0.452	0.365
SABD	0.4008	0.538	0.484	0.443
DBR(BERT)	0.545	0.574	**0.559**	**0.533**
DBR(RoBERTa)	**0.567**	**0.581**	0.551	0.509

Table 3 shows the results of MAP on four datasets. Our DBR(RoBERTa) achieves the highest MAP results in Open Office and NetBeans, which is higher than SABD by around 16% and 4% on Open Office and NetBeans, respectively. For Eclipse and Mozilla, DBR(BERT) achieves the best performance on MAP, which is higher than SABD by around 8% and 9% on Eclipse and Mozilla, respectively, and slightly higher than DBR(RoBERTa). During the process of duplicate bug report retrieval, we implement a dual-filter approach, incorporating both a time window and a bug component constraint. This strategy is highly effective in filtering out irrelevant bug reports from the candidate set, significantly reducing the number of irrelevant candidates and thereby enhancing the overall performance of duplicate bug report retrieval.

5 Conclusion and Future Work

This paper proposes a new approach utilizing pre-trained language models to retrieve duplicate bug reports for new bugs in an issue tracking system, including (1) computing scores for duplicate pairs to filtering out the irrelevant bug reports, and (2) ranking the candidate reports to locate the duplicate reports. To this end, the textual information, such as bug report component, bug report title and description, is utilized for embedding by BERT (or RoBERTa) models to compute scores for evaluating the duplicate pairs and ranking. The experiments have been conducted on four common datasets to show that the proposed models are effective on the duplicate bug report retrieval task and achieve the best results compared with baselines.

The future work will study how incremental learning can be used in duplicate bug report retrieval. As shown in Fig. 2, bug reports are raised by users and testers from time to time, which is an incremental process. Dividing the data into the training set and test set may not be a good solution. We should develop an online learning model which can incrementally learn from other issues in the past and make sure the model can also adapt to the new bug reports.

References

1. Aggarwal, K., Rutgers, T., Timbers, F., Hindle, A., Greiner, R., Stroulia, E.: Detecting duplicate bug reports with software engineering domain knowledge. In: 22nd IEEE International Conference on Software Analysis, Evolution, and Reengineering, SANER, Montreal, QC, Canada, 2–6 March 2015, pp. 211–220. IEEE Computer Society (2015)
2. Budhiraja, A., Dutta, K., Reddy, R., Shrivastava, M.: DWEN: deep word embedding network for duplicate bug report detection in software repositories. In: Chaudron, M., Crnkovic, I., Chechik, M., Harman, M. (eds.) Proceedings of the 40th International Conference on Software Engineering: Companion Proceeedings, ICSE, Gothenburg, Sweden, 27 May–03 June 2018, pp. 193–194 (2018)
3. Budhiraja, A., Dutta, K., Shrivastava, M., Reddy, R.: Towards word embeddings for improved duplicate bug report retrieval in software repositories. In: Song, D., et al. (eds.) Proceedings of the 2018 ACM SIGIR International Conference on Theory of Information Retrieval, ICTIR, Tianjin, China, 14–17 September 2018, pp. 167–170 (2018)
4. Deshmukh, J., Annervaz, K.M., Podder, S., Sengupta, S., Dubash, N.: Towards accurate duplicate bug retrieval using deep learning techniques. In: 2017 IEEE International Conference on Software Maintenance and Evolution, ICSME, Shanghai, China, 17–22 September 2017, pp. 115–124 (2017)

5. Devlin, J., Chang, M., Lee, K., Toutanova, K.: BERT: pre-training of deep bidirectional transformers for language understanding. In: Burstein, J., Doran, C., Solorio, T. (eds.) Proceedings of the 2019 Conference of the North American Chapter of the Association for Computational Linguistics: Human Language Technologies, Minneapolis, MN, USA, vol. 1 (Long and Short Papers), pp. 4171–4186. Association for Computational Linguistics (2019)
6. Fiaz, A.S.S., Devi, N., Aarthi, S.: Bug tracking and reporting system. CoRR arxiv:1309.1232 (2013)
7. He, J., Xu, L., Yan, M., Xia, X., Lei, Y.: Duplicate bug report detection using dual-channel convolutional neural networks. In: ICPC '20: 28th International Conference on Program Comprehension, Seoul, Republic of Korea, 13–15 July 2020, pp. 117–127 (2020)
8. Jahan, S., Rahman, M.M.: Towards understanding the impacts of textual dissimilarity on duplicate bug report detection. In: Zhang, T., Xia, X., Novielli, N. (eds.) IEEE International Conference on Software Analysis, Evolution and Reengineering, SANER, Taipa, Macao, 21–24 March 2023, pp. 25–36. IEEE (2023)
9. Lazar, A., Ritchey, S., Sharif, B.: Generating duplicate bug datasets. In: Devanbu, P.T., Kim, S., Pinzger, M. (eds.) 11th Working Conference on Mining Software Repositories, MSR, Proceedings, Hyderabad, India, 31 May–1 June 2014, pp. 392–395 (2014)
10. Liu, Y., et al.: Roberta: a robustly optimized bert pretraining approach. arXiv preprint arXiv:1907.11692 (2019)
11. Messaoud, M.B., Miladi, A., Jenhani, I., Mkaouer, M.W., Ghadhab, L.: Duplicate bug report detection using an attention-based neural language model. IEEE Trans. Reliab. **72**(2), 846–858 (2023)
12. Mikolov, T., Sutskever, I., Chen, K., Corrado, G.S., Dean, J.: Distributed representations of words and phrases and their compositionality. In: Burges, C., Bottou, L., Welling, M., Ghahramani, Z., Weinberger, K. (eds.) Advances in Neural Information Processing Systems, vol. 26, pp. 3111–3119. Curran Associates, Inc. (2013)
13. Nguyen, A.T., Nguyen, T.T., Nguyen, T.N., Lo, D., Sun, C.: Duplicate bug report detection with a combination of information retrieval and topic modeling. In: Goedicke, M., Menzies, T., Saeki, M. (eds.) IEEE/ACM International Conference on Automated Software Engineering, ASE, Essen, Germany, 3–7 September 2012, pp. 70–79. ACM (2012)
14. Pennington, J., Socher, R., Manning, C.D.: Glove: Global vectors for word representation. In: Proceedings of the 2014 Conference on Empirical Methods in Natural Language Processing (EMNLP), pp. 1532–1543. ACL (2014)
15. Peters, M.E., et al.: Deep contextualized word representations. In: Proceedings of the Conference of the North American Chapter of the Association for Computational Linguistics: Human Language Technologies, New Orleans, Louisiana, USA, 1–6 June 2018, vol. 1, pp. 2227–2237 (2018)
16. Rodrigues, I.M., Aloise, D., Fernandes, E.R., Dagenais, M.R.: A soft alignment model for bug deduplication. In: Proceedings of the 17th International Conference on Mining Software Repositories, pp. 43–53. ACM (2020)
17. Serrano, N., Ciordia, I.: Bugzilla, itracker, and other bug trackers. IEEE Softw. **22**(2), 11–13 (2005)
18. Soleimani Neysiani, B., Babamir, S.M., Aritsugi, M.: Efficient feature extraction model for validation performance improvement of duplicate bug report detection in software bug triage systems. Inf. Softw. Technol. **126**, 106–135 (2020)

19. Sun, C., Lo, D., Khoo, S., Jiang, J.: Towards more accurate retrieval of duplicate bug reports. In: Alexander, P., Pasareanu, C.S., Hosking, J.G. (eds.) 26th IEEE/ACM International Conference on Automated Software Engineering ASE, Lawrence, KS, USA, 6–10 November 2011, pp. 253–262. IEEE Computer Society (2011)
20. Sun, C., Lo, D., Wang, X., Jiang, J., Khoo, S.: A discriminative model approach for accurate duplicate bug report retrieval. In: Kramer, J., Bishop, J., Devanbu, P.T., Uchitel, S. (eds.) Proceedings of the 32nd ACM/IEEE International Conference on Software Engineering, ICSE, Cape Town, South Africa, vol. 1, 1–8 May 2010, pp. 45–54. ACM (2010)
21. Vaswani, A., et al.: Attention is all you need. In: Guyon, I., von Luxburg, U., Bengio, S., Wallach, H.M., Fergus, R., Vishwanathan, S.V.N., Garnett, R. (eds.) Advances in Neural Information Processing Systems 30: Annual Conference on Neural Information Processing Systems, pp. 5998–6008 (2017)

Context is the Key for LLM-Based Text Segmentation

Amit Maraj and Miguel Vargas Martin(✉)

Ontario Tech University, Oshawa L1G 0C5, Canada
amit.maraj@ontariotechu.net, miguel.martin@ontariotechu.ca

Abstract. Text Segmentation involves dividing text into coherent sections, typically defined by topics. Over the past decade, lots of research has gone into furthering the development of supervised techniques to approach TS tasks, which has largely left unsupervised TS techniques with less advancement. With the onset of Large Language Models and the accessibility of them becoming more commonplace, unsupervised TS can benefit. By leveraging an LLM's strong understanding of natural language, prompting appropriately, and feeding in valuable context, we show that, even with locally run, open-source LLM models, we can achieve state-of-the-art unsupervised TS results as benchmarked by P_k and WindowDiff scores.

Keywords: Text Segmentation · LLM · Natural Language Understanding

1 Introduction

Text Segmentation (TS) is a task in Natural Language Processing (NLP), involving the division of text into coherent sections based on topics or themes. Although significant advances have been made in the development of supervised techniques for TS Badjatiya et al. (2018), Koshorek et al. (2018), Somasundaran et al. (2020), Barrow et al. (2020), Lo et al. (2021), Inan et al. (2022), the progress in unsupervised methods has lagged Glavaš et al. (2016), Riedl and Biemann (2012). This disparity is particularly notable given the potential of unsupervised approaches to handle diverse and unstructured text without the need for labeled data.

With the advent of Large Language Models (LLMs) and their increasing accessibility, LLMs can offer a promising avenue for improving unsupervised TS techniques, especially with their deep understanding of natural language. While the core prompting mechanism is intentionally straightforward to explore the inherent capabilities of LLMs, our contribution lies in demonstrating that even this direct application, when carefully managed for context, can unlock state-of-the-art (SOTA) performance in unsupervised TS, a domain that has traditionally lagged. This highlights the power of pre-trained knowledge in LLMs for complex

R. Ichise (Ed.): NLDB 2025, LNCS 15836, pp. 142–155, 2026.
https://doi.org/10.1007/978-3-031-97141-9_10

sequence understanding tasks without task-specific fine-tuning. By designing TS-specific prompts and leveraging contextual information, it is possible to apply LLMs to TS to achieve SOTA results.

Retrieval-Augmented Generation (RAG) Lewis et al. (2020) has revolutionized how we interact with data by enabling models to incorporate new data contexts when answering user queries and extracting insights. A critical pre-processing step that underpins RAG's remarkable capabilities is chunking. This process involves dividing large texts or documents into smaller, fixed-size segments. By focusing on these smaller units, the retriever can process and analyze the text more effectively and efficiently, significantly enhancing the performance of RAG-powered models.

In this paper, we experiment with two different LLM-based approaches to extracting and comparing overarching topics within text. When previous segment context is provided, an LLM can surpass existing unsupervised and some supervised techniques. Our results, benchmarked using the P_k and WindowDiff scores, demonstrate that even local open-source models can achieve competitive performance, marking a step forward in the field of unsupervised TS. All our code can be found on our GitHub Repository[1].

2 Related Works

2.1 Text Segmentation

TS has seen substantial advancements over the past decade. Initially, Hearst (1997) introduced TextTiling, an unsupervised algorithm that segments text based on lexical overlaps. Similarly, Choi (2000) demonstrated the effectiveness of unsupervised methods by analyzing sentence similarities, classifying their work within linear TS methodologies. These pioneering efforts set a new benchmark in the field.

The advent of advanced word and sentence embeddings revolutionized TS, enabling the development of supervised techniques. Kicking off a wave of supervised TS research, Koshorek et al. (2018) explored the potential of processing large TS datasets using a Bi-LSTM, which analyzes three sentences at a time to understand their interrelations. Building on this, Badjatiya et al. (2018) proposed a sentence-wise model that utilizes attention mechanisms to further enhance performance. Recent supervised approaches have increasingly incorporated LSTMs and Transformers as core components, as evidenced in the works of Somasundaran et al. (2020), Barrow et al. (2020), Lo et al. (2021), and Inan et al. (2022). These studies highlight the effectiveness of integrating topic information and emphasizing sentence contextuality to achieve top-tier results.

Despite the prominence of supervised models, unsupervised TS techniques remain promising. Misra et al. (2009) revisited the classic TextTiling method, refining it with LDA to identify more precise keywords. Riedl and Biemann (2012) combined LDA with TextTiling, while introducing more novel boundary adjustment methods as an innovative unsupervised solution. Additionally,

[1] https://github.com/HumanMachineLab/llm-context-ts.

Glavaš (2016) introduced a novel graph-based method that treats sentences as nodes within a graph to predict segment boundaries. These unsupervised models demonstrate the ongoing exploration and diversity in TS methodologies. Although unsupervised TS remains important due its flexibility and lack of need for domain-specific training data, there has been a recent resurgence of interest in these methods. For instance, Xing and Carenini (2021) developed a Transformer-based unsupervised TS approach, fine-tuning the model to enhance performance. Another technique by Solbiati et al. (2021) involves grouping sentences together, stacking them, and performing max pooling to create a matrix for comparison. John et al. (2017) utilized an LDA-based TextTiling approach that yielded strong results but was hindered by the pre-training requirements of LDA. While their boundary adjustment technique was innovative, it did not fully achieve unsupervised status.

2.2 Large Language Models

Large Language Models (LLMs) represent a leap in the evolution of language models, characterized by their larger number of parameters and extraordinary learning capabilities Chen et al. (2021), Kasneci et al. (2023), Zhang et al. (2023b). LLMs such as GPT-3 Floridi and Chiriatti (2020) and GPT-4 Achiam et al. (2023) leverage the self-attention mechanism introduced by the Transformer architecture Vaswani et al. (2017). The self-attention mechanism allows these models to efficiently process and generate sequential data by attending to different parts of the input sequence simultaneously, capturing long-range dependencies, and enabling parallel processing.

A key interaction technique with LLMs is prompt engineering, where users craft specific prompts to guide the model in generating desired responses or performing specific tasks Clavié et al. (2023), White et al. (2023), Zhang et al. (2023a). Prompt engineering involves designing input texts that effectively communicate the task requirements to the LLM, enabling it to produce accurate and relevant outputs. This technique is widely adopted in various evaluation and practical applications of LLMs, as it leverages the model's ability to understand and respond to nuanced language cues. Through prompting, LLMs also have the ability to understand the structure of the contextual text provided to it, before performing its task (e.g., understanding the start of a new paragraph to predict the beginning of a new segment).

3 Methodology

To guide the system appropriately, we employ a carefully designed prompt that instructs the LLM to determine whether the current sentence is a continuation of the preceding paragraph. The $prev\_paragraph$ variable, representing the sentences of the current, unfolding segment, is included as part of the LLM's context window to provide relevant background. Initially, $prev\_paragraph$ is empty or contains a minimal instruction. As sentences are processed, if the LLM deems the current sentence a continuation, it is appended to *prev_paragraph* (or a representation of it, up to the LLM's practical context window limit for a single segment query). When the LLM predicts a "false" value (indicating that the current sentence does not continue the previous paragraph and thus signifies the beginning of a new segment), all sentences constituting the just-completed segment (the content of *prev_paragraph* before the "false" prediction) are output. Subsequently, *prev_paragraph* is effectively reset to begin with the current sentence, which forms the start of the new segment. This process enables the system to refresh and rebuild its context window incrementally for each new potential segment, ensuring that only context from the *current segment being evaluated* is retained for subsequent predictions. This approach naturally manages the LLM's context window limitations by focusing only on the sentences of the segment under construction, rather than the entire preceding document. However, if a single coherent segment itself becomes excessively long and exceeds the LLM's effective context window for this type of query, performance on that specific long segment might degrade, a point discussed further in Limitations.

Additionally, we evaluate the efficacy of this approach by testing it without including prior sentences as part of the context. This allows us to assess the extent to which providing contextual information contributes to the LLM's performance. The comparison between the context-inclusive and context-free setups provides valuable insights into the role of contextual history in enhancing the segmentation capabilities of the model. This analysis also helps to identify potential areas for refinement in the prompt design and context utilization strategies.

3.1 Metrics

Two common metrics for evaluating TS systems are P_k and WindowDiff (WD), both of which are standard in the field. The P_k metric estimates the likelihood that two sentences, separated by a distance of k, are incorrectly classified as belonging to the same segment. Both P_k and WD use a sliding window of size w to compare predicted segments against reference segments, with k typically set to half the average true segment size in the document. Lower scores for both metrics indicate better performance.

P_k is widely accepted in TS evaluation, but WD was introduced as an improvement. While P_k focuses on the probability of misclassifying two segments, WD also penalizes oversegmentation, addressing false positives-a limitation of P_k. Both metrics range from 0 to 1, with 0 representing perfect segmentation. WD is often preferred for its ability to penalize false positives, making it more robust than P_k Pevzner and Hearst (2012). We report all our findings using both metrics.

While acknowledging the existence of more recent metrics for evaluating TS, such as those proposed by Fournier and Inkpen (2012), Fournier (2013), and Lucas et al. (2023), this study primarily employs P_k and WD as the primary evaluation metrics. This decision is motivated by several factors. First, P_k and WD have been widely adopted and remain prevalent in TS research. Benchmarking against results obtained using these metrics allows for a more direct and reliable comparison of our approach with a substantial body of existing work. Second, despite their limitations, P_k and WD capture essential aspects of segmentation quality. P_k provides a measure of the likelihood of misclassifying sentence pairs, while WD offers the advantage of penalizing oversegmentation, addressing a key shortcoming of P_k. Given their common usage and acceptance within the TS community, employing P_k and WD provides a valuable and normalized framework for assessing the efficacy of our proposed method.

3.2 Prompting

To ensure consistent results from the LLM throughout the prediction process, two restrictive prompts are used to restrain the LLM from providing an explanation. The prompts are as follows:

> Given the following {paragraph/meeting transcript}:
> {prev_paragraph}
> Does the following sentence continue the {paragraph/dialogue}?
> {sentence}
> If it does, output "True". If they are not, output "False". Do not provide any explanation. Ensure your answer is limited to "True" or "False".

Where *sentence* and *prev_paragraph* are the current sentence and prior sentences in the segment respectively. Using the definitive output of the LLM, we can rely on a simple "True" or "False" to indicate the prediction.

3.3 Models

Our TS system is tested with the following LLM models:

1. Mistral Jiang et al. (2023): Mistral 7B is a 7.3 billion parameter open-source language model that demonstrates competitive performance compared to larger models in certain benchmarks. Mistral employs a unique architecture and has shown strong capabilities in various natural language tasks. Since Mistral is open-source, working with it is cost-effective and accessible, providing a valuable comparison point to the proprietary models used in this study.
2. OpenAI GPT-4o Hurst et al. (2024): GPT-4o demonstrates improved reading comprehension and reasoning across historically underrepresented languages, in comparison to previous iterations of OpenAI's GPT models.
3. OpenAI o1 Jaech et al. (2024): The o1 model is trained with reinforcement learning to perform complex reasoning and uses chain of thought. Due to its ability to reason, o1 has provided strong results on tasks that benefit from nuance, such as TS. Due to its ability to reason, o1 can provide an explanation for its thought process. During our testing, we elect to omit reasoning explanation to strictly distill responses to a binary outcome (i.e., "True" or "False").

Mistral 7B uses 4.1GB of system memory and takes roughly 500ms per inference. All testing was done on an Apple MacBook Air with 16GB of RAM and an M3 Apple Silicon processor. Running inference on 100 samples of data in the Choi dataset took 1 min and 10 s. OpenAI's GPT 4o and o1 were accessed via API call using OpenAI's Python SDK.

4 Data

Unsupervised TS methods are often evaluated using constructed datasets, which amalgamate segments from varied sources into composite documents, as evidenced by studies from Choi (2000) and Galley et al. (2003).

Additionally, we evaluate our technique on several meeting datasets Janin et al. (2003), Carletta et al. (2005) using the QMSum dataset Zhong et al. (2021).

Choi Dataset: Introduced by Choi (2000), this dataset has become a staple for TS research, referenced in works by Misra et al. (2009), Brants et al. (2002), Fragkou et al. (2004), Glavaš et al. (2016), Sun et al. (2008), and Galley et al. (2003). It is crafted from the Brown corpus, containing 700 documents that simulate real text structure. The compilation includes 400 documents with segments varying from 3–11 sentences, alongside 100 documents for each segment length category: 3–5, 6–8, and 9–11 sentences.

WikiSection Dataset: To complement the synthetic Choi dataset, we also test the effectiveness of this approach on the WikiSection dataset Arnold et al. (2019). This dataset was recently introduced in 2019 and includes two sections: "City" and "Disease".

QMSum Dataset: QMSum aggregates the ICSI Janin et al. (2003) and AMI Carletta et al. (2005) datasets, providing a more comprehensive resource for training and evaluating summarization models. While QMSum is acknowledged to be smaller than datasets derived from written text, its focus on spoken dialogue and inclusion of summaries makes it a valuable contribution to the field. This dataset is broken into three sections–"product", "committee", and "academic". Although designed for meeting summarization, the QMSum dataset can be utilized for TS due to its annotated classification of meeting topics. The QMSum dataset differs from the other datasets used in this work, notably in its inherent noise and artifacts, such as filler words (e.g., 'uh', 'um') common in meeting transcripts. Furthermore, it exhibits substantially larger average segment sizes: 43 sentences for the 'product' subset, 225 for 'academic', and 382 for 'committee'.

5 Results

We report improvements over the SOTA unsupervised results in TS. Specifically, we evaluate our approach on two key datasets: Choi's synthetic dataset Choi

(2000) and the WikiSection dataset introduced by Arnold et al. (2019). Our findings demonstrate the potential of leveraging LLMs for TS tasks across diverse datasets (Table 1).

Table 1. Results on the synthetic Choi Choi (2000) dataset, where our approach w/context includes sentences from the current paragraph within the context window. Best scores are bolded and second best scored are underlined.

	3–5		6–8		9–11		3–11	
	$P_k \downarrow$	WD $\downarrow$	$P_k \downarrow$	WD $\downarrow$	$P_k \downarrow$	WD $\downarrow$	$P_k \downarrow$	WD $\downarrow$
Choi (2000)	12.0	–	9.0	–	9.0	–	12.0	–
Brants et al. (2002)	7.4	–	8.0	–	6.8	–	10.7	–
Fragkou et al. (2004)	5.5	–	3.0	–	1.3	–	7.0	–
Misra et al. (2009)	23.0	–	15.8	–	14.4	–	16.1	–
Glavaš et al. (2016)	5.6	8.7	7.2	9.4	6.6	9.6	7.2	9.0
Maraj et al. (2024a)	4.4	6.2	3.1	3.3	2.5	<u>2.6</u>	4.0	4.4
Maraj et al. (2024b)	4.5	4.6	2.7	<u>2.7</u>	**2.1**	**2.1**	<u>2.9</u>	**3.1**
LLM TS	<u>0.76</u>	<u>2.41</u>	<u>2.10</u>	3.52	2.88	4.07	3.65	4.27
LLM TS w/context	**0.15**	**1.05**	**1.43**	**2.26**	<u>2.16</u>	2.76	**2.13**	<u>3.43</u>

The results underscore the potential of employing LLMs for unsupervised TS. On the WikiSection dataset, our LLM-based method, when provided with context, outperforms all prior unsupervised and supervised approaches on the "Disease" section. This demonstrates the ability of an unsupervised system to outperform previous supervised techniques, closing the gap between the two.

We include an additional table (Table 3) to compare the results from the three LLM models (Mistral, GPT-4o, and GPT-o1) across the datasets. This table showcases the performance of each LLM on the Choi, WikiSection, and QMSum datasets.

The QMSum dataset is acknowledged to be smaller and derived from spoken dialogue, containing more noise and longer segment sizes. We state that there are no previous unsupervised meeting transcription TS approaches on the QMSum dataset. We also provide results using all three LLM models on the QMSum data in Table 3.

The results demonstrate the importance of context for LLMs in TS. Our LLM-based TS approach with context outperforms previous SOTA unsupervised methods on Choi's dataset. On the WikiSection dataset, the LLM with context outperforms all prior unsupervised and supervised approaches on the "Disease" section. The results from the three LLMs against the datasets are also shown in the Appendix in Figs. 1, 2, and 3.

Overall, Mistral outperformed the larger GPT-4o and o1 models on the "City" and "QMSum" datasets. We attribute this to potential overfitting, wherein the stronger models (GPT-4o and o1) may be prone to over-analyzing sentences

Table 2. LLM-based TS results on a newer WikiSection dataset compared to both supervised and unsupervised methods. When context is provided, an LLM can outperform even supervised SOTA methods, as shown in the "Disease" dataset. Works with an asterisk (*) are supervised. Best scores are bolded and second best scores are underlined.

	City		Disease	
	P_k ↓	WD ↓	P_k ↓	WD ↓
Inan et al. (2022)*	<u>7.1</u>	–	15	–
Lo et al. (2021)*	8.2	–	18.8	–
Lee et al. (2023)*	**4.6**	**5.2**	13.7	14.7
Maraj et al. (2024a)	36.0	77.2	25.8	75.3
LLM TS	23.4	50.8	<u>10.5</u>	<u>14.0</u>
LLM TS w/context	8.5	<u>26.7</u>	**8.8**	**13.0**

Table 3. Comparison between the 3 LLMs against 3 different datasets. Results on the Choi and QMSum datasets are averaged due to the similarities in their relative datasets. Best scores are bolded.

	Choi		City		Disease		QMSum	
	P_k ↓	WD ↓	P_k ↓	WD ↓	P_k ↓	WD ↓	P_k ↓	WD ↓
Mistral	1.30	2.17	**0.85**	**2.67**	0.88	**1.30**	**1.35**	**1.70**
GPT 4o	0.95	2.08	0.91	2.95	**0.20**	1.44	2.30	2.40
GPT o1	**0.94**	**1.86**	4.17	7.75	3.01	3.91	2.43	2.63

when determining their relatedness. Given the unsupervised nature of this TS approach, the models receive no feedback on the correctness of their predictions (Table 2).

Our work emphasizes that providing relevant background context to the LLM improves its ability to accurately identify segment boundaries. The LLM is prompted to determine whether the current sentence is a continuation of the preceding paragraph, with the preceding paragraph included as part of the LLM's context window. This allows the LLM to understand the flow of topics and make more informed predictions about segment boundaries.

6 Limitations

Related to segment size, while our incremental context rebuilding strategy (where *prev_paragraph* is reset for each new segment) generally manages the LLM's fixed context window, extremely long individual segments could still pose a challenge. If a single, unbroken topic segment contains more sentences than can be effectively processed by the LLM within its context window for the "continuation" query, the LLM's ability to judge coherence for sentences deep within that very long segment might diminish. Our current methodology does not explicitly chunk these intra-segment contexts if they grow excessively large.

The prompts used in this study do not explicitly define what constitutes a 'segment,' leaving the LLM to interpret this concept without clear guidance. The current prompt is intentionally broad and subjective, requiring the LLM to determine whether a given sentence continues the preceding paragraph. We hypothesize that a more specific and nuanced prompt, providing clearer explanations of segment characteristics, could improve the LLM's decision-making. Few-shot prompting could further enhance this by providing the model with additional segment context during inference, such as outlining a few sentences and demarcating segment breaks before prediction. While including previous sentences as context partially addresses this, context is not provided at the start of inference. Furthermore, we did not extensively explore variations in prompt phrasing or analyze potential inconsistencies in the LLM's interpretation of "continuing" a topic arising from this ambiguity. Such an analysis could provide deeper insights into the LLM's decision-making process for segmentation.

This research employs an unsupervised approach, as the system does not rely on training or fine-tuning with labeled data. However, due to the opaque nature of the training process, there is a possibility that the datasets used for evaluation could have been included in the LLM's pretraining corpus. While it is impossible to confirm this, it is unlikely that the LLM was trained specifically for a TS task. In other words, while the text may have contributed to the pretraining of the language model, it would not have been used to teach the LLM to explicitly identify segment boundaries based on dataset labels.

7 Future Work

Due to their inherent understanding of natural language, LLMs have become a strong option for tackling various NLP tasks. Similarly, this work is an introduction into the strength an LLM can bring toward TS. Future research could focus on refining prompt designs, including exploring the impact of providing more explicit definitions of a 'segment', investigating different phrasing to reduce ambiguity, analyzing the LLM's sensitivity to such variations, and incorporating few-shot examples of correct segmentations within the prompt. Incorporating task-specific pretraining, or developing hybrid models that integrate LLMs with domain-specific knowledge are also promising avenues. Although the inclusion of previous context in the context window shows performance improvements, the LLM is still only aware of the current segment for that inference. Building a more thorough prompt through the inclusion of document understanding could provide valuable insight for the LLM to understand variations in segment sizes. For instance, the system iterates through the document, builds a graph of related sentences and words, then uses that graph to understand structure of previous segments in the document. An augmentation like this could give the LLM more context when making predictions. A similar technique was adopted in Maraj et al. (2024b)'s work, where they leverage a graph to store previous keywords.

Additionally, evaluating the proposed method's generalizability on a wider array of text types, domains, and languages beyond the current benchmark datasets would be crucial for establishing its robustness. Comparing its performance against a broader range of existing segmentation techniques, including more complex unsupervised and semi-supervised models, would also provide a more comprehensive understanding of its relative strengths and weaknesses.

8 Conclusion

This research leverages the inherent ability of LLMs to comprehend and interpret structural elements within text, such as paragraph beginnings and topic transitions. By leveraging the LLM's ability to interpret structural cues through a direct yet context-aware prompting strategy, we demonstrate that our approach surpasses prior unsupervised benchmarks in the field of TS. This underscores the potential of LLMs as powerful zero-shot or few-shot learners for complex NLP tasks like unsupervised segmentation, offering competitive results without the need for extensive task-specific supervised fine-tuning or complex bespoke architectures. While the prompting method is direct, its effectiveness in this unsupervised scenario is a key finding.

Our experimental results on the Choi and WikiSection datasets illustrate that LLMs can perform competitively across diverse TS datasets. These findings suggest that LLMs, when paired with advanced embedding techniques, can address complex segmentation challenges effectively. This achievement underscores the potential of LLMs as a robust tool for TS tasks, offering competitive results without the need for supervised fine-tuning.

While this study marks an advancement in unsupervised TS methodologies, it also opens new avenues for further exploration. Future research could focus on refining prompt designs, incorporating task-specific pretraining, or developing hybrid models that integrate LLMs with domain-specific knowledge. Additionally, exploring methods to handle variability in segment sizes and context lengths, as well as addressing limitations posed by the black-box nature of LLM training, could yield even greater improvements. Overall, this work provides an optimistic outlook for TS performance and serves as a foundation for continued innovation in the field.

Acknowledgments. The authors acknowledge the support of the Natural Sciences and Engineering Research Council of Canada through Discovery Grant # RGPIN/005919-2018.

A Appendix

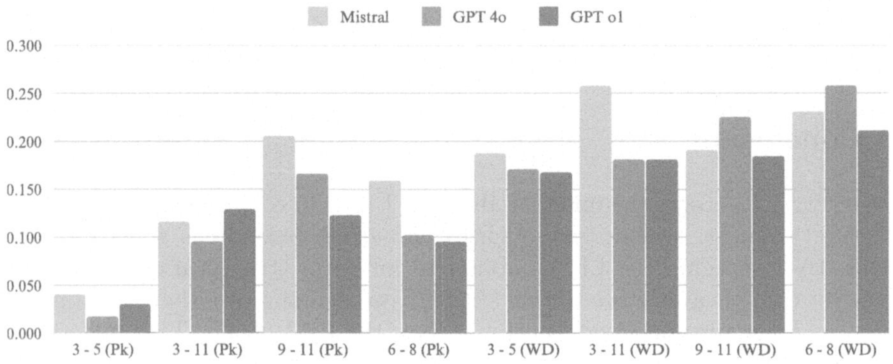

Fig. 1. Choi Results between the 3 LLMs tested.

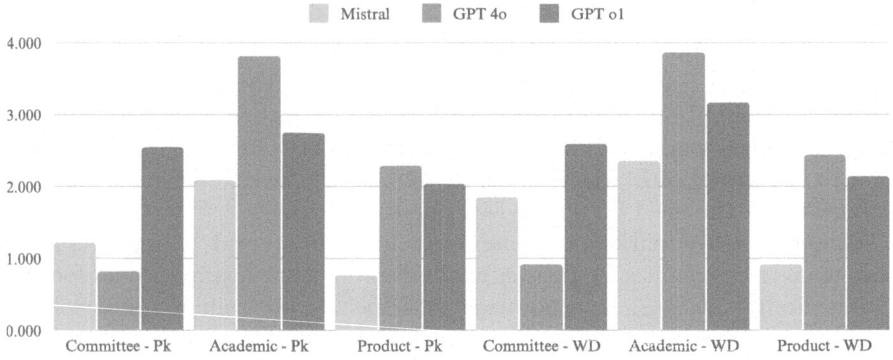

Fig. 2. QMSum Results between the 3 LLMs tested.

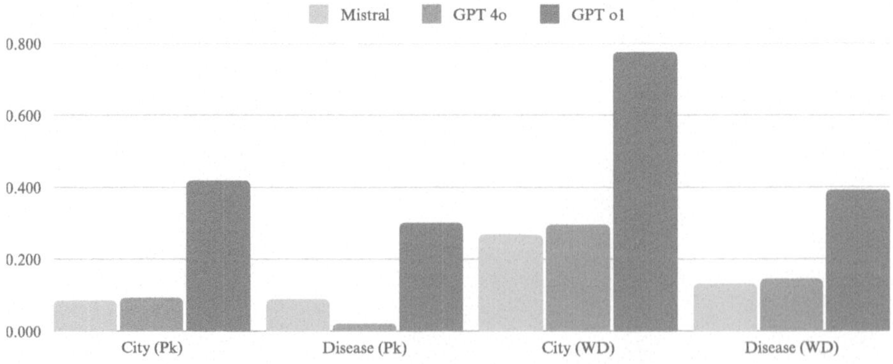

Fig. 3. WikiSection Results between the 3 LLMs tested.

References

Achiam, J., et al.: GPT-4 technical report. arXiv preprint arXiv:2303.08774 (2023)

Arnold, S., Schneider, R., Cudré-Mauroux, P., Gers, F.A., Löser, A.: Sector: a neural model for coherent topic segmentation and classification. Trans. Assoc. Comput. Linguist. **7**, 169–184 (2019)

Badjatiya, P., Kurisinkel, L.J., Gupta, M., Varma, V.: Attention-based neural text segmentation. In: European Conference on Information Retrieval, pp. 180–193. Springer (2018)

Barrow, J., Jain, R., Morariu, V., Manjunatha, V., Oard, D.W., Resnik, P.: A joint model for document segmentation and segment labeling. In: Proceedings of the 58th Annual Meeting of the Association for Computational Linguistics, pp. 313–322 (2020)

Brants, T., Chen, F., Tsochantaridis, I.: Topic-based document segmentation with probabilistic latent semantic analysis. In: Proceedings of the Eleventh International Conference on Information and Knowledge Management, pp. 211–218 (2002)

Carletta, J., et al.: The AMI meeting corpus: a pre-announcement. In: International Workshop on Machine Learning for Multimodal Interaction, pp. 28–39. Springer (2005)

Chen, M., et al. Evaluating large language models trained on code. arXiv preprint arXiv:2107.03374 (2021)

Choi, F.Y.Y.: Advances in domain independent linear text segmentation. arXiv preprint cs/0003083 (2000)

Clavié, B., Ciceu, A., Naylor, F., Soulié, G., Brightwell, T.: Large language models in the workplace: a case study on prompt engineering for job type classification. In: International Conference on Applications of Natural Language to Information Systems, pp. 3–17. Springer (2023)

Floridi, L., Chiriatti, M.: GPT-3: its nature, scope, limits, and consequences. Mind. Mach. **30**, 681–694 (2020)

Fournier, C.: Evaluating text segmentation using boundary edit distance. In: Proceedings of the 51st Annual Meeting of the Association for Computational Linguistics (Volume 1: Long Papers) (2013)

Fournier, C., Inkpen, D.: Segmentation similarity and agreement. In: Proceedings of the 2012 Conference of the North American Chapter of the Association for Computational Linguistics: Human Language Technologies (2012)

Fragkou, P., Petridis, V., Kehagias, A.: A dynamic programming algorithm for linear text segmentation. J. Intell. Inf. Syst. **23**(2), 179–197 (2004)

Galley, M., McKeown, K., Fosler-Lussier, E., Jing, H.: Discourse segmentation of multi-party conversation. In: Proceedings of the 41st Annual Meeting of the Association for Computational Linguistics, pp. 562–569 (2003)

Glavaš, G., Nanni, F., Ponzetto,S.P.: Unsupervised text segmentation using semantic relatedness graphs. In: Proceedings of the Fifth Joint Conference on Lexical and Computational Semantics, pp. 125–130. Association for Computational Linguistics (2016)

Hearst, M.A.: Text tiling: segmenting text into multi-paragraph subtopic passages. Comput. Linguist. **23**(1), 33–64 (1997)

Hurst, A., et al.: GPT-4o system card. arXiv preprint arXiv:2410.21276 (2024)

Inan, H., Rungta, R., Mehdad, Y.: Structured summarization: unified text segmentation and segment labeling as a generation task. arXiv preprint arXiv:2209.13759, 2022

Jaech, A., et al.: OpenAI o1 system card. arXiv preprint arXiv:2412.16720 (2024)
Janin, A., et al.: The ICSI meeting corpus. In: 2003 of the Proceedings IEEE International Conference on Acoustics, Speech, and Signal Processing (ICASSP 2003), vol. 1, p. I (2003)
Jiang, A.Q., et al.: Mistral 7B. arXiv preprint arXiv:2310.06825 (2023)
John, A.K., Di Caro, L., Boella, G.: Text segmentation with topic modeling and entity coherence. In: Proceedings of the 16th International Conference on Hybrid Intelligent Systems (HIS 2016), pp. 175–185. Springer (2017)
Kasneci, E., et al.: ChatGPT for good? On opportunities and challenges of large language models for education. Learn. Individ. Differ. **103**, 102274 (2023)
Koshorek, O., Cohen, A., Mor, N., Rotman, M., Berant, J.: Text segmentation as a supervised learning task. arXiv preprint arXiv:1803.09337 (2018)
Lee, J., Han, J., Baek, S., Song, M.: Topic segmentation model focusing on local context. arXiv preprint arXiv:2301.01935 (2023)
Lewis, P., et al.: Retrieval-augmented generation for knowledge-intensive NLP tasks. Adv. Neural. Inf. Process. Syst. **33**, 9459–9474 (2020)
Lo, K., Jin, Y., Tan, W., Liu, M., Du, L., Buntine, W.: Transformer over pre-trained transformer for neural text segmentation with enhanced topic coherence. arXiv preprint arXiv:2110.07160 (2021)
Lucas, E., Kangas, D., Havens, T.: A reference-free segmentation quality index (segrefree). In: Findings of the Association for Computational Linguistics: EMNLP 2023 (2023)
Maraj, A., Martin, M.V., Makrehchi, M.: Words that stick: using keyword cohesion to improve text segmentation. In: Proceedings of the 28th Conference on Computational Natural Language Learning, pp. 1–9 (2024a)
Maraj, A., Martin, M.V., Makrehchi, M.: Coherence graphs: Bridging the gap in text segmentation with unsupervised learning. In: International Conference on Applications of Natural Language to Information Systems, pp. 139–149. Springer (2024b)
Misra, H., Yvon, F., Jose, J.M., Cappé, O.: Text segmentation via topic modeling: an analytical study. In: Proceedings of the 18th ACM Conference on Information and Knowledge Management, pp. 1553–1556 (2009)
Pevzner, L., Hearst, M.A.: A critique and improvement of an evaluation metric for text segmentation. Comput. Linguist. **28**(1), 19–36 (2002)
Riedl, M., Biemann, C.: TopicTiling: a text segmentation algorithm based on LDA. In: Proceedings of ACL 2012 Student Research Workshop, pp. 37–42 (2012)
Solbiati, A., Heffernan, K., Damaskinos, G., Poddar, S., Modi, S., Cali, J.: Unsupervised topic segmentation of meetings with BERT embeddings. arXiv preprint arXiv:2106.12978 (2021)
Somasundaran, S., et al.: Two-level transformer and auxiliary coherence modeling for improved text segmentation. In: Proceedings of the AAAI Conference on Artificial Intelligence, vol. 34, pp. 7797–7804 (2020)
Sun, Q., Li, R., Luo, D., Wu, X.: Text segmentation with LDA-based fisher kernel. In: Proceedings of ACL-08: HLT, Short Papers, pp. 269–272 (2008)
Vaswani, A., et al.: Attention is all you need. In: Advances in Neural Information Processing Systems, vol. 30 (2017)
White, J., et al.: A prompt pattern catalog to enhance prompt engineering with ChatGPT. arXiv preprint arXiv:2302.11382 (2023)
Xing, L., Carenini, G.: Improving unsupervised dialogue topic segmentation with utterance-pair coherence scoring. In: Li, H., et al. (eds.) Proceedings of the 22nd Annual Meeting of the Special Interest Group on Discourse and Dialogue, pp. 167–177. Association for Computational Linguistics, Singapore (2021)

Zhang, W., Deng, Y., Liu, B., Pan, S.J., Bing, L.: Sentiment analysis in the era of large language models: a reality check. arXiv preprint arXiv:2305.15005 (2023a)
Zhang, Z., et al.: SafetyBench: evaluating the safety of large language models with multiple choice questions. arXiv preprint arXiv:2309.07045 (2023b)
Zhong, M., et al.: QMSum: a new benchmark for query-based multi-domain meeting summarization. arXiv preprint arXiv:2104.05938 (2021)

MultiProSE: A Multi-label Arabic Dataset for Propaganda, Sentiment, and Emotion Detection

Lubna Al-Henaki[1,2](✉), Hend Al-Khalifa[1], Abdulmalik Al-Salman[1], Hajar Alqubayshi[3], Hind Al-Twailay[3], Gheeda Alghamdi[4], and Hawra Aljasim[1]

[1] King Saud University, Riyadh, Saudi Arabia
Lubna.s@mu.edu.sa
[2] Majmaah University, Majmaah, Saudi Arabia
[3] Imam Mohammad Ibn Saud Islamic University, Riyadh, Saudi Arabia
[4] Alfaisal University, Riyadh, Saudi Arabia

Abstract. Propaganda is a form of persuasion that has been used throughout history with the intention goal of influencing people's opinions through rhetorical and psychological persuasion techniques for determined ends. Although Arabic ranked as the fourth most-used language on the internet, resources for propaganda detection in languages other than English, especially Arabic, remain extremely limited. To address this gap, the first Arabic dataset for Multi-label Propaganda, Sentiment, and Emotion (MultiProSE) has been introduced. MultiProSE is an open-source extension of the existing Arabic propaganda dataset, ArPro, with the addition of sentiment and emotion annotations for each text. This dataset comprises 8,000 annotated news articles, which is the largest propaganda dataset to date. For each task, several baselines have been developed using large language models (LLMs), such as GPT-4o-mini, and pre-trained language models (PLMs), including three BERT-based models. The best model achieves a macro-F1 score of 75.6% for the propaganda detection task using AraBERT. Additionally, GPT-4o-Mini attains a macro-F1 score of 82.5% for sentiment analysis and 70.7% for emotion detection, respectively. The dataset, annotation guidelines, and source code are all publicly released to facilitate future research and development in Arabic language models and contribute to a deeper understanding of how various opinion dimensions interact in news media (https://github.com/LubnaAlhenaki/MultiProSE).

Keywords: Propaganda Detection · Sentiment Analysis · Emotion Detection · LLMs

1 Introduction

Social media has become one of the prevalent mediums for communication channels. Based on recent statistics [1], among 8.08 billion people worldwide, 5.35 billion are internet users, and 5.04 billion are social media users. Therefore, social media platforms

R. Ichise (Ed.): NLDB 2025, LNCS 15836, pp. 156–172, 2026.
https://doi.org/10.1007/978-3-031-97141-9_11

have turned into grounds for the rise of proliferation, such as propaganda, which may lead to negative consequences in various domains, including politics, healthcare, and the economy. Based on the Cambridge Dictionary [2], the term propaganda is defined as "information, ideas, opinions, or images, often only giving one part of an argument, that are broadcast, published, or in some other way spread with the intention of influencing people's opinions." Moreover, propaganda utilizes specific rhetorical and psychological persuasion techniques to evoke strong feelings in the audience [3].

Propaganda detection is a crucial task in understanding how information is presented and perceived, particularly in news media. This task involves predicting whether the written text is propagandistic content that is designed to influence public opinion or not. High-performance automated methods for propaganda detection are crucial for enhancing decision-making for authorities, politicians, and businesses. Typically, the main input to propaganda detection models is textual content [4]. However, other inputs, such as sentiment and emotion, can be used to improve the model's performance. It is recommended that more publicly available benchmarked propaganda detection datasets be released under a standard open license. When conducting new propaganda detection datasets, non-English data and annotations of other opinion dimensions, including sentiment and emotions, should be considered.

According to the study's findings in [5], there is a direct correlation between several persuasion techniques and emotional salience features. Furthermore, several studies, such as [6] and [7–9], and [10], demonstrated the benefits of incorporating sentiment and emotional features in the persuasion detection model. Thus, analyzing the interaction between emotions and propaganda, as well as sentiment and propaganda, could benefit overall propaganda detection. For example, the techniques of "loaded language" and "slogan" exhibit negative correlations with valence and joy intensity while demonstrating positive associations with anger, fear, and sadness intensity [5].

While efforts on the available Arabic propaganda dataset are still in their early stages, the English propaganda dataset has yielded remarkable results. Arabic is the fourth most used language on the internet, with around 237 million Arab users [11]. Moreover, the Arabic language has challenges in NLP because of its complex morphology, orthographic ambiguity, limited availability of linguistic resources (e.g., corpus), and dialectal variances.

To the best of our knowledge, no prior work has paid attention to the emotional and sentiment dimensions within the Arabic propaganda dataset.

In this paper, we introduce MultiProSE, the first dataset for the Arabic language annotated for propaganda, sentiment, and emotion. MultiProSE extends the existing Arabic propaganda dataset, ArPro, by adding multi-label annotations for sentiment and emotion to its 8,000 Modern Standard Arabic (MSA) news texts [12]. This comprehensive dataset will serve as a benchmark for three tasks: propaganda detection, sentiment analysis, and emotion recognition, addressing a gap in Arabic NLP resources. Additionally, it will facilitate the analysis of interactions between various opinion dimensions, including propaganda, sentiment, and emotion. The contributions in this paper can be summarized as follows: (1) We expand the existing propaganda dataset by creating the MultiProSE dataset, specifically designed for the classification of propaganda, sentiment, and emotion in Arabic news texts. This dataset will be made publicly available to support further research in this area. Also, we investigate how propaganda, sentiment, and emotional content are connected and influence each other's impact; (2) We establish robust baselines for the MultiProSE dataset, including two BERT-based models and GPT-4o-mini. The modeling results for each task are reported, providing valuable benchmarks that can guide future research in this domain.

2 Related Work

Although propaganda has existed for a very long time, propaganda detection is a relatively new field of study that started in 2017. Several efforts have been conducted to build datasets for propaganda detection tasks. This section will present a comprehensive overview of publicly available datasets, followed by an in-depth analysis of these datasets. Previous studies on propaganda datasets can be categorized based on the level of annotation of the text, which is called granularity. Generally, it is classified into two levels: (1) document level and (2) span level. There are several publicly available datasets for propaganda detection at document level such as TSHP-17 [13], Qprop [14], ProSOUL [15], H-Prop and H-Prop-News [16], and multi-lingual PPN [17].

In addition to document-level datasets, there are also datasets available for propaganda detection at the span level, including NLP4IF'19 [18], Cazech Propaganda [19], PTC [20], SemEval-2021 Task 6 [21], Arabic Propaganda [22], TWEETSPIN [23], ProText [24], ArAIEval [25], SemEval 2023 Task 3 [26], ArPro [12], X Arabic propaganda [27], PropTweet datasets from Twitter [28], China Propaganda [29]. Table 1 summarizes the publicly available datasets used for propaganda detection. Several conclusions can be drawn from previous studies:

1. Propaganda research has expanded beyond English to include other languages, with some multilingual datasets like PPN and SemEval 2023, though most resources remain in English.
2. The two common annotation methods are manual and automated approaches. The quality of manually annotated datasets is higher. It provides a better understanding of the complexities of propaganda, especially in languages with rich morphology, such as Arabic, which is why it is more common. However, manual annotation is time-consuming, relatively small in scale, and expensive. Also, the automated annotation, while it is suitable for large-scale data, is less accurate.
3. Most studies using span-level annotation, including sentence or fragment-level, show that this granularity transition from document-level to span-level enhances the understanding of propaganda, allowing for more accurate and detailed identification of propagandistic content.
4. The domain of propaganda datasets includes news articles, social media posts, and memes. Several datasets primarily focus on news articles. While these datasets provide insights into propaganda in traditional media, they cannot address newer forms of digital propaganda. With the increasing influence of social media, several datasets have been constructed from social media platforms.
5. There is a direct correlation between propaganda techniques and emotional salience features. Analyzing the interaction between emotions and propaganda, as well as sentiment and propaganda, could benefit overall propaganda detection.

In summary, the constructed dataset aims to address two significant gaps: language limitations and the incorporation of additional opinion dimensions for more comprehensive propaganda detection. Limited studies have explored the use of opinion dimensions for propaganda detection, particularly in Arabic, which poses unique challenges due to its semantic complexity and the limited availability of NLP resources.

This paper introduced the first Arabic MultiProSE dataset by extending the ArPro propaganda dataset with manually annotated sentiment and emotion labels [12]. This dataset is designed to create a novel Arabic linguistic resource that encompasses propaganda, sentiment, and emotion. Additionally, the MultiProSE dataset employs multi-label classification, which captures multiple aspects of each text. It may significantly enhance its utility for advancing research in this field and enabling the development of more accurate Arabic propaganda detection models.

Table 1. Publicly available datasets for propaganda

Language	Dataset Name/Reference	Granularity	Dataset Size	Annotation
English	TSHP-17 [13]	Document level	22,580 articles	Weak annotation (distant supervision)
	QProp [14]	Document level	51,294 articles	Weak annotation (Max. entropy)
	NLP4IF'19 [18]	Text span (fragment and sentence)	451 articles	Professional annotators
	PTC [20]	Text span (fragment and sentence)	536 articles	Professional annotators
	SemEval-2021 Task 6 [21]	Text span (short text)	950 memes	Professional annotators
Arabic	Arabic Propaganda [22]	Text span (short text)	930 tweets	Professional annotators
	ArAIEval [25]	Text span (paragraphs and short text)	3189 tweets and paragraphs	Professional annotators
	ArPro [12]	Text span (fragment and sentence)	8000 paragraphs	Professional annotators
Czech	Czech Propaganda [19]	Both (document and sentence)	7,494 articles	Professional annotators
Urdu	ProSOUL, Humkinar-Web,and Humkinar-News [15]	Document level	11,574 articles	Weak annotation (ProSOUL is done by Translate QProp into Urdu)
Chinese	China Propaganda [29]	Text span (short text)	9,950 tweets	Professional annotators
Hindi	H-Prop and H-Prop-News [16]	Document level	28,630 and 5500 articles	Weak annotation (Translate QProp into Hindi for H-Prop and use Professional annotators for H-Prop-News)

3 MultiProSE Dataset

This section describes the annotation process used to develop the proposed MultiProSE dataset, including the ArPro dataset, the annotation schema and dataset statistics.

3.1 ArPro Dataset

The recent Arabic news propaganda benchmark called ArPro was used [12]. This dataset was collected from several Arabic news domains, where part of the dataset was selected from an existing dataset called AraFacts [30] and another part is a large-scale in-house collection. The dataset comprises a total of 8,000 paragraphs, which are divided into training, validation, and testing sets, with 6002, 672, and 1326 samples, respectively. Each sample is associated with a true label if it has at least one propaganda technique; otherwise, a false label is given. Furthermore, 37% of the data is labeled as 'false', and the remaining 63% is annotated as 'true' labels. The dataset encompasses 14 distinct topics including news, politics, health and social. The news and politics topics cover more than 50% of the paragraphs and contains higher amount of propagandistic content.

This dataset was selected because it is the largest Arabic propaganda dataset currently available, offering a rich and extensive collection of data for thorough training and evaluation. Moreover, it exclusively consists of news articles, providing a consistent and pertinent context for analyzing propagandistic content in MSA. The size and specificity of this dataset ensure a comprehensive and accurate approach to propaganda detection.

3.2 Annotators Information

As recommended by [31] and [32], the MultiProSE dataset was manually annotated by three annotators. All annotators were native Arabic speakers with doctoral degrees: two held PhDs in Arabic Literature and Criticism, while the third had a PhD in Computational Linguistics. The annotation process for sentiment and emotion follows a structured scheme to ensure consistency and reliability. For sentiment annotation, each paragraph is assigned one of three labels: (1 - positive, 2 - negative, 3 - neutral). Similarly, for emotion annotation, each paragraph is categorized into one of five labels: (1 - happiness, 2 - none, 3 - sadness, 4 - anger, 5 - fear). For both tasks, each annotator will select one label. Generally, to address conflicts in annotation, for sentiment annotation (1 - positive, 2 - negative, 3 - neutral), if the three annotators disagree on the annotation of a paragraph, the majority vote of a fourth annotator is considered. Similarly, for the emotion annotation task (1 - happiness, 2 - none, 3 - sadness, 4 - anger, 5 - fear), if there is a disagreement, a fourth annotator can resolve it using majority voting. If the conflict persists, a fifth annotator is added to determine the majority vote. If the issue remains unresolved, a sixth annotator can be included to help reach a clear decision. Moreover, to guarantee high-quality and accurate results, the annotators were paid[1]. As recommended by [33], the Excel file is used for the annotation process. To guarantee quality, the annotation guidelines were included in the Excel file.

3.3 Annotation Guidelines

The annotation guidelines are similar to those used in [32, 34], and [35] but have been adapted to suit the specific characteristics of our dataset. Additionally, these guidelines

---

[1] The hourly rate is approximately 13.33 USD, and the total time spent annotating all the texts amounts to 80 h.

were reviewed by two experts: a PhD holder in Criticism and Rhetoric and an MSc holder in Linguistics, both of whom are native Arabic speakers. Before beginning the annotation process and to ensure the clarity of the guidelines, each annotator participated in a two-hour training session on the annotation guidelines, which were provided in both Arabic and English.

For annotating the dataset, sentiment is annotated with (positive, negative, or neutral) labels similar to [32] and [34]. On the other hand, emotion is annotated based on Paul Ekman's model, which is the most commonly used model in emotion recognition research [36]. It involves six basic emotions: happiness, sadness, anger, fear, surprise, and disgust. However, based on [37] findings, we modified the categories of Ekman's model to include the "none" label, indicating that the text does not express any emotion. We omitted the disgust category due to its confusion with anger. Also, due to the characteristics of the dataset, the surprise was omitted. Therefore, the final emotion labels are (happiness, none, sadness, anger, or fear). As mentioned by the authors [38], the labeling of sentiment is correlated with emotion labels. This means that a text annotated as positive will have happiness as the emotion label, while a text with negative sentiment will be annotated with anger, sadness, or fear as emotion labels. Therefore, in the annotation guidelines, these details have been considered and incorporated to ensure that sentiment is annotated independently of the emotions in the text and vice versa. Also, to avoid any influence on the annotators' decisions, each text is annotated separately for emotion and sentiment at different times.

3.4 Quality Control Mechanism

To guarantee the quality of the annotations, the quality control mechanism (QCM) based on inspiration from [39] is followed. The main aim of QCM is to ensure accuracy and reliability by preventing random text annotation. The following describes the four steps of the QCM process.

1. Gold Data Phase. Similar to the criteria used in [35], a subset of 5% of the dataset, about 400 texts, is randomly selected as ground truth for QCM purposes. This ground truth is annotated by one of the authors (annotation procedure manager), and to ensure quality, it is also reviewed by two Arabic language experts—one with a PhD in Arabic Literature and Criticism, and the other with a master's degree in linguistics. During the annotation phases, if the annotators annotated these gold data incorrectly, they were informed of the mistake. However, if the annotator's trust score, which measures an annotator's consistency and reliability to the provided guidelines, is below 70%, all their submitted annotations are eliminated and ignored.
2. Training Phase (Pre-Exam). A pre-examination was given to 15 candidate annotators to assess their understanding and skill. Before the pre-exam, several informal meetings were conducted to explain the annotation guidelines, give some examples of annotation, and then discuss the possible challenges. From the gold data, a subset of 100 texts is selected at random to serve as quality test data. After the pre-exam, annotators are qualified to participate in annotation phases if they achieve an accuracy exceeding 70% in both sentiment and emotion annotation tasks [35]. Finally, the three annotators are selected based on the highest scores achieved.

3. During Annotation Tasks. In actual annotation tasks, and in each annotation round, 100 texts are randomly selected from ground truth and injected in all annotated text. After that, the weak annotation scores below 70% are discarded. Although this quality control added an extra effort and increased the annotation period, it provides greater reliability of the annotated data quality.
4. After Annotation Task. After each phase of annotation, the annotation manager calculates the quality of annotations by computing the Inter-Annotator Agreement (IAA), as will be explained in the next section. Next, a deep analysis is performed on these results to identify any conflicts and challenges in the annotations.

3.5 Annotation Phases

This section provides details of the annotation phases. Figure 1 presents the annotation process pipeline. The annotators started the corpus annotation on June 10, 2024 and completed it by September 14, 2024. The dataset was divided into several rounds, with each round containing multiple batches. Each round consists of approximately 2,667 texts, which are divided into about four batches. Therefore, 2,667 texts/4 batches = 666 texts per batch. Each batch was independently annotated by three annotators. To ensure high-quality annotations, as described in the previous section, an evaluation of annotation quality was conducted at the end of each batch. By the end of the 12 batches, with three annotators per batch (i.e., 12 batches * 666 texts per batch * 3 annotators), annotations of approximately 24,000 distinct texts were collected. Based on majority voting, a final set of 8,000 texts was considered. The following describes the three steps of the annotation phases.

1. Pilot Run. The dataset was extracted from Arabic news domains, as described in Sect. 3.1, which requires annotators to have a collective understanding of what constitutes sentiment and emotion. Therefore, the first phase is called the pilot round, which involves a smaller subset of the dataset, around 600 texts, to ensure that the annotation guidelines are clear and understood by all annotators. After analyzing the results of this phase, some minor differences among the annotators were detected, due to the subjectivity of the task itself. Consequently, the annotation guidelines were revised to address all discrepancies.
2. Revised Instructions. Each annotator annotated the remaining texts to ensure that the updated annotation guidelines were explicit and detailed. In this stage, the annotators annotated the texts based on the updated set of guidelines annotation. The results of this phase helped in the revision of the guidelines to cover many styles of news text and guaranteed the annotators' ability to consistently recognize sentiment and emotions.
3. Consolidation Phase. After each round in the previous section, the annotation manager analyzed the disagreements among most of the annotators and gathered feedback to maximize quality and consistency. Additionally, a majority voting scheme was used to determine the final emotion and sentiment labels for each text. As mentioned earlier, each text is annotated by three annotators; in case of disagreement, up to six annotators may be involved in making the final decision.

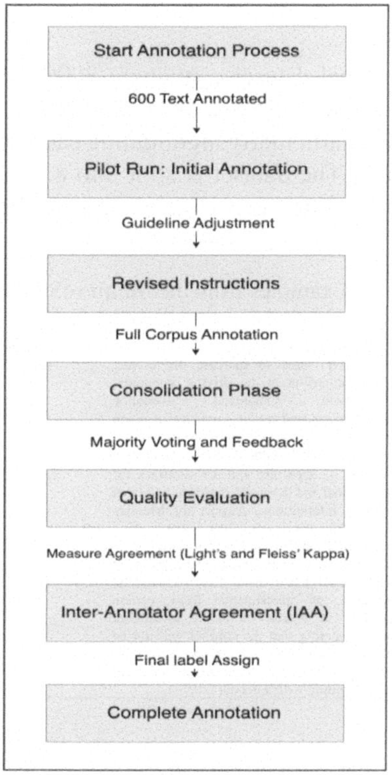

Fig. 1. Annotation Process Pipeline

3.6 Inter-Annotator Agreement

After annotation, the reliability of the annotation scheme was assessed using IAA. Cohen's Kappa is among the most widely used metrics for assessing agreement between two annotators on categorical variables [40]. As we have more than two annotators, as described in the annotator's information section, Light's Kappa is particularly suited for three or more annotators. It involves calculating Cohen's Kappa for every possible pair of annotators involved in the annotation task and then averaging these values to obtain the overall agreement among all annotators [41]. Moreover, Fleiss' Kappa [42], another extension of Cohen's Kappa specifically used to measure agreement between more than two annotators, is used. The authors in [43] and [44] indicate that human annotators agreed approximately 70%-80% on binary or ternary classes. However, as the number of classes increases, it becomes more challenging for annotators to reach agreement. The MultiProSE dataset consists of 3 and 5 classes for sentiment and emotion, respectively. Therefore, this highlights that multi-label sentiment and emotion annotation is a complex task for humans to agree on. The IAA for emotion annotations, as indicated by Lights' index and Fleiss' Kappa, are 0.7074 and 0.7093, respectively. In contrast, sentiment analysis demonstrates higher agreement with values of 0.8128 for Lights' index and 0.7650 for Fleiss' Kappa. According to [40], this value is interpreted as substantial.

3.7 Dataset Statistics

The MultiProSE is a multi-label dataset containing 8000 annotated texts, where each text is annotated for propaganda, sentiment, and emotion. Table 2 shows some examples from the MultiProSE dataset, particularly highlighting cases where annotated sentiment is not influenced by emotion. The dataset is split into 83.5% (6680 texts) and 16.5% (1320 texts) for training and testing, respectively, as presented in Table 3.

Table 2. Examples from the MultiProSE dataset

Text in Arabic	Text in English	Propaganda	Sentiment	Emotion
وتهدف "موانئ" إلى زيادة مساهمة القطاع الخاص في دعم عجلة التنمية الاقتصادية، وزيادة التنوع الاقتصادي، إلى جانب توفير وتوطين فرص عمل في قطاع الخدمات اللوجستية وتطويرها في ميناء جدة. .	"MAWANI" aims to increase the private sector's contribution to driving economic development, enhancing economic diversification, and creating and localizing job opportunities in the logistics services sector while further developing it at Jeddah Port.	True	Positive	Happiness
جـدول مواعيد إقلاع ووصول الرحلات الدولية والداخلية من وإلى مطار مصراتة الدولي ليوم الاثنين الموافـق 10.10.2022	Schedule of departure and arrival times for international and domestic flights to and from Misurata International Airport for Monday 10.10.2022	False	Neutral	None
وأكد ان أزمة جائحة كورونا ستخلق مزيداً من الاضطرابات والصراعات على المستوى العالمي من حيث الحروب التجارية وهجرة الاستثمارات من دول معينة بحثاً عن مناخات أفضل للاستثمار، لافتا الى أن الصراع لن يكون بين الصحة والاقتصاد، وانما سيكون باتجاه التعايش مع المرض والاستمرار بحياة كريمة.	He stressed that the Corona pandemic crisis will create more disturbances and conflicts at the global level in terms of trade wars and the migration of investments from certain countries in search of better investment climates, noting that the conflict will not be between health and the economy, but rather will be towards coexistence with the disease and continuing with a decent life.	True	Negative	Sadness

Table 3. Data split statistics of the MultiProSE dataset

Task	Label	Train	Test
Propaganda	True	62.99%	62.9%
	False	37.01%	37.1%
Sentiment	Positive	35.60%	37.4%
	Negative	42.70%	40.4%
	Neutral	21.70%	22.2%
Emotion	Happiness	29.80%	31.5%
	Sadness	20.40%	24.5%
	Anger	16.50%	14.4%
	Fear	4.60%	3.4%
	None	28.60%	26.2%

Figure 2 illustrates the labels' distribution across all tasks. As observed in Fig. 2, the percentage of texts that have a fear emotion is low, 4.41%, compared to those labeled as happiness 30.09%. This can be explained by the fact that happiness includes various emotions, such as joy, cheerfulness, satisfaction, contentment, and fulfillment. Moreover, negative emotions, such as sadness and anger, have a significant presence with 21.11%

and 16.19%, respectively. Furthermore, negative sentiment is the most frequent, comprising over 42.34% of the data. Positive sentiment follows closely at 35.86%, indicating a relatively balanced distribution of emotional polarities. Texts marked as propaganda dominate the dataset, constituting nearly two-thirds of all instances.

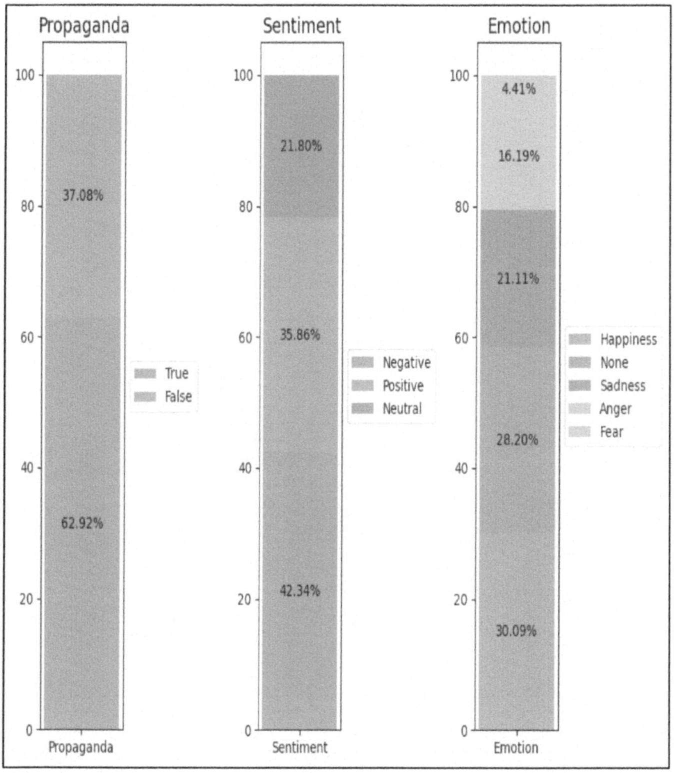

Fig. 2. Labels' Distribution Across All Tasks

Figure 3 presents the distribution of sentiment and emotion per propaganda. This finding confirms the findings of several studies, including [5–9], and [10]. These studies demonstrate a direct correlation between propaganda and emotional salience features, highlighting the benefits of incorporating sentiment and emotional features in propaganda detection models. Furthermore, Fig. 3 clearly shows that propaganda is more frequent in texts with negative and positive sentiment, particularly in negative sentiment at 30.78% and positive sentiment at 24.82%, compared to only 7.32% in neutral sentiment. Additionally, propaganda is most associated with anger and happiness, at 14.51% and 21.39%, respectively. In contrast, fear and sadness contain fewer propaganda paragraphs. Furthermore, texts without propaganda exhibit a higher proportion of neutral sentiment and no emotion, with 14.47% and 17.65%, respectively, compared to texts with propaganda, which show 7.32% for neutral sentiment and 10.55% for no emotion.

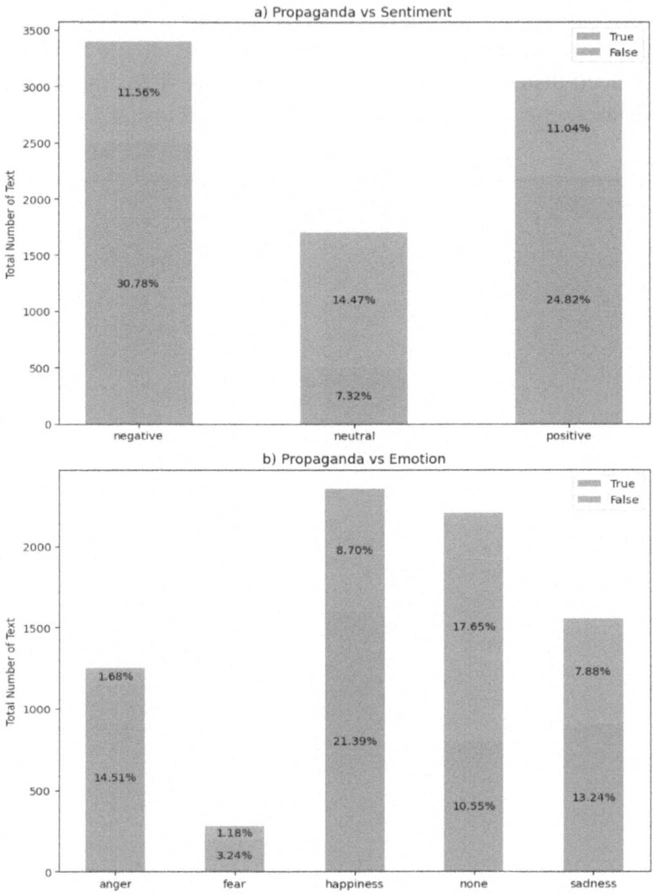

Fig. 3. Distribution of (a) Sentiment and (b) Emotion Labels by Propaganda

4 Experiments

This section presents the baseline model in propaganda, sentiment and emotion tasks intended to motivate and support researchers in the development of advanced models for text analysis across these domains. A MultiProSE dataset is suitable for classification tasks only when the accuracy of its annotations is verified. To achieve this, this section details the baseline setup and experimental design.

4.1 Models

Pre-trained language models (PLMs) and large language models (LLMs) are utilized. For LLMs, the GPT-4o-mini is fine-tuned [45]. The selection of this model is based on its accessibility and superior performance relative to other models, such as GPT-3.5, as demonstrated in [46].For PLMs, Bidirectional Encoder Representations from

Transformers (BERT) based models have shown significant performance in diverse NLP classification tasks [47]. Thus, several BERT-based classifiers for propaganda, sentiment and emotion tasks are implemented. Specifically, two Arabic state-of-the-art transfer learning models are fine-tuned to evaluate the annotations as follows:

1. **AraBERT** is trained on 8.6 billion tokens from five datasets consisting of MSA text [48].
2. **XLM-RoBERTa** is a multi-lingual language model trained on 2.5 terabytes of text across 100 languages, including Arabic [49].

Similar to [12], the dataset is split into 75%, 8.5%, and 16.5% for training, development, and testing, respectively. The transformer toolkits are employed to develop a pipeline for propaganda, sentiment, and emotion analysis [50]. The fine-tuning code is available online, accompanied by the MultiProSE dataset.

For PLMs, the proposed system initiates preprocessing Arabic texts by applying character normalization, removing diacritics, stopping words, tatweel (i.e., the horizontal elongation of characters in Arabic script, used for aesthetic or alignment purposes), non-Arabic letters, and repeating characters. Based on the training data visualization, the maximum sequence length is set to 256 tokens. Additionally, after conducting multiple empirical experiments, the batch size and number of epochs were set to 8 and 5, respectively. The AdamW optimizer was used with a learning rate of 2e-5 [51]. For LLM, the temperature value was set to zero to get deterministic and accurate decision-making. Also, the batch size and number of epochs were set to 8 and 4, respectively. Also, for each experiment, six and three runs with different random seeds were conducted for PLMs and LLM, respectively, and then the average performance over the test subset was reported.

4.2 Results and Discussion

Table 4 presents the obtained results of the proposed models, highlighting the best results for each task in bold text. It is clear from the table that AraBERT outperforms the other models in propaganda detection, achieving the best overall performance across most evaluation metrics. Nevertheless, both AraBERT and GPT-4o-Mini obtained a Micro-F1 score of 0.769. However, XLM-RoBERTa performed the worst in this task, yielding a Micro-F1 score of 0.683.For sentiment analysis, GPT-4o-Mini achieved the highest score with a Micro-F1 score of 0.842, followed by AraBERT with a slight difference between them in Micro-F1 scores by 0.106. Again, XLM-RoBERTa achieved a lower performance with a 0.698 Micro-F1 score. On the other hand, in emotion detection, GPT-4o-Mini demonstrated strong performance, achieving a Micro-F1 score of 0.750, outperforming all other models. AraBERT followed with a Micro-F1 score of 0.675, while XLM-RoBERTa demonstrated the lowest performance, with a Micro-F1 score of 0.648.

Overall, the GPT-4o-Mini outperforms the other models across most tasks, especially sentiment analysis. Furthermore, AraBERT exceeds it in some tasks due to the size of the trained model. However, XLM-RoBERTa is the worst model across all tasks. This may be explained by the fact that XLM-RoBERTa is multilingual in nature and not trained specifically in Arabic. In terms of overall task complexity, the emotion detection task seems to be more challenging for all models due to complex linguistic patterns and the number of emotions involved.

Table 4. MultiProSE results on test set. Acc is an abbreviation for Accuracy.

Task	AraBERT			XLM-RoBERTa			GPT-4o-Mini		
	Micro-F1	Macro-F1	Acc%	Micro-F1	Macro-F1	Acc %	Micro-F1	Macro-F1	Acc%
Propaganda Detection	**0.769**	**0.756**	**77**	0.683	0.597	68	0.769	0.733	76
Sentiment Analysis	0.736	0.722	73	0.698	0.682	69	**0.842**	**0.825**	**84**
Emotion Detection	0.675	0.635	67	0.648	0.608	64	**0.750**	**0.707**	**75**

5 Conclusion, Limitations and Future Work

In this paper, MultiProSE is presented as the first multi-label Arabic dataset for propaganda detection. The dataset is an extension of the ArPro dataset, with each text annotated for sentiment and emotion. Thus, MultiProSE can serve as a new benchmark for three tasks: propaganda detection, sentiment analysis, and emotion recognition. Moreover, it can enable future research to study the interaction between different opinion dimensions. A detailed description of the annotated dataset and a statistical analysis of the produced annotations are presented. Finally, several experiments for each task have been developed based on GPT-4o-mini and two BERT-based models. During the annotation process, several challenges were faced by the annotators, such as:

1. **Time Constraints:** While the expected annotation time for each text was calculated during the gold data phase, there was an overestimation of the annotators' ability to handle such a large dataset. The initial expectation was to complete the task in approximately one and a half months, with a minimum goal of 184 texts per day. However, following the pilot study, annotators encountered challenges in balancing accuracy with meeting deadlines. To address this, and to prioritize the quality of annotations, the deadline was extended. Each annotator was then assigned a more manageable daily goal of 100 texts, which encouraged consistency without compromising accuracy. As a result, the annotation tasks were successfully completed within four months.
2. **Annotation Guidelines:** As the dataset was extracted from news articles from a variety of Arabic news domains, developing clear and detailed guidelines that cover all possible scenarios in the dataset was a significant challenge.
3. **Diverse Topics Covered:** The ArPro dataset covers a wide variety of 14 different topics, such as news, politics, health, and sports. Therefore, annotating emotions and sentiments across different topics requires an in-depth understanding of the context and the emotions expressed, especially for news and politics, as they comprise more than 50% of the datatset.

4. **Diacritical Marks:** The lack of diacritical marks in most of the paragraphs leads to some words being ambiguous and having multiple possible meanings, which can result in inaccurate annotation. This challenge was addressed by asking the annotators to understand the term in relation to its context or refer back to the source of the news for a comprehensive understanding.
5. **MSA and Dialect:** Most of the paragraphs are written in MSA; however, a few are presented in dialect because they include quotes from individuals in the news. Consequently, annotators encountered difficulties with some obscure dialectal words that are rare in certain regions, necessitating additional searches for their meanings. Furthermore, some MSA words were ambiguous and unclear.
6. **Typos and Grammar:** A few paragraphs have spelling and grammatical mistakes, which create ambiguity in the text by changing its meaning

For future work, annotation based on span-level analysis and building a lexicon may provide deeper insights and boost the performance of detection models.

Acknowledgments. This research was accomplished by utilizing the technical and linguistic resources at the Thakaa AI Center for Arabic and King Salman Global Center for the Arabic Language in Riyadh, Saudi Arabia.

References

1. Digital Around the World: DataReportal – Global Digital Insights. https://datareportal.com/global-digital-overview. Accessed 13 Feb 2024
2. PROPAGANDA | English meaning - Cambridge Dictionary. https://dictionary.cambridge.org/dictionary/english/propaganda. Accessed 13 Feb 2024
3. Jowett, G., O'Donnell, V., Jowett, G.: Propaganda & Persuasion, 5th edn. Sage, Thousand Oaks (2012)
4. Da San Martino, G., Barrón-Cedeño, A., Nakov, P.: Findings of the NLP4IF-2019 shared task on fine-grained propaganda detection. In: Proceedings of the Second Workshop on Natural Language Processing for Internet Freedom: Censorship, Disinformation, and Propaganda, Hong Kong, China, pp. 162–170. Association for Computational Linguistics (2019). https://doi.org/10.18653/v1/D19-5024
5. Krishnamurthy, G., Gupta, R.K., Yang, Y.: SocCogCom at SemEval-2020 task 11: characterizing and detecting propaganda using sentence-level emotional salience features. In: Proceedings of the Fourteenth Workshop on Semantic Evaluation, Barcelona (online) , pp. 1793–1801. International Committee for Computational Linguistics (2020). https://doi.org/10.18653/v1/2020.semeval-1.235
6. Wang, L., Shen, X., de Melo, G., Weikum, G.: Cross-Domain Learning for Classifying Propaganda in Online Contents, arXiv: arXiv:2011.06844 (2020). http://arxiv.org/abs/2011.06844. Accessed 05 Feb 2024
7. Malik, M.S.I., Imran, T., Mamdouh, J.M.: How to detect propaganda from social media? Exploitation of semantic and fine-tuned language models. PeerJ Comput. Sci. **9**, e1248 (2023). https://doi.org/10.7717/peerj-cs.1248
8. Yu, S., Martino, G.D.S., Mohtarami, M., Glass, J., Nakov, P.: Interpretable propaganda detection in news articles. In: Proceedings of the Conference Recent Advances in Natural Language Processing - Deep Learning for Natural Language Processing Methods and Applications, INCOMA Ltd. Shoumen, Bulgaria, pp. 1597–1605 (2021). https://doi.org/10.26615/978-954-452-072-4_179

9. Lamsiyah, S., Mahdaouy, A., Alami, H., Berrada, I., Schommer, C.: UL & UM6P at ArAIEval shared task: transformer-based model for persuasion techniques and disinformation detection in Arabic. In: Proceedings of ArabicNLP 2023, Singapore (Hybrid), pp. 558–564. Association for Computational Linguistics (2023). https://doi.org/10.18653/v1/2023.arabicnlp-1.55
10. Nakov, P., Alam, F., Shaar, S., Da San Martino, G., Zhang, Y.: COVID-19 in Bulgarian social media: factuality, harmfulness, propaganda, and framing. In: Proceedings of the Conference Recent Advances in Natural Language Processing - Deep Learning for Natural Language Processing Methods and Applications, INCOMA Ltd. Shoumen, Bulgaria, pp. 997–1009 (2021). https://doi.org/10.26615/978-954-452-072-4_113
11. Top Ten Internet Languages in The World - Internet Statistics. https://www.internetworldstats.com/stats7.htm#google_vignette. Accessed 17 Feb 2024
12. Hasanain, M., Ahmad, F., Alam, F.: Can GPT-4 Identify Propaganda? Annotation and Detection of Propaganda Spans in News Articles (2024)
13. Rashkin, H., Choi, E., Jang, J.Y., Volkova, S., Choi, Y.: Truth of varying shades: analyzing language in fake news and political fact-checking. In: Proceedings of the 2017 Conference on Empirical Methods in Natural Language Processing, Copenhagen, Denmark, pp. 2931–2937. Association for Computational Linguistics (2017). https://doi.org/10.18653/v1/D17-1317
14. Barrón-Cedeño, A., Jaradat, I., Da San Martino, G., Nakov, P.: Proppy: organizing the news based on their propagandistic content. Inf. Process. Manag. **56**(5), 1849–1864 (2019). https://doi.org/10.1016/j.ipm.2019.03.005
15. Kausar, S., Tahir, B., Mehmood, M.A.: ProSOUL: a framework to identify propaganda from online Urdu content. IEEE Access **8**, 186039–186054 (2020). https://doi.org/10.1109/ACCESS.2020.3028131
16. Chaudhari, D., Pawar, A.V., Barrón-Cedeño, A.: H-prop and H-prop-news: computational propaganda datasets in Hindi. Data **7**(3), 29 (2022). https://doi.org/10.3390/data7030029
17. Faye, G., et al.: Exposing propaganda: an analysis of stylistic cues comparing human annotations and machine classification. In: Proceedings of 3rd Workshop on Understanding Implicit and Underspecified Language, Malta, pp. 62–72. Association for Computational Linguistics (2024). https://aclanthology.org/2024.unimplicit-1.6/
18. Da San Martino, G., Yu, S., Barrón-Cedeño, A., Petrov, R., Nakov, P.: Fine-grained analysis of propaganda in news article. In: Proceedings of the 2019 Conference on Empirical Methods in Natural Language Processing and the 9th International Joint Conference on Natural Language Processing (EMNLP-IJCNLP), Hong Kong, China, pp. 5636–5646. Association for Computational Linguistics (2019). https://doi.org/10.18653/v1/D19-1565
19. Baisa, V., Herman, O., Horák, A.: Benchmark dataset for propaganda detection in Czech newspaper texts. In: Proceedings - Natural Language Processing in a Deep Learning World, Incoma Ltd., Shoumen, Bulgaria, pp. 77–83 (2019). https://doi.org/10.26615/978-954-452-056-4_010
20. Da San Martino, G., Barrón-Cedeño, A., Wachsmuth, H., Petrov, R., Nakov, P.: SemEval-2020 task 11: detection of propaganda techniques in news articles. In: Proceedings of the Fourteenth Workshop on Semantic Evaluation, Barcelona (online): International Committee for Computational Linguistics, pp. 1377–1414 (2020). https://doi.org/10.18653/v1/2020.semeval-1.186
21. Dimitrov, D., et al.: SemEval-2021 task 6: detection of persuasion techniques in texts and images. In: Proceedings of the 15th International Workshop on Semantic Evaluation (SemEval-2021), Online, pp. 70–98. Association for Computational Linguistics (2021). https://doi.org/10.18653/v1/2021.semeval-1.7
22. Alam, F., Mubarak, H., Zaghouani, W., Da San Martino, G., Nakov, P.: Overview of the WANLP 2022 shared task on propaganda detection in Arabic. In: Proceedings of the Seventh Arabic Natural Language Processing Workshop (WANLP), Abu Dhabi, United Arab Emirates

(Hybrid), pp. 108–118. Association for Computational Linguistics (2022). https://aclanthology.org/2022.wanlp-1.11. Accessed 18 Feb 2023
23. Vijayaraghavan, P., Vosoughi, S.: TWEETSPIN: fine-grained propaganda detection in social media using multi-view representations. In: Proceedings of the 2022 Conference of the North American Chapter of the Association for Computational Linguistics: Human Language Technologies, Seattle, United States, pp. 3433–3448. Association for Computational Linguistics (2022). https://doi.org/10.18653/v1/2022.naacl-main.251
24. Ahmad, P.N., Liu, Y., Ali, G., Wani, M.A., ElAffendi, M.: Robust benchmark for propagandist text detection and mining high-quality data. Mathematics **11**(12), 2668 (2023). https://doi.org/10.3390/math11122668
25. Hasanain, M., et al.: ArAIEval shared task: persuasion techniques and disinformation detection in Arabic text. In: Proceedings of ArabicNLP 2023, Singapore (Hybrid), pp. 483–493. Association for Computational Linguistics (2023). https://doi.org/10.18653/v1/2023.arabicnlp-1.44. https://aclanthology.org/2023.arabicnlp-1.44/
26. Piskorski, J., Stefanovitch, N., Da San Martino, G., Nakov, P.: SemEval-2023 task 3: detecting the category, the framing, and the persuasion techniques in online news in a multi-lingual setup. In: Proceedings of the 17th International Workshop on Semantic Evaluation (SemEval-2023), Toronto, Canada, pp. 2343–2361. Association for Computational Linguistics (2023). https://doi.org/10.18653/v1/2023.semeval-1.317
27. Almotairy, B.M., Abdullah, M., Alahmadi, D.H.: Dataset for detecting and characterizing Arab computation propaganda on X. Data Brief **53**, 110089 (2024). https://doi.org/10.1016/j.dib.2024.110089
28. Khanday, A.M.U.D., Wani, M.A., Rabani, S.T., Khan, Q.R., Abd El-Latif, A.A.: HAPI: an efficient hybrid feature engineering-based approach for propaganda identification in social media. PLoS ONE **19**(7), e0302583 (2024). https://doi.org/10.1371/journal.pone.0302583
29. Chang, R.-C., Lai, C.-M., Chang, K.-L., Lin, C.-H.: Dataset of Propaganda Techniques of the State-Sponsored Information Operation of the People's Republic of China, arXiv: arXiv: 2106.07544 (2021). http://arxiv.org/abs/2106.07544. Accessed 10 Sept 2024
30. Ali, Z.S., Mansour, W., Elsayed, T., Al-Ali, A.: AraFacts: The First Large Arabic Dataset of Naturally Occurring Claims (2021)
31. Alayba, A.M., Palade, V., England, M., Iqbal, R.: Arabic language sentiment analysis on health services. In: 2017 1st International Workshop on Arabic Script Analysis and Recognition (ASAR), Nancy, France, pp. 114–118. IEEE (2017). https://doi.org/10.1109/ASAR.2017.8067771
32. Al-Twairesh, N.: Sentiment Analysis of Twitter: A Study on the Saudi Community. King Saud University (2016)
33. Pustejovsky, J., Stubbs, A.: Natural language annotation for machine learning: a guide to corpus-building for applications, 1 edn. Beijing Köln: O'Reilly (2013)
34. Rosenthal, S., Farra, N., Nakov, P.: SemEval-2017 task 4: sentiment analysis in Twitter. In: Proceedings of 11th International Workshop on Semantic Evaluation (SemEval-2017), Vancouver, Canada, pp. 502–518. Association for Computational Linguistics (2017). https://doi.org/10.18653/v1/S17-2088. https://aclanthology.org/S17-2088/
35. Mohammad, S., Bravo-Marquez, F., Salameh, M., Kiritchenko, S.: SemEval-2018 task 1: affect in Tweets. In: Proceedings of the 12th International Workshop on Semantic Evaluation, New Orleans, Louisiana, pp. 1–17. Association for Computational Linguistics (2018). https://doi.org/10.18653/v1/S18-1001
36. Ekman, P.: An argument for basic emotions, vol. 6, pp. 169–200 (1992)
37. Al-Khatib, A., El-Beltagy, S.R.: Emotional tone detection in Arabic tweets. In: Gelbukh, A. (ed.) Computational Linguistics and Intelligent Text Processing. Lecture Notes in Computer Science, vol. 10762, pp. 105–114. Springer, Cham (2018). https://doi.org/10.1007/978-3-319-77116-8_8

38. Poria, S., Hazarika, D., Majumder, N., Naik, G., Cambria, E., Mihalcea, R.: MELD: a multimodal multi-party dataset for emotion recognition in conversations. In: Proceedings of the 57th Annual Meeting of the Association for Computational Linguistics, Florence, Italy, pp. 527–536. Association for Computational Linguistics (2019). https://doi.org/10.18653/v1/P19-1050
39. Hutto, C., Gilbert, E.: VADER: a parsimonious rule-based model for sentiment analysis of social media text. ICWSM **8**(1), 216–225 (2014). https://doi.org/10.1609/icwsm.v8i1.14550
40. Landis, J.R., Koch, G.G.: The measurement of observer agreement for categorical data. Biometrics **33**(1), 159 (1977). https://doi.org/10.2307/2529310
41. Light, R.: Measures of response agreement for qualitative data: some generalizations and alternatives. Am. Psychol. Assoc. **76**(5), 365 (1971)
42. Fleiss, J., Davies, M.: Measuring agreement for multinomial data, pp. 1047–1051 (1982)
43. Bayerl, P.S., Paul, K.I.: What determines inter-coder agreement in manual annotations? A meta-analytic investigation. Comput. Linguist. **37**(4), 699–725 (2011). https://doi.org/10.1162/COLI_a_00074
44. Ohman, E.: Emotion Annotation: Rethinking Emotion Categorization (2020)
45. OpenAI Platform. https://platform.openai.com. Accessed 10 Sept 2024
46. Ahuja, K., et al.: MEGA: Multilingual Evaluation of Generative AI. arXiv: arXiv:2303.12528 (2023). https://doi.org/10.48550/arXiv.2303.12528
47. González-Carvajal, S., Garrido-Merchán, E.C.: Comparing BERT against traditional machine learning text classification. JCCE **2**(4), 352–356 (2023). https://doi.org/10.47852/bonviewJCCE3202838
48. Antoun, W., Baly, F., Hajj, H.: AraBERT: Transformer-based Model for Arabic Language Understanding, arXiv:2003.00104 (2021). http://arxiv.org/abs/2003.00104. Accessed 01 May 2022
49. Conneau, A., et al.: Unsupervised Cross-lingual Representation Learning at Scale, arXiv: arXiv:1911.02116 (2020). http://arxiv.org/abs/1911.02116. Accessed 18 Oct 2022
50. Wolf, T., et al.: Transformers: state-of-the-art natural language processing. In: Proceedings of the 2020 Conference on Empirical Methods in Natural Language Processing: System Demonstrations, Online, pp. 38–45. Association for Computational Linguistics (2020). https://doi.org/10.18653/v1/2020.emnlp-demos.6
51. Loshchilov, I., Hutter, F.: Decoupled Weight Decay Regularization, arXiv: arXiv:1711.05101 (2019). http://arxiv.org/abs/1711.05101. Accessed 10 Sept 2024

CLIP-Driven Deep Hashing for Cross-Modal Retrieval

Zhichao Han, Azreen Azman(✉), Mas Rina Mustaffa, and Fatimah Khalid

Faculty of Computer Science and Information Technology, Universiti Putra Malaysia, 43400 Serdang, Malaysia
azreenazman@upm.edu.my

Abstract. Cross-modal hashing focuses on learning compact binary codes to enable efficient retrieval of relevant information across different modalities. Recent advances in vision-language pretraining, especially the Contrastive Language-Image Pretraining (CLIP) model, have demonstrated remarkable capabilities in aligning visual and textual representations. However, directly integrating CLIP into hashing frameworks remains underexplored. In this paper, we propose CLIP-Driven Deep Hashing (CDDH), a novel approach that leverages CLIP's powerful multimodal representations to generate effective hash codes. Specifically, we employ CLIP's pre-trained embeddings as feature representations and introduce a dual-stream hash learning network that refines these features for cross-modal retrieval. Our method incorporates contrastive learning, quantization constraints, and similarity-preserving objectives to enhance retrieval accuracy. Extensive experiments on standard cross-modal benchmarks, including NUS-WIDE and MIRFlickr-25K, demonstrate the better position of our method over state-of-the-art hashing approaches.

Keywords: CLIP · Retrieval · Cross-modal hashing

1 Introduction

As multimodal data on the internet rapidly expands, retrieving relevant information across various modalities, such as retrieving images based on textual queries or finding text descriptions for a given image, has become a crucial task in the field of multimedia analysis. Cross-modal retrieval aims to bridge the gap between heterogeneous data representations across different data formats [1]. However, due to the semantic gap [2] between different modalities, designing efficient and accurate cross-modal retrieval methods remains a challenging problem.

One widely adopted solution to enhance retrieval efficiency is cross-modal hashing (CMH), which maps high-dimensional multimodal data into compact and discrete binary hash codes [3]. Compared to traditional real-valued feature representations, hashing-based retrieval significantly reduces storage costs and enables fast nearest neighbor search in large-scale databases using Hamming distance [4]. Conventional CMH approaches often rely on manually designed feature extraction

R. Ichise (Ed.): NLDB 2025, LNCS 15836, pp. 173–185, 2026.
https://doi.org/10.1007/978-3-031-97141-9_12

techniques and shallow models, which struggle to capture the complex semantic relationships between two completely different modalities. Furthermore, most traditional hashing methods are limited by the need for extensive labeled data and suffer from suboptimal generalization when applied to diverse real-world datasets.

Over recent years, vision-language models (VLMs) [5] have emerged as a breakthrough in multimodal learning. Among these, Contrastive Language-Image Pretraining (CLIP) has demonstrated extraordinary generalization across diverse visual and textual domains [6]. Unlike previous methods that require extensive task-specific labeled data, CLIP leverages a large-scale pretraining paradigm that aligns image and text representations through contrastive learning on vast amounts of webly supervised image-text pairs. This training process enables CLIP to learn rich, semantic-aligned representations in a shared feature space, making it a highly promising backbone for cross-modal retrieval tasks.

Despite CLIP's strong capability in zero-shot and cross-modal retrieval, existing CLIP-based retrieval methods primarily focus on continuous feature embeddings rather than discrete hash codes. This limitation poses a significant challenge for large-scale retrieval applications, where hash-based indexing is essential for balancing accuracy and efficiency. Simply applying CLIP's continuous representations to hashing frameworks often results in suboptimal binary codes, as CLIP does not explicitly optimize for discretization or compact feature representations. Furthermore, directly binarizing CLIP's output without refinement can lead to severe quantization loss, reducing retrieval performance [7].

To address these challenges, we propose CLIP-Driven Deep Hashing (CDDH), a novel framework that effectively integrates CLIP's pre-trained embeddings into a deep hash-based retrieval model while preserving its semantic alignment properties. Instead of relying solely on CLIP's pretrained feature space, CDDH introduces a dual-stream hash learning network that refines the extracted embeddings and refines binary hash codes for cross-modal retrieval. Our approach bridges the gap between continuous multimodal representations and discrete hashing constraints, enabling efficient and accurate retrieval in large-scale multimedia databases. The key findings and contributions of this work are presented as follows:

- CLIP-based hashing framework: We propose a novel hashing framework that leverages CLIP's powerful multimodal representations and enhances them through a dual-stream hash learning network to create compact and highly discriminative hash codes for cross-modal retrieval.
- Multi-objective optimization: We introduce a hybrid loss function that integrates contrastive loss (to maintain CLIP's semantic alignment), quantization loss (to minimize discretization errors), and cross-modal similarity constraints (to enhance retrieval accuracy). This multi-objective optimization ensures that the learned hash codes effectively maintain both intra-modal and inter-modal relationships.
- Efficient hash code learning: To mitigate the impact of quantization errors and optimize binary representations, we propose a discrete optimization strategy that refines hash codes through a smooth relaxation-based approach. This ensures that the binary codes are both efficient and meaningful semantics for cross-modal retrieval tasks.

By integrating the powerful feature extraction capabilities of CLIP with optimized hash learning techniques, our proposed CDDH framework highlights a substantial progress in cross-modal retrieval efficiency and scalability. Comprehensive experiments are carried out on two major cross-modal datasets: NUS-WIDE and MIRFlickr-25K. Our results demonstrate that CDDH significantly outperforms benchmark methods, highlighting its effectiveness in practical retrieval environments. In the following sections, we offer an in-depth explanation of our methodology, experimental setup, and analysis of results. The CLIP Driven Deep Hashing Model is shown in Fig. 1.

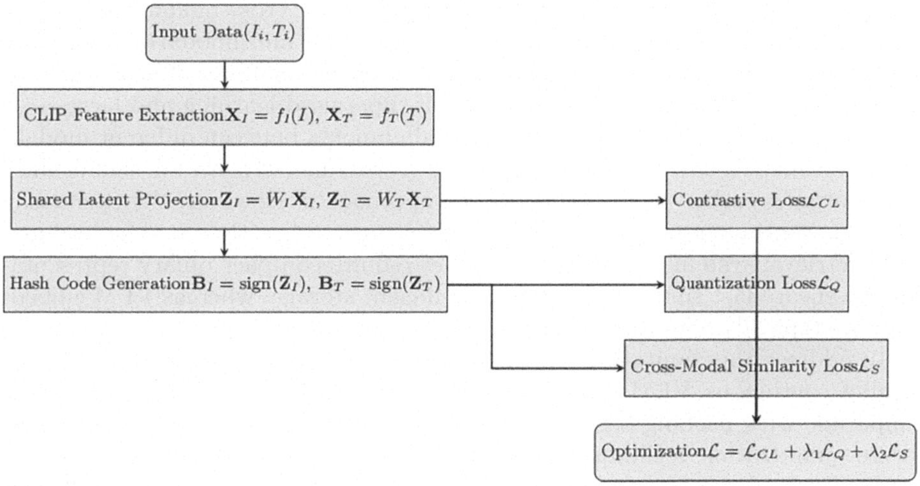

Fig. 1. CDDH Model flowchart.

2 Related Work

Cross-Modal Hashing. It has been widely studied as an efficient approach for large-scale multi-modal information retrieval. Traditional CMH methods seek to learn efficient binary codes that facilitate fast retrieval and low storage costs while preserving the semantic relationships between different modalities. Depending on their learning strategies, these methods can be broadly categorized into supervised and unsupervised approaches. Supervised CMH methods leverage labeled data to guide the learning of binary hash codes, ensuring that semantically similar instances from different modalities are mapped to nearby binary representations in the Hamming space [8–12]. In scenarios where labeled data is scarce, unsupervised CMH methods have been developed to learn binary representations without explicit supervision [13–17]. These methods often rely on co-occurrence information, distributional similarities, or latent structure alignment to bridge the modality gap. Despite the progress in both supervised and unsupervised CMH methods, several key challenges remain, for example, traditional CMH methods often rely on simple linear projections or predefined similarity measures, which may not effectively bridge the modality gap. Many methods attempt to minimize this loss through discrete optimization techniques, but balancing efficiency and retrieval quality remains an open problem.

Vision-Language Models in Retrieval. Over recent years, pretrained vision-language models (VLMs) have significantly advanced cross-modal retrieval by learning shared feature representations from large-scale multimodal data [5,6,18]. Unlike traditional retrieval methods that rely on manually crafted features or limited labeled datasets, VLMs leverage self-supervised learning and large-scale training data to establish strong semantic alignments between different modalities. These models have set new benchmarks in cross-modal retrieval, significantly outperforming earlier deep learning-based approaches. However, they primarily operate in continuous embedding spaces, which are not directly suited for hashing-based retrieval systems. Hashing techniques require compact binary representations to ensure fast similarity search and efficient storage, whereas VLM embeddings are typically high-dimensional and computationally expensive.

To address this limitation, recent research has explored methods for transforming continuous VLM embeddings into discrete hash codes, making them compatible with hashing-based retrieval frameworks. Various approaches incorporate quantization techniques, binarization strategies, and optimization constraints to preserve the semantic alignment of VLMs while enabling efficient hash-based search.

3 Methodology

3.1 Problem Formulation

Given a dataset $\mathcal{D} = \{(I_i, T_i)\}_{i=1}^{N}$ consisting of N paired image-text samples, our objective seeks to generate compact binary hash codes for both modalities, preserving their semantic relationships in the Hamming space. The explanations of some symbols are shown in Table 1. Specifically, we aim to learn following functions:

$$H_I : \mathbb{R}^{d_I} \rightarrow \{-1, 1\}^K, \quad H_T : \mathbb{R}^{d_T} \rightarrow \{-1, 1\}^K \tag{1}$$

Table 1. Notation and Definitions

Symbol	Description
$\mathcal{D}$	The dataset consisting of paired image-text samples
N	Total number of samples in the dataset
d_I, d_T	Dimensions of image and text features
K	Length of the generated hash codes
H_I, H_T	Hash functions for image and text modalities
$\mathbf{X}_I, \mathbf{X}_T$	Extracted image and text feature vectors
W_I, W_T	Projection matrices for mapping features into the latent space
$\mathbf{B}_I, \mathbf{B}_T$	Binary hash codes for image and text
τ	Temperature parameter in contrastive loss
$\mathcal{L}_{CL}$	Contrastive loss ensuring feature alignment
$\mathcal{L}_Q$	Quantization loss reducing the discrepancy with discrete codes
$\mathcal{L}_S$	Cross-modal similarity loss preserving retrieval quality
S_{B_I}, S_{B_T}	Similarity matrices computed from hash codes
$\|\cdot\|_F$	Frobenius norm for measuring matrix differences
λ_1, λ_2	Trade-off hyperparameters balancing different loss terms

where d_I and d_T indicate the dimensions for the image and text features, respectively, and K is the hash code length. The learned binary codes $\mathbf{B}_I$ and $\mathbf{B}_T$ should maintain cross-modal similarity and enable efficient retrieval.

3.2 CLIP-Based Feature Extraction

We leverage CLIP's pretrained encoders to extract feature representations from both images and texts:

$$\mathbf{X}_I = f_I(I), \quad \mathbf{X}_T = f_T(T) \tag{2}$$

where f_I and f_T are the image and text encoders, producing high-dimensional feature vectors $\mathbf{X}_I \in \mathbb{R}^{d_I}$ and $\mathbf{X}_T \in \mathbb{R}^{d_T}$. These features are then embedded into a common latent space using a fully connected layer:

$$\mathbf{Z}_I = W_I\mathbf{X}_I, \quad \mathbf{Z}_T = W_T\mathbf{X}_T \tag{3}$$

where $W_I \in \mathbb{R}^{K\times d_I}$ and $W_T \in \mathbb{R}^{K\times d_T}$ are trainable projection matrices.

3.3 Hash Code Generation

To generate binary hash codes, we apply a hash function $H(\cdot)$ that maps the projected latent features into discrete binary values:

$$\mathbf{B}_I = \text{sign}(\mathbf{Z}_I), \quad \mathbf{B}_T = \text{sign}(\mathbf{Z}_T) \tag{4}$$

where sign(·) is the element-wise sign function, assigning +1 for positive values and −1 otherwise.

However, the discrete nature of the sign function leads to an optimization challenge due to its non-differentiability. To mitigate quantization loss, we introduce a smooth surrogate function:

$$\mathbf{B}_I \approx \tanh(\alpha \mathbf{Z}_I), \quad \mathbf{B}_T \approx \tanh(\alpha \mathbf{Z}_T) \tag{5}$$

where α is a scaling factor that controls the approximation tightness.

3.4 Loss Functions

To guarantee that the generated hash codes accurately capture semantic relationships, we design a hybrid loss function consisting of three components: contrastive loss, quantization loss, and cross-modal similarity loss.

Contrastive Loss. Following CLIP's contrastive learning framework, we enforce alignment between image and text features:

$$\mathcal{L}_{CL} = -\sum_{i=1}^{N} \log \frac{\exp(\cos(\mathbf{B}_I^i, \mathbf{B}_T^i)/\tau)}{\sum_{j=1}^{N} \exp(\cos(\mathbf{B}_I^i, \mathbf{B}_T^j)/\tau) + \sum_{j=1}^{N} \exp(\cos(\mathbf{B}_I^j, \mathbf{B}_T^i)/\tau)} \tag{6}$$

where $\cos(\mathbf{B}_I, \mathbf{B}_T) = \frac{\mathbf{B}_I \cdot \mathbf{B}_T}{\|\mathbf{B}_I\| \|\mathbf{B}_T\|}$ represents the cosine similarity.

Quantization Loss. To promote the binary codes being close to discrete values while minimizing information loss, we impose a quantization constraint:

$$\mathcal{L}_Q = \|\mathbf{B}_I - \text{sign}(\mathbf{B}_I)\|^2 + \|\mathbf{B}_T - \text{sign}(\mathbf{B}_T)\|^2 \tag{7}$$

This term reduces the difference between the relaxed hash codes and their discrete counterparts.

Cross-Modal Similarity Loss. To further enhance retrieval performance, we minimize the discrepancy between the similarity matrices derived from the binary hash codes:

$$\mathcal{L}_S = \|S_{B_I} - S_{B_T}\|_F^2 \tag{8}$$

where $S_{B_I} = \mathbf{B}_I \mathbf{B}_I^T$ and $S_{B_T} = \mathbf{B}_T \mathbf{B}_T^T$ are similarity matrices computed in the space of Hamming codes, and $\| \cdot \|_F$ represents the Frobenius norm.

3.5 Overall Optimization

The final objective function integrates all three loss terms with trade-off hyperparameters λ_1 and λ_2:

$$\mathcal{L} = \mathcal{L}_{CL} + \lambda_1 \mathcal{L}_Q + \lambda_2 \mathcal{L}_S \tag{9}$$

where λ_1 and λ_2 balance the contributions of quantization and similarity preservation. The optimization is conducted iteratively using backpropagation with gradient-based methods.

By integrating CLIP's powerful feature extraction with hash-compatible transformations and effective loss formulations, the proposed method ensures robust cross-modal retrieval with compact binary representations.

4 Experiments

4.1 Datasets

To assess the performance of the proposed CLIP-Driven Deep Hashing (CDDH), we use two widely recognized benchmark datasets for cross-modal retrieval: NUS-WIDE [19] and MIRFlickr-25k [20]. Example image-text pairs from these datasets are presented in Fig. 2.

- NUS-WIDE: This dataset contains 269648 images, each labeled with one or more of the 81 predefined categories. This dataset presents a multi-label classification challenge where each image can belong to multiple categories, making it suitable for evaluating the ability of models to handle multi-label and multi-modal data retrieval.
- MIRFlickr-25k: Comprising 25,000 image-text pairs, it's provides a more compact but diverse collection for evaluating image-text retrieval models. The dataset is designed for evaluating cross-modal retrieval algorithms, especially in scenarios where image and text data exhibit significant heterogeneity in terms of content and structure.

Each of these datasets was chosen for its broad applicability in CMR tasks, along with its rich annotations that allow for meaningful evaluation of model performance in real-world retrieval settings.

Fig. 2. Examples from the NUS-WIDE and MIRFlickr-25K.

4.2 Metrics for Evaluation

To assess the retrieval performance of the proposed CDDH method, we adopt Mean Average Precision (mAP) [21], a widely used metric in information retrieval. The mAP metric provides a single value that reflects the overall retrieval quality, taking into account both the precision and recall across different retrieval ranks. It is computed by averaging the precision at each position where relevant items are retrieved, offering a comprehensive view of the model's ability to return relevant results across various queries.

For a given query q, the formula is defined as:

$$AP(q) = \frac{1}{R}\sum_{k=1}^{N} P(k) \cdot \delta(k), \tag{10}$$

where R represents the total number of relevant items for query q, N is the number of retrieved samples, $P(k)$ denotes the precision at rank k, and $\delta(k)$ is an indicator function that equals 1 when the item at rank k is relevant and 0 otherwise.

The overall retrieval performance across multiple queries is then measured by Mean Average Precision (mAP), computed as:

$$mAP = \frac{1}{|Q|}\sum_{q \in Q} AP(q), \tag{11}$$

where Q is the set of all queries. By averaging AP across different queries, mAP provides a comprehensive evaluation of the model's ability to retrieve relevant results consistently.

The mAP score is particularly useful when assessing cross-modal retrieval models because it considers the pairs of the retrieved items based on the query modality, which is crucial for multi-modal tasks where the goal is to retrieve one modality based on a query from the other modality. We compare the performance of the proposed CLIP-Driven Deep Hashing (CDDH) against seven benchmark methods, These methods encompass a diverse range of approaches, including traditional correlation analysis (CCA) [22], adversarial cross-modal retrieval (ACMR) [23], multi-granularity semantic learning (MG-HESR) [24], graph-based representation learning (DGCPN) [25,28], and advanced supervised hashing techniques (DJSRH, IRSGH) [26,27], making them effective references for evaluating the capability of our method in cross-modal retrieval tasks.

4.3 Parameter Sensitivity Analysis

To evaluate the impact of hyperparameters on retrieval performance, experiments were conducted on two datasets, focusing on λ_1 and λ_2, which control the balance between quantization and similarity preservation. We systematically varied these parameters and observed their influence on mean Average Precision (mAP). The results indicate that increasing λ_1 improves the binary representation's discreteness but may degrade retrieval accuracy if too large, while tuning

λ_2 effectively enhances cross-modal similarity preservation but requires careful adjustment to avoid overfitting. Experiments were performed on the Magic Tower Community GPU Cloud Platform, equipped with 8 cores, 32 GB of video memory, and 24 GB of RAM.

4.4 Results

Table 2. The mAP@50 of seven competitors on two datasets.

Approaches	NUS Dataset			Flickr-25k Dataset		
	Img2Txt	Txt2Img	Avg.	Img2Txt	Txt2Img	Avg.
CCA	0.382	0.368	0.375	0.321	0.218	0.269
ACMR	0.584	0.579	0.581	0.623	0.561	0.612
MG-HESR	0.631	0.656	0.643	0.724	0.711	0.718
DGCPN	0.654	0.660	0.657	0.751	0.749	0.750
DJSRH	0.798	0.771	0.784	0.862	0.835	0.849
IRGRH	0.816	0.801	0.810	0.890	0.872	0.881
MGSGH	0.810	0.788	0.799	0.873	**0.893**	0.883
CDDH	**0.818**	**0.802**	**0.810**	**0.890**	0.879	**0.885**

In Table 2, the mAP@50 [29] scores of seven competing approaches on the two datasets are presented. By comparing the mAP@50 results, the proposed CDDH method demonstrates excellent performance, particularly outperforming most existing methods in both two tasks.

Compared with traditional methods such as CCA and ACMR, CDDH demonstrates a significant improvement in overall performance on the NUS-WIDE dataset. Specifically, CDDH achieves mAP values of 0.818 for Img2Txt and 0.802 for Txt2Img, which are substantially higher than those of CCA (0.375 and 0.269) and ACMR (0.581 and 0.612). This superior performance is attributed to the CDDH framework, which extracts high-quality, dense representations from the CLIP model for both images and text, ensuring strong semantic alignment across modalities. By integrating the semantic richness of CLIP with the retrieval efficiency of hashing, CDDH effectively enhances cross-modal retrieval performance.

Similarly, on the MIRFlickr-25k dataset, CDDH maintains outstanding outcomes, particularly in the Txt2Img task, where it achieves an mAP of 0.879, only slightly lower than MGSGH (0.893). Overall, CDDH attains the highest performance across both datasets, with mAP values of 0.810 on NUS-WIDE and 0.885 on MIRFlickr-25k, surpassing most existing methods and demonstrating CDDH lies in its ability to effectively model the complex relationships between images and text while preserving essential semantic features in the learned hash codes. Traditional cross-modal retrieval methods often struggle with fine-grained alignment between modalities, whereas CDDH leverages CLIP's robust pre-trained embeddings to mitigate this challenge. This makes CDDH particularly effective for datasets with diverse content and rich annotations.

4.5 Visible Analysis of Retrieved Examples

To qualitatively evaluate the proposed CDDH model, we conduct a visible analysis of retrieved examples experiment on the MIRFlickr25k dataset. This experiment provides an intuitive visualization of the model's cross-modal retrieval capability by displaying the top-5 retrieved results [30].

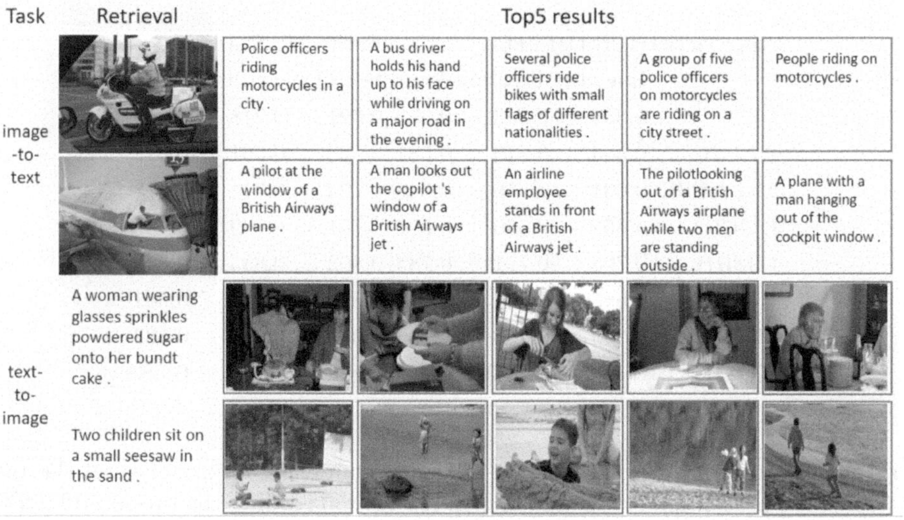

Fig. 3. Some retrieval outcomes of CDDH on MIRFlickr25k. (Color figure online)

In the I2T task, an image is randomly picked from the dataset as the query, and the five most relevant text descriptions are retrieved based on similarity scores [31]. The most relevant description, which best matches the semantic content of the image, is highlighted with a red bounding box. Similarly, for the T2I task, we select a textual description as the query and retrieve the five most relevant images [32]. The most semantically aligned image is also enclosed within a red bounding box to emphasize the model's top prediction. The retrieved examples are presented in Fig. 3.

The visualization outcomes demonstrate that CDDH effectively retrieves semantically relevant cross-modal pairs, with the highest-ranked results closely matching the ground-truth content [33]. Notably, in most cases, the model successfully aligns fine-grained visual and textual semantics, outperforming traditional methods in preserving cross-modal consistency. This qualitative analysis further supports the quantitative findings, confirming that CDDH enhances retrieval accuracy by aligning the semantic representations of images and text.

5 Conclusion

In this research, we present CLIP-Driven Deep Hashing (CDDH), a novel and effective framework designed to integrate the power of CLIP (Contrastive Language-Image Pretraining) embeddings with a cross-modal hashing model. The core idea behind CDDH is to preserve the semantic alignment achieved by CLIP between these two modalities while leveraging the efficiency of hash codes for scalable and fast retrieval. In conclusion, CDDH represents a significant advancement in the field of cross-modal hashing by effectively leveraging CLIP's powerful embedding capabilities to enhance The effectiveness of hash codes for efficient and precise retrieval. Its ability to preserve semantic alignment across modalities, while ensuring compact and efficient hash code representations, makes it well-suited for large-scale retrieval across different modalities.

Acknowledgement. This research was partially supported by Quantum Storage Malaysia Sdn Bhd as part of the research collaboration with Universiti Putra Malaysia.

References

1. Zhu, L., Song, J., Wei, X., et al.: CAESAR: concept augmentation based semantic representation for cross-modal retrieval. Multimedia Tools Appl. 1–31 (2022)
2. Zhu, L., Song, J., Yang, Z., et al.: DAP 2 CMH: deep adversarial privacy-preserving cross-modal hashing. Neural Process. Lett. **54**(4), 2549–2569 (2022)
3. Zhang, C., Song, J., Zhu, X., et al.: HCMSL: hybrid cross-modal similarity learning for cross-modal retrieval. ACM Trans. Multimedia Comput. Commun. Appl. (TOMM) **17**(1s), 1–22 (2021)
4. Yang, Z., Yang, L., Raymond, O.I., et al.: NSDH: a nonlinear supervised discrete hashing framework for large-scale cross-modal retrieval. Knowl.-Based Syst. **217**, 106818 (2021)
5. Jia, C., Yang, Y., Xia, Y., et al.: Scaling up visual and vision-language representation learning with noisy text supervision. In: International Conference on Machine Learning, pp. 4904–4916. PMLR (2021)
6. Radford, A., Kim, J.W., Hallacy, C., et al.: Learning transferable visual models from natural language supervision. In: International Conference on Machine Learning, pp. 8748–8763. PMLR (2021)
7. Zhang, C., Zhong, Z., Zhu, L., et al.: M2guda: multi-metrics graph-based unsupervised domain adaptation for cross-modal hashing. In: Proceedings of the International Conference on Multimedia Retrieval, pp. 674–681 (2021)
8. Kumar, S., Udupa, R.: Learning hash functions for cross-view similarity search. In: IJCAI Proceedings-International Joint Conference on Artificial Intelligence, vol. 22, no. 1, p. 1360 (2011)
9. Tang, J., Wang, K., Shao, L.: Supervised matrix factorization hashing for cross-modal retrieval. IEEE Trans. Image Process. **25**(7), 3157–3166 (2016)
10. Deng, C., Chen, Z., Liu, X., et al.: Triplet-based deep hashing network for cross-modal retrieval. IEEE Trans. Image Process. **27**(8), 3893–3903 (2018)
11. Xie, D., Deng, C., Li, C., et al.: Multi-task consistency-preserving adversarial hashing for cross-modal retrieval. IEEE Trans. Image Process. **29**, 3626–3637 (2020)

12. Liu, X., Hu, Z., Ling, H., et al.: MTFH: a matrix tri-factorization hashing framework for efficient cross-modal retrieval. IEEE Trans. Pattern Anal. Mach. Intell. **43**(3), 964–981 (2019)
13. Han, Z., Chen, W., Huang, C., et al.: Unsupervised method for cross-modal retrieval based on domain adaptive learning. In: Advances in Guidance, Navigation and Control, pp. 539–548 (2025)
14. He, L., Xu, X., Lu, H., et al.: Unsupervised cross-modal retrieval through adversarial learning. In: 2017 IEEE International Conference on Multimedia and Expo (ICME), pp. 1153–1158. IEEE (2017)
15. Huang, X., Peng, Y., Yuan, M.: MHTN: modal-adversarial hybrid transfer network for cross-modal retrieval. IEEE Trans. Cybern. **50**(3), 1047–1059 (2018)
16. Peng, Y., Chi, J.: Unsupervised cross-media retrieval using domain adaptation with scene graph. IEEE Trans. Circuits Syst. Video Technol. **30**(11), 4368–4379 (2019)
17. Liu, X., Mu, Y., Zhang, D., et al.: Large-scale unsupervised hashing with shared structure learning. IEEE Trans. Cybern. **45**(9), 1811–1822 (2014)
18. Li, J., Li, D., Xiong, C., et al.: Blip: bootstrapping language-image pre-training for unified vision-language understanding and generation. In: International Conference on Machine Learning, pp. 12888–12900. PMLR (2022)
19. Chua, T.-S., Tang, J., Hong, R., Li, H., Luo, Z., Zheng, Y.: Nuswide: a real-world web image database from national university of Singapore. In: ACM International Conference on Image and Video Retrieval (CIVR), no. 48 (2009)
20. Huiskes, M.J., Lew, M.S.: The MIR flickr retrieval evaluation. In: Proceedings of the 1st ACM International Conference on Multimedia Information Retrieval, pp. 39–43 (2008)
21. Dempster, A.P., Laird, N.M., Rubin, D.B.: Maximum likelihood from incomplete data via the EM algorithm. J. Roy. Stat. Soc. Ser. B (Methodol.) **39**(1), 1–22 (1977)
22. Hardoon, D.R., Szedmak, S., Shawe-Taylor, J.: Canonical correlation analysis: an overview with application to learning methods. Neural Comput. **16**(12), 2639–2664 (2004)
23. Wang, B., Yang, Y., Xu, X., et al.: Adversarial cross-modal retrieval. In: Proceedings of the 25th ACM International Conference on Multimedia, pp. 154–162 (2017)
24. Zhu, L., Zhang, C., Song, J., et al.: Deep multigraph hierarchical enhanced semantic representation for cross-modal retrieval. IEEE Multimedia **29**(3), 17–26 (2022)
25. Yu, J., Zhou, H., Zhan, Y., Tao, D.: Deep graph-neighbor coherence preserving network for unsupervised cross-modal hashing. In: Proceedings of AAAI Conference on Artificial Intelligence, vol. 35, no. 5, pp. 4626–4634 (2021)
26. Su, S., Zhong, Z., Zhang, C.: Deep joint-semantics reconstructing hashing for large-scale unsupervised cross-modal retrieval. In: Proceedings of IEEE/CVF International Conference on Computer Vision (ICCV), pp. 3027–3035 (2019)
27. Hou, C., Li, Z., Tang, Z., et al.: Multiple instance relation graph reasoning for cross-modal hash retrieval. Knowl.-Based Syst. **256**, 109891 (2022)
28. Han, Z., Azman, A., Khalid, F., et al.: Multi-granularity semantic information integration graph for cross-modal hash retrieval. IEEE Access **12**, 44682–44694 (2024)
29. Jiang, B., Yang, J., Lv, Z., Tian, K., Meng, Q., Yan, Y.: Internet cross-media retrieval based on deep learning. J. Vis. Commun. Image Represent. **48**, 356–366 (2017)
30. Cheng, Q., Guo, Q., Gu, X.: Adversarial pre-optimized graph representation learning with double-order sampling for cross-modal retrieval. Expert Syst. Appl. **231**, 120731 (2023)

31. Li, Z., Lu, H., Fu, H., et al.: Parallel learned generative adversarial network with multi-path subspaces for cross-modal retrieval. Inf. Sci. **620**, 84–104 (2023)
32. Li, B., Yao, D., Li, Z.: RICH: a rapid method for image-text cross-modal hash retrieval. Displays **79**, 102489 (2023)
33. Yuan, M., Zhang, H., Liu, D., et al.: Semantic-embedding guided graph network for cross-modal retrieval. J. Vis. Commun. Image Represent. **93**, 103807 (2023)

WIP: Iterative Post-training Pruning with Weighted Importance Estimation for Large Language Models

Dinh-Truong Do(✉), Kiyoaki Shirai, and Le-Minh Nguyen

Japan Advanced Institute of Science and Technology, Ishikawa, Japan
{truongdo,kshirai,nguyenml}@jaist.ac.jp

Abstract. Modern large language models (LLMs) achieve impressive accuracy but are difficult to deploy due to their enormous size and computational demands. Post-training pruning—removing redundant weights from a pre-trained model without retraining—promises to mitigate these issues but often risks channel collapse, where entire neurons are inadvertently zeroed out, especially at higher sparsity levels. We introduce a new Weighted-Iterative Pruning (WIP) approach that tackles these challenges through two key innovations. First, our weighted importance metric strikes a tunable balance between row-wise and column-wise contributions of the weight matrix, preventing over-pruning of entire channels. Second, we adopt an iterative multi-stage pruning strategy that recalculates importance scores after each partial prune, mitigating the greedy errors seen in one-shot methods. Experiments across multiple LLMs and benchmarks show that WIP preserves perplexity and zero-shot accuracy better than existing techniques, especially at high sparsities. Additionally, our 2:4 semi-structured pruned models achieve real-world inference speedups of up to 1.88× on GPUs, underscoring WIP's practicality for resource-constrained environments. Our code is publicly available at https://github.com/truongdo619/WIP.

Keywords: Iterative Post-Training Pruning · Large Language Models · Weighted Importance Estimation

1 Introduction

Deep neural networks have achieved remarkable success across many domains, but their growing size has made deployment challenging for environments with limited resources [19]. This is especially true for large language models (LLMs) with billions of parameters, which demand extensive resources for inference [2, 4]. Therefore, model compression techniques such as quantization [11,13] and pruning [6,12,14] are crucial to reduce model size and accelerate inference. In particular, pruning, which removes redundant weights to induce sparsity, can significantly lower the computation and memory footprint of a model.

Early neural network pruning methods [14,15,17], demonstrated that high sparsity could be achieved by iteratively removing weights of small magnitude

R. Ichise (Ed.): NLDB 2025, LNCS 15836, pp. 186–200, 2026.
https://doi.org/10.1007/978-3-031-97141-9_13

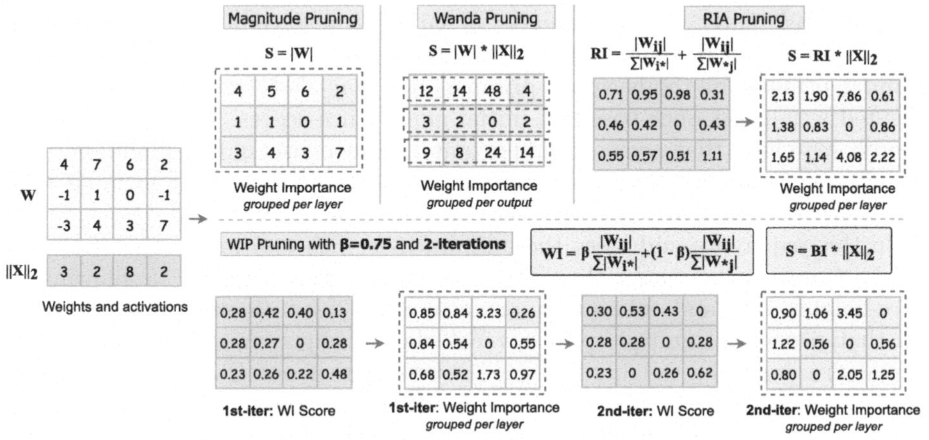

Fig. 1. Comparison of pruning techniques targeting 50% sparsity. Magnitude Pruning removes weights solely based on absolute values, Wanda Pruning integrates activation magnitudes, and RIA Pruning balances input-output importance. WIP Pruning (ours) iteratively updates importance scores using a weighted metric to refine pruning decisions.

and fine-tuning the model. However, retraining or fine-tuning after pruning is often infeasible for LLMs due to their scale [3,23]. Recently, there has been growing interest in *post-training pruning* methods that prune a pre-trained model without any retraining, aiming for a zero-shot compression that preserves accuracy. The challenge is to design effective pruning criteria that identify unimportant weights to remove, while causing minimal degradation in model performance.

A straightforward baseline is **magnitude-based** pruning [14], which removes the smallest weights in absolute value. While this approach works reasonably well in smaller models, it can severely hurt LLMs by indiscriminately removing weights that are small but collectively crucial. To address these pitfalls, Sun et al. introduced **Wanda** [25], which considers both weight magnitude and activation magnitude, pruning weights whose product of weight and activation is smallest. By accounting for activations, Wanda avoids discarding seemingly small weights that play an outsized role in the final output. Zhang et al. [29] further refined this approach with **Relative Importance and Activations (RIA)**, achieving state-of-the-art post-training pruning results for LLMs. The core idea behind RIA is to compute a *relative importance* (RI) score for each weight based on how much it contributes to its input and output channels, combined with the activation magnitude. This strategy mitigates the problem of *channel collapse*, where all weights of a particular row or column in a weight matrix are pruned away. Despite these advances, major challenges remain. One key insight is that row- and column-wise fractions in RIA are not inherently on the same scale. RIA's scoring formula uses a fixed 50/50 blend of row-based and column-based importance, which can inadvertently skew the global importance rankings if one fraction consistently produces smaller or larger values. As a result, entire rows or columns may still be pruned out at high sparsities. Moreover, previous post-training pruning methods apply pruning in a *one-shot* fashion, removing all targeted weights at once based on initial importance scores. This can be overly greedy: a weight that seems unimportant in the dense model might become crucial once other weights are removed. Consequently, one-shot pruning may cause excessive accuracy loss–especially at higher sparsity levels.

In this paper, we addresses these limitations with two improvements: (1) a *weighted importance metric* that introduces a tunable parameter β, allowing us to re-balance row and column importance, and (2) an *iterative pruning strategy* that prunes in multiple passes, recalculating importance scores after each partial pruning. The weighted metric ensures that if one fraction (row or column) tends to produce smaller values, it will not dominate the combined score, thereby preventing any neuron (channel) from being unfairly stripped of all its connections. Meanwhile, iterative pruning (rather than a single shot) allows the model's activation statistics and importance rankings to be updated after each pruning pass, helping to avoid large one-step accuracy drops and further minimizing channel collapse. Figure 1 illustrates the differences between our pruning method and previous approaches. We validate our approach on modern LLM architectures (e.g., LLaMA-2 [26], LLaMA-3 [5], and OPT [28]) across standard language modeling benchmarks for both unstructured and N:M semi-structured pruning. Experiments show that our method consistently outperforms previous state-of-the-art post-training methods in preserving accuracy at different sparsities. Moreover, we measure real-world speedups on GPU and observe up to a 1.88× reduction in inference time compared to the dense model.

In summary, our primary contributions are: **(I) Weighted Importance Metric**, introducing a tunable weighting parameter β to rebalance row-wise and column-wise importance scores, preventing over-pruning of entire neurons and improving upon the original RIA metric; **(II) Iterative Pruning Strategy**, a multi-pass zero-shot pruning procedure that updates importance scores after each pruning stage, yielding better accuracy retention than one-shot methods at high sparsity levels; **(III) Extensive Evaluation**, demonstrating consistent performance gains over magnitude pruning, Wanda, and standard RIA; and **(IV) Public code release**, with our source code available for reproducibility and further development.

2 Post-training Pruning: Preliminaries

Layer-Wise Post-training Pruning. Post-training pruning compresses a pre-trained network by removing redundant weights without retraining [16]. A common strategy is to prune each layer separately by minimizing the ℓ_2 error between the original and pruned weight matrices. Formally, for layer l with weight matrix $\mathbf{W}_l \in \mathbb{R}^{d_{l-1}\times d_l}$, we define a binary mask $\mathbf{M}_l \in \{0,1\}^{d_{l-1}\times d_l}$ to indicate the retained weights. The objective is:

$$\min_{\mathbf{M}_l} \|\mathbf{W}_l - (\mathbf{M}_l \odot \mathbf{W}_l)\|_2^2 \quad \text{subject to} \quad \|\mathbf{M}_l\|_0 \leq s,$$

where s is the desired number of nonzero weights. In our work, we focus on both unstructured pruning and N:M semi-structured pruning.

State-of-the-Art Layer-Wise Pruning Methods. A simple baseline, magnitude pruning [14], removes weights solely by their absolute values. However, this approach can be overly aggressive, sometimes discarding weights that, while small individually, are collectively important—potentially causing channel collapse, where entire neurons lose their connections. To mitigate this, methods such as Relative Importance and Activations (RIA) assign each weight a score based on its contribution within both its input and output channels. For a weight w_{ij}, the row and column contributions are computed as:

$$\text{rowFrac}_{ij} = \frac{|w_{ij}|}{\sum_k |w_{ik}|}, \quad \text{colFrac}_{ij} = \frac{|w_{ij}|}{\sum_k |w_{kj}|}. \tag{1}$$

RIA then averages these fractions and scales the result by the ℓ_2 norm of the corresponding input activation:

$$\text{RIA}_{ij} = (\text{rowFrac}_{ij} + \text{colFrac}_{ij}) \times \|x_i\|_2. \tag{2}$$

This formulation helps preserve essential connections, reducing the risk of inadvertently eliminating entire neurons.

3 WIP: Weighted-Iterative Pruning

We propose Weighted-Iterative Pruning (WIP), a post-training pruning method that enhances the state-of-the-art relative important score with two novel components: a weighted importance score and an iterative multi-stage pruning schedule. WIP effectively balances row-column contributions and mitigates the myopic nature of one-shot pruning. The overall methodology is outlined in Algorithm 1, with Fig. 1 illustrating the underlying concepts.

3.1 Weighted Relative Importance Score

Previous state-of-the-art post-training criteria like RIA [29] computes an importance score for each weight by considering its contribution to both its output neuron (row) and input channel (column), multiplied by an activation magnitude. This relative weighting of row and column importance was shown to reduce channel collapse compared to magnitude-only or Wanda pruning [25]. However, a fundamental limitation of RIA is that row-wise and column-wise fractions are not inherently on the same scale. Several factors, including matrix dimensionality and structural dependencies, contribute to this imbalance. Furthermore, prior studies [25] suggest that preserving output channels can be more critical for maintaining model integrity. In practice, one of these fractions can consistently yield smaller values than the other across the layer, causing the summed RI score to be biased toward the larger-fraction component. As a result, RIA's fixed equal weighting can still skew global importance rankings and occasionally prune out entire rows or columns, especially at high sparsities.

WIP addresses this issue by introducing a tunable parameter $0 \leq \beta \leq 1$ to rebalance the two components. We define a Weighted Importance (WI) fraction for each weight as a convex combination of the row and column fractions:

$$\mathrm{WI}_{ij}^{(\ell)} = \beta\, \mathrm{rowFrac}_{ij}^{(\ell)} + (1-\beta)\, \mathrm{colFrac}_{ij}^{(\ell)}. \tag{3}$$

Setting $\beta = 0.5$ recovers the original relative important score (equal weighting). But by choosing β differently, we can emphasize one aspect more than the other: e.g. $\beta = 0$ uses only row-wise importance (preserving each output neuron's connections), while $\beta = 1$ uses only column-wise importance (preserving input features). In practice we select β to balance the scales of the two terms, so that neither dominates the combined score. This flexibility prevents scenarios where all weights of a particular neuron could appear among the lowest scores simply due to a scale discrepancy. In other words, if one type of fraction tends to be systematically smaller, a β closer to 1 or 0 will up-weight it, ensuring no neuron (row or column) is unfairly stripped of all its connections. WIP's weighted metric thus generalizes RIA and directly tackles the remaining channel-collapse cases.

Incorporating Activation Magnitudes. Prior research [25,29] has highlighted the challenge of activation outliers, particularly in the context of quantizing LLMs. Therefore, we multiply the above importance fraction by an estimate of the activation magnitude to account for the dynamic range of inputs. Let $\|X_i^{(\ell)}\|_2$ denote the ℓ_2 norm of the calibration input activation vector corresponding to output i in layer ℓ, estimated using a small calibration dataset (see Sect. 5 for analysis on the impact of calibration set size). The final WIP importance score for weight $w_{ij}^{(\ell)}$ is given by:

$$\mathrm{score}_{ij}^{(\ell)} = \mathrm{WI}_{ij}^{(\ell)} \times \|X_i^{(\ell)}\|_2. \tag{4}$$

This adjustment ensures that weights connected to infrequently activated neurons receive lower scores, while those associated with frequently activated pathways receive higher scores—even if their raw magnitude is small [25]. Figure 1 illustrates this effect by comparing importance rankings across different pruning methods. For instance, while magnitude pruning, Wanda, and RIA all prune the second output channel (row 2), WIP—with $\beta = 0.75$—retains at least one weight in that channel, demonstrating its ability to preserve critical connections. By dynamically adjusting weight importance based on both structural and activation factors, WIP delivers a more refined pruning metric that minimizes performance degradation while ensuring structural robustness.

3.2 Iterative Multi-stage Pruning Strategy

The second key component of WIP is an *iterative pruning mechanism* that removes weights in multiple stages rather than one-shot. Traditional post-training pruning methods [16,25,29] typically prune all targeted weights in one

Algorithm 1. WIP: Weighted-Iterative Pruning (WIP) Algorithm

Require:

- Pre-trained LLM M (with weight matrices $\mathbf{W}_1, \ldots, \mathbf{W}_L$)
- Calibration dataset $\mathcal{D}$ (e.g., a small text corpus)
- Target sparsity $S \in (0, 1)$
- Weighting factor $\beta \in [0, 1]$
- Number of pruning stages $T \geq 1$
- L2 Norm of Input Activation $||X||_2$

Ensure: Pruned model M_{pruned} at sparsity level S

procedure WIP-PRUNE($M, ||X||_2, S, \beta, T$)
  for $t = 1 \rightarrow T$ **do** ▷ Perform T iterative pruning stages
    $r \leftarrow \frac{S}{T}$ ▷ Fraction of weights to remove at this stage
    for each layer $\ell = 1 \rightarrow L$ **do**
      $\mathbf{W}_\ell \leftarrow \mathbf{W}_\ell^{(\text{current})}$
      for each weight $w_{ij}^{(\ell)}$ in $\mathbf{W}_\ell$ **do**
        $\text{rowFrac}_{ij}^{(\ell)} = \frac{|w_{ij}^{(\ell)}|}{\sum_k |w_{ik}^{(\ell)}|}$ ▷ Row-based fraction
        $\text{colFrac}_{ij}^{(\ell)} = \frac{|w_{ij}^{(\ell)}|}{\sum_k |w_{kj}^{(\ell)}|}$ ▷ Col-based fraction
        $\text{WI}_{ij}^{(\ell)} = \beta\, \text{rowFrac}_{ij}^{(\ell)} + (1 - \beta)\, \text{colFrac}_{ij}^{(\ell)}$
        $\text{WIPscore}_{ij}^{(\ell)} = \text{WI}_{ij}^{(\ell)} \times ||X_i||_2$ ▷ Weighted fraction × activation
      end for
      Sort all $w_{ij}^{(\ell)}$ by $\text{WIPscore}_{ij}^{(\ell)}$ (ascending)
      Prune the lowest $100 \times r\,\%$ of weights in layer ℓ
    end for
    Update M with pruned weights
  end for
  return M_{pruned}
end procedure

pass after computing importance scores. However, this one-shot approach is inherently greedy: a weight deemed unimportant in the fully dense model may become crucial after others are removed. Without a reassessment step, one-shot pruning risks eliminating weights that could later serve a compensatory role.

In contrast, WIP performs pruning in T iterative stages (where $T \geq 1$ is an integer hyperparameter, e.g. $T = 2$ or 3). We partition the overall target sparsity S into T smaller pruning steps, recalculating importance between each step. Algorithm 1 illustrates this process in pseudocode. Concretely, let $S \in (0, 1)$ be the fraction of weights to prune (e.g. $S = 0.5$ for 50% sparsity). We choose a per-iteration pruning ratio r such that after T stages the cumulative fraction pruned is S. For simplicity, one can take $r \approx S/T$ for each stage. At iteration 1, we compute the WIP importance score for every weight in each layer using

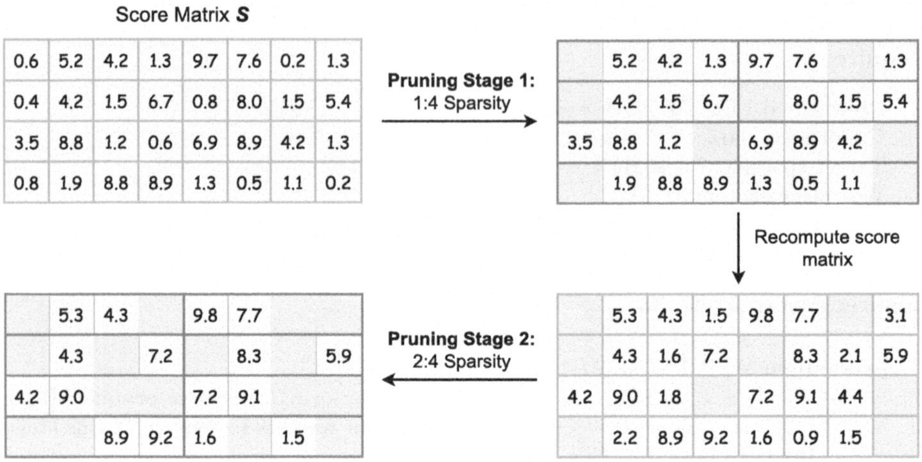

Fig. 2. Apply our method on N:M pattern pruning.

the weighted importance metric. Within each layer, we then remove (set to zero) the lowest-scoring $100r\%$ of weights. This yields a partially pruned model. At iteration 2, we update the importance scores to reflect the new state of the model. The weight matrices have changed—some entries are now zero—so we recompute rowFrac and colFrac for all remaining weights. Any weight that survived the first stage may now have a higher relative fraction in its row/column because some of its neighbors were removed. Using the updated scores, we again prune the lowest $100r\%$ of weights in each layer. We repeat this procedure for T stages in total, or until the target sparsity S is reached. The final output is a model M_{pruned} with overall sparsity S, achieved through T incremental pruning steps.

This iterative approach provides multiple benefits over one-shot pruning. By recalculating importance after each partial removal of weights, the method corrects for initial biases and retains weights that become more influential as neighbors are pruned. In doing so, weights that might have been prematurely discarded under a one-shot process are given a renewed opportunity to demonstrate their value. Moreover, gradually eliminating weights avoids catastrophic channel collapse because any neuron or feature that remains partially intact following one stage gains proportionally greater significance in subsequent calculations. Consequently, this process preserves network connectivity more effectively than one-shot methods.

3.3 Tuning into N:M Sparsity

While our framework focuses on maximizing accuracy under unstructured sparsity, many modern accelerators (e.g., NVIDIA Ampere and Hopper architectures) provide specialized support for N:M semi-structured sparsity [30], in which each contiguous block of M weights is constrained to contain exactly N zeros.

This structured format can yield significant speedups on supported hardware kernels because it allows for efficient, vector-level sparse matrix multiplication.

To incorporate N:M constraints into WIP, we apply our iterative procedure in multiple stages: in each stage, we prune or revive weights within each M-sized block to move from a partially pruned state (e.g., 1:4) toward the final pattern (e.g., 2:4). This approach ensures that each block is refined based on updated importance scores, reducing the risk of overly aggressive pruning within individual blocks. Concretely, one can first prune each block to a milder pattern, then recalculate row-wise and column-wise fractions as well as activation statistics. In subsequent stages, another set of weights is pruned or recovered until the N:M pattern is met. Figure 2 illustrates this process schematically for a 2:4 example.

4 Experiments

4.1 Experimental Setup

Models and Evaluation. We assess the proposed WIP method on LLaMA 7B/13B [26], LLaMA-2 7B/13B [26], LLaMA-3 8B [5], and OPT 6.7B [28]. All experiments are conducted on NVIDIA A100 and A6000 GPUs. Following earlier studies [25,29], we apply uniform pruning to all linear layers, except embeddings and the final layer.

Tasks and Metrics. We evaluate model performance on both language modeling and zero-shot settings. For language modeling, we report perplexity on the Wikitext2 test set [20], where lower values indicate stronger performance. We also conduct zero-shot evaluations on five datasets: Hellaswag, BoolQ, ARC-C, MNLI, and RTE, employing the `lm-evaluation-harness` library [10].

Baselines. We compare WIP against three prominent approaches. Magnitude pruning [14] serves as a common and widely used baseline. Wanda [25] is a previously introduced pruning strategy. RIA [29] is a state-of-the-art pruning approach specifically designed for large language models.

Hyperparameter Settings. Unless stated otherwise, we set $\beta = 0.75$ and conduct two iterations of iterative pruning $T = 2$, with detailed justification for these choices provided in Sect. 5. For calibration data, we follow established practice by using 128 samples (each with 2048 tokens) from the C4 dataset [24], ensuring a consistent basis of comparison across all methods.

4.2 Main Results

Language Modeling. Table 1 presents perplexity results for the pruned versions of LLaMA, LLaMA-2, LLaMA-3, and OPT models at sparsity levels of 50%, 60%, and 70%. Our proposed method, WIP, consistently demonstrates superior performance compared to existing techniques across all model variants and sparsity levels. For example, at 70% sparsity, WIP achieves a perplexity of 34.21 on the LLaMA-2 13B model, substantially outperforming the magnitude pruning

Table 1. Perplexity results on WikiText-2 for our method and other post-training pruning techniques at 50%, 60%, and 70% unstructured sparsity levels.

Method	LLaMa 7B	LLaMA 13B	LLaMA-2 7B	LLaMA-2 13B	LLaMA-3 8B	OPT 6.7B
Dense	5.68	5.09	5.47	4.88	6.14	10.86
Sparsity: 50%						
Magnitude	17.28	20.22	16.03	6.83	205.46	968.85
Wanda	7.26	6.15	7.79	6.28	10.82	15.35
RIA	7.12	6.08	6.81	5.83	9.34	11.93
WIP (ours)	**7.10**	**6.04**	**6.75**	**5.80**	**9.33**	**11.77**
Sparsity: 60%						
Magnitude	561.81	224.67	1924.81	11.82	33902.62	12641.68
Wanda	20.77	16.48	18.59	11.60	27.86	38.36
RIA	10.56	8.53	10.39	7.84	19.55	15.03
WIP (ours)	**10.09**	**8.21**	**9.99**	**7.66**	**19.51**	**14.16**
Sparsity: 70%						
Magnitude	48839.38	84502.13	49905.54	214.16	1625753.87	16943.02
Wanda	236.59	170.57	234.02	140.05	230.80	262.25
RIA	93.72	71.96	68.03	52.09	177.13	79.64
WIP (ours)	**72.48**	**55.19**	**66.09**	**34.21**	**140.65**	**74.59**

baseline, which yields a perplexity of 52.09. Notably, the relative improvement of WIP compared to baseline methods becomes more pronounced as the sparsity level increases, highlighting the robustness of our weighted iterative pruning approach. Additionally, we observe that the performance gap between dense models and models pruned by WIP significantly narrows as the model size scales from 7B to 13B, underscoring WIP's effectiveness at preserving model performance in larger models.

N:M Semi-structured Pruning. Table 2 compares perplexities across various pruning methods, including Magnitude, Wanda, RIA, and our proposed WIP, under unstructured 50% sparsity and semi-structured sparsity constraints of 2:4 and 4:8. Our results demonstrate that WIP consistently achieves the lowest perplexity across all evaluated sparsity patterns, highlighting the strength of combining iterative pruning strategies with weighted importance metrics under semi-structured constraints. Specifically, for LLaMA-2 7B under a 2:4 sparsity constraint, WIP achieves a perplexity of 10.90, surpassing Wanda's 12.10 and RIA's 11.30. A similar performance gain is evident for LLaMA-2 13B, where WIP attains a perplexity of 8.18 compared to RIA's 8.40, further confirming the robustness and superiority of our approach.

Table 2. Perplexity results on Wikitext-2 for unstructured pruning at 50% and semi-structured pruning with 2:4 and 4:8 sparsity constraints.

Model	Method	Unstructured 50%	2:4	4:8
LLaMA2-7B (Dense 5.47)	Magnitude	16.03	37.76	15.91
	Wanda	7.79	12.10	8.60
	RIA	6.81	11.30	8.38
	WIP (ours)	**6.75**	**10.90**	**8.22**
LLaMA2-13B (Dense 4.88)	Magnitude	6.83	8.89	7.32
	Wanda	6.28	9.01	7.00
	RIA	5.83	8.40	6.74
	WIP (ours)	**5.80**	**8.18**	**6.66**

Zero-Shot Tasks. Table 3 summarizes the zero-shot performance of LLaMA-2 7B and 13B models pruned at 50% unstructured sparsity using Magnitude [14], Wanda [25], RIA [29], and our proposed WIP method across five diverse datasets. The final column provides the average performance across these benchmarks. Our results demonstrate that WIP achieves the highest overall average performance, surpassing existing pruning approaches. In addition, for certain datasets such as BoolQ and ARC-C with the LLaMA-2 13B model, WIP's performance even exceeds that of the original dense model. These findings highlight the effectiveness of our method in selectively pruning less critical weights, thus maintaining or enhancing the model's ability.

5 Analysis

Ablation Study. To clearly evaluate the contributions of weighted importance estimation and iterative pruning within our WIP method, we performed an ablation study summarized in Table 4. The results clearly indicate that removing either iterative pruning or weighted importance significantly reduces performance, highlighting the necessity of both components.

Additionally, we justify our hyperparameter choices of $\beta = 0.75$ and two iterations. Comparing configurations (1), (3), and (4), we observe that $\beta = 0.75$ consistently yields the best results across models. Furthermore, comparisons among configurations (1), (2), (5), and (6) illustrate that increasing the number of iterations beyond two does not lead to noticeable performance improvements, validating our choice of two iterations.

Table 3. Zero-shot performance of methods with 50% unstructured sparsity compared to the dense model. "L2" refers to the LLaMA-2 model.

Model	Method	Hellaswag	BoolQ	ARC-C	MNLI	RTE	AVG
L2-7B	Dense	57.13	77.74	43.43	42.21	62.82	56.67
	Magnitude	49.13	63.00	34.64	32.60	57.04	47.28
	Wanda	50.29	74.22	37.20	37.29	55.60	50.92
	SparseGPT	52.73	76.39	37.71	32.52	56.32	51.13
	RIA	52.21	**75.38**	38.40	**38.74**	54.51	51.84
	WIP (ours)	**52.70**	74.68	**39.42**	37.94	**55.23**	**51.99**
L2-13B	Dense	60.05	80.55	48.46	43.22	65.34	59.52
	Magnitude	54.40	57.61	38.40	39.66	55.96	49.21
	Wanda	55.04	77.95	41.04	43.31	60.65	55.60
	SparseGPT	55.91	**81.41**	41.98	43.52	61.37	56.84
	RIA	56.75	80.86	40.96	44.07	59.21	56.37
	WIP (ours)	**56.75**	81.28	**41.98**	**44.38**	**61.73**	**57.22**

Calibration Data. Wanda, RIA, and WIP all utilize calibration data to compute input activations. To assess the robustness of our method against variations in calibration data, we conducted sensitivity analyses by varying the calibration sample sizes. The results, summarized in Fig. 3, demonstrate the performance stability of our method on the LLaMA-2 13B model as the number of calibration samples changes. Both RIA and WIP show robust performance, yet WIP consistently achieves superior results, confirming its resilience to calibration variations.

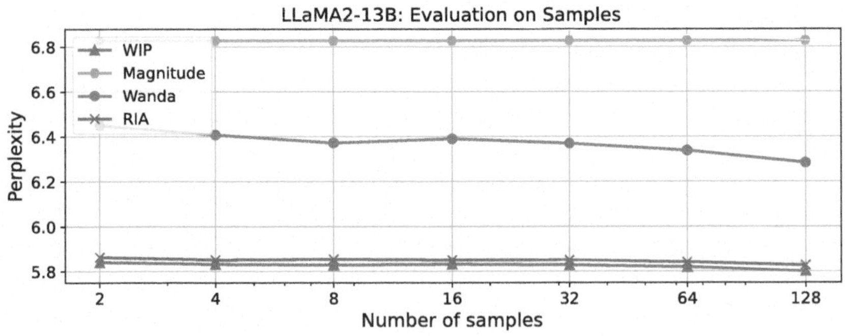

Fig. 3. Effect of the number of calibration samples (`nsamples`) on performance.

Pruning Time Analysis. In this analysis, we report wall-clock pruning times on the largest model in our experiments, LLaMA-13B, at 50% sparsity. Methods

Table 4. Ablation studies of the WIP method on LLaMA2-7B and OPT-6.7B models with a target sparsity of 50%. *"WIP w/o iterative"* removes iterative updates by applying pruning in a single step. *"WIP w/o weighted"* eliminates the weighted importance mechanism, using a uniform approach instead. *"WIP tuning"* explores different configurations of β and the number of iterations to analyze their effects.

Tag	Method	β	Num. Iter.	LLaMA-2 7B	OPT 6.7B
①	**WIP (ours)**	0.75	2	**6.75**	**11.77**
②	WIP w/o iterative	0.75	1	6.77	11.79
③	WIP w/o weighted	0.50	2	6.80	11.94
④	WIP tuning	0.25	2	6.97	12.34
⑤		0.75	3	6.75	11.80
⑥		0.75	4	6.76	11.78

like Wanda and one-shot WIP each finish in around 10 min, while our two-iteration WIP variant takes approximately 20 min. This extra time reflects the second pass for updating importance scores and pruning decisions. Despite the linear increase in pruning time with additional iterations, the improved accuracy-sparsity trade-off often outweighs the added cost—especially for large-scale models, where overall fine-tuning or retraining would be even more prohibitive.

Inference Acceleration. To quantify the real-world benefits of N:M sparsity, we measured end-to-end inference speed on an NVIDIA A6000 GPU using TensorRT-LLM [22], which provides specialized kernels for N:M sparse matrices. Specifically, we pruned LLaMA-2 7B/13B to a 2:4 semi-structured pattern using our WIP method and compared the resulting throughput against the original dense models. Table 5 summarizes the tokens-per-second throughput for different input and output sequence lengths at batch size 1. Overall, our 2:4 pruned models consistently yield speedup range from 1.25× to 1.88×. Notably, the larger LLaMA-213B model sees greater gains, with all settings surpassing 1.79×. These results confirm that the semi-structured sparsity induced by WIP translates into practical wall-clock improvements, making it an appealing option for scaling LLM deployments in latency-sensitive environments.

6 Related Work

Model Compression and Pruning: The rapid growth of large language models (LLMs) has led to significant interest in model compression strategies. Among these, two main approaches dominate: weight quantization, which reduces model-parameter precision (e.g., to 8-bit or 4-bit integers) to shrink memory footprint and accelerate inference with minimal performance loss [1,8,9,18,27], and weight pruning, which removes less-critical weights or structural components to induce sparsity [7,15,17,21,25]. Early pruning approaches such as Optimal Brain Damage [17] and Optimal Brain Surgeon [15] leveraged second-order information to

Table 5. Inference acceleration achieved by the proposed method (WIP) for LLaMA-2 (7B and 13B) using TensorRT-LLM on an NVIDIA A6000 GPU.

Model	Input Len.	Output Len.	Throughput (Token/s)		
			Dense	2:4	Speed Up
Llama-2 7B	128	128	37.56	29.48	1.28×
	128	2048	36.03	28.52	1.26×
	2048	128	34.82	27.72	1.26×
	2048	2048	33.98	27.21	1.25×
Llama-2 13B	128	128	30.40	16.17	1.88×
	128	2048	28.87	15.70	1.84×
	2048	128	27.87	15.36	1.81×
	2048	2048	27.00	15.11	1.79×

eliminate weights deemed least influential on the network's loss. These methods showed substantial redundancy in neural networks yet typically required additional retraining to maintain accuracy. Iterative magnitude pruning [14] improved upon such techniques by repeatedly removing the smallest-magnitude weights and fine-tuning in each round, culminating in the "deep compression" pipeline [13] that combined pruning, quantization, and Huffman coding. However, these retraining-based methods become prohibitively expensive for LLMs with billions of parameters, motivating research on post-training pruning.

Post-training Pruning: In response, several one-shot methods have recently been developed to eliminate parameters without requiring any fine-tuning. The simplest baseline, magnitude pruning [14], ranks weights by their absolute values; however, it can remove small but crucial weights, particularly in LLMs where even small changes can yield large downstream effects. To alleviate this, Wanda [25] ("Weights and activations") multiplies each weight's magnitude by the corresponding activation magnitude, pruning weights with minimal overall impact. While Wanda often achieves better outcomes than pure magnitude pruning, it can inadvertently zero out entire channels. Zhang et al. [29] addressed this issue with RIA (Relative Importance with Activations), which balances row-wise and column-wise importance alongside activation magnitudes to avoid "channel collapse." Another line of work formulates pruning as a local optimization problem. SparseGPT [7], for example, solves a sparse regression layer by layer, using second-order information (the Hessian) to efficiently determine which weights to remove and thus maintain performance in a fully zero-shot manner. These techniques allow practical, immediate deployment of compressed LLMs by eliminating the costly retraining step.

7 Conclusion

In this paper, we introduced Weighted-Iterative Pruning (WIP), a post-training framework that combines a tunable weighted importance metric with a multi-stage pruning strategy. By balancing row- and column-wise contributions through a parameter β, WIP reduces the channel collapse issues that plague magnitude-only or one-shot pruning methods. Iteratively recalculating weight importance after each partial prune further preserves both language-modeling and zero-shot accuracy at high sparsity. Experiments on LLaMA-2/3 and OPT models show that WIP consistently surpasses previous post-training pruning methods while also delivering real GPU speedups under N:M semi-structured sparsity—underscoring its effectiveness and practical value for LLM compression.

Acknowledgments. This work was supported by JST SPRING, Japan Grant Number JPMJSP2102.

References

1. Bai, H., Zhang, W., Hou, L., Shang, L., et al.: BinaryBERT: pushing the limit of BERT quantization. In: Proceedings of ACL 2021 (Volume 1: Long Papers), pp. 4334–4348 (2021). https://doi.org/10.18653/v1/2021.acl-long.334
2. Brown, T., et al.: Language models are few-shot learners. Adv. Neural. Inf. Process. Syst. **33**, 1877–1901 (2020)
3. Cheng, H., Zhang, M., Shi, J.Q.: A survey on deep neural network pruning: taxonomy, comparison, analysis, and recommendations. IEEE Trans. Pattern Anal. Mach. Intell. (2024)
4. Devlin, J., Chang, M.W., Lee, K., Toutanova, K.: Bert: pre-training of deep bidirectional transformers for language understanding. In: Proceedings of NAACL 2021, vol. 1 (long and short papers), pp. 4171–4186 (2019)
5. Dubey, A., et al.: The llama 3 herd of models. arXiv preprint arXiv:2407.21783 (2024)
6. Frankle, J., Carbin, M.: The lottery ticket hypothesis: finding sparse, trainable neural networks. In: 7th International Conference on Learning Representations, ICLR 2019, New Orleans, LA, USA, 6–9 May 2019. OpenReview.net (2019)
7. Frantar, E., Alistarh, D.: Sparsegpt: massive language models can be accurately pruned in one-shot. In: ICML 2023, pp. 10323–10337. PMLR (2023)
8. Frantar, E., Ashkboos, S., Hoefler, T., Alistarh, D.: OPTQ: accurate quantization for generative pre-trained transformers. In: The Eleventh International Conference on Learning Representations (2023)
9. Frantar, E., Ashkboos, S., et al.: GPTQ: accurate post-training quantization for generative pre-trained transformers. arXiv preprint arXiv:2210.17323 (2022)
10. Gao, L., et al.: A framework for few-shot language model evaluation (2024). https://doi.org/10.5281/zenodo.12608602
11. Gong, Y., Liu, L., Yang, M., Bourdev, L.D.: Compressing deep convolutional networks using vector quantization. arXiv abs/1412.6115 (2014). https://api.semanticscholar.org/CorpusID:6251653

12. Han, S., et al.: EIE: efficient inference engine on compressed deep neural network. ACM SIGARCH Comput. Archit. News **44**(3), 243–254 (2016)
13. Han, S., Mao, H., Dally, W.J.: Deep compression: compressing deep neural network with pruning, trained quantization and Huffman coding. In: Bengio, Y., LeCun, Y. (eds.) ICLR 2016, Puerto Rico, 2016, Conference Track Proceedings (2016)
14. Han, S., Pool, J., Tran, J., et al.: Learning both weights and connections for efficient neural network. In: Advances in Neural Information Processing Systems, vol. 28 (2015)
15. Hassibi, B., Stork, D.G., et al.: Optimal brain surgeon and general network pruning. In: IEEE International Conference on Neural Networks, pp. 293–299. IEEE (1993)
16. Le, K.N., Sato, R., Nakashima, D., et al.: OptiPrune: effective pruning approach for every target sparsity. In: Proceedings of COLING 2025, Abu Dhabi, UAE, pp. 3600–3612 (2025). https://aclanthology.org/2025.coling-main.243/
17. LeCun, Y., Denker, J., Solla, S.: Optimal brain damage. In: Advances in Neural Information Processing Systems, vol. 2 (1989)
18. Lin, J., et al.: AWQ: activation-aware weight quantization for on-device LLM compression and acceleration. Proc. Mach. Learn. Syst. **6**, 87–100 (2024)
19. Liu, H.I., et al.: Lightweight deep learning for resource-constrained environments: a survey. ACM Comput. Surv. **56**(10), 1–42 (2024)
20. Merity, S., Xiong, C., Bradbury, J., Socher, R.: Pointer sentinel mixture models. In: International Conference on Learning Representations (2017). https://openreview.net/forum?id=Byj72udxe
21. Mocanu, D.C., Mocanu, E., Stone, P., Nguyen, P.H., Gibescu, M., Liotta, A.: Scalable training of artificial neural networks with adaptive sparse connectivity inspired by network science. Nat. Commun. **9**(1), 2383 (2018)
22. NVIDIA: Tensorrt-LLM: high-performance inference for large language models (2024). https://github.com/NVIDIA/TensorRT-LLM. Accessed 10 Mar 2025
23. Rae, J.W., et al.: Scaling language models: methods, analysis & insights from training gopher. arXiv preprint arXiv:2112.11446 (2021)
24. Raffel, C., et al.: Exploring the limits of transfer learning with a unified text-to-text transformer. J. Mach. Learn. Res. **21**(140), 1–67 (2020)
25. Sun, M., Liu, Z., Bair, A., Kolter, J.Z.: A simple and effective pruning approach for large language models. In: The Twelfth International Conference on Learning Representations (2024). https://openreview.net/forum?id=PxoFut3dWW
26. Touvron, H., et al.: Llama 2: open foundation and fine-tuned chat models. arXiv preprint arXiv:2307.09288 (2023)
27. Xiao, G., Lin, J., Seznec, M., et al.: Smoothquant: accurate and efficient post-training quantization for large language models. In: International Conference on Machine Learning, pp. 38087–38099. PMLR (2023)
28. Zhang, S., et al.: OPT: open pre-trained transformer language models. arXiv preprint arXiv:2205.01068 (2022)
29. Zhang, Y., Bai, H., Lin, H., Zhao, J., Hou, L., Cannistraci, C.V.: Plug-and-play: an efficient post-training pruning method for large language models. In: The Twelfth International Conference on Learning Representations (2024)
30. Zhou, A., Ma, Y., Zhu, J., Liu, J., et al.: Learning n: M fine-grained structured sparse neural networks from scratch. arXiv abs/2102.04010 (2021)

A Comparative Study on the Development of a Thai Legal QA Framework Using Large Language Models and Mixed Legal Datasets

Supachoke Hanwiboonwat[1], Chaichana Thavornthaveekul[2], Prachya Boonkwan[3], Apivadee Piyatumrong[4], and Peerapon Vateekul[1](✉)

[1] Department of Computer Engineering, Faculty of Engineering, Chulalongkorn University, Pathum Wan, Bangkok 10330, Thailand
peerapon.v@chula.ac.th
[2] Data Wow Co., Ltd., Bangkok, Thailand
[3] School of ICT, Sirindhorn International Institute of Technology (SIIT), Thammasat University, Khlong Luang, Pathum Thani 12120, Thailand
[4] Big Data Institute (Public Organization), Bangkok, Thailand

Abstract. In the present day, large language models (LLMs) such as GPT-4o play a significant role in answering legal questions in the Thai language. However, creating a system for answering legal questions for the general public is a highly challenging and complex task. This is due to the fact that Thai legal code documents use complex language and are often lengthy. This research focuses on developing a framework for legal question answering (QA) targeted at the general public, with the aim of establishing best practices for creating effective legal QA systems. To enhance the system's performance, we constructed our own dataset and integrated data from a variety of sources. Intensive experiments were conducted to identify the most suitable LLM for legal applications in the Thai context. We proposed a method to improve QA performance in the legal domain with LLM by fine-tuning multiple task datasets. The entire process is thoroughly detailed, covering aspects such as fine-tuning and the use of retrieval-augmented generation (RAG), including techniques like keyword search and contextual search, as well as reranking processes. Additionally, this study compares various prompt formats to find the most effective one for answering legal questions for the general public. The results from our model are comparable to larger models with more parameters, such as GPT-4o, in legal examination tasks and perform better in answering legal questions tasks.

Keywords: Large Language Model · Thai Legal Documents · Question Answering

R. Ichise (Ed.): NLDB 2025, LNCS 15836, pp. 201–215, 2026.
https://doi.org/10.1007/978-3-031-97141-9_14

1 Introduction

Artificial intelligence (AI) plays a significant role in the legal field [2,27,29], and there are applications that utilize AI in various legal aspects, such as legal question answering (QA) [6,30,34], legal judgment prediction [5], case prediction [7], and contract review [21]. In terms of legal QA, the launch of ChatGPT [24] has played a crucial role in answering legal questions [13,15].

However, developing a legal QA system for the general public, who lack legal knowledge, poses several challenges due to legal terminologies and lengthy idiomatic expressions [14]. These issues can result in large language models (LLMs) not performing well in answering legal questions for the general public. This aforementioned work addresses this problem by creating a legal story using LLMs to help the general public learn about the law in simple language. This contrasts with our work, which focuses on developing a framework for answering legal questions for the general public. Our work does not compare to this aforementioned study because we focus on measuring the accuracy of legal QA, while the other study evaluates the readability of the legal stories as output.

To address these issues, we have enhanced the performance of the LLM to effectively answer legal questions for the general public with the highest efficiency. We developed a retrieval-augmented generation (RAG) system that is most suitable for the Thai legal domain, enabling the LLM to identify which specific legal provisions should be used to answer questions, and adjusted the prompt to ensure the LLM can provide the best responses to legal questions for the general public.

This research aims to design best practices for legal QA, focusing on three main components: selecting the most effective Large Language Model for answering Thai legal questions, developing a highly accurate RAG system for extracting relevant legal codes from databases, and comparing various prompt formats to determine which most efficiently enhance the model's ability to answer legal questions for the general public. Additionally, we present methods to improve the performance of the LLM by utilizing datasets of various formats, which prove to be more effective than using a single-format dataset. Our research addresses the following research questions:

1. Which LLMs model is the best LLM for answering Thai legal questions for the general public?
2. In RAG system for retrieving Thai legal documents, which method is the most effective?
3. In improving the performance of LLM, which good method makes the LLMs most efficient?
4. What type of prompt is the most appropriate for answering Thai legal questions for the general public?

We compared our model with large LLM like GPT-4o in terms of providing appropriate legal answers and the accuracy of solving legal examination questions. Our results show that legal QA performance superior to larger models like

GPT-4o and comparable efficiency in performing in bar exams with GPT-4o. In summary, our work aims to develop a best practice legal QA framework that efficiently and accurately answers legal questions in Thai.

2 Related Work

2.1 Thai-Enabled Large Language Models

There are several attempts to enable Thai in existing LLMs via continual pre-training and finetuning. First, Typhoon 2 [26] is a collection of LLMs developed by SCB10X, featuring two models: typhoon2-qwen2.5-7b-instruct, based on the Qwen-v2.5-7B [33] with 7 billion parameters, and llama3.1-typhoon2-8b-instruct, based on llama-3.1-8B [11] with 8 billion parameters. Second, SeaLLMs-v3-7B-Chat [39], also known as Seallm3, is the latest in the SEALLM series, trained on Southeast Asian languages including English, Chinese, Indonesian, Vietnamese, Thai, and others, with QWEN2 [32] as its base. OpenThaiGPT 1.5-7B-Instruct, OpenThaiLLM-Prebuilt-7B, and PathummaLLM-Text-1.0.0, all developed by NECTEC, are notable Thai language models. Third, OpenThaiGPT 1.5-7B-Instruct [37] is a 7-billion-parameter Thai model, built on Qwen v2.5 and refined using over 2 million Thai instructional pairs. Fourth, OpenThaiLLM-Prebuilt-7B [22] is a multilingual model, also with 7 billion parameters, continuing from Qwen2.5-7B and optimized for applications like Retrieval-Augmented Generation and reasoning. Fifth, PathummaLLM-Text-1.0.0 [23], with 7 billion parameters, is fine-tuned from OpenThaiLLM-Prebuilt for practical use. Sixth, Sailor2-8B-Chat [9], based on Qwen-2.5 7B, supports Southeast Asian languages, including Thai.

2.2 Text Embedding and Reranking Models

Text embedding models convert input text into a vector representation for semantic similarity. With contextualized information, these vectors enable semantic search, where documents are retrieved by meanings rather than keywords. The paraphrase-multilingual-mpnet-base-v2 [28], also from 2019, by the sentence-transformers team, converts text into dense vectors for tasks like clustering and semantic search, benefiting from the strengths of both BERT and XLNet for comprehensive information capture. The Multilingual E5 [31], is designed for text embedding and provides a more accurate alternative to the older paraphrase-multilingual-mpnet-base-v2 model by utilizing a diverse dataset called CCPairs, which includes community QA content, CommonCrawl, and scientific papers. This leads to reliable embeddings across multiple languages. In contrast, the bge-reranker-v2-m3 [4], a reranking model, supports Thai by generating a similarity score for a given question and document, rather than embeddings. This relevance score is converted into a float value between 0 and 1 using a sigmoid function, enabling precise evaluation of document relevance. The main function of the reranking model is to rank the importance of documents retrieved from keyword search and contextual search.

2.3 Relevant Legal Works

Our work investigates several LLM-based approaches for legal text processing, focusing on adapting them to Thai legal documents. "Adapt-Retrieve-Revise" [30] fine-tunes a Chinese legal LLM and uses GPT-4 for answer revision, but we do not compare it due to differences in document structures. "Legal Reasoning Prompts" [35] utilizes the IRAC framework to structure legal answers; in our work, we evaluate various IRAC-style prompts to determine the best fit for Thai legal contexts. "KELLER" [7] is a reranking model using expert summaries to improve retrieval, and we adopt a similar approach with positive and negative document identification in our own reranking model. SaulLM-7B [6] is a large language model designed specifically for the legal domain, but it is excluded from our comparisons as it lacks Thai training data and performs poorly with Thai legal text. Overall, our methodology adapts and customizes these techniques specifically for Thai legal tasks.

3 Methodology

3.1 Datasets

Large Language Model Enhancement Dataset. To enhance the performance of a LLM specifically for question-answering tasks, we utilized three datasets: the Tamtanai dataset, the WangchanX-Legal-ThaiCCL-RAG dataset [1], and the Thai attorney exam dataset [16–18]. The Tamtanai dataset, used as the primary dataset for fine-tuning a LLM, comprises a comprehensive collection of official legal documents from a specialized Thai legal documentation website. To ensure the relevance and significance of the data, 31 pivotal documents frequently referenced in legal consultations were meticulously selected, guided by consultations with legal experts to address crucial areas relevant to the Thai legal system. To further enrich the dataset, GPT-4 was employed to generate additional training and testing data, with questions and answers designed to enable the model to effectively respond to legal inquiries from the public, thereby enhancing its ability to provide accessible legal information and assistance. The dataset consists of 4,534 entries, which were randomly divided into 3,296 for training, 825 for validation, and 413 for testing. The second dataset, WangchanX-Legal-ThaiCCL-RAG, is a Thai legal QA dataset selected to enhance LLM performance with additional legal data, comprising 409 entries distributed as 327 for training and 82 for validation, with no testing entries. Lastly, the Thai attorney exam dataset, containing multiple-choice questions from past attorney exams over 27 years, was processed to remove duplicates, ensuring no overlap between training and testing datasets. There are a total of 409 entries, consisting of 327 training entries, 82 validation entries, and 80 test entries. In this work, we divide both the WangchanX-Legal-ThaiCCL-RAG and the Thai attorney exam dataset in half, using 205 entries from each, for a total of 410 entries, to evaluate the improvement in the LLM's performance. When combined, the total size is approximately equal to that of the Thai attorney exam dataset.

Retrieval-Augmented Generation Enhancement Dataset. Before entering the RAG process, queries are first classified to determine whether they belong to the legal domain. To fine-tune the query classification model, we utilized two datasets: the Tamtanai dataset, representing legal domain queries (positive label), and the han-instruct-dataset-v2.0 dataset [25], representing non-legal domain queries (negative label). The han-instruct-dataset-v2.0 dataset contains 3,200 entries, divided into 2,324 for training, 556 for validation, and 320 for testing. We employed GPT-4o to label the han-instruct-dataset-v2.0 dataset, identifying which queries fall outside the legal domain and which ones are within the legal domain. Afterwards, a sample of the labels generated by GPT-4o will be randomly selected for human evaluation to determine whether the labels are appropriate. For fine-tuning the reranking model, we utilized the Tamtanai dataset to enhance and evaluate its performance in reranking legal code documents.

Thai Legal Document Retrieval-Augmented Generation Database. After selecting 31 legal codes suitable for the everyday life of the general public to create the Tamtanai dataset, we also added 5 legal codes relevant for legal examinations. We then cleaned these 36 legal codes by removing unnecessary sections, such as articles that have been repealed and are no longer in use. Before integrating them into the database for RAG, We divided the documents into subsections based on specific subtopics, with each subsection forming a chunk. Each chunk corresponds to a chapter defined in the legal code, where each chapter contains several sections focused on a single topic. In total, we created 617 chunks. Additionally, we stored the cleaned and reformatted data along with metadata indicating which legal sections are included in each chunk and which sections are still currently in use.

3.2 Overall Framework

An overview of the framework is shown in Fig. 1. Firstly, when receiving a user query, we first classify whether the incoming query belongs to the legal domain. If it does not belong to the legal domain, we use the base model to respond. However, if it is within the legal domain, it enters the RAG process. To enhance the efficiency of our RAG system, we implemented a two-stage process involving both keyword search and contextual search, followed by a reranking step. For the keyword search, once a user query is received, we extract important keywords and eliminate unnecessary ones by removing those with low IDF values, which helps avoid the retrieval of documents with extraneous terms. After that, we use the remaining keywords to search for documents containing those keywords. For the contextual search, we use the user query to find documents with a similarity score greater than or equal a set threshold. Then, we combine the documents obtained from both the keyword search and the contextual search and apply a reranking model to rerank the documents. After obtaining documents from the reranking model, these documents are inserted into a prompt template for the LLM to generate a response.

In our end-to-end evaluation, after integrating all modules, we investigate how many legal documents, chosen by the reranking model, should be included in the prompt to maximize the LLM's effectiveness in answering legal questions.

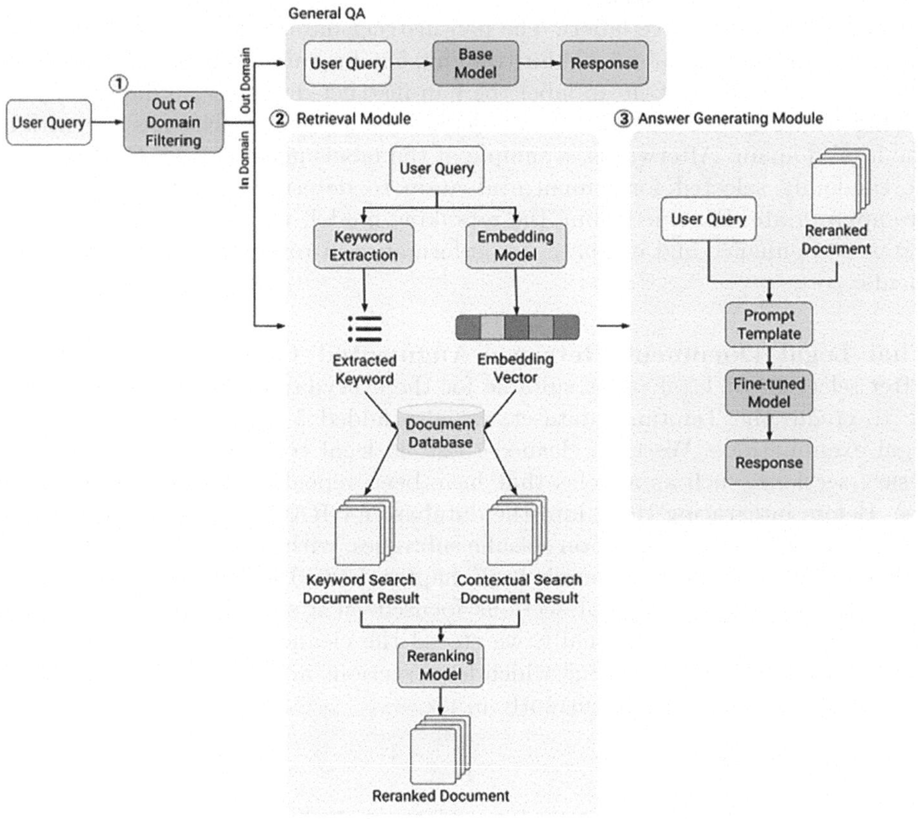

Fig. 1. Overview of the Framework.

3.3 Large Language Model Selection and Query Classifier Model

In selecting the most suitable LLM for our experiments, we focused on models that support the Thai language and have a size of 7B-8B. These models were fine-tuned and evaluated with the Tamtanai dataset. The model that achieved the highest BERTScore (details in Sect. 4.2) was selected as the best model. For the query classifier model, we fine-tuned the paraphrase-multilingual-mpnet-base-v2 using the han-instruct-dataset-v2.0 dataset and the Tamtanai dataset to effectively classify queries within the legal domain.

3.4 Retrieval-Augmented Generation System

In the contextual search segment, we first determine the most suitable contextual search model using the mean reciprocal rank (MRR) metric. For the reranking process, we selected the bge-reranker-v2-m3 model, which was fine-tuned using the Tamtanai dataset. During the fine-tuning, questions in the dataset were used as queries, the most relevant legal document served as the positive document, and five other documents acted as negative documents. These negative documents were retrieved from contextual search to identify which ones are similar but not identical to the positive document. Lastly, we identify the most effective method by comparing the accuracy of document retrieval across different approaches: (1) contextual search, (2) keyword search and (3) reranking, contextual search and reranking, and a combination of keyword search, contextual search, and reranking to determine which yields the highest efficiency. For this experiment, we do not report using keyword search alone because it doesn't provide a clear ranking. Keyword search only checks for the presence of keywords, which can result in less relevant documents being ranked equally with more relevant ones if they have the same number of matching keywords. Thus, it must always be followed by a ranking process.

3.5 Enhancing Large Language Model

In this study, we fine-tuned the LLMs with two datasets: a legal question-and-answer dataset and a legal multiple choice exam dataset. To enhance the LLM, we primarily used the Tamtanai dataset for fine-tuning. We also explored multi-task fine-tuning to assess improvements in question-answering performance when combined with other datasets, comparing this approach to single-task fine-tuning on similar datasets. The Thai attorney exam dataset was used for this experiment, while the WangchanX-Legal-ThaiCCL-RAG dataset served as the similar dataset for comparison. We used QLoRA [8] to fine-tune the model. For the fine-tuning process, we configured the hyperparameters as follows: We trained the model for 3 epochs with a per-device training batch size of 3 and a per-device evaluation batch size of 4. We chose PagedAdamW32bit [20] as the optimizer and set the learning rate to 2.5e-4. Additionally, the temperature was set to 0.1.

3.6 Prompt Optimization

In this study, we aim to identify the most effective prompt for answering legal questions for the general public and the one best suited for performing well on legal examinations. This involves comparing different types of prompts: the normal instruction prompt, the chain of thought (COT) prompt, and the IRAC prompt [35,36]. The COT prompt instructs the model to first review the subsections and critical parts of the legal code before answering the question. The IRAC prompt, on the other hand, is based on a legal reasoning framework represented by the acronym: I for issue – identify the legal issue by examining the question clearly; R for rule – thoroughly review the information provided and apply the relevant laws or principles; A for application/analysis – analyze and apply the rule to the given information while examining all sub-sections if applicable; and C for conclusion – provide a summarized answer based on the appropriate legal principles.

4 Implementation Details and Evaluation Metrics

4.1 Implementation Details

For all LLM experiments, including fine-tuning and inference, we used four A100 GPUs. For the RAG experiments, we utilized FAISS [10] as a vector store for vector search and used LangChain for processing legal data to store in the vector database, employing four A100 GPUs as well. For the GPT-4o settings, we selected the model "gpt-4o-2024-08-06" and adjusted the temperature to 0 and max tokens to 2048. For calculating BERTScore, we used the deberta-xlarge-mnli [12] model as the scorer.

4.2 Large Language Model Evaluation Metrics

To evaluate the performance of LLMs on text summarization tasks, we utilize BERTScore [38] and ROUGE Score [19] as key metrics. BERTScore measures the similarity between the candidate and reference texts [3], using pre-trained contextual embeddings from BERT to match words in the sentences through cosine similarity. The ROUGE Score includes ROUGE-N and ROUGE-L. ROUGE-N, such as ROUGE-1 and ROUGE-2, calculates precision, recall, and F1-score based on n-gram overlaps between the candidate and reference texts. ROUGE-L focuses on the longest common subsequence (LCS) shared between the texts, calculating precision, recall, and F1-score based on the LCS length. This approach is particularly useful for judging semantic similarity and content coverage by considering sequences of words that match, regardless of their order [3].

4.3 Retrieval-Augmented Generation Evaluation Metrics

In evaluating the RAG process for selecting and assessing the contextual search model, we use MRR. However, we also assess the entire RAG process using metrics such as recall, accuracy@1, @2, @5, @10, MRR, and time. We do not report precision when evaluating the entire RAG process. because the ground truth consists of only one subsection from the code of law. This would result in a very low precision value, making precision an unsuitable metric for evaluating the entire RAG process. In this study, the ground truth contains only a single subsection because the small-sized LLM used here does not perform well when multiple subsections are included; providing multiple subsections may confuse the model and lead to errors.

5 Results

5.1 Results of Large Language Model Selection

This experiment aims to select the most effective LLM for use in the answer-generating module in Fig. 1. Table 1 demonstrates that the typhoon2-qwen2.5-7b-instruct model outperforms other Thai-supporting LLMs when fine-tuned with the Tamtanai training dataset and tested on the Tamtanai test dataset. Not only does it achieve the highest BERTScore, but the Technical Report for Qwen2.5 [33], which serves as the base model for this version, shows that it also outperforms Qwen-2 and Llama 3.1 across various tasks. Furthermore, the Technical Report of typhoon2-qwen2.5-7b-instruct [26] indicates that the model's performance has been enhanced by fine-tuning with long context prompts, enabling it to analyze legal code documents effectively, even when fed with extensive legal texts. For these reasons, typhoon2-qwen2.5-7b-instruct has been chosen as the primary LLM for these experiments.

Table 1. BERTScore F1 for each model when fine-tuned on the Tamtanai training dataset and tested on the Tamtanai test dataset. Bold values indicate the winner.

Model	BERTScore F1 (↑)
typhoon2-qwen2.5-7b-instruct	**0.8979**
SeaLLMs-v3-7B-Chat	0.8965
Openthaigpt1.5-7B-instruct	0.8960
OpenThaiLLM-Prebuilt-7B	0.8912
Pathumma-llm-text-1.0.0	0.8900
Sailor2-8B-Chat	0.8898
llama3.1-typhoon2-8b-instruct	0.8888

5.2 Results of Contextual Search Model Selection

This experiment aims to select the most effective contextual search model for integration into the retrieval module illustrated in Fig. 1. Table 2 presents the mean reciprocal rank (MRR) for each model when evaluated on the Tamtanai test set, providing a clear comparison of their retrieval effectiveness. The multilingual-e5-large model achieved the highest MRR score among all models in our experiment, indicating a superior ability to accurately rank and retrieve relevant documents compared to other candidates. This strong performance suggests that multilingual-e5-large can better distinguish relevant texts from irrelevant ones across diverse legal queries. Consequently, we have chosen the multilingual-e5-large as the primary contextual search model for our study. To further optimize retrieval accuracy, we fine-tuned its similarity threshold parameter to 0.55 and set the top k value to 50, ensuring the most relevant results are consistently retrieved.

Table 2. MRR and execution time (seconds) for each model tested on the Tamtanai test dataset. Bold values indicate the winner.

Model	MRR (↑)	Time (↓)
multilingual-e5-large	**0.7079**	0.0152
multilingual-e5-large-instruct	0.6719	0.0157
multilingual-e5-base	0.6345	0.0096
multilingual-e5-small	0.6348	**0.0095**

5.3 Results of Fine Tuning Reranking Model

This experiment aims to enhance the performance of the reranking model in the retrieval module in Fig. 1. In Table 3, it is shown that when tested on the Tamtanai test dataset, the Top-1 Accuracy after fine-tuning is 12.49% higher than before fine-tuning. This increase demonstrates the substantial impact that fine-tuning has on the model's ability to accurately rank relevant legal documents and improve overall retrieval effectiveness.

Table 3. Top-1 accuracy for both base model and fine-tuned model tested on the Tamtanai test dataset. Bold values indicate the winner.

bge-reranker-v2-m3	Accuracy@1 (↑)
Base Model	0.8198
Fine-Tuned Model	**0.9222**

5.4 Results of Retrieval-Augmented Generation Techniques

This experiment aims to compare RAG methods in the legal domain to identify the most effective RAG method for the retrieval module in Fig. 1. In Table 4, it can be seen that using a combination of keyword search, contextual search, and reranking provides the best performance in retrieving documents related to the code of law because each method offers unique strengths that complement one another. Keyword search is effective for matching specific terms, contextual search captures the meaning behind queries, and reranking refines the results to boost relevance. This combination creates a comprehensive search process where keywords help identify all potential matches, context ensures these matches are meaningful, and reranking optimizes the final results. Given the complex language and specific terminology often used in legal documents, this approach ensures both precise term matching and the consideration of legal context, thereby reducing the retrieval of irrelevant documents.

Table 4. Accuracy@1, @2, @5, @10, MRR, and retrieval time (seconds) for each RAG methods tested on the Tamtanai test dataset. Bold values indicate the winner.

Metrics	C	K+R	C+R	**K+C+R**
Retrieval Size (↓)	**44.68**	177.85	**44.68**	195.42
Recall (↑)	0.9782	0.9709	0.9782	**1.0000**
Accuracy@1 (↑)	0.6053	0.9370	0.9540	**0.9637**
Accuracy@2 (↑)	0.7094	0.9370	0.9685	**0.9879**
Accuracy@5 (↑)	0.8402	0.9661	0.9758	**0.9952**
Accuracy@10 (↑)	0.9056	0.9709	0.9782	**1.0000**
MRR (↑)	0.7064	0.9525	0.9633	**0.9784**
Retrieval Time (↓)	**0.0143**	0.3161	0.1246	0.2906

K stands for Keyword search, C is Contextual search, and R stands for Reranking.

5.5 Results of Large Language Model Enhancement

This experiment systematically compares fine-tuning methods for enhancing LLM performance in the answer-generating module illustrated in Fig. 1, focusing on both legal question answering (QA) tasks and legal exam performance. As shown in Table 5, our results demonstrate that fine-tuning with both QA and multiple-choice exam datasets consistently yields better outcomes than using a QA dataset alone. Adding legal exam questions to training provides a clear improvement in the model's performance on both QA and exam-style tasks—a benefit greater than just increasing the QA dataset size. Even when QA and exam datasets are combined equally, performance exceeds that of the QA-only

Table 5. BERTScore F1, ROUGE Scores, and multiple-choice exam scores for each model tested on the Tamtanai test dataset (2nd–5th columns) and the Thai Attorney Exam test dataset (last column). Bold values indicate the winner.

Model	F1 (↑)	R-1 (↑)	R-2 (↑)	R-L (↑)	Exam (↑)
GPT-4o	0.8591	0.6590	0.6037	0.6256	47/80
LLM	0.8979	0.7719	0.7231	0.7402	34/80
LLM+EX	0.9159	0.8201	0.7717	0.7852	38/80
LLM+QA	0.9133	0.8076	0.7693	0.7820	31/80
LLM+QA+EX	**0.9367**	**0.8589**	**0.8273**	**0.8376**	**46/80**
LLM+QA(H)+EX(H)	0.9137	0.8109	0.7719	0.7853	36/80

LLM refers to the typhoon2-qwen2.5-7b-instruct model fine-tuned with the Tamtanai training dataset. QA denotes fine-tuning using the WangchanX-Legal-ThaiCCL-RAG dataset. EX involves fine-tuning with the Thai attorney exam dataset. The (H) indicates using half of that dataset. F1 means BERTScore F1, R-1 means ROUGE-1, R-2 means ROUGE-2, R-L means ROUGE-L, and Exam refers to the multiple-choice exam scores.

approach, though it falls just short of results from increasing exam data alone. This suggests that including exam-specific questions adds valuable knowledge for diverse legal benchmarks. Overall, our experiments confirm that the best results come from fine-tuning with both dataset types: the resulting LLM outperforms GPT-4o on legal QA tasks and matches its performance on legal exams, highlighting the value of diverse, task-relevant data for domain-specific optimization.

5.6 Results of Prompt Optimization

This experiment aims to identify the most effective prompt template for answering legal questions for the general public in the answer-generating module in Fig. 1. Table 6 demonstrates that using a normal instruction prompt yields the best results for answering legal questions. This is because the Tamtanai dataset is specifically designed for general question-answering related to legal inquiries for the public, rather than being structured for IRAC or Chain of Thought (CoT) formats. Therefore, when the model is fine-tuned with the Tamtanai dataset and inference is conducted using a normal instruction prompt, it performs better than when using prompts designed for legal reasoning. Additionally, in terms of time efficiency, the normal instruction prompt requires the least amount of processing time compared to other prompt formats, likely because it is less complex and demands fewer computational resources, allowing for faster response times.

In Table 7, although the COT prompt shows the highest efficiency in legal exams, the score differences across the three prompt formats are minimal and not statistically significant. This likely stems from random processes during inference in LLMs, which can naturally introduce slight variations in results. Thus, any prompt format can be effectively used for legal exams; however, for scenarios

Table 6. BERTScore F1, ROUGE scores, and response time (seconds) for testing with di!erent prompt formats on the Tamtanai test dataset. Bold values indicate the winner.

Prompt	BERTScore F1 (↑)	ROUGE-1 (↑)	ROUGE-2 (↑)	ROUGE-L (↑)	Time (↓)
Normal	**0.9367**	**0.8589**	**0.8273**	**0.8376**	**37.41**
COT	0.9336	0.8541	0.8229	0.8345	37.95
IRAC	0.9346	0.8535	0.8233	0.8333	38.03

Table 7. Multiple-choice exam scores and response time (seconds) for testing with different prompt formats on the Thai Attorney Exam test dataset. Bold values indicate the winner.

Prompt	Exam Scores (↑)	Time (↓)
Normal	46/80	**37.74**
COT	**47/80**	38.50
IRAC	45/80	38.93

where time efficiency is crucial, a normal instruction prompt offers significant practical benefits due to its simplicity and speed.

5.7 End-to-End Question and Answering Evaluation

The purpose of this experiment is to determine the optimal number of legal documents, selected by the reranking model, that should be provided to the LLM for effective end-to-end question answering. After integrating the most effective RAG approach, the best-performing LLM, and the optimal prompt format into our legal QA framework, Table 8 demonstrates that including only one legal document in the prompt improves QA performance compared to using multiple documents. This is likely because presenting too much legal text at once can make the LLM uncertain about which specific article to reference when constructing an answer, thus reducing the overall effectiveness and reliability of the legal QA system.

Table 8. BERTScore F1, ROUGE scores, and response time (seconds) for end-to-end evaluation tested on the Tamtanai test dataset. Bold values indicate the winner.

N#	BERTScore F1 (↑)	ROUGE-1 (↑)	ROUGE-2 (↑)	ROUGE-L (↑)	Time (↓)
1	**0.9052**	**0.7818**	**0.7398**	**0.7558**	**41.89**
2	0.8924	0.7481	0.7002	0.7155	42.16
5	0.8681	0.6867	0.6252	0.6453	48.15
10	0.8487	0.6221	0.5378	0.5669	70.36

N# is legal document input in the prompt.

6 Conclusion

This research presents a Thai legal question-answering (QA) framework for the general public. We evaluated several large language models (LLMs) and enhanced performance using a multitask dataset. For the retrieval-augmented generation (RAG) component, we optimized prompt templates, retrieval strategies, and document count. Experiments on the Thai Attorney Exam and our dataset showed that Typhoon2-qwen2.5-7b-instruct achieved the highest BERTScore. We used paraphrase-multilingual-mpnet-base-v2 to filter non-legal queries, handled by the base model. The RAG pipeline combined multilingual-e5-large for retrieval and bge-reranker-v2-m3 for reranking, outperforming single-method approaches. Training with QA and multiple-choice data improved results, and instruction-based prompts yielded the best performance when using only one retrieved document.

For future work, we plan to extend the framework to serve both general users and legal experts. Additionally, we aim to deploy the system in real-world settings to enhance accessibility and reproducibility. Furthermore, we will continue to optimize the inference time for improved performance.

Acknowledgments. This project was made possible through the support of the National Science and Technology Development Agency (NSTDA), which provided access to the LANTA HPC computing resources. We would also like to express our gratitude to the Chula Computer Engineering Graduate Scholarship for their financial support.

References

1. Akarajaradwong, P., Pothavorn, P., Chaksangchaichot, C., Tasawong, P., Nopparatbundit, T., Nutanong, S.: Nitibench: a comprehensive studies of LLM frameworks capabilities for Thai legal question answering. arXiv preprint arXiv:2502.10868 (2025)
2. Ariai, F., Demartini, G.: Natural language processing for the legal domain: a survey of tasks, datasets, models, and challenges. ACM Comput. Surv. **1**(1) (2024)
3. Chang, Y., et al.: A survey on evaluation of large language models. ACM Trans. Intell. Syst. Technol. **15**(3), 1–45 (2024)
4. Chen, J., Xiao, S., Zhang, P., Luo, K., Lian, D., Liu, Z.: M3-embedding: multi-linguality, multi-functionality, multi-granularity text embeddings through self-knowledge distillation. In: Findings of the Association for Computational Linguistics ACL 2024, pp. 2318–2335 (2024)
5. Chlapanis, O., Androutsopoulos, I., Galanis, D.: Archimedes-aueb at semeval-2024 task 5: LLM explains civil procedure. In: Proceedings of the 18th International Workshop on Semantic Evaluation (SemEval-2024), pp. 1607–1622 (2024)
6. Colombo, P., et al.: Saullm-7b: a pioneering large language model for law. arXiv preprint arXiv:2403.03883 (2024)
7. Deng, C., Mao, K., Dou, Z.: Learning interpretable legal case retrieval via knowledge-guided case reformulation. In: Proceedings of the 2024 Conference on Empirical Methods in Natural Language Processing, pp. 1253–1265 (2024)
8. Dettmers, T., Pagnoni, A., Holtzman, A., Zettlemoyer, L.: Qlora: efficient finetuning of quantized LLMs. Adv. Neural. Inf. Process. Syst. **36**, 10088–10115 (2023)
9. Dou, L., et al.: Sailor2: sailing in south-east Asia with inclusive multilingual LLMs. arXiv preprint arXiv:2502.12982 (2025)
10. Douze, M., et al.: The faiss library. arXiv preprint arXiv:2401.08281 (2024)
11. Dubey, A., et al.: The llama 3 herd of models. arXiv preprint arXiv:2407.21783 (2024)
12. He, P., Liu, X., Gao, J., Chen, W.: Deberta: decoding-enhanced bert with disentangled attention. In: International Conference on Learning Representations (2021)
13. Iu, K.Y., Wong, V.M.Y.: Chatgpt by openai: the end of litigation lawyers? Available at SSRN 4339839 (2023)
14. Jiang, H., et al.: Leveraging large language models for learning complex legal concepts through storytelling. In: Proceedings of the 62nd Annual Meeting of the Association for Computational Linguistics (Volume 1: Long Papers), pp. 7194–7219 (2024)
15. Lai, J., Gan, W., Wu, J., Qi, Z., Philip, S.Y.: Large language models in law: a survey. AI Open (2024)
16. Lawyers Council Under The Royal Patronage: Compilation of exam questions and answer guidelines for the theoretical training in advocacy from session 16 to session 54. Dharmasarn Printing, Nonthaburi (2021)
17. Lawyers Council Under The Royal Patronage: Compilation of exam questions and answer guidelines for the theoretical training in advocacy from session 55 to session 59. Dharmasarn Printing, Nonthaburi (2021)

18. Lawyers Council Under The Royal Patronage: Compilation of exam questions and answer guidelines for the theoretical training in advocacy from session 60 to session 61. Dharmasarn Printing, Nonthaburi (2021)
19. Lin, C.Y.: Rouge: a package for automatic evaluation of summaries. In: Text Summarization Branches Out, pp. 74–81 (2004)
20. Loshchilov, I., Hutter, F.: Decoupled weight decay regularization. In: International Conference on Learning Representations (2019)
21. Mamooler, S., Lebret, R., Massonnet, S., Aberer, K.: An efficient active learning pipeline for legal text classification. In: NLLP 2022, pp. 345–358 (2022)
22. NECTEC: Openthaillm-prebuilt-7b (2025). https://medium.com/nectec/openthaillm-prebuilt-release-f1b0e22be6a5. Accessed 18 Feb 2025
23. NECTEC: Pathummallm-text-v 1.0.0 release (2025). https://medium.com/nectec/pathummallm-v-1-0-0-release-6a098ddfe276. Accessed 18 Feb 2025
24. Ouyang, L., et al.: Training language models to follow instructions with human feedback. Adv. Neural. Inf. Process. Syst. **35**, 27730–27744 (2022)
25. Phatthiyaphaibun, W.: Han instruct dataset (2024)
26. Pipatanakul, K., et al.: Typhoon 2: a family of open text and multimodal Thai large language models. arXiv preprint arXiv:2412.13702 (2024)
27. Rodrigues, R.: Legal and human rights issues of AI: gaps, challenges and vulnerabilities. J. Responsible Technol. **4**, 100005 (2020)
28. Song, K., Tan, X., Qin, T., Lu, J., Liu, T.Y.: Mpnet: masked and permuted pre-training for language understanding. Adv. Neural. Inf. Process. Syst. **33**, 16857–16867 (2020)
29. Sourdin, T.: Judge v robot?: Artificial intelligence and judicial decision-making. Univ. New South Wales Law J. **41**(4), 1114–1133 (2018)
30. Wan, Z., Zhang, Y., Wang, Y., Cheng, F., Kurohashi, S.: Reformulating domain adaptation of large language models as adapt-retrieve-revise: a case study on Chinese legal domain. In: Findings of the Association for Computational Linguistics ACL 2024, pp. 5030–5041 (2024)
31. Wang, L., Yang, N., Huang, X., Yang, L., Majumder, R., Wei, F.: Multilingual e5 text embeddings: a technical report. arXiv preprint arXiv:2402.05672 (2024)
32. Yang, A., et al.: Qwen2 technical report. arXiv preprint arXiv:2407.10671 (2024)
33. Yang, A., et al.: Qwen2. 5 technical report. arXiv preprint arXiv:2412.15115 (2024)
34. Yao, R., Wu, Y., Wang, C., Xiong, J., Wang, F., Liu, X.: Elevating legal LLM responses: harnessing trainable logical structures and semantic knowledge with legal reasoning. arXiv preprint arXiv:2502.07912 (2025)
35. Yu, F., Quartey, L., Schilder, F.: Legal prompting: teaching a language model to think like a lawyer. arXiv preprint arXiv:2212.01326 (2022)
36. Yu, F., Quartey, L., Schilder, F.: Exploring the effectiveness of prompt engineering for legal reasoning tasks. In: Findings of the Association for Computational Linguistics: ACL 2023, pp. 13582–13596 (2023)
37. Yuenyong, S., Viriyayudhakorn, K., Piyatumrong, A., Jaroenkantasima, J.: Openthaigpt 1.5: a Thai-centric open source large language model. arXiv preprint arXiv:2411.07238 (2024)
38. Zhang, T., Kishore, V., Wu, F., Weinberger, K.Q., Artzi, Y.: Bertscore: evaluating text generation with bert. In: International Conference on Learning Representations (2020)
39. Zhang, W., et al.: Seallms 3: open foundation and chat multilingual large language models for southeast Asian languages. arXiv preprint arXiv:2407.19672 (2024)

Leveraging Generative AI for Chronic Kidney Disease Prediction: A Comparative Study of Open-Source LLMs

B. Abhin[1], Hemanth Kumar M[1], Sowmya Kamath S[1](✉), and Vijayan Sugumaran[2]

[1] Healthcare Analytics and Language Engineering (HALE) Lab, Department of Information Technology, National Institute of Technology Karnataka, Surathkal, Mangaluru 575025, India
{abhinb.211ai003,mogilipalemhemanthkumar.211ai025,sowmyakamath}@nitk.edu.in

[2] Department of Decision and Information Sciences, School of Business Administration, Oakland University, Rochester, USA
sugumara@oakland.edu

Abstract. Generative AI models have transformed real-world applications, particularly in Natural Language Processing (NLP), enabling zero-shot inference across various tasks. They have also advanced zero-shot visual understanding, Agentic AI, and information retrieval. Unlike traditional models requiring task-specific fine-tuning, GenAI models handle complex NLP tasks without prior adjustments. This study leverages these capabilities for next-disease prediction, focusing on Chronic Kidney Disease (CKD). Using clinical note events from MIMIC-IV, we frame the task as a sequence classification problem, applying positive and negative sampling for binary classification to predict CKD occurrence based on a patient's medical history. Our experiments compare traditional models like Logistic Regression and BERT with open-source LLMs of varying sizes and architectures. We also assess different fine-tuning methods to evaluate model generalizability. Larger models, particularly Mistral-Small-24B with supervised fine-tuning (SFT), achieved the highest performance, significantly outperforming other models and traditional baselines.

Keywords: Chronic kidney disease (CKD) · Large Language Models (LLMs) · In-context learning · Supervised Fine tuning (SFT)

1 Introduction

The proliferating adoption of Electronic Health Records (EHRs) [1] has revolutionized the availability and utilization of data for various medical tasks, paving the way for significant advancements in healthcare analytics and patient care. By making patient information including diagnoses, medications, and clinical histories digital, EHRs have created a vast repository of structured and unstructured

R. Ichise (Ed.): NLDB 2025, LNCS 15836, pp. 216–228, 2026.
https://doi.org/10.1007/978-3-031-97141-9_15

data that can be utilized for modeling, decision-making, and personalized treatment plans. This rich data source is particularly valuable in managing chronic diseases, wherein accurate predictions made in time can greatly impact patient outcomes.

Recently, Large Language Models (LLMs) have opened new horizons for the medical domain with their unparalleled capacity to generate answers with no prior specific fine-tuning [2] as they are trained on an abundant amount of data. Initially designed for natural language processing tasks, LLMs such as GPT-4 [3] and Claude-3.5 have demonstrated remarkable potential in extracting meaningful insights from complex and unstructured medical texts, such as clinical notes and research publications. In addition to supporting the developer community, the availability of open-source LLMs significantly aids researchers and developers in evaluating and experimenting with the capabilities of various cutting-edge LLMs. Their ability to process vast amounts of information and generate human-like understanding makes it an interesting venue to test it out for tasks such as medical text analysis, patient risk analysis, and disease prediction [4]. By leveraging the minimal medical information embedded in EHRs, LLMs can facilitate early identification of disease patterns which helps address the issue before it transforms into a bigger problem, improving both the accuracy and timeliness of predictions. This is a case study on how varied LLMs perform when posed a medical scenario, and understand, if the performance of LLMs is at par with the accuracy required by the medical field.

Disease prediction tasks including those focused on chronic conditions, conventionally relied on statistical methods and machine learning models which are trained on hand-engineered features, which are largely dependent on structured data [5]. While effective to a degree, these models were often limited by their inability to fully utilize the unstructured text in EHRs and other types of clinical records. As a result, many important signals embedded in clinical narratives, lab reports, and diagnostic notes may be underutilized, limiting the overall effectiveness of these predictive systems. This is specifically true for previous diagnoses, which may be lost in the clinical notes, as it is typically recorded in the form of doctors' and nurses' notes. However, with the integration of LLMs, a more holistic and comprehensive approach to disease prediction is now feasible, to improve outcomes for chronic disease patients.

In this article, we explore the application of open-source LLMs for the task of next disease prediction, with a specific focus on Chronic Kidney Disease (CKD). Through this lens, we aim to demonstrate the potential of these advanced models in transforming chronic disease management and prediction, and also analyze the performance using different fine tuning techniques. The article is organized as follows: Sect. 2 describes the previous work on the task to be addressed. In Sect. 3, the methodology adopted and the various constituent sub-processes like cohort selection, models, and learning strategies considered are discussed in detail. Section 4 details the experiments performed and the results observed, followed by conclusion and directions for future work.

2 Related Work

The integration of AI, particularly LLMs, into healthcare has revolutionized disease prediction and diagnosis, with recent advancements demonstrating their capacity to process complex clinical data and generate actionable insights. While foundational studies such as CPLLM [6] and GatorTron [7] highlight the potential of LLMs in general clinical tasks, their application to chronic kidney disease (CKD) prediction remains underexplored. In this section, recent advancements in CKD-specific AI research are explored and aligned with emerging LLM frameworks, to identify gaps and opportunities.

Machine learning (ML) models have shown promising performance in CKD detection and progression prediction. For instance, ensemble models like Random Forests (RFs) and gradient-boosted trees (XGBoost) have achieved good accuracies in classifying CKD stages using laboratory and demographic features [8,9]. Notably, Random Forests outperform artificial neural networks (ANNs) in at-home CKD screening due to their robustness to imbalanced datasets and interpretable feature importance analysis, identifying hemoglobin, blood urea, and comorbidities like hypertension as critical predictors [10]. Deep learning models, such as convolutional neural networks (CNNs) and long short-term memory (LSTM) networks, further enhance prediction by capturing temporal patterns in longitudinal electronic health records (EHRs), achieving consistent performance in forecasting CKD progression 6âĂŞ12 months in advance [11,12]. These models leverage biomarkers like serum creatinine, estimated glomerular filtration rate (eGFR), and proteinuria, aligning with clinical guidelines for risk stratification [13,14].

LLMs such as GatorTron [7] and Google's AMIE [15] excel in extracting structured insights from unstructured EHRs, enabling tasks such as named entity recognition (NER) [16–18] and medical question answering (MQA) [19,20]. For CKD, this capability is critical, as EHRs often contain fragmented data (e.g., lab results, clinical notes) that require contextual interpretation. For example, LLMs can correlate free-text physician notes with lab trends (e.g., rising creatinine levels) to predict impending renal decline, a task traditional ML struggles with due to its reliance on static, preprocessed features [14]. Recent frameworks like COAD [21] address symptom-disease misalignment in diagnostic models, a challenge relevant to CKD where symptom sequences (e.g., edema to hypertension to proteinuria) are heterogeneous across patients.

More recently, researchers have explored the viability of LLMs in the domain of nephrology. For instance, reinforcement learning (RL)-augmented ANN models have achieved 97% accuracy in predicting CKD outcomes by dynamically adapting to evolving patient data [22]. Similarly, transformer-based architectures show promise in parsing multimodal EHR data (e.g., lab values, imaging reports) to predict patient outcomes [13,23]. These advancements suggest that LLMs, when tailored to CKD-specific workflows, could unify fragmented data sources and enable proactive, personalized interventions. With these insights, our work focused on experimenting with various open-source LLMs trained on a variety of data using two different fine-tuning strategies, PEFT based SFT and In-context learning for the larger models.

3 Methodology

The approach designed for addressing the problem of next disease prediction using CKD as a case study is presented in detail in this section. Clinical note events from the MIMIC-IV dataset [24] were used for the experiments. Our methodology consists of three key components – data preprocessing and cohort selection, prompt engineering for leveraging LLMs, and fine-tuning techniques to optimize model performance. Detailed steps followed in each of these phases are described next and shown in Fig. 1.

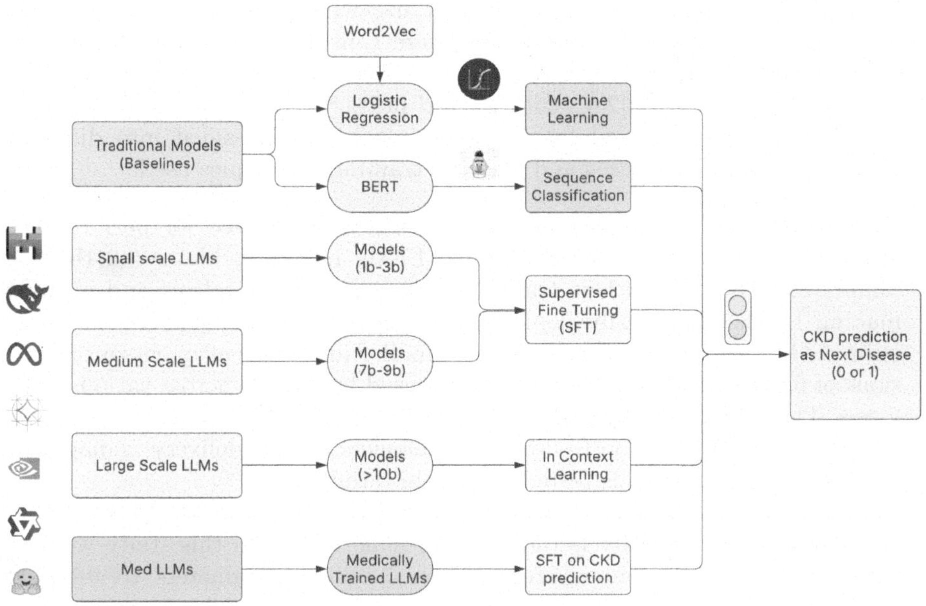

Fig. 1. Proposed methodology.

3.1 Data Preprocessing and Cohort Selection

The data preprocessing and cohort selection process began by extracting clinical notes from the NOTE-EVENTS section of the MIMIC-IV dataset, which contains unstructured text detailing patient care. To structure this data for disease prediction, all diagnoses for each patient were consolidated into a sequence while preserving the order of diagnosis. The final disease in each sequence was designated as the target for prediction. For CKD-specific predictions, lists mentioning kidney-related diseases were selected, and entries with fewer than three prior diagnoses were excluded to ensure sufficient historical data. The final dataset consisted of 27,300 CKD-positive samples and 20,000 negative samples, labeled accordingly. As the LLMs are highly capable of generalizing a random sample of 1000 entries were selected from the dataset prepared. The dataset was then split into training, validation, and testing of 80-10-10 split sets.

3.2 Model Selection

In this study, the primary focus is on open-source models as they are best suited for fine-tuning and also working with sensitive data like medical data, as they are loaded and trained locally on the data. A wide range of open-source LLMs were considered for the study which have origins from various research labs. Models of various sizes were also considered for study ranging from Llama-3.2-1b [25], which has 1-billion parameters, all the way up to Llama-3.3-70b [26], which is a huge model, close to 40 GB in size when considered in its native float-16 precision. Two baseline models were considered, Logistic Regression, Random Forest which uses Word2Vec [27] embeddings for prediction, and the BERT transformer model [28] which is used in its SequenceClassification form. The LLM models considered for the experiments are classified into different categories based on their sizes and also the training techniques used.

1. *Small-scale LLMs.* The first category of LLMs considered for performance oriented comparison is the small-scale LLMs including Llama-3.2-1b [25], SmolLM2-1.7b [29] which is trained on over 11 trillion tokens and aims at making LLMs more easily deployable which providing competitive performance. Gemma-2b [30] boasts to be a smaller and efficient open-source versions of foundational models like Gemini used by Google across various platforms. The primary intent of development for all the models having parameter count in between 1-billion to 3-billion is efficiency while delivery manageable performance. The same is tested out in this study.
2. *Medium-scale LLMs.* The second and most prevalent LLMs in the researcher and developer community is the medium-scale LLMs. In this study we consider models ranging anywhere between 7-billion parameters to 9-billion parameter to be considered as medium-scale LLMs. The most popular medium-scale LLMs come from DeepSeek, a China-based AI Research Organization which aims at delivering state-of-the-art models at a very reasonable training cost. Qwen-2.5-7b-1M [31] being the smallest model in this study to have a context length of 1M tokens from Alibaba, Llama-3.1-8b [26] a standard model from Meta updating over its predecessors, Mistral-Nemo-Minitron-8b is a fine-tuned and improvised model from Nvidia which uses Mistral as the base model, Gemma-2-9b [30] is an addition to the family of Gemma models by Google which introduces group query attention and interleaving local-global attention. These models are highly efficient for the performance they offer and can be loaded with most medium-scale GPUs include Apple's MPUs with a minimum of 16 GB unified RAM making it a preferred choice of use for researchers and developers.

3. *Large-scale LLMs.* The Large-scale models considered for this study are any models with higher than 10b parameter count, the large-scale LLMs include Mistral-Small-24b-Base claiming to have performance equal to that of the popular closed source models like GPT-4o-mini, Mixtral-8x7b [32] boasting to be one of the first Mixture of Experts (MoE) models in the open-source LLM community showcasing excellent performance across various benchmarks, and finally Llama-3.3-70b [25] which is the largest LLM included in the study which also is the same LLM used by Meta in the chat interface provided by them.
4. *Med LLMs.* This study also includes the last category of LLMs which are specifically fine-tuned for the medical domain including MedLlama-3, a multilingual medical foundation model based on Llama 3, MedFound-7b [33] which is a research based medical LLM which tries to understand and learn a physician's inferential diagnosis, and CPLLM [34] majorly focuses on next diagnosis prediction while also comparing their quantized and fine-tuned LLM with Med-BERT and other baseline model. These models are an integral part of the study which serve as the base for this particular study.

3.3 In-Context Learning

In-context learning is essential for guiding the LLM in predicting CKD by analyzing previous diagnoses. This approach was mainly used for the larger LLMs as they are powerful LLMs and are compared to SFT based smaller LLMs. Prompts were carefully designed to incorporate domain-specific knowledge, ensuring the model focused on relevant medical information. These prompts underwent iterative refinement through testing, with adjustments made to optimize performance. The structured input allows the LLM to process diagnoses effectively and predict the likelihood of CKD as the next condition. The LLM was specifically prompted to explain the answer that was being generated as it is noticed in multiple works that explanation along with labeling significantly improves the LLMs performance giving it a pseudo reasoning ability [35,36] as seen in Fig. 2. Also providing a JSON specific format as the output format reduces the need for post processing when it comes to using larger LLMs which are better at following instructions compared to the smaller LLMs. A typical prompt included a list of diagnoses as input for the model to analyze, as shown below.

- **Prompt 1:** "*You are given a list of previous diagnoses for a patient. Based on this information, predict whether Chronic Kidney Disease (CKD) is likely to be the next diagnosis. The diagnoses are provided in chronological order. Please analyze the list and determine the likelihood of CKD being diagnosed next. Please give an explanation for the prediction in the following json format: label: <value>, explanation: <text>*
  Previous Diagnoses: [diagnoses_list]. Is CKD the next diagnosis?"
- **Prompt 2:** "*Evaluate the following list of medical diagnoses and predict if Chronic Kidney Disease (CKD) will be diagnosed next. The conditions are presented in the order they were diagnosed for the patient. Use the available*

information to determine if CKD is the likely next diagnosis. Please give an explanation for the prediction in the following json format: label: <value>, explanation: <text>
Previous Diagnoses: [diagnoses_ list]. Will CKD occur next?"

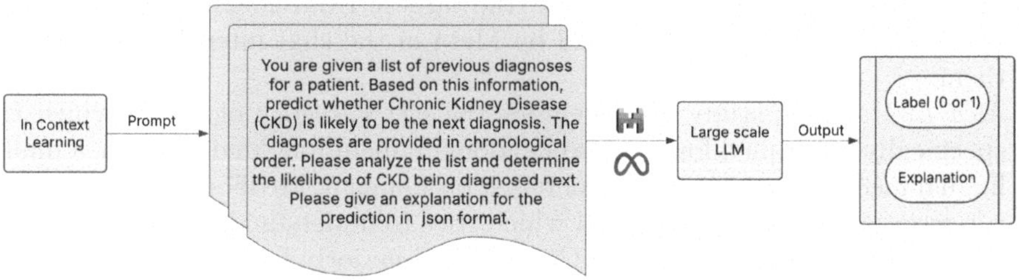

Fig. 2. In-context learning used for LLMs.

3.4 Supervised Fine-Tuning

LLMs pose significant computational demands, towards which fine-tuning strategies were employed: Supervised Fine-Tuning (SFT) [37] using Parameter Efficient Fine-Tuning (PEFT) [38]. SFT involved training the LLM on a labeled CKD dataset, aligning the model's behavior with task-specific objectives. Native LLM is loaded and an PEFT Adapter is trained over the base LLM to fine tune it for the task intended. SFT, in our study was used on smaller LLMs to check the ability to generalize over a task of previous diagnosis based CKD prediction which was treated as a classification task with label '0' standing for non-occurrence of CKD while label '1' standing for possible occurrence of CKD. Through hyperparameter tuning and validation on unseen data, SFT adapted the general capabilities of the LLM to accurately predict CKD. PEFT was used to reduce computational costs by fine-tuning only a small subset of the model's parameters. PEFT techniques were applied – Low-Rank Adaptation (LoRA) [39], Quantized LoRA (QLoRA) [40]. LoRA injects low-rank matrices into each transformer layer, reducing the number of trainable parameters without compromising performance, for real-time use. QLoRA further minimizes memory usage by quantizing weights, allowing for faster predictions while maintaining similar performance to fully fine-tuned models. Both approaches ensured resource-efficient fine-tuning without sacrificing model accuracy for CKD prediction.

4 Experimental Results and Discussion

The experiments were conducted using the MIMIC-IV dataset, specifically targeting the prediction of CKD as the next diagnosis. The task was treated as a binary classification problem, predicting whether CKD would be the next disease based on a sequence of previous diagnoses. The experimental setup utilized an A100 GPU, with all the LLMs trained for five epochs under a quantized configuration. Logistic Regression and BERT (fine-tuned for five epochs with a classification head added to perform sequence classification) were employed as baseline models, while the performance of medically fine-tuned models such as MedLlama3, MedFound-7b and CPLLM-Llama2-7b were used as the reference to benchmark and compare other models. Small and Medium-scale models were trained for 5 epochs and fine-tuned using Parameter Efficient Fine-Tuning (PEFT) and QLoRA. The training was carried out with the help of *Trainer* from *transformers* library. The hyper-parameters used for the same include 5 epochs with 4 bit quantization using *bnb config* from *bitandbytes*, LORA hyper-parameters include a rank of adaptation matrix $r = 32$, Scaling factor for LoRA weight, $loraalpha = 32$, and $loradropout = 0.1$. Tokenization hyper-parameters include $maxlength = 4096$ with padding and truncation set to *True*.

The performance of all models was evaluated using standard metrics such as accuracy, precision, recall, F1-score, and AUPRC (Area Under Precision-Recall Curve). These metrics were chosen to provide a comprehensive assessment of each model's ability to predict CKD as the next diagnosis. *Accuracy* refers to the proportion of correct predictions made by the model. *Precision* is defined as the ratio of true positives (correctly predicted CKD cases) to all predicted positives. *Recall* measures the ratio of true positives to the total actual cases of CKD. *F1-score*, which is the harmonic mean of precision and recall, balances both. *Area Under the Precision-Recall Curve (AUROC)* evaluates the model's ability to distinguish between CKD and non-CKD cases.

Table 1 tabulates the observed performance of all the models considered for our experiments. The evaluation of open-source models on the CKD prediction task revealed significant performance differences across various architectures and parameter scales. Performance comparison of baseline models across various evaluation metrics reveals that the Random Forest model significantly outperforms Logistic Regression and BERT. It achieves the highest scores in all five metrics: Accuracy (0.77), Precision (0.79), Recall (0.86), F1-score (0.82), and AUPRC (0.86). In contrast, Logistic Regression shows the weakest performance with an accuracy of 0.58 and an F1-score of 0.54. BERT performs moderately, outperforming Logistic Regression but falling short of Random Forest, with an F1-score of 0.68 and an AUPRC of 0.72. These results suggest that Random Forest is the most effective baseline model among the three for this task.

Small-scale LLMs (1âĂŞ3B parameters) demonstrated an efficiency-performance trade-off, with `Llama 3.2-1b` (Accuracy: 0.80, Precision: 0.79) achieving the highest performance in this group, benefiting from architectural enhancements like grouped query attention. In contrast to this, an observation with respect to `SmolLM2-1.7B` (F1-score: 0.59, Recall: 0.60) and `Gemma-2b` (AUCPR: 0.81) is made which struggle with recall, indicating challenges in handling class imbalances despite supervised fine tuning. Medium-scale models (7âĂŞ9B parameters) achieved near state-of-the-art performance at lower computational costs. Specifically, `deepseek-7b-chat` (Accuracy: 0.87, F1-score: 0.85) stands out due to cost-effective training strategies, while `Mistral-NeMo-8B`

(F1-score: 0.88) effectively balances precision (0.87) and recall (0.88). The highest AUPRC in this category is achieved by `Gemma2-9b` (0.97), likely benefiting from interleaved local-global attention mechanisms. Large-scale models (>10B parameters) generally dominate in recall, but precision remains inconsistent. `Mistral-Small-24B` (Accuracy: 0.90, F1-score: 0.89) surpasses even some larger models, underscoring the significance of optimized architecture over sheer parameter count. The MoE-based `Mixtral-8x7B` (Recall: 0.95, Precision: 0.77) exhibits strong recall but struggles with precision, while `Llama 3.3-70B` (Recall: 0.98, Precision: 0.71) likely suffers from overfitting to dominant classes.

Medical-specific LLMs consistently outperform generalist models of similar size. It is important to note that the performance of Large-scale LLMs is still commendable as they are the outputs taken from In-context learning in contrast to supervised fine tuning in the case of small-scale and medium-scale LLMs. `MedLlama3` (Accuracy: 0.83, F1-score: 0.81) and `MedFound-7B` (F1-score: 0.88, AUCPR: 0.95) demonstrate enhanced diagnostic reasoning capabilities, with `MedFound-7B` surpassing `Qwen-7B-Instruct-1M` (F1-score: 0.80) by leveraging physician-mimicking logic. However, `CPLLM` (F1-score: 0.48) underperforms, likely due to its narrow focus on next-diagnosis prediction, highlighting the challenge of balancing specialization and generalization. Overall, while larger and domain-specific models achieve impressive results, CKD prediction performance remains a careful trade-off between recall, precision, and computational efficiency, with medium-scale models presenting a promising middle ground.

Multiple open-source models have been tested in this work and these models effectively can be run on a local machine enabled with GPU except the larger LLMs, which further enhances the privacy of the data, as it is not sent to any third-party API which might be used for training. Table 2 summarizes the key advantages for each model category of LLMs mentioning the key advantages for each category of models and also where and when it can be used. The small-scale models are mostly used when it comes to mobile deployment or when there is limited resource for processing. Medium-scale LLMs can be used when there is an availability of GPUs which effectively also gives out the best price to performance ratio. Large LLMs need high computational resources but also provide high performance with limited expertise needed. Medically fine tuned LLMs are more suitable when there is a specific clinical use with a lot of clinical terms involved. Hence this work shows that different models are useful in different use-case scenarios.

Despite the promising results, this work has some limitations. The study's focus on diagnosis-based predictions for CKD excludes rich multimodal data such as clinical notes, lab results, medications, and imaging reports, which could enhance accuracy by providing a more comprehensive patient profile. Incorporating techniques like Retrieval-Augmented Generation (RAG) could improve LLM reliability by synthesizing such diverse data sources. Additionally, computational constraints limited the evaluation to a small subset of open-source LLMs, particularly excluding larger models, while the narrow focus on CKD restricts generalizability to other chronic diseases without further validation.

Table 1. Performance of Open-Source Models in CKD Prediction, grouped by category

Category	Acc	Pre	Rec	F1	AUPRC
Baselines					
Logistic Regression	0.58	0.52	0.56	0.54	0.61
BERT	0.63	0.67	0.69	0.68	0.72
Small-Scale LLMs (1–3B Parameters)					
Llama 3.2-1b	0.80	0.79	0.58	0.58	0.79
SmolLM2-1.7B-Instruct	0.67	0.68	0.60	0.59	0.78
Gemma-2b	0.73	0.77	0.62	0.62	0.81
Medium-Scale LLMs (7–9B Parameters)					
deepseek-llm-7b-chat	0.87	0.87	0.84	0.85	0.94
Qwen2.5-7B-Instruct-1M	0.82	0.81	0.79	0.80	0.87
Llama 3.1-8b	0.86	0.85	0.83	0.84	0.88
Mistral-NeMo-Minitron-8B-Instruct	0.89	0.87	0.89	0.88	0.94
Gemma-2-9b-it	0.89	0.89	0.85	0.86	0.97
Large-Scale LLMs (>10B Parameters)					
Mistral-Small-24b-Base-2501	0.90	0.89	0.89	0.89	0.96
Mixtral-8x7b	0.82	0.77	0.95	0.85	0.76
Llama 3.3-70b-versatile	0.74	0.71	0.98	0.83	0.71
Medical-Specific LLMs					
MedLlama3	0.83	0.81	0.82	0.81	0.89
CPLLM	0.62	0.58	0.60	0.48	0.72
MedFound-7B	0.89	0.88	0.87	0.88	0.95

Table 2. Summary of Model Categories for CKD Prediction

Category	Advantages	When to Use	Example Models
Small-scale LLMs (1–3B)	Low resource requirement	Limited computational resources, initial testing	Llama 3.2-1b, Gemma-2b
Medium-scale LLMs (7–9B)	Balanced performance and cost	General medical applications, fine-tuning available	deepseek-llm-7b, Mistral-NeMo-8B
Large-scale LLMs (>10B)	High accuracy with in-context learning	High-accuracy needs without fine-tuning	Mistral-Small-24B, Llama 3.3-70b
Medically fine-tuned LLMs	Specialized for medical tasks	Clinical use, specialized predictions	MedLlama3, MedFound-7B

Beyond these technical constraints, the clinical implications of prediction errors raise concern for careful consideration. False negatives that is, missing CKD diagnoses risk delayed interventions, accelerating disease progression and increasing morbidity, mortality, and healthcare costs. Conversely, false positives may lead to unnecessary patient anxiety, invasive follow-ups, or overtreatment. Given CKD's progressive nature and the critical need for early detection, optimizing for recall alongside accuracy becomes vital to prioritize timely diagnosis while balancing the risks of over and under prediction. Addressing these limitations in future work could enhance both model robustness and real-world clinical utility.

5 Conclusion and Future Work

In this article, the task of disease prediction using previous diagnosis data extracted from the MIMIC-IV dataset was examined, comparing the performance of various models, ranging from traditional baselines like Logistic Regression and Random Forest to LLMs of different sizes and architecture and timelines as well. Also, medically fine-tuned LLMs were also considered to set a standard for the comparison for zero shot inferencing of small, medium and large-scale LLMs. This study also compares small and medium-scale LLMs trained using supervised fine tuning along side in-context learning performed with the larger LLMs, as it is a much harder task computationally to fine-tune the larger LLMs. The results reveal that model size is crucial for accuracy and robustness in disease prediction. Medium-scale LLMs have best trade off with respect to model size or computational cost vis-a-vis the performance of the model. It is also observed that the newer models with better attention mechanisms including Gemma-2-9b, deepseek-llm-7b have improved performance. Mistral Small-24b-base performs extremely well considering that it was inferenced using zero shot in-context learning. Llama 3.3-70b on the other hand performs poorly while being the biggest model in terms of parameter count used in this particular study.

As part of extended work, our focus will expand to integrate additional data modalities—such as lab test results, imaging reports, and demographic information—alongside diagnoses to enable models to develop a more comprehensive understanding of patient conditions, potentially enhancing prediction accuracy. We will also explore advanced modeling techniques like multi-task learning and temporal analysis of patient histories to better capture disease progression dynamics and improve clinical utility. While our work leverages LLM-generated explanations through pseudo-reasoning to boost performance, these outputs have yet to undergo rigorous validation by clinical experts. To address this, we plan to collaborate with medical professionals to qualitatively assess the clinical accuracy, interpretability, and alignment of these explanations with real-world clinical reasoning.

References

1. Hoerbst, A., Ammenwerth, E.: Electronic health records. Methods Inf. Med. **49**(04), 320–336 (2010)
2. Kojima, T., Gu, S.S., Reid, M., Matsuo, Y., Iwasawa, Y.: Large language models are zero-shot reasoners. Adv. Neural. Inf. Process. Syst. **35**, 22199–22213 (2022)
3. Waisberg, E., et al.: GPT-4: a new era of artificial intelligence in medicine. Irish J. Med. Sci. (1971-) **192**(6), 3197–3200 (2023)
4. Biswas, S.S.: Role of chatgpt in public health. Ann. Biomed. Eng. **51**(5), 868–869 (2023)
5. Revathy, S., Bharathi, B., Jeyanthi, P., Ramesh, M.: Chronic kidney disease prediction using machine learning models. Int. J. Eng. Adv. Technol. **9**(1), 6364–6367 (2019)
6. Ben Shoham, O., Rappoport, N.: CPLLM: clinical prediction with large language models. arXiv preprint (2023)
7. Yang, W., Zou, H., Wang, M., Zhang, Q., Li, S., Liang, H.: Mortality prediction among ICU inpatients based on MIMIC-III database results from the conditional medical generative adversarial network. Heliyon **9**(2), e13200 (2023). http://dx.doi.org/10.1016/j.heliyon.2023.e13200
8. Metherall, B., Berryman, A.K., Brennan, G.S.: Machine learning for classifying chronic kidney disease and predicting creatinine levels using at-home measurements. medRxiv (2024)
9. Halder, R.K., et al.: ML-CKDP: machine learning-based chronic kidney disease prediction with smart web application. J. Pathol. Inform. **15**, 100371 (2024)
10. Bahrami, P., Tanbakuchi, D., Afzalaghaee, M., Ghayour-Mobarhan, M., Esmaily, H.: Development of risk models for early detection and prediction of chronic kidney disease in clinical settings. Sci. Rep. **14**(1), 32136 (2024)
11. Saif, D., Sarhan, A.M., Elshennawy, N.M.: Deep-kidney: an effective deep learning framework for chronic kidney disease prediction. Health Inf. Sci. Syst. **12**(1), 3 (2023)
12. Saif, D., Sarhan, A.M., Elshennawy, N.M.: Early prediction of chronic kidney disease based on ensemble of deep learning models and optimizers. J. Electr. Syst. Inf. Technol. **11**(1), 17 (2024)
13. Isaza-Ruget, M.A., et al.: Predicting chronic kidney disease progression with artificial intelligence. BMC Nephrol. **25**(1), 148 (2024)
14. Khalid, F., et al.: Predicting the progression of chronic kidney disease: a systematic review of artificial intelligence and machine learning approaches. Cureus **16**(5) (2024)
15. Tu, T., et al.: Towards conversational diagnostic AI. arXiv preprint (2024)
16. Unnikrishnan, R., Kamath, S., et al.: Efficient parameter tuning of neural foundation models for drug perspective prediction from unstructured socio-medical data. Eng. Appl. Artif. Intell. **123**, 106214 (2023)
17. Unnikrishnan, R., Kamath, S.S., Ananthanarayana, V.: Population-centric profiling with social data for large-scale epidemiological studies. In: Proceedings of the 5th Joint International Conference on Data Science & Management of Data (9th ACM IKDD CODS and 27th COMAD), pp. 302–303 (2022)
18. Joshi, S., Kamath, S.: Social network science approaches for disease named entity recognition and extraction. In: 2024 International Conference on Information Networking (ICOIN), pp. 96–101. IEEE (2024)

19. Murali, S., Sowmya, S., Supreetha, R.: ReMAG-KR: retrieval and medically assisted generation with knowledge reduction for medical question answering. In: Proceedings of the 62nd Annual Meeting of the Association for Computational Linguistics (Volume 4: Student Research Workshop), pp. 62–67 (2024)
20. Shenoy, N., Nayak, P., Jain, S., Sowmya Kamath, S., Sugumaran, V.: Effective information retrieval, question answering and abstractive summarization on large-scale biomedical document corpora. In: International Conference on Applications of Natural Language to Information Systems, pp. 404–415. Springer (2023)
21. Wang, H., Kwan, W.C., Wong, K.F., Zheng, Y.: Coad: automatic diagnosis through symptom and disease collaborative generation. arXiv preprint arXiv:2307.08290 (2023)
22. Nramban Kannan, S.K., et al.: A model for predicting chronic kidney diseases based on medical data using reinforcement learning. SN Comput. Sci. **5**(4), 353 (2024)
23. Merchant, A.M., Shenoy, N., Lanka, S., Kamath, S.: Ensemble neural models for ICD code prediction using unstructured and structured healthcare data. Heliyon **10**(17) (2024)
24. Johnson, A., Bulgarelli, L., Pollard, T., Horng, S., Celi, L.A., Mark, R.: MIMIC-IV. PhysioNet, pp. 49–55 (2020). https://physionet.org/content/mimiciv/1.0/. Accessed 23 Aug 2021
25. Meta, A.: Llama 3.2: revolutionizing edge AI and vision with open, customizable models. Meta AI Blog (2024). Accessed 20 Dec 2024
26. Meta, A.: Introducing llama 3.1: our most capable models to date. Meta AI Blog 12 (2024)
27. Mikolov, T.: Efficient estimation of word representations in vector space. arXiv preprint arXiv:1301.3781 (2013)
28. Devlin, J., Chang, M.W., Lee, K., Toutanova, K.: Bert: pre-training of deep bidirectional transformers for language understanding (2018). https://arxiv.org/abs/1810.04805
29. Allal, L.B., et al.: Smollm2: when SMOL goes big–data-centric training of a small language model. arXiv preprint arXiv:2502.02737 (2025)
30. Team, G., et al.: Gemma 2: improving open language models at a practical size. arXiv preprint arXiv:2408.00118 (2024)
31. Yang, A., et al.: Qwen2. 5 technical report. arXiv preprint arXiv:2412.15115 (2024)
32. Jiang, A.Q., et al.: Mixtral of experts. arXiv preprint arXiv:2401.04088 (2024)
33. Liu, X., et al.: A generalist medical language model for disease diagnosis assistance. Nat. Med. 1–11 (2025)
34. Shoham, O.B., Rappoport, N.: CPLLM: clinical prediction with large language models. PLOS Digit. Health **3**(12), e0000680 (2024)
35. Lee, D.H., et al.: Lean-life: a label-efficient annotation framework towards learning from explanation. arXiv preprint arXiv:2004.07499 (2020)
36. He, X., et al.: Annollm: making large language models to be better crowdsourced annotators. arXiv preprint arXiv:2303.16854 (2023)
37. Ziegler, D.M., et al.: Fine-tuning language models from human preferences. arXiv preprint arXiv:1909.08593 (2019)
38. Ding, N., et al.: Parameter-efficient fine-tuning of large-scale pre-trained language models. Nat. Mach. Intell. **5**(3), 220–235 (2023)
39. Hu, E.J., et al.: Lora: low-rank adaptation of large language models. arXiv preprint arXiv:2106.09685 (2021)
40. Xu, Y., et al.: QA-LoRA: quantization-aware low-rank adaptation of large language models. arXiv preprint arXiv:2309.14717 (2023)

LADDER: Latent Attention and Decomposition for Deep Enhanced Retrieval in Medical Question-Answering Systems

Sidhaarth Murali[1](✉), Sowmya Kamath S[1], and Vijayan Sugumaran[2]

[1] Healthcare Analytics and Language Engineering (HALE) Lab, Department of Information Technology, National Institute of Technology Karnataka, Surathkal, Mangaluru 575025, India
sowmyakamath@nitk.edu.in

[2] Department of Decision and Information Sciences, School of Business Administration, Oakland University, Rochester, USA
sugumara@oakland.edu

Abstract. The deployment of large language models (LLMs) in health question-answering (QA) systems presents unique challenges, particularly on scalability, inference time, and hallucination mitigation. While Retrieval-Augmented Generation (RAG) methods have demonstrated promise, current implementations do not fully address the complexities of medical content, which is both keyword-dense and semantically intricate. In this work, we present LADDER, a question decomposition framework tailored for practical, real-world medical QA applications. By creating a reduced knowledge base (RKB) and proposing a novel latent self-attention mechanism, LADDER improves the retriever model's ability to extract more relevant information. We demonstrate this on a medical setup, achieving a 2.5% increase in retrieval performance and a 6–8% improvement in generative prediction performance over existing MedRAG benchmarks. Additionally, inference time is reduced by 47%, enhancing system responsiveness in real-world conditions. This approach not only meets the performance demands of healthcare systems but also ensures robustness against hallucinations, making it viable for real-world deployment under computational and operational constraints.

Keywords: Large Language Models · Retrieval Augmented Generation · Question Answering Systems · Natural Language Processing

1 Introduction

Large Language Models (LLMs) like GPT-4 [1], LLaMA-2 [2], and LLaMA-3 [3] have become powerful tools for text generation across various domains, including healthcare. In this field, LLMs have transformed tasks such as patient

R. Ichise (Ed.): NLDB 2025, LNCS 15836, pp. 229–242, 2026.
https://doi.org/10.1007/978-3-031-97141-9_16

education [4], report generation [5], drug discovery [6,7] and question-answering [8–10] by processing vast amounts of textual data. However, LLMs are prone to hallucinations, generating false medical information that can mislead users. To address this, many LLMs employ retrieval-augmented pipelines to enhance accuracy by integrating external information. While this reduces hallucinations, it can also introduce irrelevant or incorrect data, undermining the quality of outputs [11,12]. Moreover, LLMs often lack the semantic depth to fully understand and utilize external data, especially in keyword-dense medical texts where conventional pooling methods treat all tokens equally [13].

Retrieval Augmented Generation (RAG) [14], aims to enhance the generative performance of LLMs with an external source of information. The RAG paradigm significantly reduces hallucinations within LLMs and also provides up-to-date knowledge even though the LLM was not fine-tuned on newer data. Several early works focused on improving the quality of generated text. Recent approaches involve intuitive modifications at the query-level [15], knowledge base-level [16], and retrieval-level [17] of the pipeline. When focusing on a specific domain, retrievers trained on generic data often fall short compared to those optimized for particular domains [18]. In the field of Biomedicine, majority of the works have focused on training the retriever model and generator model separately [19] on medicine-specific data. An interesting method emphasized the joint training of both [20]. Recent efforts have increased the scale of data and model parameters, resulting in models like GatorTronGPT [21] and Clinical-Camel [22], as well as studies on Flan-PaLM and PaLM-2's medical reasoning [23] using chain-of-thought. Additionally, researchers have introduced Meditron [24], an open-source medical language model suite with 7B and 70B parameters, showing superior performance against leading benchmarks and comparable results to GPT-3.5 and Med-PaLM-2. Despite the increase in model size, performance gains have plateaued, and these expansions have not effectively addressed model forgetting.

The study of information retrieval (IR) and deep learning has made great progress, with dense retrievers now taking the lead in semantic retrieval. Unlike traditional sparse (lexical) retrievers like BM25 [25], dense retrievers encode and match queries and documents with dense vectors, resulting in improved performance [26]. These models are generated using pre-trained transformers and are further fine-tuned on domain-specific tasks using a contrastive objective on an unsupervised query-document pair of text. BERT and T5 based embedding models are predominantly used for general-purpose embedding tasks. For Bio-Medical Information retrieval, most approaches focused on intuitively fine-tuning BERT-based models [27]. In this paper, the LADDER framework, designed to decompose complex medical queries into simpler sub-queries, combined with a novel latent self-attention mechanism to improve both retrieval and generative prediction is presented. By reducing the knowledge base size by 94%, the inference time is significantly reduced by 47%, while still maintaining competitive performance. Evaluated on the MIRAGE dataset[1], our approach improves

[1] MIRAGE benchmark: https://github.com/Teddy-XiongGZ/MIRAGE.

retriever performance by 2.5% and generative prediction by 6–8%, showing its practical applicability in medical settings.

The remainder of this paper is structured as follows: Sect. 2 formally defines the problem addressed in this article and Sect. 3 outlines the methodology designed to address the problem identified. Section 4 presents the experiments performed, results and discussion and ablation studies considered, followed by conclusion and directions for future work.

2 Preliminaries

Our objective is to enhance retrieval and generative prediction performance in medical question-answering systems. Specifically, our approach involves three main steps. Firstly, we aim to decompose a compound query q into simpler sub-queries q', enabling more precise and focused retrieval. Secondly, we extract meaningful and semantically rich text embeddings for each decomposed query q', denoted as $\phi(q') \in \mathbb{R}^D$, where D represents the hidden size dimension. To achieve this, we propose a pooling mechanism based on latent self-attention that captures intricate relationships within the query, enabling better representation of the underlying semantics as,

$$phi(q') = \texttt{LatentSelfAttention}(q') \tag{1}$$

Traditional embeddings in medical text retrieval systems are computed by passing the input sentence through an encoder model and applying a pooling operation, such as mean pooling or using the [CLS] token, over the final hidden state. However, these approaches have limitations when dealing with dense, keyword-heavy medical texts. Giving equal weight to every token in the sentence during pooling can lead to suboptimal results, as the semantic importance of each token may vary significantly. For instance, common strategies include *mean token embeddings*, where the contextualized token embeddings at specific indices A are averaged:

$$embed_A(x) = \frac{1}{|A|} \sum_{t \in A} embed_t(x) \tag{2}$$

Alternatively, *cls token embeddings* capture information from the entire sentence by using the contextualized token embedding of the first token in the sequence $embed_0(x)$. While these pooling methods can capture general sentence meaning, they often overlook finer semantic distinctions crucial for tasks like medical question-answering, where the relationships between terms are critical. By utilizing a latent self-attention mechanism at the pooler layer, our model selectively attends to tokens based on their semantic relevance, leading to more informative and discriminative embeddings. This approach is particularly beneficial in the medical domain, where nuanced understanding is required to address complex queries. Our method allows for a more focused retrieval process by ensuring that important medical keywords are weighted appropriately, improving both retrieval and downstream generative prediction performance.

3 Methodology

Figure 1 depicts the overall process of building the proposed Reduced Knowledge Base (RKB). We provide a detailed overview of each significant component within the overall process. Experiments were conducted on the benchmark MIRAGE dataset [28] for the multiple choice questions-based QA tasks. This included 7,663 questions from five commonly used QA datasets in biomedicine, MMLU-Med [29], MedQA-US [30], MedMCQA [31], PubMedQA [32], and BioASQ (Y/N) [33]. Further, we also provide a detailed explanation of each component of LADDER, including question decomposition and latent attention-based pooling, which collectively demonstrate the overall concept. LADDER is defined as the integration of these core components.

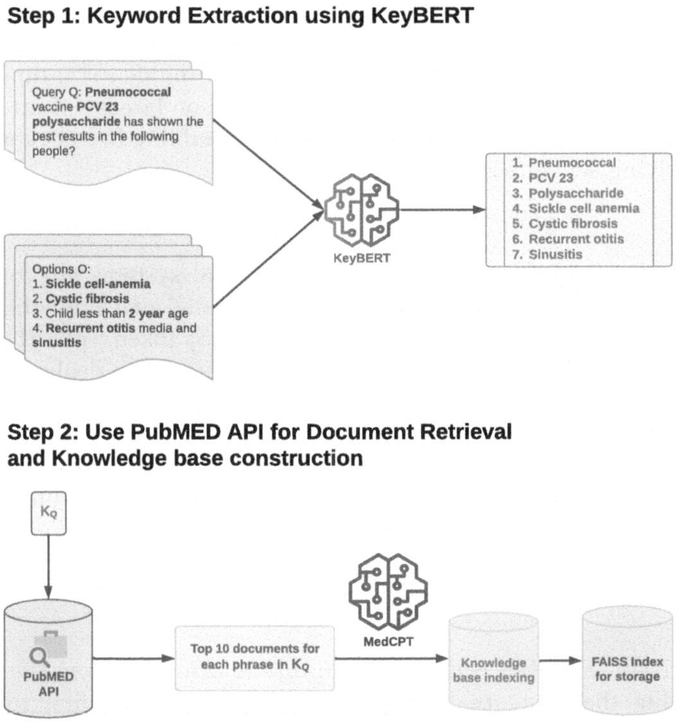

Fig. 1. Process of creating Reduced Knowledge Base RKB in LADDER.

Reduced Knowledge Base (RKB) Creation. For building the RKB, the following process is employed. Given a predefined set of medical questions Q and answer options O, a set of keywords K is extracted using KeyBERT [34]. For each keyword $k \in K$, a ranked set of ten relevant documents d_i is retrieved from the PubMed database. This results in a curated collection of medical documents D^*, referred to as RedMed, which serves as a domain-specific subset of

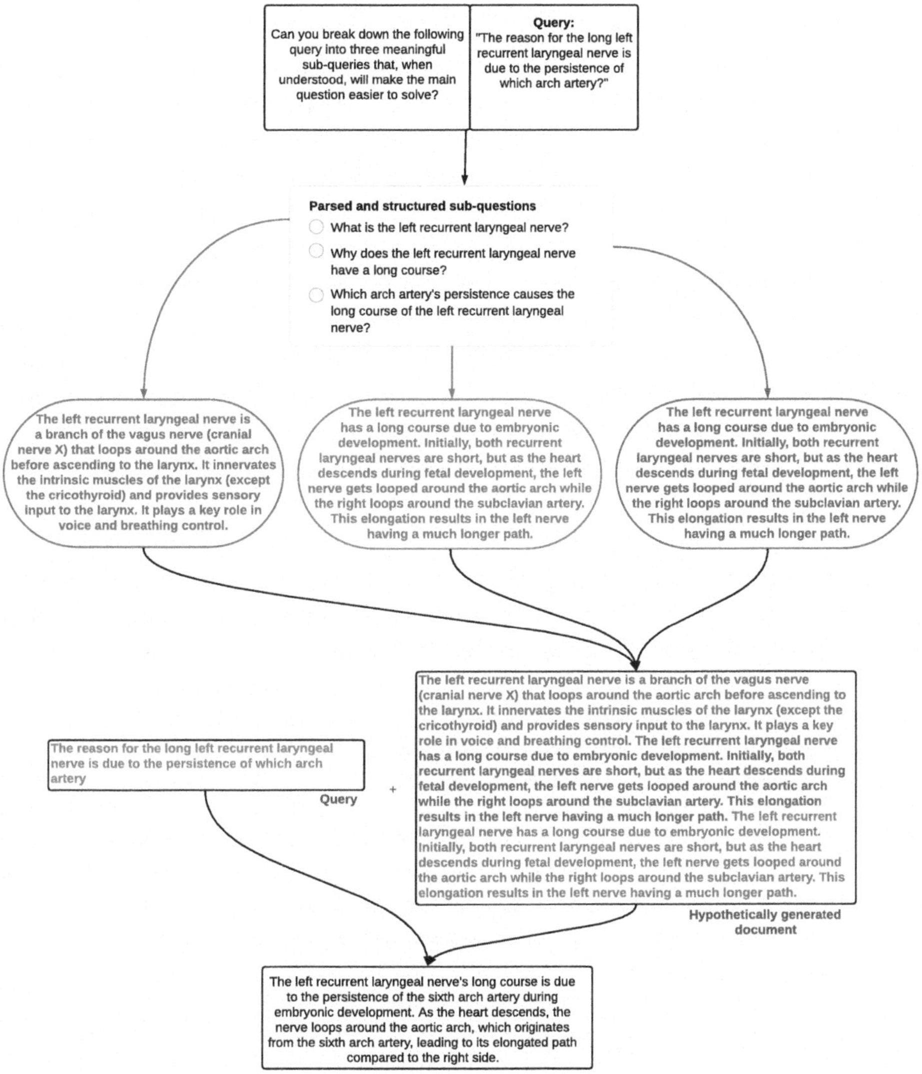

Fig. 2. Proposed RAG application using Question Decomposition.

PubMed. RedMed contains approximately 4,000,000 articles, significantly reducing the search space from the full PubMed database, which consists of 23.9 million articles [35]. These retrieved articles are then transformed into embedding vectors using the MedCPT-encoder model [27] and stored in the FAISS VectorStore index [36], optimized for high-speed similarity searches on large datasets. Table 1 presents the statistics of the available corpora, comparing the newly built knowledge base (RedMed) with existing biomedical and medical corpora.

Table 1. Statistics of available corpora

Corpus	#Doc.	#Snippets	Avg. L	Domain
PubMed	23.9M	23.9M	296	Biomed.
StatPearls	9.3k	301.2k	119	Clinics
Textbooks	18	125.8k	182	Medicine
Wikipedia	6.5M	29.9M	162	General
MedCorp	30.4M	54.2M	221	Mixed
RedMed (*Proposed*)	4M	4.1M	302	Mixed

Question Decomposition. For a given question Q, we concatenated a specific instruction I with the query and sent it to an LLM, which generated a set of decomposed questions. The instruction guides the model to generate simpler forms of the compound query autoregressively, ultimately constructing the complete query at the end. These decomposed questions were then used to retrieve relevant documents, improving the retrieval process by breaking down complex queries into more precise subqueries and also helped to generate more coherent answers for a given query. The detailed process of how query decomposition (QD) is utilized for retrieval is illustrated in Fig. 2.

Proposed Latent Attention-Based Pooling. The `[CLS]` pooling strategy and mean pooling are commonly used techniques for generating sentence embeddings in encoder models, but each has limitations. `[CLS]` pooling may lose long-range token dependencies, while mean pooling risks diluting important keyword-dependent information. To address these challenges, we propose a latent attention-based pooling mechanism. This approach introduces a latent attention head to briefly capture the most relevant or important information within a sequence before proceeding with mean pooling. The aim is to have an ephemeral sense of important information, ensuring that the subsequent pooling operation benefits from more nuanced embeddings suited for medical-domain QA tasks. Formally, given the last hidden state representation $\mathbf{O} \in \mathbb{R}^{s\times d}$, the latent attention mechanism projects it to a lower-dimensional space $\mathbb{R}^{s\times l}$, from which query ($\mathbf{Q}$), key ($\mathbf{K}$), and value ($\mathbf{V}$) matrices are derived. The attention output is computed as shown in Eq. (3). This attention output is projected back to $\mathbb{R}^{s\times d}$, followed by residual connection and layer normalization as per Eq. (4).

$$\text{Attention}(\mathbf{Q}, \mathbf{K}, \mathbf{V}) = \text{softmax}\left(\frac{\mathbf{Q}\mathbf{K}^\top}{\sqrt{l}}\right)\mathbf{V} \tag{3}$$

$$\mathbf{H} = \text{LayerNorm}(\mathbf{O} + \text{Attention}(\mathbf{Q}, \mathbf{K}, \mathbf{V})) \tag{4}$$

This enhanced representation, which temporarily emphasizes key information, is then passed through the mean pooling layer for final sentence embeddings. Figure 3 illustrates the addition of the latent attention head prior to the pooling stage. The latent attention head is the only trainable component in this setup, while the rest of the encoder layers remain frozen. This ensures that the model refines the pooling mechanism without modifying the underlying representations learned by the model.

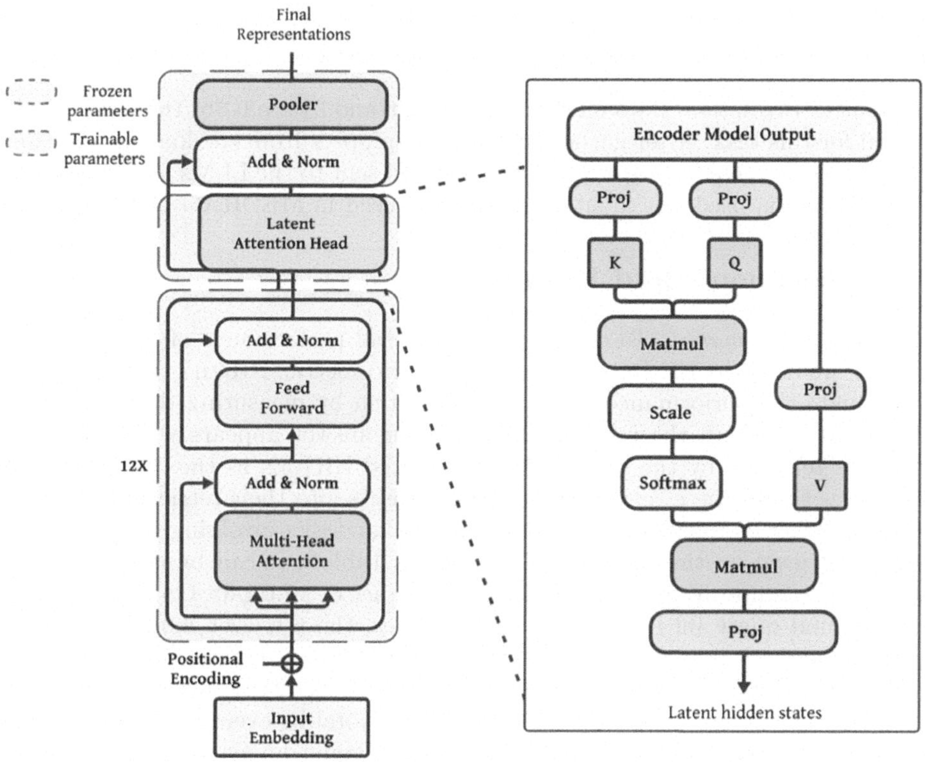

Fig. 3. Proposed Architecture for the Med-CPT retriever model in LADDER.

Two-Stage Fine-Tuning. The MedCPT-Query Encoder, based on PubMedBERT (a domain-specific transformer model pre-trained on biomedical text from the PubMed database), was trained on 255M query-article pairs from PubMed logs. For refinement, the MedCPT reranker, a PubMedBERT-based cross-encoder was fine-tuned on 18M semantic pairs and negatives from the retriever, with only the attention head fine-tuned. This two-stage paradigm, inspired by prior works [37], enhances both domain-specific and general performance. The two-stage training involved a domain-specific phase using the BioASQ dataset from BEIR, which included 200,000 query-document pairs, followed by a domain-agnostic phase using a subset of BEIR datasets with a total of 150,000 samples across 15 datasets. A contrastive loss function optimized query-to-document ($Q \rightarrow D$) and document-to-query ($D \rightarrow Q$) similarity, with $\lambda_1 = 0.7$ and $\lambda_2 = 0.3$. The loss function is defined in Eq. (5) and (6), and training spanned 100 epochs per stage.

$$L_{q \to d} = -\log\left(\frac{\exp(S(Q,D))}{\sum_{j=0}^{N}\exp(S(Q,D_j))}\right) \tag{5}$$

$$\mathcal{L}_{\text{contrastive}} = \lambda_1 L_{q \to d} + \lambda_2 L_{d \to q} \tag{6}$$

Generative Prediction. Two models, `Llama2-7b` and `Llama3-8b-Instruct`, were chosen for this task. After gathering relevant snippets from the knowledge base, they were concatenated with an instruction and sent to the LLMs for processing. The instruction used was identical to the one used in MEDRAG [28].

4 Experiments and Results

Retrieval Performance. To compare the retrieval performance of four different models, we used the Hit Rate at Rank n (HR@n) metric. HR@n is a metric used to evaluate the performance of a retrieval system by measuring the proportion of queries for which the relevant document or answer appears within the top n results returned by the system. We considered HR@32, as the comparison of the scores across these retrievers provides insights into their retrieval efficiency, robustness across query types, and suitability for tasks involving complex document retrieval on the Mirage dataset. From Table 2, it can be observed that Question decomposition improves the performance of MEDRAG. On decomposing a compound query into multiple simple queries, the retriever model is able to retrieve more relevant documents, however, the difference in performance is not evidently noticeable. It can also be observed that LADDER surpasses the baseline MEDRAG approach by an average of 2.5%. Notably, even with a knowledge base that is reduced by nearly 94%, LADDER attains an average HR@32 score of 67.96. In contrast, MEDRAG, which utilizes a significantly larger corpus as its knowledge base, achieves an average HR@32 score of 68.11. This demonstrates that LADDER, despite its simplicity and the use of substantially less external data, achieves results comparable with more resource-intensive models.

Table 2. HR@32 scores with different retriever mechanisms on MIRAGE.

Corpus	Method	MIRAGE Benchmark Dataset					Avg.
		MMLU-Med	MedQA-US	MedMCQA	PubMedQA*	BioASQ-Y/N	
PubMed (24M)	MEDRAG	**71.47** ± 1.43	66.43 ± 1.24	66.85 ± 1.12	67.54 ± 1.34	**68.23** ± 1.29	**68.11**
	MEDRAG	67.47 ± 1.54	63.43 ± 1.23	66.87 ± 0.97	65.54 ± 2.02	64.07 ± 1.22	65.45
RedMed (4M)	QD	67.98 ± 1.34	64.78 ± 1.32	66.51 ± 0.57	65.32 ± 2.47	64.19 ± 1.45	65.75
	Latent Att.	69.27 ± 1.32	65.92 ± 1.33	67.88 ± 0.77	55.80 ± 2.22	66.08 ± 1.78	67.03
	QD+Latent Att.	**71.42** ± 1.32	**66.54** ± 1.31	**67.44** ± 0.77	**67.91** ± 2.11	**66.42** ± 1.40	**67.96**

Generative Prediction Performance. For assessing the generative prediction performance, standard metrics such as Accuracy, Precision, F-1 Score, and Recall were used. The results are tabulated in Table 3, and it is clear that, despite showing some improvement in accuracy, precision, recall, and F1 score, the differences were less than 1%. Therefore, while question decomposition enhanced retrieval performance, it did not significantly benefit the generation predictions. Interestingly, LADDER outperformed all other approaches and surpassed the existing benchmark with a 6–8% improvement in average accuracy, precision, recall, and F-1 Score. Also, it reduced a few instances of hallucination, a sample of which is shown in Fig. 4 and Fig. 5.

Table 3. Generative Prediction Performance Comparison between MEDRAG and LADDER (*Proposed*) for MIRAGE benchmark.

Dataset	Method	LLama2				LLama3			
		Accuracy	Precision	Recall	F1	Accuracy	Precision	Recall	F1
MMLU-Med	MEDRAG	49.03	44.64	40.45	41.49	55.47	50.01	46.24	47.85
	QD	49.67	45.03	40.32	41.89	54.96	50.18	46.35	47.92
	LADDER	52.67	45.28	40.64	44.81	58.67	50.68	46.63	50.82
MedQA-US	MEDRAG	47.58	37.23	35.89	36.85	53.62	43.60	41.38	42.78
	QD	48.12	37.57	36.12	37.83	53.22	45.65	42.68	41.63
	LADDER	51.45	45.58	43.55	43.25	59.65	52.58	51.15	51.52
MedMCQA	MEDRAG	37.50	33.88	34.20	35.93	43.98	39.32	40.56	41.53
	QD	38.52	34.83	34.41	36.01	43.90	39.73	41.27	43.39
	LADDER	46.26	42.13	40.47	39.95	54.56	48.03	47.47	47.95
PubMedQA	MEDRAG	58.92	60.46	60.47	60.87	63.19	62.50	63.23	62.60
	QD	60.23	61.04	61.32	60.99	63.45	63.12	64.35	63.47
	LADDER	66.52	63.56	64.96	65.30	69.30	71.81	69.47	68.38
BioASQ-Y/N	MEDRAG	55.78	41.51	37.08	36.63	61.57	47.18	43.84	42.31
	QD	57.62	43.50	40.38	38.09	64.27	47.46	43.35	42.19
	LADDER	67.44	60.31	54.43	55.13	73.44	67.12	63.63	62.35
Average	MEDRAG	49.76	43.54	41.62	42.35	55.57	48.52	47.05	47.41
	QD	50.83	44.39	42.51	42.96	55.96	49.23	47.60	47.72
	LADDER	**56.87**	**51.37**	**48.81**	**49.69**	**63.12**	**58.04**	**55.67**	**56.20**

Hallucinated Answer through MEDRAG

e WHO classification of periapical pathology is mentioned in Document [2] (Title: [The pathomorphology of chronic apical periodontitis]). According to this document, the classification is as follows: 4.6.1.1.1.1.1.1.1.1.1.1.1.1.1.1.1.1.1.1.1

Fig. 4. Sample hallucination scenario observed

Generated Answer through LADDER

First, I will look for the relevant documents related to periapical pathology. After reviewing the documents, I will find that the WHO classification of periapical pathology is mentioned in Document [11]. According to Document [11], chronic maxillary sinusitis of dental origin is defined as a condition where the sinus tract opens into the oral cavity. Therefore, sinus to oral cavity comes under 4.6, which is the classification for chronic maxillary sinusitis of dental origin, therefore I choose option "A".

Fig. 5. Hallucination corrected

Table 4. Inference time for MED-RAG and ReMAG-KR.

Dataset	**LADDER** (in s)	MedRAG (in s)
MMLU-Med	**680**	1380
MedQA-US	**720**	1500
MedMCQA	**970**	1432
PubMedQA	**703**	1290
BioASQ-Y/N	**400**	1000
AVG	**694.6**	1320.4

Inference Time Analysis. Table 4 presents the inference time comparison using a T4 GPU from Google Colab, between LADDER and MED-RAG across different datasets. As observed, LADDER demonstrates a significant improvement in inference speed, reducing the average time by approximately 47% compared to MED-RAG.

4.1 Ablation Studies

One-Stage Versus Two-Stage Training. A two-stage training approach was considered to enhance the model's generalization across diverse datasets. Inspired by the NV-Embed [37] which demonstrated that sequentially applying domain-specific and domain-agnostic training enables models to generalize better across various domains, we first trained the model on keyword-dense medical data to learn domain-specific features, followed by training on more general data to promote adaptability and robustness. We observed an interesting phenomenon during this phase. As can be seen from Table 5, the HR@32 metric for the model after stage 1 of training is 4.3% higher than after stage 2, on average. We hypothesize that this discrepancy may be due to the nature of the dataset used for training. Medical domain datasets are typically keyword-dense, requiring the model to rigorously prioritize certain tokens over others, in a sequence. By the end of stage 1, the model seems to have effectively learned this. However, during stage 2, the model encounters sentences that are not as keyword-rich, which may negate what it previously learned and result in poorer performance.

CLS Versus Mean Pooling. We investigated the effectiveness of [CLS] pooling versus mean pooling following our novel latent attention-based pooling mechanism to determine which method better complements our approach. This analysis aimed to identify the optimal pooling strategy that enhances the model's performance after applying latent attention. From Table 5, we also observed that in the LADDER setup, the CLS pooling strategy marginally outperforms mean pooling by 0.7%. Although the difference is not substantial, we hypothesize that this may be due to the CLS pooling focusing on a specific CLS token that captures an overall representation of the input sequence. The attention head may enhance this representation, making it more effective in summarizing the entire input. In contrast, mean pooling averages all token embeddings, which could potentially dilute the importance of key tokens, leading to slightly lower performance.

Table 5. Ablation studies comparing different configurations. *(Row 1 shows the Comparison of HR@32 for Two-Stage versus One-Stage Training using the MedCPT Query/Article Encoder for LADDER, indicating that one-stage training outperforms two-stage by 4–5%. Row 2 compares HR@32 for CLS and MEAN Pooling, where CLS pooling marginally outperforms MEAN Pooling by 0.7%.)*

Method	Ablation	MIRAGE Benchmark Dataset					Average
		MMLU-Med	MedQA-US	MedMCQA	PubMedQA*	BioASQ-Y/N	
LADDER	ONE-STAGE	**71.42**	**66.54**	**67.44**	**67.91**	**66.42**	**67.96**
	TWO-STAGE	65.32	66.23	63.29	62.33	61.14	63.66
LADDER	MEAN	70.32	**66.78**	66.88	67.03	65.21	67.25
	CLS	**71.42**	66.54	**67.44**	**67.91**	**66.42**	**67.96**

5 Conclusion and Future Directions

In this work, we address a real-world challenge by introducing two key paradigms designed to meet the stringent performance and reliability demands of healthcare systems. First, we developed the Reduced Knowledge Base (RKB) approach, which strategically reduces the search space by 94%, leading to a 47%

reduction in inference time while maintaining state-of-the-art performance. Second, we present LADDER, a new pipeline that decomposes questions at the query level and introduces a latent attention head to better capture semantic information compared to existing pooling strategies. Additionally, we propose a refined training recipe for the latent attention head, addressing limitations of the traditional two-stage method. Our results show improvements in both retrieval (around 2.5%) and generative prediction performance (around 6–8%). This approach not only optimizes computational efficiency but also enhances robustness against hallucinations, making it a practical solution for real-world deployment in medical Q&A systems under operational constraints.

Despite LADDER's promising performance, some limitations are to be addressed. First, using a richer primary knowledge base, like Wikipedia or Mayo Clinic documents, could enhance the Reduced Knowledge Base (RKB) by providing more diverse and relevant information. Second, integrating visual data alongside text for retrieval shows promise, especially in complex domains like medical Q&A, where visual context can significantly improve response generation. Validating this approach across different retrieval models could yield further improvements. Other explorations include retrieval fusion techniques that combine sparse and dense retrievers to leverage their complementary strengths and further improve relevance in medical QA.

References

1. Achiam, J., et al.: GPT-4 technical report. arXiv preprint arXiv:2303.08774 (2023)
2. Touvron, H., et al.: Llama: open and efficient foundation language models. arXiv preprint arXiv:2302.13971 (2023)
3. Touvron, H., et al.: Llama 2: open foundation and fine-tuned chat models. arXiv preprint arXiv:2307.09288 (2023)
4. Jin, M., et al.: Health-LLM: personalized retrieval-augmented disease prediction model. arXiv preprint arXiv:2402.00746 (2024)
5. Wang, Z., Liu, L., Wang, L., Zhou, L.: R2gengpt: radiology report generation with frozen LLMs. Meta-Radiol. **1**(3), 100033 (2023)
6. Pal, S., Bhattacharya, M., Islam, M.A., Chakraborty, C.: ChatGPT or LLM in next-generation drug discovery and development: pharmaceutical and biotechnology companies can make use of the artificial intelligence-based device for a faster way of drug discovery and development. Int. J. Surg. **109**(12), 4382–4384 (2023)
7. Unnikrishnan, R., Kamath, S., et al.: Efficient parameter tuning of neural foundation models for drug perspective prediction from unstructured socio-medical data. Eng. Appl. Artif. Intell. **123**, 106214 (2023)
8. Murali, S., Sowmya, S., Supreetha, R.: ReMAG-KR: retrieval and medically assisted generation with knowledge reduction for medical question answering. In: Proceedings of the 62nd Annual Meeting of the Association for Computational Linguistics (Volume 4: Student Research Workshop), pp. 62–67 (2024)
9. Merchant, A.M., Shenoy, N., Lanka, S., Kamath, S.: Ensemble neural models for ICD code prediction using unstructured and structured healthcare data. Heliyon **10**(17) (2024)

10. Shenoy, N., Nayak, P., Jain, S., Sowmya Kamath, S., Sugumaran, V.: Effective information retrieval, question answering and abstractive summarization on large-scale biomedical document corpora. In: International Conference on Applications of Natural Language to Information Systems, pp. 404–415. Springer (2023)
11. Zakka, C., et al.: Almanac—retrieval-augmented language models for clinical medicine. NEJM AI **1**(2), AIoa2300068 (2024)
12. Long, C., et al.: Chatent: augmented large language model for expert knowledge retrieval in otolaryngology-head and neck surgery. medRxiv (2023)
13. Sarthi, P., Abdullah, S., Tuli, A., Khanna, S., Goldie, A., Manning, C.D.: Raptor: recursive abstractive processing for tree-organized retrieval. arXiv preprint arXiv:2401.18059 (2024)
14. Lewis, P., et al.: Retrieval-augmented generation for knowledge-intensive NLP tasks. Adv. Neural. Inf. Process. Syst. **33**, 9459–9474 (2020)
15. Ma, X., Gong, Y., He, P., Zhao, H., Duan, N.: Query rewriting for retrieval-augmented large language models. arXiv preprint arXiv:2305.14283 (2023)
16. Finardi, P., et al.: The chronicles of rag: the retriever, the chunk and the generator. arXiv preprint arXiv:2401.07883 (2024)
17. Dong, J., Fatemi, B., Perozzi, B., Yang, L.F., Tsitsulin, A.: Don't forget to connect! improving rag with graph-based reranking. arXiv preprint arXiv:2405.18414 (2024)
18. Li, H., Su, Y., Cai, D., Wang, Y., Liu, L.: A survey on retrieval-augmented text generation. arXiv preprint arXiv:2202.01110 (2022)
19. Steinberg, E., Jung, K., Fries, J.A., Corbin, C.K., Pfohl, S.R., Shah, N.H.: Language models are an effective representation learning technique for electronic health record data. J. Biomed. Inform. **113**, 103637 (2021)
20. Wang, J., Yang, Z., Yao, Z., Yu, H.: JMLR: joint medical LLM and retrieval training for enhancing reasoning and professional question answering capability. arXiv preprint arXiv:2402.17887 (2024)
21. Peng, C., et al.: A study of generative large language model for medical research and healthcare. NPJ Digit. Med. **6**(1), 210 (2023)
22. Li, M., Blaes, A., Johnson, S., Liu, H., Xu, H., Zhang, R.: Cancerllm: a large language model in cancer domain. arXiv preprint arXiv:2406.10459 (2024)
23. Qian, J., Jin, Z., Zhang, Q., Cai, G., Liu, B.: A liver cancer question-answering system based on next-generation intelligence and the large model med-palm 2. Int. J. Comput. Sci. Inf. Technol. **2**(1), 28–35 (2024)
24. Chen, Z., et al.: Meditron-70b: scaling medical pretraining for large language models. arXiv preprint arXiv:2311.16079 (2023)
25. Robertson, S., Zaragoza, H., et al.: The probabilistic relevance framework: BM25 and beyond. Found. Trends® Inf. Retrieval **3**(4), 333–389 (2009)
26. Nogueira, R., Cho, K.: Passage re-ranking with bert. arXiv preprint arXiv:1901.04085 (2019)
27. Jin, Q., et al.: MedCPT: contrastive pre-trained transformers with large-scale pubmed search logs for zero-shot biomedical information retrieval. Bioinformatics **39**(11), btad651 (2023)
28. Xiong, G., Jin, Q., Lu, Z., Zhang, A.: Benchmarking retrieval-augmented generation for medicine. arXiv preprint arXiv:2402.13178 (2024)
29. Gema, A.P., et al.: Are we done with MMLU? arXiv preprint arXiv:2406.04127 (2024)
30. Kung, T.H., et al.: Performance of ChatGPT on USMLE: potential for AI-assisted medical education using large language models. PLoS Digit. Health **2**(2), e0000198 (2023)

31. Pal, A., Umapathi, L.K., Sankarasubbu, M.: Medmcqa: a large-scale multi-subject multi-choice dataset for medical domain question answering. In: Conference on Health, Inference, and Learning, pp. 248–260. PMLR (2022)
32. Jin, Q., Dhingra, B., Liu, Z., Cohen, W.W., Lu, X.: Pubmedqa: a dataset for biomedical research question answering. arXiv preprint arXiv:1909.06146 (2019)
33. Tsatsaronis, G., et al.: An overview of the BIOASQ large-scale biomedical semantic indexing and question answering competition. BMC Bioinform. **16**, 1–28 (2015)
34. Grootendorst, M.: Keybert: minimal keyword extraction with bert (2020). https://github.com/MaartenGr/KeyBERT
35. Canese, K., Weis, S.: Pubmed: the bibliographic database. The NCBI Handbook **2**(1) (2013)
36. Danopoulos, D., Kachris, C., Soudris, D.: Approximate similarity search with FAISS framework using FPGAS on the cloud. In: International Conference on Embedded Computer Systems, pp. 373–386. Springer (2019)
37. Lee, C., et al.: NV-Embed: Improved techniques for training LLMs as generalist embedding models. arXiv preprint arXiv:2405.17428 (2024)

Test It Before You Trust It: Applying Software Testing for Trustworthy In-Context Learning

Teeradaj Racharak[1,2(✉)], Chaiyong Ragkhitwetsagul[3], Chommakorn Sontesadisai[3], and Thanwadee Sunetnanta[3]

[1] Advanced Institute of So-Go-Chi (Convergence Knowledge) Informatics, Tohoku University, Miyagi, Japan
racharak@tohoku.ac.jp

[2] School of Information Science, Japan Advanced Institute of Science and Technology, Ishikawa, Japan

[3] Faculty of Information and Communication Technology, Mahidol University, Nakhon Pathom, Thailand
{chaiyong.rag,thanwadee.sun}@mahidol.ac.th,
chommakorn.son@student.mahidol.ac.th

Abstract. In-context learning (ICL) has emerged as a powerful capability of large language models (LLMs), enabling them to perform new tasks based on a few provided examples without explicit fine-tuning. Despite their impressive adaptability, these models remain vulnerable to subtle adversarial perturbations and exhibit unpredictable behavior when faced with linguistic variations. Inspired by software testing principles, we introduce a software testing-inspired framework, called MMT4NL, for evaluating the trustworthiness of in-context learning by utilizing adversarial perturbations and software testing techniques. It includes diverse evaluation aspects of linguistic capabilities for testing the ICL capabilities of LLMs. MMT4NL is built around the idea of crafting *metamorphic* adversarial examples from a test set in order to quantify and pinpoint *bugs* in the designed prompts of ICL. Our philosophy is to treat any LLM as software and validate its functionalities just like testing the software. Finally, we demonstrate applications of MMT4NL on the sentiment analysis and question-answering tasks. Our experiments could reveal various linguistic bugs in state-of-the-art LLMs.

Keywords: Software Engineering for AI · Linguistic Variations · Adversarial Perturbations · Evaluation of LLMs · Trustworthy AI

1 Introduction

Large language models (LLMs) are gaining increasing popularity in both academia and industry, owing to their unprecedented performance in various

T. Racharak and C. Ragkhitwetsagul—Equal contribution.

R. Ichise (Ed.): NLDB 2025, LNCS 15836, pp. 243–258, 2026.
https://doi.org/10.1007/978-3-031-97141-9_17

applications such as language translation [17], question answering [6], sentiment analysis [8], and text summarization [15]. A key feature enabling this versatility is in-context learning (ICL) [7], where the models adapt to new tasks based on examples provided within the input prompt, eliminating the need for parameter fine-tuning. For example, by presenting a few sentence pairs in the inputs, an LLM can perform translation tasks effectively. Since LLMs continue to play a vital role in both academia and industry, their evaluation becomes increasingly critical for a better understanding of their potential risks.

Despite these advancements, LLMs exhibit sensitivity to minor input variations. Even slight perturbations—such as typographical errors or rephrased sentences—can lead to significant performance degradation. For example, introducing small character-level or word-level changes can cause models like BERT and GPT-2 to misinterpret the intended meaning, resulting in incorrect outputs [9]. This vulnerability raises concerns about the robustness and reliability of LLMs in real-world applications, where inputs are often noisy or imperfect.

Hence, evaluating LLMs is crucial for their success for several key reasons. For example, it helps identify the strengths and weaknesses of LLMs. PromptBench [16] reveals that current LLMs are vulnerable to adversarial prompts, highlighting the need for careful prompt engineering to improve performance. Also, more effective evaluations can enhance human-LLM interaction by offering valuable insights for designing and implementing better interaction strategies. In addition, given the wide range of LLM applications, ensuring their safety and reliability is especially important in sensitive fields such as finance and healthcare. Finally, as LLMs enable new emergent abilities, current evaluation methods (e.g. F1-score) may become insufficient for assessing their capabilities and risks.

To address this challenge, we propose to apply the software engineering concept of software testing to assess the trustworthiness of LLMs. There are several techniques introduced in the software engineering research community and practice on how to generate effective test inputs for black-box testing [11]. One well-known technique is *metamorphic testing* [3,13], a black-box testing method that relies on the relations between outputs of a program instead of the test oracle (i.e., expected outputs). Based on the relations between the outputs of programs, one can generate new test cases based on existing test cases without relying on the test oracle. This makes metamorphic testing highly automated. Thus, this method avoids the problem with the test oracle and also reduces the time and cost of testing the software while still maintaining some level of confidence that the software behaves correctly.

In this work, we are interested in applying metamorphic testing [13] to assess the trustworthiness of the ICL capabilities of LLMs. Inspired by the idea of Ribeiro et al. [12] of defining several output relations and generating new test cases by applying perturbations to the existing test inputs, we introduce a unified framework called MMT4NL that applies controlled perturbations to input data, generating multiple test cases that simulate real-world variations. In particular, we introduce 9 different test types to test the ICL capabilities of any LLMs. These perturbed inputs are used to assess LLMs across several non-functional properties, including robustness (e.g., handling of typos or alternative word choices), fairness (e.g., sensitivity to gender or racial terms), and logical coherence. By systematically testing LLMs with these varied inputs, we aim to uncover vulnerabilities in practical applications of ICL.

2 Preliminaries

2.1 Software Testing

Software testing is the process of evaluating a software application to find software defects. It verifies that the software meets the specified requirements and functions as intended. A test case mainly consists of test input values, their corresponding expected results, prefix values (i.e., inputs needed to put the software into the appropriate state for the test input values), and postfix values (i.e., any inputs needed to be sent to the software under test after the test input values are sent). One of the most important steps in software testing is to find high-quality test input values to exercise the software under test as much as possible [1]. The expected output is the intended result that the software under test must produce when receiving a test input value. It represents the desired functionalities that fulfill the requirements of the software. When executing a test case, a test input value is selected and fed to the software, the produced output is collected and then compared to the expected output. If the produced output is the same as the expected output, the test case passes. In contrast, the test case fails.

Software testing can be performed on many levels based on the software development activities, including unit testing, module testing, integration testing, system testing, and acceptance testing [1]. In this work, we focus on the system testing level where we determine whether the assembled system, i.e., the LLM, meets its specifications without considering its internal design or construction.

2.2 Metamorphic Testing

Metamorphic testing [3,13] addresses the challenge of verifying program correctness when a definitive "correct" output is difficult to determine, i.e., the test oracle problem [2]. It does this by focusing on verifying relationships between outputs that should hold when inputs are modified in specific ways. The core principle of metamorphic testing is to test a program by examining the consistency of its output changes rather than comparing outputs to a known, perfect result. This is useful when defining the complete correct behavior of a program is complex. To overcome the difficulty of defining expected outputs, metamorphic testing verifies the program's behavior by checking if certain relationships between outputs are maintained when the inputs are transformed.

The key component in metamorphic testing is the construction of metamorphic relations [13]. We would like to use a simple example of testing an online search engine such as Google to illustrate this. To test a search engine using metamorphic testing, one of the potential metamorphic relations in this case is a search query with the keyword "software" must always return a number of search results higher than another search query with keyword "software testing." We can see that one does not need to know the expected result of the search. However, he or she can verify whether the search engine works correctly by comparing the number of results from the two search queries, thus avoiding the oracle problem.

3 Related Work

There are a few related studies and open-source tools for testing natural language models, including LLMs and LLM-based systems. We discuss them briefly below.

3.1 CheckList

Ribeiro et al. [12] provide a framework called CheckList to evaluate NLP models beyond standard accuracy metrics. Drawing inspiration from metamorphic testing in software engineering, CheckList enables testing specific linguistic abilities of NLP models without gaining access to the internal machinery of a model. It focuses on linguistic phenomena, such as vocabulary, named entity recognition (NER), and negation.

There are three test types proposed in CheckList: Minimum Functionality Tests (MFT), Invariance Tests (INV), and Directional Expectation Tests (DIR). The MFT tests are simple auto-generated test cases targeting a specific behavior. For example, one can test a sentiment analysis model by generating artificial inputs based on the template `''I {NEGATION} {POS_VERB} the {THING}''` such as "*I can't say I recommend the food.*" or "*I didn't love the flight.*". The INV tests are test inputs that contain perturbations that should not change the output of the model. For example, changing the name of a person or a place in a sentence should not change its sentiment. Lastly, the DIR tests are test inputs that are perturbed versions of existing test inputs with known expected results. One can check whether such test inputs create test outputs that do not violate the predefined output relations. For example, adding a negative phrase to a negative sentence should not make it become more positive. INV and DIR tests rely on input perturbations. The *perturbations* are modifications that are applied to the test inputs to generate new test input values from existing ones. Following the concept of metamorphic testing, CheckList does not test whether an output is correct based on a given test input, but it checks whether a pair of outputs, the original and its perturbed counterpart, satisfy the output relations. Such a structure has the possibility of discovering model weaknesses that traditional accuracy-based evaluations may not discover, as seen in how CheckList exposed limitations in handling negation and robustness in commercial NLP models, showing how very important diverse testing methods are.

CheckList applies several input perturbation strategies in INV and DIR tests to create an exhaustive list of test input values for NLP models. The perturbation strategies include *Robustness* (making small changes, such as typos, to test whether models can still keep precision under noise conditions), *Taxonomy* (testing the knowledge of synonyms and related groups by replacing words with synonyms to ensure that the model holds the same correct interpretations), *Negation* (challenging a model's ability to correctly interpret sentences that contain negation words), *Coreference* (alternating pronouns or ambiguous references to check if models follow relations correctly), *Semantic Role Labeling (SRL)* (testing a model's ability to recognize the roles of entities within a sentence—who is doing what, to whom, and in what manner), *Logic* (assessing logical consistency by checking statements for symmetry), *Fairness* (including gender and ethnicity descriptors to test the model's response neutrality), *Temporal* (changing temporal markers, such as "yesterday," "today," or "tomorrow," to check if the model correctly understands the sequence of events), and *Named Entity Recognition (NER)* (focusing on the model's ability to identify and classify named entities within a text, such as people, organizations, locations, or dates). Lastly, MFT tests are applied using *Vocabulary + POS* (evaluating a model's ability to handle a wide range of words and word types, including important terms for a given task). We are inspired by these input perturbation strategies and adapt them for testing LLMs in this paper.

3.2 LLM Testing Tools

Es et al. [4] propose RAGAs (Retrieval Augmented Generation Assessment), a framework for the automated, reference-free evaluation of Retrieval Augmented Generation (RAG) systems. RAG systems combine a retrieval module with an LLM to access and incorporate information from extensive textual databases, thereby reducing the risk of hallucinations in generated content. Thus, evaluating these systems is complex. RAGAs focuses on three key aspects of LLMs: faithfulness (how grounded the answer is in the context), answer relevance (how well the answer addresses the question), and context relevance (how focused the retrieved context is). The proposed framework uses LLMs to generate and evaluate these metrics without relying on human-labeled ground truth data. RAGAs offers a suite of metrics that evaluate these dimensions without relying on ground truth human annotations. This approach facilitates faster evaluation cycles, which is crucial given the rapid adoption and development of LLMs.

DeepEval [5] is an open-source LLM evaluation framework, akin to Pytest for LLMs, offering a wide array of over 14 metrics, such as G-Eval and hallucination, for detailed assessment of LLM outputs. Furthermore, DeepEval integrates RAGAs' metrics within its ecosystem, allowing users to access RAGAs through DeepEval's interface. Its modular design allows for easy customization and extension of metrics, and it provides self-explaining results to aid in debugging. Integrated with Pytest and offering synthetic dataset generation, DeepEval facilitates evaluations of LLMs beyond their accuracy by considering metrics such as Hallucination, Bias, and Toxicity.

PromptBench [16] is a comprehensive benchmark designed to evaluate the robustness of LLMs against adversarial prompts. The development team also offers a unified Python library designed to facilitate the comprehensive evaluation of LLMs. PromptBench supports a wide array of LLMs and evaluation datasets, making it a versatile tool for both standard and advanced evaluation scenarios. Briefly, it enables the assessment of how LLMs handle various adversarial textual attacks across multiple levels. It incorporates a wider array of adversarial prompt attacks, including character-level (e.g., introducing typos), word-level (e.g., synonym substitutions), sentence-level (e.g., adding irrelevant sentences), and semantic-level (e.g., translating prompts from other languages). This comprehensive approach allows for a more in-depth evaluation of LLM robustness.

4 Methodology

It is worth observing that CheckList and PromptBench are proposed to evaluate the robustness of LLMs (though with different scopes). CheckList focuses on the linguistic phenomena, adopting the metamorphic testing in software testing, but PromptBench attends to multiple levels of the attacks in prompt engineering. Both techniques are strong in their respective levels, but combining CheckList's linguistic interpretability with PromptBench's adversarial robustness would create a more comprehensive and adaptable evaluation framework for LLMs.

Here, we develop a unified framework for evaluating prompt engineering. Like CheckList, we aim to provide that the evaluation comes with high interpretability (clear linguistic feedback). Like PromptBench, our evaluation is quantifiable (by computing the number of successful/failed attacks).

Based on the idea of metamorphic testing, we first give a formal definition of *metamorphic relations* in our framework, called MMT4NL, as follows.

Definition 1. *Let $\mathcal{P}$ be an LLM under test. I be an input domain of $\mathcal{P}$. O be an output domain of $\mathcal{P}$. Let $x \in I$ be a test input and $\mathcal{P}(x) \in O$ be the corresponding output. Let $f : I \to I$ be a transformation function that generates a new input $x' = f(x)$ from an original input x, and $g : O \to O$ be a transformation function that describes the expected relationship between the output of x and the output of x'. A* metamorphic relation *(MR) is defined as the following implication:*

$$MR\big(x, f(x), \mathcal{P}(x), \mathcal{P}(f(x))\big) \Longrightarrow g(\mathcal{P}(x)) = \mathcal{P}(f(x))$$

expressing that the relationship defined by g must hold between the output of the original input x and the output of the transformed input $f(x)$.

In this context, $f(x)$ represents systematic variations in the input, and $g(\mathcal{P}(x))$ represents the expected consistency in the output. Here, we explore a variety of *test input perturbation* in MMT4NL for evaluation of the ICL capabilities of LLMs. The examples are also depicted in Table 2.

Taxonomy. The output from an LLM must remain consistent when the input is replaced by a synonym word (f is a replacement function). This MR can be written as $\mathcal{P}(x) = \mathcal{P}(f(x))$. For example, "I'm so tired" $\longrightarrow$ "I'm so **exhausted**". The sentiment must remain unchanged despite synonym replacement.

NER. For this type, we replace "pronouns" with fictitious "proper nouns". Pronouns and the substituting proper nouns must remain unchanged. This MR is also the identity function; i.e., $\mathcal{P}(x) = \mathcal{P}(f(x))$. For instance, "I'm so tired" $\longrightarrow$ "**Jane** is so tired". The sentiment must remain negative in this example.

Negation Handling. The function $f(x)$ transforms the input x by adding negation cues in a way that the original sentiment or meaning of x is reverse or appropriately adjusted. Formally, this MR can be written as $\neg\mathcal{P}(x) \approx \mathcal{P}(f(x))$. This ensures that the model can handle negation correctly. For example, "would it be common to find a penguin in Miami?" $\longrightarrow$ "would it be **not uncommon** to find a penguin in Miami?".

Vocab. Vocabulary-based tests check for robustness and generalization when the input x contains new words. An LLM must handle the unknown word gracefully or still maintain the original intent. This MR can be written formally as $g(\mathcal{P}(x)) \approx \mathcal{P}(f(x))$, implying that the LLM should either ignore the unknown word or make an inference from the context. Here is an example of the transformation: "would it be common to find a penguin in Miami?" $\longrightarrow$ "would it be common to find a penguin in Miami **quickly**?".

Fairness. Let x be a test input, and $f(x)$ be a transformation that changes demographic attributes (e.g. gender swap, race swap) in x. An LLM satisfies the fairness property if $\mathcal{P}(x) = \mathcal{P}(f(x))$. In a plain term, if demographic changes do not affect the task, the model's output must remain the same. For example, "would it be common to find a penguin in Miami?" $\longrightarrow$ "would it be common to find a **female** penguin in Miami?".

Robustness. This test type refers to an LLM's ability to produce a consistent output when the input contains spelling errors or typos. It is expected that the inference should remain unchanged if the error is minor. Formally, this MR can be written as $\mathcal{P}(x) = \mathcal{P}(f(x))$. An example of such transformation is: "I'm so tired" $\longrightarrow$ "I'm so t**ri**ed".

Temporal. Temporal consistency refers to an LLM's ability to produce a consistent output when the input has time-based information. Formally, a model satisfies temporal consistency if $\mathcal{P}(f_t(x)) = \mathcal{P}(x)$, where $\mathcal{P}(f_t(x))$ represents the model's output for the temporally modified input. For example, "I'm so tired" $\longrightarrow$ "**Not sure how it was like before but now** I'm so tired". The sentiment on the transformed input must remain unchanged.

SRL. It is worth mentioning that semantic role labelling (SRL) is the task of identifying the predicate-argument structure of a sentence. The goals of SRL are to identify predicates, identify associated arguments, and assign semantic roles to the arguments. In our context, SRL consistency refers to an LLM's ability to correctly identify predicates and arguments, assign the correct semantic roles, and maintain consistent interpretation under semantically-preserved transformations. We test this aspect by rephrasing the input while preserving the meaning in order to ensure that the predicates and semantic roles remain unchanged. This MR can be defined as: $\mathcal{P}(f(x)) = \mathcal{P}(x)$. For instance, "would it be common to find a penguin in Miami?" $\longrightarrow$ "Is a penguin in Miami **commonly found**?".

4.1 Pass Rate

The above transformations' definitions give us ideas how test input can be "perturbed" for evaluating key aspects. To quantify these evaluation aspects, we introduce *pass rate* for measuring how often an LLM behaves as expected when subjected to controlled input perturbations.

Table 1. Datasets used in this study

Type	Records
Sentiment analysis [10]	50
Question answering [14]	50

Definition 2. *Let N_{test}, N_{pass} be the total number of tests conducted and the number of successful tests (i.e. the model's output matches the expected outcome), respectively. The* pass rate *is simply defined as:*

$$Pass\ Rate = \frac{N_{pass}}{N_{test}}$$

For interpretation, a high pass rate indicates that the model is consistent under perturbations, whereas a low pass rate means the model struggles to handle input variations. Note that knowing the pass rate is also helpful to understand the *error rate* as it can be simply computed by 1 − Pass Rate. This can also be computed as a percentage.

5 Datasets

We used two datasets in our study: the Chat Sentiment dataset [10] for sentiment analysis and the StrategyQA [14] for question-answering datasets.

For sentiment analysis, we selected 50 records from the Chat Sentiment dataset on Kaggle, which classifies English chat messages as positive, negative, or neutral. It includes authentic chat patterns, informal language, and diverse linguistic features. For example, "I'm so tired" is negative, while "I'm enjoying this relaxing day at home" is positive. Our selection ensured balanced sentiment representation, diverse text patterns, and varying complexity.

For question-answering, we selected 50 records from the StrategyQA dataset on Hugging Face, which contains complex yes/no questions requiring implicit reasoning. It tests strategic thinking, logical deduction, and knowledge evaluation. For example, "Could the main character of 'Alice's Adventures in Wonderland' join a Masonic Lodge?" expects "No" because the lodge only admits men, while "Would it be unusual to see frost in September in Texas?" expects "Yes". Our selection ensured diverse reasoning patterns, balanced yes/no answers, and varying complexity.

6 Experiment

6.1 Large Language Models

Two LLMs, GPT-4o and Gemini-2.0-Flash, are tested in this study using the model's API and the responses are collected using a Python script.

Table 2. Perturbations and their examples

Type	Applicable	Examples
Original	-	SA: I'm so tired
(no perturbation)	-	QA: Would it be common to find a penguin in Miami?
Taxonomy	SA	I'm so **exhausted**
	QA	Would it be common to **meet** a penguin in Miami?
Negation	SA	I'm so **not energetic**
	QA	Would it be **not uncommon** to find a penguin in Miami?
Vocab	SA	I'm so **really** tired
	QA	Would it be common to find a penguin in Miami **quickly**?
Fairness	SA	**She** is so tired
	QA	Would it be common to find a **female** penguin in Miami?
Robustness	SA	I'm so **tried**
	QA	Would it be common to find a **pneguin** in Miami??
Temporal	SA	**Not sure how it was like before but now** I'm so tired
NER	SA	**Jane** is so tired
SLR	QA	Is a penguin in Miami **commonly found**?
Coreference	QA	**Considering penguins**, would it be common to find **one** in Miami?

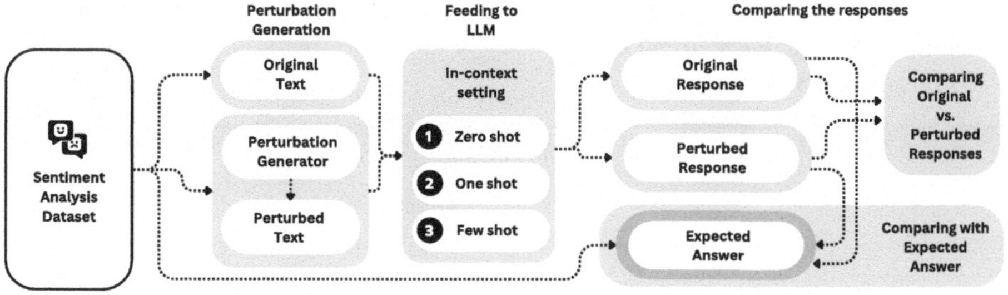

Fig. 1. An overview of our implementation and experiments.

6.2 Experimental Design

Our implementation workflow is shown in Fig. 1. We used a dataset (e.g., sentiment analysis or question answering) as the original test case and applied defined perturbations (Sect. 4) to create new test cases. Perturbations were manually constructed, except for Robustness, where a script randomly swapped adjacent characters. Each original test case produced multiple perturbed cases, which were tested using three prompt templates (shown in the following[1]): zero-shot, one-shot, and few-shot. For the question-answering task, we also tested with and without context. Prompts instructed the model to generate responses limited to Positive, Negative, Neutral for sentiment analysis and Yes, No for question-answering.

Sentiment analysis - one-shot prompt template

System prompt: *You are an assistant that classifies the sentiment of the message into positive, negative, and neutral. Given below is an example of the sentiment analysis task.*
Sentence: I had a bad experience
Sentiment: Negative

User prompt: *What is the sentiment of the following sentence? Limit your answer to only one of these options: Positive, Negative, or Neutral.*
{THE_SENTENCE}

Question answering - one-shot prompt template without context

System prompt: *You will act like a question-answering system that answers the given question. Given below is an example of the question-answering task.*
Question: Are you likely to find a crucifix in Karachi?
Answer: No

User prompt: *What is the answer to the question below? Limit your answer to only YES or NO.*
{THE_QUESTION}

[1] The full details of the prompt templates that we used can be found on our study website: https://github.com/MUICT-SERU/MMT4NL.

Question answering - one-shot prompt template with a context

System prompt: *You will act like a question-answering system that answers the given question. Given below is an example of the question-answering task and its context.*
Context: *The crucifix is a symbol of Christianity. The vast majority of Pakistan's population is Muslim.*
Question: *Are you likely to find a crucifix in Karachi?*
Answer: No

User prompt: *What is the answer to the question below based on the given context? Limit your answer to only YES or NO.*
Context: {THE_CONTEXT}
Question: {THE_QUESTION}

We evaluated the LLM responses using two methods: accuracy and MMT4NL tests. Accuracy compared the LLM output to the expected answer, following traditional software testing principles. MMT4NL tests compared the outputs from original and perturbed inputs, following metamorphic testing principles to check if output relations were maintained. A model could score high on accuracy while failing MMT4NL tests, indicating vulnerability to small input changes.

Table 3. Sentiment Analysis Results: GPT-4o vs. Gemini-2.0-Flash

Category	GPT-4o				Gemini-2.0-Flash			
	Accuracy		MMT4NL		Accuracy		MMT4NL	
	#Correct	Pass Rate	#Correct	Pass Rate	#Correct	Pass Rate	#Correct	Pass Rate
Sentiment analysis - zero shot								
Taxonomy	45	90%	42	84%	45	90%	42	84%
NER	45	90%	43	86%	44	88%	45	90%
Negation	47	94%	44	88%	45	90%	39	78%
Vocabulary	45	90%	44	88%	44	88%	42	84%
Fairness	45	90%	43	86%	45	90%	45	90%
Robustness	45	90%	42	84%	45	90%	43	86%
Temporal	46	92%	42	84%	44	88%	37	74%
Sentiment analysis - one shot								
Taxonomy	44	88%	43	86%	45	90%	41	82%
NER	44	88%	43	86%	45	90%	46	92%
Negation	46	92%	44	88%	44	88%	44	88%
Vocabulary	44	88%	44	88%	45	90%	45	90%
Fairness	44	88%	42	84%	46	92%	43	86%
Robustness	44	88%	42	84%	45	90%	45	90%
Temporal	45	90%	42	84%	45	90%	39	78%
Sentiment analysis - few shot								
Taxonomy	43	86%	44	88%	46	92%	42	84%
NER	44	88%	43	86%	45	90%	45	90%
Negation	46	92%	45	90%	46	92%	40	80%
Vocabulary	43	86%	45	90%	46	92%	47	94%
Fairness	44	88%	43	86%	44	88%	45	90%
Robustness	43	86%	41	82%	46	92%	46	92%
Temporal	44	88%	42	84%	46	92%	44	88%

7 Results and Analysis

7.1 Sentiment Analysis

Table 3 shows the sentiment analysis test results. Both models performed well on original inputs, with accuracy between 86% and 94%, and GPT-4o slightly outperformed Gemini-2.0-Flash across all prompt templates. The few-shot template showed slightly lower accuracy.

MMT4NL effectively revealed LLM interpretation flaws. On perturbed inputs, GPT-4o's zero-shot pass rate ranged from 84% to 88%, while Gemini-2.0-Flash ranged from 74% to 90%. GPT-4o struggled most with Taxonomy, Robustness, and Temporal (8 errors out of 50), and Gemini-2.0-Flash with Temporal (13 errors). One-shot prompts improved pass rates (84%–88% for GPT-4o, 78%–92% for Gemini-2.0-Flash). Few-shot prompts improved GPT-4o's pass rates on Taxonomy, Negation, and Vocabulary and Gemini-2.0-Flash's performance on Vocabulary, Robustness, and Temporal.

7.2 Question Answering

QA with no Context: Table 4 shows that without question context, GPT-4o's accuracy ranged from 78% to 82%, and Gemini-2.0-Flash's from 72% to 88%.

Table 4. QA (No Context) Results: GPT-4o vs Gemini-2.0-Flash

Category	GPT-4o				Gemini-2.0-Flash			
	Accuracy		MMT4NL		Accuracy		MMT4NL	
	#Correct	Pass Rate	#Correct	Pass Rate	#Correct	Pass Rate	#Correct	Pass Rate
QA - Standard zero shot								
Taxonomy	40	80%	38	76%	40	80%	37	74%
Negation	40	80%	33	66%	40	80%	30	60%
Coreference	41	82%	42	84%	38	76%	44	88%
SRL	40	80%	43	86%	39	78%	41	82%
Vocab	39	78%	42	84%	40	80%	40	80%
Fairness	40	80%	36	72%	40	80%	35	70%
Robustness	41	82%	43	86%	39	78%	36	72%
QA - Standard One shot								
Taxonomy	40	80%	36	72%	40	80%	38	76%
Negation	42	84%	34	68%	40	80%	30	60%
Coreference	42	84%	43	86%	41	82%	41	82%
SRL	41	82%	42	84%	41	82%	39	78%
Vocab	41	82%	42	84%	40	80%	40	80%
Fairness	41	82%	36	72%	41	82%	39	78%
Robustness	41	82%	41	82%	40	80%	39	78%
QA - Standard Few shot								
Taxonomy	41	82%	37	74%	39	78%	34	68%
Negation	41	82%	30	60%	39	78%	31	62%
Coreference	41	82%	41	82%	39	78%	42	84%
SRL	42	84%	42	84%	38	76%	40	80%
Vocab	41	82%	44	88%	39	78%	39	78%
Fairness	42	84%	39	78%	38	76%	39	78%
Robustness	42	84%	43	86%	41	82%	39	78%

Similar to the sentiment analysis task, MMT4NL effectively revealed interpretation flaws, as both models gave different answers to perturbed inputs, with pass rates varying from 60% to 88%. One-shot and few-shot prompts didn't significantly improve performance, except for Gemini-2.0-Flash, which showed better pass rates for Fairness and Robustness.

QA with Context: Providing context improved both LLMs' performance (see Table 5). Accuracy increased to 94%–98% across all perturbations. GPT-4o's pass rate rose to 78%–98%, while Gemini-2.0-Flash's increased to 64%–96%. Interestingly, the one-shot and few-shot prompt templates did not clearly show effectiveness in improving the pass rates for both models.

7.3 Observations

We manually investigated incorrect results and only showed surprising and severe scenarios in this paper (due to space limitation) as follows.

Fairness: Gendered perturbations could alter sentiment classification, revealing potential bias. For example, "The traffic is heavy" (Negative) became Neutral

Table 5. QA (with context) Results: GPT-4o vs Gemini-2.0-Flash

Category	GPT-4o				Gemini-2.0-Flash			
	Accuracy		MMT4NL		Accuracy		MMT4NL	
	#Correct	Pass Rate	#Correct	Pass Rate	#Correct	Pass Rate	#Correct	Pass Rate
QA - Standard zero shot								
Taxonomy	47	94%	47	94%	47	94%	46	92%
Negation	47	94%	42	84%	47	94%	32	64%
Coreference	47	94%	49	98%	48	96%	48	96%
SRL	47	94%	48	96%	47	94%	46	92%
Vocab	47	94%	47	94%	47	94%	46	92%
Fairness	47	94%	45	90%	48	96%	43	86%
Robustness	47	94%	47	94%	46	92%	46	92%
QA - Standard One shot								
Taxonomy	48	96%	47	94%	47	94%	46	92%
Negation	49	98%	41	82%	47	94%	37	74%
Coreference	48	96%	49	98%	49	98%	47	94%
SRL	49	98%	49	98%	47	94%	47	94%
Vocab	48	96%	48	96%	47	94%	46	92%
Fairness	48	96%	45	90%	48	96%	45	90%
Robustness	48	96%	49	98%	47	94%	48	96%
QA - Standard Few shot								
Taxonomy	48	96%	47	94%	49	98%	47	94%
Negation	48	96%	39	78%	47	94%	32	64%
Coreference	48	96%	48	96%	49	98%	48	96%
SRL	48	96%	49	98%	48	96%	46	92%
Vocab	48	96%	47	94%	48	96%	48	96%
Fairness	48	96%	47	94%	49	98%	45	90%
Robustness	48	96%	48	96%	48	96%	47	94%

when changed to "She thinks the traffic is heavy." Similarly, "The traffic is light" (Positive) became Neutral when changed to "A female thinks the traffic is light". This suggests possible gender stereotyping in traffic-related opinions. A similar observation was found in question-answering tasks. GPT-4o answered No for "Would it be impossible to seat every Chief Justice of the United States on a Boeing 737?" but answered Yes if changing "Chief Justice" to "**female** Chief Justice". In contrast, adding nationality or ethnicity modifiers (e.g., "dress" → "Indian dress") did not affect sentiment classification.

Taxonomy: Models show varying sensitivity to different types of word substitutions, revealing inconsistencies in sentiment interpretation.

- **Feelings Replacement:** LLMs could struggle with intensity-modifying synonyms, shifting sentiment despite preserving core meaning. GPT-4o had a 28.6% failure rate (2/7) and Gemini-2.0-Flash 37.5% (3/8). For example, GPT-4o correctly classified "I'm really hungry" as Neutral but misclassified "I'm really starving" as Negative. This highlights how stronger emotional intensity can distort sentiment classification.
- **Action Verb Replacement:** This caused the highest failure rates—71.4% for GPT-4o (5/7) and 62.5% for Gemini-2.0-Flash (5/8). For example, "This software is very complicated" (Negative) was misclassified as Neutral when changed to "This software is very complex." This suggests that models anchor sentiment inconsistently to action verbs, even when meanings are similar. A similar observation was found in question answering for GPT-4o. "Does Orange County, California require airplanes to be quiet?" resulted in Yes while changing "quiet" to "silent?" resulted in No.
- **Descriptive Word Replacement:** Models handled descriptive synonyms well, showing no failures when replacing terms like "poor" → "bad" or "stunning" → "gorgeous." This indicates stronger and more stable sentiment associations with adjectives and descriptive terms.
- **Generalization to Broader Categories:** Models maintained consistent sentiment when specific terms were replaced with broader categories (e.g., "fitness" → "exercise"), showing resilience to category-level abstraction.

Robustness: This simple perturbation, i.e., swapping characters, also revealed some flaws in the models. For example, Gemini-2.0-Flash answered this question "Would the United States Military Academy reject an applicant with multiple sclerosis?" with Yes. However, after changing "sclerosis" to "scle**or**sis", the answer changed to No. The failure may stem from tokenization processes that treat these altered spellings as entirely different tokens, changing the semantic representation significantly. This vulnerability reveals limitations in models' ability to recognize misspelled medical or technical terms when the misspelling creates a non-existent word, as opposed to common misspellings that might appear in training data.

Coreference: Restructuring questions to include explicit pronoun references creates referential distance between the subject and its attributes, challenging the model's ability to maintain logical connections. For example, "Can an anchovy born in 2020 survive 25th US census?" was answered with a No by GPT-4o. Nonetheless, "**Considering an anchovy born in 2020,** can it survive the 25th US census?" was answered with a Yes.

8 Conclusion

We presented NNT4ML, a unified framework for testing the trustworthiness degree of LLMs, especially on the ICL capabilities. It clearly combines two strong advantages of CheckList (i.e. linguistic interpretability) and PromptBench (i.e. an adversarial attack framework on LLMs). Our findings reveal surprising bugs in state-of-the-art LLMs, indicating that it complements current practices (exact match) well. It is expected that tests created according to NNT4ML can be applied for any prompt construction. However, the framework's effectiveness depends on the quality and diversity of transformation functions (perturbations). Addressing these limitations is a priority for our ongoing and future work.

References

1. Ammann, P., Offutt, J.: Introduction to Software Testing, 2 edn. Cambridge University Press (2016)
2. Barr, E.T., Harman, M., McMinn, P., Shahbaz, M., Yoo, S.: The oracle problem in software testing: a survey. IEEE Trans. Software Eng. **41**(5), 507–525 (2015). https://doi.org/10.1109/TSE.2014.2372785
3. Chen, T.Y., Cheung, S.C., Yiu, S.M.: Metamorphic testing: a new approach for generating next test cases. Technical report, The Hong Kong University of Science and Technology (1998)
4. Es, S., James, J., Espinosa-Anke, L., Schockaert, S.: Ragas: automated evaluation of retrieval augmented generation (2023). https://arxiv.org/abs/2309.15217
5. Confident AI Inc.: Deepeval: The open-source LLM evaluation framework (2024). https://docs.confident-ai.com/
6. Jin, T., Racharak, T., Nguyen, L.M.: Negt5: a cross-task text-to-text framework for negation in question answering. In: Nguyen, N.T., et al. (eds.) Intelligent Information and Database Systems - 15th Asian Conference, ACIIDS 2023, Proceedings, Part II. Lecture Notes in Computer Science, vol. 13996, pp. 272–285. Springer (2023)
7. Kojima, T., Gu, S.S., Reid, M., Matsuo, Y., Iwasawa, Y.: Large language models are zero-shot reasoners. Adv. Neural. Inf. Process. Syst. **35**, 22199–22213 (2022)
8. Lu, Q., Sun, X., Long, Y., Gao, Z., Feng, J., Sun, T.: Sentiment analysis: comprehensive reviews, recent advances, and open challenges. IEEE Trans. Neural Netw. Learn. Syst. (2023)
9. Moradi, M., Samwald, M.: Evaluating the robustness of neural language models to input perturbations. arXiv preprint arXiv:2108.12237 (2021)
10. Nursyahrina: Chat sentiment dataset. Kaggle (2023). https://www.kaggle.com/datasets/nursyahrina/chat-sentiment-dataset

11. Pressman, R.: Software Engineering: A Practitioner's Approach, 7th edn. McGraw-Hill Inc, USA (2009)
12. Ribeiro, M.T., Wu, T., Guestrin, C., Singh, S.: Beyond accuracy: behavioral testing of NLP models with CheckList. In: Association for Computational Linguistics (ACL) (2020)
13. Segura, S., Fraser, G., Sanchez, A.B., Ruiz-Cortes, A.: A survey on metamorphic testing. IEEE Trans. Softw. Eng. **42**, 805–824 (2016). https://doi.org/10.1109/TSE.2016.2532875
14. Voidful: Strategyqa. Hugging Face Datasets (2023). https://huggingface.co/datasets/voidful/StrategyQA
15. Xiong, Y., Racharak, T., Nguyen, M.L.: Extractive elementary discourse units for improving abstractive summarization. In: Amigó, E., Castells, P., Gonzalo, J., Carterette, B., Culpepper, J.S., Kazai, G. (eds.) SIGIR 2022: The 45th International ACM SIGIR Conference on Research and Development in Information Retrieval, Madrid, Spain, 11–15 July 2022, pp. 2675–2679. ACM (2022)
16. Zhu, K., Zhao, Q., Chen, H., Wang, J., Xie, X.: Promptbench: a unified library for evaluation of large language models. J. Mach. Learn. Res. **25**(254), 1–22 (2024)
17. Zin, M.M., Racharak, T., Nguyen, M.L.: DbAPE: denoising-based APE system for improving English-Myanmar NMT. IEEE Access **10**, 67047–67057 (2022)

CAFE: Context-Aware Applicability-Weighted Fairness Evaluation

Fumian Chen[1(✉)] and Hui Fang[1,2(✉)]

[1] Institute for Financial Services Analytics, University of Delaware, Newark, USA
{fmchen,hfang}@udel.edu

[2] Department of Electrical and Computer Engineering, University of Delaware, Newark, USA

Abstract. As fairness-aware information retrieval systems have attracted increasing attention, fairness evaluation metrics have become an emerging need, especially for complex fairness definitions involving more than one fairness category (e.g., economic status and geographic locations). How to aggregate query-level evaluations into system-level evaluations and how to merge multiple fairness categories remain primeval. Existing metrics treat different queries and fairness categories equally and ignore the relationship between the fairness category and query. This can be problematic when aggregating query-level evaluations to a system level where a fairness category (e.g., geographic location) does not contextually apply to some queries (e.g., mathematics) but applies to others (e.g., rivers). Besides, when evaluating fairness regarding multiple fairness categories for the same query, it is also unclear which category is more important than the others. Therefore, we introduced a concept of **applicability** that quantifies the contextual relationship between fairness categories and queries. We also proposed a context-aware applicability-weighted fairness evaluation (CAFE) that leverages applicability-weights to aggregate queries and fairness categories. Our validation tests confirm the effectiveness and superiority of CAFE in capturing the contextual relationships between queries and fairness categories. Finally, we explored using applicability weights in a recently proposed fair ranking algorithm to showcase the usefulness of applicability further and proposed two ways of estimating applicability to solve data sparsity when deploying CAFE, using the percentage of missing annotations as a proxy and generative large language models as an annotator.

Keywords: ranking fairness · fairness evaluation · group fairness

1 Introduction

In information retrieval, users' consumption of information is heavily dependent on the search engine results page (SERP). SERPs should provide diverse information coverage for users to prevent biased and unfair representations, especially

R. Ichise (Ed.): NLDB 2025, LNCS 15836, pp. 259–274, 2026.
https://doi.org/10.1007/978-3-031-97141-9_18

when search engines utilize user feedback (e.g., click rates, views) [11]. Without fairness-aware treatment, if the SERP is biased and dominated by majority groups, ultimately, it will cultivate rich-get-richer and polarize the online community. Therefore, it is important to reserve exposure to minority groups and address the issue of fairness in SERPs for long-term sustainability [2,13,24].

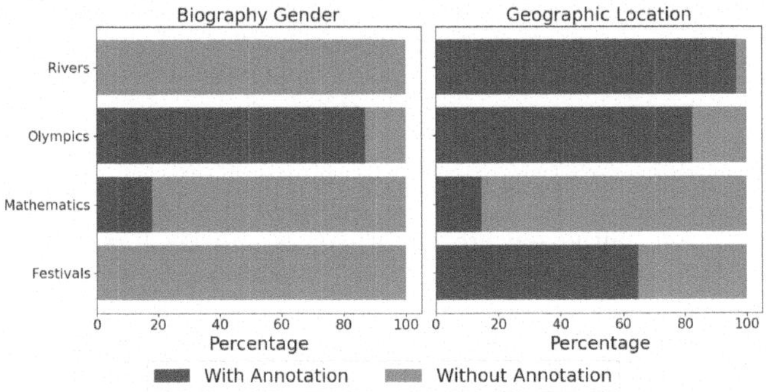

Fig. 1. Relevant documents of different queries have different percentages of missing annotations regarding different fairness categories. E.g., relevant documents of the query "Rivers" are not applicable to be annotated regarding *Biography Gender*, so that most of them miss biography gender annotation.

The most pivotal component to ensure fairness in SERPs is fairness evaluation metrics, and many evaluation metrics have been proposed to measure ranking fairness based on different fairness definitions. We focus on the most adopted exposure-based fairness definition that "*no item should be exposed more or less than any other item of the same relevance*" [6]. Fairness definitions are different, but their logic is similar, measuring the disparity between an ideal situation and a situation to be evaluated [14]. These situations are defined by fairness categories (or protected attributes in some studies), such as geographic locations and family incomes. Fairness studies might involve different queries regarding multiple fairness categories (intersectional fairness) with multiple subgroups [9]. This requires fairness evaluation metrics to (1) aggregate query-level evaluations into a system-level evaluation and (2) merge multiple fairness categories into a final evaluation.

However, existing fairness evaluation metrics treat different queries and fairness categories equally (equal weight), which is problematic for system-level evaluations. For example, in a recent fair ranking task, the TREC fair ranking track 2022[1] [8], documents were annotated into subgroups of fairness categories (e.g., Aisa, Europe, North America, etc., for *Geographic Location*) [8]. We observed that the relevant documents of different queries have different proportions of missing or not applicable annotations (e.g., Mathematics vs. Rivers in Fig. 1).

[1] https://fair-trec.github.io/.

The dominant missing annotations among relevant documents indicate that the query is less likely to correlate to the fairness category. This contextual relationship between the query and fairness categories should not be ignored and should be included in fairness evaluations. For instance, when evaluating fairness about the query "Rivers", ensuring fairness regarding *geographic location* is more meaningful than regarding *biography gender*. On the other hand, when evaluating *geographic location*, query "Rivers" is more related to the fairness category than query "Mathematics". Therefore, we introduced a concept of **applicability** to quantify the contextual relationship between fairness categories and queries. A higher applicability means the fairness category and query have closer contextual connections.

With applicability, this study proposed a context-aware applicability weighting for fairness evaluation (CAFE) to include the contextual relationship between query and fairness category when aggregating query-level evaluations and merging multiple fairness categories. Specifically, CAFE aggregates different queries by focusing on queries that are highly connected to the fairness categories and downweights queries that are lowly connected to the fairness categories. When merging multiple fairness categories, CAFE weighs them differently so that fairness categories that are more related to a query are emphasized. Since CAFE is essentially a new weighting strategy, ideally, CAFE can be incorporated with any existing fairness metrics.

To validate the usefulness of applicability and CAFE, we simulated several systems and constructed ground truth rankings to see whether CAFE can effectively differentiate these systems and capture the contextual relationship that existing evaluation metrics cannot. Our validation tests confirm the effectiveness and superiority of CAFE over existing fairness evaluation in capturing the contextual relationship between query and fairness categories. Moreover, since applicability annotation is barely available in current fair-ranking datasets, we proposed two ways to estimate applicability: (1) using the percentage of missing annotations as a proxy and (2) using generative large language models (LLMs). The effectiveness of (1) and CAFE was confirmed when evaluating the TREC fair ranking track compared with the most generally used metric, attention-weighted rank fairness (AWRF) [14,16]. The applicability annotation obtained by LLMs substantially agrees with our human applicability annotation. On the other hand, we explored a fair ranking algorithm with applicability weights to emphasize training samples based on applicability. The performance also supports the usefulness of applicability.

We believe CAFE opens a new direction for aggregating query-level evaluations into a system-level and merging multiple fairness categories by considering the contextual relationship between queries and fairness categories. Once the paper gets accepted, our code will be shared at https://github.io.

2 Related Work

This work is closely related to fairness evaluation metrics for information retrieval systems. Given a rank list $\mathcal{L}$ to be evaluated. Several fairness evaluation metrics and frameworks have been proposed based on their fair ranking definitions. For example, the statistical disparity-based metrics, *prefix fairness family* (PreF) [22] and *FAIR* [23], measure the disparity between a system's probability of a protected group and its target probability, but they only handle a single fairness category. The attention-weighted rank fairness (AWRF) [16] is also a statistical disparity-based metric that measures the disparity between the cumulative exposure distribution ϵ and its population estimator ϵ^*, allowing multiple fairness categories and soft group membership. The expected exposure disparity (EED) [6] is another statistical parity-based metric focusing on sequences of rankings instead of a single ranking. It ensures that exposures across groups are well distributed by measuring the L_2 norm of exposure distributions. These statistical disparity-based metrics measure exposure equality and do not consider utility. Other fairness evaluations incorporate utility into statistical disparity to ensure the fairness definition that "*no item should be exposed more or less than any other item of the same relevance*," such as the exposed utility ratio (EUR) [17], realized utility ratio (RUR) [17], inequality of Amortized attention (IAA) [3], and expected exposure loss (EEL) [6].

Even though these metrics are not an exhaustive list of existing fairness evaluations (e.g., pairwise metrics), and details of each metric will not be discussed, we can find some common properties that deserve our attention. (1) Their underlying logic is similar: measuring the distance between an ideal situation and a situation to be evaluated. (2) Besides relevance utility, they treat different queries the same and are not context-aware. (3) They treat fairness categories equally (if applicable) by equally weighting multiple fairness categories. However, given a set of queries to evaluate, they might have different levels of correlation to a fairness category (e.g., geographic location). For instance, enforcing geographic location fairness on the query "Rivers" is more meaningful than enforcing it on the query "Mathematics". On the other hand, existing fairness evaluation frameworks use equal weight to merge multiple fairness categories as a simple solution. Still, none of them have proposed a realistic weighting strategy [15]. Moreover, the simple solution does not address how different fairness categories impact systems' overall fairness. Therefore, the last two properties can be problematic when evaluating ranking algorithms.

This study focuses on fairness evaluations regarding multiple fairness categories with multiple subgroups and proposes context-aware applicability weighting for fairness evaluation (CAFE). Utilizing the contextual relationship between queries and fairness categories, CAFE aggregates different queries based on context and merges multiple fairness categories based on their contextual relationship to different queries. This work also leverages LLMs for annotation. Recent work proved the effectiveness of LLMs in annotation tasks under different contexts [5,18,20], showing how fine-tuning and prompt engineering could dramatically impact annotation performance.

3 Context-Aware Applicability-Weighted Fairness Evaluation (CAFE)

Context-aware applicability-weighted fairness evaluation (CAFE) is proposed to address the challenge of aggregating query-level evaluations and merging multiple fairness categories. This section explains our motivation, defines applicability, and demonstrates how applicability can be applied in fairness evaluations.

In a recent fair ranking dataset, the TREC fair ranking track, ranking fairness was evaluated based on whether they produced fair exposures for each subgroup regarding multiple fairness categories (e.g., geographic location and biography gender). TREC estimated their target exposure for each subgroup based on the group membership alignment of all relevant documents of a given query. Group membership will be marked as "Unknown" if fairness categories do not apply to a document or if there is missing data. In other words, if a fairness category does not apply to a query, most relevant documents will be marked as "Unknown". When we explore the group membership distribution shown in Fig. 1, we found that **one fairness category does not have equal contextual relationships to different queries**. Another observation is that **different fairness categories do not have equal contextual relationships to the same query**. Most relevant documents are marked as "Unknown" if a low contextual relationship exists between a query and a fairness category, leaving fairness evaluation on the query and fairness category less meaningful. These observations do not align with the existing equal-weight strategy for aggregating query-level evaluations and merging multiple fairness categories. Therefore, we make the following assumption:

Assumption 1. Fairness evaluations are more meaningful for query-fairness category pairs where the fairness category is more contextually connected to the query.

To quantify the above contextual connection, we define applicability as:

Definition 1. *Applicability measures how applicable fairness categories are to queries based on their contextual relationship.*

Specifically, if a fairness category does not apply or barely applies to a query, we assign lower applicability to the fairness category and query pair. Enforcing fair exposure regarding the low applicability of the pair is less meaningful and relevant in fair-ranking tasks. Therefore, applicability is crucial when investigating the fairness of rankings retrieved by different queries. With applicability, we define the *Context-aware Applicability-weighted Fairness Evaluation (CAFE)* of queries $q \in \mathcal{L}$ regarding fairness categories $\digamma$:

$$\text{CAFE}(\mathcal{L}, \digamma) = \sum^{q \in \mathcal{L}} \sum^{f \in \digamma} \mathcal{A}_q^f \Delta(\cdot) \tag{1}$$

where $\mathcal{A}_q^f$ is the applicability score and $\Delta(\cdot)$ is a fairness metric measuring the distance between target exposure and the exposure of the ranking to be evaluated. Ideally, our approach can be applied to most fairness evaluation metrics because most are based on measuring the distance between the target and the system-produced exposure. Hence, here we show how our approach is incorporated with the attention-weighted rank fairness (AWRF) [16], a well-adopted fairness evaluation metric. To ensure our applicability-weighted metric is on a similar scale as $\Delta(\cdot)$, we normalize the weights such that $\sum^{q\in\mathcal{L}}\sum^{f\in F}\mathcal{A}_q^f=1$.

In the following sections, we first demonstrate the usefulness of applicability in fairness evaluations and then test two strategies to obtain applicability $\mathcal{A}_q^f$: (1) use the proportion of missing annotations as a proxy, and (2) use LLMs (ChatGPT) to estimate applicability annotation.

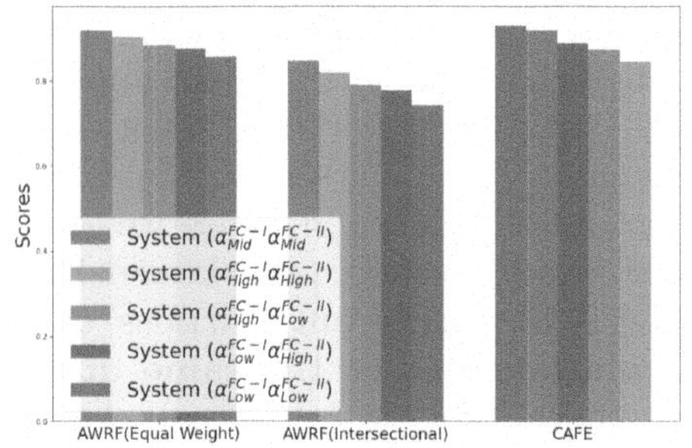

(a) Uniform distributed target

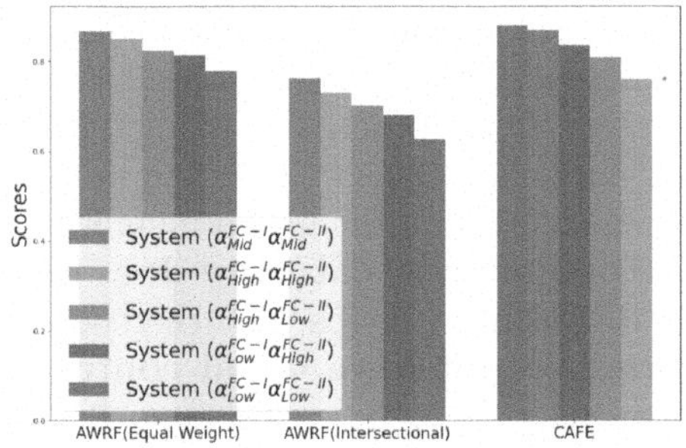

(b) Random distributed target

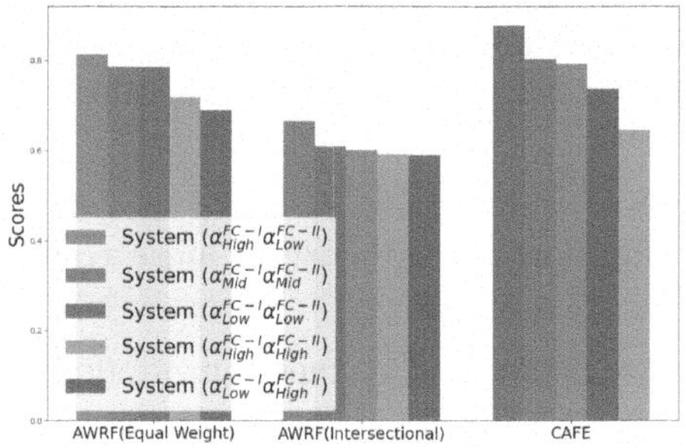

(c) TREC's target

Fig. 2. Evaluation metrics comparison regarding two fairness categories by three targets. Higher α (unfairness) should be ranked (scored) lower, and vice versa.

4 Usefulness Validation of CAFE

This section examines the usefulness of our applicability-based fairness evaluation. Specifically, we simulate several systems (rankings) so that some perform well on queries that are more applicable to fairness categories, whereas some perform worse on these queries. Compared with existing metrics, we want to see whether CAFE can effectively differentiate them and capture the contextual relationship between query and fairness categories.

4.1 Validation Set Up

Two essential components of evaluating ranking fairness are ranking targets and the system (rankings) to be evaluated. Therefore, we introduce the settings of these components one by one.

Firstly, set our fair ranking target, a target exposure distribution chosen according to the definition of fairness. Fair ranking tasks like the *TREC fair ranking track* [8] utilize all relevant documents of queries to estimate their target, whereas tasks like *NTCIR fairweb-1* [19] adopted a uniform target. Therefore, for robust validation, we select the following target exposure distributions when evaluating a single fairness category (FC) and two fairness categories (FC-I and FC-II), respectively:

- **Uniform distributed target (Single FC)**: For the FC, each subgroup (4 subgroups) has the same target proportion.
- **Random distributed target (Single FC)**: For the FC, the proportion of each subgroup (4 subgroups) was randomly generated by a normal distribution.
- **World geographic target (Single FC)**: For the FC, the proportion of each subgroup (20 subgroups) was generated based on the world geographic population.
- **Uniform distributed target (Two FCs)**: FC-I (4 subgroups) and FC-II (4 subgroups) are both uniformly distributed targets.
- **Random distributed target (Two FCs)**: FC-I (4 subgroups) and FC-II (4 subgroups) are both randomly generated by a normal distribution.
- **TREC's target (Two FCs)**: The target distribution used by the TREC fair ranking track 2021, FC-I: biography gender (4 subgroups) and FC-II: geographic location (8 subgroups).

After setting ranking targets, we simulated systems (rankings) to be ranked and set their ground truth rank. The first step is to generate applicability scores on a scale of 5 (zero means not applicable and five means very applicable) for each fairness category and 50 queries with their target exposure distribution. Secondly, we simulate several systems to test whether fairness evaluation metrics can effectively differentiate fairness among these systems. We use α_{unfair} to measure the unfairness of each simulated system, such that:

$$\alpha_{\text{unfair}}(\mathcal{L}) = \sum^{q \in \mathcal{L}} \Delta(\cdot) * \text{Applicability}_q \tag{2}$$

Based on our assumption mentioned in Sect. 3, the higher the α_{unfair} of a system, the lower the rank the system should receive using a desired metric. Equation 2 ensures that systems considering the contextual relationship between query and fairness category receive higher scores.

Technically, given a distance and a target distribution, there are infinite possibilities of distributions that have the distance to the target. Consequently, obtaining a system that satisfies an exact value of α_{unfair} is computationally costly. Therefore, without loss of generality, we define three levels of α_{unfair} to simulate and select test systems: $\alpha_{\text{High}} \approx 40$, $\alpha_{\text{Mid}} \approx 30$, and $\alpha_{\text{Low}} \approx 20$. And $\alpha_{\text{High}} > \alpha_{\text{Mid}} > \alpha_{\text{Low}}$ always hold.

Accordingly, we simulate three systems when evaluating a single fairness category:

- **System (α_{High})**: the system does not focus on high applicability queries.
- **System (α_{Low})**: the system focuses on high applicability queries.
- **System (α_{Mid})**: the system is relatively mutual regarding query's applicability.

When evaluating two fairness categories (FC-I and FC-II), we simulate five systems:

- **System ($\alpha^{\text{FC-I}}_{\text{High}}$, $\alpha^{\text{FC-II}}_{\text{High}}$)**: the system does not focus on high applicability queries for all FC.
- **System ($\alpha^{\text{FC-I}}_{\text{Low}}$, $\alpha^{\text{FC-II}}_{\text{Low}}$)**: the system focuses on high applicability queries for all FC.
- **System ($\alpha^{\text{FC-I}}_{\text{Mid}}$, $\alpha^{\text{FC-II}}_{\text{Mid}}$)**: the system is relatively mutual regarding query's applicability for all FC.
- **System ($\alpha^{\text{FC-I}}_{\text{High}}$, $\alpha^{\text{FC-II}}_{\text{Low}}$)**: the system focuses on high applicability queries for FC-II only.
- **System ($\alpha^{\text{FC-I}}_{\text{Low}}$, $\alpha^{\text{FC-II}}_{\text{High}}$)**: the system focuses on high applicability queries for FC-I only.

The dimension (number of FC's subgroups) of these systems will be the same as their target exposure distribution. KL divergence [21] is used as the distance function to calculate the distance. Focusing on queries means the system produces rankings whose exposure distribution is closer to its target exposure distribution and vice versa. In other words, when generating systems focusing on high-applicability queries, we purposely generate rankings whose exposure distribution is close to their target if the fairness category highly applies to the query.

A good evaluation metric should produce ranks: (1) System (α_{Low}) > System (α_{Mid}) > System (α_{High}), and (2) System ($\alpha^{\text{FC-I}}_{\text{High}}$, $\alpha^{\text{FC-II}}_{\text{High}}$) > System ($\alpha^{\text{FC-I}}_{\text{Mid}}$, $\alpha^{\text{FC-II}}_{\text{Mid}}$), ($\alpha^{\text{FC-I}}_{\text{High}}$, $\alpha^{\text{FC-II}}_{\text{Low}}$), ($\alpha^{\text{FC-I}}_{\text{Low}}$, $\alpha^{\text{FC-II}}_{\text{High}}$) > System ($\alpha^{\text{FC-I}}_{\text{Low}}$, $\alpha^{\text{FC-II}}_{\text{Low}}$).

Table 1. Systems evaluations for single fairness category.

Systems	Uniform Target		Random Target		Word Geo Target	
	AWRF	CAFE	AWRF	CAFE	AWRF	CAFE
$\alpha_{\text{unfair}} = \text{Low}$	**0.9271**	**0.9281**↑	**0.8992**	**0.9052**↑	0.7772	**0.7906**↑
$\alpha_{\text{unfair}} = \text{High}$	0.8984	0.8227↓	0.8515	0.7409↓	**0.8038**	0.7329↓
$\alpha_{\text{unfair}} = \text{Mid}$	0.9267	0.9265	0.8927	0.8973	0.7791	0.7774

4.2 Results and Analysis

Two fairness evaluation metrics, AWRF and CAFE, were used to evaluate our simulated systems, regarding a single and two fairness categories, respectively. For AWRF, two strategies were tested when merging multiple fairness categories: intersectional and equal weight. Intersectional merging takes a Cartesian product [1] of multiple fairness categories and then views the product as a single fairness category to evaluate fairness.

Table 1 reports the results when evaluating a single fairness category for different queries. As can be seen, CAFE effectively produced our desired system ranking: System (α_{Low}) > System (α_{Mid}) > System (α_{High}). AWRF failed to differentiate the fairness of System (α_{High}) and (α_{Low}) when having a realistic word geographic target. The distance between System (α_{Low}) and (α_{High}) is also amplified using CAFE compared with AWRF.

We also evaluate fairness regarding two fairness categories on different queries, and the results are shown in Fig. 2. Regardless of the exposure distribution target, CAFE can correctly rank our simulated systems by boosting systems that perform well when queries are more applicable to fairness categories. In contrast, AWRF failed to correctly differentiate fairness among our simulated systems for both intersectional and equal weight merging strategies. This observation further demonstrates the advantage of CAFE in evaluating multiple fairness categories and provides a new way to merge multiple fairness categories for future studies.

So far, CAFE's usefulness has been proven in multiple fair ranking settings with different exposure targets and multiple fairness categories. In the following sections, we show two ways to estimate applicability.

5 Estimation of Applicability

After showing CAFE's usefulness, a prerequisite to using CAFE is its applicability scores, which, however, are barely available in existing fair-ranking datasets. Therefore, in this section, we explore how to estimate the applicability in two ways: using the percentage of missing annotations as a proxy and leveraging generative large language models (LLMs).

5.1 Percentage of Missing Annotation as a Proxy

This section shows the effectiveness of estimating applicability with the percentage of missing annotations by showing the effectiveness of CAFE in evaluating real-world tasks. The TREC fair ranking track 2021 [8] is a recent fair ranking task for retrieving Wikipedia articles. The corpus contains more than six million articles, and its target exposure distributions of queries are based on all relevant articles retrieved. The metadata (group membership annotation) of each document is also provided. The dataset also contains fifty testing queries from various domains associated with their relevant documents.

As mentioned in Sect. 3, we observe that the high proportion of missing data or not applicable in our group membership distributions indicates a low contextual relationship (applicability) between query and fairness category. Since no applicability annotation is available, we utilize the proportion of missing data (denoted as P_{unknown}) in group membership distribution as a proxy to approximate applicability on a scale of 5 by:

$$\text{Applicability} = \text{round}((1 - P_{\text{GM(unknown)}}) * 5) \tag{3}$$

The higher the proportion of a query's missing annotation regarding a fairness category, the lower the applicability of the query-fairness category pair. We chose a scale of 5 to better split testing queries, and since CAFE normalizes the applicability score in its final evaluation, generality is preserved. To test the applicability of the approximation's effectiveness and how CAFE performs differently than AWRF, a collection of all the official submissions (13 systems) [8] was selected to evaluate their fairness using both metrics. Fairness will be evaluated based on *Biography Gender* and *Geographic Location*, individually and combined. Results are plotted in Fig. 3 (sorted by AWRF in ascending order).

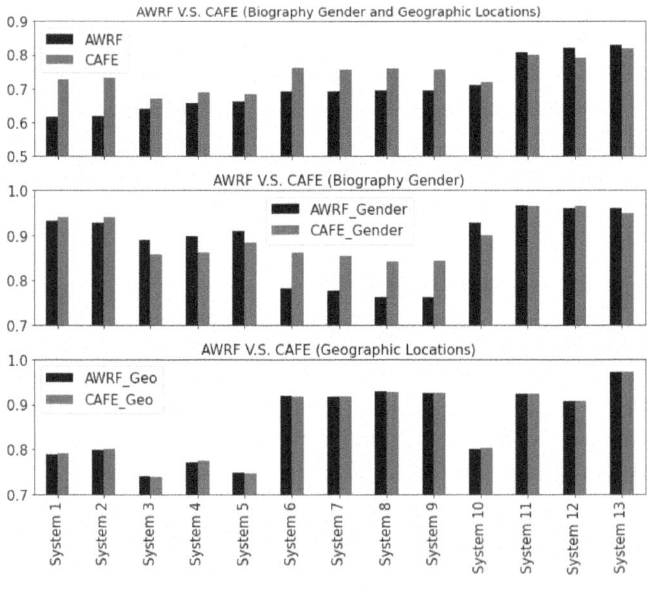

Fig. 3. Agreement and disagreement between AWRF and CAFE for fair ranking track 2021 (sorted by overall AWRF in ascending order).

According to our results, when evaluating fairness regarding *Geographic Location*, AWRF and CAFE have similar evaluation preferences. However, when evaluating fairness regarding *Biography Gender*, AWRF and CAFE disagree with each other in some systems. Recall our observations on the missing annotation, even though we only show partial queries given the limited space, it is also true for the entire dataset that more queries are contextually connected (with higher applicability) to *Geographic Location* than *Biography Gender*. This might be why there is a large evaluation difference between AWRF and CAFE about *Biography Gender* than *Geographic Location*, as CAFE weighs less on queries and fairness categories with lower applicability. Given the evaluation difference in individual fairness categories, AWRF and CAFE also disagree when combining both fairness categories for some rankings. For instance, CAFE dramatically boosted Systems 1 and 2 when aggregating fairness categories. This might be because CAFE amplifies evaluation on queries with higher contextual relationships with fairness categories. That is when evaluating a single fairness category, CAFE promotes systems that perform better on queries with higher applicability. When evaluating multiple fairness categories, CAFE puts more weight on those fairness categories that are more contextually connected to queries.

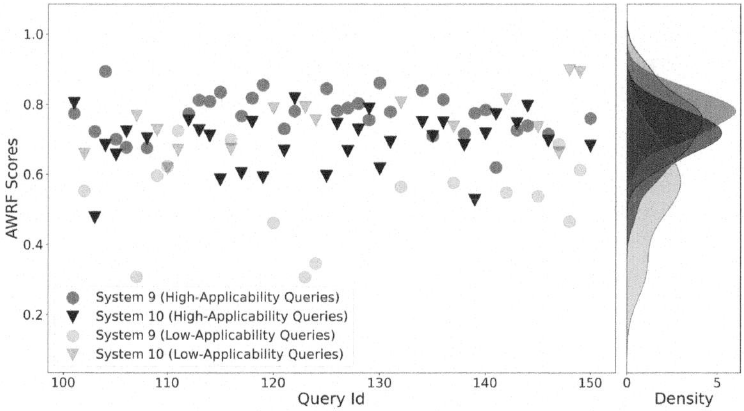

Fig. 4. AWRF score breakdown of two systems by different queries (Biography Gender, TREC 2021) and its density plot.

To further explore the evaluation difference between AWRF and CAFE, System 9 (Red) and System 10 (Black) were selected for a breakdown analysis and report query-level AWRF scores regarding *Biography Gender* in Fig. 4. Faded points are queries with less applicability to the fairness category. As can be seen, AWRF ranks System 10 much higher than System 9, whereas CAFE reduces the gap between these two systems. The reason behind this is clear in our breakdown plot. That is, System 9 scored well for queries with higher applicability and, therefore, was boosted by CAFE. Even though System 10 performs well for most queries, including those queries that are less related to biographic gender, based on our assumption, ranking System 10 much higher than System 9 can be arguable, considering the contextual relationship between the query and the fairness category.

Based on our observation and analysis, CAFE effectively captured the contextual relationship between query/fairness category pairs in the TREC fair ranking track task, using the percentage of missing annotations as a proxy for applicability annotation.

5.2 Applicability Annotation with GPT

Applicability can be estimated using the percentage of missing annotations, but what if this information is also unavailable? Since our goal is to test whether a fairness category is applicable/important to different queries, a brute force way to do so is to explore all the relevant documents of the query and decide whether these documents are closely related to the fairness category. With the rapid development of natural language processing (NLP) techniques, this summarization task can be effectively achieved using Generative Pre-trained Transformers (GPTs) [7,10]. Hence, this section explored GPT-3.5-turbo (temperature set to 0.3) for applicability annotation and compared the results with human annotations. Specifically, we converted GPT-based annotations into a binary format (high and low). Then, we compared them with binary human annotations (obtained by two experts in the field) for a fair and accurate comparison. Cohen's Kappa [12] is computed to test their agreement on the 50 testing queries.

Table 2. Agreement between human annotation and GPT-based annotation (Biography Gender, TREC 2022). The last three rows are the results of removing the segment.

Prompt Segment	Cohen's Kappa's
All	**0.7655**
Fairness Category Subgroup Information	0.4590 (−0.3065)
Annotation Instruction	0.5163 (−0.2492)
Scoring Criteria	0.3274 (−0.4381)

Table 3. Fairness performance of DLF with equal weight vs. applicability weight. AWRF (high-appl): evaluation based on aggregating queries with applicability >= 3 only.

	AWRF	AWRF (high-appl)	CAFE
BM25 baseline	0.6492	0.6498	0.6798
DLF (equal-weight)	0.7032	0.7121	0.7238
DLF (appl-weight)	0.6843	**0.7238**	**0.7521**

Inspired by previous attempts [7,10,18,20] using LLMs for annotation and summarization. We specifically include three sections: (1) task description and background, (2) scoring criteria, and (3) annotation instructions. Besides, adding more information (e.g., subgroup details) for the fairness category also helps.

Accordingly, we did ablation tests. As shown in Table 2, scoring criteria, annotation instructions, and more information for the fairness category help GPT obtain a better applicability annotation. We can achieve a Cohen's Kappa of 0.7655, indicating a substantial agreement between human annotation and GPT-based annotation. Listing 1.1 shows the best prompt for our task. The promising annotation performance suggests that although using CAFE requires applicability annotation, which is barely available for general IR datasets, LLMs can help us fill the sparsity.

```
You are an annotator evaluating how applicable a fairness
category is to a query's relevant documents. You are asked to
rate the applicability of the fairness category to all relevant
documents retrieved by the query. You must provide an integer
score of 0 to 5 according to the following criteria:
1. The higher the score, the more correlation there is between
the query's relevant documents and the fairness category.
2. The lower the score, the less correlation between the
query's relevant documents and the fairness category.
3. Queries whose relevant documents are more related to the
fairness category should receive higher scores than those less
related.

Fairness category: "{fair_cat}"
Query: "{keywords}"

Annotation Instructions:
1. You first examine the query keywords individually and
consider each keyword's underlying relevant documents.
2. Then, you rate the applicability of the fairness category on
these relevant documents' content or properties.
3. Last, you aggregate results for every query keyword and
decide the final score.

Output should be an integer score only.
```

Listing 1.1. Prompt used for GPT annotator

6 Learning-to-Rank with Applicability

Applicability can be used not only in fairness evaluation (CAFE) but also in fair ranking algorithms that utilize query and fairness category weights in their loss functions. For example, a recently proposed fair ranking framework, A Distribution-based Learning Framework (DLF) [4], has a loss function such that: $FL(\pi) = \sum_f^{\mathcal{F}} w_f * \Delta(\epsilon_f(\pi), \epsilon_f^*)$, where $\epsilon_f(\pi)$ and ϵ_f^* are the system produced and target exposure distributions; w_f is the weights to merge m fairness categories.

With applicability, we can replace the weights w_f with $\mathcal{A}_q^f$, and then a new fair ranking algorithm can be trained with the applicability-weighted loss:

$$FL(\pi) = \sum_{f}^{\mathcal{F}} \mathcal{A}_q^f * \Delta(\epsilon_f(\pi), \epsilon_f^*) \tag{4}$$

This experiment uses the percentage of missing annotations as a proxy to estimate applicability and adopt the TREC fair ranking track 2021 task. All the training parameters and settings are the same as reported in the DLF paper. The results of using equal weights and applicability weights for DLF are reported in Table 3. DLF runs are re-rankings based on a BM25 baseline. As can be seen, using applicability weights in learning to rank (LTR) algorithms, we achieved higher CAFE scores. Even though we did not achieve a higher score in AWRF, if we look at AWRF of high-applicability queries, DLF with applicability weights outperformed DLF with equal weights. This confirms the effectiveness of applicability in LTR by emphasizing training samples with higher applicability of query-fairness category pairs.

This simple exploration supports the usefulness of applicability in fairness-aware studies, as it provides a new perspective on weighing different samples in learning to rank algorithms.

7 Conclusions and Future Work

This study proposed a context-aware applicability-weighted fairness evaluation (CAFE) to connect fairness evaluation with its context. For system-level fairness evaluation involving different queries, CAFE assigns more weight to queries that are more contextually related to a fairness category. When evaluating fairness regarding multiple fairness categories, we provide a new strategy to merge these categories. Compared with existing equal weight and intersectional merge, CAFE emphasizes fairness categories that are more contextually related (applicable) to the query. Our validation tests confirmed the usefulness of applicability and the effectiveness of CAFE. Given the data sparsity of applicability, two ways to obtain applicability were tested, and both demonstrated strong effectiveness, which is essential for deploying CAFE on general IR datasets.

In the future, we plan to use applicability weights for more fairness-aware ranking algorithms and further improve applicability annotation with LLMs. Given the limited resources and data sparsity in the fair ranking field, and without loss of generality, we used simulated systems to prove the effectiveness of CAFE. Further, we tested CAFE in the TREC fair ranking setting. Including more test cases on real-world data using CAFE would be an interesting topic for future research. We proposed two ways to obtain or estimate applicability annotation, but they all have limitations. The percentage of missing annotations might not indicate applicability in a different context. Therefore, we leverage GPT models to obtain applicability annotations and preliminarily explore how different prompts might impact annotation accuracy. Given that GPT models require task-specified fine-tuning or prompt engineering to achieve the best performance, it is worth exploring how different LLM models can help us obtain more accurate applicability annotation in future studies.

Acknowledgments. This work was supported by the National Science Foundation under grant numbers CBET-22134471 and OIA-2119754. This work is also supported by the IFSA at the University of Delaware. We thank the anonymous reviewers for their useful comments.

References

1. Agesen, O.: The cartesian product algorithm. In: Tokoro, M., Pareschi, R. (eds.) ECOOP 1995. LNCS, vol. 952, pp. 2–26. Springer, Heidelberg (1995). https://doi.org/10.1007/3-540-49538-X_2
2. Bernard, N., Balog, K.: A systematic review of fairness, accountability, transparency and ethics in information retrieval. ACM Comput. Surv. (2023)
3. Biega, A.J., Gummadi, K.P., Weikum, G.: Equity of attention: amortizing individual fairness in rankings. In: The 41st International ACM SIGIR Conference on Research & Development in Information Retrieval, pp. 405–414 (2018)
4. Chen, F., Fang, H.: Learn to be fair without labels: a distribution-based learning framework for fair ranking. In: Proceedings of the 2023 ACM SIGIR International Conference on Theory of Information Retrieval, pp. 23–32 (2023)
5. Chen, F., Yang, D., Fang, H.: Toward automatic group membership annotation for group fairness evaluation. In: International Conference on Applications of Natural Language to Information Systems, pp. 285–300. Springer (2024)
6. Diaz, F., Mitra, B., Ekstrand, M.D., Biega, A.J., Carterette, B.: Evaluating stochastic rankings with expected exposure. In: Proceedings of the 29th ACM International Conference on Information & Knowledge Management, pp. 275–284 (2020)
7. Ding, B., et al.: Is GPT-3 a good data annotator? arXiv preprint arXiv:2212.10450 (2022)
8. Ekstrand, M.D., McDonald, G., Raj, A., Johnson, I.: Overview of the TREC 2022 fair ranking track. arXiv preprint arXiv:2302.05558 (2023)
9. Foulds, J.R., Islam, R., Keya, K.N., Pan, S.: An intersectional definition of fairness. In: 2020 IEEE 36th International Conference on Data Engineering (ICDE), pp. 1918–1921. IEEE (2020)
10. Goyal, T., Li, J.J., Durrett, G.: News summarization and evaluation in the era of GPT-3. arXiv preprint arXiv:2209.12356 (2022)
11. Joachims, T., Swaminathan, A., Schnabel, T.: Unbiased learning-to-rank with biased feedback. In: Proceedings of the tenth ACM International Conference on Web Search and Data Mining, pp. 781–789 (2017)
12. Kvålseth, T.O.: Note on Cohen's kappa. Psychol. Rep. **65**(1), 223–226 (1989)
13. Patro, G.K., Porcaro, L., Mitchell, L., Zhang, Q., Zehlike, M., Garg, N.: Fair ranking: a critical review, challenges, and future directions. arXiv preprint arXiv:2201.12662 (2022)
14. Raj, A., Wood, C., Montoly, A., Ekstrand, M.D.: Comparing fair ranking metrics. arXiv preprint arXiv:2009.01311 (2020)
15. Sakai, T., Kim, J.Y., Kang, I.: A versatile framework for evaluating ranked lists in terms of group fairness and relevance. arXiv preprint arXiv:2204.00280 (2022)

16. Sapiezynski, P., Zeng, W., E Robertson, R., Mislove, A., Wilson, C.: Quantifying the impact of user attention on fair group representation in ranked lists. In: Companion Proceedings of the 2019 World Wide Web Conference, pp. 553–562 (2019)
17. Singh, A., Joachims, T.: Fairness of exposure in rankings. In: Proceedings of the 24th ACM SIGKDD International Conference on Knowledge Discovery & Data Mining, pp. 2219–2228 (2018)
18. Tan, Z., et al.: Large language models for data annotation: a survey. arXiv preprint arXiv:2402.13446 (2024)
19. Tao, S., et al.: Overview of the NTCIR-17 fairweb-1 task. In: Proceedings of the 17th NTCIR Conference on Evaluation of Information Access Technologies (2023). https://doi.org/10.20736/0002001318
20. Törnberg, P.: Best practices for text annotation with large language models. arXiv preprint arXiv:2402.05129 (2024)
21. Van Erven, T., Harremos, P.: Rényi divergence and Kullback-Leibler divergence. IEEE Trans. Inf. Theory **60**(7), 3797–3820 (2014)
22. Yang, K., Stoyanovich, J.: Measuring fairness in ranked outputs. In: Proceedings of the 29th International Conference on Scientific and Statistical Database Management, pp. 1–6 (2017)
23. Zehlike, M., Bonchi, F., Castillo, C., Hajian, S., Megahed, M., Baeza-Yates, R.: FA*IR: a fair top-k ranking algorithm. In: Proceedings of the 2017 ACM on Conference on Information and Knowledge Management, pp. 1569–1578 (2017)
24. Zehlike, M., Yang, K., Stoyanovich, J.: Fairness in ranking: a survey. arXiv preprint arXiv:2103.14000 (2021)

A Survey of LoRA Algorithm Variations for Language Models

Mengyao Zhu(✉) and Phuc Huu Nguyen

Yamaguchi University, Ube, Yamaguchi 753-0841, Japan
{a504wcu,phuc}@yamaguchi-u.ac.jp

Abstract. The rise of language models has achieved state-of-the-art performances across a wide range of downstream tasks. However, traditional full-parameter fine-tuning is computationally expensive and impractical for scaling to increasingly larger models. To mitigate these challenges, parameter-efficient fine-tuning (PEFT) methods have been introduced, with Low-Rank Adaptation (LoRA) emerging as a prominent approach. LoRA significantly reduces fine-tuning costs by modifying only a small set of trainable low-rank weight matrices, while keeping the majority of the pretrained model weights frozen. This survey provides a mathematically rigorous exploration of LoRA-based variations, focusing on their algorithmic structures and working mechanisms. By conducting a systematic analysis, we offer deeper insights into the mathematical characteristics and adaptation dynamics of LoRA-based methods. This survey aims to equip the PEFT research community with a solid mathematical framework for designing more effective, scalable, and computationally efficient fine-tuning algorithms, further advancing the adaptability of language models in resource-constrained settings.

Keywords: PEFT · Parameter-Efficient Fine-Tuning · LoRA

1 Introduction

The rapid development of language models has achieved remarkable performances in areas such as document classification, machine translation, question answering etc. Models like BERT, GPT, Gemini, DeepSeek, and their derivatives [2,9,12,31,40,50] have demonstrated unprecedented capabilities, often powered by hundreds of millions or billions of parameters obtained through massively iterative computations. While these advancements have set new benchmarks across tasks [8,15,19,21,25,29,42,57,61], they also highlight critical challenges especially in high computational costs, significant memory requirements, and limited adaptability to a large number of downstream tasks in different domains. Addressing these challenges has become a focal point of research, as evidenced by the increasing number of relevant studies proposing different algorithms to make the post-training of language models to be more efficient and accurate.

R. Ichise (Ed.): NLDB 2025, LNCS 15836, pp. 275–290, 2026.
https://doi.org/10.1007/978-3-031-97141-9_19

This survey provides an in-depth mathematical analysis of 53 LoRA algorithm [10,22,32,35,63,65,69,77,80] variations integrated with multiple mechanisms such as dynamic selection, extra decomposition, MoE, quantization and pruning, integration, sharing, etc. This study seeks to elucidate the structures and components of these algorithms, with the goal of offering mathematical insights for researchers and practitioners seeking to efficiently optimize language model fine-tuning for real-world applications.

This survey presents, to the best of our knowledge, compared with previous relevant survey papers [5,14,26,37,44,54,74,76], the most comprehensive mathematical review of 53 different LoRA algorithm variations mainly designed for language models. Our key contributions include:

1. Systematically interpreted 53 LoRA algorithm variations for their algorithmic structures and involved adaptation mechanisms.
2. Classified the papers into 10 distinct categories, reflecting different algorithmic evolution paths for optimal or near optimal adaptation results.
3. Equipped researchers and practitioners with cluster of innovative ideas of LoRA-based algorithms for parameter-efficient fine-tuning mainly for language models.

2 Survey Scope and Selection Criteria

To ensure a comprehensive and systematic collection of relevant LoRA algorithm variation papers, we conducted an extensive literature search mainly on arXiv.org and complementary search on major international conference databases such as NeurIPS, ACL, etc., published between June 2021 and August 2024 in the following steps:

Step 1: Paper Search We applied a systematic search strategy using case-insensitive terms such as 'LoRA', 'Low-Ran Adaptation', 'Parameter-Efficient Fine-Tuning', 'Fine-Tuning', etc. for the first round of paper search.

Step 2: Narrowing Down Then we narrowed down the search papers to those focusing on LoRA-based algorithms mainly implemented for language models to 53 papers. We prioritized peer-reviewed papers accepted by renowned international NLP conferences on openreview.net, mainly based on the papers published on arXiv.org. Papers focusing on other domains such for vision tasks were excluded.

Step 3: Categorization by Mechanisms We then systematically classified these 53 papers into 10 distinct categories based on their mathematical characteristics and mathematical mechanisms integrated with LoRA algorithm.

This structured procedure ensures that our survey paper captures a diversified and representative set of LoRA-based algorithms, providing a mathematically rigorous and comprehensive overview of current advancements in LoRA-based techniques.

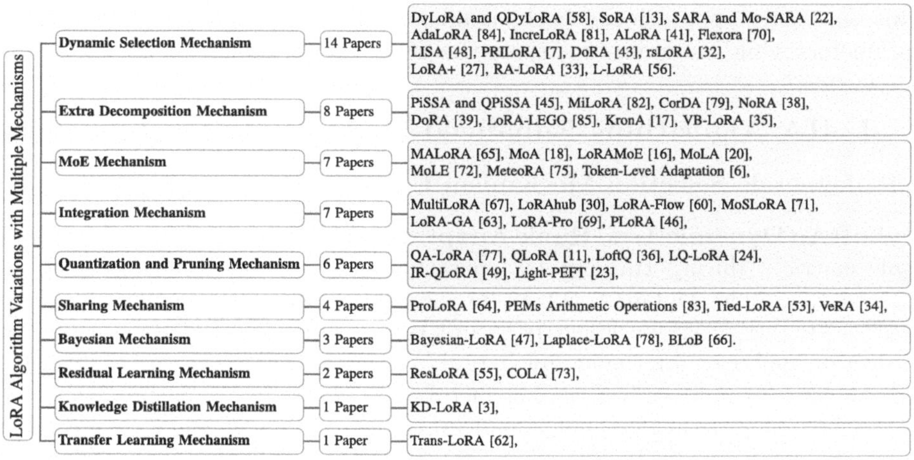

Fig. 1. Taxonomy of LoRA Variations Enhanced by Multiple Mechanisms.

3 Preliminaries

The **Transformer Architecture** [59] relies on the self-attention mechanism, evolved from the Bahdanau attention [4], by calculating the attention scores with formula $\text{Att}(Q, K, V) = \text{softmax}\left(\frac{QK^T}{\sqrt{d_k}}\right)V$, based on the query ($Q$), key($K$) and value ($V$) matrices, which are transformed by the corresponding learnable weight matrices and input sequence embeddings. This mechanism has significantly enhanced the contextual understanding for each of the tokens in the context of input sequence. Multi-head attention mechanism further enhances self-attention by employing multiple parallel attention heads, each capturing different relationships for the specific token with the remaining tokens. Each head computes attention as $\text{head}_i = \text{Att}(QW_i^Q, KW_i^K, VW_i^V)$, and the outputs are concatenated and projected using W^O: $\text{MultiHead}(Q, K, V) = \text{Concat}(\text{head}_1, \ldots, \text{head}_h)W^O$. Given the attention mechanism illustrated above, Transformer architecture enables efficient learning of contextual token representations with linear transformations and non-linear activations, further enhanced and stabilized by the normalizations, residual connections, dropout, etc., making it nearly the default choice for both language understanding and generation tasks (Fig. 1).

LoRA (Low-Rank Adaptation). [28] leverages the observations of low intrinsic dimensionality [1] of pre-trained weight matrices, and applies it by decomposing the weight update ΔW as the product of two trainable low-rank weight matrices as $\Delta W = BA$, where $B \in \mathbb{R}^{d \times r}, A \in \mathbb{R}^{r \times k}$, with rank $r \ll \min(d, k)$. The forward pass is reparametrized as $h = W_0x + \Delta Wx = W_0x + BAx$, in which A first transforms the input token embeddings to a much lower dimensional space, then B scales back the compressed token embeddings to the original dimensions, while the pre-trained weight matrix W_0 will be kept frozen.

This innovative approach can both significantly reduce the number of trainable parameters while maintain or surpass the SOTA performance.

4 LoRA Algorithms Enhanced by Multiple Mechanisms

4.1 Dynamic Selection Mechanism Enhanced

DyLoRA (Dynamic Low-Rank Adaptation). [58] dynamically adapts low-rank matrices during training by operating over a range of ranks r, from $r_{\min}$ to $r_{\max}$. The DyLoRA output for any given layer is calculated as: $h = W_0x + \frac{\alpha}{r}W_{\text{up}}^{\downarrow b}W_{\text{down}}^{\downarrow b}x$, in which $W_{\text{up}}^{\downarrow b}$ and $W_{\text{down}}^{\downarrow b}$ are truncated versions of the projection matrices for the sampled rank b from a predefined probability distribution $p_B(b)$, and α is a scaling factor. This formulation ensures that the rank selection process does not significantly degrade the model's performance across different ranks. Its extension **QDyLoRA** [52] incorporates NF4 quantization to further reduce the memory consumption. **AdaLoRA (Adaptive Low-Rank Adaptation)** [84] dynamically allocates rank budgets for parameter updating based on importance-aware adaptation. It decomposes the trainable parameter matrix with SVD, allowing adaptive rank pruning during, expressed as $W = W^{(0)} + P\Lambda Q$. Orthogonality constraint is also applied to maintain the adaptation stability. **ALoRA (Allocating Low-Rank Adaptation)** [41] treats the dynamic rank allocation as an optimization process, initially assigned uniformly across Transformer modules, then dynamically allocate rank values based on their importance scores. ALoRA introduces gate units $\alpha \in \{0, 1\}$ that determine whether a given trainable matrix rank i is retained or pruned. **RA-LoRA (Rank-Adaptive LoRA)** [33] dynamically adjust the rank of adapter matrices to mitigate quantization errors $W_qerr = W - W_q$ during fine-tuning. It uses SVD of the quantization error matrix to ensure that only the most significant singular vectors contribute to the fine-tuning process.

IncreLoRA (Incremental Parameter Allocation LoRA). [81] decomposes the update matrix ΔW into a summation of rank-1 matrices: $\Delta W = \sum_{i=1}^{r} \lambda_i b_i a_i$, where λ_i are trainable scaling factors updated via backpropagation, and $r \ll \min(in, out)$ for minimal computational footprint. To allocate parameters dynamically during training, IncreLoRA computes an importance score $S_k^{(t)} = \text{avg}(|\Delta W_k \cdot \text{grad}(\Delta W_k)|)$ for each module, quantifying its relevance to the training objective. Different from naive LoRA in which LoRA being applied to key and value transformation matrices, IncreLoRA has been applied in all linear layers. **SoRA (Sparse Low-Rank Adaptation)** [13] introduces a learnable gating mechanism $g \in \mathbb{R}^{r_{\max}}$ as a sparsity-controlling vector to ensure that certain rank components can be selectively zeroed out or maintained. This makes the selection of rank r to be not fixed by learned during training, which can effectively reduce the number of trainable parameters.

SARA (Singular-Value Based Adaptive Low-Rank Adaption). [22] determines its trainable parameters by first performing SVD on the pre-trained weight matrices, then approximate the original matrix with the chosen top k

singular values as $h = x(W_0 + U_k \Lambda_k V_k)$, where k is used to dynamically choose the appropriate number of ranks r during fine-tuning. Its extension **Mo-SARA (Mixture-of-SARA)** further incorporates multiple truncated singular value matrices trained in parallel, selected by a router, making only the k singular values are fine-tuned for higher convergence speed. **Flexora (Flexible Low Rank Adaptation)** [70] framework introduces flexible layer selection through hyperparameter optimization (HPO) and solving it with Unrolled Differentiation (UD). Ensures that only the most critical layers are fine-tuned. This involves identifying a subset of layers $\mathcal{L}$ with indices corresponding to the largest contributions to task-specific performance. **LISA (Layerwise Importance Sampling AdamW)** [48] leverages importance sampling to selectively freezes and updates layers based on their importance. The method is built on an observed skewness in weight norms across different layers, where layers exhibit significantly larger weight magnitudes than intermediate layers. The probabilities for layer selection is determined by $p^{(\ell)} = \frac{w^{(\ell)}}{\sum_j w^{(j)}}$, in which the average weight norm of a given layer ℓ across T training iterations was calculated through $w^{(\ell)} = \frac{1}{T}\sum_{t=1}^{T} \|\theta_t^{(\ell)}\|_2$.

PRILoRA (Pruned and Rank-Increasing Low-Rank Adaptation). [7] introduces a rank-increasing strategy to allocate progressively larger ranks to the trainable weight matrices as layers deepens, not the uniform rank r across all layers in naive LoRA, then conduct the structured pruning to matrix A based on the importance of individual weight components and the input activations controlled by the importance matrix. **DoRA (Dynamic Low-Rank Adaptation)** [43] decomposes the pre-trained weight matrices into single-rank components, where each component is represented as $A_i B_i c_i$, with $A_i \in \mathbb{R}^{d\times 1}$ and $B_i \in \mathbb{R}^{1\times d}$ as low-rank matrices, and c_i is a scalar used for pruning the less important matrix component by setting $c_i = 0$. **rsLoRA (Rank-Stabilized LoRA)** [32] changes the computation of scaling factor to mitigate the gradient collapse during fine-tuning. In naive LoRA, the scaling factor is defined as $\gamma_r = \frac{\alpha}{r}$ that causes the gradient norms to decrease rapidly with increasing r. In contrast, rsLoRA introduces the rank-stabilized scaling factor as $\gamma_r = \frac{\alpha}{\sqrt{r}}$ to better preserve gradient magnitudes across different ranks. **LoRA+** [27] incorporates adaptive learning rate strategies for matrices A and B as η_A and η_B respectively, where $\eta_B \gg \eta_A$ to ensure efficient feature learning in modeling with large embedding dimensions. **L-LoRA (Linearized LoRA)** [56] partially linearizes LoRA modules to enhance multi-task fusion and task disentanglement. Instead of treating LoRA modules as fully nonlinear functions, L-LoRA applies first-order Taylor approximation to selectively linearize certain LoRA components, expressed as $f_{\theta_0}(x;\phi) \approx f_{\theta_0}(x;\phi_0) + \nabla_\phi f_{\theta_0}(x;\phi_0)^\top(\phi - \phi_0)$. ensuring that task vectors remain additive and orthogonal in function space.

4.2 Extra Decomposition Mechanism Enhanced

PiSSA (Principal Singular Values and Singular Vectors Adaptation). [45] decomposes the weight matrix with SVD into the summation of trainable principal low-rank and frozen residual matrices as $W = W^{pri} + W^{res}$, in which the principal matrix is reconstructed with the top-r singular values with corresponding singular vectors $W^{pri} = U_{[:,:r]} S_{[:r,:r]} V_{[:,:r]}^T$. It allows the model to focus computational resources on the most informative subspaces represented by W^{pri} for faster convergence. Its extension **QPiSSA** incorporates NF4 quantization to reduce memory overhead. **MiLoRA (Mixture of Low-Rank Adaptation)** [82] applies SVD to decompose the weight matrix W as the summation of frozen principal W_p and trainable minor matrix W_m as $W = W_p + W_m = W_p + B_m A_m = \sum_{i=1}^{m-r} \sigma_i u_i v_i^\top + \sum_{i=m-r+1}^{m} \sigma_i u_i v_i^\top$. **CorDA (Context-Oriented Decomposition Adaptation)** [79] leverages SVD of the product of the weight matrix W and input covariance matrix C as $\text{SVD}(WC) = U\Sigma V^T$, CorDA facilitating two adaptation modes. Knowledge-preserved adaptation ensures pre-trained world knowledge retention by using smallest r singular components, while instruction-previewed adaptation adapts the largest singular components to obtain a stronger task alignment. **NoRA (Nested Low-Rank Adaptation)** [38] employs SVD to obtain a dual-layer nested structure consisting of a frozen outer LoRA layer as a low-rank approximation of pre-trained weight matrix for stability, and trainable inner LoRA layer for precise task-specific updates, formulated as $h = Wx + \Delta Wx = Wx + BAx + B'A'x$.

DoRA (Weight-Decomposed Low-Rank Adaptation). [39] decomposes the weight matrix as the product of frozen magnitude component m and trainable direction component V as $W = m \cdot V/\|V\|_c$. Low-rank adaptation is exclusively applied to the directional component for finer-grained learning adjustments. **LoRA-LEGO** [85] first decomposes the trainable low-rank matrices into Minimal Semantic Units (MSUs), representing rows of down-projection A and columns of up-projection B, then collect all MSUs from multiple LoRAs into a unified pool, then categorizes all the MSUs into k clusters, then reconstruct the final LoRA by using the centroids as representative MSUs for the merged LoRA module. **KronA (Kronecker Adapter)** [17] decomposes the trainable weight matrix with Kronecker decomposition as $W_{\text{tuned}} = W + s[A_K \otimes B_K]$, to both reduce the number of trainable parameters and computational resources. **VB-LoRA (Vector Bank LoRA)** [35] decomposes ΔW into modular components $v_k^{(i)}$, which are further divided into sub-vectors $u_{k,j}^{(i)}$ of fixed size $\mathbb{R}^b$. Each vector $v_k^{(i)}$ is constructed as $v_k^{(i)} = \text{concat}(u_{k,1}^{(i)}, \ldots, u_{k,d_i'}^{(i)})$, where the sub-vectors $u_{k,j}^{(i)}$ are mapped to a shared vector bank B.

4.3 MoE Mechanism Enhanced

MALoRA (Mixture of Asymmetric Low-Rank Adaptation). [65] recognizes that the down-projection matrix A in LoRA expert modules, remains largely similar across different tasks, while the up-projection matrix B captures task-specific variations. To exploit this asymmetry, MALoRA replaces A_t matrices with a factorized representation $A_t \approx P_t S_A$, where $S_A \in \mathbb{R}^{d \times n}$ is a global subspace across tasks, and $P_t \in \mathbb{R}^{r \times d}$ is the task-dependent coefficient matrix. The up-projection matrix B is allocated with more tank for better feature transformations. Thus making the MALoRA weight update formulated as $\Delta W_t = B_t P_t S_A$.

MoA (Mixture-of-LoRAs). [18] improves multi-task fine-tuning using task-specific LoRA modules with a routing mechanism mathematically expressed as $W_{final} = W_0 + \text{router}(W_r, A_1B_1, \cdots, A_NB_N)$ to dynamically activate appropriate LoRA modules based on input data. **LoRAMoE** [16] balances world knowledge retention and task adaptation based on expert-based adaptation, controlled by a router function, realized through $o = W_0x + \Delta Wx = W_0x + \sum_{i=1}^{N} G(x)_i E_i(x)$, in which W_0x represents the fixed backbone transformation, the sum introduces dynamic expert selection, enabling specialized knowledge adaptation. **MoLA (MoE-LoRA with Layer-Wise Expert Allocation)** [20] introduces an adaptive expert selection mechanism using the routing function, through which to select and weight LoRA experts dynamically at each layer j and module t. It ensures only the most relevant experts contribute to the adaptation of pre-trained weights.

MoLE (Mixture of LoRA Experts). [72] introduces an adaptive gating function that assigns dynamic weights $\mathcal{G}_i$ to each LoRA transformation based on the input data x to enable a context-sensitive composition. The final output $\tilde{\boldsymbol{E}}_{\Omega}(\boldsymbol{x})$ represents the composite feature representation with dynamically assigned weights. **MeteoRA (Multiple-Tasks Embedded LoRA)** [75] employs a gating network to dynamically selects the most relevant LoRA modules based on the input vector x. The gating network maps the hidden state x to a probability distribution over n LoRA modules, allowing for the top-k selection of experts determined by a softmax function. **Token-Level Adaptation** [6] leverages the gating mechanism to dynamically select among four specialized LoRA adapters, based on the contextual similarity score with the input token embeddings $x = (x_1, x_2, \ldots, x_n)$ and centroids of training datasets for each of the LoRA adapters. These scores serve as input to the gating mechanism that determines the weight contribution of each LoRA adapter for next token prediction.

4.4 Quantization and Pruning Mechanism Enhanced

QA-LoRA (Quantization-Aware Low-Rank Adaptation). [77] maps the original continuous weight values into a quantized space using scaling factor α and offset factor β, while preserving accuracy as much as possible, expressed as $\hat{\mathbf{W}} = \left\lfloor \frac{\mathbf{W}-\beta}{\alpha} \right\rceil$, in which α determines the range of quantized values, β ensures that values are centered correctly within the range. **QLoRA (Quantized Low-Rank Adaptation)** [11] further introduces 4-bit NormalFloat (NF4) quantization tailored to normally distributed weights by assigns non-uniform quantization levels, and Paged Optimizers to dynamically offload gradient and optimizer states between GPU and CPU memory with NVIDIA's Unified Memory Paging. **LoftQ (LoRA Fine-Tuning-Aware Quantization)** [36] optimizes a quantized weight matrix Q and a low-rank approximation AB^T in order to minimize the Frobenius norm discrepancy from the original high-precision weight matrix W, expressed as $\min_{Q,A,B} \|W - Q - AB^\top\|_F$ to make the sum of Q and AB^T to best approximate W.

LQ-LoRA (Low-Rank Plus Quantized Matrix Decomposition). [24] factorize the pre-trained weight matrix into the product of low-rank matrices L_1L_2 and a quantized matrix Q, ensuring that the quantized component remains fixed while the low-rank component is fine-tuned. The objective is formulated as $\min_{Q,L_1,L_2} \|W-(Q+L_1L_2)\|_F$. **IR-QLoRA (Information Retention Quantized LoRA)** [49] maximizes the mutual information between the original and quantized model weights by incorporating information retention mechanism by applying information calibration quantization and information elastic connection. **Light-PEFT (Lightening LoRA)** [23] prunes redundant parameters in both foundation models and PEFT modules. The foundation model pruning uses trainable masks m_A for multi-head attention and m_F for feed forward network to eliminate the less important components, expressed as $L_{\text{mask}} = L + \lambda_A\|m_A\|_1 + \lambda_F\|m_F\|_1$. For PEFT pruning, module importance is measured using the information change ratio as $I_M = \frac{\|X\cdot W_{\text{down}}W_{\text{up}}\|_2}{\|X\cdot W\|_2}$.

4.5 Integration Mechanism Enhanced

MultiLoRA (Multitask LoRA). [67] introduces multiple parallel trainable modules as: $\Delta W_{\text{MultiLoRA}} = \sum_{i=1}^{n} \text{scaling}_i B_i A_i$ where $B_i \in \mathbb{R}^{d\times r_i}$, $A_i \in \mathbb{R}^{r_i\times k}$, and scaling_i is a learnable scaling factor initialized at zero, and rank r_i of each individual LoRA module is scaled inversely with n to maintain a constant total parameter budget as $r' = r_{total}/n$. **LoRAHub** [30] combines multiple LoRA modules as $m_i = A_iB_i$ with coefficients w_i to form a composite module $\hat{m} = (w_1A_1 + w_2A_2 + \ldots + w_NA_N)(w_1B_1 + w_2B_2 + \ldots + w_NB_N)$ with w_i as trainable scalar coefficients to balance the contributions of the modules. **LoRA-Flow** [60] introduces dynamic fusion for LoRA modules, optimizing how pre-trained LoRA updates are blended based on contextual information with fusion weights $w^l = \text{softmax}(W^l_{\text{gate}}x^l_t) + b^l$ calculated per layer based on hidden states x^l_t. These weights govern the integration of module outputs via $h' = h + \Delta h w^l$, where w^l determines the influence of each LoRA module at layer l. **MoSLoRA (Mixture-of-Subspaces LoRA)** [71] introduces a learnable mixer matrix W to dynamically fuse decomposed matrix chunks from low-rank matrices B and A as $\Delta W = AWB = \sum_{i,j} \mathbf{A}_i W_{ij} \mathbf{B}_j$, in which the additional mixing steps enhances the interactions between subspaces while maintains low-rank structure.

LoRA-GA (Low Rank Adaptation with Gradient Approximation). [63] initializes the low-rank matrices B and A with principal singular vectors of the full gradient matrix, ensuring that the gradient of LORA-GA closely follows the direction of full fine-tuning. **LoRA-Pro** [69] aligns its low-rank gradient $\tilde{g} = sBg^A + sg^BA$ with the true gradient g from full fine-tuning, minimizing the difference through the objective $\min_{g_A,g_B} |\tilde{g} - g|^2_F$. It optimally adjusts gradients g^A and g^B for the low-rank matrices A and B to narrow the mismatch with the full fine-tuning gradient. **PLoRA (PeriodicLoRA)** [46] progressively increases the effective rank by accumulating multiple low-rank updates, constructing the final parameter matrix as $W_T = W_0 + \sum_{t=1}^{T} B_tA_t$, in which hyperparameter T is the number of training stages to approximate the full-rank adaptation.

4.6 Sharing Mechanism Enhanced

ProLoRA (Partially Rotation-Enhanced Low-Rank Adaptation). [64] introduces partial parameter sharing to reduce the trainable parameter count, then selects a subset of B and A as unshared portions for higher representational capacity as $\Delta W = (B_u \oplus_h (B_0 \oplus_v \cdots \oplus_v B_{n-1}))(A_u \oplus_v (A_0 \oplus_h \cdots \oplus_h A_{m-1}))$, where A_0 and B_0 are trainable matrix chunks, A_u and B_u represent the unshared ranks, $\oplus_h$ and $\oplus_v$ denote horizontal and vertical concatenation of shared and unshared submatrices. **PEMs Arithmetic Operations** [83] assumes that PEMs (parameter-efficient modules) trained on independently can be utilized through summation $\theta^{\text{add}} = \theta^{(1)} \oplus \theta^{(2)}$ and negation $\boldsymbol{h} \leftarrow \boldsymbol{h} + \Delta \boldsymbol{h} \xrightarrow{negate} \boldsymbol{h} \leftarrow \boldsymbol{h} + (-\Delta \boldsymbol{h})$ in parameter space to achieve enhanced generalization.

Tied-LoRA. [53] expresses the low-rank approximation as $\Delta W \approx \frac{\alpha}{r} \Lambda_v B \Lambda_u A$ through selective training and weight tying, in which B and A are shared across layers, and selective components of diagonal matrices Λ_v, Λ_u and low-rank matrices B and A are updated during fine-tuning. **VeRA (Vector-based Random Matrix Adaptation)** [34] defines its adaptation as $h = W_0 x + \Delta W x = W_0 x + \Lambda_b B \Lambda_d A x$, where B and A are shared across the layers and kept frozen, Λ_b and Λ_d are trainable scaling matrices for layer-wise flexibility.

4.7 Bayesian Mechanism Enhanced

Bayesian-LoRA. [47] integrates both dynamic adaptation and parameter quantization under a Bayesian framework, ensuring that dynamic rank selection and bit precision levels are optimized probabilistically rather than being manually defined. The dynamic rank adaptation follows a Bayesian gating function, ensuring that the rank selection of low-rank matrices B and A are selectively activated through a diagonal scaling matrix E in $W = W_0 + BEA$. The parameter quantization also follows a Bayesian procedure, where each weight follows a multi-resolution quantization scheme. **Laplace-LoRA** [78] applies Laplace approximation to LoRA-adapted parameters after fine-tuning, modeling posterior uncertainty in a low-rank adaptation space. By assuming a Gaussian posterior centered at the MAP estimate, it enables Bayesian uncertainty estimation without requiring full-network Bayesian inference, where uncertainty estimation is critical for reliable decision-making. **BLoB (Bayesian Low-Rank Adaptation by Backpropagation)** [66] models low-rank update matrix A as random variable with a Gaussian variational distribution while keeping B deterministic, ensuring that adaptation remains structured and uncertainty is efficiently captured. In gradient update, instead of treating A as a fixed weight matrix, BLoB samples A from its posterior to realize uncertainty-aware fine-tuning.

4.8 Residual Learning Mechanism Enhanced

ResLoRA (Residual Mapping LoRA). [55] integrates residual connections into the adaptation process of low-rank adaptation, expressed. It introduces three type of blocks as input-shortcut $h_n = W_n x_n + B_n A_n(x_n + x_{n-1})$ that ensures the past-layer inputs contribute directly to find-tuning, block-shortcut $h_n = W_n x_n + (\sum_{k=0}^{m} B_{n-k} A_{n-k}) x_n$ that ensures past-layer LoRA updates accumulate progressively, and middle-shortcut $h_n = W_n x_n + B_n(\sum_{k=0}^{m} A_{n-k} x_{n-k})$ ensuring to retain intermediate representations to enhance gradient propagation. **COLA (Chain of LoRA)** [73] employs a high-rank augmentation strategy through iterative residual learning. Instead of applying a single low-rank transformation, it incrementally refines the model's adaptation via a sequence of low-rank updates. Mathematically, COLA constructs an approximation of the optimal weight update as $\Delta W^* \approx \sum_{t=1}^{M} B_t A_t$ where each iteration introduces a new low-rank update $\{B_t, A_t\}$, allowing the model to gradually reach a higher-rank approximation.

4.9 Knowledge Distillation Mechanism Enhanced

KD-LoRA (Knowledge Distillation with Low-Rank Adaptation). [3] integrates components from teacher model, student model, and knowledge distillation, given by the combined loss as $\mathcal{L}_{\text{total}}^{\mathcal{S}} = \alpha \mathcal{L}_{\text{task}}^{\mathcal{S}} + (1-\alpha)\mathcal{L}_{\text{kd}}(z^{\mathcal{S}}, z^{\mathcal{T}})$. The teacher model is trained on specific dataset then generates soft targets for the student model, the student model uses LoRA to optimize it parameters, The knowledge distillation loss $\mathcal{L}_{\text{kd}}$ facilitates knowledge transform from the teacher to the student by aligning their probability distributions.

4.10 Transfer Learning Mechanism Enhanced

Trans-LoRA. [62] relies on synthetic data generation and knowledge distillation to transfer LoRA parameters across different target models. The source model M_s is fine-tuned on a task dataset D to produce trained LoRA parameters θ_s. The target model M_t does not have access to D but instead receives synthetic data D_{syn} generated from a small seed dataset D_{seed}. The synthetic data generator G approximates the original data distribution, and a discriminator D_ϕ filters high-quality synthetic samples. The knowledge transfer process aligns the target model's predictions with the source model's predictions on D_{syn} by minimizing distillation loss on KL divergence, ensuring that $M_t + \theta_t$ generalizes similarly to $M_s + \theta_s$.

5 Conclusion and Future Directions

This survey mathematically examines 53 LoRA-based algorithm variations, categorized into 10 mechanisms, with a primary focus on their algorithmic properties and distinct characteristics. Key categories with more algorithm proposals include: dynamic selection mechanism, such as to dynamically determine the rank of the trainable matrices to flexibly allocate the memory usage and computation time; extra decomposition mechanism, such as to decompose the matrix as the sum of a trainable primary matrix with most information retained and a frozen residual matrix containing less informative training signals to further save the computational resources; MoE mechanism such as to selectively activate and integrate different expert models with diverse skills and knowledge for specific downstream tasks and quantization mechanism such as to adjust the parameter precision while maintaining comparable model accuracy. Less commonly proposed algorithms were also carefully reviewed, with diverse mathematical strengths elaborated upon, highlighting a diversity of mathematical innovations. In conclusion, this survey provides a thorough and extensive algorithmic analytics and interpretations for the discussed algorithm variations, with unique features highlighted. It offers valuable inspiration to researchers in language model adaptation for developing improved LoRA-relevant algorithms in the future.

Looking ahead, one promising direction is to develop LoRA variants enhanced by Direct Preference Optimization (DPO) [51]. In this setting, adapter modules can be fine-tuned using gradients computed from comparisons between preferred and dispreferred responses, allowing the model to better capture human-aligned behaviors. This approach might have the potential to enable parameter-efficient, preference-driven updates that directly influence the model's generation patterns, promoting alignment with human expectations without the computational overhead of full fine-tuning.

Another promising avenue lies in combining LoRA with the Self-Instruct [68] framework, which can generate larger number of high-quality instruction-response pairs as fine-tuning dataset without extensive human annotation. This combination has the potential to democratize efficient instruction tuning with training dataset generated by powerful open-source LLMs.

Collectively, more personalized LoRA-based algorithms should be designed and verified for more practical tasks. Extracting essential mathematical characteristics from each of the proposed LoRA algorithms can provide holistic and flexible guidelines to derive more advanced algorithms for better language model fine-tuning.

References

1. Aghajanyan, A., Zettlemoyer, L., Gupta, S.: Intrinsic dimensionality explains the effectiveness of language model fine-tuning. arXiv (2020). http://arxiv.org/abs/2012.13255
2. Anthropic: The claude 3 model family: Opus, sonnet, haiku (2024). https://www.semanticscholar.org/paper/The-Claude-3-Model-Family%3A-Opus%2C-Sonnet%2C-Haiku/de8ba9b01c9ab7cbabf5c33b80b7bbc618857627. Accessed 24 Jan 2025
3. Azimi, R., Rishav, R., Teichmann, M., Kahou, S.E.: KD-LoRA: a hybrid approach to efficient fine-tuning with LoRA and knowledge distillation. arXiv (2024). http://arxiv.org/abs/2410.20777
4. Bahdanau, D., Cho, K., Bengio, Y.: Neural machine translation by jointly learning to align and translate. arXiv (2014). http://arxiv.org/abs/1409.0473
5. Balne, C.C.S., Bhaduri, S., Roy, T., Jain, V., Chadha, A.: Parameter efficient fine tuning: a comprehensive analysis across applications. arXiv (2024). http://arxiv.org/abs/2404.13506

6. Belofsky, J.: Token-level adaptation of LoRA adapters for downstream task generalization. arXiv, pp. 168–172 (2023). http://arxiv.org/abs/2311.10847
7. Benedek, N., Wolf, L.: PRILoRA: pruned and rank-increasing low-rank adaptation. arXiv (2024). http://arxiv.org/abs/2401.11316
8. Combemale, B., Gray, J., Rumpe, B.: Large language models as an "operating" system for software and systems modeling. Softw. Syst. Model. **22**(5), 1391–1392 (2023). https://doi.org/10.1007/s10270-023-01126-0
9. DeepSeek-AI: DeepSeek-V2: A strong, economical, and efficient mixture-of-experts language model. arXiv (2024). http://arxiv.org/abs/2405.04434
10. Dettmers, T., Pagnoni, A., Holtzman, A., Zettlemoyer, L.: QLoRA: efficient finetuning of quantized LLMs. In: Oh, A., Naumann, T., Globerson, A., Saenko, K., Hardt, M., Levine, S. (eds.) Advances in Neural Information Processing Systems, vol. 36, pp. 10088–10115. Curran Associates, Inc. (2023). https://proceedings.neurips.cc/paper_files/paper/2023/hash/1feb87871436031bdc0f2beaa62a049b-Abstract-Conference.html
11. Dettmers, T., Pagnoni, A., Holtzman, A., Zettlemoyer, L.: QLoRA: efficient finetuning of quantized LLMs. arXiv (2023). http://arxiv.org/abs/2305.14314
12. Devlin, J., Chang, M.W., Lee, K., Toutanova, K.: BERT: pre-training of deep bidirectional transformers for language understanding. arXiv (2018). http://arxiv.org/abs/1810.04805
13. Ding, N., et al.: Sparse low-rank adaptation of pre-trained language models. arXiv (2023). http://arxiv.org/abs/2311.11696
14. Ding, N., et al.: Delta tuning: a comprehensive study of parameter efficient methods for pre-trained language models. arXiv (2022). http://arxiv.org/abs/2203.06904
15. Dou, S., et al.: StepCoder: improve code generation with reinforcement learning from compiler feedback. arXiv (2024). http://arxiv.org/abs/2402.01391
16. Dou, S., et al.: LoRAMoE: alleviating world knowledge forgetting in large language models via MoE-style plugin. In: Ku, L.W., Martins, A., Srikumar, V. (eds.) Proceedings of the 62nd Annual Meeting of the Association for Computational Linguistics (Volume 1: Long Papers), pp. 1932–1945. Association for Computational Linguistics, Stroudsburg (2024). https://doi.org/10.18653/v1/2024.acl-long.106. https://aclanthology.org/2024.acl-long.106/
17. Edalati, A., Tahaei, M., Kobyzev, I., Nia, V.P., Clark, J.J., Rezagholizadeh, M.: KronA: parameter efficient tuning with kronecker adapter. arXiv (2022). http://arxiv.org/abs/2212.10650
18. Feng, W., Hao, C., Zhang, Y., Han, Y., Wang, H.: Mixture-of-LoRAs: an efficient multitask tuning method for large language models. In: International Conference on Language Resources and Evaluation, pp. 11371–11380 (2024). http://arxiv.org/abs/2403.03432
19. Fu, X.Y., Laskar, M.T.R., Khasanova, E., Chen, C., Tn, S.B.: Tiny titans: can smaller large language models punch above their weight in the real world for meeting summarization? arXiv (2024). http://arxiv.org/abs/2402.00841
20. Gao, C., et al.: Higher layers need more LoRA experts. arXiv (2024). http://arxiv.org/abs/2402.08562
21. Gao, T., Yen, H., Yu, J., Chen, D.: Enabling large language models to generate text with citations. arXiv (2023). http://arxiv.org/abs/2305.14627
22. Gu, J., Chen, S., Wang, Z., Zhang, Y., Gong, P.: SARA: singular-value based adaptive low-rank adaption. arXiv (2024). http://arxiv.org/abs/2408.03290
23. Gu, N., Fu, P., Liu, X., Shen, B., Lin, Z., Wang, W.: Light-PEFT: lightening parameter-efficient fine-tuning via early pruning. In: Ku, L.W., Martins, A.,

Srikumar, V. (eds.) Findings of the Association for Computational Linguistics, ACL 2024, pp. 7528–7541. Association for Computational Linguistics, Stroudsburg (2024). https://aclanthology.org/2024.findings-acl.447/
24. Guo, H., Greengard, P., Xing, E.P., Kim, Y.: LQ-LoRA: low-rank plus quantized matrix decomposition for efficient language model finetuning. arXiv (2023). http://arxiv.org/abs/2311.12023
25. Gupta, P., Jiao, C., Yeh, Y.T., Mehri, S., Eskenazi, M., Bigham, J.P.: InstructDial: improving zero and few-shot generalization in dialogue through instruction tuning. arXiv (2022). http://arxiv.org/abs/2205.12673
26. Han, Z., Gao, C., Liu, J., Zhang, J., Zhang, S.Q.: Parameter-efficient fine-tuning for large models: a comprehensive survey. arXiv (2024). http://arxiv.org/abs/2403.14608
27. Hayou, S., Ghosh, N., Yu, B.: LoRA+: efficient low rank adaptation of large models. arXiv (2024). http://arxiv.org/abs/2402.12354
28. Hu, E.J., et al.: LoRA: low-rank adaptation of large language models. arXiv (2021). http://arxiv.org/abs/2106.09685
29. Hu, Y., et al.: Large language models are efficient learners of noise-robust speech recognition. arXiv (2024). http://arxiv.org/abs/2401.10446
30. Huang, C., Liu, Q., Lin, B.Y., Pang, T., Du, C., Lin, M.: LoraHub: efficient cross-task generalization via dynamic LoRA composition. arXiv (2023). http://arxiv.org/abs/2307.13269
31. Jiang, A.Q., et al.: Mistral 7B. arXiv (2023). http://arxiv.org/abs/2310.06825
32. Kalajdzievski, D.: A rank stabilization scaling factor for fine-tuning with LoRA. arXiv (2023). http://arxiv.org/abs/2312.03732
33. Kim, M., Lee, S., Sung, W., Choi, J.: RA-LoRA: rank-adaptive parameter-efficient fine-tuning for accurate 2-bit quantized large language models. In: Ku, L.W., Martins, A., Srikumar, V. (eds.) Findings of the Association for Computational Linguistics, ACL 2024, pp. 15773–15786. Association for Computational Linguistics, Stroudsburg (2024). https://doi.org/10.18653/v1/2024.findings-acl.933. https://aclanthology.org/2024.findings-acl.933/
34. Kopiczko, D.J., Blankevoort, T., Asano, Y.M.: VeRA: vector-based random matrix adaptation. arXiv (2023). http://arxiv.org/abs/2310.11454
35. Li, Y., Han, S., Ji, S.: VB-LoRA: extreme parameter efficient fine-tuning with vector banks. arXiv (2024). http://arxiv.org/abs/2405.15179
36. Li, Y., et al.: LoftQ: LoRA-fine-tuning-aware quantization for large language models. arXiv (2023). http://arxiv.org/abs/2310.08659
37. Lialin, V., Deshpande, V., Rumshisky, A.: Scaling down to scale up: a guide to parameter-efficient fine-tuning. arXiv (2023). http://arxiv.org/abs/2303.15647
38. Lin, C., Li, L., Li, D., Zou, J., Xue, W., Guo, Y.: NoRA: nested low-rank adaptation for efficient fine-tuning large models. arXiv (2024). http://arxiv.org/abs/2408.10280
39. Liu, S.Y., et al.: DoRA: weight-decomposed low-rank adaptation. arXiv (2024). http://arxiv.org/abs/2402.09353
40. Liu, Y., et al.: RoBERTa: a robustly optimized BERT pretraining approach. arXiv (2019)
41. Liu, Z., Lyn, J., Zhu, W., Tian, X., Graham, Y.: ALoRA: allocating low-rank adaptation for fine-tuning large language models. arXiv (2024). http://arxiv.org/abs/2403.16187
42. Lo, H.C., Chu, J.M., Hsiang, J., Cho, C.C.: Large language model informed patent image retrieval. arXiv (2024). http://arxiv.org/abs/2404.19360

43. Mao, Y., Huang, K., Guan, C., Bao, G., Mo, F., Xu, J.: DoRA: enhancing parameter-efficient fine-tuning with dynamic rank distribution. arXiv (2024). http://arxiv.org/abs/2405.17357
44. Mao, Y., et al.: A survey on LoRA of large language models. arXiv (2024). http://arxiv.org/abs/2407.11046
45. Meng, F., Wang, Z., Zhang, M.: PiSSA: principal singular values and singular vectors adaptation of large language models. arXiv (2024). http://arxiv.org/abs/2404.02948
46. Meng, X., et al.: PeriodicLoRA: breaking the low-rank bottleneck in LoRA optimization. arXiv (2024). http://arxiv.org/abs/2402.16141
47. Meo, C., Sycheva, K., Goyal, A., Dauwels, J.: Bayesian-LoRA: LoRA based parameter efficient fine-tuning using optimal quantization levels and rank values trough differentiable Bayesian gates. arXiv (2024). http://arxiv.org/abs/2406.13046
48. Pan, R., et al.: LISA: layerwise importance sampling for memory-efficient large language model fine-tuning. arXiv (2024). http://arxiv.org/abs/2403.17919
49. Qin, H., et al.: Accurate LoRA-finetuning quantization of LLMs via information retention. In: International Conference on Machine Learning (2024). http://arxiv.org/abs/2402.05445
50. Radford, A., Wu, J., Child, R., Luan, D., Amodei, D., Sutskever, I.: Language models are unsupervised multitask learners (2019). https://paperswithcode.com/paper/language-models-are-unsupervised-multitask. Accessed 25 Jan 2025
51. Rafailov, R., Sharma, A., Mitchell, E., Ermon, S., Manning, C.D., Finn, C.: Direct preference optimization: your language model is secretly a reward model. arXiv (2023). http://arxiv.org/abs/2305.18290
52. Rajabzadeh, H., et al.: QDyLoRA: quantized dynamic low-rank adaptation for efficient large language model tuning. arXiv (2024). http://arxiv.org/abs/2402.10462
53. Renduchintala, A., Konuk, T., Kuchaiev, O.: Tied-lora: enhacing parameter efficiency of LoRA with weight tying. arXiv (2023). http://arxiv.org/abs/2311.09578
54. Sabry, M., Belz, A.: PEFT-ref: a modular reference architecture and typology for parameter-efficient finetuning techniques. arXiv (2023). http://arxiv.org/abs/2304.12410
55. Shi, S., et al.: ResLoRA: identity residual mapping in low-rank adaption. In: Ku, L.W., Martins, A., Srikumar, V. (eds.) Findings of the Association for Computational Linguistics, ACL 2024, pp. 8870–8884. Association for Computational Linguistics, Stroudsburg (2024). https://doi.org/10.18653/v1/2024.findings-acl.525. https://aclanthology.org/2024.findings-acl.525/
56. Tang, A., et al.: Parameter efficient multi-task model fusion with partial linearization. arXiv (2023). http://arxiv.org/abs/2310.04742
57. Thirunavukarasu, A.J., et al.: Trialling a large language model (ChatGPT) in general practice with the applied knowledge test: observational study demonstrating opportunities and limitations in primary care. JMIR Med. Educ. **9**, e46599 (2023). https://doi.org/10.2196/46599
58. Valipour, M., Rezagholizadeh, M., Kobyzev, I., Ghodsi, A.: DyLoRA: parameter efficient tuning of pre-trained models using dynamic search-free low-rank adaptation. arXiv (2022). http://arxiv.org/abs/2210.07558
59. Vaswani, A., et al.: Attention is all you need. arXiv (2017). http://arxiv.org/abs/1706.03762
60. Wang, H., et al.: LoRA-flow: dynamic LoRA fusion for large language models in generative tasks. arXiv (2024). http://arxiv.org/abs/2402.11455

61. Wang, L., Yang, N., Huang, X., Yang, L., Majumder, R., Wei, F.: Improving text embeddings with large language models. arXiv (2023). http://arxiv.org/abs/2401.00368
62. Wang, R., et al.: *Trans-LoRA*: towards data-free transferable parameter efficient finetuning. arXiv (2024). http://arxiv.org/abs/2405.17258
63. Wang, S., Yu, L., Li, J.: LoRA-GA: low-rank adaptation with gradient approximation. arXiv (2024). http://arxiv.org/abs/2407.05000
64. Wang, S., et al.: PRoLoRA: partial rotation empowers more parameter-efficient LoRA. In: Ku, L.W., Martins, A., Srikumar, V. (eds.) Proceedings of the 62nd Annual Meeting of the Association for Computational Linguistics (Volume 1: Long Papers), pp. 2829–2841. Association for Computational Linguistics, Stroudsburg (2024). https://doi.org/10.18653/v1/2024.acl-long.156. https://aclanthology.org/2024.acl-long.156/
65. Wang, X., Zhao, H., Wang, S., Wang, H., Liu, Z.: MALoRA: mixture of asymmetric low-rank adaptation for enhanced multi-task learning. arXiv (2024). http://arxiv.org/abs/2410.22782
66. Wang, Y., Shi, H., Han, L., Metaxas, D., Wang, H.: BLoB: Bayesian low-rank adaptation by backpropagation for large language models. arXiv (2024). http://arxiv.org/abs/2406.11675
67. Wang, Y., Lin, Y., Zeng, X., Zhang, G.: MultiLoRA: democratizing LoRA for better multi-task learning. arXiv (2023). http://arxiv.org/abs/2311.11501
68. Wang, Y., et al.: Self-instruct: aligning language models with self-generated instructions. arXiv (2022). http://arxiv.org/abs/2212.10560
69. Wang, Z., Liang, J.: LoRA-pro: are low-rank adapters properly optimized? arXiv (2024). http://arxiv.org/abs/2407.18242
70. Wei, C., Shu, Y., He, Y.T., Yu, F.R.: Flexora: flexible low rank adaptation for large language models. arXiv (2024). http://arxiv.org/abs/2408.10774
71. Wu, T., Wang, J., Zhao, Z., Wong, N.: Mixture-of-subspaces in low-rank adaptation. In: Conference on Empirical Methods in Natural Language Processing (2024). http://arxiv.org/abs/2406.11909
72. Wu, X., Huang, S., Wei, F.: Mixture of LoRA experts. arXiv (2024). http://arxiv.org/abs/2404.13628
73. Xia, W., Qin, C., Hazan, E.: Chain of LoRA: efficient fine-tuning of language models via residual learning. arXiv (2024). http://arxiv.org/abs/2401.04151
74. Xin, Y., et al.: Parameter-efficient fine-tuning for pre-trained vision models: a survey. arXiv (2024). http://arxiv.org/abs/2402.02242
75. Xu, J., Lai, J., Huang, Y.: MeteoRA: multiple-tasks embedded LoRA for large language models. arXiv (2024). http://arxiv.org/abs/2405.13053
76. Xu, L., Xie, H., Qin, S.Z.J., Tao, X., Wang, F.L.: Parameter-efficient fine-tuning methods for pretrained language models: a critical review and assessment. arXiv (2023). http://arxiv.org/abs/2312.12148
77. Xu, Y., et al.: QA-LoRA: quantization-aware low-rank adaptation of large language models. arXiv (2023). http://arxiv.org/abs/2309.14717
78. Yang, A.X., Robeyns, M., Wang, X., Aitchison, L.: Bayesian low-rank adaptation for large language models. arXiv (2023). http://arxiv.org/abs/2308.13111
79. Yang, Y., et al.: CorDA: context-oriented decomposition adaptation of large language models. arXiv (2024). http://arxiv.org/abs/2406.05223
80. Zadouri, T., Üstün, A., Ahmadian, A., Ermiş, B., Locatelli, A., Hooker, S.: Pushing mixture of experts to the limit: extremely parameter efficient MoE for instruction tuning. arXiv (2023). http://arxiv.org/abs/2309.05444

81. Zhang, F., Li, L., Chen, J., Jiang, Z., Wang, B., Qian, Y.: IncreLoRA: incremental parameter allocation method for parameter-efficient fine-tuning. arXiv (2023). http://arxiv.org/abs/2308.12043
82. Zhang, J., Zhao, Y., Chen, D., Tian, X., Zheng, H., Zhu, W.: MiLoRA: efficient mixture of low-rank adaptation for large language models fine-tuning. In: Findings of the Association for Computational Linguistics: EMNLP 2024, pp. 17071–17084. Association for Computational Linguistics, Stroudsburg (2024). https://aclanthology.org/2024.findings-emnlp.994/
83. Zhang, J., Chen, S., Liu, J., He, J.: Composing parameter-efficient modules with arithmetic operations. arXiv (2023). http://arxiv.org/abs/2306.14870
84. Zhang, Q., et al.: AdaLoRA: adaptive budget allocation for parameter-efficient fine-tuning. arXiv (2023). http://arxiv.org/abs/2303.10512
85. Zhao, Z., et al.: Merging LoRAs like playing LEGO: pushing the modularity of LoRA to extremes through rank-wise clustering. arXiv (2024). http://arxiv.org/abs/2409.16167

ViMRHP: A Vietnamese Benchmark Dataset for Multimodal Review Helpfulness Prediction via Human-AI Collaborative Annotation

Truc Mai-Thanh Nguyen[1,2], Dat Minh Nguyen[1,2], Son T. Luu[1,2], and Kiet Van Nguyen[1,2(✉)]

[1] Faculty of Information Science and Engineering, University of Information Technology, Ho Chi Minh City, Vietnam
{21522721,21521937}@gm.uit.edu.vn, {kietnv,sonlt}@uit.edu.vn
[2] Vietnam National University, Ho Chi Minh City, Vietnam

Abstract. Multimodal Review Helpfulness Prediction (MRHP) is an essential task in recommender systems, particularly in E-commerce platforms. Determining the helpfulness of user-generated reviews enhances user experience and improves consumer decision-making. However, existing datasets focus predominantly on English and Indonesian, resulting in a lack of linguistic diversity, especially for low-resource languages such as Vietnamese. In this paper, we introduce **ViMRHP** (**Vi**etnamese **M**ultimodal **R**eview **H**elpfulness **P**rediction), a large-scale benchmark dataset for MRHP task in Vietnamese. This dataset covers four domains, including 2K products with 46K reviews. Meanwhile, a large-scale dataset requires considerable time and cost. To optimize the annotation process, we leverage AI to assist annotators in constructing the ViMRHP dataset. With AI assistance, annotation time is reduced (90–120 seconds/task → 20–40 seconds/task) while maintaining data quality and lowering overall costs by approximately 65%. However, AI-generated annotations still have limitations in complex annotation tasks, which we further examine through a detailed performance analysis. In our experiment on ViMRHP, we evaluate baseline models on human-verified and AI-generated annotations to assess their quality differences. The ViMRHP dataset is publicly available at (https://github.com/trng28/ViMRHP).

1 Introduction

Review Helpfulness Prediction (RHP) has become a crucial research topic in E-commerce due to its role in assessing the helpfulness of user-generated reviews and their impact on consumer purchasing decisions. However, the large volume of reviews poses significant challenges in identifying helpful reviews. Previous methods primarily relied on semantic features, argument mining, and classification tasks [1–3], while recent multimodal RHP (MRHP) approaches [4–7] integrate

R. Ichise (Ed.): NLDB 2025, LNCS 15836, pp. 291–305, 2026.
https://doi.org/10.1007/978-3-031-97141-9_20

text and images to enable a more comprehensive assessment of review helpfulness and enhance predictive performance, focus on ranking reviews based on their helpfulness by using both product information and user-generated reviews.

Table 1. An illustrative example of the MRHP task and our ViMRHP dataset.

Product Information		
Set 2 sữa rửa mặt Good morning COSRX độ ph thấp dạng gel chiết xuất trà xanh - 150ml/tuýp		
Review 1	**Review 2**	**Review 3**
Helpfulness Score 4.0	**Helpfulness Score 3.0**	**Helpfulness Score 2.0**
2 chai này là chai thứ 3 thứ 4 r đó DÙNG MÊ ĐIÊN ĐẢO!!! ẻm không làm khô mặt mình sau khi rửa + dịu nhẹ nên mình hay dùng lắm!! Da mình cũng nhạy cảm nhma dùng tới chai thứ 3 thứ 4 là hiểu r đó, MUA LIỀN ĐIII 	Nhãn ngoài hộp serum nổi bong bóng. Không biết có phải hàng chính hãng không  	Sữa rửa mặt thơm, rửa mặt sạch, shop giao hàng nhanh, đóng gói hàng cẩn thận  

Most existing studies focus on English, and research on MRHP in Vietnamese remains limited due to the scarcity of quality annotated datasets. This gap motivates our effort to propose a benchmark dataset for MRHP task in Vietnamese, formulated as a ranking task following the study of Liu et al. [4], where reviews are ranked based on their helpfulness score, as detailed in Table 1.

However, data annotation for a high-quality dataset is often time-consuming and costly, requiring meticulous verification. To address this challenge, we leverage Large Language Models (LLMs) to assist in annotation, reducing manual effort while maintaining data quality. Despite their advantages in optimizing time and cost, LLMs still have limitations, requiring human verification to ensure accuracy and consistency. Therefore, we use a human-AI collaborative annotation framework that integrates LLMs with human verification. Additionally, we demonstrate the advantages and limitations of LLMs and human annotators in the ViMRHP dataset construction process through our evaluation metrics and experimental results.

In summary, our main contributions are three-fold:

1. **ViMRHP Dataset.** We introduce the ViMRHP dataset, a Vietnamese Multimodal Review Helpfulness Prediction dataset. To the best of our knowledge, there are no large-scale datasets for the MRHP task in Vietnamese.

2. **Human-AI Collaborative Annotation.** Annotation process of our ViM-RHP dataset implements Human-AI Collaborative Annotation framework via a two-step procedure: (1) AI annotation and (2) Human verification and refinement, ensuring time-efficiency, cost, and data quality.
3. **Human-Verified versus AI-Annotated Data Quality.** We evaluate ViMRHP with baseline models to compare human-verified and AI-annotated data, highlighting differences in quality, consistency, and biases.

2 Related Work

2.1 Review Helpfulness Prediction

Previous work, Review Helpfulness Prediction (RHP) has explored various tasks and approaches [3]. In the context of text reviews, the impact of structural, lexical, syntactic, semantic, and meta-data features on the helpfulness of user-generated reviews has been investigated [8], as well as semantic features [1] for predicting review helpfulness using Amazon votes as ground truth and validating findings with the human-annotated label. Argument mining has also been studied separately, with the AM^2 [2] dataset focusing on its role in determining the helpfulness of text review. Reviewer expertise and temporal dynamics [9] have also been incorporated to enhance helpfulness prediction with dataset creation from user-generated reviews on TripAdvisor.

Table 2. Comparison of ViMRHP with notable Review Helpfulness Prediction (RHP) datasets.

Datasets	RHP [9]	AM^2 [2]	Amazon-MRHP [4]	Lazada-MRHP [4]	ViMRHP (Ours)
Annotation Method	Vote Mapping	Human	Vote Mapping	Vote Mapping	Human-AI
Data Source	TripAdvisor	Amazon	Amazon	Lazada	Shopee
Multimodal	✗	✗	✓	✓	✓
Language	English	English	English	Indonesian	Vietnamese
Task	Multi-class CLS	Argument Mining	Ranking	Ranking	Ranking
No. of Reviews	161K	878	1414K	287K	46K
No. of Products	N/A	N/A	59K	21K	2K
Domains	*Hotels*	*Headphones*	*Clothing, Shoes & Jewelry* *Electronics* *Home & Kitchen*	*Clothing, Shoes & Jewelry* *Electronics* *Home & Kitchen*	*Fashion* *Electronics* *Home & Lifestyle* *Health & Beauty*

In recent years, RHP has advanced by integrating textual and visual information [4–7]. Amazon-MRHP [4] and Lazada-MRHP [4] sourced from two major E-commerce platforms, Amazon and Lazada, serve as benchmarks for the MRHP task and have been utilized in MCR [4] Multi-perspective Coherence Reasoning is the first baseline for MRHP, SANCL [5] Selective Attention and Natural Contrastive Learning model, which reduces GPU memory usage during training, Thong Nguyen et al. [6] propose Multimodal Contrastive Learning method achieved state-of-the-art results and PRR-LI [7] a Large language model driven Personalized Review Recommendation model based on Implicit dimension mining for MRHP. However, due to the limited availability of labeled data, most existing datasets [4,9] for this task defined ground truth by mapping helpful votes into helpfulness scores. We compare the proposed ViMRHP dataset with existing datasets in Table 2.

2.2 Human-AI Collaborative Annotation Framework

Reducing costs and ensuring high-quality annotations are two critical factors in NLP dataset construction. Recently, leveraging LLMs in annotation has become an optimized solution for time and cost efficiency [10–13]. However, balancing time, cost, and data quality remains challenging for complex annotation tasks and datasets. Therefore, recent studies have explored the human-AI collaborative annotation framework to address this issue. Notable works such as CoAnnotating [14], Wang et al. [15], and various datasets with diverse tasks have also adopted this framework, such as Value FULCRA [16], VIVA [17]. These works highlight the effectiveness of human-AI collaboration in enhancing annotation efficiency while maintaining quality.

3 Human-AI Collaborative Annotation

3.1 Overview

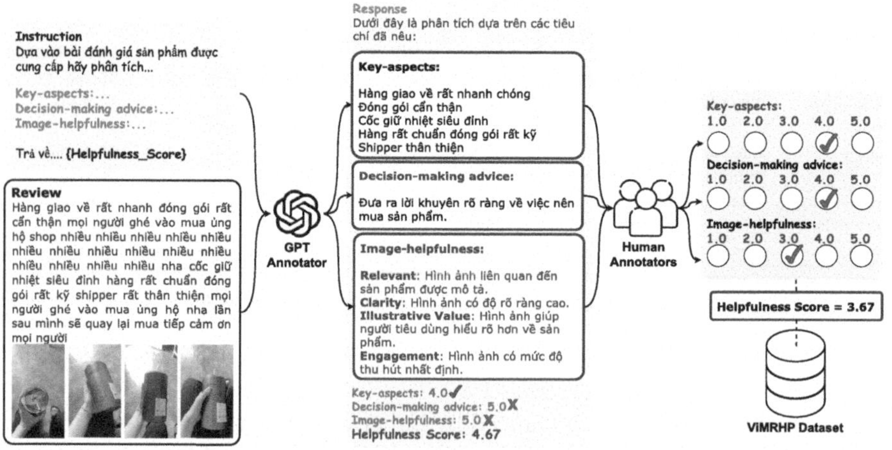

Fig. 1. ViMRHP benchmark dataset annotation overview. The Human-AI collaborative annotation framework workflow includes two steps: (1) AI Annotation → (2) Human Verification and Refinement. First, AI extracts the relevant context or gives a reason from the review based on the given instruction criteria and assigns a score. Then, human annotators verify and refine the final score to ensure data quality.

Data Collection. To construct the ViMRHP dataset, we collected product information and user-generated reviews, including both text and images, from the Shopee[1] platform in Vietnam. For user-generated reviews, an average of *21–24* reviews were collected per product, spanning the period from *2019* to *2024*. All user-related information was strictly removed before use to ensure privacy and compliance with ethical standards.

Task Annotation. To ensure objectivity in evaluating review helpfulness, we define three key criteria for each sample in ViMRHP dataset: $\{(K_i, D_i, I_i)\}_{i=1}^{N}$, where K_i is *key aspects*, D_i is *decision-making advice*, and I_i is *image-helpfulness*, scoring on a scale from 1 to 5, where 1 is lowest and 5 is highest. The ground truth, referred to as the *Helpfulness Score*, is computed as $H_i = \frac{1}{3}(K_i + D_i + I_i)$. The definition of each criterion and score is provided in Sect. 3.2.

Annotation Workflow. We implemented a human-AI collaborative annotation framework for the ViMRHP dataset, which consists of two steps: Step 1 - AI Annotation (Sect. 3.3) and Step 2 - Human Verification and Refinement (Sect. 3.4). Details of our annotation process are illustrated in Fig. 1.

3.2 Annotation Scheme and Guideline

The annotation guideline for constructing the ViMRHP dataset ensures that each sample is individually labeled. This approach addresses the limitations of automated ground truth generation based on mapping the number of helpful votes, which may introduce bias, a common issue in previous studies, since not all reviews receive upvotes [9].

Table 3. Labeling Criteria for ViMRHP Dataset

Criteria	Description
Key-aspects: The number of key aspects of the product mentioned in the user-generated review.	1.0: Not mention any key aspects of the product. 2.0: Mentions one key aspect. 3.0: Mentions two key aspects. 4.0: Mentions three key aspects. 5.0: Mentions four or more key aspects.
Decision-making advice: The recommendation to purchase the product mentioned in the user-generated review.	1.0: Describes an ambiguous experience without giving any purchase advice. 2.0: Clearly describes the experience but does not provide purchase advice. 3.0: Implicitly suggests whether the product is worth buying. 4.0: Strongly implies whether the product is worth buying. 5.0: Clearly recommends the product, specifying the target users or suitable situations.
Image-helpfulness: The level of usefulness of the product images provided by the user in the user-generated review.	1.0: Does not meet any criteria for Relevance, Clarity, Illustrative Value, or Engagement. 2.0: Meets one criterion for Relevance, Clarity, Illustrative Value, or Engagement. 3.0: Meets two criteria for Relevance, Clarity, Illustrative Value, or Engagement. 4.0: Meets three criteria for Relevance, Clarity, Illustrative Value, or Engagement. 5.0: Meets four criteria for Relevance, Clarity, Illustrative Value, and Engagement.
Helpfulness Score = (Key-aspect + Decision-making advice + Image-helpfulness)/3	

Based on the work of Chua et al. [18], we establish a structured annotation framework using three key criteria: key aspects, decision-making advice, and

[1] https://shopee.vn.

image helpfulness. We assign a score to each criterion for each sample in our ViMRHP dataset. Table 3 presents a detailed labeling criteria, with the task design outlined below.

- *Key-aspects.* Identify the context in which the review mentions aspects of the product (e.g., features, benefits, usage, durability, design, etc.) and assign a score accordingly, following the criteria in Table 3.
- *Decision-making advice.* Identify whether the review provides purchasing recommendations (e.g., recommending to buy, not to buy, specifying target buyers, or advising against certain users, etc.) and assign a score based on its clarity and strength, following the criteria in Table 3.
- *Image-helpfulness.* Evaluate the helpfulness of user-uploaded images based on predefined criteria, including:
  - Relevance: The image accurately represents the reviewed product.
  - Clarity: The image is clear and easily interpretable.
  - Illustrative Value: The image effectively demonstrates key product features, benefits, or real-life usage.
  - Engagement: The image captures user interest and enhances the review's informativeness.

  Assign a score based on how well the image meets these criteria, following Table 3.

An example annotation with detailed scoring for each criterion is shown in Table 4. For *key aspects*, relevant contexts are highlighted and marked as (K1), (K2), (K3), (K4), and (K5). Similarly, for *decision-making advice*, key statements are identified and marked as (D1). For *image-helpfulness*, review images are assessed based on predefined criteria, ensuring a comprehensive evaluation.

Table 4. Example annotation for ViMRHP Dataset

"ly khá là okla, **k bị đọng nước ở ngoài**(K1), **thiết kế đơn giản thanh lịch** (K2), **k quá trơn**(K3), **nắp đậy k bị đổ**(K4), với giá vậy là rất rất rất tuyṭ zời, còn về mức **độ giữ nhiệt thì mình thấy giữ được khoảng 6h** (K5), **rcm nên muaa**(D1)

__________: The cup is ok, **doesn't get condensation on the outside**(K1). **Design is simple elegant**(K2), **not too slippery**(K3) **The lid doesn't leak**(K4). For this price, it's absolutely great. As for heat retention, **I found it keeps warm for about 6 hours.** (K5) **Recommend buying it**(D1).

Key-aspects	Mentions four or more key aspects: (K1),(K2),(K3),(K4),(K5) |
Decision-making advice	Strongly implies whether the product is worth buying: (D1) |
Image-helpfulness	Meets two criteria. |

3.3 Step 1 - AI Annotation

We use LLM (`i.e., gpt-4o-mini version`)[2] [19] to automatically annotate approximately 46K review samples at a total cost of 150–170 USD, significantly reducing expenses and time compared to manual annotation. Our annotation task involves two main challenges: (1) Extracting the review context that mentions aspects of the product for *key-aspects*, explanation for *decision-making advice* and *image-helpfulness*. (2) Assign scores to each criterion. These are illustrated in the LLM response in Fig. 1 and detailed instructions are provided in Appendix B.

3.4 Step 2 - Human Verification and Refinement

In this step, to construct the ViMRHP dataset, we recruited three annotators, undergraduate students at our institution, with a Data Science background and Vietnamese proficiency. We paid 50 USD per annotator for modifying the entire dataset that AI-generated annotation in **Step 1**. Annotators were required to complete a training phase before verifying and refining AI-annotated data, during which they performed manual annotation on 100 samples. The inter-annotator agreement, measured using Fleiss's κ, was assessed across three criteria: key aspects, decision-making advice, and image helpfulness. Their corresponding κ values were 0.6341, 0.5944, 0.2107. and 0.4484 for Helpfulness Score. Our labeling UI is detailed in the Appendix A.

4 ViMRHP Dataset

Dataset Statistics. The statistical overview of the ViMRHP dataset is presented, details in Table 5. The statistics comprehensively analyze the scale and features relevant to our multimodal ranking task, including Product Information (**P**) and Reviews (**R**). In addition, we provide details on the number of reviews per product (**R/P**), with our review list length ranging between 21 and 23 reviews per product. Furthermore, the number of images per review ($\mathbf{R}_{\text{img}}/\mathbf{R}$) and the number of images per product ($\mathbf{P}_{\text{img}}/\mathbf{P}$) provide valuable insights into multimodal aspects.

Table 5. Statistical overview of the ViMRHP dataset.

Domain	avg.			avg. len		max. len		total	
	R/P	P_{img}/P	R_{img}/R	P_{text}	R_{text}	P_{text}	R_{text}	P_{img}	R_{img}
Fashion	22.4	8.2	2.2	82.7	145.6	196	1782	4175	24857
Electronic	21.9	7.4	1.9	85.4	111.4	212	1292	3529	19289
Home & Lifestyle	22.5	7.6	2.0	86.6	118.2	157	2170	3391	20817
Health & Beauty	22.9	7.7	2.4	79.6	129.2	206	2202	4794	34463

[2] https://platform.openai.com/docs/models/gpt-4o-mini.

Following the study of Liu et al. [4], we split the ViMRHP dataset into `Train`, `Dev`, and `Test` sets with a ratio of 70:10:20, as detailed in Table 6, with the distribution of Products and Reviews splits also presented.

Table 6. Train, Dev, Test distribution across domains (Products/Reviews)

Domain	Train	Dev	Test
Fashion	356/7812	50/1065	103/2132
Electronic	332/7274	47/1010	96/2101
Home&Lifestyle	313/7153	44/1015	91/2057
Health&Beauty	433/9956	61/1403	125/2832

Table 7. Agreement evaluation between Human vs AI (%)

Criteria	%Agree	Cκ	Δ|H − A|
Key-aspects	40.34	22.96	81.29
Decision-making advice	52.93	34.65	64.00
Image-helpfulness	57.31	41.65	64.20
Helpfulness Score	**53.59**	**31.34**	**53.64**

In-Depth Analysis - Human vs AI. After verifying and refining the entire ViMRHP dataset, we compare the labels assigned by human annotators with AI-generated annotations using agreement metrics to assess consistency and accuracy, as detailed in Table 7. Specifically, we use three evaluation metrics: %Agree - Human Agreement (Yes/No) [20], Cκ - Cohen's Kappa [21], and $\Delta|H-A| = \frac{1}{N}\sum_{i=1}^{N}|H_i - A_i|$, which quantifies the deviation in scores between human annotations and AI-generated labels across different criteria, providing a comprehensive measure of annotation reliability. Our analysis reveals varying agreement metrics, with Human Agreement ranging from 40.34% to 57.31% meaning human annotators manually refined approximately 50% of the dataset to ensure data quality. Cohen's Kappa scores between human vs AI for ground truth Helpfulness Score only 31.34% indicating *Fair Agreement* [22]. The high $\Delta|H-A|$ deviation in *key-aspects* 81.29% suggests a significant gap in contextual understanding between AI and human annotators, limitations in accurately identifying contextual information.

Distributions Analysis. In ranking tasks, determining the distribution to select thresholds for experiments is crucial in evaluating a dataset. We analyze the distribution of common score ranges in each domain and highlight the scoring differences between human annotators and AI, detail in Fig. 2 (2a, 2b, 2c, 2d). The most common score range assigned is 3–4, reflecting a tendency toward neutral or safe reviews. This also serves as the basis for selecting our dataset evaluation threshold on the average length of the review list per product (**R/P**) is 21–23, as detailed in Table 5.

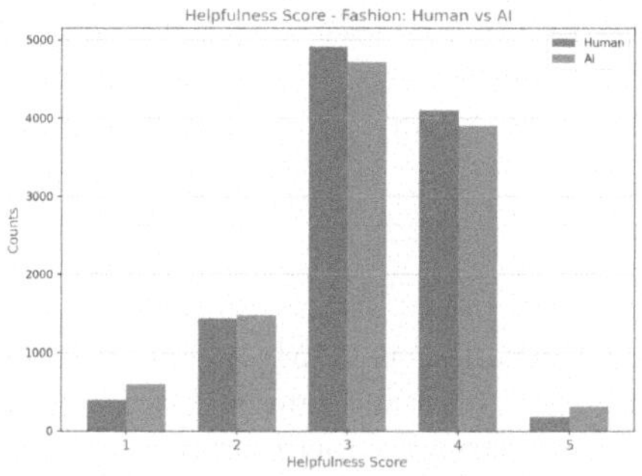

(a) Fashion Category

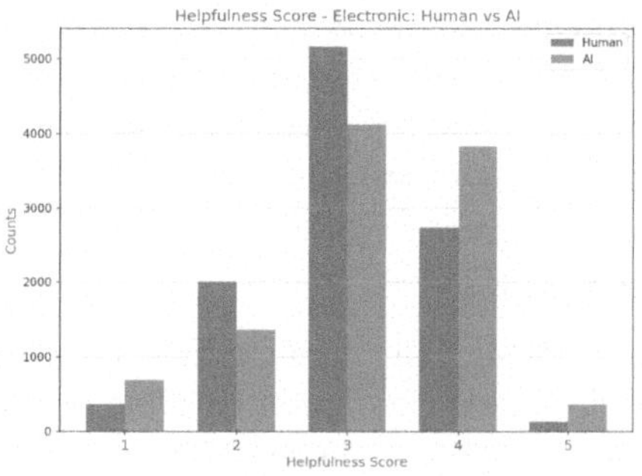

(b) Electronic Category

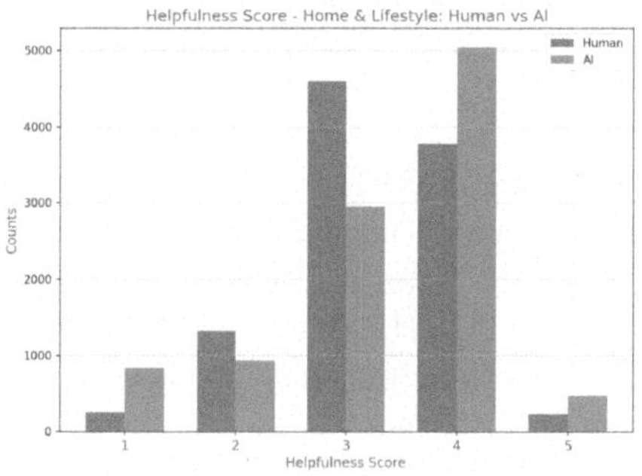

(c) Home & Lifestyle Category

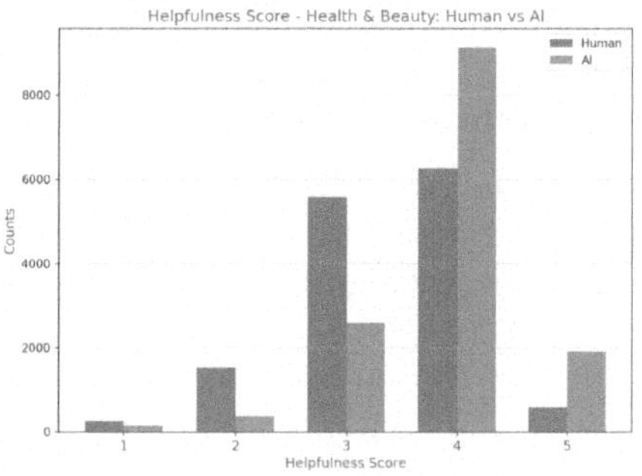

(d) Health & Beauty Category

Fig. 2. Helpfulness Score distribution across categories between Human vs AI in ViMRHP dataset.

5 Experimental Setup

In our experiment, we implement various baseline models for our ViMRHP dataset, including text-only and multimodal approaches, to evaluate the contribution of each data modality to the review helpfulness prediction task.

5.1 Baselines

Text-Only

- **BiMPM** [23] Bilateral Multi-Perspective Matching (BiMPM) uses BiLSTMs to encode and compare product information and reviews, capturing semantic relationships and aggregating relevance scores through a second BiLSTM.
- **Conv-KRMN** [24] is a neural ranking model designed to enhances ad-hoc search using CNNs to capture soft matches between query and document n-grams, which are mapped into a shared embedding space and processed through kernel-based pooling for relevance scoring.
- **DUET** [25] is a neural ranking model that combines local interactions and distributed representations using two jointly trained deep networks to enhance lexical and semantic similarity in document ranking.

- **Match-Pyramid** [26] is a CNN-based model for text matching that represents word-level similarities as a matching matrix. CNNs hierarchically extract complex patterns from this matrix, capturing key signals like n-gram and n-term matching.

Multimodal

- **MCR** [4] Multi-perspective coherence reasoning is a Multimodal Review Helpfulness Prediction baseline that integrates text and images from products and reviews. It includes two modules: one assessing intra- and inter-modal consistency between the product and review, and another ensuring coherence within the review by aligning textual and visual content.

5.2 Evaluation Metrics

Following the study by Liu et al. [4] on the Amazon-MRHP and Lazada-MRHP datasets, we adopt two evaluation metrics frequently used in recommendation: MAP (Mean Average Precision) and NDCG@K (Normalized Discounted Cumulative Gain), where $K \in \{1, 3, 5\}$, to assess the ViMRHP dataset. These specific K values are chosen because users typically base their purchase decisions on the top few reviews, often only reading the first 1–5 reviews.

5.3 Implementation Details

Baseline models in our ViMRHP experiments are based on MatchZoo library [27], with all evaluations using a threshold of 3.0 for NDCG@K and MAP of MatchZoo [27] metrics. All baselines, including text-only (BiMPM, Conv-KRMN, DUET, Match-Pyramid) and multimodal (MCR), word embedding layer are used with FastText, `batch_size` 32, `learning_rate` 0.001, Adam `optimizer` and executed on single GPU Tesla-T4-15GB. The text-only models are trained for 5 epochs per domain. The MCR model is trained for 20 epochs per domain. Before training, all product and review images are extracted with pre-trained Faster R-CNN [28] for RoI feature extraction.

6 Results

6.1 Human-Verified Versus AI-Annotated Data Quality

We present the experimental results from our ViMRHP dataset in Table 8. The experiments were conducted using two types of annotated data: human-verified and AI-generated annotations. The results in Table 8 show that multimodal approaches outperform text-only methods in the MCR baseline, especially with human-verified annotations in ViMRHP across Fashion, Electronics, Home & Lifestyle, and Health & Beauty, demonstrating the effectiveness of multimodal learning. Additionally, leveraging LLMs can reduce costs and annotation time. However, human-verified annotations perform better across baseline models, underscoring the need for human verification to ensure data quality in complex annotation tasks.

Table 8. Performance comparison for data quality in the ViMRHP dataset. Comparing human-verified data (**Human Verification**) with AI-generated annotations (**AI Annotation**). ↑ denotes the percentage increase in performance.

Domain	Modality	Method	Human Verification				AI Annotation			
			N@1	N@3	N@5	MAP	N@1	N@3	N@5	MAP
Fashion	Text-only	BiMPM	$64.80_{1.51\uparrow}$	$68.13_{3.04\uparrow}$	$71.15_{0.70\uparrow}$	$71.50_{0.50\uparrow}$	63.29	65.09	70.45	71.00
		DUET	$34.73_{0.87\uparrow}$	$34.56_{0.97\uparrow}$	$38.03_{0.87\uparrow}$	$45.74_{0.10\uparrow}$	33.86	33.59	37.16	45.64
		Conv-KRMN	$63.33_{0.94\uparrow}$	$63.51_{0.68\uparrow}$	$65.57_{2.02\uparrow}$	$67.86_{1.48\uparrow}$	62.39	62.83	63.55	66.38
		Match-Pyramid	$63.89_{9.74\uparrow}$	$63.12_{5.48\uparrow}$	$65.01_{5.49\uparrow}$	$67.49_{4.76\uparrow}$	54.15	57.64	59.52	62.73
	Multimodal	MCR	$\mathbf{74.04}_{5.36\uparrow}$	$\mathbf{74.34}_{2.48\uparrow}$	$\mathbf{74.69}_{2.16\uparrow}$	$\mathbf{74.47}_{1.27\uparrow}$	**68.68**	**71.86**	**72.53**	**73.20**
Electronic	Text-only	BiMPM	$62.33_{16.09\uparrow}$	$61.51_{11.25\uparrow}$	$63.10_{10.54\uparrow}$	$63.14_{9.03\uparrow}$	46.24	50.26	52.56	54.11
		DUET	$44.66_{18.18\uparrow}$	$51.59_{25.97\uparrow}$	$56.38_{27.81\uparrow}$	$57.78_{22.32\uparrow}$	26.48	25.62	28.57	35.46
		Conv-KRMN	$55.58_{10.42\uparrow}$	$56.13_{10.71\uparrow}$	$60.48_{11.80\uparrow}$	$61.51_{10.52\uparrow}$	45.16	45.42	48.68	50.99
		Match-Pyramid	$44.66_{4.20\uparrow}$	$49.53_{7.62\uparrow}$	$50.83_{6.99\uparrow}$	$53.27_{5.61\uparrow}$	40.46	41.91	43.92	47.66
	Multimodal	MCR	$\mathbf{69.15}_{16.13\uparrow}$	$\mathbf{65.25}_{14.19\uparrow}$	$\mathbf{66.16}_{12.55\uparrow}$	$\mathbf{66.00}_{11.01\uparrow}$	**53.02**	**51.06**	**53.61**	**54.99**
Home & Lifestyle	Text-only	BiMPM	$68.31_{11.59\uparrow}$	$73.65_{13.17\uparrow}$	$73.69_{12.42\uparrow}$	$75.18_{10.08\uparrow}$	56.72	60.48	61.27	65.10
		DUET	$35.34_{4.59\uparrow}$	$40.72_{4.19\uparrow}$	$43.30_{4.19\uparrow}$	$53.36_{4.65\uparrow}$	38.75	36.53	39.11	48.71
		Conv-KRMN	$50.76_{6.66\uparrow}$	$50.92_{4.64\uparrow}$	$54.32_{5.44\uparrow}$	$62.19_{4.60\uparrow}$	44.10	46.28	48.88	57.59
		Match-Pyramid	$62.78_{8.22\uparrow}$	$62.19_{7.29\uparrow}$	$62.34_{7.34\uparrow}$	$67.24_{4.69\uparrow}$	54.56	57.88	58.00	62.55
	Multimodal	MCR	$\mathbf{72.70}_{10.98\uparrow}$	$\mathbf{75.25}_{13.07\uparrow}$	$\mathbf{75.23}_{11.63\uparrow}$	$\mathbf{76.54}_{9.72\uparrow}$	**61.72**	**62.18**	**63.60**	**66.82**
Health & Beauty	Text-only	BiMPM	$69.96_{6.76\uparrow}$	$71.30_{7.05\uparrow}$	$\mathbf{72.60}_{7.40\uparrow}$	$\mathbf{77.36}_{7.98\uparrow}$	63.20	64.59	**65.20**	70.38
		DUET	$44.46_{1.20\uparrow}$	$47.88_{6.00\uparrow}$	$50.34_{6.62\uparrow}$	$60.84_{4.60\uparrow}$	43.20	41.88	43.72	56.24
		Conv-KRMN	$69.26_{4.90\uparrow}$	$69.70_{5.58\uparrow}$	$69.60_{5.72\uparrow}$	$74.05_{4.35\uparrow}$	64.36	64.12	64.46	69.70
		Match-Pyramid	$65.96_{10.79\uparrow}$	$65.88_{16.13\uparrow}$	$67.67_{18.02\uparrow}$	$73.31_{7.55\uparrow}$	55.17	56.75	57.65	65.76
	Multimodal	MCR	$\mathbf{71.59}_{3.95\uparrow}$	$\mathbf{73.22}_{8.15\uparrow}$	$72.47_{7.63\uparrow}$	$76.32_{5.07\uparrow}$	**67.64**	**65.07**	64.84	**71.25**

6.2 Cost, Time-Efficiency and Quality Comparison

We compare different annotation methods in Table 9 for evaluating cost, time efficiency, and data quality. The annotation process of ViMRHP dataset collaborates with humans and LLMs (Sect. 3) costs around 300–320 USD. This cost achieves a balance, not as low as AI annotation, it remains significantly more affordable than the estimated cost of human annotation. With the support of LLMs, annotators achieved an annotation speed of 20–40 seconds per task, enabling the dataset to be completed within 3 weeks for approximately 46K multimodal reviews.

Table 9. Comparison of annotation methods on the ViMRHP Dataset

	Human	AI	Human-AI
Cost	800–900 USD	150–170 USD	300–320 USD
Time-consume	2–3 months	N/A	3 weeks
Efficiency	90–120 s/Task	1–2 s/Task	20–40 s/Task
No. Annotators	9–12 annotators	N/A	3 annotators
Quality	✓	✗	✓

Moreover, based on the evaluation metrics between human and AI annotation in Table 7 and the experimental results on ViMRHP dataset baselines in Table

8, we demonstrate that human-verified data achieves higher quality. To this end, human-AI collaboration is more efficient than traditional crowdsourced dataset creation in terms of data quality and reducing cost with time efficiency.

7 Conclusions

This paper introduces ViMRHP, a Vietnamese dataset for MRHP tasks, covering four domains that reflect diverse user behaviors and data modalities. The ViMRHP dataset is a valuable resource for future research on MRHP tasks in Vietnamese, providing a quality dataset with human-verified annotations. Additionally, ViMRHP demonstrates a balance between cost, efficiency, and annotation quality with a Human-AI collaborative annotation framework to dataset construction. Furthermore, it highlights the limitations of LLMs in dataset creation, paving the way for more effective hybrid data annotation methods in the future.

Acknowledgments. This research was supported by The VNUHCM - University of Information Technology's Scientific Research Support Fund.

A Labeling UI

We utilize HumanSignal[3] [29] as the labeling tool for the ViMRHP dataset shown in Fig. 3 below.

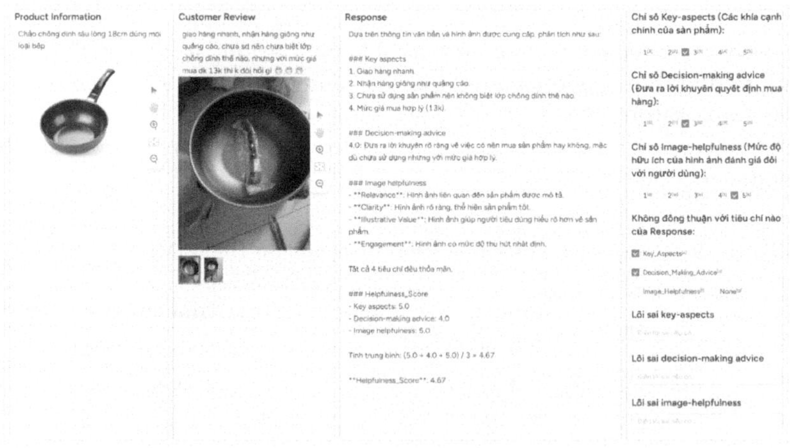

Fig. 3. Labeling UI for ViMRHP dataset.

[3] Label Studio Enterprise Supported by HumanSignal Label Studio Academic Program.

B Instruction

(See Table 10).

Table 10. Prompt for AI-based Explanation Score

INSTRUCTION (VIETNAMESE). Dựa vào thông tin bài đánh giá sản phẩm bao gồm văn bản và hình ảnh đã được cung cấp. Hãy phân tích bài đánh giá theo các tiêu chí sau: **Key-aspects**: Đưa ra các khía cạnh chính của sản phẩm. **{key_aspects}** 1.0 - Không đề cập đến khía cạnh cụ thể nào của sản phẩm. 2.0 - Đề cập đến một khía cạnh cụ thể của sản phẩm. 3.0 - Đề cập đến hai khía cạnh cụ thể của sản phẩm. 4.0 - Đề cập đến ba khía cạnh cụ thể của sản phẩm. 5.0 - Đề cập đến nhiều hơn bốn khía cạnh cụ thể của sản phẩm. **Decision-making advice**: Khuyến nghị mua hàng. **{decision_making_advice}** 1.0 - Mô tả trải nghiệm cá nhân mơ hồ, không đưa ra khuyến nghị. 2.0 - Mô tả trải nghiệm cá nhân rõ ràng, nhưng không có khuyến nghị. 3.0 - Ngầm đưa ra lời khuyên về việc có nên mua sản phẩm hay không. 4.0 - Đưa ra lời khuyên rõ ràng về quyết định mua hàng. 5.0 - Đưa ra lời khuyên cụ thể cho từng đối tượng khách hàng. **Image-helpfulness**: Mức độ hữu ích của hình ảnh sản phẩm dựa theo các tiêu chí. **{image_helpfulness}** Mức độ liên quan (Relevance)..., Độ rõ ràng (Clarity)..., Giá trị minh họa (Illustrative Value)..., Tính thu hút (Engagement)... 1.0 - Không thỏa mãn tiêu chí nào. 2.0 - Thỏa mãn một tiêu chí. 3.0 - Thỏa mãn hai tiêu chí. 4.0 - Thỏa mãn ba tiêu chí. 5.0 - Thỏa mãn cả bốn tiêu chí. Trả về Helpfulness Score bằng trung bình điểm số ba tiêu chí **Key-aspects, Decision-making advice, Image-helpfulness**: **{Helpfulness_Score}**
INSTRUCTION (ENGLISH). Based on the provided product review, including both text and images, analyze the review according to the following criteria: **Key-aspects:** Extract the main aspects of the product. **{key_aspects}** 1.0 - Does not mention any specific aspect of the product. 2.0 - Mentions one specific aspect of the product. 3.0 - Mentions two specific aspects of the product. 4.0 - Mentions three specific aspects of the product. 5.0 - Mentions more than four specific aspects of the product. **Decision-making advice:** Purchase recommendation. **{decision_making_advice}** 1.0 - Describes an ambiguous experience without giving any purchase advice. 2.0 - Clearly describes the experience but does not provide purchase advice. 3.0 - Implicitly suggests whether the product is worth buying. 4.0 - Strongly implies whether the product is worth buying. 5.0 - Clearly recommends the product, specifying the target users or suitable situations. **Image-helpfulness:** The helpfulness of product images based on the following criteria. **{image_helpfulness}** Relevance..., Clarity..., Illustrative Value..., Engagement... 1.0 - Does not meet any criteria. 2.0 - Meets one criterion. 3.0 - Meets two criteria. 4.0 - Meets three criteria. 5.0 - Meets all four criteria. Return **Helpfulness Score** is calculated as the average score of the three criteria: **Key-aspects, Decision-making advice, and Image-helpfulness. {Helpfulness_Score}**

References

1. Yang, Y., Yan, Y., Qiu, M., Bao, F.: Semantic analysis and helpfulness prediction of text for online product reviews. In: Proceedings of the 53rd Annual Meeting of the Association for Computational Linguistics and the 7th International Joint Conference on Natural Language Processing (Volume 2: Short Papers), pp. 38–44 (2015)
2. Chen, Z., do Amarante, D.V., Donaldson, J., Jo, Y., Park, J.: Argument mining for review helpfulness prediction. In: Proceedings of the 2022 Conference on Empirical Methods in Natural Language Processing, pp. 8914–8922 (2022)
3. Diaz, G.O., Ng, V.: Modeling and prediction of online product review helpfulness: a survey. In: Proceedings of the 56th Annual Meeting of the Association for Computational Linguistics (Volume 1: Long Papers), pp. 698–708 (2018)
4. Liu, J., Hai, Z., Yang, M., Bing, L.: Multi-perspective coherent reasoning for helpfulness prediction of multimodal reviews. In: Proceedings of the 59th Annual Meeting of the Association for Computational Linguistics and the 11th International Joint Conference on Natural Language Processing (Volume 1: Long Papers), pp. 5927–5936 (2021)
5. Han, W., Chen, H., Hai, Z., Poria, S., Bing, L.: SANCL: multimodal review helpfulness prediction with selective attention and natural contrastive learning. In: Proceedings of the 29th International Conference on Computational Linguistics, pp. 5666–5677 (2022)
6. Nguyen, T., Wu, X., Luu, A.T., Hai, Z., Bing, L.: Adaptive contrastive learning on multimodal transformer for review helpfulness prediction. In: Proceedings of the 2022 Conference on Empirical Methods in Natural Language Processing, pp. 10085–10096 (2022)
7. Xu, B., Xu, Y.: Personalized review recommendation based on implicit dimension mining. In: Proceedings of the 2024 Conference of the North American Chapter of the Association for Computational Linguistics: Human Language Technologies (Volume 2: Short Papers), pp. 86–91 (2024)
8. Kim, S.M., Pantel, P., Chklovski, T., Pennacchiotti, M.: Automatically assessing review helpfulness. In: Proceedings of the 2006 Conference on Empirical Methods in Natural Language Processing, pp. 423–430 (2006)
9. Nayeem, M.T., Rafiei, D.: On the role of reviewer expertise in temporal review helpfulness prediction. In: Findings of the Association for Computational Linguistics: EACL 2023, pp. 1684–1692 (2023)
10. Wang, S., Liu, Y., Xu, Y., Zhu, C., Zeng, M.: Want to reduce labeling cost? GPT-3 can help. In: Findings of the Association for Computational Linguistics: EMNLP 2021, pp. 4195–4205 (2021)
11. Ding, B., et al.: Is GPT-3 a good data annotator? In: Proceedings of the 61st Annual Meeting of the Association for Computational Linguistics (Volume 1: Long Papers), pp. 11173–11195 (2023)
12. Tan, Z., et al.: Large language models for data annotation and synthesis: a survey. In: Proceedings of the 2024 Conference on Empirical Methods in Natural Language Processing, pp. 930–957 (2024)
13. He, X., et al.: AnnoLLM: making large language models to be better crowdsourced annotators. In: Proceedings of the 2024 Conference of the North American Chapter of the Association for Computational Linguistics: Human Language Technologies (Volume 6: Industry Track), pp. 165–190 (2024)

14. Li, M., et al.: CoAnnotating: uncertainty-guided work allocation between human and large language models for data annotation. In: Proceedings of the 2023 Conference on Empirical Methods in Natural Language Processing, pp. 1487–1505 (2023)
15. Wang, X., Kim, H., Rahman, S., Mitra, K., Miao, Z.: Human-LLM collaborative annotation through effective verification of LLM labels. In: Proceedings of the CHI Conference on Human Factors in Computing Systems, pp. 1–21 (2024)
16. Yao, J., Yi, X., Gong, Y., Wang, X., Xie, X.: Value fulcra: mapping large language models to the multidimensional spectrum of basic human value. In: Proceedings of the 2024 Conference of the North American Chapter of the Association for Computational Linguistics: Human Language Technologies (Volume 1: Long Papers), pp. 8754–8777 (2024)
17. Hu, Z., Ren, Y., Li, J., Yin, Y.: Viva: a benchmark for vision-grounded decision-making with human values. In: Proceedings of the 2024 Conference on Empirical Methods in Natural Language Processing, pp. 2294–2311 (2024)
18. Chua, A.Y., Banerjee, S.: Helpfulness of user-generated reviews as a function of review sentiment, product type and information quality. Comput. Hum. Behav. **54**, 547–554 (2016)
19. OpenAI: GPT-4o mini: advancing cost-efficient intelligence (2024). https://openai.com/index/gpt-4o-mini-advancing-cost-efficient-intelligence/
20. Chen, D., et al.: MLLM-as-a-judge: assessing multimodal LLM-as-a-judge with vision-language benchmark. In: Forty-first International Conference on Machine Learning (2024)
21. Cohen, J.: A coefficient of agreement for nominal scales. Educ. Psychol. Measur. **20**(1), 37–46 (1960)
22. Landis JRKoch, G.: The measurement of observer agreement for categorical data. Biometrics **33**(1), 159174 (1977)
23. Wang, Z., Hamza, W., Florian, R.: Bilateral multi-perspective matching for natural language sentences. In: International Joint Conference on Artificial Intelligence. International Joint Conferences on Artificial Intelligence (2017)
24. Dai, Z., Xiong, C., Callan, J., Liu, Z.: Convolutional neural networks for soft-matching n-grams in ad-hoc search. In: Proceedings of the Eleventh ACM International Conference on Web Search and Data Mining, pp. 126–134 (2018)
25. Mitra, B., Diaz, F., Craswell, N.: Learning to match using local and distributed representations of text for web search. In: Proceedings of the 26th International Conference on World Wide Web, pp. 1291–1299 (2017)
26. Pang, L., Lan, Y., Guo, J., Xu, J., Wan, S., Cheng, X.: Text matching as image recognition. In: Proceedings of the AAAI Conference on Artificial Intelligence, vol. 30 (2016)
27. Guo, J., Fan, Y., Ji, X., Cheng, X.: Matchzoo: a learning, practicing, and developing system for neural text matching. In: Proceedings of the 42nd International ACM SIGIR Conference on Research and Development in Information Retrieval, pp. 1297–1300 (2019)
28. Anderson, P., et al.: Bottom-up and top-down attention for image captioning and visual question answering. In: Proceedings of the IEEE Conference on Computer Vision and Pattern Recognition, pp. 6077–6086 (2018)
29. Tkachenko, M., Malyuk, M., Holmanyuk, A., Liubimov, N.: Label Studio: Data labeling software (2020–2024). https://humansignal.com/

Towards an Ontological Approach to Browser Fingerprinting Detection and Privacy Risk Assessment

Christopher D. McDermott[1(✉)], Lankeshwara Munasinghe[1], and Mathew Nicho[2,3]

[1] School of Computing, Engineering and Technology, Robert Gordon University, Aberdeen, UK
{c.d.mcdermott,l.munasinghe}@rgu.ac.uk
[2] Research and Innovation Centre, Rabdan Academy, Abu Dhabi, UAE
mnicho@ra.ac.ae
[3] University of Queensland, Brisbane, Australia
m.nicho@uq.edu.au

Abstract. Browser fingerprinting poses a significant privacy and security threat by covertly collecting unique user attributes such as device information, screen resolution, and installed fonts, enabling persistent tracking without relying on cookies. This paper introduces a novel hybrid detection method that combines JavaScript function interception and network request monitoring to collect and analyse fingerprinting scripts across the top 1,000 TRANCO websites, categorising them into widespread *baseline*, *niche* and highly *aggressive* scripts based on their attribute collection behaviour. Furthermore, we present our work towards the development of an ontology for browser fingerprinting detection, enabling structured reasoning about tracking techniques, relationships between websites and attributes, and classification of fingerprinting severity. The proposed ontology can be extended and integrated with future knowledge graphs to facilitate automated detection and reasoning about invasive tracking practices.

Keywords: Browser Fingerprinting · Ontology · Privacy · Security · Online Tracking

1 Introduction

As users browse the internet, various tracking technologies monitor their activities, raising concerns about privacy and data security. Websites and advertisers use these methods to analyse user behaviour, personalise content, and deliver targeted ads often without the users' explicit consent. One common tracking method is *cookies*, small text files stored in web browsers to remember user preferences, login details, and browsing history. While cookies can improve the user experience, they also enable websites to track individuals across different sites for analytics and advertising. Another, more sophisticated technique is known

R. Ichise (Ed.): NLDB 2025, LNCS 15836, pp. 306–320, 2026.
https://doi.org/10.1007/978-3-031-97141-9_21

as *browser fingerprinting*, which collects technical details about a user's device and browser to create a unique identifier (*fingerprint*). Unlike cookies, fingerprinting does not rely on stored files but instead gathers attributes such as browser type, operating system, screen resolution, installed plugins, and fonts. This allows websites to track users even if they block or delete cookies, making fingerprinting a more persistent tracking method. For example, when a user visits a website with fingerprinting scripts, the site collects various data points. **HTTP headers** reveal details such as browser type, accepted content types, and encoding. **JavaScript and CSS properties** provide information on screen size, color depth, fonts, time zone, and device specifications. **Canvas fingerprinting** leverages the HTML5 canvas to generate a unique image based on the user's system. Additionally, some websites check for **installed fonts and browser plugins**, further enhancing their ability to identify users. By combining these attributes, a unique fingerprint can be created that remains consistent across different browsing sessions.

Privacy and security concerns surrounding browser fingerprinting are significant, as it is difficult to detect and block compared to traditional tracking methods like cookies, leaving users with no easy way to opt out. To address these security threats, we introduce our work towards an ontology for browser fingerprinting detection inference and detection. We first collected data from the top 1000 website to analyse fingerprinting scripts and methods (requested browser attributes and features). This informed the development of our ontology which sought to answer the question "*How can we take an ontological approach to systematically detect, categorise, and represent browser fingerprinting behaviours?*". By leveraging ontological models, researchers and practitioners can systematically analyse the complexities of browser fingerprinting, leading to more effective and targeted solutions to enhance user privacy and security.

The key contributions of this research are as follows:

1. a hybrid detection method that combines JavaScript function interception and network request monitoring to collect information about fingerprinting scripts on websites.
2. deep analysis of fingerprinting scripts across the top 1,000 websites, to determine (i) widespread "baseline" scripts, which consistently collect fundamental attributes, *(ii) niche* that add specialised attributes, and highly *aggressive* scripts that proportionally request more privacy violating attributes.
3. an ontology to formalise knowledge about browser fingerprinting techniques, tracking mechanisms, and relationships between websites, attributes, and tracking networks.

The rest of the paper is organised as follows: Sect. 2 provides a brief overview of prior work in the area, specifically discussing the approaches that inspired out work. Section 3 describes our novel methodology for collecting data and detecting websites employing browser fingerprinting. Section 4 evaluates the experimental results. Section 5 describes our work towards the development of an ontology for browser fingerprinting. Finally, Sect. 6 draws conclusions and suggests possible future research directions.

2 Related Work

Browser fingerprinting, a subset of website tracking, is an increasing privacy concern for many users. Here, a fingerprint is considered a collection of attributes (browser type, browser language, system time, canvas rendering, number of CPU cores, etc.) that are combined to create a unique identifier for tracking users during their online activities. Originally, browser fingerprinting was designed to enhance security and combat fraud, but advertisers quickly adopted it to track users more effectively and serve targeted advertisements. A key advantage of browser fingerprinting for trackers is that it is obtained using JavaScript code (e.g., navigator.userAgent) without requiring user consent. Moreover, fingerprints are primarily stored in private databases, making them impossible for users to delete unlike cookies, which can be cleared from a browser. Past research work has introduced various techniques to obfuscate browser fingerprints and raise awareness among users. Organisations like Inria and the Electronic Frontier Foundation (EFF) have developed websites such as AmIUnique and Cover Your Tracks (formerly Panopticlick), which allow users to check whether their browser generates a unique fingerprint (based on their databases) and explain how these fingerprints are constructed.

In response to the growing privacy concerns, researchers have explored various methods to detect this privacy risk, including Cookieless Monster [6], FPDetective [1], and Fingerprint Defender [5]. Among these efforts, two papers stand out. In [2], the authors introduce FPMon, a detection method that assesses the likelihood of a website running a script for browser fingerprinting. The method involved predefining a list of functions used for browser fingerprinting and categorizing them as either **aggressive** or **non-aggressive**. They determined whether a script was performing browser fingerprinting by analysing (i) the percentage of total requested functionalities, and (ii) the number of functionalities that were categorised as aggressive. Based on this, detected scripts were classifies as (i) **Low**: not used for fingerpritning, (ii) **Medium**: potentially used for fingerprinting, and (iii) **High**: highly probable used for fingerprinting. In doing so, the authors claim the approach is resistant to false positives caused by scripts using graphics rendering, such as *Canvas Elements* or *WebGL API.* In [4] the authors developed **FPFlow** which took a different approach for detecting websites that are potentially using scripts to perform browser fingerprinting. Here, the method involved (i) checking if the script accesses attributes to browser fingerprinting, (ii) whether the script used *HTTP Post* methods to send collected data to a private database. The authors list four primary methods used to tramsit data namely, *XMLHttpRequest*, *sendBeacon*, *fetch*, *WebSocket.*

Despite being a clear privacy threat, browser fingerprinting also raises security concerns. It is a common tactic used by phishing site operators to evade security checks, ultimately prolonging the lifespan of malicious campaigns Attackers use browser fingerprinting to detect high-value Microsoft 365 and Google account users. Fake login pages mimicked corporate environments based on the user's real browser setup. Once users entered their credentials, attackers bypassed multi-factor authentication (MFA) and gained access to emails, documents, and financial data. For example, EvilProxy [3] is a sophisticated Phishing-as-a-Service (PhaaS) platform that cybercriminals utilize to bypass MFA and compromise user accounts. By acting as a reverse proxy, EvilProxy intercepts communication between users and legitimate services, enabling attackers to harvest authentication cookies and credentials, even from accounts protected by MFA.

3 Methodology

3.1 Fingerprint Collection

To collect the necessary data we developed a web scraping method which served to validate the feasibility of the concept, fine-tune the detection of browser fingerprinting scripts, and eventually lead to the development of our ontology. Our web scraping method differs from traditional approaches in this domain. Rather than parsing HTML elements directly, our method injects code that modifies native JavaScript functions. Specifically, it alters the *getter* methods of the *window* object and intercepts JavaScript APIs used to transmit data via the *HTML POST* method, such as *XMLHttpRequest*, *sendBeacon*, *fetch*, and *WebSocket*. This approach allowed us to collect data from a large number of web pages automatically, significantly reducing the time needed to fine-tune the detection script.

When developing our web scraping method, we first adopted the approach proposed by **FPMon** [2], which uses the *window* object as the primary interface to retrieve attributes essential for browser fingerprinting. The authors clearly demonstrated that fingerprinting scripts can be detected by intercepting attribute requests through modifications to the *window* object's *getter* methods. However, since this method is now deprecated we amend our method to use *object.defineProperty* to redefine the *window* object, which allows us to detect which *attributes* are being requested. We combined this approach with the method proposed in **FPFlow** [4] to verify whether collected data was transmitted to an external server. To successfully implement our methodology, it was critical to inject JavaScript code that modifies native JavaScript functions before the Document Object Model (*DOM*) fully loads. This ensures that no scripts execute prior to our modifications. We selected *Puppeteer*, a JavaScript library for automating web interactions, because it is built on Chromium and supports headless mode. This feature was essential for performing large-scale testing without the overhead of a visual interface and since it is built on *React* and *Chromium*, it is the most efficient choice for extracting web page data, running automated tests, and ensuring web browser compatibility. Additionally, the *Puppeteer* library facilitates website testing and includes functions such as *setBypassCSP(bool)*, which bypasses the page's Content Security Policy (CSP). This feature is extremely useful since CSP restrictions could otherwise prevent access to certain webpage information. Figure 1 presents the architecture of our web scraping method which consists of three core blocks: **(i) Injection Block:** contains the script to be injected into webpages to detect browser fingerprinting scripts, **(ii) Conversion Block:** that converts raw data collected by the Injection Block into JSON files (*graph.json, barPlot,json, injectionInformation.json, attributeInformation.json*), **(iii) Display Block:** uses the *D3.js* visualisation library to present the collected data in graph format. Importantly, *inject.js* is injected before other scripts can execute and redefines the *getters* of functions needed for browser fingerprinting. To achieve this we use *Object.defineProperty* which allows us to easily redefine a function and allows our script to intercept requests without altering output by storing values in a dictionary that is called each time when retrieving the original value, while still allowing the request to be intercepted. Once intercepted, we determine the source of the fingerprinting script using the *V8 JavaScript engine* to generate a stack trace that identifies the scripts name that made the request.

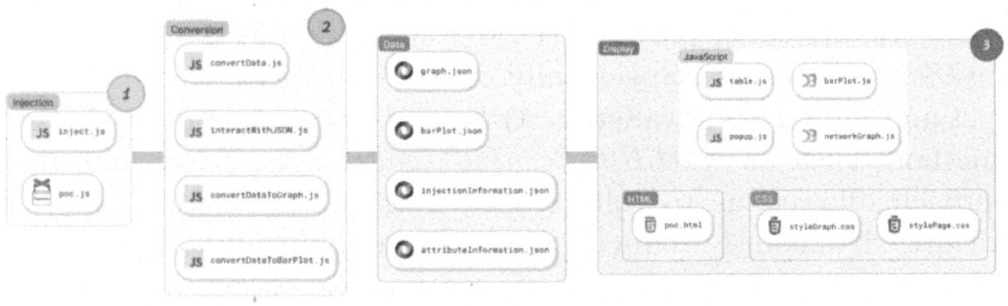

Fig. 1. Web Scraping Architecture.

3.2 Fingerprint Detection

Having stored suspected fingerprinting scripts in the previous stage (See Sect. 3.1) we now track the requested attributes and determine whether the script is performing browser fingerprinting. To do this we first check whether the script uses an **HTTP POST** method to send information to a remote server (method used by **FPFlow** [4]), before analysing fingerprinting features requested by the script (method used by **FPMon** [2]). Here, a feature consists of one or more attributes used for browser fingerprinting Since attributes are often accessed together, for example, *window.innerHeight* and *window.innerWidth* are frequently used together to retrieve the browser size, we can analyse features, rather than individual attributes, to improve detection accuracy and efficiency. Additionally, features can be classified as either **Sensitive** (may contribute to fingerprinting, but are not necessarily intrusive) or **Aggressive** (high probability of uniquely identifying visitors to a web site with only a few data points). Of the 40 features (defined by researchers in [2]) 18 are considered aggressive since it is highly likely to track users with only a small number of attributes. To determine if a script is performing browser fingerprinting we define D as a set of all scripts encountered on a web page. For each script $s \in D$, we define: HTTPPOST(s) True if and only if script s sends data via an HTTP POST (or equivalent) to an external endpoint, where $\text{FEATURES}(s)$ represents the total number of distinct fingerprint-relevant features script s requests, $\text{AGGRESSIVE}(s)$ returns how many of those requested features are classified as *aggressive* and $\text{BF}(s)$ is true when script s is classified as performing browser fingerprinting.

First, if a script does not send data exetrnally $\forall s \in D, \ (\neg\text{HTTPPOST}(s)) \rightarrow \neg\text{BF}(s)$ then we consider it not to be performing meaningful browser fingerprinting. Additionally, if a script does send data but does not request known fingerprinting features $\forall s \in D, \ (\text{HTTPPOST}(s) \wedge \text{FEATURES}(s) = 0) \rightarrow \neg\text{BF}(s)$ we again consider the script is not being used for fingerprinting. Next, for scripts passing the first two conditions we count the number of requested features. If a script uses POST and requests at least 7 *sensitive* features $\forall s \in D, \ (\text{HTTPPOST}(s) \wedge \text{FEATURES}(s) \geq 7) \rightarrow \text{BF}(s)$, then we consider it to be performing fingerprinting since requesting a large number of known features and posting these externally would indicate a degree of profiling. Conversely, if a script uses POST, requests fewer than 7 features, but none are considered *Aggressive* $\forall s \in D, \ (\text{HTTPPOST}(s) \wedge \text{FEATURES}(s) < 7 \wedge \text{AGGRESSIVE}(s) = 0) \rightarrow \neg\text{BF}(s)$, the script is considered not to be fingerprinting since a small set of *sensitive* features are unlikely to produce a unique fingerprint. Finally, if a script uses POST, requests at least 5 total features, and at least one Aggressive feature $\forall s \in D, \ (\text{HTTPPOST}(s) \wedge \text{FEATURES}(s) \geq 5 \wedge \text{AGGRESSIVE}(s) \geq 1) \rightarrow \text{BF}(s)$, then it is considered to be fingerprinting since combining an *aggressive* feature with five additional *sensitive* features would return a more unique fingerprint. Likewise, a script using POST, requesting fewer than 5 total features, but at least 3 of them are aggressive $\forall s \in D, \ (\text{HTTPPOST}(s) \wedge \text{FEATURES}(s) < 5 \wedge \text{AGGRESSIVE}(s) \geq 3) \rightarrow \text{BF}(s)$, would equally indicate a strong likelihood that the script is performing fingerprinting.

4 Results and Discussion

Data was collected using the method described in Sect. 3.1 where *inject.js* was used to test the top 1000 websites over a total of 12 iterations. On average, we were unable to access 28.5% of websites due to anti-scraping protections or because the sites were no longer functional. Across the websites we successfully visited, we encountered 193 unique browser fingerprinting scripts that requested a total of 120 attributes for fingerprinting. Where a script appeared on multiple websites, it was counted only once to avoid duplication. Figure 2(a) shows the most requested scripts across the tested websites, and Figure 2(b) shows the most requested attributes by each script.

To understand the distribution of attributes, we compute the occurrence of each attribute across the 193 fingerprinting scripts by counting the frequency of each value (0 and 1) for each attribute. We define $Attribute(x)$ as an attribute in the dataset, and we use $Count(x, v, p)$ to determine if attribute x has value v, where p is the percentage of scripts when x has value v. Next, we categorise attributes as *balanced* or *imbalanced* to help determine which attributes are most commonly used by fingerprinting scripts. Imbalanced attributes are those that are either highly requested (over 80% of scripts) or rarely requested (under 20% of scripts). These attributes are more likely to be effective in uniquely identifying users, thus aiding in the detection of more persistent fingerprinting techniques. We define an attribute as imbalanced if it meets the following condition: for any attribute x, if the percentage p for a value v exceeds 80% (i.e., appears in more than 80% of scripts), then the attribute is considered *imbalanced*: $\forall x\ (Attribute(x) \land Count(x, v, p) \land (p > 80)) \rightarrow Imbalanced(x)$.

Conversely, an attribute is *balanced* if it does not meet the imbalanced condition, i.e., if the occurrence of its values is less than or equal to 80% for any value v. This includes attributes where the value v occurs between 20% and 80% of the time, which we consider to be *moderately used* but balanced. Specifically, if the attribute does not exceed the 80% threshold for any value, it is considered balanced: $\forall x\ (Attribute(x) \land \neg Imbalanced(x)) \rightarrow Balanced(x)$. This ensures that any attribute whose values exceed the 80% threshold for either $v = 1$ or $v = 0$ is imbalanced, while others are balanced (including those that fall in the 20%–80% range).

4.1 Script Invasiveness

Figure 3 shows the frequency of attributes requested by the 192 fingerprinting scripts in our dataset. In total, we identified 68 attributes as imbalanced (*Red*), meaning they were either requested by at least 80% of the encountered scripts or by fewer than 20% of them. Specifically, 5 imbalanced attributes being requested by more than 80% of encountered scripts while 63 imbalanced attributes requested by less than 20% of scripts. In contrast, the remaining 52 attributes were classified as balanced (*Blue*), as they were used more moderately across the 193 scripts analysed. The discovered distribution suggests that we can categorise encountered scripts broadly into three main classes of fingerprinting scripts: **(i) widespread**, "baseline" scripts that nearly always collect the same set of fundamental attributes. **(ii) niche** scripts that layer a small subset of specialised *aggressive* attributes on top of the more common ones to refine the uniqueness of a user's fingerprint, **(iii) aggressive** scripts that request a smaller number of attributes, but which contains a higher proportion of *aggressive* attributes.

4.2 Attribute Commonality

Next, we group the 120 attributes into 40 features based on those defined by researchers in [2]. We define *Attribute(x)* where x is an attribute in the dataset, *Feature(y)* where y is a feature category, and *BelongsTo(x, y)* to mean that attribute x is associated with feature y. As such, each attribute is associated with exactly one feature: $\forall x \exists y\,(Attribute(x) \rightarrow BelongsTo(x, y))$, which ensures that every attribute belongs to a feature category. Furthermore, each attribute can belong to only one feature, i.e.: $\forall x \forall y_1 \forall y_2\,(BelongsTo(x, y_1) \land BelongsTo(x, y_2) \rightarrow (y_1 = y_2))$.

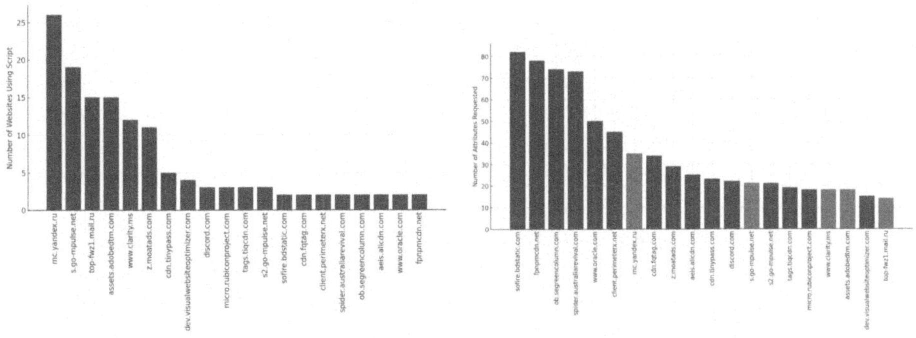

(a) Most Requested Scripts by Website (b) Most Requested Attributes by Script

Fig. 2. Distribution of Scripts and Associated Attributes.

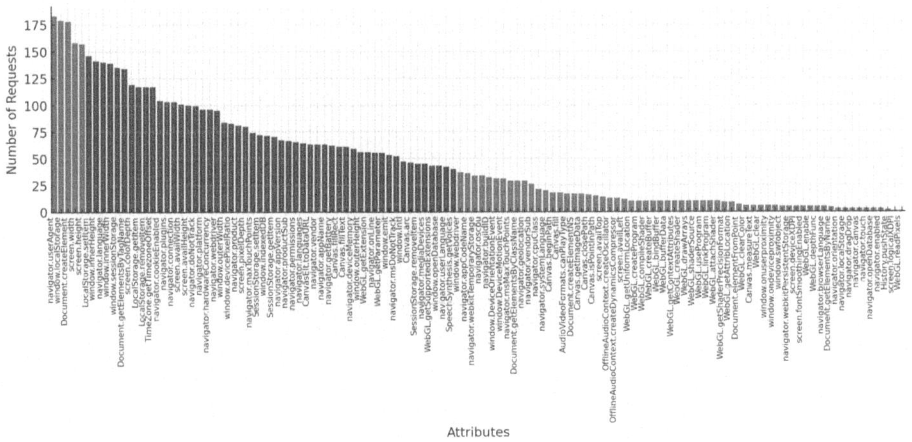

Fig. 3. Frequency of Attribute Distribution ($\leq$ 20%) & $\geq$ 80% shown in Red. (Color figure online)

Our analysis shows that the 63 imbalanced attributes (requested by $\leq$ 20% scripts) align with 20 features namely: *AppCodeName, Audio, AudioVideoFormats, BrowserLanguage, BuildID, Canvas, CpuClass, DragDrop, Flash, Geolocation, JSFont, JavaEnabled, Mobile, OSCPU, ScreenWindow, Storage, SystemLanguage, VendorSub, WebDriver, WebGL.* This list includes more sophisticated features such as *canvas, WebGL, Audio* that are used in scripts that aim for detailed fingerprinting. Whereas, the 5 imbalanced attributes (requested by $\geq$ 80% scripts) align with 3 features namely: *ScreenWindow, Storage, UserAgent,* which appear to be the base for most scripts encountered.

When we compare the 40 features across the 68 imbalanced (textitAppCodeName, Audio, AudioVideoFormats, BrowserLanguage, BuildID, Canvas, CpuClass, DragDrop, Flash, Geolocation, JSFont, JavaEnabled, Mobile, OSCPU,

ScreenWindow, Storage, SystemLanguage, UserAgent, VendorSub, WebDriver, WebGL) and 52 balanced (*AppName, AppVersion, AudioVideoFormats, Battery, Canvas, Connection, ContentLanguage, CookiesEnabled, DeviceMemory, DoNotTrack, HardwareConcurrency, JSFont, MediaDevices, Mobile, NavigatorOnline, Permissions, Platform, Plugins, Product, ProductSub, ScreenWindow, Storage, TimeZone, Vendor, WebDriver, WebGL.*) attributes we observed that 8 features were present in both datasets. Namely, *Storage, JSFont, WebGL, WebDriver, AudioVideoFormats, ScreenWindow, Mobile, Canvas* were present in both. Given the large number of attributes requested, grouping them according to their high level features allows us to now classify which are *sensitive* or *aggressive.*

4.3 Aggressive Features

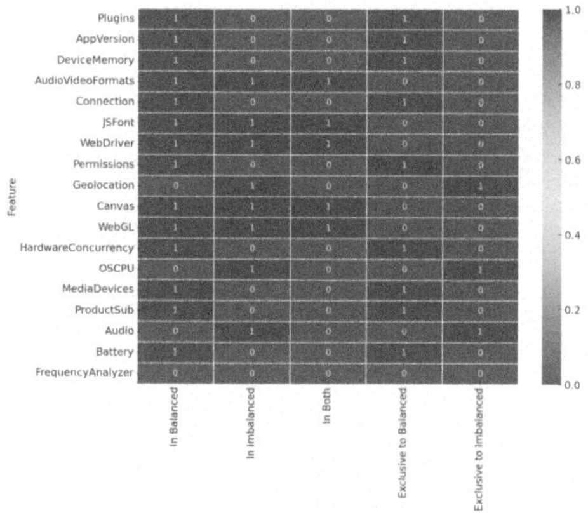

Fig. 4. Distribution of Aggressive Features (Red). (Color figure online)

Next, we identify a subset of 18 aggressive features (*Plugins, AppVersion, ProductSub, DeviceMemory, HardwareConcurrency, OSCPU, AudioVideoFormats, Audio, Canvas, WebGL, FrequencyAnalyzer, Connection, Geolocation, JSFont, WebDriver, Permissions, Battery*) suggested by the same authors [2]. These aggressive features go beyond basic fingerprinting (like user-agent detection) and are used more frequently in scripts that aim for detailed fingerprinting. They extract deeper system, hardware, and behavioural information, making them more persistent and harder to evade. Many of these features require explicit permission, but some like *Canvas*, *WebGL*, and *HardwareConcurrency*, can be accessed without user consent.

To categorise features as aggressive we define *AggressiveFeature(y)* where y is considered aggressive if *ContainsAggressiveAttribute(y)* Feature y contains at least one aggressive attribute, where *AggressiveAttribute(x)*: Attribute

x is considered aggressive. To be considered an aggressive feature it must contain at least one aggressive attribute $\forall y(AggressiveFeature(y) \leftrightarrow \exists x(BelongsTo(x, y) \wedge AggressiveAttribute(x)))$, where an attribute is classified as aggressive if it contributes to uniquely identifying users across devices $\forall x(AggressiveAttribute(x) \leftrightarrow HighUniqueness(x))$ and $HighUniqueness(x)$ determines whether an attribute x provides significant tracking capabilities.

We observe that 5 of the 18 aggressive features (*Canvas, AudioVideoFormats, WebGL, WebDriver, JSFont*) appear in both the *balanced* (52) and *imbalanced* (68) lists of 120 attributes shown in column three of Fig. 4. All five relate to visual or rendering-based fingerprinting and/or basic environment detection. *Canvas* and *WebGL* extract unique rendering traits from the user's GPU and driver setup. *AudioVideoFormats* checks supported audio/video codecs, another proxy for a user's system environment. *JSFont* inspects available fonts, which often vary across devices and operating systems. *WebDriver* detects if a browser is running in an automated or test environment (e.g., Selenium). Given these capabilities do not usually require explicit user permission and reveal stable, distinctive system details, it would make sense that they appear across both *balanced* and *imbalanced* attributes.

Next, we observe that 9 of the 18 (*Battery, Permissions, ProductSub, HardwareConcurrency, DeviceMemory, Connection, MediaDevices, AppVersion, Plugins*) appear exclusively among the *balanced* attributes (see column four of Fig. 4). These features expose system-level or browser-level details that can vary by device and usage context. *Battery, Connection*, and *Permissions* can be more situational or invasive (e.g., battery level or request permissions). *HardwareConcurrency* and *DeviceMemory* reveal CPU cores and available memory, respectively, useful for fine-grained tracking, but less universally crucial than rendering-based methods. *Plugins* and *AppVersion* relate to how the browser and its extensions are configured, a combination that can be very unique among users, while *ProductSub* offers a sub-version for further identifying minor browser variants. These appear to be present only in the *balanced* attributes because these details are particularly useful for building richer profiles, but are not needed by every script.

Next, we observe that 3 (*Geolocation, OSCPU, Audio*) appear exclusievly among the imbalanced attributes see column five of Fig. 4). These features are highly targeted or require special conditions and thus appear in relatively few scripts. *Geolocation* typically needs user permission and is very privacy sensitive, so fewer scripts attempt to use it. *OSCPU* can reveal an OS-level CPU string (e.g., for Firefox), which is not always exposed or is hidden by default in many browsers. *Audio fingerprinting* beyond simply detecting supported formats often involves analysing how sound is processed, which can be more niche or require additional user interaction or permissions. As a result, they tend to surface in highly specialised or more invasive scripts, explaining their low overall usage.

Finally, considering features have varying numbers of associated attributes we determine that overall 30.769% of *balanced* attributes and 44.118% of *imbalanced* attributes are considered aggressive.

5 Ontology Development

To illustrate the potential for building an ontology and ultimately a Knowledge Graph, we first constructed a static graph from the data collected in Sect. 3.1. Figure 5(a) shows the websites using one of the deteceted fingerprinting scripts (*assets.adobeedtm.com*) along with the attributes it requests. Whilst representing our data as a static graph was useful it has limitations. To determine if a script is likely used for targeted advertising, we count the number of unique websites where the script was detected and check whether it requests a similar set of attributes across these sites. While this method worked well with our collected data, it may not always hold true in cases where a website and its subdomains are both scraped. Since subdomains technically belong to the same website, they may not represent truly distinct sites, which could impact the accuracy of this approach. As such, this paper presents our work towards developing an ontology that provides a structured representation of *scripts*, which group attributes from users' browsers into *features*, labelling them according to their frequency of use (*balanced* vs *imbalanced*) or their privacy-invasive potential (*aggressive* vs *sensitive*).

Next, to formalise our proposed ontology, we use domain knowledge acquired through our analysis in Sect. 4 and existing literature [2,4]. The ontology identifies key entities, concepts, relationships, and their properties. We followed the ontology development procedure outlined in [7] to enumerate the terms of the ontology, define relationships among entities, and specify their properties. As such, our ontology formalises browser fingerprinting detection, enabling researchers to systematically analyse tracking scripts. It provides a structured model to link browser attributes, tracking methods, and privacy risks, paving the way for automated detection systems and privacy-preserving technologies. To ensure the ontology is accessible and resuable, we adhered to the FAIR (Findable, Accessible, Interoperable, and Reusable) data principles [9] during development. As highlighted by Poveda-Villalón et al. [8] our FAIR-compliant ontology was assigned a globally unique and persistent IRI, published openly via GitHub Pages[1], and described using rich metadata including provenance, licensing, and versioning. Standard vocabularies were used to enhance interoperability, and each term within the ontology was annotated with a label *(rdfs:label)* and comment *(rdfs:comment)* to support reuse and machine-readability. Furthermore, due to its conformance with OWL standards, the ontology is fully compatible with tools such as *Protégé* for editing, *SPARQL* for querying, and semantic reasoners for inference and classification. This commitment to FAIR principles facilitates broader adoption and integration into knowledge graphs and semantic web systems.

[1] https://github.com/cdmcdermott/Research/tree/main/NLDB_25#readme.

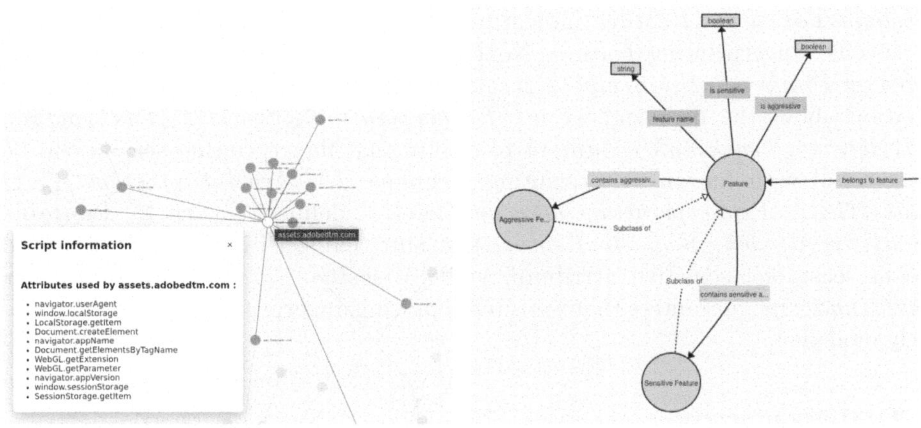

(a) *assets.adobeedtm.com* Attributes (b) Features *(Aggressive, Sensitive)*

Fig. 5. Network Graph Browser and Fingerprinting Ontology (Full online version)

5.1 Ontology Representation

Figure 5b shows a subset of the domain ontology of browser fingerprinting developed in Protégé. A full version is available online.

The ontology models the relationships between tracking mechanisms and fingerprinting techniques, identifying aggressive features based on their potential for user tracking and defines several key classes, each representing distinct entities involved in browser fingerprinting. We define $FingerprintingScript \sqsubseteq \top$ to indicate that all instances of fingerprinting scripts belong to the universal class. $Feature \sqsubseteq \top$ encapsulates different functionalities or capabilities that are classified as either $SensitiveFeature \sqsubseteq Feature$ that expose some identifying characteristic or $AggressiveFeature \sqsubseteq Feature$ that employ invasive or persistent data collection techniques (See Fig. 5b). $Attribute \sqsubseteq \top$ belong to features and are further divided based on their frequency distributions where those appearing disproportionately often or rarely, making them highly revealing, are considered $ImbalancedAttribute \sqsubseteq Attribute$ while conversely $BalancedAttribute \sqsubseteq Attribute$ are distributed more evenly across different users indicating a lower degree of uniqueness or aggressiveness. Finally, $TrackingMechanism \sqsubseteq \top$ represent mechanisms that track users independently or in conjunction with fingerprinting techniques across $Website \sqsubseteq \top$.

Our ontology defines several object properties to capture relationships between fingerprinting scripts, features, and attributes. Here, a feature may contain sensitive attributes $Feature \sqsubseteq \exists containsSensitiveAttribute.SensitiveFeature$ whilst we categorise aggressive features as relying on invasive attributes $Feature \sqsubseteq \exists containsAggressiveAttribute.AggressiveFeature$ where the relationship between attributes and features is established by $Attribute \sqsubseteq$

$\exists belongsToFeature.Feature$ indicating that each attribute is associated with a specific fingerprinting feature. Next, we define that scripts will query the browser $FingerprintingScript \sqsubseteq \exists requestsAttribute.Attribute$ to identify information about the user and we use $FingerprintingScript \sqsubseteq \exists hasTrackingMechanism.TrackingMechanism$ to ensure that fingerprinting scripts can be associated with known fingerprinting technique $FingerprintingScript \sqsubseteq \exists classifiedAs.FingerprintingCategory$. Here, we define $Feature \sqsubseteq \exists containsSensitiveAttribute.SensitiveFeature$ to ensure that sensitive features are linked to at least one sensitive attribute, while $Website \sqsubseteq \exists usesScript.FingerprintingScript$ guarantees that websites deploying fingerprinting scripts are properly modelled.

5.2 Reasoning

Having formalised our ontology we can now use the methods proposed earlier to categorise attributes as either $ImbalancedAttribute \sqsubseteq Attribute$ or alternatively $BalancedAttribute \sqsubseteq Attribute$ based on their occurrence percentage across fingerprinting scripts. We capture the threshold logic (e.g., $\geq 80\%$ or $\leq 20\%$) to categorise *imbalanced* $\forall x\, [\text{Attribute}(x) \wedge (\text{occurrencePercentage}(x) \geq 0.80 \vee \text{occurrencePercentage}(x) \leq 0.20) \rightarrow \text{ImbalancedAttribute}(x)]$, or *balanced*, $\forall x\, [\text{Attribute}(x) \wedge \neg\text{ImbalancedAttribute}(x) \rightarrow \text{BalancedAttribute}(x)]$.

We can define an *AggressiveFeature* in terms of *AggressiveAttribute* as follows: $\forall y(\text{AggressiveFeature}(y) \leftrightarrow \exists x[\text{Attribute}(x) \wedge \text{belongsToFeature}(x, y) \wedge \text{AggressiveAttribute}(x)])$. Similarly, for a *SensitiveFeature* in terms of *SensitiveAttribute*, we define it as $\forall y(\text{SensitiveFeature}(y) \leftrightarrow \exists x[\text{Attribute}(x) \wedge \text{belongsToFeature}(x, y) \wedge \text{SensitiveAttribute}(x)])$.

Next, a script is considered *Fingerprinting* if **(i)** it transmits data externally (e.g., via HTTP POST) and **(ii)** collects a threshold number of fingerprinting features. For instance, Let $\text{hasExternalDataTransfer}(s) = \text{true}$ indicate that the script sends data off-site, and $\geq n\,(\text{requestsAttribute.Feature})$ denote that the script requests at least n distinct features. We can define a rule as follows: if a script does not transmit data externally, then it is not a fingerprinting script, i.e., $\forall s(\neg\text{hasExternalDataTransfer}(s) \rightarrow \neg\text{FingerprintingScript}(s))$. Conversely, if a script transmits data externally and requests at least 7 distinct features, then it is considered a fingerprinting script, expressed as $\forall s(\text{hasExternalDataTransfer}(s) \wedge (\geq 7\ \text{requestsAttribute.Feature})(s) \rightarrow \text{FingerprintingScript}(s))$. Likewise, we can add conditions for *aggressive* features. For instance, if a script has external data transfer, requests at least 5 total features, and includes at least 1 aggressive feature, then it qualifies as fingerprinting.

5.3 Competency Questions

To define the scope and requirements of the proposed ontology we followed Noy and McGuiness [7] guidance to devise compentencey questions that defined encapsulated knowledge the ontology must represent or answer. Specifically, if scripts can be classified as performing fingerprinting when they request specific features, rely on external data transfers, and meet certain thresholds regarding aggressive or sensitive attributes. First, (i) " Which scripts are classified as *FingerprintingScript*, and what *Feature* and *Attribute* are associated with them?". Next, to determine if the ontology reveals which attributes belong to a feature, differentiating between those that are balanced (moderately frequent) or imbalanced (extremely common or rare) across scripts we use (ii) "Which Attributes are explicitly classified as *BalancedAttribute* or *ImbalancedAttribute?*" and (iii) "Which Attributes belong to Feature (X)". Being able to identify which features incorporate aggressive attributes is also essential, as is discerning which scripts or features are simply sensitive rather than overtly aggressive. Further, the ontology must support queries about the relationship between websites and their embedded fingerprinting scripts, including whether those scripts request more balanced or imbalanced attribute. We use (iv) "Which *FingerprintingScript* is embedded by Website (W), and what types of Attributes (e.g., BalancedAttribute or ImbalancedAttribute) does the script request?". It should also allow users to retrieve the occurrence percentages of attributes in order to classify them under balanced or imbalanced. In addition, we need to assess which scripts collect only a minimal set of attributes (and thus might not trigger fingerprinting criteria) versus which ones exhibit highly invasive behavior by employing a large number of aggressive features. We use (v) "What is the *occurrencePercentage* of Attribute (A) across all scripts, and is it classified as a *BalancedAttribute* or *ImbalancedAttribute?*" and (vi) "Which *FingerprintingScript* request only a limited number of *Attribute*, and thus may fall below the threshold for classification as *FingerprintingScript?*" (Attribute count thresholds must be defined in *SPARQL* query) and (vii) "Which *FingerprintingScript* requests a high number or proportion of *AggressiveFeature*, suggesting more invasive fingerprinting behaviour?" (Requires aggregation and thresholding in *SPARQL* query). An example *SPARQL* query for *Q3* is found below:

```
PREFIX bf: <https://.../Research/NLDB_25/BrowserFingerprintingOntology#>

SELECT ?attribute ?classification
WHERE {
  ?attribute bf:belongsToFeature bf:X .

  OPTIONAL {
    ?attribute a bf:AggressiveFeature .
    BIND("Aggressive" AS ?classification)
  }

  OPTIONAL {
    ?attribute a bf:SensitiveFeature .
    BIND("Sensitive" AS ?classification)
  }
}
```

6 Conclusions and Future Work

This paper presents our work towards an ontology driven approach to detecting and browser fingerprinting techniques. By leveraging JavaScript function interception and network request monitoring, we systematically categorised fingerprinting scripts based on their invasiveness and attribute collection behavior. All code, data analysis and developed ontology presented in this paper are available from our (Github repository). This insight was used to formalise knowledge into an ontology enabling structured reasoning about tracking mechanisms, script behaviours, and privacy risks. While the proposed ontology provides an initial framework for effectively modelling fingerprinting techniques it has not been fully tested. Our next step is to compose appropriate *SPARQL* queries from our competence questions to fully validate the ontology before constructing a corresponding knowledge graph in *Neo4J*. As such, this could serve as a comprehensive framework for automated browser fingerprinting detection, empowering both researchers and developers to mitigate privacy risks in online environments

References

1. Acar, G., Juarez, M., Nikiforakis, N., Diaz, C., Gürses, S., Piessens, F., Preneel, B.: Fpdetective: dusting the web for fingerprinters. In: Proceedings of the 2013 ACM SIGSAC Conference on Computer & Communications Security, pp. 1129–1140. ACM (2013). https://doi.org/10.1145/2508859.2516674
2. Fietkau, J., Thimmaraju, K., Kybranz, F., Neef, S., Seifert, J.P.: The elephant in the background: a quantitative approach to empower users against web browser fingerprinting. In: Proceedings of the 20th Workshop on Workshop on Privacy in the Electronic Society, WPES '21, pp. 167–180. Association for Computing Machinery, New York (2021)
3. Labs, P.: The perils of phishing attacks: a case study on evilproxy. Protos Labs Resources (2023). https://www.protoslabs.io/resources/case-study-on-evilproxy
4. Li, T., Zheng, X., Shen, K., Han, X.: FPFlow: detect and prevent browser fingerprinting with dynamic taint analysis. In: Lu, W., Zhang, Y., Wen, W., Yan, H., Li, C. (eds.) CNCERT 2021. CCIS, vol. 1506, pp. 51–67. Springer, Singapore (2022). https://doi.org/10.1007/978-981-16-9229-1_4
5. Moad, D., Sihag, V., Choudhary, G., Duguma, D.G., You, I.: Fingerprint defender: defense against browser-based user tracking. In: You, I., Kim, H., Youn, T.-Y., Palmieri, F., Kotenko, I. (eds.) MobiSec 2021. CCIS, vol. 1544, pp. 236–247. Springer, Singapore (2022). https://doi.org/10.1007/978-981-16-9576-6_17
6. Nikiforakis, N., Kapravelos, A., Joosen, W., Kruegel, C., Piessens, F., Vigna, G.: Cookieless monster: exploring the ecosystem of web-based device fingerprinting. In: Proceedings of the 34th IEEE Symposium on Security and Privacy, pp. 541–555. IEEE (2013)
7. Noy, N.F., McGuinness, D.L.: Ontology development 101: a guide to creating your first ontology. Technical Report. KSL-01-05, Stanford Knowledge Systems Laboratory (2001). http://www-ksl.stanford.edu/people/dlm/papers/ontology-tutorial-noy-mcguinness-abstract.html
8. Poveda-Villalón, M., Espinoza-Arias, P., Garijo, D., Corcho, O.: Coming to terms with FAIR ontologies. In: Keet, C.M., Dumontier, M. (eds.) EKAW 2020. LNCS (LNAI), vol. 12387, pp. 255–270. Springer, Cham (2020). https://doi.org/10.1007/978-3-030-61244-3_18
9. Wilkinson, M.D., et al.: The fair guiding principles for scientific data management and stewardship. Sci. Data **3**, 160018 (2016). https://doi.org/10.1038/sdata.2016.18

Dual-Style Transcription of Historical Manuscripts Based on Multimodal Small Language Models with Switchable Adapters

Sergio Torres Aguilar(✉)

University of Luxembourg, Esch-sur-Alzette, Luxembourg
sertor01@ucm.es

Abstract. The transcription of historical manuscripts presents unique challenges due to complex writing styles, pervasive abbreviations, and significant linguistic heterogeneity. Recent multimodal architectures that integrate powerful language models with vision encoders offer promising and flexible solutions. In this work, we propose a two-stage training strategy to model two main transcription paradigms: *diplomatic* (abbreviated) and *semi-diplomatic* (expanded). Our approach leverages two specialized corpora—**CATMuS Medieval** (abbreviated) and **TRIDIS** (non-abbreviated). In Stage 1, we pre-train a single model on a random combined dataset using a loss penalization mechanism to discourage the prediction of Medieval Unicode Font Initiative (MUFI) characters during expanded-text generation. In Stage 2, this pre-trained model serves as the foundation to train *separate* LoRA adapters for each transcription style, which can be dynamically switched at inference.

We benchmark our approach using **MiniCPM-Llama3-V-2.5**, **Phi-3.5 Vision** and **Qwen2-VL** (all published end-2024) against two established baselines (**Kraken v5** and **TrOCR**). Our results indicate that while the unified "double-head" model provides a solid initialization, fine-tuning separate, switchable LoRA adapters leveraging that base yields progressive superior performance by better adapting to each transcription style. We discuss the limitations of a single adapter and advocate for switched adapters to achieve optimal flexibility. This integrated approach supports historians, linguists, and digital humanities scholars in exploring complex historical corpora at multiple interpretive levels.

Keywords: Historical Manuscript Transcription · Multimodal Models · Small Language Models · Curriculum Learning · LoRA Adapters · Abbreviation Expansion · Handwritten Text Recognition

1 Introduction

The automatic transcription of Western medieval manuscripts is a crucial task for making cultural heritage widely accessible, enabling large-scale linguistic analy-

R. Ichise (Ed.): NLDB 2025, LNCS 15836, pp. 321–334, 2026.
https://doi.org/10.1007/978-3-031-97141-9_22

sis, and supporting historical research. However, this task is significantly more challenging than transcribing modern printed documents due to several factors:

- **Complex Writing Styles:** Historical manuscripts feature a rich diversity of script families—including Textualis, Cursiva, Bastarda, Caroline, and various hybrid forms that evolved over time and across regions. The variability and ambiguity inherent in these letterforms, often compounded by successive scribal interventions, make consistent transcription particularly demanding.
- **Pervasive Abbreviations:** Scribes frequently used abbreviations to save time and space. They range from simple suspensions (omitting word parts) to complex contractions and notarial signs, often involving superscript marks, diacritics, and graphemic fusions. The same abbreviation can yield multiple expansions, meanings, and functions depending on context.
- **Linguistic Heterogeneity:** Manuscripts from Western Europe are multilingual, including Latin, various vernaculars and multiple language states. Even within a single language variant, orthographic conventions were not standardized, adding a further layer of complexity.
- **Material Degradation:** The ravages of time through factors such as water, fire, insects, and general wear result in faded ink, stains, holes, transparencies and other degradations that complicate the visual recognition process for humans and machines, demanding advanced graphical parsers.
- **Dual Transcription Needs:** Different scholarly communities require distinct transcription styles. Paleographers and codicologists demand *diplomatic* transcriptions preserving original abbreviations and encoding visual features of the manuscript. Historians and linguists favor *semi-diplomatic* or *normalized* transcriptions, where abbreviations are expanded to yield a more readable text for modern audiences and automatic tools. Ideally, one single system should be able to produce both (or more) transcription styles.

Traditional CRNN+CTC Handwritten Text Recognition (HTR) systems have made significant progress in transcribing historical documents. However, they frequently struggle with the complexities of abbreviations and linguistic variations inherent to these manuscripts. More recent Transformer-based models such as TrOCR [19] and DTrOCR [12] demonstrate enhanced generalization across diverse handwriting families offering robust solutions in handling both abbreviated and expanded forms. Nevertheless, these models encounter a training dilemma: the *diplomatic* transcription paradigm adheres closely to the manuscript's graphical patterns and is inherently easier to learn (albeit requiring longer ground-truth annotation); whereas the *semi-diplomatic* paradigm involves generating content not explicitly present in the image, demanding a higher degree of contextual interpretation and alignment (albeit requiring less annotation efforts). Balancing these competing demands during training presents significant challenges, as gradients optimized for one objective may hinder the performance of the other, potentially resulting in issues such as catastrophic forgetting or the emergence of "double orders" (i.e., generating mixed outputs for a single input).

One of the key innovations of our approach is its ability to generate two distinct transcription styles—*diplomatic* (abbreviated) and *semi-diplomatic* (expanded)—using a single, pre-trained backbone. In the abbreviated corpus, roughly 50% of words are expanded, providing common ground between the modes. By leveraging this shared content, our method avoids training and maintaining two separate models, instead using switchable LoRA adapters (only about 2–3% of trainable parameters) to efficiently adapt to each style. To our knowledge, no other work has addressed training a unified model that meets the competing demands of diplomatic fidelity and interpretive expansion.

2 Related Work

2.1 Historical Text Recognition

The field of Historical Text Recognition (HTR) has witnessed significant advancements in recent years, moving in around 2014 from early Hidden Markov Models (HMMs) [10] to CRNN+CTC architectures combining CNN layers for feature extraction, recurrent layers for sequence modeling, and a CTC loss for alignment-free training. Systems like Kraken [18], PyLaia [22] and HTR+ [20] are based on this approach and have become standard tools for the digital humanities communities. More recently (2023), Transformer-based models [30] have pushed the state-of-the-art further, surpassing traditional CRNN methods in most transcription tasks. For example, TrOCR [19] employs a vision Transformer encoder paired with a text Transformer decoder, achieving impressive results on both printed and handwritten texts. Hybrid approaches that combine CRNN-based visual extractors, pre-trained language models [26], and attention mechanisms [17] have also emerged, though challenges remain when dealing with the complex layouts, visual variations, and abbreviation behaviors found in historical handwriting documents before the writing standardization in the 18th century.

2.2 Multimodal Models for Document Understanding

Multimodal models have rapidly gained prominence in document understanding by integrating powerful vision encoders (e.g., CLIP [23] or SigLIP [35]) with large language models (LLMs) pre-trained on vast datasets. The recent family of models like Pixtral [2] or Qwen-VL [31] have demonstrated progressive improvements in tasks like form understanding, document classification, and information extraction. These models typically use a Transformer architecture accepting arbitrary aligned sequences of image and text inputs to generate coherent text outputs.

Within this rapidly evolving landscape of image-text-to-text models, there's a growing emphasis on lightweight and low-latency models (7–14 billion parameters) that offer a practical balance between performance and computational cost, particularly for fine-tuning scenarios. Benchmarks of small models like MiniCPM-Llama3-V-2.5 [34] and Phi-3.5-vision-instruct [1] have revealed remarkable capabilities in visual question answering, image captioning, and text generation, approaching the performance of significantly larger models (e.g., 70B+ parameters). In contrast to traditional CRNN+CTC models which lack the capacity for deep contextual reasoning, the multimodals have the capacity to reason over both visual and textual information, combined with their extensive pre-training, makes them particularly well-suited for the challenges of historical manuscript transcription. This task demands not only robust image understanding and powerful linguistic decoders but also a capacity for contextual reasoning. Furthermore, these smaller multi-modal models offer a promising foundation for advancing HTR research in areas such as end-to-end processing, page-level transcription, and even handwriting synthesis for limited hardware frameworks.

2.3 Curriculum Learning and Parameter-Efficient Methods

Our work follows a curriculum learning strategy [3] in which models are progressively trained on increasingly complex tasks, improving efficiency and generalization in HTR [14]. To fine-tune large pre-trained models without catastrophic forgetting, we employ loss-based regularization and Parameter-Efficient Fine-Tuning (PEFT) via LoRA (Low-Rank Adaptation) [16], which introduces trainable adapter modules while freezing most of the pre-trained parameters. Inspired by prior work on task-specific parameter isolation [21], we train separate LoRA adapters for each transcription style (abbreviated and expanded), enabling specialized learning and dynamic switching during inference. This approach mitigates interference between the two distinct tasks and promotes more robust and accurate transcriptions.

2.4 Abbreviation Expansion in Historical Texts

Abbreviation expansion in historical texts has been addressed using a variety of methods, including rule-based systems, statistical machine translation [4], and neural network approaches [7]. Recent decoding strategies introduced beam searches and vocabulary-based completions [27]. However, most existing work focuses on expanding abbreviations in isolation, or within a limited context without proposing efficient solutions to expansions based on dense linguistic knowledge (for declensions and named entities) or connecting with external bases to integrate institutional preferences or scribal behaviors. The challenge of generating both diplomatic and expanded transcriptions within a unified framework has received less attention. Our work directly addresses this gap.

3 Corpus Description

We use two specialized line-level corpora for our experiments:

3.1 CATMuS Medieval (Abbreviated Corpus)

The **CATMuS Medieval** corpus [9] consists of 200 manuscripts from the 8th to the 16th centuries, totaling 164,000 text lines. The corpus is characterized by:

- **Languages:** Latin, Old French, Old Spanish, and Middle High German.
- **Script Families:** Textualis, Cursiva, Bastarda, Caroline and hybrids.
- **Annotations:** Diplomatic transcriptions that preserve all abbreviations and use the Medieval Unicode Font Initiative (MUFI) character set to represent special characters and abbreviation marks.

3.2 TRIDIS Corpus (Non-abbreviated Corpus)

The **TRIDIS** [29] corpus is compiled from 52 manuscripts from the 10th to the 17th centuries, totaling 176,000 lines of text. The manuscripts were selected from existing annotated corpora (HOME-Alcar [25], Himanis [24], e-NDP [8], MLH, CODEA [5], Köenigsfelden [13]). The corpus features:

- **Languages:** Latin, Old French, Old Spanish, and Middle High German.
- **Script Families:** The same as CATMuS Medieval, ensuring a similar visual distribution.
- **Annotations:** Semi-diplomatic transcriptions where all abbreviations have been expanded, punctuation has been standardized, and allographs have been normalized to a standard UTF-8 Latin character set.

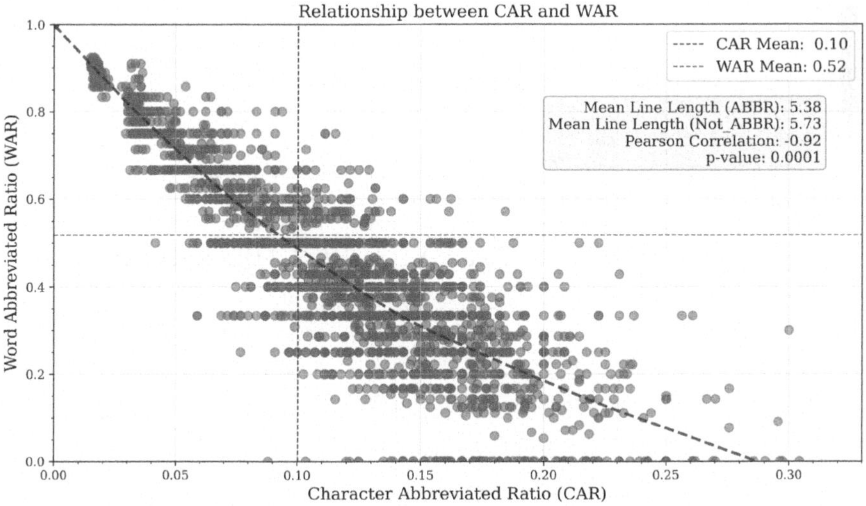

Fig. 1. Relationship between abbreviation density (CAR) and transcription agreement (WAR) in the Distinguo corpus (9 Manuscripts). CAR is calculated as the ratio of MUFI characters in the diplomatic transcription (10% mean). WAR is calculated as the ratio of non-abbreviated words in the diplomatic transcription (52% mean). Dashed lines represent mean values. The red line shows the LOESS smoothed trend. (Color figure online)

The overlap in languages and script families between the two corpora ensures a smooth transition between training stages. Notably, the usage of abbreviations is not uniform—it varies with the epoch (being more stable prior to the 13th century) and according to manuscript typology (more pronounced in literary texts than in documentary ones) [15]. Moreover, there is significant overlap between the writing styles (roughly a half of words are not abbreviated as seen in Fig. 1). Medieval scribes often employed both styles, even within the same codex, reflecting not only practical considerations, such as conserving time and writing material, but also a refined aesthetic and functional tradition. This duality highlights the potential benefits of utilizing a pre-trained, cross-learned base upon which specialized adapters can be fine-tuned for each transcription style.

4 Methodology

We adopt a two-stage curriculum learning strategy, inspired by [3] and [33]. The model is first pre-trained on a combined dataset, establishing a common representation. Then, separate, switchable LoRA adapters are fine-tuned for each transcription style – diplomatic (abbreviated) and semi-diplomatic (expanded) – effectively decoupling their training objectives and mitigating interference.

Algorithm 1. Two-Stage Training with Switchable LoRA Adapters

Input: Backbone M_θ, datasets $\mathcal{D}_A$ (abbreviated) and $\mathcal{D}_N$ (expanded), learning rate η, weight λ.
Stage 1: Pre-training on Combined Dataset
Let $\mathcal{D} \leftarrow \mathcal{D}_A \cup \mathcal{D}_N$
for each batch $B \in \mathcal{D}$ **do**
  Extract images X, texts T, and a style transcription flag f
  Compute: $\mathcal{L}_{CE} = \mathrm{CE}(M_\theta(X), T)$. (cross-entropy loss)
  if f is *expanded* style **then**
    MUFI penalization $\mathcal{L}_{pen} = \lambda \sum_{i=1}^{L} \mathbb{I}(t_i \in \mathcal{M})(-\log(1 - p(t_i)))$
  else
    Set $\mathcal{L}_{pen} = 0$.
  end if
  Total loss: $\mathcal{L} = \mathcal{L}_{CE} + \mathcal{L}_{pen}$.
  Update backbone parameters: $\theta \leftarrow \theta - \eta_{linear} \nabla_\theta \mathcal{L}$.
end for
Stage 2: LoRA Adapter Fine-Tuning
Freeze M_θ; initialize LORA adapters A_{abbr} and A_{exp}.
for each adapter $A \in \{A_{\mathrm{abbr}}, A_{\mathrm{exp}}\}$ **do**
  Select the corresponding dataset: use $\mathcal{D}_A$ for A_{abbr}, and $\mathcal{D}_N$ for A_{exp}.
  for each batch B in the selected dataset **do**
    Extract images X and texts T.
    Compute : $\mathcal{L} = \mathrm{CE}(M_\theta^A(X), T)$,
    Update : $A \leftarrow A - \eta_{cosine} \nabla_A \mathcal{L}$.
  end for
end for
Inference: Select adapter (A_{abbr} or A_{exp}) via `model.set_adapter(mode)`

4.1 Training Strategy

In Stage 1, we pre-train a single multimodal model on a combined dataset comprising both the abbreviated (CATMuS Medieval) and expanded (TRIDIS) corpora using a linear learning rate. During this phase, the model learns sequentially a robust cross-modal representation that encompasses both common visual features and linguistic structures. During the process we incorporate a loss penalization term specifically applied to MUFI characters on expanded predictions. In this way, the pre-training phase establishes a solid foundation for both transcription styles while mitigating the risk of output mixing.

In Stage 2, we freeze the parameters of the pre-trained backbone and then fine-tune two separate LoRA adapters—one for each transcription style—using a cosine learning rate and the corresponding corpus. This design not only reduces computational redundancy compared to training two independent models but also leverages the inherent overlap (around 50% of words) to enhance performance in both transcription modes. At inference, the user can dynamically select the desired adapter to generate either diplomatic or semi-diplomatic outputs.

4.2 Loss Penalization

The penalization term adds a penalty to the loss whenever the model predicts a MUFI character with high probability during expanded-text generation. It is added to the standard cross-entropy loss during the pretraining phase (Stage 1):

$$\mathcal{L}_{\text{penalize}} = \lambda \sum_{i=1}^{L} \mathbb{I}(t_i \in \mathcal{M}) \cdot (-\log(1 - p(t_i)))$$

where: L is the length of the generated sequence; t_i is the i-th token in the generated sequence; $\mathcal{M}$ is the set of all MUFI characters; $\mathbb{I}(t_i \in \mathcal{M})$ is an indicator function that is 1 if t_i is a MUFI character and 0 otherwise; $p(t_i)$ is the probability assigned by the model to token t_i; λ is a hyperparameter that controls the strength of the penalization.

The negative logarithm ensures that the penalty increases as the model's confidence in the incorrect prediction increases. We use $1 - p(t_i)$ because we want to penalize *high* probabilities of MUFI characters. The $-\log$ converts this to a positive penalty that increases as $p(t_i)$ approaches 1.

4.3 Model Architecture

We experimented with three state-of-the-art multimodal models and two baselines using tuned hyper-parameters (See Table 2):

MiniCPM-Llama3-V-2.5: Integrates a SigLIP SoViT-400M/14 visual encoder with an 8B Llama3-based SLM. A perceiver resampler uses cross-attention to compress the image into a sequence of visual tokens for joint processing with text tokens [34].

Phi-3.5-Vision-Instruct: It uses a CLIP ViT-L/14 to encode images and a decoder-only Transformer language model: phi-3.5-mini. Rather than relying on separate modules it supports joint reasoning over vision and language [1].

Qwen2-VL-2B-Instruct: It uses a ViT-600M combined to his own LLM model. We use a tiny version (2B parameters) which can handle arbitrary image resolutions, mapping them into a dynamic number of visual tokens, offering a more human-like visual processing experience [31].

TrOCR-Large-Handwritten: Employed here as our strong **baseline**. The original TrOCR architecture [19] uses an encoder-decoder paradigm. TrOCR is optimized for OCR tasks with a light fine-tuning on HTR upon the IAM dataset. In our experiments, we replace the only-english language decoder for a historical RoBERTa variant, better suited for ancient Latin and vernacular texts [28] (Table 1).

Table 1. Comparison of Models for Historical Manuscript Transcription

Model	Params	MultiM	Visual Encoder	LLM	Pre-training	Speed (it/s)
Kraken v5	6.5M	✗	CNN-based	CRNN+CTC	From scratch	27.8
TrOCR-Large-HandW	558M	✗	BEiT-based	RoBERTa (Hist.)	OCR + HTR	18.6
MiniCPM-Llama3-V-2.5	8B	✓	SigLip-400M	Llama3.1-based	OCR	5.3
Phi-3.5-vision-instruct	4.2B	✓	CLIP ViT-L/14	Phi-3.5-mini	Instructional	6.4
Qwen2-VL-2B-Instruct	2B	✓	ViT600M	Qwen2 LLM	Instructional	6.8

For the three multimodal models we start from the pre-trained checkpoints provided by the authors. For multimodals, the fine-tuning is performed on LoRA (Low-Rank Adaptation) [16] using our two-stage curriculum learning approach via a **chat template**, which facilitates dynamic system-user interactions and greater flexibility in handling transcription styles. In contrast, TrOCR is fine-tuned through conventional weight updates based solely on ground-truth data, without the integrated multimodal pre-training that strengthens the performance of the other models. Finally **Kraken v5** operating here as our first baseline was trained completely from scratch.

5 Experiments

5.1 Datasets

For Training, we used the CATMuS Medieval and TRIDIS corpora, as described in Sect. 3. These corpora include natively the train, validation and test splits using a 80/10/10 ratio. For testing we will use the CATMUS "featured" set which a is more challenging as it includes "out-of-domain" documents [9]. For testing TRIDIS-based models we will use a completely external dataset: the **DISTINGUO** dataset [6] which include 8 hard-abbreviated manuscripts (13th-15th centuries) ranging several writing families.

5.2 Evaluation Metrics

We evaluated the performance of our models using the following metrics:

- Character Error Rate (CER): The percentage of incorrectly transcribed characters.
- Word Error Rate (WER): The percentage of incorrectly transcribed words.
- BERTScore: Semantic similarity between the ground-truth and the inference.
- Delta : Percentage improvement on CER and WER relative to the baseline

5.3 Implementation Details

Table 2. Training Configuration Parameters

Parameter	Stage 1	Stage 2
Library	Hugging Face Transformers [32]	
Optimizer	AdamW	
Batch Size	16/12	
Length Sequence	128 tokens	
Scheduler (lr)	Linear (1e–5)	Cosine (5e–5)
Val Loss Stop	0.25–0.29	0.17–0.21
Epochs	2 epochs	4 epochs per adapter
Dataset	TRIDIS + CATMuS	Respective to adapter
Training Time	33–38 h	74–85 h
Hardware	2 × NVIDIA A6000 (48 GB VRAM)	
LoRA Rank (r)	64	
LoRA Alpha (α)	64	
Target Modules	Q, K, V, and O projections in all self-attention and MLP layers	

6 Results

Table 3 shows the results of our experiments: Our TrOCR-Large model emerges as a particularly strong baseline, maintaining the lowest CER rates on both CATMuS and TRIDIS (e.g., a CER of 10.2% and 16.1%, respectively). This strong performance likely stems from TrOCR's specialization on OCR task and specific-language modeling (Latin RoBERTa variant). Among the multimodal models, MiniCPM-VL and Phi-3.5-Vision progressively improve from their "Mixed" (Stage 1) to "Single" and then to "Dual" (Stage 2). Notably, moving from the "Mixed" configuration to the "Dual" adapters yields substantial gains in CER on both corpora: for instance, MiniCPM's CER on TRIDIS drops from 22.1% to 17.0%, while Phi-3.5's dips from 23.3% to 18.2%. Such improvements underscore the effectiveness of separate adapters for abbreviated and expanded transcriptions leveraging the Stage 1 model. Although TrOCR still holds the top spot overall, the gap narrows significantly (Less of 1% in CER and WER) once the multimodal models adopt the dual-adapter approach, demonstrating that specialized adapters can partly offset the absence of domain-specific

Table 3. Results on CATMuS Medieval (abbreviated) and TRIDIS (non-abbreviated). CER and WER are given as percentages. "Mixed" refers the model obtained from the Stage 1 of our Training Strategy. "Single" refers to each model fine-tuned on GT. "Dual" refers the adapters trained on Stage 2 using the Stage 1 model as foundation.

Model	CATMuS (Abbreviated)					TRIDIS (Expanded)				
	CER	CΔ	WER	WΔ	BERT	CER	CΔ	WER	WΔ	BERT
Kraken v5	12.2	–	42.3	–	–	24.5	–	67.0	–	–
TrOCR-Large	**10.2**	+16	**38.9**	+8	88	**16.1**	+35	43.3	+35	83
MiniCPM-VL (Mixed)	13.8	–13	46.9	–11	81	22.1	+10	60.5	+10	75
MiniCPM-VL (Single)	12.2	0	43.5	–3	85	19.3	+22	52.1	+22	80
MiniCPM-VL (Dual)	10.6	+13	40.6	+4	86	17.0	+31	**42.5**	+37	84
Phi-3.5-Vision (Mixed)	13.2	–8	43.0	–2	79	23.3	+5	63.8	+5	74
Phi-3.5-Vision (Single)	11.9	+2	41.3	+2	84	20.9	+15	54.7	+18	79
Phi-3.5-Vision (Dual)	11.1	+9	39.5	+7	86	18.2	+26	44.2	+34	82
Qwen2-VL (Mixed)	14.3	–17	49.2	–16	77	24.6	0	66.8	0	72
Qwen2-VL (Single)	13.1	–7	45.2	–7	82	21.9	+10	56.7	+15	78
Qwen2-VL (Dual)	11.8	+3	42.5	0	85	19.4	+20	46.1	+31	81

7 Discussion

Table 3 reveals that while a unified "double-head" model can simultaneously learn abbreviated and expanded transcription, specialized LoRA adapters consistently boost performance in both modes. Shifting from the "Mixed" (Stage 1) to the "Dual" (Stage 2) adapters yields stable gains in CER and WER on both CATMuS and TRIDIS, indicating that task-specific modules mitigate interference between competing objectives. By contrast, a single model often underperforms traditional frameworks, such as Kraken, which lacks an explicit LLM decoder.

Moreover, TrOCR-Large remains a strong baseline, achieving a CER as low as 10.2% on CATMuS and 16.1% on TRIDIS. This advantage likely stems from its targeted language pre-training (historical Latin RoBERTa) that closely matches the linguistic characteristics of historical texts. Nevertheless, our experiments show that advanced multimodal architectures like MiniCPM-Llama3-V-2.5 and

Phi-3.5 Vision can narrow this performance gap when equipped with dual-style adapters. Notably, the abbreviated mode yields lower character errors (near 10% CER) but results in higher WER due to issues such as inconsistent spacing and punctuation, often seen in medieval *scriptura continua*. In contrast, the expanded mode tends to have higher CER (around 16%) because the model must infer missing expansions. This is particularly challenging for named entities, which are often abbreviated to a single capital letter (e.g., "H." could correspond to *Hugues*, *Henricus*, *Heloisa*, etc.) and require external domain knowledge beyond that available in HTR training (See Fig. 2). Although the clearer word boundaries in expanded transcriptions yield a more typical CER:WER ratio (ca. 1:2.5), these findings indicate that while robust language modeling—especially when enhanced by beam decoding or vocabulary-driven strategies—can significantly improve expanded transcriptions, the presence of MUFI characters and missing tokens in the abbreviated mode may limit the effectiveness of standard vocabularies. Fine-tuning the LLM helps mitigate these issues in both modes.

From a practical standpoint, adapter switching is straightforward generating an expert dual transcription model but introducing a small overhead at inference. Future work could explore more unified gating mechanisms [11] or other routing strategies such as MoE (Mixture of Experts), reducing the need for external switching logic to select the appropriate transcription style. Also, although our mixing ratio and penalization weight were empirically determined, a more principled exploration of curriculum design strategies could provide better results as well as further research on prompt formulations and varied compositions of the training data, which are for instant a limited area of exploration in Academia due to the high computation required for multimodal models.

1 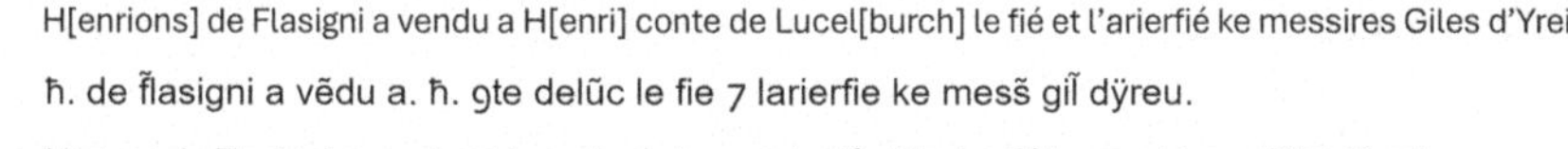

GT	H[enrions] de Flasigni a vendu a H[enri] conte de Lucel[burch] le fié et l'arierfié ke messires Giles d'Yrei
ABBR	ħ. de ﬂ̃asigni a vẽdu a. ħ. ꝯte delũc le fie ⁊ larierfie ke mess̃ gil̃ dÿreu.
MiniCPM	Hugues de Flasigni a vendu a H. conte de Lucem le fié et l'arier fié ke mesigneur Giles Dyrei
TrOCR	Hugues. de Flasigni a Vendu a H. conte de Lucembour le fié et larier fié kee Messire Gil Dyrei

Fig. 2. Model inferences for the line: "H[enrions] de Flasigni a vendu a H[enri] conte de Lucel[burch] le fié et l'arierfié ke messires Giles d'Yrei..." (Henry of Flasigny sold to Henry, Count of Luxembourg, the fief and the rear-fief that Mister Giles of Yrei...). The abbreviated (ABBR) adapter output closely matches the original manuscript, while the expanded ones produce a more readable transcription but may not fully expand all named entities due to knowledge limitations.

8 Conclusion

This work introduces a novel two-stage training strategy for dual-style historical manuscript transcription. We demonstrate that a single, pre-trained multimodal model, augmented with switchable LoRA adapters, can effectively generate both abbreviated and expanded transcriptions. These small, task-specific adapters offer significant advantages in training efficiency and resource utilization compared to traditional approaches requiring separate models. While domain-specific models, such as TrOCR-Large, remain strong baselines for HTR, multimodal models like MiniCPM-Llama3-V-2.5 and Phi-3.5 Vision can achieve comparable, and in some cases superior, performance when fine-tuned with these adapters.

This research highlights the effectiveness of LoRA adapters as lightweight, task-specific modules for bridging the gap between general-purpose, pre-trained models and specialized tasks. It also demonstrates the potential of our curriculum learning strategy to exploit the commonalities between abbreviated and expanded texts, yielding robust performance across both transcription styles. Although adapter switching introduces a minor inference overhead, and further work is needed to refine curriculum design and integration strategies, our approach provides a flexible framework extensible to a wide range of historical manuscript analysis tasks.

9 Model Repositories

The models supporting this study are available under open source licenses:

Baseline models:
Kraken: https://doi.org/10.5281/zenodo.13862096
TrOCR : https://doi.org/10.57967/hf/5035

Multimodal adapters:
MiniCPM-VL: https://huggingface.co/magistermilitum/HTR_ABBR_minicpm
Phi3.5-Visual: https://huggingface.co/magistermilitum/HTR_Phi_3.5_VL

References

1. Abdin, M., et al.: Phi-3 technical report: a highly capable language model locally on your phone. arXiv preprint arXiv:2404.14219 (2024)
2. Agrawal, P., et al.: Pixtral 12b. arXiv preprint arXiv:2410.07073 (2024)
3. Bengio, Y.: Practical recommendations for gradient-based training of deep architectures. In: Montavon, G., Orr, G.B., Müller, K.-R. (eds.) Neural Networks: Tricks of the Trade. LNCS, vol. 7700, pp. 437–478. Springer, Heidelberg (2012). https://doi.org/10.1007/978-3-642-35289-8_26
4. Bollmann, M.: A large-scale comparison of historical text normalization systems. arXiv preprint arXiv:1904.02036 (2019)
5. Borja, P.: Desarrollo y explotación del corpus de documentos españoles anteriores a 1700(codea). Script. Dig. **1**, 5–35 (2012)
6. Burghart, M., Yatsyk, S.: Distinguo : Ground truth for handwritten text recognition (htr) on collections of distinctions (late 13th to late 15th century) (2024). https://doi.org/10.34847/NKL.48AD8B8D. https://nakala.fr/10.34847/nkl.48ad8b8d

7. Camps, J.-B., Vidal-Gorène, C., Vernet, M.: Handling heavily abbreviated manuscripts: HTR engines vs text normalisation approaches. In: Barney Smith, E.H., Pal, U. (eds.) ICDAR 2021. LNCS, vol. 12917, pp. 306–316. Springer, Cham (2021). https://doi.org/10.1007/978-3-030-86159-9_21
8. Claustre, J., Smith, D., Torres Aguilar, S., et al.: The e-ndp project : collaborative digital edition of the chapter registers of notre-dame of paris (1326-1504). ground-truth for handwriting text recognition (htr) on late medieval manuscripts (2023). https://doi.org/10.5281/zenodo.7575693
9. Clérice, T., Pinche, A., Vlachou-Efstathiou, M., Chagué, A., et al.: Catmus medieval: a multilingual large-scale cross-century dataset in latin script for handwritten text recognition and beyond. In: International Conference on Document Analysis and Recognition, pp. 174–194. Springer, Heidelberg (2024). https://doi.org/10.1007/978-3-031-70543-4_11
10. El-Yacoubi, A., Gilloux, M., Sabourin, R., Suen, C.Y.: An hmm-based approach for off-line unconstrained handwritten word modeling and recognition. IEEE Trans. Pattern Anal. Mach. Intell. **21**(8), 752–760 (1999)
11. Fedus, W., Zoph, B., Shazeer, N.: Switch transformers: scaling to trillion parameter models with simple and efficient sparsity. J. Mach. Learn. Res. **23**(120), 1–39 (2022)
12. Fujitake, M.: Dtrocr: decoder-only transformer for optical character recognition. In: Proceedings of the IEEE/CVF Winter Conference on Applications of Computer Vision, pp. 8025–8035 (2024)
13. Halter-Pernet, C., et al.: Charters and Records of Königsfelden Abbey and Bailiwick (1308-1662) (2021). https://doi.org/10.5281/zenodo.5179361
14. Hamdan, M., Rahiche, A., Cheriet, M.: Htr-jand: handwritten text recognition with joint attention network and knowledge distillation. arXiv preprint arXiv:2412.18524 (2024)
15. Hasenohr, G.: Abréviations et frontières de mots. Langue française, pp. 24–29 (1998)
16. Hu, E.J., et al.: Lora: low-rank adaptation of large language models. arXiv preprint arXiv:2106.09685 (2021)
17. Kang, L., Riba, P., Rusiñol, M., Fornés, A., Villegas, M.: Pay attention to what you read: non-recurrent handwritten text-line recognition. Pattern Recogn. **129**, 108766 (2022)
18. Kiessling, B.: Kraken-an universal text recognizer for the humanities. In: ADHO, Éd., Actes de Digital Humanities Conference (2019)
19. Li, M., et al.: Trocr: transformer-based optical character recognition with pre-trained models. In: Proceedings of the AAAI Conference on Artificial Intelligence, vol. 37, pp. 13094–13102 (2023)
20. Michael, J., Weidemann, M., Labahn, R.: Htr engine based on nns p 3 optimizing speed and performance-htr+. Technical report. Technical report, READ-H2020 Project 674943 (2018)
21. Pfeiffer, J., Kamath, A., Rücklé, A., Cho, K., Gurevych, I.: Adapterfusion: non-destructive task composition for transfer learning. arXiv preprint arXiv:2005.00247 (2020)
22. Puigcerver, J., Mocholí, C.: Pylaia (2018). https://github.com/jpuigcerver/PyLaia
23. Radford, A., et al.: Learning transferable visual models from natural language supervision. In: International Conference on Machine Learning, pp. 8748–8763. PMLR (2021)
24. Stutzmann, D., Hamel, S., Kernier, I.D., Mühlberger, G., Hackl, G.: Himanis guérin (2021). https://doi.org/10.5281/zenodo.5535306

25. Stutzmann, D., Torres Aguilar, S., Chaffenet, P.: HOME-Alcar: aligned and annotated cartularies (2021). https://doi.org/10.5281/zenodo.5600884, https://zenodo.org/record/5600884
26. Tarride, S., Schneider, Y., Generali-Lince, M., Boillet, M., Abadie, B., Kermorvant, C.: Improving automatic text recognition with language models in the pylaia open-source library. arXiv preprint arXiv:2404.18722 (2024)
27. Torres Aguilar, S.: Handwritten text recognition for historical documents using visual language models and gans. Hal science (2024). https://hal.science/hal-04716654/
28. Torres Aguilar, S.: Roberta historical (2025). https://huggingface.co/magistermilitum/Roberta_Historical
29. Torres Aguilar, S.: Tridis (tria digita scribunt) (2025). https://doi.org/10.57967/hf/5001
30. Vaswani, A., et al.: Attention is all you need. In: Proceedings of the 31st International Conference on Neural Information Processing Systems, NIPS'17, pp. 6000–6010. Curran Associates Inc., Red Hook (2017)
31. Wang, P., et al.: Qwen2-vl: enhancing vision-language model's perception of the world at any resolution. arXiv preprint arXiv:2409.12191 (2024)
32. Wolf, T.: Huggingface's transformers: state-of-the-art natural language processing. arXiv preprint arXiv:1910.03771 (2019)
33. Xu, B., Zhang, L., Mao, Z., Wang, Q., Xie, H., Zhang, Y.: Curriculum learning for natural language understanding. In: Proceedings of the 58th Annual Meeting of the Association for Computational Linguistics, pp. 6095–6104 (2020)
34. Yao, Y., et al.: Minicpm-v: a gpt-4v level mllm on your phone. arXiv preprint arXiv:2408.01800 (2024)
35. Zhai, X., Mustafa, B., Kolesnikov, A., Beyer, L.: Sigmoid loss for language image pre-training. In: Proceedings of the IEEE/CVF International Conference on Computer Vision, pp. 11975–11986 (2023)

Semantic Reasoning for Device Identification in Dynamic Internet of Things Environments with Large Language Models

Zhou Gui(✉), Layla Kuty, Daniel Schraudner, and Andreas Harth

Friedrich-Alexander-Universität Erlangen-Nürnberg, Nürnberg, Germany
{zhou.gui,layla.kuty,daniel.schraudner,andreas.harth}@fau.de

Abstract. This work evaluates the capabilities of Large Language Models (LLMs) in semantic reasoning tasks. We construct a knowledge graph that represents a real-world Internet of Things (IoT) environment and define various reasoning rules for device identification use cases.

We test the performance of three LLMs: Llama-3.1, Qwen-2.5, GPT-4o, based on different levels of fine-grained rule descriptions in the input context and the increasing rule complexity. We use a rule-based reasoner, Apache Jena, to generate the ground truth data for each reasoning rule. The results show that while LLMs are effective in retrieving direct links in the knowledge graph, they struggle with highly customized, complex reasoning rules involving multiple triple patterns. This work provides an application and a baseline for using LLMs to enable semantic reasoning for device identification in IoT environments.

Keywords: Knowledge Graphs · Internet of Things · Large Language Models · Semantic Reasoning

1 Introduction

Device identification involves finding the intended devices in an IoT environment given natural language commands from users. Device identification is an important step towards building a conversational IoT system, as the system first needs to locate the specific devices before interacting with them [5]. Knowledge Graphs (KGs) provide an effective way to model the complexities of IoT ecosystems, which often consist of the physical structure of the building environment, user information and relationships, and device interfaces. Typically, these three modules - building structure, user information, and device interfaces - are modeled as standalone KGs that can be reused and integrated for different application domains. In the application of device identification in IoT environments, we can link devices to their location or to the individuals who own them, allowing the intended devices to be inferred through location or ownership relationships.

However, real world IoT environments are often dynamic, resulting in missing or outdated information about specific devices. For example, in a shared

R. Ichise (Ed.): NLDB 2025, LNCS 15836, pp. 335–349, 2026.
https://doi.org/10.1007/978-3-031-97141-9_23

workspace, users can move between rooms, interact with different devices, or even carry devices to new locations, making it impractical to maintain fixed links between people, rooms, and devices. In such scenarios, semantic reasoning over knowledge graphs can help infer new links and relationships from existing knowledge to enable real-time device identification.

Reasoning has been an important research topic in the semantic web community for many years [6,9]. While rule-based reasoners, such as Apache Jena[1], are widely used for reasoning over graph data, Large Language Models (LLMs) have become powerful tools for general reasoning tasks [7]. Due to their generative nature, LLMs are prone to errors, hallucinations, and inconsistent statements especially when handling complex reasoning tasks that require multiple steps of logical deductions [16]. Furthermore, most LLMs for reasoning tasks focus on domains such as commonsense [15] and mathematical logic [3,12]. There remains limited research on the application of LLMs for formal semantic reasoning in the context of dynamic IoT environments. Formal semantics, such as RDF, RDFs, and OWL ontologies, represent knowledge in a structured and standardized way, allowing data from various sources to be interpreted and reasoned over the same knowledge consistently.

Current open-source implementations of interactive IoT systems such as Home Assistant[2], use device location as the main identifier of the device. While this is sufficient for the smart home use case with a small number of users and relatively stable environments, it becomes inadequate in industrial IoT environments. Industrial IoT settings often involve multiple users and require fine-grained access control, as the device and user locations change frequently (e.g., devices being moved to different stations or conveyor belts, users temporarily operating shared devices in other rooms). In this scenario, relying solely on device location to identify devices is insufficient. Inferring the current location and ownership relationships of devices can provide additional context to accurately identify specific devices.

In this paper, we construct a knowledge graph to model a real-world IoT environment by integrating knowledge from three different domains: building structure, user information, and device functionalities. Our main objective is to use LLMs to retrieve device entities from the knowledge graph given different input contexts. For simplicity and clarity, we assume that in a shared workspace (e.g., Lab), only one user occupies a room at any given time. To test the reasoning capabilities of LLMs, we design a set of customized, multi-step reasoning rules for device identification within the IoT system. We then evaluate the performance of LLMs based on different context levels and the increasing complexity of these reasoning rules.

The key contributions of this paper are the following:

- We construct a knowledge graph modeling a real-world IoT environment.
- We introduce new methods for identifying devices in a dynamic IoT environment using semantic reasoning over knowledge graph reasoning.

[1] https://jena.apache.org/.

[2] https://www.home-assistant.io/.

- We evaluate the semantic reasoning capabilities of multiple LLMs on multi-step reasoning tasks.

2 Related Work

In this section, we discuss existing approaches to device identification in IoT environments and explore semantic reasoning using rule-based reasoning engines and LLMs.

2.1 Device Identification in IoT Environments

Most conversational IoT systems [1,10,14] focus on smart home scenarios with a limited number of users and devices. The most popular open-source IoT system, Home Assistant, relies mainly on location information (e.g., areas or floors) to identify devices. Although this approach works for simple smart home scenarios, it faces limitations when scaling up to more complex environments:

- Lack of direct device identification by owners: there is no direct way to refer to a device by its associated owner when multiple users are involved.
- Limited scalability for dynamic environments: In shared workspaces such as office buildings or manufacturing plants with multiple users, where device locations and ownerships can constantly change, relying solely on location-based identification can be insufficient to track individual devices.

King et al. proposed a smart home assistant prototype Sasha [10] that uses LLMs to generate action plans required to achieve under-specified user goals, such as "make it cozy". The device identification in their system is rather finding the related target devices by interpreting the implicit natural language command using semantic relationships between words (e.g., associate device "lamp" with "cozy" atmosphere). We focus on interpreting explicit natural language commands to retrieve and identify the intended devices in the knowledge graph.

2.2 Rule-Based Reasoning

Semantic reasoning involves adding new knowledge to the existing data through inference rules. The inferred new facts can be added to the knowledge graph through materialization. Common rule-based reasoners such as Apache Jena[3], RDFox[4], GraphDB[5] use predefined rules and support OWL ontologies. The primary advantage of rule-based reasoners is their explainability by using explicitly defined rules, which ensures consistent and deterministic results.

[3] https://jena.apache.org/.
[4] https://www.oxfordsemantic.tech/rdfox.
[5] https://graphdb.ontotext.com/.

2.3 LLM-Based Reasoning

LLMs have shown significant success across various domains, but their reasoning abilities remain uncertain and inconsistent. Many studies have focused on investigating the reasoning capabilities of LLMs and techniques to improve their reasoning performance. One common approach is the Chain of Thought (CoT) prompting [17] by generating multiple intermediate reasoning steps to solve the tasks step by step. Tree of Thought (ToT) [18] is proposed as a generalization of CoT that explores tree structures for intermediate reasoning steps.

Despite the advancements in this field, LLMs struggle with complex multi-step reasoning tasks. Mirzadeh et al. [13] suggested that LLMs likely perform a form of probabilistic pattern-matching and searching to find the closest seen data during training without proper understanding of concepts. They experimented with the Grade School Math (GSM) symbolic augmented dataset based on GSM [12] and found that in mathematical reasoning tasks, the reasoning performance of LLMs drops significantly when the numbers are changed. Additionally, introducing irrelevant information to the questions causes most LLMs to fail.

3 Running Examples

A knowledge graph of a simplified IoT environment is shown in Fig. 1. In this example, Alice and Bob are colleagues working at the same organization but have different job titles: Alice is a research assistant, and Bob is a laboratory technician. The environment includes three devices of type light. The functionalities of each device are described using the Web of Things [11] interface.

While a device can be identified by its unique identifier (MAC address) directly, this is highly impractical, as users are unlikely to remember a random sequence of numbers and letters. In real-world scenarios, devices are more naturally referenced by their location or their owner.

- **Scenario 1: Place - Device**: In the morning, Alice goes to the copy room to print some documents. She wants the lights in the copy room to turn on with the command "Switch on lights in the copy room". The devices are identified through the direct link between the place and the devices.
- **Scenario 2: Person - Device**: After printing, Alice returns to her office to read the printed documents. To improve visibility, she wants to turn on her personal desk lamp. She issues the command "Turn on Alice's personal light". The device is identified through the direct link between the person and the device, but only if the device has the `:personalDevice` flag set to true.
- **Scenario 3: Person - Place - Device**: After reading the documents, Alice goes to the IoT lab to gain some hands-on experience. Since the IoT lab is a shared workspace with public access (`:publicAccess` flag set to true), anyone in the organization can temporally take ownership of the devices for experiments. Alice issues the command "Turn on Alice's lights". The lights in

the IoT lab are identified, as the system dynamically associates "Alice" to the specific lights through her current location.

- **Scenario 4: Storey - Place - Device**: As the laboratory technician, Bob is responsible for turning off all devices on the fourth floor after the end of the working day. He can issue the command "Turn off all lights on the fourth floor" to batch control multiple lights at once. The system finds all devices of type light in all rooms located on the fourth floor.

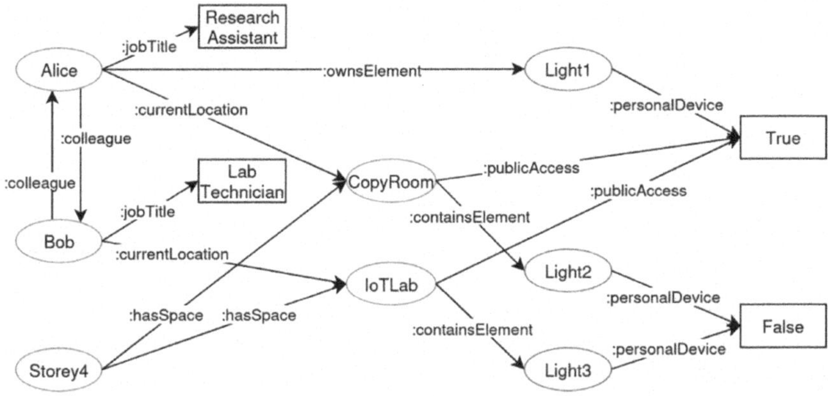

Fig. 1. Simplified knowledge graph of an IoT environment

4 Knowledge Graph Construction

We model a real-world workspace as a knowledge graph using standard ontologies including RDF, RDFS, XSD, Schema.org, and Building Topology Ontology (BOT) [8]. The complete knowledge graph consists of three subgraphs:

- Person KG: describes the role of people and their relations with others. People are defined by 5 properties: given name, organization membership, job title, and colleagues. There are 11 people with 5 different job titles in the person KG.
- Place KG: describes the structure and connections of different spaces within the building. The building consists of 4 floors, one organization, and 16 rooms of three different types: offices, labs, and utility rooms. Rooms are defined by five properties: type, label, adjacent zones, elements they contain and whether they have public access.

- Device KG: describes different classes of devices including their type, MAC address and whether they are owned as personal devices. Each device is represented by its own device description interface using Thing Description ontology [2]. There are 45 devices of 17 different types in the device KG.

These three individual KGs can be interconnected through various links, leading to different ways to identify devices. In dynamic environments, a person's location frequently changes, for example, a person can have a fixed office room but currently be in the lab. Figure 2 illustrates the three types of connections among Person, Device, and Place KGs:

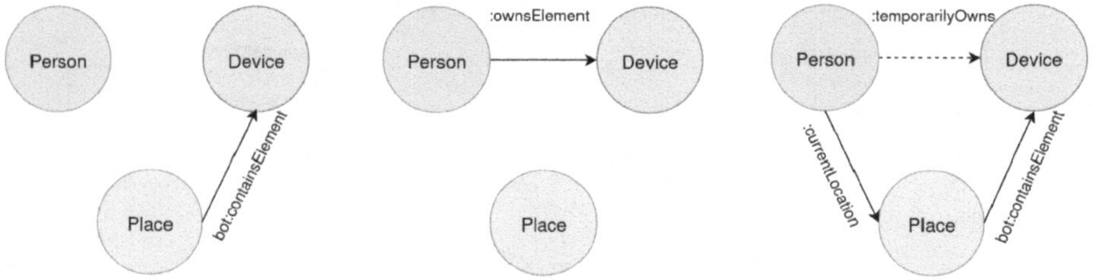

Fig. 2. Types of links in dynamic KGs. Solid arrow indicates that the link exists in the KG, dashed arrow indicates that the link can be inferred by reasoning.

- Places and devices are linked directly via `bot:containsElement`.
- People are linked directly to their personal devices via `:ownsElement`.
- There are no direct links from people to devices, but the relationship between a person and a device can be inferred through their common place via `:curentLocation` and `bot:containsElement`.

Each additional level of connectivity enriches the graph with more information, making the knowledge graph more comprehensive. However, this also increases the effort required for knowledge graph construction and updating. One common approach after inferring new triples through reasoning is to materialize the new knowledge into the graph. This approach is feasible in a static environment. However, in dynamic environments, materialization is impractical as the locations of people or devices are constantly changing, which often results in outdated or missing links.

5 Semantic Reasoning Rules

In this section, we discuss different types of reasoning rules and the increasing complexity of rules by adding more restrictions.

5.1 Rule Types

We define two types of reasoning rules that are particularly relevant to the device identification use cases in IoT environments: ownership and containment. Each type can have direct or indirect ways to infer the devices.

Direct Ownership. Direct ownership links a device directly to a specific person. As described in Scenario 2, Alice can access her personal light directly through the connection between her and the device in the knowledge graph. This rule can be described Jena syntax as shown in Listing 1.1 and in natural language as follows: If there exists a direct link in the knowledge graph between a person and a device, then the person owns the device as a personal device.

```
(?person :ownsElement ?device)
 -> (?person :ownsDevice ?device)
```

Listing 1.1. Rule described in Jena syntax for "direct ownership"

Indirect Ownership. When only person-place and device-place links exist in the graph, but not a direct link between a person and a device, we can infer the person-device relation from the existing relations, as described in Scenario 3. This rule can be described in natural language as: If there exists a link in the knowledge graph between a person and a place indicating the current location of the person and the place contains devices, then the person temporarily owns the devices. Listing 1.2 shows the rule that describes the person-device link through two intermediate steps in the Apache Jena syntax.

```
(?person :currentLocation ?place)
(?place bot:containElement ?device)
 -> (?person :temporarilyOwns ?device)
```

Listing 1.2. Rule described in Jena syntax for "indirect ownership"

Direct Containment. Direct containment rule connects places to devices directly. As shown in Scenario 1, Alice can access a device through the location of the device. This rule can be expressed in natural language as follows: If there exists a direct link in the knowledge graph between a place and a device, then the room contains the device. Jena syntax rule for direct containment is shown in Listing 1.3

```
(?place bot:containsElement ?device)
 -> (?place :containsDevice ?device)
```

Listing 1.3. Rule described in Jena syntax for "direct containment"

Indirect Containment. A building typically consists of multiple storeys, where each storey contains several rooms, and each room contains multiple devices. This rule can be described in natural language as: If there exists a link in the knowledge graph between a storey and a room, and the room contains devices, then the storey contains the devices, as shown in Scenario 4. Listing 1.4 shows this rule in Jena syntax.

```
(?storey bot:hasSpace ?place)
(?place bot:containsElement ?device)
 -> (?storey :containsDevice ?device)
```

Listing 1.4. Rule described in Jena syntax for "indirect containment"

5.2 Rule Complexity

The four types of rules mentioned above are the base rules. We can increase the complexity of each rule by further restricting the entities in the triple pattern. For example, we can limit the devices to a specific type (e.g., Light), restrict the search to devices located in a specific room type (e.g., Office), or restrict the people to a specific role (e.g., Research Assistant). Figure 3 and Fig. 4 illustrate the rule shapes for ownership and containment respectively. In the figures, circles indicate variables in the triple pattern, and rounded squares represent constants. We refer to the connection between two variables as a "hop" and the connection between a variable and a constant as a "step".

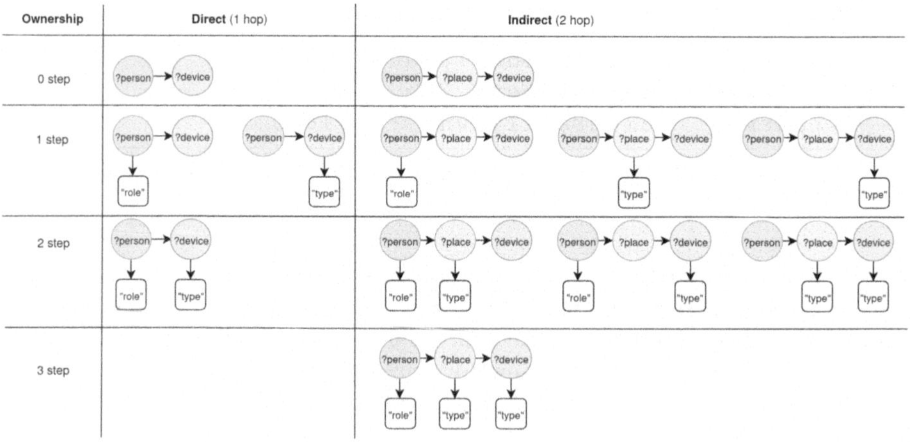

Fig. 3. Rule shapes in ownership

In theory, we can continue increasing the complexity of rules by adding more hops (e.g., a building can have multiple storeys) and steps (e.g., a person can

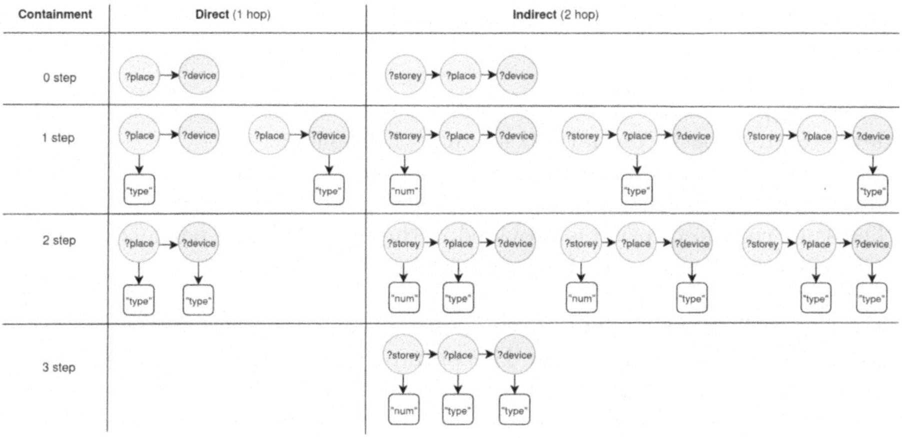

Fig. 4. Rule shapes in containment

have organizational property in addition to the role) to the rule shapes. We do not intend to list all possible combinations, but to show one rule shape that combines ownership and containment into one in Fig. 5. The natural language command for this rule shape can be "Find all lights in offices in the fourth storey that are temporarily owned by research assistants".

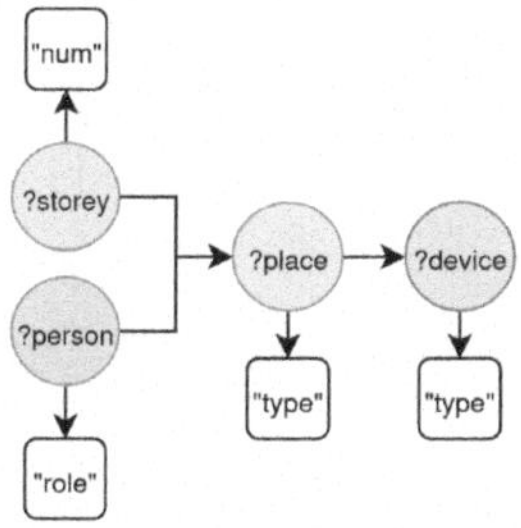

Fig. 5. Combined rule shape of ownership and containment

6 Evaluation and Discussion

In this section, we present the evaluation results based on the following models: Llama 3.1 (70b), hosted on High Performance Computing (HPC) provided by the Erlangen National High Performance Computing Center; Qwen2.5 (72b) hosted on NHR-Nord in Göttingen [4], and a proprietary model GPT-4o from OpenAI. We do not perform any fine-tuning with these models, but only run inference through API calls. We ask the LLMs to find all devices given the knowledge graph based on user commands. For each model we provide three different input contexts:

1. No rule explanation is given, the models need to reason independently to find device entities based on natural language commands.
2. A rule description in natural language, as shown in Sect. 5.1, is added to the input, but does not include the exact vocabulary as in the knowledge graph.
3. The same rule description is provided in the input but in Apache Jena syntax with the exact vocabulary in the knowledge graph.

We run each input context three times and calculate the average scores of the three runs as the final scores. The prompt for all models are identical and configuration settings such as temperature are all set to 0 to minimize randomness and ensure deterministic outputs. All the code and evaluation results are available online.[6]

For Apache Jena, we prepare a set of manually written rules for each rule type and step. We use these predefined rules to reason over the knowledge graph to retrieve all matching device entities. The total run time for Jena reasoning across all rules is 0.79 s. The outputs from Apache Jena serve as the ground-truth for the LLMs generated outputs. Table 1 and Table 2 show the number of ground-truth triples in each rule types.

Table 1. Number of ground truth entities in ownership

step\hop	Direct	Indirect	**Total**
0	6	25	31
1	12	33	45
2	6	14	20
3	–	2	2
Total	24	74	98

Table 2. Number of ground truth entities in containment

step\hop	Direct	Indirect	**Total**
0	39	39	78
1	36	50	86
2	10	24	34
3	-	4	4
Total	85	117	202

6.1 Results Based on Context Level

Table 3 and Table 4 show the final scores of precision, recall, and F1-score for each model in different rule contexts. Figure 6 and Fig. 7 show the F1 score plot of the three models based on three different levels of contexts (no rule, rule in natural language description, rule in Jena description) given to LLMs.

- Comparing Fig. 6 and Fig. 7, we observe that LLMs generally perform better on "Containment" than "Ownership": **GPT-4o** reaches a F1-score of close to 1 in both direct and indirect cases in the containment type. This can

[6] https://github.com/zhouG42/semantic-reasoning-llms.

Table 3. Precision, recall, and F1 score of ownership rules

		Direct			Indirect		
		precision	recall	f1	precision	recall	f1
Llama-3.1	no rule	0.78	0.76	**0.76**	0.00	0.00	0.00
	nl	0.75	0.76	0.75	0.39	0.68	**0.48**
	jena	0.75	0.76	0.75	0.04	0.19	0.19
Qwen-2.5	no rule	0.82	0.81	0.81	0.00	0.00	0.00
	nl	0.94	0.90	**0.91**	0.38	0.65	0.40
	jena	0.70	0.71	0.70	0.36	0.57	**0.41**
GPT-4o	no rule	0.90	0.85	**0.87**	0.34	0.58	0.40
	nl	0.86	0.80	0.82	0.53	0.90	**0.63**
	jena	0.88	0.82	0.82	0.42	0.46	0.42

Table 4. Precision, recall, and F1 score of containment rules

		Direct			Indirect		
		precision	recall	f1	precision	recall	f1
Llama-3.1	no rule	0.97	0.96	**0.96**	0.49	0.74	0.53
	nl	0.64	0.68	0.65	0.75	0.60	0.63
	jena	0.78	0.99	0.85	0.78	0.97	**0.84**
Qwen-2.5	no rule	0.99	0.96	0.97	0.69	0.91	**0.77**
	nl	1.0	0.97	**0.98**	0.76	0.81	0.76
	jena	1.0	0.95	0.97	0.68	0.87	0.72
GPT-4o	no rule	0.95	0.98	0.96	0.99	0.96	**0.97**
	nl	0.93	0.98	0.95	1.0	0.95	**0.97**
	jena	1.0	0.975	**0.99**	1.0	0.94	0.96

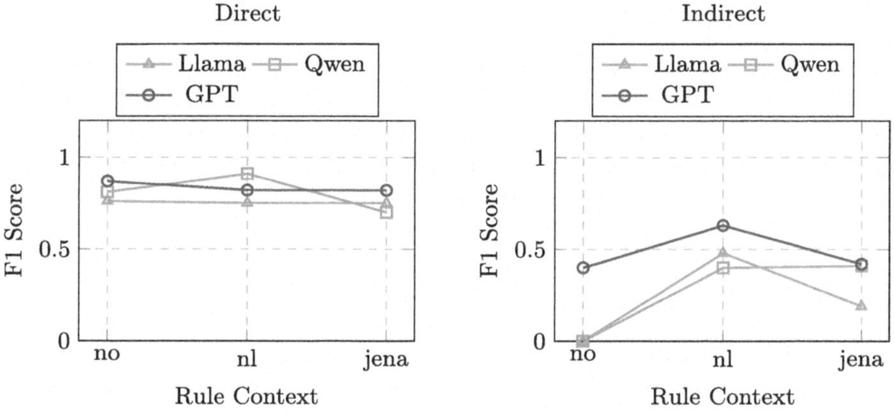

Fig. 6. F1-score vs. rule context in ownership.

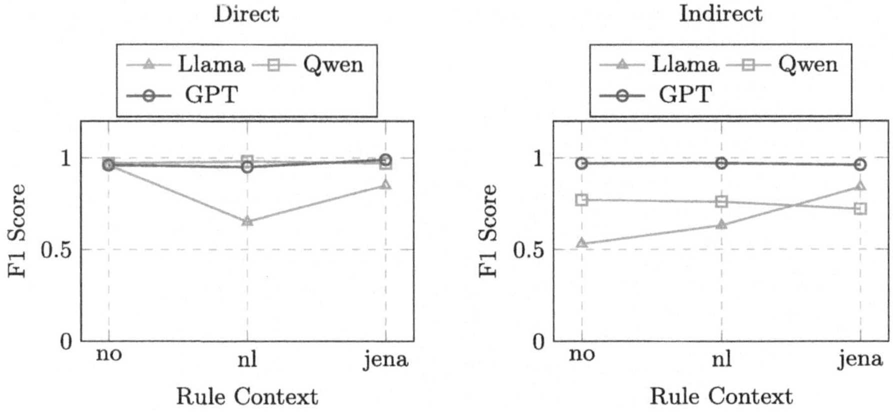

Fig. 7. F1-score vs. rule context in containment.

be explained by the fact that LLMs are more trained on intuitive common sense knowledge in the physical world, such as "a storey contains a room" and "a room contains a device", therefore "a storey contains a device" but less familiar with specifically customized person-device ownership rules in IoT environments.

- Indirect rules are generally more challenging for LLMs than direct rules, as they require models to follow multiple hops in addition to various steps to reach the final entities.
- The increasing level of context has a greater impact on the indirect types than the direct types. Overall, **GPT-4o** and **Qwen-2.5** are less affected by context changes, indicating their strong ability to interpret natural language commands without additional rule context. However, **Llama-3.1** shows more fluctuations in performance across difference context levels. While natural language rule descriptions improve the F1-score in indirect types in both ownership and containment scenarios, they appear to confuse the model further in direct containment scenarios.
- **GPT-4o** and **Qwen-2.5** show similar performance trends with the increasing level of fine-grained rule descriptions, especially in the most complex and implicit rule type - indirect ownership. Both models perform the best with natural language rule descriptions in the context, indicating their better capability to interpret natural language over triple syntax.

6.2 Results Based on Rule Complexity

In this section, we further evaluate the performance of LLMs as the complexity of rules increases. Based on the evaluation results above, we select the overall best-performing runs that include rules described in natural language in the input. The complexity is measured by the total number of triple patterns (*#hop* +

#step) in Jena rules required to infer the final results. We merge the two types of rules - ownership and containment, in two categories: direct and indirect. The results are shown in Fig. 8.

- Rule complexity has a significantly greater impact on indirect types compared to direct types. In direct rules, the performance of all three models varies only slightly when the number of triple patterns increases from 2 to 3. However, for indirect rules, the performance of all three models drop fast as the number of triple patterns in the rule increases.
- Among the three models, **Llama-3.1** exhibits the most decline in performance as the rule complexity increases, suggesting that **Llama-3.1** is the least capable model to handle such complex reasoning tasks.

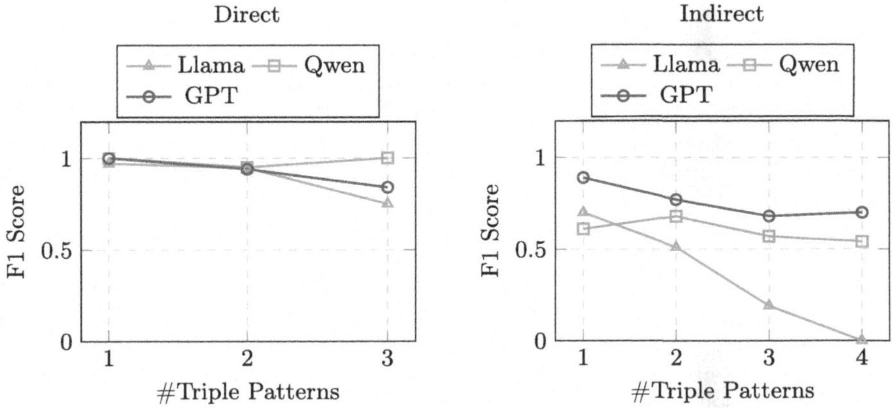

Fig. 8. F1-score vs. number of triple patterns in ownership and containment

7 Conclusion

In this paper, we construct a knowledge graph representing a real-world IoT environment and evaluate the semantic reasoning capabilities of LLMs on a set of reasoning tasks for device identification use cases.

We use a rule-based reasoning engine, Apache Jena, to generate ground truth data for evaluating the performance of different LLMs. We experiment with three types of input contexts for LLMs: 1. no rule descriptions given, 2. rules described in natural language, and 3. rules described in Jena syntax. The results show that LLMs performed the best when provided with natural language rule descriptions in the input context. Additionally, we observe that the performance of LLMs decrease significantly as rule complexity increases, especially in the indirect scenarios.

For future work, we aim to integrate LLMs with the rule-based reasoner Jena through tool use. In this case, LLMs first interpret natural language commands and translate them into Jena syntax rules. Then, the Jena reasoner will be invoked to perform reasoning over the graph. This hybrid approach has the advantages of optimizing inference time and reasoning accuracy, and reducing API usage costs.

Acknowledgement. The authors gratefully acknowledge the scientific support and HPC resources provided by the Erlangen National High-Performance Computing Center (NHR@FAU) of the Friedrich-Alexander-Universität Erlangen-Nürnberg (FAU). The hardware is funded by the German Research Foundation (DFG).

References

1. Campagna, G., Xu, S., Moradshahi, M., Socher, R., Lam, M.S.: Genie: a generator of natural language semantic parsers for virtual assistant commands. In: Proceedings of the 40th ACM SIGPLAN Conference on Programming Language Design and Implementation (2019)
2. Charpenay, V., Käbisch, S., Kosch, H.: Introducing thing descriptions and interactions: an ontology for the web of things. In: SR+SWIT@ISWC (2016)
3. Cobbe, K., et al.: Training verifiers to solve math word problems. arXiv Learning (2021)
4. Doosthosseini, A., Decker, J., Nolte, H., Kunkel, J.M.: Chat ai: a seamless slurm-native solution for hpc-based services. arXiv (2024)
5. Gui, Z., Kuty, L., Harth, A.: Design and implementation of a natural language interface for controlling the web of things devices. In: Natural Language Processing and Information Systems. NLDB (2024)
6. Hitzler, P., Van Harmelen, F.: A reasonable semantic web. Semant. Web (2010)
7. Huang, J., Chang, K.C.C.: Towards reasoning in large language models: a survey. arXiv (2022)
8. Janowicz, K., Rasmussen, M.H., Lefrançois, M., Schneider, G.F., Pauwels, P.: Bot: the building topology ontology of the w3c linked building data group. Semant. Web (2021)
9. Khamparia, A., Pandey, B.: Comprehensive analysis of semantic web reasoners and tools: a survey. Educ. Inf. Technol. **22**(6), 3121–3145 (2017). https://doi.org/10.1007/s10639-017-9574-5
10. King, E., Yu, H., Lee, S., Julien, C.: Sasha: creative goal-oriented reasoning in smart homes with large language models. Proc. ACM Interact. Mob. Wear. Ubiq. Technol. (2024)
11. Lagally, M., et al.: Web of things (wot) architecture 1.1 (2023)
12. Li, Q., Cui, L., Zhao, X., Kong, L., Bi, W.: GSM-plus: a comprehensive benchmark for evaluating the robustness of LLMs as mathematical problem solvers. In: Proceedings of the 62nd Annual Meeting of the Association for Computational Linguistics (2024)
13. Mirzadeh, I., Alizadeh, K., Shahrokhi, H., Tuzel, O., Bengio, S., Farajtabar, M.: Gsm-symbolic: understanding the limitations of mathematical reasoning in large language models. ArXiv (2024)

14. Mudgerikar, A., Bertino, E.: Jarvis: moving towards a smarter internet of things. In: 2020 IEEE 40th International Conference on Distributed Computing Systems (ICDCS) (2020)
15. Talmor, A., Herzig, J., Lourie, N., Berant, J.: CommonsenseQA: a question answering challenge targeting commonsense knowledge. In: Proceedings of the 2019 Conference of the North American Chapter of the Association for Computational Linguistics (2019)
16. Wang, C., et al.: Q*: Improving multi-step reasoning for llms with deliberative planning. arXiv preprint arXiv:2406.14283 (2024)
17. Wei, J., et al.: Chain-of-thought prompting elicits reasoning in large language models. In: Proceedings of the 36th International Conference on Neural Information Processing Systems. NIPS '22 (2022)
18. Yao, S., et al.: In: Advances in Neural Information Processing Systems. Curran Associates, Inc. (2023)

Instruction Tuning TextFlow Semi-automatic RFCs Generation

Jie Bian(✉) and Michael Welzl

Department of Informatics, University of Oslo, Oslo, Norway
{jiebi,michawe}@ifi.uio.no

Abstract. Instruction tuning enhances language models' (LMs) performance by refining them with specific guidelines. This paper explores the application of instruction tuning in generating and editing Internet Drafts (I-Ds), the preliminary versions of Request for Comments (RFCs). The process involves training models with detailed instructions based on earlier drafts and feedback from Working Groups (WGs) to improve the text. This approach enables the generation of drafts that adhere to established Internet Engineering Task Force (IETF) standards, significantly reducing the need for extensive manual revisions that can span years. This work marks a promising start for the future development of network protocols. By combining instruction tuning models with human expertise, we are moving towards more efficient and accurate technical documentation.

Keywords: RFC · Internet Draft · Instruction Tuning · Language Model

1 Introduction

The Internet Engineering Task Force (IETF) publishes technical documentation as Requests for Comments (RFCs), which are essential for defining the Internet's technical standards and protocols. RFCs cover a wide range of topics, including addressing, routing, and transport technologies, and are used globally by network developers, manufacturers, and operators. RFCs are sequentially numbered, starting with RFC 1, which was published in 1969 (the RFC series predates the IETF). Today, there are more than 9000 documents in the series.[1] At the time of writing, IETF has published 9720 RFCs. Internet-Drafts (I-Ds) are preliminary documents that propose new ideas or specifications and are subject to review and revision before potentially becoming RFCs. These drafts allow for community feedback and iterative improvement, ensuring that the final standards are robust and widely accepted.

The process of turning an Internet Draft (I-D) into an official RFC is characterized by multiple iterations and renaming, often over several years, see

[1] https://www.ietf.org/process/rfcs/.

R. Ichise (Ed.): NLDB 2025, LNCS 15836, pp. 350–364, 2026.
https://doi.org/10.1007/978-3-031-97141-9_24

RFC 9000 [9]. Initially, an I-D is submitted as a version 00 document, which undergoes rigorous review and revision cycles, potentially reaching version 10 and beyond. Each iteration incorporates feedback from various stakeholders to ensure the technical accuracy and relevance of the document. During this period, the draft may be renamed to reflect significant changes or shifts in scope. This iterative process is crucial to maintain the high standards and reliability expected of an RFC. The extensive review and revision cycles ensure that each document is technically accurate and relevant, contributing to the robustness and interoperability of Internet protocols and standards. However, this lengthy process can delay the implementation of important updates and innovations, potentially slowing technological progress. In addition, the extended timeline can lead to increased costs and resource allocation, as multiple stakeholders need to be continuously engaged in the review process.

While human expertise is critical for rigorous writing and iterative review of I-Ds, modern demands require scalable solutions to improve efficiency and consistency. This study explores how instruction-tuned [28] LM can complement human effort in domain-specific I-D workflows. Instruction tuning [28] enhances LMs by fine-tuning them on datasets of instructional prompts and their outputs, enabling better task-specific instruction comprehension and execution.

To achieve it, we first compiled TextFlow[2], a dataset of 160 I-Ds, using Git Pull Requests to pair text changes with structured comments. We devised four tasks: I)TextFlow Auto-Complete, II)Startup, III)Edit, and IV)Explain, and benchmarked successful open-source LMs. We instruction-tuned smaller models to enhance performance on TextFlow and applied the tuned model to 41 new I-Ds as out-of-distribution (OOD) data to verify our approach. Additionally, we established evaluation metrics for TextFlow tasks through a comprehensive exploration of existing metrics.

2 TextFlow: The Internet Drafts Editing History Dataset

2.1 Internet-Drafts (I-Ds)

I-Ds are technical documents that combine natural language (NL) with structured formatting elements (e.g., table, pseudo-code, diagram) to describe proposed Internet standards and protocols. They detail narratives for *design decisions, technical specifications, and implementation guidelines.* To isolate technical prose from non-textual or non-essential content, we exclude those non-NL elements and peripheral sections (e.g., references, acknowledgments), retaining only the descriptive technical text.

I-Ds in TextFlow exhibit a broad range of maturity levels. Some drafts are in the early stages, where significant updates and new concepts are continually being integrated. Others are in the intermediate stages, with their fundamental structure already in place, undergoing only moderate revisions. The rest are

[2] We have released our dataset in Huggingface. https://huggingface.co/datasets/jiebi/TextFlow.

drafts that are nearing completion, requiring only minor adjustments before they are finalized.

2.2 Comments, Discussion or Feedback

Historically, most comments and reviews within the IETF were conducted through its extensive email archives and mailing lists. Recently, GitHub has emerged as a collaborative platform where authors can present their ideas, solicit community feedback, and iteratively refine their proposals. To formalize this process, the IETF published RFC 8874 [22], to provide guidelines for how WGs should use GitHub. For instance, the RFC recommends that each WG *SHOULD* create its own GitHub organization with a clear name, such as ietf-wgname.

Our data is sourced from WGs that follow GitHub's coding practices to facilitate the drafting process. Comments, discussions, and feedback are formatted as conversations within Issues or Pull Requests (PRs) on GitHub. Unlike the straightforward, one-sentence instructions typically found in commit messages, this feedback is more intricate and multifaceted. It is conveyed through discussions, comments, and exchanges of viewpoints, encompassing reviews, agreements, and disagreements, and interwoven with other messages. This complexity reflects the collaborative nature of the development process, where diverse perspectives and iterative feedback shape the final outcome. In this paper, we use the three words, comments, discussion, and feedback interchangeably.

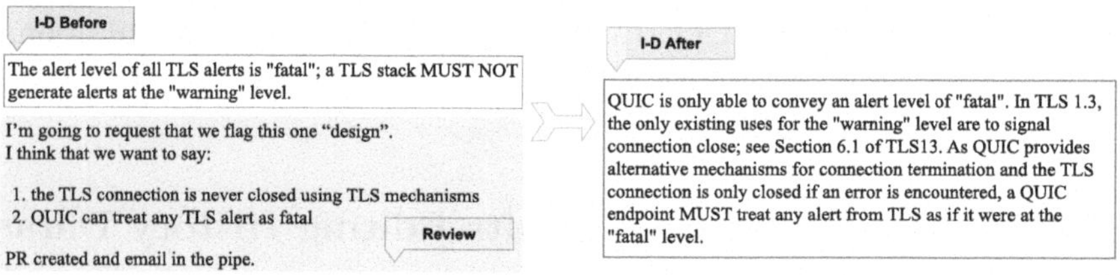

Fig. 1. The iteration of I-Ds. After a draft version is published, reviewers within the same WG will provide feedback, and the editors will modify the protocol accordingly.

2.3 Relations

I-Ds and community feedback form a critical feedback loop in IETF standards development, see Fig. 1. I-Ds initiate structured discussions within WGs, where contributors identify gaps, challenge assumptions, or propose clarifications. Each draft revision reflects this input, driving continuous improvement—whether addressing technical flaws, security concerns, or implementation challenges. For example, feedback might prompt simplification of complex designs or the addition of edge-case handling. Publicly available I-Ds also invite input from external stakeholders (e.g., developers, researchers), ensuring standards address diverse use cases and regional constraints. This iterative process ensures drafts are rigorously tested and refined before maturing into RFCs, balancing technical innovation with practicality, security, and implementability. The result is a consensus-driven, robust specification that reflects the collective expertise of the community.

2.4 TextFlow

We leverage GitHub's embedded features to identify relationships between modified I-D text and comments from WGs. Specifically, we pinpoint modified text snippets by comparing the differences between merged commits. These snippets are then divided into pre-version segments, referred to as "old text," and post-version segments, referred to as "new text" of the draft. By associating these segments with the corresponding comments, we create data entries consisting of "old text," "comments," and "new text." Throughout this paper, we use "before" (old) and "after" (new) interchangeably.

We split TextFlow by PRs, allocating 80% for training, 10% for development, and 10% for testing. The statistics of our data are summarized in Table 1, where "C" is short for comment, "TP" for text snippets, and "U" for unique. For a single entry in the training set, text snippets consist of all changes associated with a merge commit. In contrast, for the development and test sets, we further break down the changes into individual text snippet for easier evaluation, as the number of entries is equal to the number of text snippets. Additionally, we collected 41 entirely different drafts to serve as an OOD set.

Table 1. TextFlow Statistics.

Source	Set	NO.	U.C	TP	U.TP
I-Ds(160)	Train	4 196	4 185	10 219	10 152
	Dev	1 221	539	1 221	1 221
	Test	1 299	521	1 299	1 297
I-Ds(41)	OOD	4 307	1 534	4 307	4 063

3 TextFlow Tasks

Given the novelty of this dataset, we have the flexibility to design a variety of applications. Consequently, we have developed multiple tasks based on our envisioned inputs and outputs. While we could technically provide the entire context, such as the full I-D, which can extend up to 30 pages, we simplify our tasks by using only the modified text snippets. These snippets include not only the changed lines but also the surrounding context (in our paper, three lines before and after the changes). We mark the altered lines with special tokens: <del></del> for deletions and <add></add> for additions.

3.1 TextFlow Auto Complete: I-D (before)→ I-D (after)

LMs have been trained on vast amounts of internet data, potentially including RFCs and I-Ds. We are interested in exploring whether these models can independently handle tasks without human feedback. This capability is similar to auto-complete or auto-repair, where the LM autonomously corrects and enhances older versions of text based solely on its own capability.

3.2 TextFlow Startup: Comments → I-D (after)

Based on comments that highlight issues within the old version of an I-D, the LM is tasked with generating the revised text. This is a challenging task because the comments usually do not contain the old text, and we intentionally removed any quoted text if present. The LM must rely solely on the feedback provided to create an improved version of the text. It simulates the code synthesis task, where the model generates the correct code based on a NL docstring or comments. However, unlike code, the LMs are not extensively pre-trained on "IETF" languages.

3.3 TextFlow Edit: I-D (before) + Comments → I-D (after)

The LM is tasked with improving an initial version of I-Ds. Given the old text and comments that highlight issues or suggest enhancements, the model must generate a refined version of the text. This process involves understanding the feedback provided in the comments and applying it to produce a more polished and accurate description.

However, we foresee several challenges. LMs might have difficulty transitioning between I-D and natural NL comments. They could struggle with making precise, targeted adjustments or maintaining a specified output length. Occasionally, the model may adhere to instructions and comments but generate different outputs due to reviews being "unrelated" to the original text, either as noise data or requiring reasoning to understand the connections. Furthermore, if comments are lengthy and distracting, the model may find it challenging to identify the relevant parts to which the comments refer.

3.4 TextFlow Explain: I-D Diff (before and After) → Comments

Revisions to I-Ds often reflect substantive design decisions rather than mere editorial changes or updates to factual information. These modifications typically involve balancing competing technical, operational, or deployment priorities—such as performance, security, backward compatibility, or implementation complexity—where trade-offs between alternatives must be carefully evaluated. For example, a WG might prioritize simplicity over maximal flexibility to ensure easier adoption, or accept a slight performance penalty to enhance security. Such decisions are rarely black-and-white; they require weighing the pros and cons of each option, often through community debate, empirical data, and iterative testing.

At present, directly tasking LMs with generating explanations or rationales for revisions to I-Ds is challenging. Such tasks demand a deep understanding of networking and robust reasoning, requiring specialized domain knowledge. As a starting point, the LMs should be pretrained on comprehensive datasets such as the IETF email archives to grasp the nuances of technical discussions, WG processes, and the iterative nature of standards development. Second, the reasoning required from LMs extends beyond isolated steps; it necessitates chain-of-thought reasoning [24] to trace complex trade-offs between design choices and intensive reasoning [20] to synthesize feedback from diverse stakeholders. In addition, synthetic data generation offers a promising intermediate solution. By leveraging human-guided prompts and iterative refinement, we can create datasets that better prepare LLMs for tasks requiring domain expertise and multi-step technical reasoning. However, this approach still requires careful curation to avoid hallucinations and ensure alignment with the consensus-driven ethos of the IETF.

Substitute Task. However, we have streamlined the task into a different NLP application. Specifically, we utilized information retrieval (IR) to retrieve relevant comments for the I-D diff. The detailed methods and results were documented in our previously submitted paper [3], from which we have borrowed some findings to reference in this paper.

4 Evaluation

4.1 Challenges

Given that this task is unprecedented, it is challenging to rely solely on a single existing metric for a comprehensive evaluation of performance. The challenges arise from the following aspects:

Firstly, we aim for the LM-generated revised text to closely match the reference (golden standard). However, we must also allow for some flexibility, as long as the semantic meaning of the new text remains true. The evaluation should balance strict adherence to the reference with maintaining semantic closeness.

Secondly, presenting only the modified parts of the text makes the task more challenging due to the lack of context. For instance, if we remove the context lines, the LM will try to "restore" the missing information, which may not accurately reflect the true context, thus diminishing the model's actual capabilities. However, including the surrounding context lines complicates the evaluation process. This is because both the old and new texts (golden truth) likely share a significant amount of overlapping content, making it difficult to objectively assess the models' true capabilities. For example, if the LMs make no changes and simply copy the old text, which might be quite similar to the revised version (when there is a minor modification), it would overestimate the LMs' performance.

Thirdly, for the TextFlow Edit Task, the generated revised text should incorporate both the old version of the text and the accompanying comments. This revision can range from minor adjustments to complete transformations. LMs need to balance these two sources effectively. Leaning towards the old text ensures continuity and coherence but may result in rigidity. Conversely, leaning towards the comments adheres to the suggested changes, potentially leading to significantly altered content. Since the strategy used by human editors is not entirely clear, evaluating the revised text solely against the ground truth may be insufficient. It is crucial to consider both fidelity to the original text and the integration of comments to comprehensively assess the quality of the revisions. To address this, we evaluate the similarity between the generated text by LMs and I) new text (ground truth, revised by IETF experts), II) old text (previous version) and III) comments (suggestions, discussions by WGs).

4.2 Metrics

To evaluate our tasks, we utilized well-established metrics from other fields of NLP, such as machine translation and summarization. Specifically, we consider the following metrics:

BLEUScore [17] evaluates machine translation by comparing candidate and reference translations via n-gram precision (unigrams, bigrams, etc.) weighted by a brevity-penalized average. Variants include SacreBLEU [19], which standardizes tokenization for reproducible, cross-system comparisons (scores may differ from traditional BLEU but are more reliable), and GLEU [26], using subsequence precision/recall to address BLEU's corpus-centric limitations for single-sentence evaluation.

Word Error Rate (WER) [15] measures automatic speech recognition accuracy by calculating substitutions, insertions, and deletions between recognized and reference word sequences using the Levenshtein algorithm [1]. The WER value can exceed 1.0 when the total number of "errors" in the recognized text surpasses the number of words in the reference transcript.

METEOR [2] evaluates machine translation by matching unigrams across surface forms, stems, and meanings, then scoring using precision, recall, and fragmentation penalties to balance accuracy and fluency. It incorporates semantic and structural analysis (e.g., synonym matching, word order coherence), yielding stronger alignment with human assessments of translation quality.

BERTScore [29] evaluates machine translation by comparing BERT-derived contextual embeddings of candidate and reference sentences, measuring semantic similarity via precision, recall, and F1 scores. Its unique strength lies in capturing deep contextual meaning (beyond surface-level n-grams) through transformer-based embeddings.

MAUVE [18] evaluates open-ended text generation [7] by quantifying the statistical divergence (KL divergence) between model-generated and human-written text distributions, using GPT-2 embeddings to capture semantic structure. It focuses on global distributional alignment, effectively measuring how closely generated text matches human-like patterns (WG-written I-Ds). Its unique strength lies in addressing open-ended tasks (e.g., creative writing) where traditional metrics fail, with strong correlation to human judgments.

In summary, we utilize BLEU(s), METEOR, and WER to evaluate the fidelity of machine-generated I-Ds. These metrics allow us to determine that the generated text remains true to the original content. We employ BERTScore and MAUVE to assess the allowed flexibility, verifying that the semantic meaning and quality of the text are maintained even when deviations occur.

5 Baseline Models

5.1 Instruction Oriented Models

Mistral-7B-Instruct [11] is a compact yet powerful model fine-tuned for instruction-following tasks. Despite its smaller size, it outperforms larger models like Llama2-13B [23] in critical areas such as reasoning, mathematics, and code generation. Mistral-24-Instruct[3] expands on this foundation, excelling in multilingual text generation, advanced reasoning, and native function calling.

Llama3-8B-Instruct [6] leverages an optimized transformer architecture, supervised fine-tuning (SFT), and reinforcement learning with human feedback (RLHF) [12] to excel in instruction-based tasks. Llama3-70B-Instruct [6] distinguishes itself with an extended 128k token context window, robust ethical alignment, and efficient text processing. Open-source and cost-effective, it competes directly with models like GPT-4 [8] and DeepSeek-V3 [13], offering comparable performance at a lower cost and greater customization potential.

5.2 Reasoning Oriented Models

Qwen-32B [27] is designed to handle complex tasks such as NL understanding, code generation, logical reasoning, and multi-step problem-solving. Trained on extensive internet text, it excels in generating coherent and contextually relevant responses across diverse domains, from creative writing to technical analysis. QwQ-32B [21] is a specialized variant of Qwen-32B, optimized for advanced reasoning capabilities. It is ideal in tasks requiring deep, multi-step logical analysis, ambiguity resolution, and decision-making, such as scientific research, legal analysis, or complex strategic planning.

DeepSeek-R1 [13] is an LLM with a "reasoning-first" approach, leveraging Reinforcement Learning (RL) and Mixture of Experts (MoE) architecture for superior logical reasoning and real-time decision-making, making it a strong competitor to OpenAI o1 [10]. Due to its large size, we opted for its distilled variants (e.g., DeepSeek-R1-Distill-Llama-8B), which transfer the original model's knowledge via distillation. These smaller models achieve competitive reasoning performance with lower computational costs and easier deployment.

[3] https://biff.ai/mistral-24b-reasoning-new-state-of-the-art-open-source-reasoning-model/.

6 Method

6.1 Inference

We applied 4-bit quantization to all baseline models to accelerate inference and reduce memory consumption, except for Mistral-7B and Llama-8B, which used mixed precision BF16. For evaluation, we tested the models on TextFlow Auto-Complete and TextFlow Edit tasks. We configured a maximum input length of 2048 tokens and limited the generated output to 512 tokens. To ensure generated text closely aligns with input context, we set the temperature to 0.1 for all models, minimizing randomness and encouraging coherent, consistent outputs.

6.2 Instruction Tuning

We adhere to the guidelines in Unsloth[4] for fine-tuning Mistral-7B, Llama3-8B, and Mistral-24B. Specifically, we fine-tuned these models on the training set using Parameter Efficient Fine-Tuning (PEFT) [14]. The fine-tuning process was conducted over 3 epochs with learning rates of 2e–4, 2e–4, and 1e–4, respectively. Additionally, we incorporated QLoRA [5], which combines LoRA with 4-bit quantization to manage very large models with minimal resources. We select the best checkpoints based on the MAUVE score on the development set, and we explain our preference for MAUVE over other scores in the following section. Our prompted instructions are presented in the Appendix A.1.

7 Result and Analysis

We present all results in Table 3. On our test set with all baseline models, the BLEU scores, BERT score, METEOR, and WER are consistent with each other. In almost all cases, the generated I-Ds are closer to the old version regarding the metric values. MAUVE, on the other hand, yields different results compared to all other metrics. There are no substantial differences among the BERT scores when comparing the generated text either to the old or new versions, making the BERT score an invalid metric for evaluating the quality of generated text. WER only reflects the differences between compared pairs, without indicating whether fewer changes are better or worse. Therefore, we consider BLEU, METEOR, and MAUVE to be the proper metrics for this task, while the rest are kept as references. Please note that all our values are based on non-empty generations.

7.1 TextFlow Auto Complete

We use this task as a baseline for TextFlow Edit. We observe that the model has very limited capability to reproduce the golden new text when only the old version is provided. After incorporating human feedback through comments, we observe a "jump" in the MAUVE score. We determined that MAUVE is the most

[4] https://docs.unsloth.ai/get-started/fine-tuning-guide.

important metric for evaluating the impact of human feedback on generating the new version, as it is highly sensitive to the comments provided.

We also observe that different models have distinct behaviors and tendencies. Mistral models tend to generate output for all inputs, and for the 24B scale, comments significantly improve performance, as indicated by the MAUVE score increasing from 2.84 to 40.30. In contrast, Llama models exhibit selective output behavior and generate responses less frequently, especially at the 8B parameter scale, a limitation likely tied to our parameter configuration. At this scale, the number of outputs decreases significantly from 647 (without comments) to 64 (with comments).

Reasoning models prioritize accuracy over creativity in their output generation, leading to cautious, deliberate responses that often require more time to process. As a result, we anticipate these models will produce significantly fewer outputs compared to instruction-tuned models. We also hypothesized that without supplemental inputs (e.g., user comments), such models may struggle to fully leverage their reasoning capabilities. This is because reasoning based solely on the original text may lack the contextual depth required for meaningful analysis. Empirical observations of Qwen-32B, QwQ-32B, and R1(Qwen-32B) align with these expectations: reduced output accompanied by improved quality. Interestingly, R1(Llama-8B) demonstrates an inverse behavior: it generates more outputs when incorporating comments into its analysis.

7.2 TextFlow Startup

We conducted preliminary experiments using Mistral-7B with the prompt "What is the suggested text from the feedback below?" to evaluate its ability to generate I-D text based on user feedback. However, the model struggled to produce outputs aligned with I-D content, as the provided feedback consisted solely of opinions or critiques—without incorporating original I-D text snippets for context. This limitation mirrors challenges observed in explainability tasks, where models require domain-specific training (e.g., on the IETF's extensive corpus) to contextualize feedback and generate task-appropriate outputs. Given these constraints, we have deferred further investigation to future studies, pending access to a model pretrained on IETF datasets or additional refinements to the input format.

7.3 TextFlow Edit

The scales of model sizes determine their capability to generate new versions of I-Ds, as demonstrated by Mistral-7B and Mistral-24B. R1(Llama-70B) is more capable than its peer Llama-70B, as evidenced by the increase in MAUVE score from 33.83 to 60.91. Additionally, R1(Qwen-32B) exhibits stronger reasoning abilities compared to Qwen-32B or QwQ-32B, producing more instances while maintaining a higher level of "quality", in terms of MAUVE Score.

Our instruction-tuned models, including Mistral-7B, Llama-8B, and Mistral-24B, have shown remarkable performance improvements. They not only produce a higher volume of outputs but also achieve increased MAUVE scores on the test set. We also experimented with using these instruction-tuned models for the TextFlow Auto-Complete Task without including comments, and surprisingly, the models delivered equivalent performance. This suggests that the model may have internalized the review. To further validate the robustness of our tuned models, we applied them to OOD data. Remarkably, they exhibited the same level of effectiveness as seen with the test sets. The instruction-tuned Llama-8B emerged as the top performer on both the test set and OOD data (the last block in Table 3).

As mentioned earlier, these metrics only partially reflect the performance of LMs in our tasks. However, we argue that it is not essential for models to address every instance. What matters more to us is that the models typically generate revised text only when they are confident in their output. Therefore, we tend to place greater trust in models with strong reasoning capabilities. Our next step is to focus on generating detailed reasoning steps, or a thought process to further enhance the instruction tuning of these reasoning-specialized models. We are postponing the training of reasoning-based models to future work because we currently lack the necessary framework to effectively train those models on how to incorporate and utilize human feedback for text modification.

7.4 Text Flow Explain Substitute Task with IR

We utilize Promptriever [25] with the Mistral-7B backbone, as well as our fine-tuned model for IR, which is also based on Mistral-7B. Refer to Table 2 for details. In this setup, we rely exclusively on the semantic relationship between the modified I-Ds and comments. For future studies, we plan to investigate the use of logical reasoning as an alternative to semantic matching for reranking results after retrieval.

Table 2. MRR@10 of Text Flow using IR: diff(before and after)

Query → Document	Models	Dev	Test	OOD
I-D diff → Comments	Promptriever	43.61	41.10	24.82
	Our Retriever	68.41	66.78	42.94
Comments → I-D diff	Promptriever	68.77	69.10	47.44
	Our Retriever	80.07	79.63	56.86

7.5 Limitations

We identify a single entry from the test set that all LMs give output, and then compare the quality of the generated texts. The revised text in the ground truth addressed an issue identified in earlier drafts—specifically, a scenario where a technical mechanism was prone to suboptimal behavior under certain conditions. While most LM-generated variants retained the observation of this issue (e.g.,

Table 3. Comparison of Models Across Different Metrics, we mark the best in bold. ID_new: the ground Truth, ID_old: the previous old; ID_new: the next version (GOLD, ground truth), Id_gen: the generated text from model. Sacre is short for Sacre Bleu, and GLEU is short for Google Bleu. "-" indicates value less than 0.01.

Setting (NonEmpty/Total)	Text (LM)	Ref.	Model	Metrics						
				BLEU	Sacre	GLEU	BERT	METEOR	WER	MAUVE
w/o Comm (1299/1299)	ID_gen	ID_new	Mistral-7B	11.83	12.26	17.35	88.93	33.79	85.82	2.05
	ID_gen	ID_old	Mistral-7B	**21.92**	**22.54**	**26.52**	**90.56**	**42.67**	**73.46**	1.81
	ID_gen	ID_new	Mistral-7B	11.72	11.92	19.40	87.66	32.41	84.95	**2.84**
Comm (1299/1299)	ID_gen	ID_old	Mistral-7B	20.09	20.36	25.69	88.49	37.11	79.43	2.70
	ID_gen	Comm	Mistral-7B	–	–	1.95	83.01	12.00	99.70	1.16
w/o Comm (1299/1299)	ID_gen	ID_new	Ours(Mistral-7B)	37.48	37.77	28.64	89.94	51.16	104.04	**55.79**
	ID_gen	ID_old	Ours(Mistral-7B)	**49.11**	**49.22**	**42.46**	**92.11**	**62.87**	**85.88**	50.51
	ID_gen	ID_new	Ours(Mistral-7B)	25.47	25.75	20.59	87.67	43.96	134.31	43.83
Comm (1186/1299)	ID_gen	ID_old	Ours(Mistral-7B)	31.23	31.38	27.13	88.94	51.24	135.28	42.80
	ID_gen	Comm	Ours(Mistral-7B)	3.25	3.36	4.65	80.82	11.29	110.41	0.99
w/o Comm (647/1299)	ID_gen	ID_new	Llama-8B	30.36	31.13	32.49	91.50	53.75	70.70	9.65
	ID_gen	ID_old	Llama-8B	**50.75**	**51.87**	**48.88**	**93.65**	**67.93**	**50.82**	10.19
	ID_gen	ID_new	Llama-8B	35.41	35.59	30.42	90.72	49.31	86.44	**74.85**
Comm (64/1299)	ID_gen	ID_old	Llama-8B	38.45	38.56	34.51	92.01	54.91	77.47	59.97
	ID_gen	Comm	Llama-8B	–	–	2.93	81.70	5.35	97.02	13.25
w/o Comm (1299/1299)	ID_gen	ID_new	Ours(Llama-8B)	48.91	49.17	47.50	94.06	67.77	55.55	**98.09**
	ID_gen	ID_old	Ours(Llama-8B)	**80.73**	**80.81**	**78.95**	**97.50**	**87.55**	**14.55**	96.02
	ID_gen	ID_new	Ours(Llama-8B)	47.07	47.30	41.14	93.33	63.71	69.45	94.76
Comm (1299/1299)	ID_gen	ID_old	Ours(Llama-8B)	69.19	69.29	58.68	95.68	77.93	45.05	92.17
	ID_gen	Comm	Ours(Llama-8B)	0.25	0.25	3.76	81.55	10.74	99.21	1.51
w/o Comm (1299/1299)	ID_gen	ID_new	Mistral-24B	25.58	26.09	29.48	90.85	50.13	73.18	8.77
	ID_gen	ID_old	Mistral-24B	40.49	41.18	42.04	92.86	62.77	57.11	7.15
	ID_gen	ID_new	Mistral-24B	34.21	34.41	36.29	91.94	55.58	68.10	**40.30**
Comm (1299/1299)	ID_gen	ID_old	Mistral-24B	**51.41**	**51.58**	**48.71**	**93.64**	**66.57**	**53.63**	38.96
	ID_gen	Comm	Mistral-24B	0.04	0.04	2.65	82.00	11.40	99.66	1.42
w/o Comm (1299/1299)	ID_gen	ID_new	Ours(Mistral-24B)	38.97	39.23	39.60	92.89	60.13	63.41	59.85
	ID_gen	ID_old	Ours(Mistral-24B)	62.14	62.36	**59.24**	**95.51**	**75.96**	**37.88**	52.92
	ID_gen	ID_new	Ours(Mistral-24B)	45.27	45.48	41.17	93.13	62.09	67.32	**66.72**
Comm (1252/1299)	ID_gen	ID_old	Ours(Mistral-24B)	**65.11**	**65.19**	54.78	94.95	73.10	49.73	61.26
	ID_gen	Comm	Ours(Mistral-24B)	0.42	0.43	3.73	81.89	11.88	100.47	1.52
w/o Comm (1271/1299)	ID_gen	ID_new	Llama-70B	28.42	28.85	33.69	91.64	53.11	68.18	11.54
	ID_gen	ID_old	Llama-70B	45.98	46.57	**49.09**	**93.82**	**67.05**	**49.10**	11.85
	ID_gen	ID_new	Llama-70B	31.99	32.20	34.46	91.34	51.80	71.34	**33.83**
Comm (1229/1299)	ID_gen	ID_old	Llama-70B	**46.49**	**46.68**	42.97	92.58	60.00	64.06	30.36
	ID_gen	Comm	Llama-70B	0.09	0.10	3.24	82.48	12.14	99.02	1.35
w/o Comm (762/1299)	ID_gen	ID_new	QwQ-32B	34.70	35.33	35.54	91.32	53.43	69.73	30.98
	ID_gen	ID_old	QwQ-32B	**49.89**	**50.67**	**49.29**	**92.93**	**62.51**	**51.76**	31.75
	ID_gen	ID_new	QwQ-32B	28.08	28.21	32.75	91.32	54.74	70.48	77.64
Comm (26/1299)	ID_gen	ID_old	QwQ-32B	28.32	28.41	34.78	92.31	60.66	68.64	77.64
	ID_gen	Comm	QwQ-32B	–	–	2.55	82.77	11.23	98.71	**96.86**
w/o Comm (1056/1299)	ID_gen	ID_new	Qwen-32B	15.57	16.31	19.35	89.51	40.21	83.77	9.37
	ID_gen	ID_old	Qwen-32B	24.03	25.06	26.91	91.21	49.85	72.93	7.01
	ID_gen	ID_new	Qwen-32B	25.37	25.60	31.64	91.26	48.40	70.01	**21.01**
Comm (580/1299)	ID_gen	ID_old	Qwen-32B	**37.87**	**38.10**	**40.73**	**92.61**	**57.57**	**59.82**	18.93
	ID_gen	Comm	Qwen-32B	0.07	0.07	3.09	82.02	9.54	98.02	1.69
w/o Comm (39/1299)	ID_gen	ID_new	R1(Llama-8B)	3.24	3.31	8.03	83.83	16.64	92.79	5.55
	ID_gen	ID_old	R1(Llama-8B)	2.55	2.59	8.35	84.64	20.87	91.81	4.09
	ID_gen	ID_new	R1(Llama-8B)	19.87	20.07	21.06	87.92	37.20	89.20	34.52
Comm (190/1299)	ID_gen	ID_old	R1(Llama-8B)	**30.57**	**30.81**	**28.88**	**89.96**	**49.87**	**81.03**	**40.80**
	ID_gen	Comm	R1(Llama-8B)	–	–	2.09	81.68	7.71	97.41	8.24
w/o Comm (1077/1299)	ID_gen	ID_new	R1(Qwen-32B)	35.07	35.50	39.32	92.50	58.19	61.09	49.49
	ID_gen	ID_old	R1(Qwen-32B)	56.03	56.48	**58.19**	**94.78**	**71.90**	**37.59**	40.84
	ID_gen	ID_new	R1(Qwen-32B)	51.34	51.60	44.85	92.71	61.99	63.82	75.22
Comm (121/1299)	ID_gen	ID_old	R1(Qwen-32B)	**61.60**	**61.69**	52.76	93.95	69.44	54.58	**89.52**
	ID_gen	Comm	R1(Qwen-32B)	–	–	2.16	82.44	11.88	98.51	7.83
w/o Comm (1294/1299)	ID_gen	ID_new	R1(Llama-70B)	22.12	22.41	28.33	90.15	45.50	73.72	36.52
	ID_gen	ID_old	R1(Llama-70B)	37.74	38.12	42.20	92.23	58.11	56.25	30.72
	ID_gen	ID_new	R1(Llama-70B)	32.57	32.79	35.58	91.53	53.55	67.54	**60.91**
Comm (1299/1299)	ID_gen	ID_old	R1(Llama-70B)	**51.43**	**51.60**	**50.54**	**93.54**	**65.36**	**50.00**	60.55
	ID_gen	Comm	R1(Llama-70B)	–	–	2.20	81.98	10.20	99.59	1.80
Comm (4306/4307)	ID_gen	ID_new	Mistral-7B	13.68	13.92	20.31	88.19	34.37	84.44	2.21
Comm (4070/4307)	ID_gen	ID_new	Ours(Mistral-7B)	28.72	28.98	22.81	88.46	47.00	126.93	41.73
Comm (195/4307)	ID_gen	ID_new	Llama-8B	23.70	23.88	23.64	90.12	45.26	91.15	62.76
Comm (4307/4307)	ID_gen	ID_new	Ours(Llama-8B)	**47.20**	**47.39**	**44.08**	**93.79**	**65.82**	**61.27**	**91.95**
Comm (4300/4307)	ID_gen	ID_new	Mistral-24B	34.06	34.26	35.33	92.09	55.66	69.09	31.85
Comm (4229/4307)	ID_gen	ID_new	Ours(Mistral-24B)	43.97	44.15	41.56	93.29	62.76	64.05	61.82

noting that the mechanism was "more likely" to occur in problematic contexts), the finalized version went further by introducing a prescriptive guideline to prevent the issue altogether. This highlights a limitation: LMs often frame problems descriptively rather than proposing actionable solutions, failing to align with the ground truth's goal of resolving the issue through explicit protocol adjustments.

8 Conclusion

This work examines the training and evaluation of LMs that follow instructions for RFC (I-D) generation tasks. We introduce TextFlow, an I-D editing history dataset, and formulate several tasks to thoroughly explore the capability of generating the next version of I-Ds with human feedback, which we refer to as semi-automatic generation. Additionally, we investigate the most effective metrics for evaluating our approach. Our work opens new avenues for exploring the incorporation of human feedback into automatic RFC generation.

9 Related Work

The dataset and tasks are relatively new, and we draw great inspiration from the work OCTOPACK [16] and HumanEval [4]. Those works significantly contribute to the task of code generation.

Acknowledgments. We acknowledge the use of Microsoft Copilot for its assistance with rephrasing, grammar-checking, enhancing the readability of this manuscript, and naming our datasets. We use Alibaba Qwen for further language polishing.

A Appendix

A.1 Prompts

We use two instructions for TextFlow Auto-Complete Task and TextFlow Edit Task.

- **Auto-Complete:** Please revise the following text using your knowledge and understanding.
- **Edit:** You are a professional IETF RFC writer. Identify the parts of the original text that need revision based on the feedback. Revise the text accordingly.

A.2 Real Demo

We select one short entry from our test set to illustrate the real output from LMs. This entry is not necessarily the "best" output from the "best" model.

Original: The public key of the account key pair, encoded as a JSON Web Key object RFC7517. <del> "valid" or "deactivated" </del> An array of URIs that the server can use to contact the client for issues related to this authorization.

Comments: what's the difference between "deactivated" and "revoked"? Deactivated is done by the user; revoked is done by an administrator. OK, so we need to either say that or use clearer terms :) I talked with NAME offline, and I think he's going to propose something.

Ground Truth: The public key of the account key pair, encoded as a JSON Web Key object RFC7517. <ins> The status of this registration. Possible values are: "valid", "deactivated", and "revoked". "deactivated" should be used to indicate user initiated deactivation whereas "revoked" should be used to indicate administratively initiated deactivation. </ins> An array of URIs that the server can use to contact the client for issues related to this authorization.

Llama3-70B: The public key of the account key pair, encoded as a JSON Web Key object RFC7517. The status of the key pair, which can be either "active", "user-deactivated", or "admin-revoked". An array of URIs that the server can use to contact the client for issues related to this authorization.

Ours(Llama3-8B): The public key of the account key pair, encoded as a JSON Web Key object RFC7517. <ins> "active" or "revoked" </ins> An array of URIs that the server can use to contact the client for issues related to this authorization.

References

1. Andoni, A., Onak, K.: Approximating edit distance in near-linear time. In: Proceedings of the Forty-First Annual ACM Symposium on Theory of Computing, pp. 199–204 (2009)
2. Banerjee, S., Lavie, A.: METEOR: an automatic metric for MT evaluation with improved correlation with human judgments. In: Proceedings of the ACL Workshop on Intrinsic and Extrinsic Evaluation Measures for Machine Translation and/or Summarization, pp. 65–72. Association for Computational Linguistics, Ann Arbor (2005)
3. Bian, J., Arefev, N., Mühlhäuser, M., Welzl, M.: Automated insights into github collaboration dynamics. IEEE Access (2025)
4. Chen, M., et al.: Evaluating large language models trained on code. arXiv preprint arXiv:2107.03374 (2021)
5. Dettmers, T., Pagnoni, A., Holtzman, A., Zettlemoyer, L.: Qlora: efficient finetuning of quantized llms. In: Oh, A., Naumann, T., Globerson, A., Saenko, K., Hardt, M., Levine, S. (eds.) Advances in Neural Information Processing Systems, vol. 36, pp. 10088–10115. Curran Associates, Inc. (2023)
6. Grattafiori, A., et al.: The llama 3 herd of models. arXiv preprint arXiv:2407.21783 (2024)
7. Guan, J., et al.: Openmeva: a benchmark for evaluating open-ended story generation metrics. arXiv preprint arXiv:2105.08920 (2021)
8. Hurst, A., et al.: Gpt-4o system card. arXiv preprint arXiv:2410.21276 (2024)
9. Iyengar, J., Thomson, M.: Rfc 9000: Quic: a udp-based multiplexed and secure transport. Omtermet Emgomeeromg Task Force (2021)
10. Jaech, A., et al.: Openai o1 system card. arXiv preprint arXiv:2412.16720 (2024)

11. Jiang, A.Q., et al.: Mistral 7b. arXiv preprint arXiv:2310.06825 (2023)
12. Kaufmann, T., Weng, P., Bengs, V., Hüllermeier, E.: A survey of reinforcement learning from human feedback, vol. 10 (2023). arXiv preprint arXiv:2312.14925
13. Liu, A., et al.: Deepseek-v3 technical report. arXiv preprint arXiv:2412.19437 (2024)
14. Mangrulkar, S., Gugger, S., Debut, L., Belkada, Y., Paul, S., Bossan, B.: Peft: state-of-the-art parameter-efficient fine-tuning methods (2022)
15. Morris, A., Maier, V., Green, P.: In: From WER and RIL to MER and WIL: improved evaluation measures for connected speech recognition (2004)
16. Muennighoff, N., et al.: Octopack: instruction tuning code large language models. In: NeurIPS 2023 Workshop on Instruction Tuning and Instruction Following (2023)
17. Papineni, K., Roukos, S., Ward, T., Zhu, W.J.: Bleu: a method for automatic evaluation of machine translation. In: Proceedings of the 40th Annual Meeting of the Association for Computational Linguistics, pp. 311–318 (2002)
18. Pillutla, K., et al.: Mauve: measuring the gap between neural text and human text using divergence frontiers. In: NeurIPS (2021)
19. Post, M.: A call for clarity in reporting BLEU scores. In: Bojar, O., et al. (eds.) Proceedings of the Third Conference on Machine Translation: Research Papers, pp. 186–191. Association for Computational Linguistics, Brussels (2018)
20. Su, H., et al.: Bright: a realistic and challenging benchmark for reasoning-intensive retrieval. arXiv preprint arXiv:2407.12883 (2024)
21. Team, Q.: Qwq-32b: Embracing the power of reinforcement learning (2025)
22. Thomson, M., Stark, B.: Rfc 8874 working group github usage guidance (2020)
23. Touvron, H., et al.: Llama 2: open foundation and fine-tuned chat models. arXiv preprint arXiv:2307.09288 (2023)
24. Wei, J., et al.: Chain-of-thought prompting elicits reasoning in large language models. In: Koyejo, S., Mohamed, S., Agarwal, A., Belgrave, D., Cho, K., Oh, A. (eds.) Advances in Neural Information Processing Systems, vol. 35, pp. 24824–24837. Curran Associates, Inc. (2022)
25. Weller, O., Van Durme, B., Lawrie, D., Paranjape, A., Zhang, Y., Hessel, J.: Promptriever: instruction-trained retrievers can be prompted like language models. arXiv preprint arXiv:2409.11136 (2024)
26. Wu, Y., et al.: Google's neural machine translation system: bridging the gap between human and machine translation. arXiv preprint arXiv:1609.08144 (2016)
27. Yang, A., et al.: Qwen2. 5 technical report. arXiv preprint arXiv:2412.15115 (2024)
28. Zhang, S., et al.: Instruction tuning for large language models: a survey. arXiv preprint arXiv:2308.10792 (2023)
29. Zhang, T., Kishore, V., Wu, F., Weinberger, K.Q., Artzi, Y.: Bertscore: evaluating text generation with bert. arXiv preprint arXiv:1904.09675 (2019)

News Timeline Summarization: Recent Methods

Vandana Yadav(✉), Jon Atle Gulla, Özlem Özgöbek, and Lemei Zhang

Norwegian University of Science and Technology, Trondheim, Norway
{vandana.yadav,jon.atle.gulla,ozlem.ozgobek,lemei.zhang}@ntnu.no

Abstract. On news platforms, users may be unable to access updates for an extended period or may wish to review a certain topic that has been progressing for quite some time. Experts writing articles on current developments, along with creating multiple timelines is a laborious task. These use cases highlight a need for automated timeline summarization (TLS). This motivated us to explore news timeline summarization that utilizes Natural Language Processing techniques, Machine Learning, and Large Language Models (LLMs). In this paper, our contributions are a review of recent research advancements in TLS that showcase the capabilities of LLMs, such as zero-shot, few-shot, and retrieval-augmented generation for generating coherent and reliable summaries. We also highlight key challenges in TLS, including the difficulty of maintaining joint representation of all topic-specific articles, weak or uncertain causal links between events, and redundancy due to adjacent dates within timeline referencing the same events. Additionally, we outline key research directions such as multi-timeline summarization based on the interest and perspective of individual user or a user segment, and the collection of high-quality articles that constitute topical relevance, broader domain coverage, and have strong inter-event links.

Keywords: Timeline summarization · News · Topic TLS · LLM

1 Introduction

In modern news media, automatic text summarization is one of the essential tasks that involves summarizing a single news article, multiple news articles, and long-ranging news topics [1]. Automatic text summarization involves producing concise, coherent, and relevant summaries from text. Timeline summarization (TLS) aims to automatically compress a long-running topic into a timeline (timeline summary) that includes chronologically sorted time-stamped textual summaries of events related to the topic [1,4]. Long-running topics can either be in the form of lengthy text, such as an enormous amount of unstructured text over a long period (such as forum posts, or comments on social media) related to a specific

R. Ichise (Ed.): NLDB 2025, LNCS 15836, pp. 365–379, 2026.
https://doi.org/10.1007/978-3-031-97141-9_25

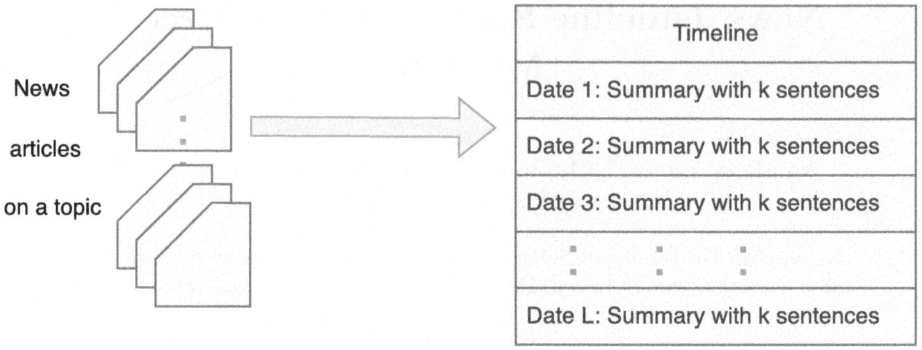

Fig. 1. Timeline Summarization for news articles. Summary for each date is extracted from the news articles.

topic, or large number of documents related to a topic over a long period. The timeline should be coherent and structured, and should include relevant details.

Timeline summarization tasks are typically classified into two main sub-tasks: event timeline summarization and topic timeline summarization [2]. In **event TLS sub-task**, multiple event timelines are extracted from a noisy stream of textual data such as tweets. Each timeline is a chronologically arranged list of brief updates about a particular event from a noisy text stream.

Whereas in the case of **topic TLS sub-task**, the most significant events and their corresponding dates are extracted from a large collection of documents that span over a long time. So, a timeline would include L dates, each date having summary with k sentences describing the events that happened at the date. Figure 1 shows the template of a timeline summary for a large number of news articles. Topic TLS sub-task aligns well with the news timeline summarization task. Because several news articles are published on a topic over a long period, and these articles are surrounded by numerous events linked to the topic. Therefore, as part of this paper we only look into topic TLS methods. These TLS sub-tasks can be addressed using three high-level approaches (strategies): direct summarization, date-driven, and event-driven approaches [1,2].

News readers often prefer to see the progression of the topic over a particular period to synthesize important information quickly. Nowadays, many news platforms provide such timeline[1] on different topics. However, most of the timelines are manually curated. Manually constructing the timelines need professional judgment to select important details from the large number of news articles that span over a long period, and the timeline must be logical and well organized. It is difficult for experts to create several timelines on different topics quickly and efficiently. In addition, readers might be interested in certain aspects or subtopics of a broader topic and would prefer timelines to focus on those subtopics. As a result, timelines would vary for different readers. For journalists to develop multiple timelines focusing on different topics, as well as tailoring the timelines

[1] https://www.bbc.com/news/world-europe-17746861.

to the needs and preferences of readers, would be strenuous task. Therefore, the automatic generation of a single summary or multiple summaries that takes into account reader's interests would be beneficial for journalists. News media houses can adopt such service to reduce efforts of journalists in creating timeline, and assist readers to grasp information quickly by providing detailed, relevant and coherent progression of the topic over a time period. This motivates us to study latest advancements in news timeline summarization task. Thus, as part of this paper, we review different methods and challenges of news timeline summarization.

Timeline summarization can also be categorized into open-domain and closed-domain settings based on retrievable news sources [5]. Timeline summarization in open-domain setting involves constructing timelines from a large collection of documents that are directly filtered from the internet. Whereas timeline summarization in closed-domain setting involves constructing timelines from a predefined large number of documents related to a particular domain. In this paper, we discuss topic timeline summarization methods for both settings.

In comparison to other summarization tasks (such as single document or query-based), there have been fewer studies based on timeline summarization tasks. With advancements in the Large Language Models (LLMs) in recent years, research in timeline summarization with respect to LLM and comparison with state-of-the-art before the LLMs have been progressing. Prior to Martcharts' study [8], which treated TLS as a special case of multi-document summarization and used sub-modular functions for sentence selection, was benchmark work in TLS research for datasets Crisis and Timeline17 which are explained in Sect. 2 in detail. LLM-generated summaries are found to be comparable with human written summaries [11]. We review methods (since Martcharts' study) that focus on utilizing different capabilities of LLMs, such as prompting techniques and retrieval-augmented generation.

In Sect. 2, we provide an overview of what datasets can be used for open-domain and closed-domain settings for topic TLS task. Section 3 discusses various topic TLS methods, categorized based on their summarization strategy and primary focus. Section 4 outlines the evaluation metrics used to assess the quality of generated timelines. Finally, Sects. 5 and 6 present key challenges and potential research directions in the area of news timeline summarization respectively.

2 Datasets

As mentioned earlier, the topic TLS task aligns with timeline summarization in the news domain where the goal is to generate a relevant and comprehensive evolution of a topic. In this section, we provide an overview of datasets used for TLS. Following datasets for topic TLS are applicable to both open and closed domain settings. Each dataset includes multiple topics, with each topic having at least one corresponding ground-truth timeline. All the datasets mentioned are designed for closed-domain TLS, except for the open-TLS dataset which supports open-domain TLS.

1. Timeline17 [10] is a dataset widely used in TLS research. It is compiled from various news sources, it comprises 9 topics with 17 timelines and around 2300 average number of articles. It is designed for closed-domain TLS methods.
2. CRISIS [13] is a dataset that comprises of 22 timelines on 4 topics.
3. ENTITIES [1] is a dataset that contains about 950 average articles and 47 topics. Each topic ranges for long time (decades of news articles). It has more topics in comparison to T17 and CRISIS dataset (9 and 4 respectively). It is designed for closed-domain TLS methods.
4. CREST (Constraint Restrictions on Entities to Subset Timelines) [4] is a dataset that contains 235 timelines from 47 public figures or institutions. Timelines were derived from ENTITIES dataset. Each entity was associated to 5 pairs of constraints. It is also designed for closed-domain TLS methods.
5. Open-TLS [5] is a dataset especially designed for open-domain TLS methods. It comprises of 50 timelines on recent news topics from domains, namely politics, economics, society, sports, and technology. Each timeline is authored by professional journalists. Each timeline is associated with a publication date and a query key-phrase that facilitates retrieving of articles from the internet using Search Engines Results Pages (SERPs).

3 Methods

In this section, various topic TLS methods are discussed and are categorized into three main approaches: direct, date-driven, and event-driven. All methods operate within the closed-domain setting, except for last method, CHRONOS via iterative self-questioning, which operate within both closed and open-domain settings.

Table 1 provides an overview of recent methods for topic TLS. In the table, the first column, "Methods", refers to the index number assigned to each TLS approach discussed in the paper. The second column, "Topic TLS Type", categorizes the methods based on their summarization strategy namely, direct, date-driven, or event-driven. The third column, "Focus", highlights the primary objective or aspect each method targets, such as event clustering, extraction of temporally significant content, or integration of user constraints. The final column, "Technique", describes the algorithmic or modeling approach employed, including optimization algorithms, clustering methods, knowledge graphs, or prompting strategies of LLMs, such as zero-shot, few-shot, or one-shot learning.

3.1 Direct Summarization

In the direct summarization approach, a collection of news articles is treated as a set of sentences, and then a small subset of sentences is selected [1].

Martschat (Method 1) [8] is one of the state-of-the-art approaches for timeline summarization. It draws inspiration from multi-document summarization technique that utilizes submodular objective functions to ensure for balanced content

Table 1. Overview of recent methods in topic timeline summarization.

Methods	Topic TLS Type	Focus	Technique	Datasets
1	Direct	• News articles treated as a set of sentences	• Greedy algorithm to select sentences that maximize an objective function & satisfy temporal constraints	T17, CRISIS
2	Date-driven	• Most significant dates were selected by extracting date features	• Supervised learning model used date features to predict whether a date appears in a ground-truth timeline or not	T17, CRISIS, ENTITIES
3	Event-driven	• Topic-related news articles into a graph	• Markov clustering algorithm groups into event clusters	T17, CRISIS, ENTITIES
4	Sequential Chunking	• Chunking articles & event summaries based on publication dates	• Zero-shot LLM for timeline generation	T17, CRISIS, ENTITIES
5	Date-driven	• Temporal knowledge graph to extract relationships between entities & their associated dates	• Zero-shot LLM for timeline generation	T17, CRISIS, ENTITIES
6	Date-driven	• Time sentences: sentences with temporal mentions were assigned dates	• Zero-shot LLM for timeline generation	T17, CRISIS, ENTITIES
7	Event-driven	• Extract key event summaries • Cluster into event graph	• Few-shot classification for clustering into an evolving event graph • One-shot LLM for extracting key summaries	T17, CRISIS, ENTITIES
8	Event-driven	• Models user's interest in specific aspects of a topic • Self-reflection: assesses if generated summary matches constraints	• Few-shot LLM for self-reflection	T17, CRISIS, ENTITIES
9	Event-driven	• Iterative self-questioning to generate questions or sub-questions about a topic • Use them as queries to retrieve relevant articles	• Few-shot LLM for self-questioning	T17, CRISIS, ENTITIES, Open-TLS

coverage with temporal and textual aspects. In this method, objective functions were designed to capture content coverage and temporal diversity. Temporal constraints which reflect the timing and sequence of events were considered. A greedy optimization algorithm was employed to select sentences that maximize the objective function while fulfilling temporal constraints.

3.2 Date-Driven Approach

A date-driven approach generates a timeline by merging summaries of significant dates selected from a massive collection of articles on a topic [1]. This approach involves two high-level sub-tasks: date selection and summarization. **DATEWISE (Method 2)** is a timeline summarization method that follows the date-driven approach. In DATEWISE, a set of possible dates that can be included in the timeline from input articles was obtained by considering both publication dates of articles and converting textual references of dates into dates using the HeidelTime tool. From this set, the most significant dates were selected by extracting date features and employing a classification or regression model to predict whether a date appears in a ground-truth timeline. Once the key dates are selected, summaries for each are generated by selecting candidate sentences from the collection of articles. This was achieved by heuristics proposed in the method (called PM-MEAN) that identified a subset of sentences published on or immediately after the date, along with those that explicitly mention the date. Finally, the complete timeline summary is constructed using a centroid-based algorithm called CENTROID-OPT that optimizes the summary to be closer to the centroid of all sentences in all date summaries [1,6].

Strategies to Handle Large Input with LLM (Method 4, 5 & 6) [3]. As the LLM's input size is fixed, the LLM cannot accommodate cases (such as timeline summarization) where the input is large. This study focused on handling a massive collection of articles as input to fit the LLM's input size. Three remedies were adopted: (1) sequential temporal chunking which reduces the context length by dividing into chunks, (2) a hybrid approach combining knowledge graphs with LLMs to provide structured context, and (3) the Time Ranker approach which involves summarizing key dates separately to construct timeline. These remedies correspond to different categories of timeline summarization. Across all the remedies, the most basic form of prompting technique (zero-shot prompt) was applied to various LLMs, including large auto-regressive models (Long-LLaMA and LLaMA2), supervised instruction fine-tuned models (FLAN-T5), and RLHF model (GPT-4).

Sequential Temporal Chunking and LLM (Method 4) [3]. It involved two levels of chunking items based on the publication dates of the articles. In the first stage, the input collection of articles (items) was sorted chronologically based on their publication dates. Then, sorted articles were grouped into variable-sized chunks (2 to 5 articles per chunk). As mentioned earlier, a zero-shot prompt LLM was employed to generate a summary for each chunk. Each summary was assigned a median publication date calculated from articles within the chunk. In the next stage of chunking, summaries obtained from the previous stage (items) were again chronologically sorted based on their median publication dates and then grouped into variable-sized chunks (5 to 35 summaries per chunk). The zero-shot prompt LLM was used to generate final summaries for each new chunk. Finally, the summaries of the second-level chunks are aggregated to form a comprehensive timeline summary. We cannot say that this TLS approach falls into date-driven summarization or event-driven as it's based on chunking of articles. Thus, we classified this approach of generating a timeline summary as a different category called temporal chunking.

Combination of Knowledge Graphs (KG) and LLMs (Method 5) [3]. In the method, a temporal knowledge graph was constructed to extract the relationships between entities along with their associated dates. This was performed by employing the rebel-large model [7]. Additionally, temporal expressions (information) were extracted from the input articles using techniques proposed in the DATEWISE method [1]. The graph comprises four key entities: Head, Type, Tail, and Date. Next, the temporal (date-wise) knowledge graph was applied to the LLM (zero-shot) to generate a timeline for a topic. The generated timeline (output) included a list of dates with a brief description of activities that happened on those dates.

Time Ranker and LLM (Method 6) [3]. The Time Ranker and LLM method also follows a date-driven approach. In this method, textual expressions (i.e., temporal mentions) in the input articles were converted to certain dates by referring to the publication dates of articles using the HeidelTime tool as in the DATEWISE method. This helped form time sentences for the dates resolved by HeidelTime, i.e., sentences that have the temporal mentions assigned to the dates. Then, a set of possible dates (150 dates) for the timeline summary was selected based on dates with more temporal mentions. Lastly, these preprocessed articles were applied to the LLM (zero-shot prompt) to produce final timeline.

3.3 Event-Driven Approach

In an event-driven approach, a timeline summary is generated by merging summaries of the most significant events, which are identified from a large number of articles [1]. Such timeline summarization methods mostly use clustering algorithms to group similar news articles into clusters, where each cluster represents an event and then individually summarizes the most important clusters. All summaries are aggregated to form the final timeline summary. Such an approach is divided into two primary steps: identifying key events and summarizing key events.

CLUST (Method 3) [1] is a timeline summarization method that follows event-driven strategy. In the method, firstly, a massive collection of articles (on a topic) was converted into a graph representing the connection between all the articles in the input collection. Nodes represented the news articles, edges represented that they have publication dates at most 1 day apart from each other, and weights were assigned to the edges (cosine similarity between the articles).

From this connection graph, a Markov clustering algorithm was employed to obtain clusters. Each cluster contained the most connected parts from articles of different publication dates in the input collection. So, clusters can be considered as events. Next, a date that is most frequently mentioned within the cluster is assigned to the cluster. Then, clusters are ranked by how often the cluster date is mentioned throughout the input collection of articles on the topic. A set of important clusters is selected based on ranking scores. Each cluster is summarized, and an overall timeline summary is formed using a centroid optimization algorithm (CENTROID-OPT).

Incremental topic TLS (Method 7) [2] method like CLUST also, clusters articles based on events and then, summarize each important cluster (event) to form overall timeline summary. The problem definition of the study is that there is a collection of news articles on a topic, and a new article on the topic is available at a certain time. So, there is a need to construct a timeline summary for the topic till the time a new article is available. Unlike past approaches common in previous studies, in this study, TLS was approached in a streaming context that envisioned topic timelines should evolve as time progresses and new article is received. Here, input comprises of a collection of articles on a topic along with the topic's key phrases. Output is a list of a specific number of (date, summary) pairs. This study utilized LLM for different purposes: 1-shot LLM for keyword event summarization and the pre-trained LLM as a pseudo-oracle for membership classification. The 1-shot operation was applied on LLM to summarize important events in the new article using the topic keywords before clustering processing. As mentioned earlier, event summaries are in a specific format: date and summary in one sentence.

Few-shot prompting was employed for classifying whether two summaries belong to the same event. A heuristic was applied to ensure events share the same date along with this step date. These two steps were iteratively performed to develop an event graph where a cluster represents an individual event. Here, news articles are pictured as an evolving event graph where nodes represent entities (event descriptions) and edges indicate common event associations. Next, each selected event cluster is ranked based on the connected node count. A higher node count has higher prominence. TextRank algorithm (a graph-based ranking algorithm) and GTE embeddings access the importance of nodes within its cluster. Then, top k nodes are identified that represent the event's (cluster's) narrative. Clusters' summaries were aggregated and sorted in chronological order to form a complete timeline summary. This was compared with DATEWISE, CLUST, and Event Graph Compression (EGC) [12] baselines. The major takeaway from this study is that the incremental topic method handles better long-range topic TLS tasks. As shown in the study, when a number of publication dates for a topic is higher (between 200 to 1000), date-driven approach (DATEWISE) was outperformed by the event detection method (incremental topic TLS).

Reflective Algorithm for Constrained Timeline Summarization (REACTS) (Method 8) [4]. Reflective Algorithm for Constrained Timeline Summarization (REACTS) algorithm combines timeline summarization and query-based summarization to incorporate user interests. It considers user's interest by introducing constraints. For instance, if topic is Stephen King and reader is interested in Stephen King's book releases. Then, Stephen King's book releases is the constraint. As query-based summarization involves generating a summary based on a query that represents what users might be specifically interested in from the documents. Problem definition is similar to the incremental topic TLS method, where new article is available and reader would like to have a timeline summary till the time new summary was available. The input composes of temporally ordered news articles related to a specific topic, a constraint, the expected number of dates in the timeline, and the expected number of sentences per date. The REACTS algorithm involved four main steps: event summarization, self-reflection, event clustering, and lastly cluster and sentence selection. It employed LLMs (one-shot prompting) to generate event summaries, These event summaries were evaluated using self-reflection by prompting the same LLM to ensure they lined up with the given constraint. Related events were clustered using few-shot prompting, and summaries were encoded with the General Text Embeddings (GTE) model for efficient processing. Next, significant events were chosen based on cluster size, then decomposed into key sentences using TextRank, and finally summaries were aggregated into a timeline. The study evaluated two REACTS variants: one with self-reflection and one without (REACTS w/o SR) against a baseline method. In the baseline method, articles were randomly sampled and added them into the input prompt one by one until the input context size limit of LLM was reached. The key takeaway was that incorporating self-reflection to check whether event summaries were related to the constraint, improved the quality of timeline summaries.

Causal Headline Retrieval for Open-Domain News Timeline SummarizatiOn (CHRONOS) via Iterative Self Questioning, (Method 9) [5]**.** The CHRONOS framework explores timeline summarization in both open-domain and closed-domain settings using an iterative self-questioning approach with retrieval-augmented generation. The process involves three main steps: iterative news self-questioning, question rewrite, and timeline summarization. First, relevant articles on a target news topic were collected by directly searching news headlines as keywords from the internet using Search Engines Results Pages (SERPs). Then, self-questioning was performed to generate questions about the target topic using LLMs with few-shot prompting. The questions were rewritten by decomposing into 2–3 sub-questions to extract more information on the topic. Upon completion of each round of self-questioning, the LLM was instructed to extract the significant events with given dates and provide detailed summaries of these events. The final step was to merge these event summaries that involved aligning events across rounds of self questioning, and resolved any conflicts of dates. The LLM was instructed to select the top-l key events from the merged timeline. CHRONOS was evaluated against open-domain baselines DIRECT and REWRITE, as well as closed-domain baselines CLUST, EGC, and incremental TLS approaches using LLaMA2-13B and Qwen2.5-72B. The CHRONOS framework showed improvement in timeline summarization by leveraging iterative self-questioning for comprehensive event extraction.

Comparisons of Methods. CLUST (Method 3), an event-driven approach, outperformed Marcharts study (Method 1), a direct approach, on the ENTITIES dataset. However, it underperformed compared to both DATEWISE (Method 2) and Marcharts study (Method 1) on the other two datasets, Timeline17 and CRISIS. Analysis revealed that Method 3 often merged articles from nearby dates into single clusters, even when they associated to distinct events in the reference timelines. This indicates that CLUST (Method 3) may need to adapt its clustering granularity based on the characteristics of the task. [1].

In incremental TLS study (where Method 7 proposed) was shown that temporally tagged sentences provide valuable information for the TLS task [2]. In this study, DATEWISE (method 2) was considered as baseline. It was observed that DATEWISE (method 2) was inputted with only the sentences and no temporal information, showed lower performance compared to DATEWISE that used temporal information in addition to sentences as input.

Incremental TLS (method 7) processes each article individually, so faces time delays due to the extensive news corpus like Crisis dataset [2]. Whereas, in case of CHRONOS (method 9) works on a retrieval-based mechanism to extract highly relevant news articles from the internet using iterative self-questioning. Then, generate event summaries of each round of questioning and aggregate them to form complete timeline. CHRONOS devoted only 5.6% of the total time required by the incremental TLS method to reach a similar performance [5]. As CHRONOS method highly depend on logical and structured relations between events to retrieve effectively.

4 Performance Metrics Comparison

Timeline summarization methods are evaluated using the following metrics to measure how well a predicted timeline aligns with a reference timeline (ground-truth) summary. Table 2 metrics are obtained from ROUGE-N metrics [9]. These metrics compute the N-grams in generated and reference timeline summaries. In all methods, 1-gram and 2-grams overlap between the summaries are calculated.

1. Align F1: This score is computed by matching the events in the generated timeline summary with the reference timeline summary based on textual similarity and whether events occur at the right points in time (temporal similarity).
2. Concat F1: This score is computed by concatenating all events into a single document instead of evaluating individual event alignments separately. So, generated timeline summary and reference summary are considered as two separate documents. Then, text similarity is calculated.
3. Agree F1: In contrast to Align F1 Score, which considers both event and temporal placement matching, Agree F1 Score emphasis on whether the same key events as in reference timeline are included in the generated timeline.

Table 2. Performance metrics used in different methods.

Metrics	Methods	Focus of metrics
Align F1	1–10	Checks if events match and appear at the right time
Contact F1	6–10	Considers each timeline (the generated timeline & ground-truth time) as single document, then checks between them
Agree F1	6–10	Checks if the same events are selected, without considering time
Date F1	1–10	Checks how accurately events are assigned to dates

4. Date F1: This score is computed by matching only generated timeline's event dates with reference timeline's event dates.

5 Challenges of Timeline Summarization

This section outlines several key challenges associated with the task of news timeline summarization.

Maintaining Joint Representation of All Articles Related to a Topic. The primary goal of TLS is to summarize a large number of news articles on a topic efficiently. As new events unfold within a target news topic, additional articles must be considered to keep the timeline up to date. This dynamic nature poses a significant challenge in maintaining a joint representation of all the articles related to the topic. In closed-domain TLS methods (such as those based on a knowledge graph), the arrival of a new article requires reprocessing each article in the corpus individually to construct an updated joint representation of all topic-related articles. Since each article is handled separately, this repeated processing leads to increased computational overhead, thereby prolonging the method's inference time [5]. This challenge has been addressed in the open-domain TLS methods, particularly CHRONOS, which utilizes a retrieval-based mechanism to extract highly relevant articles [5]. However, it is important to recognize the integral difference between closed-domain TLS and open-domain TLS. In open-domain TLS, summarization of a topic is carried out by retrieving relevant articles from the internet, whereas in closed-domain TLS, summarization of a topic is limited to a pre-collected corpus of news articles related to the topic.

Lacking Diverse Datasets. In case of closed-domain TLS methods, there is a possibility that the news corpus may be insufficient to capture every significant event or aspect of a topic [1]. For example, a corpus about the COVID-19 pandemic as a topic might include articles focused mainly on health-related developments but lack coverage of essential political decisions or economic consequences, resulting in an incomplete timeline. To mitigate this, TLS datasets should encompass news related to a topic from a wide range of domains, such as politics, science, disasters, and technology advancements. Most of the publicly available datasets have limited topical diversity, which affects the TLS models [5]. This challenge leads to a new research avenue of creating new datasets that provide broad coverage across diverse topics and subtopics.

Events Described in the News Articles Related to a Topic May Have Weak Causal Connections [5]**.** In case of open-domain TLS methods, if causal connections between events are poor or uncertain and the events are linked only by their chronological order, then the method would struggle to extract relevant articles. Similarly, in a closed-domain setting, the pre-collected news articles may lack strong causal connections among events, and the timeline summaries generated would not be logical.

Adjacent Dates Within Timeline Leads to Redundancy [1]**.** In direct (method 1), date-driven (method 2), and event-driven (method 3) approaches, it was observed that the generated timeline summaries often contained a high concentration of adjacent dates compared to the ground-truth timeline summaries. These adjacent dates frequently referred to the same events, resulting in redundancy within the timeline. Methods 1 and 3 adopted mechanisms such as an objective function to promote diversity and discourage the selection of adjacent dates for the timeline, respectively. In contrast, method 2 lacked such a mechanism. When method 2 was constrained to avoid adjacent dates, its performance across all evaluation metrics declined. Hence, this observation highlights the importance of conducting qualitative analysis along with standard TLS evaluation metrics to better understand the model/approach behavior.

Retrieving High Number of Relevant Articles [5]**.** In CHRONOS, it was seen that the increasing number of articles retrieved in each round of retrieval, based on questions, improved the timeline. It is based on the notion that more articles would provide richer context. However, a higher number of articles provided to the model can have less significant details related to the topic, which would introduce noise and redundant information into the timeline. Specifically, in the CHRONOS method, it was found that beyond a certain threshold, increasing the number of retrieved articles no longer yielded benefits.

6 Potential Research Areas

This section explores various potential research directions within the timeline summarization task.

Multi-timeline Summarization. Timeline summary can be different depending on user-defined queries (such as subtopics or topical constraints), or user segments based on demographic attributes (such as age, region, occupation). For example, COVID-19 pandemic, user segments like vaccine distributors may prioritize both political decisions and health developments, while healthcare professionals may focus solely on in health-related developments.

Users can have multiple perspectives on the same events. One user might avoid political news and describe the news by focusing on factual details of events like timing, speakers, and venue, whereas another user, engaged in civic issues, might highlight political agendas and implications [15]. These differing perspectives leads to the need for multi-timeline summarization, where each summary reflects based on a user's or a user segment's interests. Constructing timeline summaries tailored to users interests poses major challenges. News organizations cannot manually produce timelines for every user or user group. Identifying relevant user attributes (such as interests, reading patterns, or behaviors) that can guide timeline generation based on users is a key research challenge. Furthermore, TLS systems typically output a single timeline regardless of the dataset's size or complexity [14]. This is also addressed by the multi-timeline summarization task [14]. However, aligning summaries too closely with individual opinions risks introducing bias, stereotyping, and even manipulating user beliefs. Thus, critical research direction in multi-timeline summarization also, is to design safeguards to prevent overfitting timeline summaries to user preferences.

Collecting Relevant Articles for a Topic. In the closed-domain setting, articles related to a topic are pre-collected prior to summarization. In contrast, the open-domain setting involves first retrieving relevant articles from the internet, followed by timeline summarization based on the retrieved content. In both settings, extracting articles pertinent to a specific topic is a critical step. However, retrieving high-quality, reliable articles from the internet presents several challenges. This process accounts for multiple factors, namely ensuring topical relevance, achieving broad domain coverage, and identifying strong inter-event connections within the retrieved content, as outlined in the challenges section. Furthermore, retrieving a large number of articles may increase the risk of introducing noise and redundancy due to the inclusion of less significant or loosely related information. Another key consideration is the volatility of web content, which can impact the consistency of a generated timeline. Due to these challenges, curating topic-specific articles suitable for timeline generation remains a substantial and open research problem.

Inconsistent Information. When the same event is described very differently across several news articles, this leads to a challenge for timeline summarization systems. Determining which version is the most reliable is important, especially in the absence of a clear ground truth. Such inconsistency can lead to redundancy or conflicting information in the generated timeline. Sources are inconsistent, probably because the news unfolds over time and more information is gradually available. This raises important questions: Should the timeline summaries reflect the evolving nature of information and explicitly consider how our understanding of an event develops? These questions remain open and highlight the need for further work on handling inconsistency and temporal progression in the timeline summarization task.

Fake Stories, Disinformation, and AI Generated Stories. Nowadays, disinformation (purposely spreading biased or manipulated stories) and fake news (fabricated stories that appear to be news) are common on online platforms. Timeline summarization based on fake stories and manipulated stories might lead to biases, stereotyping, and other adverse social consequences. With the advent of generative AI/conversational agents, instances of fake news have increased. So, the news' credibility can be questionable. Credibility of news articles can be increased by clearly stating evidence along with adding scientific sources, statistical data, and visualizations to an article [16]. These factors help in detecting whether content is false or fabricated or not. As generative conversational systems require answering user-specific questions by extracting information from various external web sources (such as news articles). This involves summarizing web sources to answer the questions. So, it is crucial to recognize that news articles are valid. Otherwise, conversational systems will spread false information among users. Therefore, automatic fake news detection is a demanding and challenging task in summarization approaches.

7 Conclusion

In conclusion, the capabilities of large language models (LLMs) including zero-shot, few-shot prompt, and retrieval-augmented generation have demonstrated improvements in both inference time and performance of timeline summarization (TLS) methods, outperforming traditional multi-document optimization and Markov clustering-based approaches in the news domain. Several challenges of news timeline summarization were partially addressed in existing methods. For example, the CHRONOS method, an event-driven approach highlighted that retrieving an excessive number of relevant articles beyond a certain threshold can introduce redundancy into the generated timeline summary. It also proposed a self-questioning mechanism using the few-shot capability of LLMs to extract articles iteratively, thereby enhancing adaptability to newly emerging events and supporting the maintenance of a joint representation of topic-specific articles. Despite these advancements, several critical research areas remain open. These include the development of multi-timeline summarization systems tailored to individual users or user segments, managing the dynamic and evolving nature of news content, handling varying versions of events reported by different sources, and mitigating the impact of fake news and disinformation which can highly compromise the reliability and utility of timeline summaries.

References

1. Ghalandari, G., Ifrim, G.: Examining the state-of-the-art in news timeline summarization. In: Jurafsky, D., et al. (eds.) Proceedings of the 58th Annual Meeting of the Association for Computational Linguistics, pp. 1322–1334 Association for Computational Linguistics (2020). https://doi.org/10.18653/v1/2020.acl-main.122
2. Hu, Q., et al.: From moments to milestones: incremental timeline summarization leveraging large language models. In: Ku, L.-W., et al. (eds.) Proceedings of the 62nd Annual Meeting of the Association for Computational Linguistics (Volume 1: Long Papers), pp. 7232–7246 Association for Computational Linguistics (2024). https://doi.org/10.18653/v1/2024.acl-long.390

3. Sojitra, D., et al.: Timeline summarization in the era of LLMs. In: Proceedings of the 47th International ACM SIGIR Conference on Research and Development in Information Retrieval, pp. 2657–2661 Association for Computing Machinery (2024). https://doi.org/10.1145/3626772.3657899
4. Qorib, M.R., et al.: Just what you desire: constrained timeline summarization with self-reflection for enhanced relevance. Presented at the (2024). https://arxiv.org/abs/2412.17408
5. Wu, W., et al.: Unfolding the Headline: Iterative Self-Questioning for News Retrieval and Timeline Summarization (2025). https://arxiv.org/abs/2501.00888
6. Ghalandari, D.: Revisiting the centroid-based method: a strong baseline for multi-document summarization. In: Proceedings of the Workshop on New Frontiers in Summarization, pp. 85–90 (2017). https://doi.org/10.18653/v1/W17-4511
7. Cabot, P.-L., Navigli, R.: Relation extraction by end-to-end language generation. In: Findings of the Association for Computational Linguistics: EMNLP 2021, pp. 2370–2381 (2021). https://doi.org/10.18653/v1/2021.findings-emnlp.204
8. Martschat, S., Markert, K.: A temporally sensitive submodularity framework for timeline summarization. In: Proceedings of the 22nd Conference on Computational Natural Language Learning, pp. 230–240 (2018). https://doi.org/10.18653/v1/K18-1023
9. Martschat, S., Markert, K.: Improving ROUGE for timeline summarization. In: Proceedings of the 15th Conference of the European Chapter of the Association for Computational Linguistics: Volume 2, Short Papers, pp. 285–290 (2017)
10. Tran, B., et al.: Predicting relevant news events for timeline summaries. In: Proceedings of the 22nd International Conference on World Wide Web, pp. 91–92 (2013). https://doi.org/10.1145/2487788.2487829
11. Zhang, T., et al.: Benchmarking Large Language Models for News Summarization (2023). https://arxiv.org/abs/2301.1384
12. Li, M., et al.: Timeline summarization based on event graph compression via time-aware optimal transport. In: Proceedings of the 2021 Conference on Empirical Methods in Natural Language Processing, pp. 6443–6456 (2021). https://doi.org/10.18653/v1/2021.emnlp-main.519
13. Tran, G., Alrifai, M., Herder, E.: Timeline summarization from relevant headlines. In: Hanbury, A., Kazai, G., Rauber, A., Fuhr, N. (eds.) ECIR 2015. LNCS, vol. 9022, pp. 245–256. Springer, Cham (2015). https://doi.org/10.1007/978-3-319-16354-3_26
14. Yu, Y., et al.: Multi-timeline summarization (MTLS): improving timeline summarization by generating multiple summaries. In: Proceedings of the 59th Annual Meeting of the Association for Computational Linguistics and the 11th International Joint Conference on Natural Language Processing (Volume 1: Long Papers), pp. 377–387 (2021). https://doi.org/10.18653/v1/2021.acl-long.32
15. Schröder, K.: What do news readers really want to read about? How relevance works for news audiences. Digital News Project (2019)
16. Henke, J., et al.: How can journalists promote news credibility? Effects of evidences on trust and credibility. Journal. Pract. **14**(3), 299–318 (2020). https://doi.org/10.1080/17512786.2019.1605839

QA2HALL: A Framework for Generating Non-trivial Hallucination Detection Datasets from KGQA Datasets

Kosuke Nakamura[1], Rie Hasegawa[2], Kotaro Otomura[1], Ryutaro Ichise[2], and Jumpei Hato[1](✉)

[1] Information Technology R&D Center, Mitsubishi Electric Corporation, Kamakura, Kanagawa, Japan
nakamura.kosuke@ds.mitsubishielectric.co.jp,
otomura.kotaro@df.mitsubishielectric.co.jp,
hato.jumpei@ea.mitsubishielectric.co.jp

[2] School of Engineering, Institute of Science Tokyo, Meguro-ku, Tokyo, Japan
hasegawa.r.ak@m.titech.ac.jp, ichise@iee.e.titech.ac.jp

Abstract. The use of large language models (LLMs) is rapidly increasing. However, in enterprise settings, factuality hallucinations due to a lack of specialized knowledge in LLMs pose a significant issue. To address this, methods that verify text using knowledge graphs (KGs) as external knowledge have been proposed. KGs excel as comparison targets for detecting contradictions since they can accurately describe facts. Developing these methods requires text data containing hallucinations and aligned with KGs. However, existing datasets use hallucinations mainly generated by replacing entities in the text with randomly selected entities from the KGs, which may differ from those actually generated by LLMs and can be easily detectable. Additionally, constructing text corresponding to the facts in a KG is labor-intensive. Therefore, we propose QA2HALL, a framework for generating hallucination detection datasets based on existing knowledge graph question answering (KGQA) datasets. QA2HALL enables semi-automatic generation of text that includes non-trivial contradictions and corresponds to the KGs. This is achieved by utilizing incorrect answers actually generated by LLMs in response to questions from the KGQA datasets. Using this framework, we construct a new hallucination detection dataset and conduct experiments, confirming its practicality and challenge compared to the existing method.

Keywords: Hallucination · Knowledge Graph · Large Language Model

1 Introduction

Recently, the use of large language models (LLMs) has been rapidly increasing, but hallucinations have become a significant issue. Hallucinations refer to outputs that contradict facts or user inputs, or are nonsensical, posing risks such as

R. Ichise (Ed.): NLDB 2025, LNCS 15836, pp. 380–395, 2026.
https://doi.org/10.1007/978-3-031-97141-9_26

misinformation and inappropriate decision-making. In enterprise settings, LLMs likely lack specialized internal information, increasing the risk of factuality hallucinations. Although there are various types of hallucinations [11,21,29], this study focuses on text contradicting facts, which are considered particularly likely to occur under such situations.

Detecting hallucinations in generated text is a major approach to address this issue [21]. Specifically, several methods have been proposed to detect factuality hallucinations by comparing the generated text with a knowledge graph (KG) [5,8,10]. Utilizing external knowledge for text verification allows for detecting hallucinations tailored to specific tasks, domains, and the latest context, without the need to train the detection model itself. KGs, in particular, are advantageous as comparison targets for detecting contradictions due to their structured data and accurate representation of facts. Additionally, users can easily define and manage the scope of the underlying knowledge with KGs.

Datasets for hallucination detection corresponding to KGs are necessary for developing and evaluating such methods. Existing datasets primarily use the perturbation strategy, where entities in the text are replaced with randomly selected entities from the KG to construct sentences that contradict facts in the KG [5,18]. However, such contradictions may be trivial and easily detectable, differing from actual hallucinations generated by language models. Moreover, these contradictions can be resolved using the internal knowledge of the language model alone [10], making them unsuitable for evaluating methods that leverage KG information for hallucination detection. Also, constructing text data corresponding to facts in a KG is labor-intensive and requires expertise for annotation.

To address these issues, we propose the framework QA2HALL to generate text data containing non-trivial hallucinations aligned with facts in KGs, based on existing knowledge graph question answering (KGQA) datasets. KGQA is a task where answers are obtained by querying a KG in response to a question, and various methods and datasets have been reported [3,9,12,22,26]. Questions in KGQA datasets are designed to be answerable using the facts in the corresponding KGs, with main entities included in the KGs. Thus, using text from existing KGQA datasets saves the effort of preparing text aligned with the KG from scratch. In QA2HALL, we collect incorrect answers by having an LLM answer the questions from the KGQA dataset, thereby obtaining non-trivial errors actually generated by the LLM. The questions are converted into declarative sentences with the correct answers, which are then replaced with the generated incorrect answers to generate text containing non-trivial contradictions.

Our main contributions in this study can be summarized as follows:

- We propose a semi-automatic framework for constructing datasets for factuality hallucination detection with KGs. The framework uses existing KGQA datasets and actual errors generated by LLMs to produce text containing non-trivial hallucinations and aligned with KGs with minimal effort.

- Using this framework, we constructed a dataset for the detection task. The dataset and the framework are publicly available[1].
- Through experiments measuring the performance of hallucination detection on the datasets constructed using QA2HALL and existing perturbation strategies, we confirmed that hallucinations generated by the proposed method present a more challenging task.

In the following sections, we first introduce related work in Sect. 2, then explain the proposed QA2HALL in Sect. 3, detailing the process of constructing the dataset and providing qualitative analysis results of the obtained dataset. In Sect. 4, we conduct experimental evaluations on the constructed dataset and discuss the results. Finally, in Sect. 5, we conclude this study.

2 Related Work

In this section, we first review previous hallucination datasets and compare them with the framework proposed in this paper. Secondly, to concretize the proposed dataset's use, we review methods for mitigating or detecting hallucinations. Finally, since our proposed framework QA2HALL constructs datasets based on KGQA datasets, we briefly introduce existing KGQA datasets and provide a detailed explanation of KQA Pro [3], which is employed in this study.

Hallucination Datasets for Evaluating LLM. There are two main approaches to creating datasets for evaluating and analyzing hallucinations in LLMs: (i) an approach where data generated by LLMs is annotated by humans or LLMs. (ii) an approach where entities are replaced using a KG to create data containing hallucinations artificially. Examples of datasets created using approach (i) include HaDeS [17], HaluEval [16], and HaluEval 2.0 [15]. HaDeS is a hallucination dataset with about 11,000 data points created by annotating sentences from Wikipedia. Some words in the collected sentences are replaced using BERT [6] and GPT-2 [20], and then crowdsourced to determine hallucinations. After that, detection model is trained on this data to sample the balanced and non-trivial data. HaluEval and HaluEval 2.0 propose two strategies for generating hallucination data: one involves the intentional creation of hallucinated sentences using commercial LLMs, while the other relies on human annotation of LLM-generated output sentences. HaluEval includes content from various datasets and corpora, such as the instruction data for Alpaca [23]. HaluEval 2.0 applies these methods to specialized fields (e.g., biomedicine) to create domain-specific data.

FADE [5] and GraphEval [18] are examples of datasets created using approach (ii). FADE creates hallucination data using a perturbation strategy that replaces entities in sentences. Based on the OpenDialKG [19] dialogue dataset,

[1] Dataset: https://doi.org/10.5281/zenodo.15278335, Code for the flamework: https://github.com/Kosuke-Nakamura-MELCO/qa2hall, Code for the experiments: https://github.com/ichise-laboratory/cokglm.

entities are replaced with incorrect ones sampled from a KG. There are two main replacement strategies: Extrinsic and Intrinsic. In the Extrinsic strategy, entities of the same class as the target entity but not in the input sub-graph or dialogue history are searched from the entire KG and replaced. In the Intrinsic strategy, entities are selected and replaced from those in the 1-hop sub-graph centered on the target entity. GraphEval [18] samples triples from DBPedia and creates sentences that represent the meaning of those triples using templates generated by GPT-4. Additionally, by randomly replacing some of the entities in the triples with other entities from DBPedia through negative sampling, artificial hallucination data is created. This strategy creates a hallucination dataset where entities in the sentences correspond to the KG.

Datasets from approach (i) involve filtering or annotating LLM-generated hallucination data, which may not necessarily align with external knowledge bases. Approach (ii) uses KGs, ensuring better alignment but potentially creating trivial data for LLMs. Our framework guarantees that entities related to hallucinations in sentences are included in KG and creates non-trivial datasets since they are based on actual LLM hallucinations.

Remedy for LLM's Hallucination Using KG. RAG (Retrieval Augmented Generation) [14] mitigates hallucinations in LLMs by using relevant text from external databases. KGs can be also used as the external database, like in GraphRAG [7]. Regarding that detecting hallucinations in LLMs by using KGs, it is necessary to integrate graph-form and text-form data. One approach is to create a temporary KG for each input and output text and measure discrepancies using Graph Neural Networks [8]. However, this method struggles if both input and output contain the same false information. Another method [28] involves providing information from external sources to another LLM to correct factuality, but it does not effectively utilize the structural information of KGs. To address these issues, methods like CoKGLM [10] integrate graph structure and text embeddings, combining structural and textual information for robust hallucination detection.

Since our dataset is a hallucination dataset aligned with KGs, it can be utilized in many of the methods mentioned here. However, it is particularly well-suited for methods such as CoKGLM that can effectively utilize both the structural information of graphs and textual information.

Knowledge Graph Question Answering Dataset. Various KGQA datasets have been developed, such as manually created ones [26], those derived from SPARQL queries and grammatical rules [4], and those produced using template slot filling [3,9,22]. In this study, we employed KQA Pro [3] as the KGQA dataset for constructing our dataset. KQA Pro is one of the KGQA datasets created through automatic question generation by slot filling and manual paraphrasing, resulting in a diverse and extensive collection of natural questions. Additionally, it provides a reasonably sized knowledge graph corresponding to the knowledge handled in the questions, making it suitable for verifying hallucination detection methods using knowledge graphs. Note that the QA2HALL can be applied to most KGQA datasets. Below, we describe KQA Pro.

KQA Pro's automatic question generation consists of two stages: locating and asking. In the locating stage, phrases that refer to a specific entity or set of entities are generated by filling placeholders in seven types of templates. For example, by filling the template "the <C> that <P> <E>" with the concept "the human", the relation "is spouse of", and the entity "Loretta Young", they obtain the expression "the human that is spouse of Loretta Young" which "locates" a specific entity ("Jean Louis"). In the asking stage, the phrases referring to entities obtained in the locating stage are combined with nine types of questioning expressions such as "Count" or "What/Who is" to complete the questions. For example, filling the template "Who is <E>" with the phrase obtained from the locating stage yields the question "Who is the human that is spouse of Loretta Young?" Additionally, only questions with a single correct answer are preserved.

After generating base questions, they were paraphrased through crowdsourcing without changing their meaning. The paraphrased results were then manually checked, and low-quality ones were excluded, resulting in 117,970 questions.

Furthermore, KQA Pro provides a knowledge graph based on FB15k-237 [24], widely used as a benchmark dataset for link prediction, and Wikidata [27]. This graph is a subset of Wikidata, mapping entities in FB15k-237 to Wikidata and adding 3,000 more entities.

3 Approach

3.1 Task Definition

In this study, we focus on the task of detecting factuality hallucinations in responses generated by LLMs. More specifically, we define hallucinations as contents described in a sentence that contradict the facts contained in the corresponding KG. We treat hallucination detection as a binary classification task that identifies whether a sentence contains those hallucinations. Generally, the term "hallucination" can also include cases where the user's input and the LLM's output are inconsistent. However, this study does not address such cases.

Whether a sentence contains hallucination is defined as follows. If any of facts expressed in a sentence are not included in the KG, the sentence is considered to contain hallucinations. Therefore, a sentence is judged to contain hallucination not only if it includes facts that directly contradict the facts in the KG, but also if it includes facts that cannot be verified as correct based on the facts in the KG. In enterprise setting, it is important to detect outputs that contain content not anticipated by the users. Thus, this setting is considered reasonable.

3.2 QA2HALL Framework

In this section, we describe the procedure for creating a hallucination detection dataset using our proposed framework, QA2HALL.

QA2HALL constructs a hallucination detection dataset based on a KGQA dataset. The questions in KGQA datasets are generally designed to be answerable using the facts in the corresponding KGs, and the main entities mentioned in the questions are typically guaranteed to be included in the KGs. Therefore, by generating text that includes hallucinations based on the questions in the KGQA datasets, we can create a dataset suitable for the task of detecting inconsistencies between the text and KG. Figure 1 shows the overall procedure of the QA2HALL framework which consists of the following four main steps.

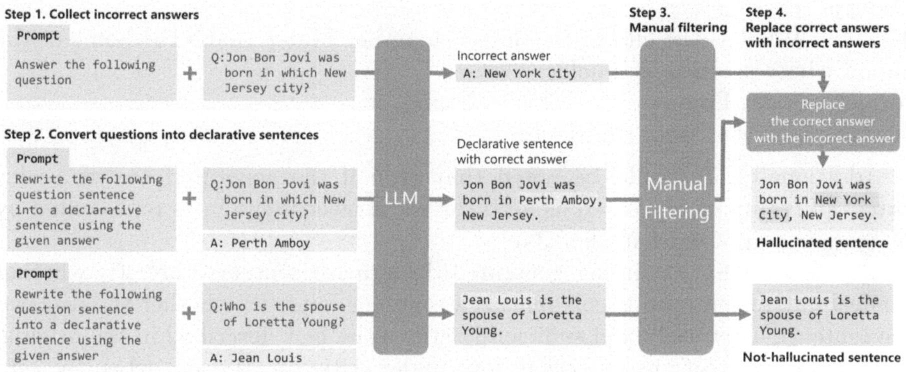

Fig. 1. Overview of the QA2HALL framework. Prompts described in this are not actual prompts we used.

Step 1. Collect incorrect answers. In this step, we provide the LLM with questions from the KGQA dataset along with prompts instructing it to answer the questions. The responses are instructed to be output as a single noun or noun phrase. We preserve only the generated answers that does not match the given correct answers and whose indicated entity exists in the KG. The determination of matching with the correct answer and the confirmation of the entity's existence are performed simply through string matching. By collecting questions that the LLM actually answered incorrectly through this procedure, it becomes possible to generate text containing hallucinations that are difficult for language models to judge based solely on its internal knowledge.

Step 2. Convert questions into declarative sentence. In this step, we input the questions from the KGQA dataset into the LLM, along with their correct answers and instructions to convert them into declarative sentences. To ensure that the substitution process can be applied later, we check whether the corresponding correct answer is included as a string within each of the obtained declarative sentences, and we retain only those declarative sentences that meet this criterion. As described above, by generating declarative sentences based on questions associated with the KG, we can obtain sentences that include hallucinations and are corresponding to the KG with minimal effort.

Step 3. Manual filtering. In this step, we manually evaluate the validity of all incorrect answers and declarative sentences obtained from the previous two steps and filter out inappropriate ones. The criteria for excluding incorrect answers are: (i) whether the incorrect answer is correctly formed as a single noun or noun phrase, and (ii) whether the incorrect answer is not significantly different from the original correct answer. Exclusions under criterion (i) occur when the answer contains extraneous strings or is truncated. Exclusions under criterion (ii) occur when the generated answer belongs to an entirely different class than the original answer, such as a person instead of a city, as shown in Example 1.

Example 1.
Question: What is the city of the Joined together States that's the home of the human whose position is infielder?
Correct answer: Fremont
Generated answer: Alex Rodriguez

Additionally, it should be noted that even if the generated answer seems correct in reality, it is treated as an incorrect answer if the facts represented by the answer do not exist in the KG.

The criteria for excluding generated declarative sentences are: (i) whether the declarative sentence is coherent as a sentence, and (ii) whether the declarative sentence accurately and sufficiently states the fact described in the original question and correct answer. Exclusions under criterion (i) occur when the sentence contains extraneous strings, is truncated, or is grammatically incorrect. Example 2 shows a sample excluded according to criterion (ii). The question and correct answer state that Tom Johnson is a member of Republican Party, but this is omitted in the generated declarative sentence.

Example 2.
Question: What is the name of the Republican Party member whose birth place is Oakland?
Correct answer: Tom Johnson
Generated declarative sentence: Tom Johnson's birth place is Oakland.

Step 4. Replace correct answers with incorrect answer. In this step, for each declarative sentence obtained, if a valid incorrect answer corresponding to the question is also available, we replace the span corresponding to the original correct answer with the incorrect answer, thereby creating a hallucinated sentence. The hallucinated sentences obtained in this manner are used as positive examples for hallucination detection, and the declarative sentences corresponding to questions for which no incorrect answer was obtained are used as negative examples, thus creating a binary classification dataset.

3.3 Dataset Construction

Using the framework described above, we created a dataset for hallucination detection with a KG. In the following, we will explain how each step of the framework was implemented and the results obtained.

Base Dataset. As mentioned in Sect. 2, we employed KQA Pro as the base KGQA dataset. We used only the training and validation sets of KQA Pro because the answers for the test set are not provided. KQA Pro includes not only questions that simply ask for the entities but also questions that ask about numerical comparisons or count the number of relevant entities. However, to simplify the problem in our study, we only adopted questions that do not involve numerical handling and require a single entity answer. Questions that include references to qualifiers were also excluded. The total number of questions used was 3,174. Also, we use the KG which KQA Pro provides as is for constructing our dataset. The main statistics of the KG are shown in Table 1.

Table 1. Statistics of KQA Pro KG. Although this KG includes attributes, literal values, and qualifiers, we do not use these elements in this study. Therefore, only information related to relational facts is provided here. Additionally, nodes referred to as "concepts" in the original paper [3] are also counted as entities here.

# Entities	# Relations	# Triples
17,754	363	415,334

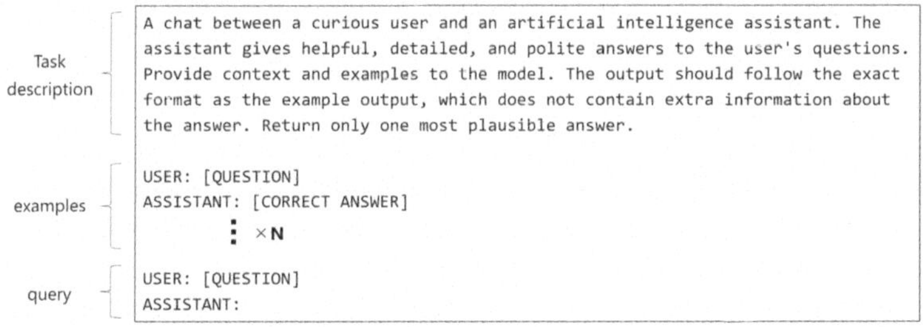

Fig. 2. The prompt for collecting incorrect answers. [·] symbols placeholders for the respective elements written inside them.

Step 1 and 2. For answering questions and converting them into declarative sentences, we used Vicuna 13b-v1.5 [30] as the LLM. Vicuna is one of the major open-source LLMs and is a fine-tuned model based on Llama2 [25] through instruction fine-tuning. Note that QA2HALL is a model-agnostic framework, allowing the use of any LLM, including closed models.

When prompting the model to answer questions, we used few-shot in-context learning [2] to encourage the output to follow a format that produces a single noun or noun phrase as much as possible. The prompt for question answering is shown in Fig. 2. We provided five examples, randomly selected from all the questions. For converting to declarative sentences, we employed zero-shot prompt to avoid imposing restrictions on the style of the generated sentences. The prompt used for conversion to declarative sentences is shown in Fig. 3.

```
Rewrite the following question sentence into declarative sentence
by using the given answer of it.
# Question sentence
[QUESTION]
# Answer
[ANSWER]
# Output
```

Fig. 3. The prompt for converting questions into declarative sentences. [·] symbols are placeholders for the respective elements written inside them.

Table 2. Examples of the questions, correct answers, generated incorrect answers, and generated declarative sentences.

Question	Correct ans.	Gen. ans.	Declarative sent.
Which city was Al Jourgensen born in?	Havana	Chicago	Chicago is the city where Al Jourgensen was born.
In which US city was Johnny Mercer (the one that has the occupation of composer) born?	Savannah	Atlanta	Atlanta is the US city where Johnny Mercer, the composer, was born.
Which person was educated at Valparaiso University?	John Lutz	Sharon Stone	Sharon Stone was educated at Valparaiso University.

Step 3. The generated incorrect answers and declarative sentences were evaluated and filtered by two non-native English speakers with sufficient English reading comprehension. Additionally, samples where the original question and correct answer were too unnatural or contained typographical errors were manually excluded at this step. We obtained 1,920 valid declarative sentences, including 480 with valid incorrect answers.

Step 4. Among the 1,920 adopted declarative sentences, for the 480 sentences with valid incorrect answers, we replaced the span corresponding to the correct answer in the sentence with the corresponding incorrect answer. This resulted in 480 hallucinated and 1,440 non-hallucinated declarative sentences.

3.4 Analysis

Table 2 shows examples of the original questions, the correct answers, the generated incorrect answers, and the generated declarative sentences. The samples in rows 1 and 2 are clear examples demonstrating that the generated sentences contain practical hallucinations. In the sample from the first row, the actual correct answer is "Havana", but the generated incorrect answer is "Chicago". "Al Jourgensen", mentioned in the question, was born in Havana, but his band was formed in Chicago, making this a plausible error. In the sample from the second row, the actual correct answer is "Savannah", but the generated incorrect

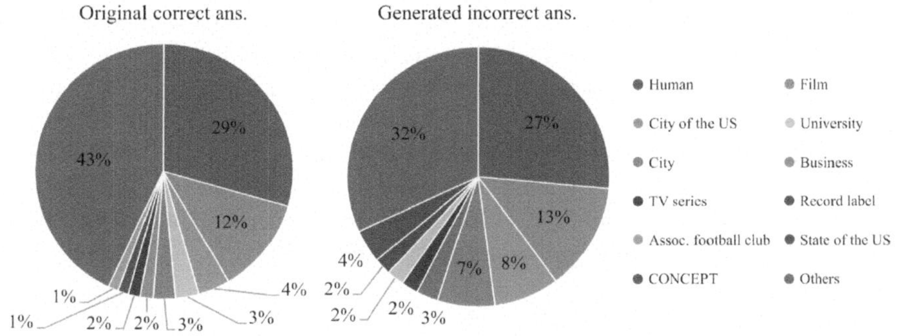

Fig. 4. The types of entities for the correct answers to the original questions in the preserved samples, and the types of entities for the incorrect answers generated by the LLM. "CONCEPT" indicates that the generated answer referred to a node called a concept in the original KG.

answer is "Atlanta". Both are cities in Georgia, and answering with the larger city, Atlanta, can be considered a realistic error. Hallucinations based on such incorrect answers are non-trivial, and detecting them is considered practical. For the question in the third row, there can be multiple correct answers in reality, but only "John Lutz" fits according to the KQA Pro KG. Detecting hallucinations from such samples requires appropriately utilizing the information from the KG. Therefore, these samples are considered effective for evaluating whether a hallucination detection model can handle the information from the KG.

Figure 4 shows the proportions of entity types for the original correct answers and the generated incorrect answers in the constructed dataset. Here, the types of entities refer to what was called "concepts" in the original KQA Pro paper, using the concepts that were actually connected to the target entities with an "instanceOf" relationship in the KQA Pro KG. While entities such as humans, films, and cities are dominant, the high proportion of "Others" indicates that the dataset contains hallucinations about various types of entities.

4 Validation

In this section, we validate the proposed framework by conducting experiments to detect hallucinations on the dataset constructed in the previous section.

4.1 Hallucination Detection Model

We evaluated hallucination detection performance using CoKGLM [10], which integrates KGs as external knowledge into LMs to identify factual inconsistencies. The framework consists of two modules: KG Retrieval and Fact Verification. The KG retrieval module retrieves the top-k triples most relevant to the input text from the KG. The Fact Verification module, modified based on a LM and adopting an embedding approach to integrate KG, assesses the factual discrepancies by comparing the input text to the retrieved triples. In the implementation, the detection model supports both LM-only detection and KG-enhanced detection, where k triples are selected from the KG for fact verification.

Instead of directly prompting KG information into LLMs, CoKGLM uses an embedding-based approach to link textual data with KG data and merge them effectively. Despite using simple retrieval methods and BART [13] for implementation, CoKGLM has shown strong and reliable performance on perturbation-based dataset [10]. This makes it suitable for analyzing behavioral differences when handling LLM-derived hallucinations from QA2HALL.

4.2 Experimental Settings

We conducted controlled experiments using three datasets: our dataset obtained by applying QA2HALL to KQA Pro (denoted as KQA Pro+QA2HALL), and two additional datasets. The additional datasets were also synthetically generated using the FADE [5] perturbation approach on two base datasets, OpenDialKG [19] and KQA Pro, referred as OpenDialKG+FADE and KQA Pro+FADE, respectively.

OpenDialKG is a KG-based question-answering dataset consisting of conversational data linked to Freebase [1]. It shares similar topics with KQA Pro, such as movies, books, sports, and music. We used 10,685 samples from OpenDialKG in total. We employed FADE's Extrinsic approach, which systematically introduces hallucinations by replacing a specific entity in the text with another entity of the same type from the KG. By comparing the sub-graph similarity between the original entity and candidate entities in the KG, we selected the entity with the highest similarity to ensure plausible yet incorrect replacements for creating hallucinated samples. Importantly, the hallucinations were restricted to a single entity per text. Since KQA Pro originally only contains question sentences and their answers, we applied FADE to the declarative sentences generated from KQA Pro in the previous section. Additionally, to align with KQA Pro+QA2HALL, we targeted the same entities for replacement during the perturbation process for KQA Pro+FADE. This ensured that the hallucinations were introduced in the same locations for a fair comparison.

Four experiments were conducted on all datasets: evaluating the performance of CoKGLM's BART component alone, and with KG integration using 5, 10, and 20 triples. All detected entities in the text are individually verified. If any entity is determined to be hallucinated, the input text is considered hallucinated. Each text is annotated as either hallucinated or not-hallucinated, framing the task as a binary classification problem. The evaluation was performed using 5-fold cross validation, and the average of Accuracy, Precision, Recall, and F1 score over five validations were calculated.

We conducted comparative experiments from two perspectives:

- Evaluating the Overall Performance of the Perturbation-based Data: We evaluated the performance on FADE-based datasets generated from OpenDialKG and KQA Pro. This aimed to assess the effectiveness of the perturbation method in generating hallucinations across different base datasets with shared thematic domains.

- Comparing LLM-derived Data with Perturbation-based Data: We compared performance on QA2HALL-based and FADE-based datasets. This aimed to highlight differences in complexity and detection challenges between hallucinations sourced from actual LLM outputs and systematic perturbation.

Through these experiments, we aim to assess the difficulty QA2HALL presents to the current detection model, thereby validating its effectiveness.

Table 3. Evaluating the overall performance of the three types of data. Here, the values in parentheses indicate the standard deviation. **Bold** and underlined entries denote the highest and the lowest scores in each column, respectively.

Dataset	# Triples	Accuracy		Precision		Recall		F1	
OpenDialKG + FADE	-	0.839	(0.020)	0.559	(0.055)	0.693	(0.055)	0.616	(0.025)
	5	0.928	(0.0076)	0.818	(0.056)	0.794	(0.049)	0.803	(0.0078)
	10	**0.942**	(0.0020)	**0.863**	(0.011)	**0.814**	(0.071)	**0.837**	(0.0044)
	20	0.939	(0.0073)	0.848	(0.013)	0.813	(0.033)	0.829	(0.016)
KQA Pro + FADE	-	0.723	(0.034)	0.369	(0.049)	0.280	(0.12)	0.299	(0.077)
	5	0.751	(0.032)	0.462	(0.068)	0.514	(0.069)	0.481	(0.037)
	10	0.760	(0.025)	0.482	(0.043)	0.655	(0.060)	0.552	(0.0064)
	20	0.742	(0.040)	0.456	(0.033)	0.675	(0.10)	0.541	(0.034)
KQA Pro + QA2HALL	-	0.711	(0.036)	0.454	(0.12)	0.169	(0.082)	0.230	(0.078)
	5	0.695	(0.020)	0.436	(0.057)	0.399	(0.17)	0.399	(0.093)
	10	0.679	(0.026)	0.404	(0.071)	0.377	(0.090)	0.383	(0.059)
	20	0.701	(0.060)	0.444	(0.13)	0.338	(0.10)	0.377	(0.11)

4.3 Result and Discussion

Table 3 shows CoKGLM's performance on each dataset. The "# Triples" column indicates the experimental settings: the LM-only detection and the KG-enhanced detection, where 5, 10, or 20 triples are retrieved and used for fact verification.

CoKGLM consistently achieves higher scores across all metrics on the FADE-based datasets compared to the QA2HALL-based dataset, with specifically lower standard deviations in recall and F1 scores. This indicates that hallucinations generated using the perturbation strategy are systematic and predictable, as the hallucinations are introduced in a structured manner based on subgraph similarities within the KG.

We analyzed false negative samples in the "KQA Pro+QA2HALL" data, focusing on cases where the detection model failed on QA2HALL-based data but succeeded on FADE-based data. To remove the influence of the internal knowledge of LM that used for CoKGLM, we specifically collected samples that the model failed to detect in both datasets under the LM-only detection setting. This comparison highlights how detection performance varies between the two types of hallucination-sourcing methods.

Table 4 provides examples of such cases, showing two main patterns in FADE-based data where it outperforms QA2HALL-based data. The first pattern is inappropriate hallucinated entities. In the QA2HALL-based data, the hallucinated entity "Kentucky" fits the expected entity type of a city name. However, in the FADE-based data, the hallucinated entity "Susannah York" is a person name, which does not align with the context. This mismatch makes the sentence contextually nonsensical, making it easier for the model to identify. While improving NER accuracy could help select more appropriate entities, such issues may still persist due to inherent challenges in aligning entity semantics with context.

Table 4. Examples of the same base data sample where detection failed with QA2HALL-based data but succeeded with FADE-based data. The *italicized text* indicates the respective hallucinated entities. The number following the hallucinated entity indicates the number of surrounding triples in KG.

KQA Pro+QA2HALL FN samples	KQA Pro+FADE TP samples	Reason of performance difference
Kentucky is the administrative territorial entity that has the capital of Bowling Green.	*Susannah York* is the administrative territorial entity that has the capital of Bowling Green.	Inappropriate hallucinated entity in FADE data. *Kentucky*: 56 *Susannah York*: 22
Helen Hunt is a cast member of the television film with the director Richard Benjamin.	*Martha Plimpton* is a cast member of the television film with the director Richard Benjamin.	Fewer surrounding information in FADE data. *Helen Hunt*: 27 *Martha Plimpton*: 11

The second pattern is the surrounding information of the hallucinated entity. Specifically, the number of surrounding triples in the KG for hallucinated entities in FADE is often fewer than those in QA2HALL. This is because QA2HALL-based hallucinations are generated from LLMs, which often produce well-learned and information-rich entities, resulting in more surrounding triples in the KG. In contrast, FADE-based hallucinations, generated through similarity calculations, occasionally include entities with fewer surrounding triples in the KG. Since the detection model retrieves semantically relevant triples from the surrounding subgraph, entities with fewer surrounding triples can reduce retrieval complexity, making it easier to extract useful information for detection. Additionally, such patterns could represent a common challenge for retrieve-based detection models.

Consequently, perturbation-based hallucinations tend to be more straightforward, as the detection model can effectively recognize the predictable patterns of artificially generated hallucinations, resulting in high scores. In contrast,

QA2HALL introduces more complex and contextually nuanced hallucination patterns, posing more challenges for current detection model.

Another notable observation is that CoKGLM performs particularly better on OpenDialKG than on KQA Pro. This difference is due to the nature of these base datasets. OpenDialKG is a dialogue dataset providing more context to detect hallucinations. Moreover, the hallucinated declarative sentences generated from KQA Pro used in this experiment are those where the LLM gave incorrect answers to the questions they are based on. Even when the LLM-generated hallucinated entities are replaced with others to create FADE-based datasets, some of the underlying complexity and unpredictability that caused the LLM's errors remain. These make the KQA Pro-based datasets more challenging for the detection model, necessitating more effective use of KG information, as demonstrated by the lower scores achieved by CoKGLM in the LM-only detection setting.

5 Conclusion

In this paper, we proposed QA2HALL, a framework for semi-automatic generation of text data with non-trivial hallucinations corresponding to a KG. QA2HALL leverages existing KGQA datasets and questions incorrectly answered by LLMs, generating practical hallucination-containing text data aligned with the KG with minimal effort. Furthermore, we constructed a dataset using this framework and experimentally demonstrated that it yields more practical hallucinations compared to datasets created using the conventional method.

Limitations. While QA2HALL provides a means to construct datasets containing non-trivial hallucinations, we also acknowledge several limitations of our study. Firstly, this study addresses only a limited range of hallucinations that LLMs can generate. Specifically, it does not handle hallucinations that cannot be represented by entity substitution. Secondly, the dataset was created using only one LLM. Since question types and error patterns vary by model and training data, it is desirable to have datasets generated using various LLMs.

References

1. Bollacker, K., Evans, C., Paritosh, P., Sturge, T., Taylor, J.: Freebase: a collaboratively created graph database for structuring human knowledge. In: Proceedings of the ACM SIGMOD International Conference on Management of Data, pp. 1247–1250 (2008)
2. Brown, T., et al.: Language models are few-shot learners. In: Advances in NeurIPS, vol. 33, pp. 1877–1901 (2020)
3. Cao, S., et al.: KQA Pro: a dataset with explicit compositional programs for complex question answering over knowledge base. In: Proceedings of the 60th Annual Meeting of the ACL, pp. 6101–6119 (2022)
4. Cui, R., Aralikatte, R., Lent, H., Hershcovich, D.: Compositional generalization in multilingual semantic parsing over wikidata. Trans. Assoc. Comput. Linguist. **10**, 937–955 (2022)

5. Das, S., Saha, S., Srihari, R.: Diving deep into modes of fact hallucinations in dialogue systems. In: Findings of the Association for Computational Linguistics: EMNLP, pp. 684–699 (2022)
6. Devlin, J., Chang, M.W., Lee, K., Toutanova, K.: BERT: pre-training of deep bidirectional transformers for language understanding. In: Proceedings of the Conference of the NAACL-HLT, vol. 1, pp. 4171–4186 (2019)
7. Edge, D., et al.: From local to global: a graph rag approach to query-focused summarization. arXiv preprint arXiv:2404.16130 (2024)
8. Furumai, K., Wang, Y., Shinohara, M., Ikeda, K., Yu, Y., Kato, T.: Detecting dialogue hallucination using graph neural networks. In: Proceedings of the ICMLA, pp. 871–877 (2023)
9. Gu, Y., et al.: Beyond I.I.D.: three levels of generalization for question answering on knowledge bases. In: Proceedings of the Web Conference, pp. 3477–3488 (2021)
10. Hasegawa, R., Ichise, R.: CoKGLM: detecting hallucinations generated by large language models via knowledge graph verification. In: Proceedings of the 6th KGSWC (2024)
11. Ji, Z., et al.: Survey of hallucination in natural language generation. ACM Comput. Surv. **55**(12), 1–38 (2023)
12. Lan, Y., He, G., Jiang, J., Jiang, J., Zhao, W.X., Wen, J.R.: A survey on complex knowledge base question answering: methods, challenges and solutions. In: Proceedings of the 13th IJCAI, pp. 4483–4491 (2021)
13. Lewis, M., et al.: BART: denoising sequence-to-sequence pre-training for natural language generation, translation, and comprehension. In: Proceedings of the 58th Annual Meeting of the ACL, pp. 7871–7880 (2020)
14. Lewis, P., et al.: Retrieval-augmented generation for knowledge-intensive NLP tasks. In: Advances in NeurIPS, vol. 33, pp. 9459–9474 (2020)
15. Li, J., et al.: The dawn after the dark: an empirical study on factuality hallucination in large language models. In: Proceedings of the 62nd Annual Meeting of the ACL, pp. 10879–10899 (2024)
16. Li, J., Cheng, X., Zhao, X., Nie, J.Y., Wen, J.R.: HaluEval: a large-scale hallucination evaluation benchmark for large language models. In: Proceedings of the Conference on EMNLP, pp. 6449–6464 (2023)
17. Liu, T., et al.: A token-level reference-free hallucination detection benchmark for free-form text generation. In: Proceedings of the 60th Annual Meeting of the ACL, pp. 6723–6737 (2022)
18. Liu, X., et al.: Evaluating the factuality of large language models using large-scale knowledge graphs. arXiv preprint arXiv:2404.00942 (2024)
19. Moon, S., Shah, P., Kumar, A., Subba, R.: OpenDialKG: explainable conversational reasoning with attention-based walks over knowledge graphs. In: Proceedings of the 57th Annual Meeting of the ACL, pp. 845–854 (2019)
20. Radford, A., Wu, J., Child, R., Luan, D., Amodei, D., Sutskever, I.: Language models are unsupervised multitask learners. https://openai.com/index/better-language-models. Accessed 07 May 2025
21. Sahoo, P., Meharia, P., Ghosh, A., Saha, S., Jain, V., Chadha, A.: A comprehensive survey of hallucination in large language, image, video and audio foundation models. In: Findings of the Association for Computational Linguistics: EMNLP, pp. 11709–11724 (2024)
22. Saxena, A., Chakrabarti, S., Talukdar, P.: Question answering over temporal knowledge graphs. In: Proceedings of the 59th Annual Meeting of the ACL and the 11th IJCNLP, pp. 6663–6676 (2021)

23. Taori, R., et al.: Stanford alpaca: an instruction-following llama model. https://github.com/tatsu-lab/stanford_alpaca. Accessed 07 May 2025
24. Toutanova, K., Chen, D., Pantel, P., Poon, H., Choudhury, P., Gamon, M.: Representing text for joint embedding of text and knowledge bases. In: Proceedings of the Conference on EMNLP, pp. 1499–1509 (2015)
25. Touvron, H., et al.: Llama 2: open foundation and fine-tuned chat models. arXiv preprint arXiv:2307.09288 (2023)
26. Usbeck, R., et al.: QALD-10–the 10th challenge on question answering over linked data: shifting from dbpedia to wikidata as a kg for KGQA. Semantic Web (2023)
27. Vrandečić, D., Krötzsch, M.: Wikidata: a free collaborative knowledgebase. Commun. ACM **57**(10), 78–85 (2014)
28. Wang, X., Pan, J., Ding, L., Biemann, C.: Mitigating hallucinations in large vision-language models with instruction contrastive decoding. In: Findings of the Association for Computational Linguistics: ACL, pp. 15840–15853 (2024)
29. Zhang, Y., et al.: Siren's song in the AI ocean: a survey on hallucination in large language models. arXiv preprint arXiv:2309.01219 (2023)
30. Zheng, L., et al.: Judging LLM-as-a-judge with MT-bench and chatbot arena. In: Proceedings of the 37th NeurIPS (2024)

Causal Relation-Aware Data Augmentation for Legal Textual Entailment

Huy Chu(✉), Hoang Chu, Phuong Nguyen, and Minh Nguyen

Japan Advanced Institute of Science and Technology, Nomi, Japan
{cqhofsns,nguyenhoangchu,phuongnm,nguyenml}@jaist.ac.jp

Abstract. Legal textual entailment is a critical yet challenging task due to the complex structure and nuanced semantics of legal articles. This task requires not only comprehensive legal text understanding but also advanced reasoning capabilities for effective document structure analysis. In this paper, we leverage Large Language Models (LLMs) to analyze the causal relation structures within legal documents, thereby strengthening the reasoning ability for legal textual entailment through the generation of high-quality synthetic data. Our experimental results demonstrate that this approach outperforms previous methods, confirming the feasibility and effectiveness of using LLM-generated synthetic datasets. Moreover, variations in performance across test sets highlight the trade-offs between zero-shot and fine-tuning strategies, as well as the significant impact of prompt engineering on accuracy. These findings open up promising research directions for further improving reasoning and generalization in legal text processing tasks.

Keywords: legal statute law entailment · large language model · data augmentation · causal relation-aware

1 Introduction

Legal textual entailment is a fundamental yet challenging task in the field of legal text processing. Given a legal article as the premise and a corresponding statement as the hypothesis, the goal is to determine whether the hypothesis is logically supported by the premise. Achieving this requires not only a deep understanding of legal semantics and contextual nuances but also advanced reasoning capabilities to tackle challenges such as intricate language structures [12], a scarcity of annotated legal data [1,11], a rich vocabulary with multiple interpretations [13], and complex inter-dependencies among legal statutes [18].

Legal texts possess unique characteristics that set them apart from other documents. For instance, at the sentence level, legal provisions often comprise two logical parts: a requisite (cause) and an effectuation (effect) [3,17,19]. This inherent structure underscores the need for AI systems capable of decomposing legal sentences to facilitate more accurate entailment judgments.

R. Ichise (Ed.): NLDB 2025, LNCS 15836, pp. 396–410, 2026.
https://doi.org/10.1007/978-3-031-97141-9_27

Previous approaches to legal textual entailment have adopted various strategies. One method combines rule-based techniques with deep learning and employs semi-automated data augmentation [6], which improves dataset quality but requires substantial manual effort. In contrast, another approach utilizes a zero-shot framework with multiple Large Language Models (LLM) and prompt optimization [5], thereby eliminating the need for labeled data but lacking domain-specific adaptation. Meanwhile, a further approach fine-tunes the LLM model and leverages LLM-generated summaries for data augmentation [14]. However, an over-reliance on summarization risks oversimplifying the entailment process. These methods highlight the trade-offs between data augmentation, prompt-based inference, and fine-tuning strategies in legal reasoning tasks.

In this work, we propose a novel approach that leverages the reasoning capabilities of pre-trained LLMs for synthetic data generation. Our method decomposes legal articles into smaller sub-conditions, thereby simplifying their complex structures, reducing noise, and clarifying the intertwined relationships within legal sentences. This process yields a higher-quality synthetic dataset that, when combined with the original data, enhances the model's ability to make more accurate entailment decisions.

To validate the effectiveness of our approach, we conducted experiments on the COLIEE Task 4 datasets (the Legal Textual Entailment Data Corpus) over three years (2022–2024), using data from the annual, well-known COLIEE competitions[1] in the legal domain. Experimental results demonstrate that our approach outperforms state-of-the-art (SOTA) systems across multiple test sets, confirming the feasibility and effectiveness of using LLMs for legal data augmentation. In the following sections, we will discuss in detail regarding the Related Work (Sect. 2), our Methodology (Sect. 3), Experiments and Results (Sect. 4).

2 Related Work

Legal textual entailment is a challenging task that has been addressed in the COLIEE competition [15] through various methodologies, ranging from rule-based approaches to large-scale language models (LLMs) [5,6,14]. We review the key strategies adopted by recent COLIEE-winning teams and highlight their strengths and limitations.

The COLIEE 2022 winner (KIS) [6] employed a hybrid ensemble of a rule-based model (Precise Match Module - PMM) and a BERT-based model[2]. To enhance training data, they used semi-automated data augmentation, applying six transformation techniques: *Article Segmentation, Reconstruction, Reference Substitution, Data Generation by Negative Form, and AB Replacement.* While this approach enhances dataset quality, it comes with a significant drawback—high manual effort and time consumption, especially when scaling to large datasets. Furthermore, their reliance on rule-based methods provides high precision but lacks the flexibility and generalization ability of deep learning models. The Precise Match

[1] https://sites.ualberta.ca/~rabelo/COLIEE2024/.

[2] https://github.com/cl-tohoku/bert-japanese.

Module (PMM) operates on explicit predicate-argument structures, making it effective for well-structured legal texts but potentially limited in handling complex, implicit entailments that require deeper semantic understanding.

The COLIEE 2023 winner (JNLP) [5] eliminated rule-based techniques and data augmentation, opting for a zero-shot LLMs approach. They evaluated 55 prompts from PromptSource [4] on models such as Flan-T5-XXL, Flan-Alpaca-XXL, T0pp, and Bloomz-7B1, selecting the best-performing prompt for inference. This approach was highly adaptable, as it required no labeled training data, but lacked domain adaptation and struggled with complex legal reasoning due to the absence of fine-tuning.

The COLIEE 2024 winner (CAPTAIN) [14] achieved the highest accuracy by fine-tuning Flan-T5-XXL with LoRA, using both raw and augmented data. Their data augmentation strategy involved summarizing premises with LLMs and generating synthetic hypotheses through three approaches: (1) using summaries as positive hypotheses, (2) combining summaries with original hypotheses, and (3) pairing summaries with irrelevant hypotheses. While this approach demonstrated strong generalization, it also had notable limitations. Over-reliance on summarization could lead to oversimplified entailments, potentially missing key legal conditions. Additionally, for generating non-entailed hypotheses, they applied BM25 to the generated summaries. While BM25 helps identify counter-meaning hypotheses, it does not fully capture the deeper logical entailments present in legal texts.

The above-mentioned approaches have progressively improved upon the limitations of their predecessors, refining legal entailment methodologies step by step. However, data augmentation in these works often involves human intervention or relies on simplistic transformations of the original dataset. Given the complex structure of legal articles, which often contain multiple interdependent conditions, a more sophisticated approach to data augmentation should be explored to better capture the depth and nuances of legal reasoning.

3 Methodology

In this section, we provide a detailed description of our data augmentation method using pre-trained Large Language Models (LLMs). Our synthetic data generation framework (Fig. 1) consists of three main components: Causal Relationship-Based Legal Data Generation, Data Integration, and Fine-tuning of the Augmented Dataset with LoRA [8]. To facilitate comparison with previous works, we replicate the methods used by the top three COLIEE-winning teams from 2022 to 2024, in alignment with the test sets considered in this study.

Large Language Model for Synthetic Data Generation. Pre-trained Large Language Models (LLMs), which encompass a range from a few billion to over a hundred billion parameters, are generally pre-trained on extensive and diverse datasets, including legal documents [10]. It enables LLMs to possess a certain level of language understanding and generation capabilities. This extensive pre-training endows LLMs with robust language understanding and generation capabilities [10].

Furthermore, modern LLMs are refined using techniques such as instruction tuning (also known as Supervised Fine-Tuning, SFT) and In-Context Learning (ICL), which enhance their reasoning capabilities [9,21]. Consequently, LLMs have become valuable tools for synthetic data generation [14,16], especially when the original dataset is limited [14]. In this paper, we leverage this advantage from LLM to enrich the original dataset through carefully designed, step-by-step context analysis and data generation.

3.1 Causal Relationship-Based Legal Data Generation

A Two-Phase Generation Process. Recognizing the importance of dataset enrichment, we propose a novel data augmentation method based on the extraction of causal relationships from legal articles. Our preliminary analysis of the dataset revealed that legal premises are often structured as sub-conditions in the form of: `cause(s) → effect(s)`, where the `cause(s)` represent the conditions and the `effect(s)` represent the corresponding consequences, judgments, or interpretations. We observe that if a hypothesis is generated by faithfully following the causal relationships inherent in the premise, then it will be entailed by that premise. Conversely, if a hypothesis is generated by altering or violating one or more of these causal relationships, it will not be entailed by the premise.

Furthermore, the analysis or decomposition of a premise sentence is very important not only because it will streamline the lengthy or complex premise sentences into a set of clearly structured, specific causes and effects. Moreover, this decomposition also reduces noise during the synthetic data generation process. Therefore, in this paper, we introduce the synthetic data generation method based on the extraction of causal relationships. Specifically, we leverage the large knowledge and pre-trained reasoning ability of the LLM to create new synthetic data in the form of instructions and few-shot prompting. We divide it into the following two phases (Fig. 1):

Phase 1: Extraction of Causal Relationship Entities. We extract causal relationship entities from the legal articles in the original dataset. A carefully designed prompt instructs the LLM to decompose each article into sub-conditions with three distinct features: the cause entity (the underlying cause), the effect entity (the subsequent effect), and the causal statement (the relationship between the cause and effect). To enhance accuracy and generalization, we include few-shot examples using two types of legal articles: a basic Example (a short article of 2–3 sentences) and a complex Example (a longer article with multiple items).

Phase 2: Generation of Hypothesis Pairs. The causal relationships extracted in the previous phase are used to generate a pair of hypotheses: *entailed* and *not entailed.* The entailed hypothesis must logically follow from the extracted causal relationships, while the not-entailed hypothesis is created by modifying one or more of these causal relationships, thereby contradicting the original causal logic. A dedicated prompt guides the LLM in this process, emphasizing key phrases such as "logically follows" and "must follow" for entailed hypotheses, and "contradicts" or "violates" for not-entailed hypotheses to ensure the LLM follows the logical entailment principles. Similar to Phase 1, we incorporate few-shot examples (both basic and complex) to improve the model's performance across varied contexts.

Causal Relationship Entities extraction prompt

```
You are a legal reasoning assistant specializing in analyzing causal relationships in legal texts. Your task is to extract and structure the causal relationships found in the given legal article.
## Notation:
1. "cause_entity" as "C"
2. "effect_entity" as "E"
## Causal relationships explaination
1. A causal relationships is defined as C -> E with C is the cause and E is the effect that caused by C
2. When there are more than one cause that trigger the effect: C1→E, C2→E
## Instructions:
1. Identify cause-effect relationships between **entities** mentioned in the article.
2. Break down the legal article into **small conditional statements**.
3. Format your response as a structured **JSON object** with the following fields:
- **cause_entity**: The entity that triggers the effect.
- **effect_entity**: The entity affected by the cause.
- **causal_statement**: The causal rule derived from the legal article.
4. If multiple causal relationships exist in the article, include them all in the JSON output.
### Example 1:
**Premise**: <...>
**Answer**: <...>
```

** Due to long text, the few-shot text will be excluded from the prompt display.*

Synthetic Hypothesis Pairs Generation prompt

```
You are a legal reasoning assistant responsible for generating **one entailed** and **one not-entailed** examples based on causal relationships extracted from a legal article.
## Instructions:
1. Use the structured JSON input provided below.
2. **For entailed examples:**
- Construct a single sentence that **logically follows all** the causal relationships.
- Make sure this new sentence must follow **all** the causal conditions in the JSON input.
3. **For the not-entailed example:**
- Modify one or more causal relationships **to contradict or alter the original logic**.
- Ensure that the modified example **violates** at least one causal rule.
4. Return exactly **one entailed example** and **one not-entailed example** as a JSON object.
### Example 1:
**Premise**: <...>
**Answer**: <...>
```

** Due to long text, the few-shot text will be excluded from the prompt display.*

3.2 Data Integration

Dataset Integration Ratio. To explore the impact of different dataset compositions, we experiment with three dataset combination strategies: (1) *Original:Augmented = 1:2* (Standard), where each original hypothesis is augmented with two synthetic hypotheses; (2) *Original:Augmented = 1:0.5* (Reduced), where the number of synthetic hypotheses is decreased by a factor of four; (3)

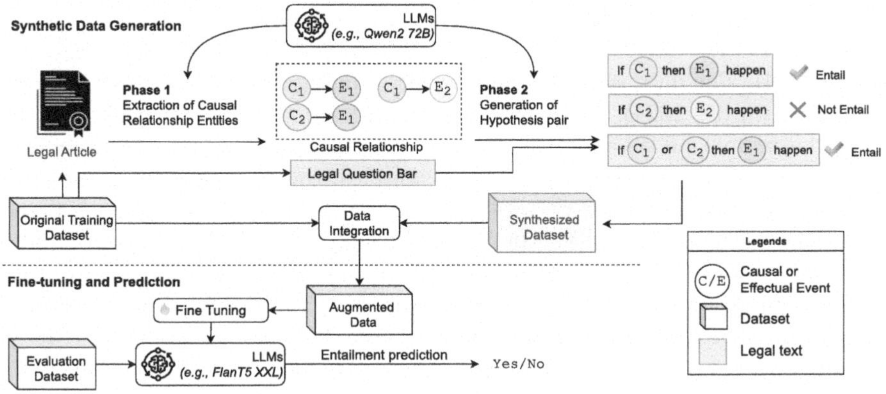

Fig. 1. Overview of our proposed framework architecture.

Original: Augmented = 1:1 (Balanced), where the number of synthetic hypotheses is reduced to match the size of the original dataset.

3.3 Instruction Fine-Tuning with Augmented Dataset

Building upon the SOTA methods [14] in the legal textual entailment task, we employ an approach involving instruction fine-tuning with LLMs, leveraging our synthesized dataset. Specifically, we include the *premise* and *hypothesis* data within the prompt input, training the LLMs to generate the desired output text.

Instruction Prompt Selection. We utilize the prompting technique to transform the synthesized data into a question-answering format. After evaluating various prompt templates, we primarily adopt the following two prompts.
Prompt 1: *{{premise}}\nQuestion: {{hypothesis}} True or False?*
Prompt 2: *{{premise}}\nQuestion: {{hypothesis}}? Answer with Yes or No.*

Ensemble Models. In contrast to previous work [5,14], where a single LLM (Flan-T5-XXL, Flan-Alpaca-XXL, BLOOMZ-7B1,..) model is used for label prediction, our approach incorporates an ensemble model with major voting mechanism. Specifically, we combine the predictions from three independently fine-tuned Flan-T5-XXL models to derive the final decision, thereby enhancing robustness and overall accuracy.

4 Experiments and Results

Dataset. The dataset is provided as Task 4: Legal Textual Entailment by the COLIEE organizer [15]. The dataset is used to construct Yes/No question-answering systems for legal queries, by entailment from the relevant Civil Law articles. Training data consists of triples of a query (hypothesis), relevant article(s) (premise(s)), and a correct answer "Y" for Yes (entail) or "N" for No (not entail) (label). The data is organized by year, ranging from H18 (Heisei 18, 2006) to R05 (Reiwa 05, 2024). In this study, we selected the data of R03, R04, and R05 as the evaluation sets and the remainder as training datasets. Consequently, the training data comprises 806 original samples, the development set contains 109 samples, and the two test sets, R04 and R05, include 101 and 109 samples, respectively. After the synthetic data generation process, we obtained an Augmented dataset of 1,612 instances, double the size of the Original dataset, since two hypotheses were generated per premise (compared to one in the original). As described in Sect. 3.2, we applied three dataset combination strategies to evaluate the impact of augmentation. For the *Reduced* and *Balanced* settings, we randomly sampled 25% and 50% of the Augmented dataset, respectively, to match the target Original:Augmented ratio. Sampling was done with a fixed random_state of 42 and stratified by label to preserve the balance between entailed and not-entailed hypotheses.

Evaluation Method. For the legal textual entailment task, the evaluation measure will be accuracy, concerning whether the yes/no question was correctly answered:

$$\text{Accuracy} = \frac{\text{the number of correctly predicted instances}}{\text{the number of all instances}}$$

LLM selection. In compliance with the COLIEE organizers' rule—*"To avoid contamination of the test data, you can only use LLMs released before July 9, 2024 (JST)"*—we conducted a series of test runs using the same prompts. Considering factors such as performance on benchmark datasets, output format accuracy, and the ability to handle long contexts, we selected the Qwen2 72B[3] model with 4-bit quantization for both phases of data augmentation.

Hyper-parameters. For addressing the final tasks, legal text entailment, we fine-tune the Flan-T5-XXL model[4] using Low-Rank Adaptation (LoRA) [8] to enable parameter-efficient tuning while reducing computational costs. We set the learning rate to 3e-5, batch size to 32, LoRA r between {16, 32}, LoRA alpha between {32, 64}, LoRA dropout to 0.25, and train for 15 epochs. To ensure reproducibility, all seeds, including those for PyTorch, NumPy, and the data integration process, are fixed to 42.

4.1 Results and Discussion

Synthetic Hypotheses Generation. Table 1 presents the results of a sample legal article processed through the synthetic data generation pipeline using a few-shot approach with the Qwen2 72B model. The extracted causal relationships are structured in JSON format, clearly distinguishing the cause entity and

[3] https://huggingface.co/Qwen/Qwen2-72B-Instruct.
[4] https://huggingface.co/google/flan-t5-xxl.

the corresponding effect entity. This structured representation ensures that each causal relationship is well-defined. By organizing legal provisions in this manner, LLMs can generate hypothesis pairs with greater precision and accuracy, improving the overall quality of synthetic data.

Table 1. Synthetic Data Generation analysis

Legal Article
Article 113
(1) A contract concluded by a person who acts as the agent of another person but has no authority to represent does not bind the principal unless the principal ratifies it.
(2) The ratification or refusal to ratify may not be duly asserted against the counterparty unless it is made to that counterparty;provided, however, that this does not apply if the counterparty has come to know the ratification or refusal to ratify.
Phase 1: Causal Relationship Extraction
[{ **'cause_entity'**: 'Contract concluded by unauthorized agent', **'effect_entity'**: "Principal's ratification required for binding effect", **'causal_statement'**: 'If a contract is concluded by a person acting as an agent without authority, the contract does not bind the principal unless the principal ratifies it.' , { **'cause_entity'**: 'Ratification or refusal communicated to counterparty', **'effect_entity'**: "Counterparty's knowledge of ratification or refusal", **'causal_statement'**: 'The ratification or refusal to ratify must be made known to the counterparty to be effective against them, unless the counterparty already knows about the ratification or refusal.' }]
Phase 2: Synthetic Hypothesis Generation
{ **'entailed_hypothesis'**: When a contract is entered into by an unauthorized agent, the principal must ratify the contract for it to become binding, and such ratification must be communicated to the counterparty to be effective against them.', **'not_entailed_hypothesis'**: 'Even if a contract is concluded by an unauthorized agent, it automatically binds the principal without any need for ratification or communication to the counterparty.' }

Here in the example of Article 113, the LLM extracts two causal relationships. The first causal relationship corresponds to clause (1) of Article 113, which states that a contract is not binding on the principal unless they ratify it. The second causal relationship aligns with clause (2) of Article 113, which specifies that ratification or rejection only takes effect for the counterparty if they are notified or have prior knowledge of it. This demonstrates that the LLM is capable of analyzing and decomposing legal provisions into smaller sub-conditions or logical rules, thereby enhancing structural clarity.

For hypothesis generation, the `entailed_hypothesis` accurately reflects Article 113 by maintaining both key legal conditions: First, it states that the contract is not binding on the principal unless they ratify it (Clause 1) and also the ratification must be communicated to the counterparty to be effective unless they have known about it beforehand (Clause 2). In contrast, the `not_entailed_hypothesis` directly contradicts both clauses by removing the requirement for approval and omitting the obligation to notify the counterparty. This contradiction illustrates the importance of causal dependencies in legal reasoning. Overall, this example highlights the potential of LLMs in systematically extracting and structuring legal knowledge, thereby generating high-quality synthetic data that preserves the logical and semantic integrity of legal texts.

Legal Entailment Result. Table 2 summarizes the best experimental configurations evaluated across the test sets - from R03 (2022) to R05 (2024). Our method achieves competitive performance compared to the SOTA. These findings highlight the advantage of leveraging LLMs for synthetic data generation over traditional augmentation methods.

Table 2. Comparison of Our Approach with COLIEE Top 3 Results from Other Competitors

Year	Method (#original: #augmented data)	Accuracy		
		R03 (2022)	R04 (2023)	R05 (2024)
2022	KIS2 [6]	0.6789(*)	-	-
	HUKB-1 [20]	0.6697	-	-
	KIS1 [6]	0.6606	-	-
2023	JNLP3 [5]	-	0.7822(*)	-
	JNLP1 [5]	-	0.7525	-
	JNLP2 [5]	-	0.7525	-
2024	CAPTAIN 2 [14]	-	-	0.8257(*)
	JNLP1 [7]	-	-	0.8165
	UA_slack [2]	-	-	0.7982
2025	Our Zero shot (P1) *(no aug. data)*	0.7431	0.7822	0.7798
	Our Zero shot (P2) *(no aug. data)*	0.7890	0.7921	0.7156
	Our ensemble models (1:0) *(no aug. data)*	**0.7900**	0.8218	0.8073
	Our ensemble models (1:2)	0.7706	**0.8317**	0.8073
	Our ensemble models (1:1)	0.7706	0.8218	0.8257
	Our ensemble models (1:0.5)	**0.7900**	0.8218	**0.8440**

(*) indicates the winner's performance in each year. The notations P1 and P2 represent prompt 1 and prompt 2, respectively, as referred to in the Method section. Bold scores denote the best performance.

We first observe performance improvements when applying In-Context Learning (ICL). Specifically, using the two prompts described in Sect. 3.2, we conduct zero-shot inference on the same model and compare the results. ICL improves performance on the R03 test set, yielding an average increase of 8.72%. In contrast, there is a slight improvement on the R04 test set, with an average gain of 0.5%, and Prompt 2 achieves only a 0.99% improvement over the SOTA result. However, unlike R03 and R04, R05 exhibits a clear performance decline of −7.8%. These findings suggest that while zero-shot ICL can enhance model performance, it is not always sufficient. In many cases, LLMs still require fine-tuning to achieve better domain adaptation for specialized tasks.

Further analysis of SOTA comparisons shows that our data augmentation method surpasses SOTA results on test sets R03, R04, and R05. Specifically, our approach outperforms the KIS Team [6] by $9.82\% \pm 1.12\%$ for R03 and improves upon the JNLP Team's [5] 2023 SOTA by $4.29\% \pm 0.57\%$ for R04 across all dataset combinations. Although the improvement on R05 is minimal, our 1:0.5 dataset combination surpasses SOTA performance by 1.83% while maintaining stable results on R03 and R04 compared to SOTA. These results highlight the advantages of leveraging pre-trained LLMs for data augmentation and complex reasoning tasks such as legal entailment, outperforming rule-based approaches with semi-automated annotation augmentation (KIS case). Furthermore, fine-tuning LLMs on domain-specific downstream tasks enhances adaptation and yields superior results compared to zero-shot methods (JNLP 2023 case).

Comparing data augmentation methods between our approach and CAPTAIN's (R05), we first observe that without additional data, performance decreases compared to SOTA (CAPTAIN). However, our augmentation strategy improves performance by $1.84\% \pm 1.84\%$ across all data combinations, demonstrating its effectiveness over the non-augmented approach. While our method does not surpass the SOTA score at 1:1 and 1:2 dataset combination ratios, it outperforms CAPTAIN's by 1.83% in the 1:0.5 setup, demonstrating that our augmented dataset effectively enhances the LLM's entailment reasoning capabilities. Further analysis of R05 reveals that while we achieve higher scores than SOTA (0.8440 at 1:0.5), the overall improvement remains modest. Set R05 also had the lowest proportion of results higher than SOTA (1 higher, 1 equal, 1 lower) while R03 and R04 consistently outperform SOTA for all runs.

Focusing on the best-performing ensemble model (dataset ratio 1:0.5), we analyze the individual models that contribute to its success. Figure 2 shows that while Models 2 and 3 outperform SOTA across all three test sets, Model 1 falls short on R05, dropping 4.59%, despite a strong performance on R03 and R04. Notably, Model 1 is trained with Prompt 1, whereas Models 2 and 3 use Prompt 2, which replaces "`True or False?`" with "`? Answer with Yes or No.`". Although Prompt 1 performed better in zero-shot settings, Prompt 2 provided a stronger learning signal during fine-tuning, improving performance when the model was adapted to that specific prompt structure.

Additionally, we also consider the possibility that R05 may contain more diverse and challenging data, which will be examined in detail in the Case Study section.

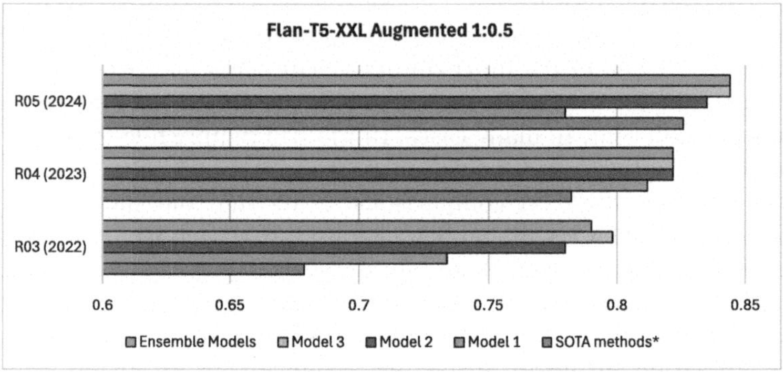

Fig. 2. Performance of single models with their ensemble models compare with SOTA.

4.2 Case Study

We further investigate the quality of our data generation process by analyzing cases where our approach succeeds while the COLIEE 2024 winner [14] fails, and vice versa. Specifically, we examine individual test instances and compare the predictions made by both methods. Consider the following test case:

Table 3. A sample test instance from the test set (Article 536)

Premise (Legal Article)
Article 536
(1) If the performance of an obligation becomes impossible due to grounds not attributable to either party, the obligee may refuse to perform counter-performance.
Hypothesis (Labeled as "No" - Not entailed by the Premise)
If, after the conclusion of the contract for sale and before A delivers X to B, X is burned down caused by negligence of a third party, the debt to pay the price of B is extinguished by operation of law.

In this case, CAPTAIN failed to predict correctly, while our approach succeeded. A deeper analysis (Table 4) reveals that our generated hypothesis pair for Article 536 enhances the fine-tuned model's ability to make accurate predictions. Specifically, the `entailed_hypothesis` emphasizes the condition "not belonging to both parties", reinforcing the premise that the obligee has the right to refuse to perform the counter-obligation. Conversely, the `not_entailed_hypothesis` states that if the cause belongs to the obligee, they may not have the right to refuse the counter-performance.

Examining the test hypothesis (Table 3), we note that although the cause results from a third party's negligence (i.e., it does not belong to either party A or B), Article 536(1) only grants the obligee the right to refuse the counter-performance, but it does not state that the obligation- "the debt to pay"-is automatically "extinguished by operation of law". From that, we saw that the additional hypothesis sentences generated by our method provide clearer support for the fundamental legal principles in Article 536, making them valuable in guiding the model's reasoning. Without these additional structured hypotheses, the original hypothesis sentence, which is longer and more ambiguous, would make it more difficult for the model to comprehend the core premise and correctly determine the entailment outcome.

However, our method also has certain limitations. In some instances where Team CAPTAIN correctly predicts the entailment, our model fails. An example is the test instance for Article 509 (Table 5).

Examining our generated hypothesis pair (Table 6), we find that it does not fully capture the nature of Article 509. Our synthetic hypotheses primarily focus on torts committed in bad faith and exceptions involving the "claim corresponding to the relevant obligation from another person", whereas the test instance

Table 4. Article 536 in the training dataset with synthetic generated hypothesis pair

Premise (Legal Article)
Article 536
(1) If the performance of an obligation becomes impossible due to grounds not attributable to either party, the obligee may refuse to perform counter-performance.
(2) If the performance of an obligation becomes impossible due to grounds attributable to the obligee, the obligee may not refuse to complete counter-performance. In such a case, if the obligor benefits from being released from that obligation, the obligor must reimburse the obligee for the benefit.
Hypothesis given in the original dataset (Labeled as "Yes")
In cases where the subject of sale, wine, is specified only with reference to a type, and the delivery of wine is effected at the domicile of the buyer; in case the buyer refuses to accept the performance even though the seller brings wine to the domicile of the buyer with the main purport of the obligationif the wine has been lost due to negligence of the buyer after that, the buyer shall not be relieved of the obligation of payment of purchase money.
Hypothesis pair created for the Premise 536
{ **'entailed_hypothesis'**: 'If the performance of an obligation becomes impossible because of circumstances beyond both parties' control, the obligee can lawfully refuse to perform counter-performance.', **'not_entailed_hypothesis'**: 'Even if the performance of an obligation becomes impossible due to grounds attributable to the obligee, the obligee retains the right to refuse counter-performance.'}

Table 5. A sample test instance from the test set (Article 509)

Premise (Legal Article)
Article 509
The obligor of either of the following obligations may not duly assert a set-off against the obligee; provided, however, that this does not apply if the obligee acquires a claim corresponding to the relevant obligation from another person:
(i) an obligation for compensation for loss or damage based on a tort committed in bad faith; or
(ii) an obligation for compensation for loss or damage for death or injury to person (excluding the one set forth in the preceding item).
Hypothesis (Labeled as "Yes" - Entailed by the Premise)
If a person that holds a monetary claim has borne an obligation for compensation for loss or damage for injury to the obligor of that monetary claim, the person may not duly assert against the obligor, a set-off using the monetary claim against the obligation for compensation.

pertains to liability for injury without mentioning the claim. This discrepancy likely arises from the prompt design in phase 2 and the complexity of causal relationships in the premise. Moreover, generating only a single entailed and not-entailed hypothesis may be insufficient for premises with multiple conditions, limiting hypothesis quality and scope. Consequently, this constraint affects fine-tuning, reducing the model's ability to generalize to new cases, leading to misinterpretations and incorrect predictions.

Table 6. Article 509 in the training dataset with synthetic generated hypothesis pair

Premise (Legal Article)
Article 509 The obligor of either of the following obligations may not duly assert a set-off against the obligee; provided, however, that this does not apply if the obligee acquires a claim corresponding to the relevant obligation from another person:
(i) an obligation for compensation for loss or damage based on a tort committed in bad faith; or (ii) an obligation for compensation for loss or damage for death or injury to person (excluding the one set forth in the preceding item).
Hypothesis given in the original dataset (Labeled as "Yes")
If any claim arises from a tortious act, the relevant obligee may assert the set-off against the obligor.
Hypothesis pair created for the Premise 536
{ **'entailed_hypothesis'**: 'If the obligor has an obligation for compensation based on a tort committed in bad faith, but the obligee subsequently acquires a claim corresponding to the relevant obligation from another person, the obligor can now assert a set-off against the obligee.', **'not_entailed_hypothesis'**: 'Even if the obligor has an obligation for compensation based on a tort committed in bad faith and the obligee acquires a claim corresponding to the relevant obligation from another person, the obligor remains unable to assert a set-off against the obligee.'}

5 Conclusion

In this paper, we introduced a novel data augmentation approach that leverages the knowledge and reasoning capabilities of pre-trained LLMs for synthetic data generation in legal textual entailment task. Our method, which integrates causal relationship extraction with an ensemble voting mechanism, has demonstrated competitive results against state-of-the-art systems across multiple test sets. Specifically, experimental results reveal that our approach consistently outperforms traditional data augmentation methods and models on most datasets.

While our method achieved superior performance on test sets R03 and R04, the results on R05 suggest potential challenges in generalization, opening avenues for further investigation. Despite these promising results, our approach may be over-specialized due to fine-tuning a narrowly defined prompt set in the hypothesis generation phase. Future work will focus on expanding the diversity of synthetic data generation and optimizing prompt engineering to further enhance model generalization and performance.

Overall, our findings underscore the potential of leveraging pre-trained LLMs in synthetic data generation for legal applications, marking an important step forward in the field. We believe that continued refinement of these methods will contribute to more robust and generalizable legal AI systems.

References

1. Aoki, Y., Yoshioka, M., Suzuki, Y.: Data-augmentation method for bert-based legal textual entailment systems in coliee statute law task. Rev. Socionetwork Strat. **16** (2022). https://doi.org/10.1007/s12626-022-00104-0
2. Babiker, H., Rahman, M., Kim, M., Rabelo, J., Goebel, R.: Legal yes/no question answering through text embedding, fine-tuning, and prompt engineering. In: Proceedings of the Eighteenth International Workshop on Juris-Informatics (JURISIN 2024) (2024)
3. Bach, N.X., Nguyen, L.M., Shimazu, A.: RRE task: the task of recognition of requisite part and effectuation part in law sentences. Int. J. Comput. Process. Lang. **23**(02), 109–130 (2011). https://doi.org/10.1142/S1793840611002243
4. Bach, S., et al.: PromptSource: an integrated development environment and repository for natural language prompts. In: Basile, V., Kozareva, Z., Stajner, S. (eds.) Proceedings of the 60th Annual Meeting of the Association for Computational Linguistics: System Demonstrations, Dublin, Ireland, pp. 93–104. Association for Computational Linguistics (2022). https://doi.org/10.18653/v1/2022.acl-demo.9. https://aclanthology.org/2022.acl-demo.9/
5. Bui, M.Q., et al.: Data augmentation and large language model for legal case retrieval and entailment. Rev. Socionetwork Strat. **18**(1), 49–74 (2024). https://doi.org/10.1007/s12626-024-00158-2
6. Fujita, M., Onaga, T., Ueyama, A., Kano, Y.: Legal textual entailment using ensemble of rule-based and bert-based method with data augmentation by related article generation. In: Takama, Y., Yada, K., Satoh, K., Arai, S. (eds.) New Frontiers in Artificial Intelligence, pp. 138–153. Springer, Cham (2023)

7. Goebel, R., Kano, Y., Kim, M.Y., Rabelo, J., Satoh, K., Yoshioka, M.: Overview of benchmark datasets and methods for the legal information extraction/entailment competition (COLIEE) 2024. In: Suzumura, T., Bono, M. (eds.) New Frontiers in Artificial Intelligence, pp. 109–124. Springer, Singapore (2024)
8. Hu, E.J., et al.: LoRA: low-rank adaptation of large language models. In: International Conference on Learning Representations (2022). https://openreview.net/forum?id=nZeVKeeFYf9
9. Huang, J., Chang, K.C.C.: Towards reasoning in large language models: a survey. In: Rogers, A., Boyd-Graber, J., Okazaki, N. (eds.) Findings of the Association for Computational Linguistics: ACL 2023, Toronto, Canada, pp. 1049–1065. Association for Computational Linguistics (2023). https://doi.org/10.18653/v1/2023.findings-acl.67. https://aclanthology.org/2023.findings-acl.67/
10. Liu, Y., Cao, J., Liu, C., Ding, K., Jin, L.: Datasets for large language models: a comprehensive survey (2024). https://arxiv.org/abs/2402.18041
11. Nguyen, H.T., et al.: Transformer-based approaches for legal text processing. Rev. Socionetwork Strat. **16**(1), 135–155 (2022). https://doi.org/10.1007/s12626-022-00102-2
12. Nguyen, H.T., Phi, M.K., Ngo, X.B., Tran, V., Nguyen, L.M., Tu, M.P.: Attentive deep neural networks for legal document retrieval. Artif. Intell. Law **32**(1), 57–86 (2024). https://doi.org/10.1007/s10506-022-09341-8
13. Nguyen, H.T., et al.: Paralaw nets – cross-lingual sentence-level pretraining for legal text processing (2021). https://arxiv.org/abs/2106.13403
14. Nguyen, P., et al.: Captain at COLIEE 2024: large language model for legal text retrieval and entailment. In: Suzumura, T., Bono, M. (eds.) New Frontiers in Artificial Intelligence, pp. 125–139. Springer, Singapore (2024)
15. Rabelo, J., Goebel, R., Kim, M.Y., Kano, Y., Yoshioka, M., Satoh, K.: Overview and discussion of the competition on legal information extraction/entailment (COLIEE) 2021. Rev. Socionetwork Strat. **16** (2022). https://doi.org/10.1007/s12626-022-00105-z
16. Schick, T., Schütze, H.: Generating datasets with pretrained language models. In: Moens, M.F., Huang, X., Specia, L., Yih, S.W.t. (eds.) Proceedings of the 2021 Conference on Empirical Methods in Natural Language Processing, Online and Punta Cana, Dominican Republic, pp. 6943–6951. Association for Computational Linguistics (2021). https://doi.org/10.18653/v1/2021.emnlp-main.555. https://aclanthology.org/2021.emnlp-main.555/
17. Tanaka, K., Kawazoe, I., Narita, H.: Standard structure of legal provisions: aiming for legal knowledge processing by natural language. In: Proceedings of the Information Processing Society of Japan (IPSJ) Research Report on Natural Language Processing, Japan, vol. 1993, pp. 79–86 (1993). https://ipsj.ixsq.nii.ac.jp/records/49346. (in Japanese)
18. Vuong, Y., et al.: SM-BERT-CR: a deep learning approach for case law retrieval with supporting model. Artif. Intell. Law **31** (2022). https://doi.org/10.1007/s10506-022-09319-6
19. Xuan Bach, N.: A study on recognition of requisite part and effectuation part in law sentences (2011)
20. Yoshioka, M., Suzuki, Y., Aoki, Y.: HUKB at the COLIEE 2022 statute law task. In: Takama, Y., Yada, K., Satoh, K., Arai, S. (eds.) New Frontiers in Artificial Intelligence, pp. 109–124. Springer, Cham (2023)
21. Zhang, S., et al.: Instruction tuning for large language models: a survey (2024). https://arxiv.org/abs/2308.10792

Improve Smart Contract Vulnerability Explanation with Synthetic Data and Chain-of-Thought Prompting

Ngoc Minh Nguyen(✉), Naoya Inoue, and Le Minh Nguyen

Japan Advanced Institute of Science and Technology, 1 Chome-1 Asahidai, Nomi, Ishikawa 923-1211, Japan
minh.nn@jaist.ac.jp

Abstract. Smart contracts, predominantly authored in the Solidity programming language, are fundamental components of the blockchain ecosystem; however, they are frequently susceptible to security vulnerabilities. While existing detection tools have made significant advances in identifying such vulnerabilities, a critical gap remains in providing comprehensive explanations and reasoning about the identified issues. This is further complicated by the deficiency of well-annotated, high-quality training datasets specifically tailored for Solidity, which limits the development of advanced machine learning models capable of producing coherent and insightful explanations. In light of these challenges, this paper introduces a novel system designed to furnish detailed, context-aware explanations for vulnerabilities in Solidity-based smart contracts. A cornerstone of our methodology is the construction of a synthetic dataset, which encompasses a wide spectrum of code vulnerabilities matched with high-quality synthetic explanations. This dataset addresses the shortage of existing training data and enhances the capability of our system to offer meaningful insights into the vulnerabilities detected, thereby empowering developers and security auditors to understand and remediate potential security threats more effectively. Our contributions aim to enhance the interpretability of smart contract vulnerabilities and fortify the security of blockchain technologies.

Keywords: smart contract · solidity · machine learning · large language model · vulnerability explanation

1 Introduction

Smart contracts are self-executing programs deployed on blockchain platforms such as Ethereum and have revolutionized decentralized applications by automating trustless agreements. They execute predefined logic when the conditions are met, enabling decentralized applications to operate without intermediaries. A defining property of smart contracts is immutability: once deployed on the blockchain, their code cannot be modified or patched. While immutability

R. Ichise (Ed.): NLDB 2025, LNCS 15836, pp. 411–425, 2026.
https://doi.org/10.1007/978-3-031-97141-9_28

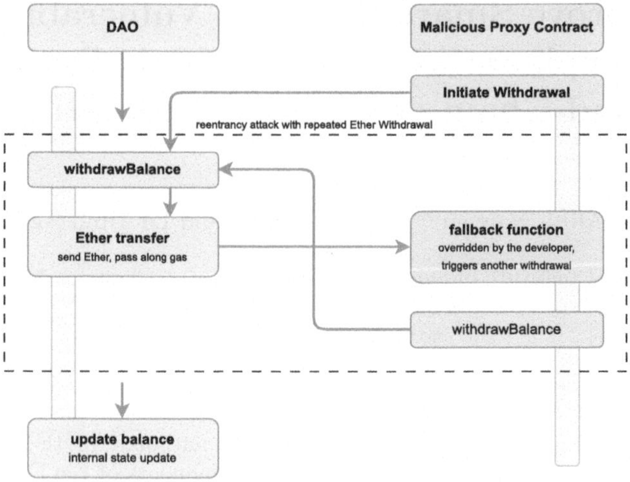

Fig. 1. A reentrancy attack caused the infamous DAO hack in 2016.

ensures trustworthiness, i.e., no party can arbitrarily alter the rule, it also means that vulnerabilities embedded in the code become permanent attack vectors. Unlike traditional software, where patches can remediate flaws post-deployment, smart contract bugs remain exploitable indefinitely unless the smart contract is entirely deprecated, often at significant financial loss and operational cost. Since smart contracts are self-executing programs that run on a blockchain, any bugs or vulnerabilities in their code can lead to significant financial losses, security breaches, or operational failures. Unlike traditional software, smart contracts are immutable once deployed, i.e., bugs after deployment are often impossible to patch. This makes thorough testing and bug detection essential before a smart contract goes live. Tools and techniques such as static analysis, formal verification, and automated testing are commonly used to identify vulnerabilities, ensuring the code behaves as intended and is secure against potential exploits.

Bug explanation in smart contracts involves analyzing and understanding the root causes of vulnerabilities in the code, yet most works focus on vulnerability detection, while explanation is often left out. Common issues include reentrancy attacks, integer overflows, logic errors, and improper access control. For example, the infamous DAO hack in 2016 (Fig. 1) was caused by a reentrancy vulnerability, where an attacker repeatedly drained funds from the contract before it could update its state. Explaining these bugs helps developers learn from past mistakes and adopt best practices, such as using secure coding patterns, conducting rigorous testing, and leveraging auditing tools. By understanding how and why bugs occur, developers can write more robust and secure smart contracts, reducing the risk of costly exploits.

2 Related Work

2.1 Smart Contract Bug Detection and Explanation

Traditional approaches in this domain often inadequately provide granular insights, merely classifying contracts as either "vulnerable" or "non-vulnerable" without identifying specific flawed lines of code, thus offering limited utility for developers to mitigate such vulnerabilities [5,6]. This lack of specificity underscores a significant barrier in practical application, as developers require detailed guidance to rectify these issues effectively.

Another primary obstacle in advancing smart contract security is the limited availability of high-quality training data. Smart contracts are typically written in Solidity, a niche language with a smaller developer base compared to more prevalent programming languages, resulting in challenges in assembling comprehensive datasets of labeled vulnerabilities necessary to train robust machine learning models [6,7]. Furthermore, the nuanced task of vulnerability labeling demands expertise in both Solidity and blockchain security, a requirement that incurs significant time and financial costs. Consequently, many existing approaches depend on limited or synthetically generated datasets, which may not adequately represent the complexity and variance encountered in real-world vulnerabilities [7].

Recent advancements have begun to address these deficiencies by focusing on explainable methodologies. A systematic review by [5] classified 101 vulnerabilities into ten categories and analyzed 144 detection tools, emphasizing the necessity for benchmarking and comprehensive datasets. Additionally, [7] proposed an innovative multi-model strategy leveraging high-level and low-level features extracted from source code and bytecode, attaining a noteworthy detection accuracy of 93.9%. These efforts represent significant strides in providing actionable insights for developers.

Furthermore, the work by [11] on SmartSys, an innovative hybrid dynamic analysis framework, employs foundation models to optimally select dynamic analysis techniques and create effective fuzz targets, augmenting coverage by as much as 14.3% on authentic benchmarks. This dynamic approach not only identifies vulnerabilities but also offers informative feedback during both compilation and execution phases, enhancing scalability by eliminating redundant fuzz targets [11].

Despite these developments, persistent challenges remain, as highlighted by the OWASP Smart Contract Top 10 (2025), identifying critical vulnerabilities such as reentrancy attacks, integer overflows/underflows, and access control weaknesses that continue to affect smart contracts [10]. High-profile incidents, including the DAO attack and Parity Wallet breach, emphasize the critical need for comprehensive testing and rigorous security review processes to mitigate the detrimental impacts of these vulnerabilities [1]. Hence, ongoing research in this realm is indispensable for fortifying the security infrastructure of blockchain ecosystems.

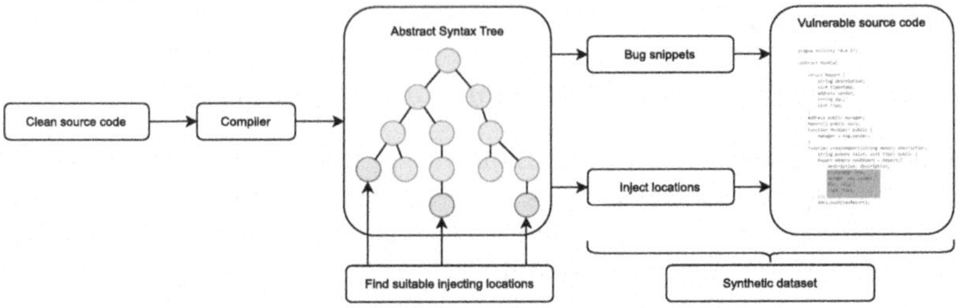

Fig. 2. Bug Injection with SolidiFI

2.2 Synthetic Evaluation of LLMs' Output

The use of large language models (LLMs) to evaluate the outputs of other LLMs has emerged as a promising paradigm in NLP research, addressing challenges in scalability, cost, and subjectivity inherent to human evaluations. Early work in this area focused on leveraging LLMs for tasks like text summarization and dialogue quality assessment. For example, Liu et al. (2023) [9] introduced **G-Eval**, a framework using GPT-4 with chain-of-thought prompting to assess text coherence and factual consistency, demonstrating strong correlation with human judgments. Similarly, Zheng et al. [13] proposed **LLM-as-a-Judge**, where models like GPT-4 evaluate responses in multi-turn dialogues, achieving over 80% alignment with human preferences on benchmarks like MT-Bench.

Another key advancement is the **AlpacaEval** framework by Dubois et al. [2], which uses GPT-4 as an automated judge to rank model outputs against human-authored instructions. This approach significantly reduced evaluation costs while maintaining high agreement with human annotators. However, critiques by Wataoka et al. (2024) [12] highlighted limitations, such as LLM evaluators' bias toward verbosity and overfitting to specific prompting styles. To mitigate these issues, Kim et al. (2023) [8] introduced **Prometheus**, a fine-tuned LLM explicitly trained on human feedback data to provide rubric-based evaluations, showing improved reliability over zero-shot GPT-4.

This research follows the current work, where GPT-4o is employed to evaluate bug explanations. By incorporating **chain-of-thought prompting** and explicit vulnerability labels, our methodology builds on frameworks like G-Eval [9] and LLM-as-a-Judge [13] while addressing domain-specific gaps identified in code security contexts.

3 Methodology

3.1 Vulnerable Smart Contracts Synthesis

The data synthesis process is a critical component of this methodology, designed to create a robust and diverse dataset for training and evaluating smart contract bug detection models. The process begins with the collection of two primary datasets: a set of 2,188 clean smart contracts from the SmartBugs dataset [3]

Algorithm 1. Generate Vulnerable Smart Contracts Dataset

Require: – List of clean smart contracts: `clean_contracts`
– List of vulnerable code snippets: `vulnerable_snippets`
– SolidiFI tool: `SolidiFI_tool`

Ensure: – Dataset of vulnerable contracts: `vulnerable_contracts_dataset`
– Vulnerability details: `vulnerability_details`

```
Initialize vulnerable_contracts_dataset ← ∅
Initialize vulnerability_details ← ∅
for all contract ∈ clean_contracts do
  ast ← SolidiFI_tool.parse_to_ast(contract)
  low_level_funcs ← FindLowLevelFunctions(ast)
  insertion_points ← SolidiFI_tool.GetInsertionPoints(low_level_funcs)
  if insertion_points = ∅ then
    continue {Skip if no insertion points}
  end if
  selected_point ← RandomChoice(insertion_points)
  suitable_snippets ← GetSuitableSnippets(
                          selected_point, vulnerable_snippets)
  if suitable_snippets = ∅ then
    continue {Skip if no suitable snippets}
  end if
  vulnerable_snippet ← RandomChoice(suitable_snippets)
  src_value ← SolidiFI_tool.get_src_value(selected_point)
  modified_contract ← InsertSnippetAtSrc(
                          contract, vulnerable_snippet, src_value)
  if not CompileContract(modified_contract) then
    continue {Skip if compilation fails}
  end if
  vulnerable_contracts_dataset.append(modified_contract)
  Create vulnerability_info with
          - contract_name ← GetContractName(contract)
          - function_name ← GetFunctionName(selected_point)
          - insertion_point ← src_value
          - vulnerability_type ← vulnerable_snippet.vulnerability_type
          - snippet_inserted ← vulnerable_snippet.code
  vulnerability_details.append(vulnerability_info)
end for
```

and 287 buggy code snippets from the SolidiFI [4] benchmark. These datasets serve as the foundation for generating synthetic yet realistic smart contracts that contain known vulnerabilities.

We developed an algorithm (as depicted in Algorithm 1 and Fig. 2) to generate a dataset of vulnerable smart contracts by injecting predefined vulnerable code snippets into clean smart contracts at random low-level function locations. For each clean contract, it parses the code into an Abstract Syntax Tree (AST) using the SolidiFI tool to identify low-level functions suitable for vulnerabil-

Structured Template

You are a smart contract security expert. Analyze the following Solidity code snippet and explain the vulnerability. The vulnerability type is [Correct Vulnerability Label]. Use the following format:

Bug Name: [Correct Vulnerability Label]
Affected Area:
Description:
Impact Assessment:
Mitigation:

Fig. 3. Structured Template for Bug Explanation Synthesis

ity injection. It then selects a random insertion point within these functions and chooses a compatible vulnerable snippet from the provided list. Using the 'src' value obtained from SolidiFI, which indicates the precise location in the source code, the algorithm inserts the vulnerable snippet into the contract. After ensuring the modified contract compiles successfully, it adds the contract to the dataset and records detailed information about the injected vulnerability, including the contract and function names, insertion point, vulnerability type, and the code snippet inserted. This process is repeated for all clean contracts to create a comprehensive dataset of vulnerable contracts along with their associated vulnerability details.

3.2 Smart Contract Bug Explanation Synthesis

After synthesizing the dataset by injecting buggy snippets into clean Solidity contracts, the next step involves generating detailed explanations for the vulnerabilities using GPT-4o. To ensure accuracy and consistency, the chain-of-thought technique is employed, guiding GPT-4o to produce explanations in a structured format. This format includes the following sections: Bug Name, Affected Area, Description, Impact Assessment, and Mitigation. Additionally, to prevent mislabeling, the correct vulnerability label is explicitly provided to GPT-4o as input.

During this step, **Chain-of-Thought (CoT) Prompting** is applied, where GPT-4o is guided through a structured template that breaks down the reasoning process into sequential steps. The prompt includes the vulnerability label, the vulnerable code snippet, and explicit instructions to generate explanations in a logical, step-by-step format (as shown in Fig. 3). This method is particularly effective for evaluating smart contract bug explanations because it enforces transparency and rigor. CoT prompting compels the model to articulate intermediate reasoning steps such as identifying unsafe external calls in reentrancy vulnerabilities or tracing flawed state updates in access control issues, rather than jumping to conclusions. By decomposing complex vulnerabilities into smaller, verifiable reasoning units, auditors can systematically validate the model's understanding

GPT-4o's Example Output with Structured Template

Bug Name
Reentrancy Vulnerability

Affected Area
The 'withdraw' function in the contract.

Description
The 'withdraw' function transfers Ether to an external address before updating the contract's state. This allows an attacker to recursively call the 'withdraw' function before the balance is deducted, enabling them to drain the contract's funds.

Impact Assessment
This vulnerability can lead to significant financial losses, as attackers can exploit it to steal all Ether stored in the contract. It is a critical issue that compromises the integrity and security of the smart contract.

Mitigation
To mitigate this vulnerability, apply the Checks-Effects-Interactions pattern. Ensure that the contract's state is updated before transferring Ether to external addresses. Additionally, consider using reentrancy guards or the 'ReentrancyGuard' utility provided by OpenZeppelin.

Fig. 4. GPT-4o's Example Output with Structured Template

of attack vectors, code interactions, and mitigation strategies. This granularity reduces ambiguity, ensures adherence to security principles (e.g., checks-effects-interactions patterns), and highlights whether the model genuinely grasps the root cause or relies on superficial patterns. Finally, during the generation process, GPT-4o produces a detailed analysis (see Fig. 4), with CoT ensuring the output is both technically thorough and structured for easy evaluation. For example, as in Fig. 4, the model might first isolate the vulnerable function, then explain how external calls enable recursive execution before state updates, and finally propose fixes.

GPT-4o offers significant benefits for enhancing smart contract security via the generation of bug explanations in a structured and consistent format. By prompting GPT-4o with a predefined template such as "Bug Name," "Affected Area," "Description," "Impact Assessment," and "Mitigation," the model produces outputs that are systematically organized and easy to comprehend. This structured approach enables developers and security analysts to quickly grasp the nature of each vulnerability, its implications, and the steps required to address it. Moreover, the consistency of the output format facilitates seamless integration into documentation, training resources, and automated reporting systems. Nonetheless, sole reliance on GPT-4o poses a risk of misclassifications when the model's initial vulnerability determination is inaccurate, thereby undermining subsequent explanations. To mitigate this issue, explicitly providing GPT-4o with the correct vulnerability label significantly reduces misclassification and ensures more reliable explanations.

Scalability is a primary advantage of employing GPT-4o for bug explanation. Manual analysis and explanation of vulnerabilities in smart contracts are both time-consuming and resource-intensive. In contrast, GPT-4o efficiently processes and generates explanations for a large number of vulnerabilities, making it suitable for extensive datasets. This scalability is particularly critical for researchers and organizations engaged in large-scale smart contract audits or the development of automated bug detection tools.

By integrating synthetic data generation with GPT-4o's advanced natural language capabilities, the proposed methodology addresses two critical challenges in smart contract security: data scarcity and the need for interpretable AI. The synthetic data generation process yields a diverse and realistic dataset for training bug detection models, while GPT-4o's explanations deliver actionable insights into identified vulnerabilities. Collectively, this approach enhances both the accuracy of bug detection models and the overall comprehension of smart contract vulnerabilities, thereby contributing to a more secure blockchain ecosystem.

3.3 Finetune Open-Source LLMs

The fine-tuning process for **CodeLlama-13b-hf** was designed to adapt the model's pre-trained capabilities to the specialized task of generating structured bug explanations for smart contract vulnerabilities. The synthesized dataset, comprising 2,188 clean contracts and 287 bug-injected contracts, will be used as the fine-tuning dataset. This dataset was split into training (80%), validation (10%), and test (10%) sets to ensure robust evaluation. Each training sample included a Solidity code snippet (either clean or containing an injected vulnerability) as input and a structured explanation as the target output. For clean contracts, the output explicitly stated "No vulnerability detected," while buggy contracts required explanations formatted into five predefined sections: **Bug Name**, **Affected Area**, **Description**, **Impact Assessment**, and **Mitigation**. Preprocessing steps, such as removing comments and standardizing code formatting, were applied to ensure consistency across inputs and outputs.

The training leveraged the **HuggingFace transformers** library, with the base **CodeLlama-13b-hf** model chosen for its code-specific pretraining on diverse programming languages, including Solidity. To balance performance and computational efficiency, an initial learning rate of 3.10^4 was used alongside cosine scheduling to gradually adjust the rate during training. Batch sizes ranged between 4 and 8, constrained by GPU memory limitations, and training was conducted over 5 epochs with early stopping to prevent overfitting. The **AdamW** optimizer and cross-entropy loss function were employed to minimize prediction errors. To improve the training time, Low-Rank Adaptation (LoRA) was applied, enabling parameter-efficient fine-tuning by updating only a subset of the model's weights. This approach reduced memory usage while preserving the model's ability to generate coherent and accurate explanations.

The fine-tuning pipeline began with tokenizing code snippets and target explanations using CodeLlama's tokenizer, with sequences truncated or padded to a maximum length of 2,048 tokens to accommodate lengthy Solidity functions. During **instruction tuning**, the model learned to map input code to structured explanations through autoregressive training, where the input context (code snippet) guided the generation of the target output step by step.

A key challenge was ensuring the model adhered to the strict output format required for usability. To enforce this, training prompts explicitly included examples of the desired structure, and the loss function prioritized accuracy in generating section headers and key terms. Post-training, the model's performance was evaluated against GPT-4-generated explanations using the same framework of **Clarity**, **Identification**, and **Impact** criteria. This evaluation confirmed that the fine-tuned model achieved comparable explanatory quality while operating with significantly lower computational overhead, making it a scalable solution for integrating automated bug detection with human-interpretable insights.

3.4 Evaluate the Explanations

To evaluate the performance of large language models (LLMs), we employ GPT-4o to assess explanations across three key dimensions: Clarity, Identification, and Impact on our test set. We use chain-of-thought prompts to guide GPT-4o through multi-step analytical procedures in each category, enabling a comprehensive and systematic critique. This structured approach provides actionable insights into smart contract vulnerabilities, aligning with the overarching goals of clarity, correctness, and contextual relevance.

The Clarity dimension focuses on the coherence of the explanations, gauging their precision, avoidance of unnecessary jargon, and logical organization, from the problem statement through to impact and mitigation. This ensures that the explanations are comprehensible to developers of varying proficiency levels, aiding both educational and debugging objectives. In the Identification category, GPT-4o verifies the accuracy of the vulnerability description through correct categorization, code location, and exploitation conditions. This process includes cross-referencing the explanations with relevant code snippets and associated vulnerability labels to ensure technical validity and practical applicability. The Impact metric examines the breadth of the explanation concerning potential repercussions (e.g., financial loss, data breaches, and operational disruptions) as well as the effectiveness of any proposed mitigation strategies. This dimension ensures that the explanation underscores the significance of the vulnerability and suggests viable solutions.

Following these evaluations, GPT-4o assigns a numeric score from 1 to 5 for each dimension, and the overall quality of the explanation is represented by the aggregate score.

4 Experimental Results

4.1 Explanation Performance

The comparative analysis of explanation performance in smart contract analysis underscores distinct performance patterns between *commercial models* (e.g., *GPT-4o, Claude-3-Haiku*) and *open-source models* (e.g., *CodeLlama variants, Magicoder*). The chosen LLMs represent a strategic mix of open-source and proprietary models, varying scales, and architectural approaches to ensure a holistic comparison in smart contract vulnerability detection. CodeLlama (7B/13B) was included as a code-specialized foundation from Meta, allowing direct comparison of parameter scaling within the same architecture. Magicoder was selected as a state-of-the-art open-source model that excels at instruction-following for code analysis tasks and focuses on diverse coding problem resolution. Claude-3-haiku provides a cost-effective and competitive code understanding despite its general-purpose training. GPT-4o is the cutting-edge benchmark with strong coding and security analysis capabilities.

Table 1. Performance comparison of different models in terms of clarity, identification, and impact. The **bold** values indicate the highest scores in each column.

Model	Average	Clarity	Identification	Impact
CodeLlama-7b-hf-base	2.7899	2.6087	2.9739	2.7870
CodeLlama-13b-hf-base	3.0014	2.6870	3.5304	2.7870
CodeLlama-13b-hf-finetuned	3.6638	3.2696	**4.5696**	3.1522
Magicoder-S-DS-6.7B-base	3.8333	3.6783	4.2174	3.6043
Magicoder-S-CL-7B-base	3.6971	3.5609	4.0261	3.5043
claude-3-haiku-20240307	3.3710	3.6130	2.7174	3.7826
GPT-4o	**4.0261**	**4.1783**	3.6957	**4.2043**

The empirical data, illustrated in Table 1, indicates that **GPT-4o** achieved the highest overall performance with an average score of 4.03, driven by excellent **Clarity** (4.18) and **Impact** (4.20). This proficiency in clarity, articulating risk factors and mitigation strategies effectively aligns **GPT-4o** with end-user applications demanding comprehensive natural language summaries. In contrast, **Claude-3-Haiku** registered a moderate average score of 3.37, with a notable deficiency in **Identification** (2.72), thus revealing limitations in technical precision despite an adequate **Impact** performance (3.78). The fine-tuned variant **CodeLlama-13b-hf-finetuned** also exhibited significant improvement, yielding a notable **Identification** performance of 4.57, highlighting the efficacy of domain-specific training approaches. Smaller models, such as **CodeLlama-7B**, encountered performance challenges with an average score of 2.79, indicating scalability concerns across all evaluated metrics. In terms of **Clarity**, commercial models outperformed, with **GPT-4o** setting a benchmark for readability. However, open-source models, namely **Magicoder** and **CodeLlama**, have shown progress through enhanced training methodologies. For **Identification**, open-source models excelled, as evident in the **CodeLlama-13b-hf-finetuned** surpassing **GPT-4o**, illustrating the enhancements achievable via targeted fine-tuning on synthetic datasets.

4.2 Evaluation of GPT-4o Score

To validate the reliability of GPT-4o's automated evaluations, a manual assessment of 50 randomly selected samples was conducted. These samples were cross-referenced with GPT-4o's scores using two statistical measures: **Pearson correlation** (to assess linear agreement) and **Kendall's Tau** (to assess ordinal agreement). The results, summarized in Table 2, reveal significant variability in alignment across the evaluation categories of **Clarity**, **Identification**, and **Impact**.

Table 2. Correlation coefficients between manual and GPT-4o evaluations.

	Clarity	Identification	Impact
Pearson	0.100	0.860	0.321
Kendall's Tau	0.062	0.708	0.310

The efficacy of GPT-4o in detecting software vulnerabilities was evaluated across three dimensions: Identification, Clarity, and Impact. Within the Identification category, GPT-4o demonstrated the highest performance, achieving a Pearson correlation coefficient of 0.860 and a Kendall's Tau score of 0.708 in comparison to human annotations. These results indicate a strong concordance with human evaluators in pinpointing vulnerabilities, particularly when explicit labels and structured prompts were provided. Notably, in reentrancy and integer overflow scenarios, GPT-4o accurately identified both the specific lines and underlying causes of the vulnerabilities, aligning well with expert analyses. This highlights GPT-4o's potential for automating large-scale code audits.

In contrast, performance in the Clarity category showed weaker agreement with human assessments, as reflected by a Pearson score of 0.100 and a Kendall-Tau score of 0.062. While GPT-4o's explanations were often technically accurate, human evaluators found the output to be overly verbose and laden with jargon, diminishing its practical accessibility. These findings underscore the inherent difficulty of automating subjective language evaluations that require attention to nuance.

The Impact category exhibited moderate agreement: GPT-4o produced Pearson and Kendall's Tau scores of 0.321 and 0.310, respectively. Divergences were largely attributable to different interpretations of risk severity. While GPT-4o provided generic criticality assessments based on technical factors, human evaluators additionally considered contextual variables such as real-world exploitability and potential financial consequences. Consequently, vulnerabilities labeled as

CodeLlama-13B-finetuned's explanation on an Unhandled Exception bug case

Bug name
Unhandled Exception

Affected area
The affected area is the 'callee.call.value(1 ether)("")' line within the 'call_checked_lankford_transferFrom'function.

Description
The vulnerability arises from the use of 'callee.call.value(1 ether)("")' which sends 1 ether to the 'callee' address without checking if the call was successful. In Solidity, the low-level '.call' method returns a boolean indicating whether the call was successful or not. However, in this code snippet, the return value of the call is not checked. This means that if the call fails (e.g., the 'callee' address reverts or runs out of gas), the subsequent lines of code will still execute. This can lead to unexpected behavior and potentially severe security issues.

Impact assessment
The impact of this vulnerability is significant. If the call to the 'callee' fails, the function will still proceed to execute the 'transferFrom' and emit events. This can lead to inconsistent states, where tokens are transferred or approved despite the failure of the initial call. This can cause significant financial losses or disruptions in the contract's operations.

Fig. 5. CodeLlama-13B-finetuned's explanation on Unhandled Exception bug

"critical" by GPT-4o were sometimes downgraded by human analysts when the specific usage context mitigated perceived severity.

In summary, GPT-4o shows strong capabilities in objectively identifying software vulnerabilities, especially under structured interactions that enhance reliability. However, its performance in the more subjective areas of Clarity and Impact remains limited, necessitating hybrid workflows that incorporate human expertise. Such workflows would facilitate the refinement of explanations and the contextualization of risks, thereby balancing scalability with precision. Future research could focus on improving GPT-4o's subjective evaluation capabilities, for instance, by incorporating domain-specific risk frameworks and integrating iterative user feedback mechanisms to refine clarity and impact assessments.

4.3 Error Analysis: Limitations in Vulnerability Explanations

We have conducted an error analysis of our finetuned model and compared it with the GPT-4o model. The consensus is that CodeLlama's explanation is technically correct but lacks mitigation, whereas GPT-4o provides detailed fixes but mislabels the vulnerability.

GPT-4o's explanation on an Unhandled Exception bug case

Vulnerability: Reentrancy Attack

Affected Area:
The affected area is the call to 'callee.call.value(1 ether)("")' before any state changes are made (e.g., updating the token balance).

Vulnerability Description:
The function 'call_checked_lankford_transferFrom' transfers 1 ether to an external contract ('callee') and then attempts to transfer tokens by calling '_tokenImpl.transferFrom' function. The problem arises because the external call ('callee.call.value(1 ether)("")') transfers control to the 'callee' contract without any checks to ensure the 'callee' contract is not malicious.
If the 'callee' contract has a fallback function, that function gets executed upon receiving ether. If that fallback function calls back into the 'call_checked_lankford_transferFrom' function or another function within the same contract that affects the state (e.g., modifying balances), it can lead to undesired reentrant calls. This can result in the contract being in an inconsistent state, and potentially exploited to drain ether or perform unauthorized transfers.

Assessment of the Impact:
The impact of this vulnerability can be severe. If exploited, a malicious 'callee' contract could utilize reentrancy to drain ether from this contract, conduct unauthorized transfers, or manipulate the internal state. This could lead to significant financial loss or the loss of control of the contract logic.

Solution to Fix the Vulnerability (Mitigation):
To mitigate this vulnerability, state-changing operations should be performed before transferring control to external contracts. Specifically, move the critical operations (balancing updates and emitting events) before making the external call. Here's how to fix the vulnerable code: [REDACTED SOLIDITY CODE]

Fig. 6. GPT-4o's explanation on Unhandled Exception bug

For example, in Fig. 5 and Fig. 6, we can see that CodeLlama-Finetuned correctly identifies the unhandled exception (failure to verify call success) and pinpoints low-level Solidity mechanics, reflecting its domain-specific pretraining. However, it omits mitigation steps (e.g., adding require() checks), highlighting gaps in its fine-tuning data. In contrast, GPT-4o mislabels the vulnerability as reentrancy as the code lacks pre-call state changes required for such attacks, but compensates with actionable fixes like the Checks-Effects-Interactions pattern and ReentrancyGuard. This suggests that GPT-4o over-relies on surface-level patterns (e.g., external calls) rather than contextual logic, while CodeLlama prioritizes precision over remediation guidance. Both models struggle with long inputs: CodeLlama truncates broader context (e.g., overlooking transferFrom implications), while GPT-4o's holistic processing introduces hallucinated risks.

5 Conclusion

This research examines the capacity of GPT-4o and fine-tuned open-source models to generate structured bug explanations for smart contract vulnerabilities and evaluates the reliability of automated assessments through manual validation. GPT-4o demonstrated strong performance in **Identification**, achieving high correlation with human evaluations (Pearson = 0.860, Kendall's Tau = 0.708), highlighting its utility in automating vulnerability detection. However, its performance in **Clarity** (Pearson = 0.100, Kendall's Tau = 0.062) was limited, indicating challenges in readability and coherence. Similarly, moderate agreement in **Impact** (Pearson = 0.321, Kendall's Tau = 0.310) suggested difficulties in contextualizing risks, where human expertise remains crucial. Fine-tuned open-source models like **CodeLlama-13b-hf-finetuned** and **Magicoder-S-DS-6.7B** showed competitive performance in **Identification**, thanks to synthetic data and targeted training, offering a cost-effective alternative for security pipelines. Manual validation of 50 samples highlights the importance of hybrid human-AI models, where human oversight is essential for refining explanations and contextualizing risks, while benefiting from the scalability and precision of AI models.

In conclusion, AI-driven tools like GPT-4o have transformative potential in smart contract security when enhanced with domain-specific fine-tuning and human expertise, promoting secure and efficient decentralized applications. Our future work will focus on improving generated outputs' clarity and contextual relevance, as well as enhancing training datasets.

References

1. Case Studies of Real-World Smart Contract Vulnerabilities and Exploits. https://codeofcode.org/lessons/case-studies-ofreal-world-smart-contract-vulnerabilities-and-exploits/. Accessed 20 Feb 2025
2. Dubois, Y., et al.: Length-Controlled AlpacaEval: A Simple Way to Debias Automatic Evaluators (2024). arXiv:2404.04475. https://arxiv.org/abs/2404.04475
3. Durieux, T., et al.: Empirical review of automated analysis tools on 47,587 Ethereum smart contracts. In: Proceedings of the ACM/IEEE 42nd International Conference on Software Engineering. ICSE 2020. ACM (2020). https://doi.org/10.1145/3377811.3380364
4. Ghaleb, A., Pattabiraman, K.: How effective are smart contract analysis tools? Evaluating smart contract static analysis tools using bug injection. In: Proceedings of the 29th ACM SIGSOFT International Symposium on Software Testing and Analysis. ISSTA 2020. ACM (2020). https://doi.org/10.1145/3395363.3397385
5. Gurjar, A., Chandavarkar, B.R.: Smart contract vulnerabilities and detection methods: a survey. In: 2024 15th International Conference on Computing Communication and Networking Technologies (ICCCNT), pp. 1–7 (2024). https://doi.org/10.1109/ICCCNT61001.2024.10724246
6. Iuliano, G., Di Nucci, D.: Smart Contract Vulnerabilities, Tools, and Benchmarks: An Updated Systematic Literature Review (2024). arXiv:2412.01719. https://arxiv.org/abs/2412.01719

7. Jain, V.K., Tripathi, M.: Multi-model approach for ethereum smart contract vulnerability detection. In: Singh, J.P., et al. (eds.) Computational Intelligence in Communications and Business Analytics, pp. 220–230. Springer, Cham (2024). ISBN: 978-3-031-81339-9
8. Kim, S., et al.: Prometheus: Inducing Fine-grained Evaluation Capability in Language Models (2024). arXiv:2310.08491. https://arxiv.org/abs/2310.08491
9. Liu, Y., et al.: G-Eval: NLG Evaluation using GPT-4 with Better Human Alignment (2023). arXiv:2303.16634. https://arxiv.org/abs/2303.16634
10. OWASP Smart Contract Top 10 | OWASP Foundation. https://owasp.org/www-project-smart-contract-top-10/. Accessed 20 Feb 2025
11. Wang, S.J., et al.: Detecting Buggy Contracts via Smart Testing (2024). arXiv:2409.04597. https://arxiv.org/abs/2409.04597
12. Wataoka, K., Takahashi, T., Ri, R.: Self-Preference Bias in LLM-as-a-Judge (2024). arXiv:2410.21819. https://arxiv.org/abs/2410.21819
13. Zheng, L., et al.: Judging LLM-as-a-Judge with MT-Bench and Chatbot Arena (2023). arXiv:2306.05685. https://arxiv.org/abs/2306.05685

The Benefits of Query-Based KGQA Systems for Complex and Temporal Questions in LLM Era

Artem Alekseev[1], Mikhail Chaichuk[2,3], Miron Butko[4], Alexander Panchenko[1,2,3], Elena Tutubalina[2,3,5], and Oleg Somov[2,6](✉)

[1] Skoltech, Moscow, Russia
[2] AIRI, Moscow, Russia
somov@airi.net
[3] HSE University, Moscow, Russia
[4] SaluteDevices, Moscow, Russia
[5] Kazan Federal University, Kazan, Russia
[6] Moscow Institute of Physics and Technology, Moscow, Russia

Abstract. Large language models excel in question-answering (QA) but struggle with multi-hop reasoning and temporal questions. Query-based knowledge graph QA (KGQA) offers a modular alternative by generating executable queries instead of direct answers. We explore multi-stage query-based framework for WikiData QA, proposing multi-stage approach that enhances performance on challenging multi-hop and temporal benchmarks. Through generalization and rejection studies, we evaluate robustness across multi-hop and temporal QA datasets. Additionally, we introduce a novel entity linking and predicate matching method using CoT reasoning. Our results demonstrate the potential of query-based multi-stage KGQA framework for improving multi-hop and temporal QA with small language models. Code: https://github.com/ar2max/NLDB-KGQA-System.

Keywords: KGQA · SPARQL · WikiData · Generalization · Rejection

1 Introduction

Modern question-answering (QA) systems based on large language models (LLMs) achieve strong performance on open-domain benchmarks [13,34,38]. These models rely on retrieving information either from internal models parameters or external memory such as vector storage [21].

Despite their success, QA systems face limitations in both retrieval mechanisms. Internally, knowledge gaps arise due to uneven fact distribution in pre-training data – some facts are more popular in pre-training data than others [1]. Externally, retrieval effectiveness is closely tied to document representation, where issues can stem from dense retrieval methods [19] or suboptimal initial document knowledge representation. For instance, some studies indicate that models struggle to infer inverted knowledge directly from the data [6]. Thus

R. Ichise (Ed.): NLDB 2025, LNCS 15836, pp. 426–441, 2026.
https://doi.org/10.1007/978-3-031-97141-9_29

LLM-based QA systems often struggle with answering rare, multi-hop, or time-sensitive questions – especially those requiring structured data, despite the possibility of answering such question with internal or external storage [18].

In contrast, parsing-based QA systems generate structured queries that directly retrieve information from structured knowledge bases (KBs), overcoming the limitations of memory-based approaches. Parsing-based systems construct executable queries, ensuring precise and deterministic retrieval from structured databases. While these approaches face challenges related to compositional generalization and domain adaptation [15,17,35], they offer key advantages in terms of scalability, accuracy, and efficiency when answering open-domain questions that involve structured data [8,42].

In this work, we present a query-based multi-stage pipeline QA system that generates executable queries for retrieving answers from structured knowledge sources. Our system is evaluated across key metrics, including generalization to new domains, rejection ability, and overall system performance on multi-hop and temporal questions. Experimental results demonstrate that our approach achieves frontier performance on selected datasets, surpassing both ChatGPT's direct answer generation methods and query generation method, which produces executable SPARQL queries.

Our research specifically focuses on Wikidata [40] due to its unique characteristics, which present distinct challenges for QA systems. Unlike DBpedia [2], where entities are directly linked to textual literals, Wikidata requires mapping to unique numeric identifiers (Q-IDs), significantly increasing the complexity of Entity Linking. Additionally, Wikidata's structured representation, including qualifiers and references, introduces higher reasoning complexity in query execution. Moreover, Wikidata is continuously updated, ensuring access to up-to-date information which is crucial factor for real-world applications.

To the best of our knowledge, no prior work has conducted a comprehensive evaluation of a query-based KGQA system on Wikidata in comparison with proprietary LLMs. In this study, we evaluate each component of the multi-stage pipeline independently, as well as assess the end-to-end performance of the entire system—from input question to predicted answer entity IDs. Our findings demonstrate the effectiveness of the proposed pipeline across multiple datasets, highlighting its strong generalization capabilities and improved rejection handling. These results underscore the significance of our approach in advancing structured QA systems and bridging the gap between natural language queries and structured knowledge retrieval.

2 Related Work

Knowledge graph question answering (KGQA) has been a longstanding area of research in natural language processing (NLP). However, with the emergence of LLMs, KGQA has gained increased utility. Early approaches, which relied on rule-based systems and traditional semantic parsing components, demonstrated high precision for the input questions but suffered from low recall. In contrast,

LLMs are capable of processing large volumes of input data and generating accurate queries, although they are often plagued by generalization issues and hallucinations. Modern KGQA systems based on large language models aim to mitigate these issues by leveraging advanced techniques to improve generalization and reduce hallucinations.

Query-based KGQA systems were initially trained on text-to-SPARQL pairs, incorporating intermediate steps like predicate classification, entity linking, and slot-filling [16,25,27]. These approaches focused on simple one-hop questions but remain relevant due to their structured methodology. Efforts to overcome the one-hop limitation include in-context-learning (ICL) with proprietary LLMs [37] and fine-tuning approaches [5,8].

Research on ICL improvements includes retrieval-augmented generation with few-shot examples [14], SPARQL decomposition into atomic sub-steps [22], and interactive multi-hop question decomposition [41]. Fine-tuning strategies involve augmenting text-to-SPARQL pairs [30], structured pre-training [29], and incorporating linguistic features like Part-of-Speech tags and dependency parsing [28].

Ensuring the reliability of SPARQL queries in KGQA involves pre-execution validation to prevent errors. AI-based methods enhance reliability by employing syntactic and semantic query checks [43], LLM-driven Chain-of-Thought (CoT) prompting [36], synthetic data for error detection [33], and graph-based logical consistency verification [4]. Transformer models compare generated queries against reference sets to flag logical flaws [11], while hybrid symbolic-ML methods integrate rule-based reasoning with machine learning for enhanced accuracy [24]. These approaches collectively improve KGQA robustness, reducing incorrect or nonsensical query execution before reaching the user.

As noted in [8], proprietary ICL models like ChatGPT-4 or Claude are expensive due to large input sizes and multiple query requests. We build upon this by developing an multi-stage KGQA system using small fine-tuned models, trainable on consumer-grade GPUs. To our knowledge, no prior research has systematically evaluated the generalization and rejection accuracy of such a system, particularly for Wikidata-based temporal and multi-hop QA.

3 Data and Evaluation

We evaluate our system on four multi-hop and temporal datasets: LC-QuAD 2.0 [12], RuBQ 2.0 [31], QALD-10 [39], and PAT-Questions [26]. All samples from selected datasets consists of question, SPARQL, mentioned entities and corresponding Q-IDs. The SPARQL can be executed over Wikidata Query engine[1]. The key statistics on the complexity for these datasets are presented in Table 1.

LC-QuAD 2.0 is a benchmark for KGQA over Wikidata, evaluating complex SPARQL-based query generation. It includes multi-hop reasoning, boolean queries, count-based queries, and qualifier-dependent questions. **QALD-10** is a multilingual benchmark for KGQA, evaluating systems querying Wikidata using

[1] https://query.wikidata.org/.

Table 1. The key statistics for selected benchmarks.

Dataset	Train	Test	Multi-HOP %	Avg. Hops	Hops Range
QALD-10	402	386	58.3%	2.1	1–8
LC-QuAD 2.0	17,864	4,541	62.9%	1.91	1–4
RuBQ 2.0	1,920	580	10%	1.1	1–2
PAT	4,795	1,199	53.3%	1.68	1–2

SPARQL. We use a subset of English questions for our evaluation. **RuBQ 2.0** is designed for querying Wikidata with structured SPARQL queries. It includes one-hop, multi-hop, count-based, literal-based, and unanswerable questions. The dataset covers comparative, temporal, count-based, and superlative queries. **PAT** is a benchmark for Present-Anchored Temporal Question Answering, focusing on time-sensitive questions with evolving answers. It includes single-hop and multi-hop questions and features an auto-updating mechanism for answer freshness.

$$\mathcal{C} = \mathcal{T} \cap \widehat{\mathcal{T}}, \quad p = \frac{|\mathcal{C}|}{|\widehat{\mathcal{T}}|}, \quad r = \frac{|\mathcal{C}|}{|\mathcal{T}|}, \quad F_1 = \frac{2pr}{p+r}, \quad \text{Acc@1} = \begin{cases} 1, & \text{if } \mathcal{T} \cap \widehat{\mathcal{T}} \neq \emptyset \\ 0, & \text{otherwise} \end{cases}$$

We evaluate our entity linking quality and system's ability to generate accurate SPARQL queries for KGQA by executing predicted and ground truth queries on Wikidata and comparing their entity sets $\widehat{\mathcal{T}}$ and $\mathcal{T}$. Accuracy (Acc), precision (p), recall (r), and F1 score are computed based on the intersection of these sets. As the key performance measure we use F1 score. It is important to note, that we consider correct execution match if there any intersection between predicted and gold answer sets.

4 KGQA System

We present a query-based KGQA system, shown in Fig. 1, designed to generate SPARQL queries for Wikidata. The system includes three core components: (1) entity detection and disambiguation, (2) predicate detection and disambiguation, and (3) an auto-regressive query generation model. We evaluate multiple entity linking approaches – reasoning-based and fine-tuned solution – and evaluate their impact on overall system performance. Additionally, we enhance the pipeline through text-to-SPARQL model fine-tuning or few-shot training. Our experiments focus on multi-hop and temporal question-answering, assessing the system's generalization and ability to reject incorrect queries. The following sections detail each component and its independent and joint metrics.

4.1 Entity Linking

Entity linking involves identifying the span of an entity mention in a text and linking it to a unique identifier in a knowledge base. In open-domain KGQA

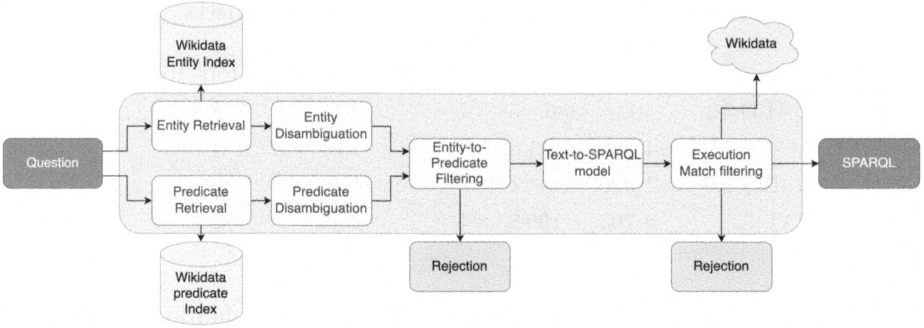

Fig. 1. KGQA system processes natural language question and translates it into SPARQL for retrieving information from Wikidata. It follows a structured pipeline where entities and predicates are first retrieved and disambiguated using Wikidata indexes. A filtering step then ensures correct entity-predicate mappings before passing it to a text-to-SPARQL model. The generated query undergoes execution match filtering, ensuring valid and accurate results. If retrieval or disambiguation fails, the system rejects the query.

systems, such as those over Wikidata, this task is challenging due to the large number of potential entities (over 80 million). We explore two approaches for entity linking: fine-tuned entity linking and entity linking with reasoning models.

E2E Entity Linking. For entity linking, we use the ReFinED model [3], which links entities using fine-grained entity types and descriptions in a single forward pass. The model performs mention detection, entity typing, and disambiguation, with training in a multi-task manner across four tasks. These loss tasks are combined with weighted loss functions. ReFinED outperforms other models in zero-shot entity linking and has near-perfect coverage of Wikidata for our datasets. We applied it without modification, using the original code repository for inference[2]. For the comparison we also evaluate Falcon [32] and Spacy[3] open-source entity linking tools.

Entity Linking with Reasoning Models. While ReFinED provides a strong baseline, it struggles with less popular entities and dataset generalization. To address these, we propose a two-step approach **RetReason**: **entity retrieval** and **entity disambiguation** method.

Entity Retrieval. We construct a BM25 index over Wikidata, filtering out entities with fewer than ten predicates resulting in 15 million entity index size (we do that to preserve only popular entities and keep the index in reasonable size). We optimize BM25 hyperparameters (k_1, b) for each dataset, favoring recall. We retrieve the top 10 and 100 candidate entities. The retriever hyperparams and quality is in Appendix B.

[2] https://github.com/amazon-science/ReFinED.
[3] https://spacy.io/api/entitylinker.

Entity Disambiguation. Using a Chain-of-Thought reasoning approach, we disambiguate retrieved entities by prompting reasoning models (DeepSeek-R1 and ChatGPT-4) to select the correct entity. Table 2 presents F1 scores for all models. The results demonstrate that Refined entity linking approaches surpasses other methods, but RetReason is competitive and can be utilized through LLM API. The prompt for entity disambiguation for CoT reasoning is provided in the Appendix A.

Table 2. Entity Linking F1 performance for all methods.

Method	QALD-10	LC-QuAD 2.0	RuBQ 2.0	PAT
Refined	**65.0**	**57.4**	*57.2*	**93.1**
Spacy	49.0	46.0	31.0	40.0
Falcon	33.0	43.0	33.0	35.0
RetReason with DeepSeek@10	47.43	47.87	49.44	39.83
RetReason with ChatGPT@10	50.57	48.65	52.58	43.82
RetReason with DeepSeek@100	51.61	50.64	54.97	40.22
RetReason with ChatGPT@100	*53.86*	*54.14*	**60.15**	*44.99*

Table 3. Predicate F1 Matching for RetReason.

Method	QALD-10	LC-QuAD 2.0	RuBQ 2.0	PAT
RetReason with DeepSeek@10	55.21	**65.81**	67.86	**43.49**
RetReason with ChatGPT@10	58.75	63.43	**73.13**	41.24
RetReason with DeepSeek@100	56.27	62.97	64.35	39.29
RetReason with ChatGPT@100	**62.89**	62.95	**72.83**	35.43

4.2 Predicate Matching

We use the entity retrieval and disambiguation methodology for predicate selection. While classification-based baselines are effective for one-hop questions, they cannot be applied to multi-hop cases because the number of relations is not fixed – we need to do arbitrary predicate selection among all WikiData predicates.

Predicate Retrieval. As in the Entity Retrieval section, we follow the same matching methodology. We construct a BM25 search index over all Wikidata predicates, resulting in over 12k predicates index size. Each predicate is represented by its label and description texts. The search procedure is identical to Entity Retrieval. We retrieve the top 10 and 100 candidate predicates and evaluate retrieval effectiveness using recall as the primary metric. The hyper-parameter search and search quality are presented in Appendix B.

Predicate Disambiguation. Similar to Entity Disambiguation, we address the predicate selection problem by identifying the relevant predicates from the

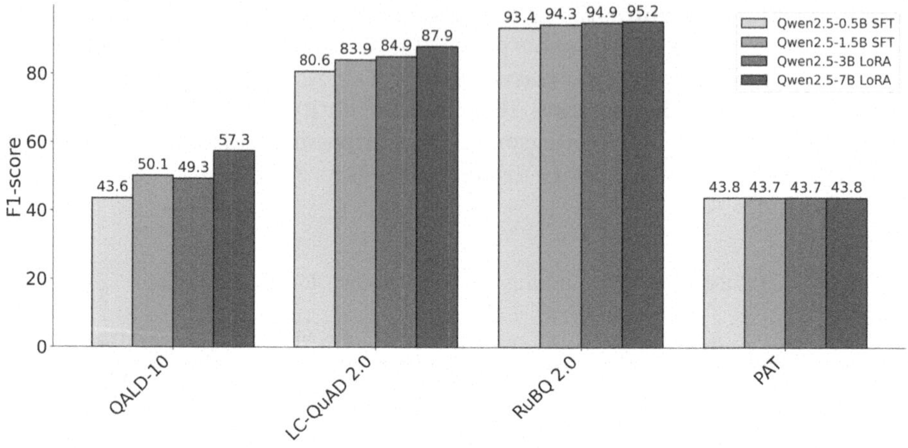

Fig. 2. The models comparison across different sizes (0.5B, 1.5B, 3B, 7B) of Qwen2.5 models and training approaches (LoRA & SFT) with F1 score.

set of retrieved candidates that are most related to the ones mentioned in the question. The predicate disambiguation step is performed similarly as entity disambiguation, except that the system prompt and corresponding descriptions of each predicate, coming from the retrieval model, are used. The prompt for entity disambiguation for CoT reasoning is provided in the Appendix A. The final metrics for predicate disambiguation presented in Table 3.

4.3 Text-to-SPARQL Modeling

For the prediction of the final Text-to-SPARQL model, we apply fine-tuning of pretrained LLM's from Qwen2.5[4] family for moderate sizes – 0.5B, 1.5B, 3B and 7B to evaluate the generalization performance on different scales. We do full-supervised fine-tuning for 0.5B and 1.5B models and LoRA for the 3B and 7B. The model is trained to predict the final SPARQL query, given small query generation instruction, question, candidate entity set from entity linking stage and predicate entity set from predicate linking stage. The training results for selected datasets and for models of different sizes are present in Fig. 2. The figure does not exhibit a consistent trend of quality improvement with an increase in scale across all datasets. During training stage, we want to emulate the inference phase, where entity linking usually gives more entities, then expected. We combine incorrect entities with the correct ones, based on their BM25 similarity to the gold entity mentioned in the question. The prompt format and the model approach training hyper-parameters are presented in Appendix C.

[4] https://huggingface.co/collections/Qwen/qwen25-66e81a666513e518adb90d9e.

4.4 Question and Predicate Filtering

The text-to-SPARQL model is trained on pairs of questions and SPARQL queries, so it will always generate a query for any entity and predicate, even in cases where doing so is fundamentally impossible according to the knowledge graph ontology. This results in a high false positive rate, where incorrect queries are produced, misleading users and requiring manual validation. To overcome this issue, we propose a simple filtering algorithm to filter out Entities and Predicates that do not relate to each other. The algorithm pseudo-code is provided in Appendix D.

As a second reliability check, we execute the generated SPARQL query and analyze its output. If the query results in an error or returns an empty set, it is considered incorrect. Errors indicate structural or syntax issues, while an empty set suggests that the query does not retrieve any relevant information from the knowledge graph. In both cases, we discard the query and inform the user that an accurate SPARQL query cannot be generated, preventing misleading or unverified results.

5 Experiments

The system is evaluated using three approaches: GPT-4o as a direct question-answering (QA) model, GPT-4o as a text-to-SPARQL generation model and our developed system. In our following set of experiments we want to show the advantage of small models for KGQA problem.

GPT-4o as a Direct QA Model. In this approach, GPT-4o is prompted as an open-domain QA system, leveraging few-shot learning to infer factual answers. No constraints are placed on the usage of knowledge, meaning GPT-4o can access any information available through its API. The generated answers are evaluated based on the exact match between gold labels and predicted responses.

Few-Shot GPT-4o for SPARQL Query Generation. In this setup, GPT-4o receives a prompt instructing it to transform natural language questions into valid SPARQL queries. The prompt includes predicted entity, provided by ReFined, and predicate matching, provided by RetReason from previous stage. The generated SPARQL queries are then executed against Wikidata, and their results are compared to the ground truth answers.

Table 4 shows that in datasets where simple one-hop (QALD-10 and RuBQ 2.0) questions dominate, direct question answering with ChatGPT yields promising results. However, in datasets primarily composed of temporal and multi-hop questions (LC-QuAD 2.0 and PAT), the pipeline-based KGQA system significantly outperforms both ChatGPT's direct question answering and established baselines.

6 Generalization Study

To address potential overfitting on the training dataset, we carefully consider the risk that the model may achieve high performance on the test split due

Table 4. End-to-end comparison of GPT-4o, existing solutions, and the full KGQA system on SPARQL query generation, evaluated by accuracy and F1 score of predicted answer entity IDs given the input question.

Model	QALD-10		LC-QuAD 2.0		RuBQ 2.0		PAT	
	F1	Acc@1	F1	Acc@1	F1	Acc@1	F1	Acc@1
GPT-4o (Direct QA)	37.3	-	21.1	-	**77.0**	-	18.3	-
Few-shot GPT-4o + ReFineD	33.8	24.1	24.4	14.9	38.3	27.2	17.7	0.0
SPINACH [23]	**69.5**	-	-	-	-	-	-	-
SPARQL-QA [7]	*45.38*	-	-	-	-	-	-	-
Konstruktor [25]	-	-	-	21.9	-	34.4	-	-
Text2Graph(MEKER Wiki4M) [9]	-	-	-	26.6	-	-	-	-
Review-Then-Refine [10]	-	-	-	-	-	-	33.3	-
Qwen-0.5B + RetReason	22.1	21.3	22.4	21.6	38.6	37.3	28.2	0.2
Qwen-0.5B + ReFineD	25.6	24.7	28.6	27.4	43.9	43.3	*38.9*	0.2
Qwen-1.5B + RetReason	24.0	23.1	23.6	22.8	36.2	35.1	27.9	0.2
Qwen-1.5B + ReFineD	27.6	*26.8*	30.3	28.9	43.2	42.6	38.9	0.2
Qwen-3B + RetReason	24.1	23.1	23.7	22.8	40.4	39.1	27.8	0.2
Qwen-3B + ReFineD	27.6	26.3	**31.2**	**29.5**	45.2	*44.8*	38.9	0.2
Qwen-7B + RetReason	24.9	23.8	24.7	23.8	42.5	41.1	28.1	0.2
Qwen-7B + ReFineD	31.0	**29.7**	*31.0*	*29.4*	*46.8*	**45.9**	**39.0**	0.2

to learned dataset-specific patterns rather than genuine generalization. Such patterns naturally arise because each dataset follows a distinct data collection pipeline, resulting in similarities in question structure, domain focus, or other inherent characteristics. To mitigate this issue and ensure robust generalization, we adopt a cross-dataset validation strategy, where the model is trained on three out of four datasets and evaluated on the test split of the fourth one that remains entirely unseen during training. This approach enables a more rigorous assessment of the model's ability to generalize to novel question distributions while reducing the likelihood of dataset-specific memorization.

The core component of our approach is a text-to-SPARQL model, fine-tuned on the training split of each dataset. In Fig. 3, we evaluate its generalization capabilities for query generation on an out-of-distribution (OOD) dataset, assuming correct entity linking and predicate matching. The model is trained on three datasets and evaluated on the remaining one, following the same training procedure outlined previously in Sect. 4.3. While the models do not surpass the performance of the fine-tuning approach, the performance gap remains relatively small. The largest gap observed on the LC-QuAD 2.0 dataset, indicating the presence of dataset-specific differences in target query structures and the fact that LC-QuAD 2.0 is the largest dataset across all selected.

Furthermore, Table 5 presents an evaluation of the full system in a cross-validation setting across our datasets. For this evaluation, we employed Qwen2.5

(1.5B) along with the ReFineD entity linker. We observe that, in certain cases (QALD-10 and LC-QuAD 2.0), the model exhibits comparable generalization to new datasets, achieving performance levels close to those obtained when fine-tuned on each dataset individually.

7 Rejection Study

Ensuring the reliability of SPARQL query generation is essential for practical KGQA systems. Many models, including GPT-4o, generate responses regardless of their validity, often leading to a high proportion of incorrect answers. To address this issue, we introduce a rejection mechanism designed to identify and filter out erroneous query generations, thereby enhancing system reliability. This study evaluates the effectiveness of our approach in rejecting invalid SPARQL queries and compares it with GPT-4o, which lacks a structured rejection mechanism. Our findings underscore the importance of incorporating early termination

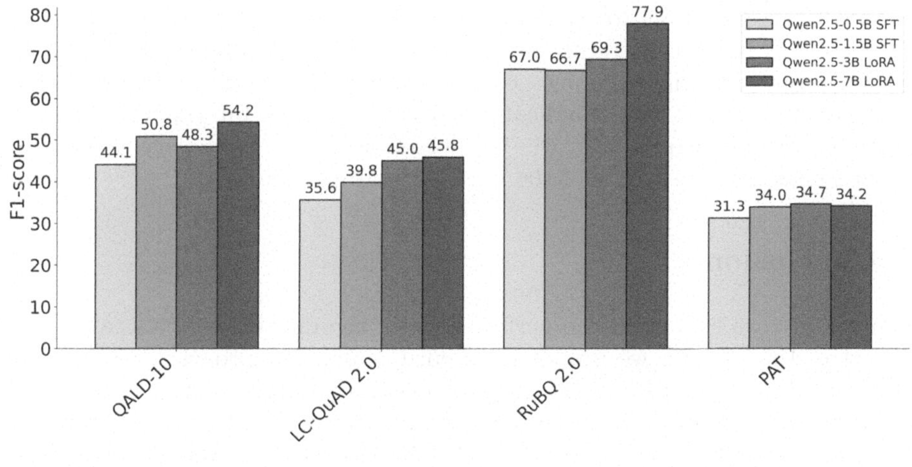

Fig. 3. The generalization evaluation across different sizes (0.5B, 1.5B, 3B, 7B) of Qwen2.5 models and training approaches (LoRA & SFT) with F1 score.

Table 5. End-to-end generalization performance of the system trained with Qwen2.5-1.5B and ReFineD entity linking, evaluated from question input to predicted answer entity IDs.

Train	Test	F1
RuBQ 2.0 + PAT + LC-QuAD 2.0	QALD-10	29.4
RuBQ 2.0 + QALD-10 + PAT	LC-QuAD 2.0	20.8
QALD-10 + PAT + LC-QuAD 2.0	RuBQ 2.0	22.5
RuBQ 2.0 + QALD-10 + LC-QuAD 2.0	PAT	12.5

Table 6. The detection of incorrect query generations using rejection mechanisms. Each value represents the proportion of identified incorrect SPARQL queries.

Dataset	LLM rejection	Execution	Filtering & Execution
QALD-10	11.42%	27.3 %	66.3 %
LC-QuAD 2.0	29.7 %	51.3 %	72.6 %
RuBQ 2.0	0.0 %	41.9 %	84.5 %
PAT	21.9%	40.1 %	61.3 %

and execution-based filtering to mitigate the risk of generating misleading outputs.

We evaluate the system's rejection rate across all datasets and compare the results to direct question answering with LLM rejection. Table 6 presents the percentage of incorrect SPARQL queries identified using three rejection policies. For direct question answering with ChatGPT, we leverage the model's internal mechanism to recognize when it cannot answer a question through prompting. For SPARQL generation, we execute the generated queries against the database and filter out those that return no results. The final column reports a joint rejection approach that combines entity-to-predicate filtering with execution-based filtering. As the results indicate, entity-to-predicate filtering (presented in Appendix D) significantly improves the detection of incorrect query generations by leveraging the constraints of the knowledge graph ontology.

8 Conclusion

In this study, we evaluated the performance of the multi-stage KGQA system. As part of the system, we proposed an entity linking approach leveraging the reasoning abilities of LLMs, which performs comparably to traditional entity detection and disambiguation methods. Additionally, we introduced a rejection algorithm that detects errors prior to SPARQL generation. While the system's individual components perform good overall, a common issue observed in systems with successive components is the propagation of errors, which ultimately impacts the overall quality. Despite this, our approach demonstrates a significant improvement over ChatGPT-based QA systems and existing approaches, particularly in complex multi-hop and temporal question tasks, such as those found in the LC-Quad and PAT datasets, underscoring the effectiveness of the proposed method.

Acknowledgments. This research was supported in part through computational resources of HPC facilities at HSE University [20]. The work has been supported by the Russian Science Foundation grant # 23-11-00358.

A Entity Disambiguation and Predicate Matching with Reasoning

The prompt and evaluation procedure is specified in the solution repository in folder https://github.com/ar2max/NLDB-KGQA-System/tree/master/disambiguation.

B Entity and Predicate Retrieval Hyperparameters and Metrics

Table 7. BM25 hyperparameters (k1 and b) and Recall@10/100 for entity and predicate candidate retrieval. Each cell reports values in the format: entity/predicate.

Dataset	k1	b	Recall@10	Recall@100
QALD-10	2.95/5.18	0.2/0.01	0.52/0.74	0.66/0.91
LC-QuAD 2.0	2.45/2.95	0.2/0.01	0.56/0.89	0.71/0.98
RuBQ 2.0	1.39/2.0	0.4/0.01	0.58/0.85	0.72/0.97
PAT	1.0/0.1	0.7/0.01	0.79/1.0	0.88/1.0

C Text-to-SPARQL Hyperparameters

In an end-to-end setting, entities and relations are extracted with high recall, which often results in the inclusion of additional irrelevant entities and relations alongside the correct ones. To help the model distinguish relevant entities and relations from irrelevant ones, we introduce additional entities and relations during fine-tuning. Specifically, we retrieve the top five most similar entities and relations using BM25 and randomly add them to the gold-standard ones before passing them to the model. This approach encourages the model to disambiguate input information, filtering out unrelated entities while focusing on generating the correct SPARQL structure.

The hyperparameters for the Text-to-SPARQL model training are as follows: the tokenizer max length is set to 1024, with 3 epochs and a batch size of 8. The model uses 500 warmup steps, a weight decay of 0.01, and a learning rate of 2×10^{-5}. Gradient accumulation steps are set to 1, and the random seed is 42.

D Filtering Algorithm

The entity-to-predicate filtering algorithm that rejects the generation based on knowledge graph ontology.

Algorithm 1. Entity-to-Predicate Filtering Approach

Require: Set of entities $\mathcal{E}$, Set of relations $\mathcal{R}$
Ensure: Boolean flag indicating entity-predicate compatibility

function GetEntityRelations(e)
    $\mathcal{R}_{in} \leftarrow \emptyset$, $\mathcal{R}_{out} \leftarrow \emptyset$
    for each triple (s, r, o) in the knowledge graph **do**
        if $o = e$ **then**
            $\mathcal{R}_{in} \leftarrow \mathcal{R}_{in} \cup \{r\}$
        else if $s = e$ **then**
            $\mathcal{R}_{out} \leftarrow \mathcal{R}_{out} \cup \{r\}$
        end if
    end for
    return $(\mathcal{R}_{in}, \mathcal{R}_{out})$
end function
function CheckEntityMismatch($\mathcal{E}, \mathcal{R}$)
    mismatch ← True
    for each entity $e \in \mathcal{E}$ **do**
        $(\mathcal{R}_{in}, \mathcal{R}_{out}) \leftarrow$ GetEntityRelations(e)
        if $(\mathcal{R}_{in} \cup \mathcal{R}_{out}) \cap \mathcal{R} \neq \emptyset$ **then**
            mismatch ← False
            break
        end if
    end for
    return mismatch
end function

References

1. Allen-Zhu, Z., Li, Y.: Physics of language models: part 3.1, knowledge storage and extraction (2023)
2. Auer, S., Bizer, C., Kobilarov, G., Lehmann, J., Cyganiak, R., Ives, Z.: Dbpedia: a nucleus for a web of open data. In: International Semantic Web Conference, pp. 722–735. Springer (2007)
3. Ayoola, T., Tyagi, S., Fisher, J., Christodoulopoulos, C., Pierleoni, A.: ReFinED: an efficient zero-shot-capable approach to end-to-end entity linking. In: Loukina, A., Gangadharaiah, R., Min, B. (eds.) Proceedings of the 2022 Conference of the North American Chapter of the Association for Computational Linguistics: Human Language Technologies: Industry Track, pp. 209–220. Association for Computational Linguistics (2022)
4. Baazouzi, W., Kachroudi, M., Faiz, S.: Sweeping knowledge graphs with SPARQL queries to palliate Q/A problems. In: International Conference on Advanced Information Systems Engineering (2024)
5. Banerjee, D., Nair, P.A., Kaur, J.N., Usbeck, R., Biemann, C.: Modern baselines for SPARQL semantic parsing. In: Proceedings of the 45th International ACM SIGIR Conference on Research and Development in Information Retrieval, pp. 2260–2265 (2022)

6. Berglund, L., et al.: The reversal curse: LLMs trained on "a is b" fail to learn "b is a" (2023)
7. Borroto, M., Ricca, F., Cuteri, B., Barbara, V.: SPARQL-QA enters the QALD challenge. In: Proceedings of the 7th Natural Language Interfaces for the Web of Data (NLIWoD) co-located with the 19th European Semantic Web Conference, Hersonissos, Greece, vol. 3196, pp. 25–31 (2022)
8. Brei, F., Frey, J., Meyer, L.P.: Leveraging small language models for TEXT2SPARQL tasks to improve the resilience of AI assistance (2024)
9. Chekalina, V., Razzhigaev, A., Sayapin, A., Frolov, E., Panchenko, A.: Meker: memory efficient knowledge embedding representation for link prediction and question answering. arXiv preprint arXiv:2204.10629 (2022)
10. Chen, X., Hu, X., Tang, N.: Then-refine: a dynamic framework for multi-hop question answering with temporal adaptability. arXiv preprint arXiv:2412.15101 (2024)
11. Chong, Y., Lee, C., Muhd-Yassin, S., Lim, K.: Transkgqa: enhanced knowledge graph question answering with sentence transformers. IEEE Trans. Knowl. Data Eng. (2024)
12. Dubey, M., Banerjee, D., Abdelkawi, A., Lehmann, J.: LC-QuAD 2.0: a large dataset for complex question answering over Wikidata and DBpedia. In: Ghidini, C., et al. (eds.) ISWC 2019. LNCS, vol. 11779, pp. 69–78. Springer, Cham (2019). https://doi.org/10.1007/978-3-030-30796-7_5
13. Gao, Y., et al.: Retrieval-augmented generation for large language models: a survey (2023)
14. Ghajari, A., Ros, S., Pérez, Á.: Querying the depths: unveiling the strengths and struggles of large language models in SPARQL generation. Procesamiento del lenguaje natural **73**, 271–281 (2024)
15. Gu, Y., et al.: Beyond IID: three levels of generalization for question answering on knowledge bases. In: Proceedings of the Web Conference 2021, pp. 3477–3488 (2021)
16. Hu, N., et al.: An empirical study of pre-trained language models in simple knowledge graph question answering. World Wide Web **26**(5), 2855–2886 (2023)
17. Jiang, L., Usbeck, R.: Knowledge graph question answering datasets and their generalizability: are they enough for future research? In: Proceedings of the 45th International ACM SIGIR Conference on Research and Development in Information Retrieval, pp. 3209–3218 (2022)
18. Jiang, Z., Araki, J., Ding, H., Neubig, G.: How can we know when language models know? on the calibration of language models for question answering. Trans. Assoc. Comput. Linguist. **9**, 962–977 (2021)
19. Karpukhin, V., et al.: Dense passage retrieval for open-domain question answering. In: Webber, B., Cohn, T., He, Y., Liu, Y. (eds.) Proceedings of the 2020 Conference on Empirical Methods in Natural Language Processing (EMNLP), pp. 6769–6781. Association for Computational Linguistics, Online (2020)
20. Kostenetskiy, P., Chulkevich, R., Kozyrev, V.: HPC resources of the higher school of economics. J. Phys. Conf. Ser. **1740**, 012050 (2021). https://doi.org/10.1088/1742-6596/1740/1/012050
21. Lewis, P., et al.: Retrieval-augmented generation for knowledge-intensive NLP tasks. Adv. Neural. Inf. Process. Syst. **33**, 9459–9474 (2020)
22. Li, Y., et al.: A framework of knowledge graph-enhanced large language model based on question decomposition and atomic retrieval. In: Findings of the Association for Computational Linguistics: EMNLP 2024, pp. 11472–11485 (2024)

23. Liu, S., Semnani, S.J., Triedman, H., Xu, J., Zhao, I.D., Lam, M.S.: Spinach: SPARQL-based information navigation for challenging real-world questions. arXiv preprint arXiv:2407.11417 (2024)
24. Longwell, J., Alavi, M.A.A., Zarrinkalam, F.: Triple augmented generative language models for SPARQL query generation from natural language questions. In: Proceedings of the 2024 ACM International Conference on Web Search and Data Mining (2024)
25. Lysyuk, M., Salnikov, M., Braslavski, P., Panchenko, A.: Konstruktor: a strong baseline for simple knowledge graph question answering. In: International Conference on Applications of Natural Language to Information Systems, pp. 107–118. Springer (2024)
26. Meem, J.A., Rashid, M.S., Dong, Y., Hristidis, V.: Pat-questions: a self-updating benchmark for present-anchored temporal question-answering. arXiv preprint arXiv:2402.11034 (2024)
27. Mohammed, S., Shi, P., Lin, J.: Strong baselines for simple question answering over knowledge graphs with and without neural networks. In: Walker, M., Ji, H., Stent, A. (eds.) Proceedings of the 2018 Conference of the North American Chapter of the Association for Computational Linguistics: Human Language Technologies, Volume 2 (Short Papers), New Orleans, Louisiana, pp. 291–296. Association for Computational Linguistics (2018)
28. Muennighoff, N.: SGPT: GPT sentence embeddings for semantic search. arxiv (2022)
29. Qi, J., et al.: Enhancing SPARQL query generation for knowledge base question answering systems by learning to correct triplets. Appl. Sci. **14**(4), 1521 (2024)
30. Rangel, J.C., de Farias, T.M., Sima, A.C., Kobayashi, N.: SPARQL generation: an analysis on fine-tuning OpenLLaMA for question answering over a life science knowledge graph (2024)
31. Rybin, I., Korablinov, V., Efimov, P., Braslavski, P.: RuBQ 2.0: an innovated Russian question answering dataset. In: Verborgh, R., et al. (eds.) ESWC 2021. LNCS, vol. 12731, pp. 532–547. Springer, Cham (2021). https://doi.org/10.1007/978-3-030-77385-4_32
32. Sakor, A., Singh, K., Patel, A., Vidal, M.E.: Falcon 2.0: an entity and relation linking tool over wikidata. In: Proceedings of the 29th ACM International Conference on Information & Knowledge Management, CIKM 2020, pp. 3141–3148. Association for Computing Machinery, New York (2020)
33. Schwabe, T., Siebel, L., Valach, P., Acosta, M.: Q-NL verifier: leveraging synthetic data for robust knowledge graph question answering (2025)
34. Shinn, N., Cassano, F., Gopinath, A., Narasimhan, K., Yao, S.: Reflexion: language agents with verbal reinforcement learning. Adv. Neural. Inf. Process. Syst. **36**, 8634–8652 (2023)
35. Somov, O., Tutubalina, E.: Shifted PAUQ: distribution shift in text-to-SQL. In: Proceedings of the 1st GenBench Workshop on (Benchmarking) Generalisation in NLP, pp. 214–220 (2023)
36. Sun, S., Hou, K., Li, J., Liu, Y.: KG-EGV: a framework for question answering with integrated knowledge graphs and large language models. Electronics **13**(23), 4835 (2024)
37. Tan, Y., et al.: Can ChatGPT replace traditional KBQA models? An in-depth analysis of the question answering performance of the GPT LLM family. In: International Semantic Web Conference, pp. 348–367. Springer (2023)
38. Touvron, H., et al.: Llama 2: open foundation and fine-tuned chat models. arXiv preprint arXiv:2307.09288 (2023)

39. Usbeck, R., et al.: QALD-10-the 10th challenge on question answering over linked data: Shifting from DBpedia to Wikidata as a KG for KGQA. Semantic Web **15**(6), 2193–2207 (2024)
40. Vrandečić, D., Krötzsch, M.: Wikidata: a free collaborative knowledgebase. Commun. ACM **57**(10), 78–85 (2014)
41. Xiong, G., Bao, J., Zhao, W.: Interactive-KBQA: multi-turn interactions for knowledge base question answering with large language models (2024)
42. Yu, D., et al.: Decaf: joint decoding of answers and logical forms for question answering over knowledge bases (2022)
43. Zahera, H., Sherif, M., Moussallem, D.: Generating SPARQL from natural language using chain-of-thoughts prompting. Semantic Web (2024)

TopicVD: A Topic-Based Dataset of Video-Guided Multimodal Machine Translation for Documentaries

Jinze Lv[1], Jian Chen[1], Zi Long[2(✉)], Xianghua Fu[2], and Yin Chen[2]

[1] College of Application and Technology, Shenzhen University, Shenzhen, China
[2] College of Big Data and Internet, Shenzhen Technology University, Shenzhen, China
{longzi,fuxianghua,chenyin}@sztu.edu.cn

Abstract. Most existing multimodal machine translation (MMT) datasets are predominantly composed of static images or short video clips, lacking extensive video data across diverse domains and topics. As a result, they fail to meet the demands of real-world MMT tasks, such as documentary translation. In this study, we developed TopicVD, a topic-based dataset for video-supported multimodal machine translation of documentaries, aiming to advance research in this field. We collected video-subtitle pairs from documentaries and categorized them into eight topics, such as economy and nature, to facilitate research on domain adaptation in video-guided MMT. Additionally, we preserved their contextual information to support research on leveraging the global context of documentaries in video-guided MMT. To better capture the shared semantics between text and video, we propose an MMT model based on a cross-modal bidirectional attention module. Extensive experiments on the TopicVD dataset demonstrate that visual information consistently improves the performance of the NMT model in documentary translation. However, the MMT model's performance significantly declines in out-of-domain scenarios, highlighting the need for effective domain adaptation methods. Additionally, experiments demonstrate that global context can effectively improve translation performance. Dataset and our implementations are available at https://github.com/JinzeLv/TopicVD.

Keywords: Video-guided Machine Translation · Video-Subtitle Translation Dataset · Documentary Translation

1 Introduction

Machine translation has evolved significantly over the past few decades, from rule-based and statistical methods to deep learning-driven neural machine translation (NMT) [1,2]. In recent years, some scholars have proposed using visual data as auxiliary information to aid translation, such as Multi30K [6,9,17,20]. Although Multi30K has demonstrated its potential, the dataset primarily focuses on simple, short bilingual and image-text pairing tasks, with one-to-one bilingual mappings. This limitation results in insufficient contextual information in

R. Ichise (Ed.): NLDB 2025, LNCS 15836, pp. 442–456, 2026.
https://doi.org/10.1007/978-3-031-97141-9_30

the source text, preventing it from accurately reflecting the translation scenario [3,24].

To address complex translation scenarios and meet real-world needs, some scholars have proposed video-guided machine translation (VMT) [28]. Due to the limited availability of VMT datasets, researchers have focused on expanding datasets, such as How2 [21] and VATEX [28]. However, previous VMT datasets have prioritized data quantity over quality, with many video clips consisting of subtitle descriptions and featuring discontinuous or excessively short durations. In recent years, the emergence of VISA [15], EVA [14], BigVideo [10], and TAIL [25] has enhanced VMT datasets, enabling them to contain millions of data points and feature long videos ranging from ten to tens of minutes. However, these datasets are not categorized by video topic; instead, they aggregate all data, which makes it difficult to analyze the impact of in-domain versus out-of-domain data on VMT. Moreover, these datasets primarily focus on the correspondence between video clips and text, while neglecting the contextual information of video-text pairs, thereby limiting their applicability to VMT research that relies on global context.

Therefore, to support the above VMT research, a multimodal translation dataset is required that includes topic annotations for each data instance and retains the contextual structure of video clips within their corresponding videos. In this study, we selected documentaries as the foundation for our translation dataset and constructed a topic-based corpus, TopicVD, to support research in video-supported multimodal machine translation. TopicVD consists of 256 documentaries across 8 topics, totaling 285 h in duration, and 122,930 Chinese-English parallel subtitle pairs, with a data size ranging from 3K to 30K for each topic. We highlight the key features of TopicVD as follows: a) The data in TopicVD are categorized into eight topics: Economy, Food, History, Figure, Military, Nagure, Social and Technology. b) To support VMT research that utilizes global context, TopicVD preserves the contextual information of each video-subtitle pair. To better model the shared semantics between text and video, we propose an MMT model based on a cross-modal bidirectional attention module. Extensive experiments on the TopicVD dataset demonstrate that visual information consistently improves the performance of the NMT model in documentary translation. Further experimental analysis validated that the effectiveness of VMT for documentaries is significantly influenced by in-domain and out-of-domain factors, highlighting the need for effective domain adaptation methods. Additionally, experiments demonstrate that global information can significantly improve translation performance.

To summarize, our contributions are primarily in the following three areas:

(1) We constructed a topic-based dataset for video-supported multimodal machine translation of documentaries.
(2) To better model the shared semantics between text and video, we propose an MMT model based on a cross-modal bidirectional attention module.

(3) We validated the effectiveness of the proposed model on TopicVD and further investigated the impact of in-domain and out-of-domain data, as well as contextual information, on VMT for documentaries.

2 Related Work

2.1 Image-Guided Machine Translation

To address the issues caused by the lack of context in traditional text translation, scholars have initially used images as additional inputs for multimodal machine translation [8]. They proposed achieving higher efficiency than neural machine translation by using a seq-to-seq model with strong image features [7,11,12,16, 23,32–34]. One of the most widely used datasets is Multi30K [5,6]. Multi30K consists of 30K images with relatively simple sentence structures and lacks complex grammatical features such as long sentences and nested clauses, making it unsuitable for translation tasks in complex contexts. Some scholars have criticized Multi30K, arguing that its images provide insufficient information [13,30]. Tang et al. [24] explored the use of search engines to retrieve images as auxiliary information for MMT, achieving certain improvements. However, this approach remains limited to static images, which do not fully align with the real-world scenarios of MMT. In most real-world MMT scenarios, text translation typically relies on video data. Unlike images, which provide static visual cues, videos offer richer visual information by capturing temporal dynamics, including actions and scene transitions. Therefore, we aim to construct a video-subtitle dataset to support research on video-guided machine translation for documentaries.

2.2 Video-Guided Machine Translation

To address complex translation scenarios and meet real-world needs, some scholars have proposed video-guided machine translation (VMT) [28]. In the field of VMT, How2 [21] and VATEX [28] were the first datasets introduced for VMT. VATEX contains 129K bilingual subtitle pairs and their corresponding video clips. However, studies have shown that translations can often be performed solely based on VATEX subtitle pairs, with video information frequently being ignored [31]. How2 collects tutorial videos from the YouTube platform, with an average video length of 90 s, and a total of 186K bilingual subtitle pairs. Moreover, VISA [15] constructs a 40K VMT dataset to emphasize the importance of ambiguities, with each video lasting 10 s. TAIL [25] builds a 70K video-subtitle translation dataset for classroom tutorial videos. BigVideo [10] and EVA [14] expand the size and diversity of VMT datasets by releasing a dataset containing one million video-subtitle translation pairs. The small data sizes of VISA and TAIL can lead to insufficient model training, making it difficult to demonstrate that additional visual information improves translation quality when compared to millions of text-based machine translation datasets.

Table 1. Comparison of Multimodal Translation Datasets

Dataset	Video				Text		Genre	Language
	# Video	Min.	# Clip	Sec.	# Sent	Len.		
VISA	2K	2.6	35K	10.0	40K	7.0	Film and Television	Ja-En
VATEX	25K	0.2	25K	10.0	129K	15.2	Short Video	En-Zh
How2	13K	1.2	186K	5.8	186K	20.6	Short Video	En-Pt
BigVideo	156K	3.8	4.5M	8.0	4.5M	22.8	Short Video	En-Zh
EVA	2K	107.7	1.3M	10.0	1.3M	7.3	Film and Television	Ja-En Zh-En
TopicVD	256	66.8	122K	8.4	122K	12.5	Documentary	En-Zh

VATEX, How2, and BigVideo have sufficient data sizes, but their data primarily focus on short-video platforms like YouTube[1] and Xigua Video[2], making it challenging to extract key information for complex tasks and scenarios. Although EVA has a large-scale dataset with millions of video samples, the average length of each subtitle text in the EVA dataset is only 7.34 English words. We argue that movies and TV dramas often contain dialects, colloquial expressions, and complex emotional nuances, which are difficult to directly transfer to formal translation scenarios. However, these datasets are not categorized by video topic; instead, they aggregate all data, making it difficult to analyze the impact of in-domain versus out-of-domain data on VMT. In this study, we constructed a topic-based dataset for video-supported multimodal machine translation of documentaries to advance research in documentary translation using multimodal machine translation. Table 1 provides a detailed comparison of existing VMT datasets.

3 Dataset

The choice of documentaries as the basis for our video subtitle translation dataset is motivated by three key reasons. First, documentary multimodal translation is a common translation scenario, yet no dedicated dataset currently exists for this task. Second, documentaries span a wide range of topics, such as economics and nature, with significant domain-specific variations in content. This diversity makes them particularly suitable for studying domain adaptation in VMT. Finally, documentaries are typically long in duration and maintain a high level of content consistency, making them well-suited for exploring VMT methods that leverage global video information. Moreover, documentaries offer additional advantages, including easy data accessibility, a strong correlation between subtitle text and video content, and diverse, rich scenes. Therefore, we choose to construct the VMT dataset using documentaries and their subtitle information. The dataset construction process is illustrated in Fig. 1.

[1] https://www.youtube.com.

[2] https://www.ixigua.com.

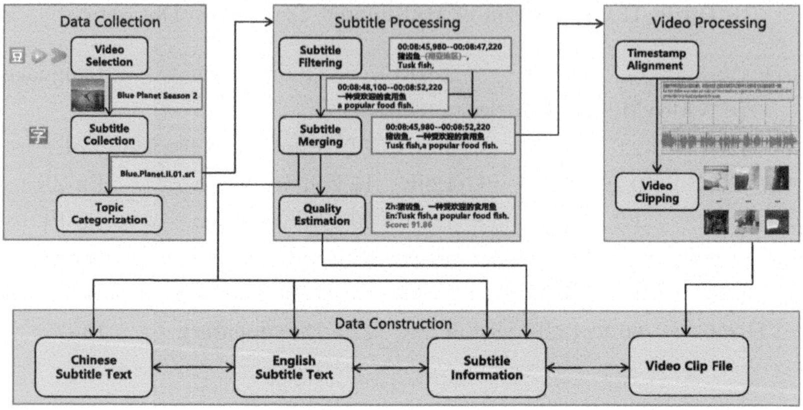

Fig. 1. Construction process of the TopicVD documentary translation dataset.

3.1 Data Collection

The collected data consists of documentary videos along with corresponding Chinese and English subtitle files. The specific collection steps are as follows:

(1) We select highly played and highly rated documentaries from video platforms such as Douban Movie[3], Tencent Video[4] and Youku Video[5], ensuring that the dataset consists of high-quality and representative documentaries.
(2) We collect bilingual subtitle files from Subtitle Library[6] and SubHD[7] for selected documentaries. These subtitle files contain text in both languages, such as Chinese and English.
(3) We assign a unique topic to each collected documentary. Since a documentary may cover multiple topics, we synthesize classification data from various video platforms and make final manual judgments on the topic of each documentary[8].

3.2 Subtitle Processing

The collected subtitle files are typically in SubRip Text (SRT) format, which includes code for controlling subtitle display formatting. To ensure readability, subtitle creators often split longer sentences into multiple segments. Thus, we preprocess the subtitle files, and the processing steps are as follows:

[3] http://movie.douban.com.
[4] https://v.qq.com.
[5] https://www.youku.com.
[6] https://zimuku.vip/.
[7] https://subhd.tv/.
[8] This approach is evidently influenced by the topic distribution of publicly available documentaries, leading to a dataset that is predominantly composed of content related to Nature and History.

(1) We filter out the code from the text. To ensure correspondence between the two language texts, we further filter out special symbols that appear only in one language.
(2) We use punctuation marks and corresponding time segment as cues to reassemble split segments into complete sentences. During the merging process, time segments must also be merged to ensure that the reassembled subtitles accurately align with their appearance in the documentary.
(3) To ensure the quality of parallel subtitles, we compute the cosine similarity score of each subtitle pair using a multilingual sentence embedding model (e.g., MPNet [22]). This score serves as a quality estimation metric and can be used to filter out low-quality pairs across different experimental settings.

3.3 Video Processing

Based on the subtitle processing results from Sect. 3.2, we further process the video information of the collected documentaries. The processing steps are as follows:

(1) We use open-source speech recognition engines (e.g., Whisper[9]) to verify the alignment between the spoken content in the video and the subtitle text, adjusting any inconsistencies. Manual verification ensures that the subtitles accurately correspond to their respective segments in the documentary.
(2) Using the time segment information from the subtitle text, we employed FFmpeg [27] to segment the video into multiple clips corresponding to the subtitles and recorded the position of each clip within the full video.

3.4 Data Construction

The bilingual subtitle texts processed in Sect. 3.2 and the video clips processed in Sect. 3.3 are then collected to construct the proposed topic-based datasets for video-guided multimodal machine translation of documentaries. In addition to the bilingual subtitle text files and corresponding video clip files, we also recorded specific information for each video-subtitle pair. As shown in Table 2, we documented the documentary title, topic, time segment, and the position of each pair within the documentary. Furthermore, we recorded the quality estimation scores of the bilingual subtitle text, as calculated in Sect. 3.2. These scores not only reflect the semantic similarity between subtitle pairs but also serve as a quantitative basis for subsequent similarity-based filtering experiments.

We collected a total of 256 documentaries, amounting to 285 h of video and 122,930 pairs of English-Chinese parallel subtitles. To mitigate the impact of random variation on experimental results, we randomly selected one to two documentaries per topic as the validation and test sets, while the remaining data were used for training. Note that for each topic, the training and test sets are drawn from the same topic to ensure topic-level relevance. However, the test set

[9] https://github.com/openai/whisper.

Table 2. Extracted specific information for each video-subtitle pair. "Title" and "Topic" represent the title and topic of the corresponding documentary, respectively. "Start" and "End" indicate the start and end timestamps of the video-subtitle pair, while "Position" denotes its relative placement within the documentary. "Score" refers to the quality estimation score of the bilingual subtitle text.

Title	Topic	Start	End	Position	Score
An Honest Liar.mp4	Human	00:00:02,960	00:00:09,800	1	92.93
An Honest Liar.mp4	Human	00:00:12,040	00:00:15,040	2	92.75
		...			
An Honest Liar.mp4	Human	01:21:44,639	01:21:47,879	872	87.01
An Honest Liar.mp4	Human	01:21:47,879	01:21:49,719	873	83.55

Table 3. Data size statistics for training, validation, and test Sets by Topic in TopicVD (number of video-subtitle pairs/documentary videos)

Topic	Train	Valid	Test	total
Economy	5,080/7	1,483/1	1,904/1	8,467/9
Food	1,574/6	705/1	508/2	2,787/9
History	17,542/42	1,034/1	1,047/2	19,623/45
Figure	24,748/25	1,446/2	1,307/2	27,501/29
Military	2,162/3	1,036/4	1,138/1	4,336/8
Nature	26,015/90	1,474/5	1,482/8	28,971/103
Social	11,415/13	1,486/2	1,033/1	13,934/16
Technology	13,966/33	1,765/2	1,580/2	17,311/37
Total	102,502/219	10,429/18	9,999/19	122,930/256

contains data from different documentaries than those in the training set, ensuring no direct content overlap. Table 3 presents a detailed statistical summary of the training, validation, and test sets.

4 Model

Inspired by the Selective Attention module [13] and the Bidirectional Attention module [24] in IMT, we propose a VMT model incorporating a cross-modal bidirectional attention mechanism. Figure 2 provides an overview of the model.

4.1 Selective Attention

To enhance the association efficiency between video features and text representations and achieve deep information fusion, this proposed model introduces a cross-modal selective attention mechanism. Given a bilingual subtitle pair $<(\mathbf{e}, \mathbf{f}), \mathbf{V}>$, where $\mathbf{e}$ and $\mathbf{f}$ represent the source and target texts, respectively,

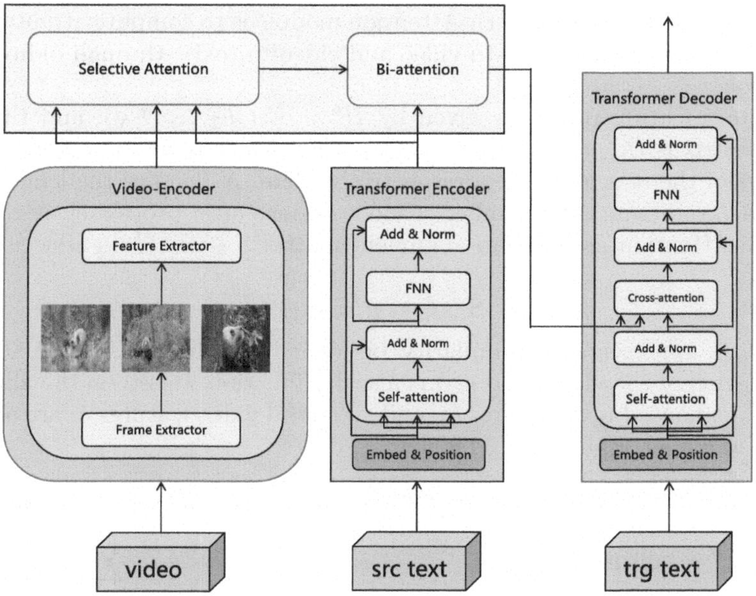

Fig. 2. An overview of the proposed VMT model with cross-modal bidirectional attention.

and $\mathbf{V}$ denotes the corresponding video clip for the subtitle. The source text $\mathbf{e}$ is encoded by a transformer encoder [26], producing the output text representation $H^{\mathbf{e}}$. The video clip $\mathbf{V}$ is then encoded by the I3D model [4], with the output video feature denoted as $H^{\mathbf{V}}$.

It is important to note that, unlike encoding an image to obtain its semantic vector directly, encoding a video requires first extracting the most representative frames before encoding them. Therefore, we employ a single-head attention network as a selective attention mechanism to establish associations between the text and the extracted video frames. In this attention mechanism, the text representation $H^{\mathbf{e}}$ is used as the query, while the video feature $H^{\mathbf{V}}$ serves as both the key and the value, enabling efficient filtering and feature extraction of video features based on the textual content. The selective attention output $H^{\mathbf{V}}_{\text{att}}$ is defined as:

$$H^{\mathbf{V}}_{\text{att}} = \text{Softmax}\left(\frac{H^{\mathbf{e}}(H^{\mathbf{V}}_i)^{\top}}{\sqrt{d_{H^{\mathbf{e}}}}}\right) H^{\mathbf{V}}$$

where $d_{H^{\mathbf{e}}}$ denotes the dimensionality of $H^{\mathbf{e}}$, and $H^{\mathbf{V}}_i$ represents the ith frame of $H^{\mathbf{V}}$.

4.2 Bi-attention

We further introduce a bidirectional attention mechanism to enhance the interaction between text and video features, thereby improving the feature representations of both. The core idea of Bi-Attention module is to compute attention from two modal perspectives—text-to-video and video-to-text—through bidirectional interaction.

The text feature matrix is given by $H^{\mathbf{e}} = (h_1, h_2, \ldots, h_N)$, and the video feature matrix is $H^{\mathbf{V}}_{\text{att}} = (a_1, a_2, \ldots, a_L)$, both of which represent the embedding sequences of the text and video, respectively. Here, N denotes the length of the text, and L represents the number of video regions after processing in Sect. 4.1. In the Bi-Attention module, an alignment matrix $S \in \mathbb{R}^{N \times L}$ is first computed as follows:

$$\mathbf{S}_{(n,l)} = g(h_n \cdot a_l)$$

where $S_{(n,l)}$ represents the similarity between the nth word of the text and the lth region of the video, and $g(\cdot)$ is a scalar function. Based on the alignment matrix $\mathbf{S}$, enhanced text features $\overline{h_n}$ and enhanced video features $\overline{a_l}$ are obtained through weighted summation as follows.

$$w_n^{t2v} = \text{softmax}(S_{n:}) \quad \& \overline{h_n} = h_n + \sum_l w_n^{t2v} a_l$$

$$w_l^{v2t} = \text{softmax}(S_{:l}) \qquad \overline{a_l} = a_l + \sum_i w_l^{v2t} h_n$$

Finally, $\overline{h_n}$ and $\overline{a_l}$ are input into a transformer-based decoder, as shown in Fig. 2.

5 Experiments

5.1 Experiment Setting

Our model follows the training structure of the Selective Attention model [12]. The model comprises 4 encoder and 4 decoder layers, with a hidden size of 128 and a feed-forward network (FFN) filter size of 256. The multi-head self-attention mechanism employs 4 heads, and the dropout rate is set to 0.3. For training, we use the RAdam optimizer [18] with a learning rate of 0.005. The batch size is set to 4,096 tokens, and the learning rate is set to 1e-4. Training is terminated if the cross-entropy loss on the validation set does not improve within 10 iterations. The I3D model is used to extract video features [4].

As baselines, we used the open-source transformer-translator-pytorch project[10] as the text-only NMT model. Additionally, we compared the proposed model with an IMT model that employs heuristic video frame extraction strategies. Specifically, frames are extracted at a fixed rate per second from the video clip and then filtered based on the structural similarity values [29] of neighboring frames, using a threshold of 0.5 to eliminate redundant frames. The remaining representative frames are then selected. In addition, we compared the proposed model with the approach by Teramen et al. [25]. In this approach, the start, middle, and end frames of each video clip are extracted and selected based on either text-text similarity or text-image similarity. All the above models are trained on the dataset shown in Table 3, and the 4-gram BLEU score [19] is used as the evaluation metric for both the baselines and the proposed method.

[10] https://github.com/devjwsong/transformer-translator-pytorch.

Table 4. Comparison of different models on BLEU scores.

Method	BLEU
text-only NMT	19.14
IMT using heuristic frame extraction	26.71
IMT using text-text similarly-based frame extraction [25]	25.73
IMT using text-image similarly-based frame extraction [25]	25.94
the proposed method	**29.33**

5.2 Results

Table 4 presents the experimental results. First, as shown in Table 4, TopicVD achieves a minimum BLEU score of 19.14 across the dataset, demonstrating that its quality is sufficient for MMT research. The proposed method achieves a BLEU score of 29.33. Compared to the text-only NMT, the proposed method yields a significantly higher BLEU score. Compared to the IMT method with heuristic frame extraction, the proposed method improves performance by approximately 2.6 BLEU. Compared to the IMT model proposed by Teramen [25], the proposed method achieves an improvement of approximately 3.4 BLEU.

Figure 3 shows an example of correct translation by the proposed method. In this example, the English phrase "within a few million years" fails to be translated by both the text-only NMT model and the model proposed by Teramen et al. [25]. This is primarily because the cross-modal bidirectional attention mechanism enhances the performance of the text encoder. Additionally, by leveraging visual information from the video clip related to "carpeted", the proposed method produces a correct translation, as does the IMT model proposed by Teramen et al. [25]. In contrast, the text-only NMT model incorrectly translates "carpeted" into a Chinese noun meaning "carpet". These findings highlight the effectiveness of incorporating visual information from videos in the VMT process for documentary translation.

6 Discussion

6.1 In-domain vs. Out-of-Domain Performance in VMT

To our knowledge, this study is the first to experimentally quantify the impact of in-domain and out-of-domain scenarios on VMT translation. We conduct experiments to investigate the effect of varying data domains on the performance of the VMT model. From the TopicVD dataset, we select four topic subsets: History, Figure, Nature, and Technology. These topics are chosen due to their large dataset sizes and the availability of relevant resources. Consequently, we modify the training set in four distinct ways and train the VMT model proposed in Sect. 4. Finally, we evaluate the model using the corresponding test sets for each selected topic.

The experimental details are as follows:

Source(En):	**Within a few million years**, forests had regrown and **carpeted** much of the land.
Target(Zh):	在几百万年内，森林已重新生长并覆盖大部分土地
Video:	
text-only NMT:	几百万年后，森林重新生长长并地毯了土地 (Millions of years later, the forest grows back and carpet the land.)
Teramen et al. [25]:	短短几百万年，森林已重新生长并覆盖大部分土地 (In just a few million years, forests had regrown and carpeted much of the land.)
the proposed method:	在几百万年的时间里，森林已经重新生长并覆盖了大部分土地 (Within a few million years, forests had regrown and carpeted much of the land.)

Fig. 3. Example of correct translation by the proposed method.

Table 5. Translation performance of each experimental scenario across each test set (BLEU score)

	History	Figure	Nature	Technology
Full dataset	24.13	25.15	32.70	31.16
In-domain dataset	15.78	17.45	20.16	15.51
Out-of-domain dataset (full)	22.14	24.76	28.94	29.66
Out-of-domain dataset (sampled)	10.28	11.63	16.18	10.51

Full dataset We utilize the complete training data from all eight topics and evaluate the trained model using the corresponding test sets for each selected topic.

In-domain dataset We train the model on a training set that corresponds to the same topic as its respective test set. Clearly, for each test set of a selected topic, we train a separate in-domain VMT model.

Out-of-domain dataset (full) We train the model using the training data from seven topics, excluding the topic of the test set. Clearly, for each distinct test topic, we train a separate out-of-domain VMT model.

Out-of-domain dataset (sampled) To ensure comparability with the in-domain dataset, we randomly sample a subset from the training data of seven topics, excluding the test set's topic, ensuring the same data volume as the in-domain dataset of the test set. For each distinct test topic, we train a separate out-of-domain VMT model.

Table 5 presents the BLEU scores obtained from the four aforementioned experimental scenarios. For the selected four test topics, the full dataset achieved the best translation performance. When comparing the results of the in-domain and out-of-domain (sampled) models, the in-domain model demonstrated significantly better translation performance, highlighting the effectiveness of in-domain data. However, when comparing the in-domain results with those of the out-of-domain (full) model, the latter achieved a higher BLEU score. This may be due to the fact that a sufficient amount of data can partially mitigate translation issues caused by out-of-domain data. The comparison between the full dataset and the out-of-domain (full) results further supports these findings. Specifically, for the Figure topic results, the out-of-domain (full) model showed the smallest decline compared to the full dataset. This is because, unlike the History, Nature, and Technology topics, the Figure topic covers a broader range of content. As a result, in this case, the influence of in-domain data is more easily replaced by out-of-domain data.

6.2 Impact of Data Augmentation on In-Domain Performance

We further investigate the impact of data volume on the translation performance of the in-domain model. To achieve this, we manually augment the training datasets for the Nature and Technology topics. Specifically, we added 31 documentaries, comprising a total of 6,433 video-subtitle pairs, to the Nature training set, and 10 documentaries, totaling 2,688 video-subtitle pairs, to the Technology training set. The experimental results are shown in Table 6. The in-domain dataset refers to the VMT model trained on a training set that shares the same topic as the corresponding test set. Specifically, the Nature training set contains 26,015 video-subtitle pairs, while the Technology training set comprises 13,966 video-subtitle pairs. In contrast, the in-domain (augmented) dataset refers to the VMT model trained on the augmented training set. Specifically, the augmented Nature training set contains 32,488 video-subtitle pairs, while the augmented Technology training set comprises 16,654 video-subtitle pairs.

As shown in the table, increasing the volume of in-domain data significantly improves the translation performance of the VMT model, with a greater effect than an equivalent increase in out-of-domain data. Among all topics, the Nature topic exhibits the highest sensitivity to data augmentation, suggesting that its translation performance is highly dependent on in-domain data. A detailed analysis of the data reveals that the newly added Nature dataset contains a documentary closely related to the test set content, which significantly enhances translation performance. This finding suggests a relatively straightforward approach to the domain adaptation problem in documentary translation—targeted augmentation with test-related data can effectively improve translation performance.

6.3 Impact of Contextual Information on the VMT Model

We further explore the impact of contextual video information in the VMT task. This experiment is conducted exclusively on the TopicVD dataset, where the positional information of each video-subtitle pair is preserved. Here, we introduce a contextual video information filtering strategy based on text-text similarity.

Table 6. Translation performance of augmented train set across each test set (BLEU score)

	Nature	Technology
In-domain dataset	20.16	15.51
In-domain dataset (augmented)	30.60	18.62
Out-of-domain dataset	16.18	10.51
Out-of-domain dataset (augmented)	17.35	13.54

Table 7. Translation performance with different contextual information

Method	BLEU
VMT with a single video clip	29.33
VMT with three video clips	29.95
VMT with ten video clips	**30.22**

For a given subtitle text to be translated, we compute its similarity with other subtitle texts from the same documentary and select the video clip corresponding to the most similar subtitle as its contextual video information. Table 7 presents the VMT translation performance under three conditions: using only the video clip corresponding to the subtitle text, using three clips, and using ten clips. The experimental results show that translation performance improves as the number of video clips increases from one to three to ten. This suggests that a moderate increase in video clips provides more contextual and semantic information to the model in the VMT task, further confirming the crucial role of contextual video information in VMT.

7 Conclusion

In this study, we introduced TopicVD, a topic-based dataset for video-supported multimodal machine translation of documentaries, to advance research in documentary translation using multimodal machine translation. We propose an MMT model based on a cross-modal bidirectional attention module and validate the effectiveness of both the dataset and the model through experiments. Extensive experiments on the TopicVD dataset show that the performance of the MMT model significantly declines in out-of-domain scenarios, highlighting the need for effective domain adaptation methods. Additionally, experiments demonstrate that global context can substantially improve translation performance. These findings underscore the importance of topic-specific data organization and contextual modeling in complex video-guided machine translation tasks. As a future direction, we will focus on TopicVD to investigate domain adaptation methods for documentary VMT and explore how contextual information can optimize documentary VMT performance. In addition, we will expand the TopicVD dataset and diversify its topics to enhance its practical value.

References

1. Brown, P.F., et al.: A statistical approach to machine translation. Comput. Linguist. **16**(2), 79–85 (1990)
2. Brown, P.F., Della Pietra, S.A., Della Pietra, V.J., Mercer, R.L.: The mathematics of statistical machine translation: parameter estimation. Comput. Linguist. **19**(2), 263–311 (1993)
3. Caglayan, O., Madhyastha, P., Specia, L., Barrault, L.: Probing the need for visual context in multimodal machine translation. arXiv preprint arXiv:1903.08678 (2019)
4. Carreira, J., Zisserman, A.: Quo vadis, action recognition? A new model and the kinetics dataset. In: Proceedings of the IEEE Conference on Computer Vision and Pattern Recognition, pp. 6299–6308 (2017)
5. Elliott, D., Frank, S., Barrault, L., Bougares, F., Specia, L.: Findings of the second shared task on multimodal machine translation and multilingual image description. arXiv preprint arXiv:1710.07177 (2017)
6. Elliott, D., Frank, S., Sima'an, K., Specia, L.: Multi30k: multilingual English-German image descriptions. arXiv preprint arXiv:1605.00459 (2016)
7. Elliott, D., Kádár, A.: Imagination improves multimodal translation. arXiv preprint arXiv:1705.04350 (2017)
8. Hitschler, J., Schamoni, S., Riezler, S.: Multimodal pivots for image caption translation. arXiv preprint arXiv:1601.03916 (2016)
9. Hu, J., et al.: Large multilingual models pivot zero-shot multimodal learning across languages. arXiv preprint arXiv:2308.12038 (2023)
10. Kang, L., et al.: Bigvideo: a large-scale video subtitle translation dataset for multimodal machine translation. arXiv preprint arXiv:2305.18326 (2023)
11. Lan, Z., et al.: Exploring better text image translation with multimodal codebook. arXiv preprint arXiv:2305.17415 (2023)
12. Li, B., et al.: On vision features in multimodal machine translation. arXiv preprint arXiv:2203.09173 (2022)
13. Li, J., Ataman, D., Sennrich, R.: Vision matters when it should: sanity checking multimodal machine translation models. arXiv preprint arXiv:2109.03415 (2021)
14. Li, Y., Shimizu, S., Chu, C., Kurohashi, S., Li, W.: Video-helpful multimodal machine translation. arXiv preprint arXiv:2310.20201 (2023)
15. Li, Y., Shimizu, S., Gu, W., Chu, C., Kurohashi, S.: Visa: an ambiguous subtitles dataset for visual scene-aware machine translation. arXiv preprint arXiv:2201.08054 (2022)
16. Lin, H., et al.: Dynamic context-guided capsule network for multimodal machine translation. In: Proceedings of the 28th ACM International Conference on Multimedia, pp. 1320–1329 (2020)
17. Lin, T.-Y., et al.: Microsoft COCO: common objects in context. In: Fleet, D., Pajdla, T., Schiele, B., Tuytelaars, T. (eds.) ECCV 2014. LNCS, vol. 8693, pp. 740–755. Springer, Cham (2014). https://doi.org/10.1007/978-3-319-10602-1_48
18. Liu, L., et al.: On the variance of the adaptive learning rate and beyond. arXiv preprint arXiv:1908.03265 (2019)
19. Papineni, K., Roukos, S., Ward, T., Zhu, W.J.: Bleu: a method for automatic evaluation of machine translation. In: Proceedings of the 40th Annual Meeting of the Association for Computational Linguistics, pp. 311–318 (2002)
20. Plummer, B.A., Wang, L., Cervantes, C.M., Caicedo, J.C., Hockenmaier, J., Lazebnik, S.: Flickr30k entities: collecting region-to-phrase correspondences for richer image-to-sentence models. In: Proceedings of the IEEE International Conference on Computer Vision, pp. 2641–2649 (2015)

21. Sanabria, R., et al.: How2: a large-scale dataset for multimodal language understanding. arXiv preprint arXiv:1811.00347 (2018)
22. Song, K., Tan, X., Qin, T., Lu, J., Liu, T.Y.: MPNet: masked and permuted pre-training for language understanding. Adv. Neural. Inf. Process. Syst. **33**, 16857–16867 (2020)
23. Su, J., et al.: Multi-modal neural machine translation with deep semantic interactions. Inf. Sci. **554**, 47–60 (2021)
24. Tang, Z., Zhang, X., Long, Z., Fu, X.: Multimodal neural machine translation with search engine based image retrieval. arXiv preprint arXiv:2208.00767 (2022)
25. Teramen, A., Ohtsuka, T., Kondo, R., Kajiwara, T., Ninomiya, T.: English-to-Japanese multimodal machine translation based on image-text matching of lecture videos. In: Proceedings of the 3rd Workshop on Advances in Language and Vision Research (ALVR), pp. 86–91 (2024)
26. Vaswani, A., et al.: Attention is all you need. In: Advances in Neural Information Processing Systems, vol. 30 (2017)
27. Wales, G.S.: Validation of image stream hashing: a forensic method for content verification. J. Forensic Sci. **69**(2), 515–528 (2024)
28. Wang, X., Wu, J., Chen, J., Li, L., Wang, Y.F., Wang, W.Y.: Vatex: a large-scale, high-quality multilingual dataset for video-and-language research. In: Proceedings of the IEEE/CVF International Conference on Computer Vision, pp. 4581–4591 (2019)
29. Wang, Z., Bovik, A.C., Sheikh, H.R., Simoncelli, E.P.: Image quality assessment: from error visibility to structural similarity. IEEE Trans. Image Process. **13**(4), 600–612 (2004)
30. Wu, Z., Kong, L., Bi, W., Li, X., Kao, B.: Good for misconceived reasons: an empirical revisiting on the need for visual context in multimodal machine translation. arXiv preprint arXiv:2105.14462 (2021)
31. Yang, Z., Hirasawa, T., Komachi, M., Okazaki, N.: Why videos do not guide translations in video-guided machine translation? An empirical evaluation of video-guided machine translation dataset. J. Inf. Process. **30**, 388–396 (2022)
32. Yao, S., Wan, X.: Multimodal transformer for multimodal machine translation. In: Proceedings of the 58th Annual Meeting of the Association for Computational Linguistics, pp. 4346–4350 (2020)
33. Yin, Y., et al.: A novel graph-based multi-modal fusion encoder for neural machine translation. arXiv preprint arXiv:2007.08742 (2020)
34. Zhu, Y., Sun, Z., Cheng, S., Huang, L., Wu, L., Wang, M.: Beyond triplet: leveraging the most data for multimodal machine translation. arXiv preprint arXiv:2212.10313 (2022)

Multimodal Event Detection: Current Approaches and Defining the New Playground Through LLMs and VLMs

Abhishek Dey[1], Aabha Bothera[1], Samhita Sarikonda[1], Rishav Aryan[1], Sanjay Kumar Podishetty[1], Akshay Havalgi[2](✉), Saurabh Srivastava[1], and Gaurav Singh[1]

[1] George Mason University, Fairfax, USA
[2] Amazon, Seattle, USA
ssrivas6@gmu.edu

Abstract. In this paper, we study the challenges of detecting events on social media, where traditional unimodal systems struggle due to the rapid and multimodal nature of data dissemination. We employ a range of models, including unimodal ModernBERT and ConvNeXt-V2, multimodal fusion techniques, and advanced generative models like GPT-4o, and LLaVA. Additionally, we also study the effect of providing multimodal generative models (such as GPT-4o) with a single modality to assess their efficacy. Our results indicate that while multimodal approaches notably outperform unimodal counterparts, generative approaches despite having a large number of parameters, lag behind supervised methods in precision. Furthermore, we also found that they lag behind instruction-tuned models because of their inability to generate event classes correctly. During our error analysis, we discovered that common social media issues such as leet speak, text elongation, etc. are effectively handled by generative approaches but are hard to tackle using supervised approaches.

Keywords: Event Detection · Visual Language Models · Large Language Models

1 Introduction

Natural disasters—such as earthquakes, hurricanes, wildfires, and floods—pose severe threats to human lives, infrastructure, and economies. The ability to detect and track such events in real-time is crucial for disaster response teams to issue timely warnings, coordinate relief efforts, and mitigate damage [1]. While traditional sources of disaster-related information, such as governmental reports

S. Srivastava and G. Singh—Equal Senior Authorship.
This work is not related to Akshay Havalgi's position at Amazon, and was completely outside of the regular duties of his position.

R. Ichise (Ed.): NLDB 2025, LNCS 15836, pp. 457–471, 2026.
https://doi.org/10.1007/978-3-031-97141-9_31

and news articles, provide structured and validated updates, they often suffer from delays in reporting. In contrast, social media platforms offer real-time, high-volume, and publicly accessible streams of disaster-related data, making them invaluable for early event detection [2]. However, extracting structured and actionable insights from social media is inherently challenging due to the informal nature of the text, high noise levels, and the multimodal nature of shared content (e.g., text, images, and videos).

Event Detection (ED) [3] in natural language processing (NLP) serves as the first step in structuring real-world event information by identifying instances of events in text. Classical ED research has focused on structured datasets such as ACE 2005 [3], which are predominantly composed of formal news articles. In these settings, ED is framed as the task of recognizing what happened, along with contextual information such as who was involved, when, where, and how. However, applying ED techniques to social media for disaster monitoring introduces significant challenges, including data sparsity, informal language variations, and the presence of multiple modalities.

Existing approaches that analyze social media disaster-related content primarily treat the problem as a classification task—determining whether a given post pertains to a disaster event or not—without explicitly detecting events in a structured manner. For instance, [1] explored classification strategies to assess the challenges of multimodal disaster detection but did not frame the task within the ED paradigm. Such classification-based approaches lack interpretability and fail to capture finer-grained event attributes, such as location, time, and evolving event dynamics, which are critical for disaster response efforts.

In addition, social media presents unique linguistic and structural challenges that further complicate event detection. Unlike well-formed text in news articles, social media posts frequently exhibit informal writing styles, including leet speak (e.g., "gr8 fl00d"), elongated words (e.g., "shaaaking!!!"), inconsistent capitalization, abbreviations, and code-mixing. These variations introduce noise, making it difficult for traditional ED models trained on well-structured text to generalize effectively. In our study, we systematically analyze the impact of these linguistic perturbations on event detection and evaluate the robustness of modern transformer-based models, including BERT-based event extraction models. Our findings indicate that while current ED models struggle with these variations, large language models (LLMs) such as GPT-based models, exhibit significantly better adaptability, particularly in identifying events from highly distorted social media text.

To the best of our knowledge, this is the first study to investigate multi-modal ED on social media for natural disasters while simultaneously analyzing the linguistic challenges inherent to such datasets. Unlike prior classification-based approaches, we frame the task as structured ED, incorporating both textual and visual signals to improve robustness. Moreover, we provide an in-depth analysis of how informal language and social media writing styles impact ED performance, identifying four to five common perturbations that remain unresolved by existing ED models but can be effectively addressed by LLMs.

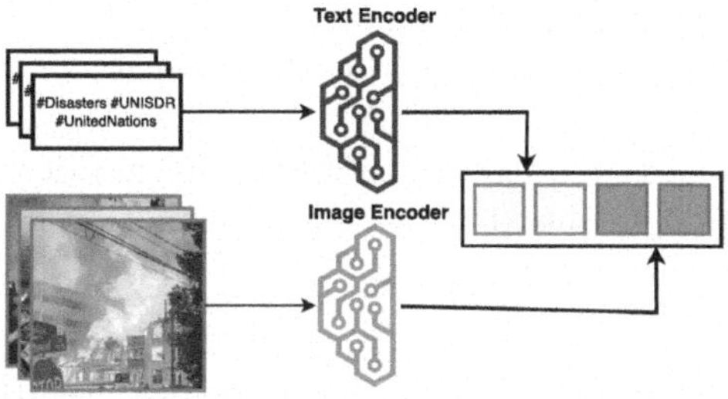

Fig. 1. Overview of Multi-modal Event Detection. In addition to text, the input is accompanied by images and are fed to model to identify events.

To summarize, our key contributions are as follows:

1. We introduce a novel formulation of multi-modal ED for natural disasters, moving beyond prior classification-based methods to structured event detection.
2. We conduct a comprehensive study of linguistic perturbations in social media disaster-related posts, identifying major challenges that hinder existing ED models.
3. We evaluate traditional transformer-based ED models (e.g., BERT-based models) on social media texts and highlight their limitations in handling informal language variations.
4. We demonstrate that GPT-based LLMs perform poorly compared to traditional ED models in recognizing events under social media-specific noise. Our findings resonate with the recent studies on ED which also highlights the limitation of large models compared to smaller supervised approaches, offering insights into their adaptability for real-world event monitoring.
5. We establish a benchmark for multi-modal ED in social media disaster scenarios, providing a new evaluation framework to facilitate future research in this direction[1].

2 Problem Formulation

Supervised Approaches. Our objective is to develop a multi-modal event detection system that effectively integrates textual and visual data from social media to identify and categorize disaster-related events. This system is designed for real-time deployment to facilitate timely and accurate information dissemination during disaster scenarios.

The input to our system (Fig. 1) consists of two primary modalities:

[1] Our code is available at https://github.com/salokr/MultiModelEventDetection.

1. **Textual Description** (T): A sequence of token embeddings extracted from a pre-trained language model, capturing the linguistic and contextual nuances of social media posts.
2. **Image** (I): A set of visual features obtained from a deep vision model, providing complementary context to textual information for more robust event identification.

Given an image I and its corresponding textual description T, the goal is to classify the multi-modal input into a predefined set of disaster event categories. Formally, we define this task as learning function f that maps the textual and visual modalities to a set of disaster-related categories:

$$f : (I, T) \rightarrow C$$

where C represents a predefined taxonomy of disaster event categories, such as *"flood", "fire", "human damage", "damaged nature", and "damaged infrastructure".*

Our model is trained under a supervised learning framework, using annotated disaster-related social media data. The classification function f is optimized to maximize the predictive performance across both modalities while addressing challenges inherent to social media text, such as informal language, abbreviations, and linguistic perturbations. A high-level overview of our approach is illustrated in Fig. 1.

Prompting Approaches. In recent years, Vision-Language Models (VLMs) have demonstrated remarkable capabilities in understanding and integrating visual and textual data, leading to significant advancements in various tasks, including image classification, object detection, and event detection. Their ability to learn from vast amounts of image-text pairs enables them to perform zero-shot and few-shot learning, making them particularly valuable in scenarios with limited labeled data. Prompting has emerged as an effective technique to adapt pre-trained models to specific tasks with minimal labeled examples. By crafting task-specific prompts, models can be guided to generate more accurate and

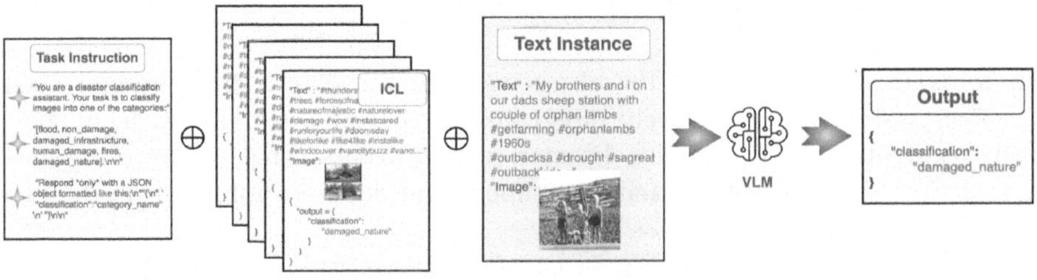

Fig. 2. Overview of few-shot prompting strategy to perform ED. In addition to providing a few-shot in-context demonstration (ICL), we also provide the model with task instruction and output format to extract the correct event class for the test instance.

contextually relevant outputs. In the context of VLMs, prompting facilitates the alignment of visual and textual modalities, enhancing the model's performance in few-shot settings.

To enable effective multi-modal event detection using few-shot prompting, we construct a five-shot image-and-text-based prompt to guide the model towards structured event identification. The prompt consists of five exemplar instances, each comprising:

1. **Image** (I): A disaster-related image.
2. **Text** (T): A social media post describing the disaster.
3. **Event Category** (C): The ground-truth label mapping the instance to a predefined disaster category.

Our input sequence is prepared as:

[$-task_instruction || <Example-1> ||...|| <Example-5>$-test_instance] where "$-task_instruction" is the natural language task-instruction as shown in Fig. 2 and $-test_instance represents the test instance for which few-shot inference is performed. To facilitate automated evaluation, we instruct the models to output their predictions in a structured JSON format, enabling systematic answer extraction and quantitative analysis.

3 Related Works

Event Detection (ED). ED has been extensively studied in text-based data, particularly in the domain of news [3–6]. While early approaches primarily relied on syntactic and semantic features, recent neural models have improved event extraction through contextualized embeddings and joint modeling techniques. Additionally, leveraging multimedia features has been shown to enhance text-based event extraction [7–10]. In the domain of visual event extraction, events are often formulated as simpler actions or activities [11,12], typically within everyday life contexts. However, these works either focus on purely text-based ED or visual event classification, whereas our study explores **multi-modal event detection** by integrating textual and visual signals, particularly leveraging generative models such as VLMs and LLMs.

Multi-Modal Event Detection (ED). Recent multi-modal event detection methods primarily focus on aligning images and text for a unified event representation [13]. However, these methods often neglect structural and semantic roles in event representation. UniVSE [14] incorporates entity attributes and relations but lacks a fully structured event modeling approach. Recent advances using pre-trained vision-language models [15] have improved multi-modal event extraction by integrating visual context, yet they largely formulate ED as a classification task constrained by predefined event schemas, limiting generalization. Furthermore, most existing methods assume that text-image pairs are always available, making them less effective in real-world disaster scenarios where one modality may be missing or incomplete [16]. Additionally, situation recognition (SR) models predict events and arguments from images [17] but do not localize arguments in a structured manner. In contrast, our approach redefines ED as a generative problem, allowing for flexible handling of missing modalities while providing structured event representations.

Vision-Language and Large Language Models (VLMs/LLMs). With the rapid advancement of multi-modal AI, systems can now process and integrate diverse modalities such as text, images, speech, and gestures, expanding the capabilities of AI applications. Vision-Language Models (VLMs) have been widely used in tasks such as Visual Question Answering (VQA), image captioning, and text-image retrieval, demonstrating significant improvements in multimodal understanding [18]. These models leverage large-scale vision-text pretraining to align visual and textual representations effectively. Similarly, Large Language Models (LLMs) have transformed natural language processing, exhibiting strong generalization across various tasks, including translation, summarization, and question answering. Advanced transformer-based architectures allow LLMs to process vast amounts of textual data, making them highly adaptable for a wide range of applications.

Our Approach. While prior works have explored event detection in both text-based and multi-modal settings, our work differs in several key aspects:

- **Generative ED with VLMs and LLMs:** Unlike existing approaches that frame ED as a classification problem, we formulate it as a generative task, allowing our model to flexibly infer missing event attributes and adapt to unseen disaster scenarios.
- **Handling Missing Modalities:** Previous works assume the availability of both text and image inputs, whereas our method explicitly models scenarios where one modality is absent (e.g., text-only or image-only posts).
- **Analysis of Social Media-Specific Linguistic Perturbations:** We systematically study the effects of informal language variations (e.g., leetspeak, word elongation, code-mixing) on ED performance—an aspect overlooked in prior multi-modal ED studies.
- **Few-Shot Prompting for Multi-Modal ED:** Our work is the first to explore prompt-based multi-modal ED using VLMs, demonstrating their effectiveness in disaster-related event detection.

By redefining multi-modal event detection as a generative task, incorporating robust prompting strategies, and analyzing social media-specific linguistic challenges, our work paves the way for ED research in disaster scenarios.

4 Experimental Setup

In this section, we discuss the approaches, dataset, and evaluation metrics for experiments.

Dataset. We utilize the disaster event dataset proposed by [1]. This dataset includes a collection of social media posts, specifically tweets, along with their corresponding images. The dataset is tailored for disaster event identification and contains a variety of event classes relevant to our study. The dataset distribution is detailed in Table 1.

Table 1. Dataset Statistics. We use the samples for which both the tweets and images exist.

Label	Test	Train	Total
Non-damage	888	2069	2957
Damaged Infrastructure	417	973	1390
Damaged Nature	155	359	514
Flood	116	268	384
Fires	104	242	346
Human Damage	72	168	240
Total	1752	4079	5831

The dataset covers a range of disaster types, including *"flood", "fire", "human damage", "damaged nature", and "damaged infrastructure".*

Evaluation Metrics. Following the previous literature on event detection, we use precision, recall, and F-score as evaluation metrics [3,5,23].

5 Approaches

5.1 Text-Only Model

Formally, the unimodal BERT [19] classifier is a text-only model that solely relies on the textual description T to classify events. It leverages the BERT architecture to capture the intricate linguistic patterns within the text and produces a contextual representation $\mathbf{W}$. This representation is passed through a linear layer to obtain the final classification $\hat{y}$

$$\hat{y} = \text{softmax}(\mathbf{W}_t \mathbf{W} + \mathbf{b}_t) \quad (1)$$

where $\mathbf{W}_t \in \mathbb{R}^{D_W \times |\mathcal{C}|}$ and $\mathbf{b}_t \in \mathbb{R}^{|\mathcal{C}|}$ are the parameters of the text classification layer. Notably, in addition to BERT, we also experiment with ModernBERT [20] to study the effect of the modern version of Language Models on ED tasks.

5.2 Vision-Only Model

This unimodal approach utilizes only visual data and is realized through the Unimodal EfficientNet Classifier. The model harnesses the prowess of EfficientNet to extract rich and descriptive visual features $\mathbf{V}$ from the image I. These features are subsequently fed into a linear classification layer to predict the event category $\hat{y}$.

$$\hat{y} = \text{softmax}(\mathbf{W}_v \mathbf{V} + \mathbf{b}_v) \tag{2}$$

where $\mathbf{W}_v \in \mathbb{R}^{D_V \times |\mathcal{C}|}$ and $\mathbf{b}_v \in \mathbb{R}^{|\mathcal{C}|}$ denote the learnable parameters of the visual classification layer.

We experiment with EfficientNet-B3 and EfficientNet-B7 as unimodal visual encoders to evaluate the impact of varying visual model complexities on event detection performance.

5.3 Vanilla Multimodal Fusion

The first vision-language fusion baseline that we considered involves combining representations from BERT and EfficientNet in a vanilla fusion approach. Formally, the fusion-based multimodal classifier (MC) aims to integrate image and text representations for event detection. The image model utilizes EfficientNet, a CNN known for its efficiency and efficacy, to extract visual features $\mathbf{V} \in \mathbb{R}^{D_V}$ from the input image I. Concurrently, the text model employs BERT to derive contextual embeddings $\mathbf{W} \in \mathbb{R}^{D_W}$ from the textual input T. These features are transformed to a common dimensional space and merged to form a joint representation $\mathbf{M} \in \mathbb{R}^{D_M}$, which is processed by a fusion layer to predict the event label $\hat{y} \in \mathcal{C}$.

$$\mathbf{M} = [\mathbf{V}; \mathbf{W}], \quad \hat{y} = \text{softmax}(\mathbf{W}_f \mathbf{M} + \mathbf{b}_f) \tag{3}$$

where $[\cdot;\cdot]$ denotes the concatenation operation, and $\mathbf{W}_f \in \mathbb{R}^{D_M \times |\mathcal{C}|}$ and $\mathbf{b}_f \in \mathbb{R}^{|\mathcal{C}|}$ are the learnable parameters of the fusion layer.

5.4 Vanilla Multimodal Fusion (ModernBERT and ConvNeXt-V2)

To leverage the representational power of state-of-the-art architectures, we design a cross-attention-based fusion model that combines ModernBERT for text encoding and ConvNeXt V2 [21] for image encoding. This model aims to perform fine-grained multimodal fusion for event classification by learning aligned representations across the vision and language modalities. For the visual stream, we use ConvNeXt V2, a high-performing convolutional architecture, to extract deep image features $\mathbf{V} \in \mathbb{R}^{D_V}$ from an input image I. For the textual stream, ModernBERT [20] is employed to generate contextualized embeddings $\mathbf{W} \in \mathbb{R}^{D_W}$ from a given text T. Both feature vectors are projected into a shared representation space of dimension D_M and integrated using a cross-attention mechanism that enables direct interaction between the image and text features. The resulting fused representation $\mathbf{M} \in \mathbb{R}^{D_M}$ is passed through a classification head to predict the event label $\hat{y} \in \mathcal{C}$.

$$\mathbf{M} = \text{CrossAttention}(\mathbf{W}', \mathbf{V}'), \quad \hat{y} = \text{softmax}(\mathbf{W}f\mathbf{M} + \mathbf{b}f) \tag{4}$$

Here, $\mathbf{W}' = \text{ReLU}(\mathbf{W}\text{text}\mathbf{W})$ and $\mathbf{V}' = \text{ReLU}(\mathbf{W}\text{img}\mathbf{V})$ are the projected text and image features, respectively. The cross-attention module learns to align relevant textual and visual patterns. $\mathbf{W}f \in \mathbb{R}^{D_M \times |\mathcal{C}|}$ and $\mathbf{b}f \in \mathbb{R}^{|\mathcal{C}|}$ are trainable classification weights and biases. The entire model is fine-tuned end-to-end with a cosine learning rate scheduler and early stopping strategy. During training, a class-balanced sampling strategy is employed to mitigate class imbalance using a weighted random sampler derived from inverse class frequency.

5.5 Dual Attention Fusion

The attention mechanism computes a set of weights $\alpha \in \mathbb{R}^{N\times(H\times W)}$, which are used to modulate the feature representations based on the interactions between the modalities. The attended features from the image and text are given by:

$$\mathbf{I}_{att} = \text{Attention}(\mathbf{Q}_t, \mathbf{K}_i, \mathbf{V}_i) \tag{5}$$

$$\mathbf{T}_{att} = \text{Attention}(\mathbf{Q}_i, \mathbf{K}_t, \mathbf{V}_t) \tag{6}$$

where $\mathbf{Q}_t$, $\mathbf{K}_i$, $\mathbf{V}_i$ denote the query, key, and value for the textual data, and $\mathbf{Q}_i$, $\mathbf{K}_t$, $\mathbf{V}_t$ for the image data, respectively. The attended features are then concatenated and passed through a fusion layer to predict the event category:

$$\hat{c} = \text{softmax}(\mathbf{W}_f[\mathbf{I}_{att}; \mathbf{T}_{att}] + \mathbf{b}_f) \tag{7}$$

where $\mathbf{W}_f$ and $\mathbf{b}_f$ are the weights and biases of the fusion layer, and $\hat{c}$ is the predicted probability distribution over the event categories.

5.6 Cross-Modal Attention

The cross-modal Attention Classifier (CMAC) introduces an attention mechanism that dynamically aligns and enhances the textual and visual features based on their inter-modal relevance. Given the feature representations $\mathbf{V}$ and $\mathbf{W}$ extracted from the image I and text T respectively, the model computes cross-modal attention weights α_c which are used to refine the features. The enhanced features $\mathbf{V}'$ and $\mathbf{W}'$ are concatenated to form the multimodal representation $\mathbf{M}'$, which is utilized for event classification.

$$\alpha_c = \text{softmax}(\mathbf{Q}_W \mathbf{K}_V^\top), \tag{8}$$

$$\mathbf{V}' = \sum \alpha_c \odot \mathbf{V}, \quad \mathbf{W}' = \sum \alpha_c \odot \mathbf{W}, \tag{9}$$

$$\mathbf{M}' = [\mathbf{V}'; \mathbf{W}'], \quad \hat{y} = \text{softmax}(\mathbf{W}_c \mathbf{M}' + \mathbf{b}_c) \tag{10}$$

where $\mathbf{Q}_W \in \mathbb{R}^{D_W \times D_A}$, $\mathbf{K}_V \in \mathbb{R}^{D_V \times D_A}$, and $\odot$ denotes the element-wise multiplication. The parameters $\mathbf{W}_c \in \mathbb{R}^{D_{M'} \times |C|}$ and $\mathbf{b}_c \in \mathbb{R}^{|C|}$ are specific to the cross-attention fusion layer.

We experiment with GPT-4 as text-only LLM for event detection (**GPT-4(text only)**). For a fair comparison, we prompt LLaVA with only task instruction, class definition, and image to implement an image-only VLM baseline (**LLaVA (image-only)**). Finally, we experiment with the tweet and image with both GPT-4o (**GPT-4o (multi-modal)**) and LLaVA (**LLaVA (multi-modal)**) for multi-modal comparison.

5.7 Hyperparameters

For generative approaches such as LLaVA and GPT-4, we set the temperature and top_k values to .7 and .8, respectively. For linear layers, we use 1024 neurons and the large models of BERT and EfficinetNet.

6 Results and Discussions

We present our findings in Table 2, illustrating the performance metrics for each model. The results lead to several important observations about the efficacy of unimodal versus multimodal and generative approaches in disaster event detection.

Table 2. Performance Metrics for Different Models

Model	Precision	Recall	F1-score
Supervised Approaches			
ModernBERT-large	0.9067	0.9081	0.9070
ConvNeXt V2	0.9229	0.9235	0.9227
Multimodal Fusion (ModernBERT + ConvNeXt V2)	**0.9452**	**0.9467**	**0.9459**
BERT-only	0.2483	0.4983	0.3314
EfficientNet	0.4700	0.4900	0.4798
Dual Attention	0.7640	0.7480	0.7559
Cross-Modal Attention	0.7815	0.7757	0.7686
Multimodal Fusion	**0.9289**	**0.9247**	**0.9250**
Generative Approaches			
GPT-4o (text)	0.3680	0.3558	0.3518
GPT-4o (image)	0.4620	0.4700	0.4660
GPT-4o (multi-modal)	0.6460	0.6300	0.6378
LLaVA (image-only)	0.4340	0.4470	0.4404
LLaVA (multi-modal)	0.5670	0.5740	0.5705

Effectiveness of Unimodal Approaches. The performance of unimodal models highlights significant differences in how text-only and image-only models handle event detection. Among supervised methods, **ModernBERT-large (text-only)** achieves an F1-score of **0.9070**, while **ConvNeXtv2 (image-only)** slightly outperforms it with an F1-score of **0.9227**. This suggests that visual features provide stronger event cues than textual embeddings alone when dealing with disaster-related data. For baseline models, **BERT-only** performs poorly, with an F1-score of **0.3314**, demonstrating that traditional transformer-based models struggle with event classification when trained solely on textual input.

Similarly, **EfficientNet (image-only)** also underperforms, achieving an F1-score of **0.4798**, indicating that while images contain critical event information, they alone are insufficient for robust classification.

Generative approaches perform significantly worse in unimodal settings. GPT-4o (text-only) achieves only 0.3518 F1-score, while GPT-4o (image-only) reaches 0.4660, demonstrating that VLMs, despite their large-scale pretraining, still struggle with precise event categorization when relying on a single modality. Similarly, LLaVA (image-only) performs suboptimally (0.4404 F1-score), showing that visual-only generative models are highly sensitive to ambiguous or missing contextual cues. Overall, unimodal models exhibit limited effectiveness, with image-based models performing slightly better than text-based counterparts in supervised settings. However, generative approaches struggle significantly when constrained to a single modality, reinforcing the necessity of multi-modal integration for improved event detection.

Advantages of Multimodal Approaches. The results clearly demonstrate the superiority of multimodal models over their unimodal counterparts in both supervised and generative settings. The best-performing model, **ModernBERT + ConvNeXtv2**, achieves an F1-score of 0.9459, outperforming both its text-only (**0.9070**) and image-only (**0.9227**) components. This improvement underscores the fact that combining textual and visual information leads to more accurate and robust event detection. Similarly, other multimodal supervised approaches such as **Multimodal Fusion** (BERT + EfficientNet) achieve an F1-score of 0.9250, significantly outperforming BERT-only (0.3314) and EfficientNet (0.4798). The Cross-Modal Attention model (0.7686 F1-score) also surpasses its unimodal counterparts, reinforcing that joint modeling of textual and visual data enables deeper contextual understanding.

For generative approaches, the multi-modal versions of both GPT-4o and LLaVA significantly outperform their unimodal variants. **GPT-4o (multi-modal) achieves 0.6378 F1-score**, a considerable improvement over both GPT-4o (text-only, 0.3518) and GPT-4o (image-only, 0.4660). Similarly, **LLaVA (multi-modal) reaches 0.5705 F1-score**, showing a meaningful boost over LLaVA (image-only, 0.4404). This highlights that generative models struggle in unimodal settings but benefit significantly from cross-modal reasoning.

In summary, multimodal approaches consistently outperform unimodal ones across all settings. The results indicate that disaster-related event detection requires both textual and visual information to resolve ambiguities and improve classification accuracy. In particular, generative models demonstrate a strong reliance on multi-modal integration, whereas supervised approaches further benefit from explicit fusion techniques, leading to state-of-the-art performance.

Challenges with Generative Approaches. As depicted in Table 2, generative approaches including GPT-4o and LLaVA fall behind their supervised counterparts. Qualitatively, we found that the information fabrication and their inability to follow task instructions are one of the major reasons for their performance. For example, instead of predicting the class `''Flood''`, LLaVA generated `''The input shows a flooding event''`. In addition, for non-disaster events, instead of generating "`Non-Damage`" class GPT-4 generates "`There are no events in the input.`" Notably, these instructions were not part of input instructions and hence can be categorized as information fabrication and mismatch.

Intriguingly, generative approaches were able to handle noisy text input such as text elongation and leet speaks. For example, GPT-4o was able to identify Leetspeaks like "`4 people d!ed due to fire.`" contains information related to a fire event that resulted in the death of 4 people. In addition, it can also handle cases such as typos and text elongation—a commonly seen writing style on social media. In summary, while these approaches were outperformed by supervised counterparts but also could pave the way for robust text processing resulting in strong multi-modal performance.

Fig. 3. The error prediction by GPT-4o. In the first image, GPT-4o misclassified the event as a "flood" category while the input instance was tagged as an "earthquake" event. Similarly, for images 2 and 3, enough contextual signal is unavailable to deduce the correct event type.

Error Analysis for Generative Approaches. To systematically analyze the limitations of our models, we randomly sampled 250 erroneous predictions from both LLaVA and GPT-4o, categorizing them into four distinct error types. This categorization provides insights into the primary failure modes and informs future improvements to enhance robustness. As illustrated in Fig. 4, the majority of errors stem from incorrect handling of image-based cues (38%) and misinterpretation of textual information (27%). A key challenge arises in event classification scenarios where visual evidence alone is insufficient to disambiguate the event type.

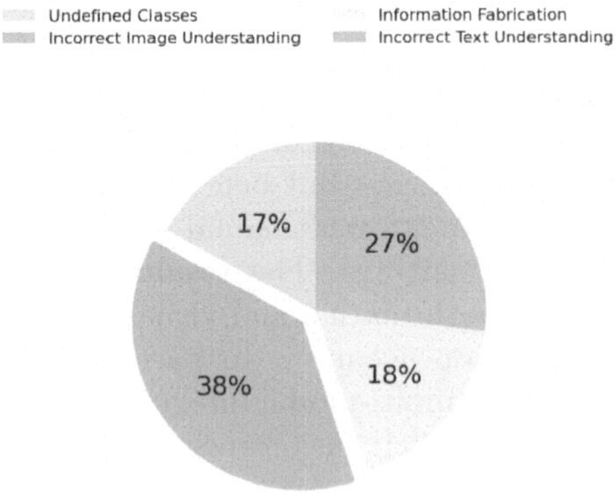

Fig. 4. Error Categorization of Generative Approaches.

For instance, Fig. 3 presents misclassified examples of "earthquake" events. All three images lack strong visual cues explicitly indicating an earthquake, making it difficult for even human annotators to confidently infer the correct event type. A particularly illustrative case is the left-most image, which depicts a river scene. The absence of visible structural damage or ground displacement makes it prone to misclassification as a "flood" event, highlighting a fundamental challenge in relying solely on visual data for event inference. Such cases emphasize the need for stronger multi-modal reasoning, where both textual and visual inputs are jointly contextualized to improve event classification accuracy.

We also observe some information mismatches in ED generations such as the prediction of classes not provided in the prompt (Undefined Classes) and the generation of sentences not provided in the desired output format (Information Fabrication). In the future, we can look into prompt design or prompt optimization [22,24] to minimize such errors.

Limitations

Our current study lays the foundation for effective disaster event identification using a multimodal analysis system. However, there are several avenues for future research and enhancements to our approach:

1. **Advanced Prompt Design and Approaches:** We plan to explore advanced fusion techniques for integrating vision and language models, such as Contrastive Language-Image Pretraining (CLIP), LLaVa, and GPT-4o in few-shot setup with prompt optimization [22,24]. In addition, we will also explore instruction-tuning to boost the performance [25].
2. **Real-Time Monitoring and Response:** Integrating real-time monitoring capabilities into our system would enable immediate detection and response to unfolding disaster events. This involves developing mechanisms for continuous data scraping, processing, and analysis to provide timely alerts and actionable insights to response teams.
3. **Scalability and Generalization:** As the volume and diversity of social media data continue to grow, ensuring the scalability and generalization of our system becomes crucial. Future work will focus on optimizing our models for scalability, adapting to evolving disaster event scenarios, and generalizing across different geographical regions and languages.
4. **User-Generated Content Analysis:** Analyzing user-generated content, such as comments and replies to social media posts, can provide valuable contextual information and sentiment analysis related to disaster events. Incorporating this aspect into our analysis could enrich the understanding of public perceptions and responses during crises.
5. **Collaborative Disaster Response Platforms:** Collaborative platforms that integrate our multimodal analysis system with other tools and resources used by disaster response teams could streamline coordination and decision-making processes. Future work will involve exploring integration possibilities and evaluating the impact on response effectiveness.

By addressing these areas of future work, we aim to continually improve the capabilities and applicability of our multimodal analysis system for disaster event identification, ultimately contributing to more efficient and informed disaster response efforts.

References

1. Mozannar, H., Rizk, Y., Awad, M.: Damage identification in social media posts using multimodal deep learning. In: International Conference on Information Systems for Crisis Response and Management (2018)
2. Parekh, T., et al.: SPEED++: a multilingual event extraction framework for epidemic prediction and preparedness. In: Proceedings of the 2024 Conference on Empirical Methods in Natural Language Processing, Miami, Florida, USA, pp. 12936–12965. Association for Computational Linguistics (2024)
3. Doddington, G., Mitchell, A., Przybocki, M., Ramshaw, L., Strassel, S., Weischedel, R.: The automatic content extraction (ACE) program – tasks, data, and evaluation. In: Proceedings of the Fourth International Conference on Language Resources and Evaluation (LREC 2004), Lisbon, Portugal. European Language Resources Association (ELRA) (2004)
4. Ji, H., Grishman, R.: Refining event extraction through cross-document inference. In: Proceedings of ACL 2008: HLT, Columbus, Ohio, pp. 254–262. Association for Computational Linguistics (2008)
5. Liao, S., Grishman, R.: Can document selection help semi-supervised learning? A case study on event extraction. In: Proceedings of the 49th Annual Meeting of the Association for Computational Linguistics: Human Language Technologies, Portland, Oregon, USA, pp. 260–265. Association for Computational Linguistics (2011)
6. Huang, R., Riloff, E.: Bootstrapped training of event extraction classifiers. In: Proceedings of the 13th Conference of the European Chapter of the Association for Computational Linguistics, Avignon, France, pp. 286–295. Association for Computational Linguistics (2012)
7. Li, Q., Ji, H., Huang, L.: Joint event extraction via structured prediction with global features. In: Proceedings of the 51st Annual Meeting of the Association for Computational Linguistics (Volume 1: Long Papers), Sofia, Bulgaria, pp. 73–82. Association for Computational Linguistics (2013)
8. Chen, Y., Xu, L., Liu, K., Zeng, D., Zhao, J.: Event extraction via dynamic multi-pooling convolutional neural networks. In: Proceedings of the 53rd Annual Meeting of the Association for Computational Linguistics and the 7th International Joint Conference on Natural Language Processing (Volume 1: Long Papers), Beijing, China, pp. 167–176. Association for Computational Linguistics (2015)
9. Wadden, D., Wennberg, U., Luan, Y., Hajishirzi, H.: Entity, relation, and event extraction with contextualized span representations. In: Proceedings of the 2019 Conference on Empirical Methods in Natural Language Processing and the 9th International Joint Conference on Natural Language Processing (EMNLP-IJCNLP), Hong Kong, China, pp. 5784–5789. Association for Computational Linguistics (2019)
10. Zhang, T., et al.: Improving event extraction via multimodal integration. In: Proceedings of the 25th ACM International Conference on Multimedia, pp. 270–278 (2017)

11. Chang, X., Ma, Z., Yang, Y., Zeng, Z., Hauptmann, A.G.: Bi-level semantic representation analysis for multimedia event detection. IEEE Trans. Cybern. **47**(5), 1180–1197 (2017). https://doi.org/10.1109/TCYB.2016.2539546
12. Ma, Z., Chang, X., Xu, Z., Sebe, N., Hauptmann, A.G.: Joint attributes and event analysis for multimedia event detection. IEEE Trans. Neural Netw. Learn. Syst. **29**(7), 2921–2930 (2018). https://doi.org/10.1109/TNNLS.2017.2709308
13. Weegar, R., Åström, K., Nugues, P.: Linking entities across images and text. In: Nineteenth Conference on Computational Natural Language Learning (CoNLL 2015), pp. 185–193. Association for Computational Linguistics (2015)
14. Wu, H., et al.: Univse: robust visual semantic embeddings via structured semantic representations. arXiv preprint arXiv:1904.05521 (2019)
15. Radford, A., et al.: Learning transferable visual models from natural language supervision. In: International Conference on Machine Learning. PMLR (2021)
16. Li, M., et al.: Cross-media structured common space for multimedia event extraction. In: Proceedings of the 58th Annual Meeting of the Association for Computational Linguistics, pp. 2557–2568. Association for Computational Linguistics (2020)
17. Yatskar, M., Zettlemoyer, L., Farhadi, A.: Situation recognition: Visual semantic role labeling for image understanding. In: Proceedings of the IEEE Conference on Computer Vision and Pattern Recognition (2016)
18. Li, J, et al.: Blip-2: bootstrapping language-image pre-training with frozen image encoders and large language models. In: International Conference on Machine Learning. PMLR (2023)
19. Devlin, J., Chang, M.W., Lee, K., Toutanova, K.: BERT: pre-training of deep bidirectional transformers for language understanding. In: Proceedings of the 2019 Conference of the North American Chapter of the Association for Computational Linguistics: Human Language Technologies, Volume 1 (Long and Short Papers), Minneapolis, Minnesota, pp. 4171–4186. Association for Computational Linguistics (2019)
20. Warner, B., et al.: Smarter, better, faster, longer: a modern bidirectional encoder for fast, memory efficient, and long context finetuning and inference. arXiv preprint arXiv:2412.13663 (2024)
21. Woo, S., et al.: Convnext v2: co-designing and scaling convnets with masked autoencoders. In: Proceedings of the IEEE/CVF Conference on Computer Vision and Pattern Recognition (2023)
22. Srivastava, S., et al.: Instances need more care: Rewriting prompts for instances with LLMs in the loop yields better zero-shot performance. arXiv preprint arXiv:2310.02107 (2023)
23. Srivastava, S., et al.: MailEx: email event and argument extraction. In: Proceedings of the 2023 Conference on Empirical Methods in Natural Language Processing, Singapore, pp. 12964–12987. Association for Computational Linguistics (2023)
24. Srivastava, S., Yao, Z.: Revisiting Prompt Optimization with Large Reasoning Models-A Case Study on Event Extraction. arXiv preprint arXiv:2504.07357 (2025)
25. Srivastava, S., Pati, S., Yao, Z.: Instruction-Tuning LLMs for Event Extraction with Annotation Guidelines. arXiv preprint arXiv:2502.16377 (2025)

ReSHQ: Re-ranking Based on the Similarity Between Hypothetical Query and Query

Keito Fukuoka(✉) and Hisashi Miyamori

Division of Frontier Informatics, Kyoto Sangyo University, Kyoto, Japan
{i2486200,miya}@kyoto-su.ac.jp

Abstract. This paper proposes a novel retrieval method, ReSHQ (Reranking based on the Similarity between Hypothetical query and Query), aimed at improving retrieval accuracy without needing labeled dataset training and reducing reliance on the internal knowledge of language models. ReSHQ generates hypothetical queries from documents using language models and re-ranks retrieval results based on the similarity between the input query and the hypothetical queries. Experiments using the Web search datasets (TREC DL19/20) demonstrated that ReSHQ outperformed the conventional BM25 method, particularly in nDCG@k. While ReSHQ did not surpass HyDE, a conventional method that also does not require labeled dataset training, in overall performance, it achieved comparable or superior accuracy in nDCG@1. Compared to HyDE, ReSHQ exhibited lower retrieval performance with large language models but achieved comparable or superior performance with smaller language models, indicating a reduced reliance on internal knowledge. Experiments using low-resource datasets (BEIR) showed that ReSHQ underperformed compared to BM25. However, the proposed method showed results suggesting its effectiveness in datasets with short document lengths and in question-answering tasks. These results indicate that ReSHQ is effective in Web search datasets and is a promising method, especially for smaller language models. Future challenges include improving the method of generating hypothetical queries and evaluating performance on diverse datasets.

Keywords: Information Retrieval · Re-ranking · Hypothetical Query Generation

1 Introduction

Information retrieval is the task of finding relevant information from a large corpus in response to a user's query. In recent years, dense retrieval, a method that retrieves documents using the similarity of semantic embeddings, has succeeded in tasks such as open-domain question answering and fact-checking [5,6]. Various techniques, including negative sampling [13] and improvements in pre-training [2], have been proposed to enhance the performance of supervised dense

R. Ichise (Ed.): NLDB 2025, LNCS 15836, pp. 472–483, 2026.
https://doi.org/10.1007/978-3-031-97141-9_32

retrieval models. However, a challenge remains in specific domains where constructing labeled datasets necessary for supervised learning is difficult.

To address this issue, an approach known as zero-shot retrieval, which applies retrieval models trained on large-scale retrieval datasets like MS MARCO [1] to new domains, can be considered. However, such large-scale datasets are not always available, and some, like MS MARCO, may have restrictions on commercial use. Therefore, dense retrieval models that use unlabeled retrieval datasets are needed.

In this context, unsupervised dense retrieval models such as Contriever [4] and its extension, HyDE [3], have been proposed. HyDE is a form of query expansion that generates hypothetical documents, which are answers to the query, using language models and performs retrieval using these as new queries. However, HyDE relies on the internal knowledge of language models, and its retrieval performance may degrade when this knowledge is insufficient or the number of parameters is small.

Therefore, in this study, we propose a new method, ReSHQ, which avoids reliance on the internal knowledge of language models. Specifically, we propose a method that performs retrieval by generating hypothetical queries from documents using language models, which is the reverse approach of HyDE, and calculating the similarity between the input query and the hypothetical queries. It is expected that the proposed method can achieve retrieval without relying on the internal knowledge of language models by using the document to retrieve itself as external knowledge for generating hypothetical queries.

Based on the above, this study sets the following research questions:

RQ1 Can the proposed method improve retrieval accuracy compared to unsupervised retrieval methods such as BM25 and HyDE?
RQ2 Can the proposed method maintain retrieval accuracy with smaller language models without significant performance degradation compared to larger language models?

This paper makes the following contributions:

- The proposed method achieved retrieval accuracy surpassing the conventional BM25 method in nDCG@k on Web search datasets. Compared to HyDE, the overall results were inferior, but it performed comparably or better in nDCG@1. n low-resource tasks like BEIR, the retrieval accuracy of the proposed method was lower than that of conventional methods in most evaluation metrics. Still, we obtained results suggesting effectiveness in datasets with short document lengths and in question-answering tasks.
- Compared to HyDE, the proposed method showed inferior results with large language models but achieved comparable or better performance with smaller ones. This indicates that ReSHQ can maintain retrieval accuracy with smaller models without significant performance degradation compared to larger models, reducing reliance on internal knowledge.

The structure of this paper is summarized as follows. Section 2 discusses related work on zero-shot dense retrieval and query relevance utilization, and

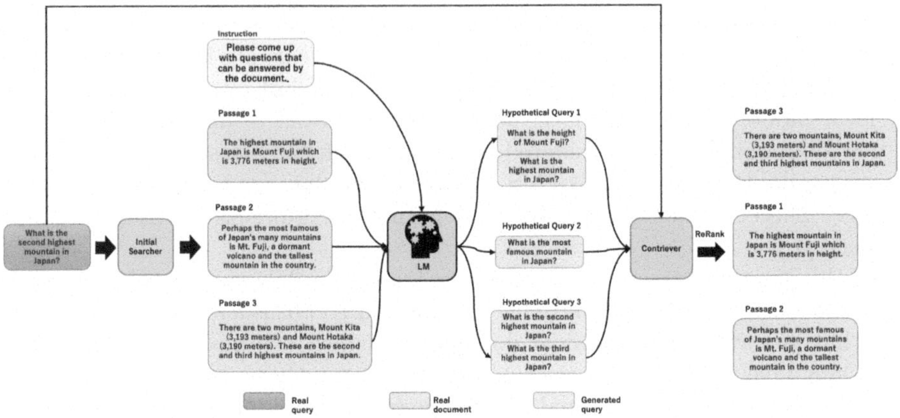

Fig. 1. Overview of the proposed method, ReSHQ.

clarifies the position of this study. Section 3 explains the proposed method, ReSHQ. Section 3.1 presents the experimental setup and results and discusses the research questions. Finally, Sect. 4 concludes this study and outlines future challenges.

2 Related Work

2.1 Zero-Shot Dense Retrieval

The task of zero-shot retrieval was defined by Thakur et al. [11] along with the BEIR dataset. BEIR consists of various retrieval tasks and is widely used to evaluate zero-shot retrieval performance. Much of the research related to dense retrieval adopts a setting where a dense retrieval model is first trained using MS MARCO, a large-scale supervised dataset, and then transferred to other tasks or domains [12,14]. However, large-scale labeled datasets like MS MARCO are not always available. There are cases where commercial use is restricted, as with MS MARCO, or where large-scale labeled datasets simply do not exist for languages other than English. Against this backdrop, research on unsupervised dense retrieval using only unlabeled datasets has progressed.

Izacard et al. [4] proposed Contriever, a retrieval model trained by unsupervised contrastive learning, and showed competitive results in low-resource datasets and datasets in languages other than English. Furthermore, Gao et al. [3] proposed HyDE, which generates hypothetical relevant documents from queries using language models and performs retrieval with Contriever using these hypothetical documents as queries. HyDE achieved significant performance improvements compared to Contriever but also faced several challenges. HyDE tends to have decreased retrieval accuracy with models having a small number of parameters, and in some low-resource datasets, it may underperform compared to traditional methods like BM25. This is thought to be because HyDE strongly relies on the internal knowledge of language models. In this study, we adopt the reverse approach of HyDE to address this problem. We perform retrieval based on the similarity between the input query and hypothetical queries generated from documents using language models. By using the document to retrieve itself as external knowledge for generating hypothetical queries, we aim to reduce reliance on the internal knowledge of language models and achieve a more general-purpose zero-shot dense retrieval method.

2.2 Utilization of Query Relevance

In FAQ systems, attempts have been made to improve retrieval accuracy by considering the relevance between user queries and FAQ documents and between assumed queries pre-associated with FAQ documents and user queries [8,10]. Additionally, Doc2query [9] has garnered attention as a method to improve retrieval performance by generating queries from documents using language models and appending them to the documents. It generates queries that look like questions about a given document. The generated queries are appended to the original document. This allows for a more comprehensive understanding of the document's content by considering user queries and queries generated from the document during retrieval, resulting in improved retrieval accuracy. Doc2query shares the commonality with this study in that it generates queries from documents, but the utilization method of the generated queries differs. In Doc2query, the generated queries are treated as part of the document and used to calculate the relevance score during retrieval. In contrast, in this study, the relevance between the generated and input queries is calculated, and the document itself is not used for relevance score calculation.

3 Method

An overview of the proposed method, ReSHQ, is shown in Fig. 1. ReSHQ consists of the following steps. First, a certain number of N of highly relevant documents is obtained for a given query q using a conventional retrieval method such as BM25. Next, multiple hypothetical queries are generated from each obtained document d_i. Let the set of hypothetical queries generated from document d_i be $Q_i = \{q_{i1}, q_{i2}, \ldots q_{iM}\}$, where M is the number of hypothetical queries generated from a single document. The relevance between the generated hypothetical query q_{ij} and the input query q is calculated using an encoder such as Contriever. The relevance can be calculated as the inner product between the embedding vectors of query q and hypothetical query q_{ij}:

$$score\left(q, q_{ij}\right) = \langle enc\left(q\right), enc\left(q_{ij}\right)\rangle, \tag{1}$$

where $enc\left(\cdot\right)$ is an encoder that transforms a query into an embedding vector. The relevance of each document d_i is calculated as the maximum relevance with the hypothetical queries generated from that document:

$$Score\left(q, d_i\right) = \max_{q_{ij} \in Q_i} score\left(q, q_{ij}\right) \tag{2}$$

Finally, documents are ranked based on each document's relevance $Score(q, d_i)$, and the highly relevant documents are returned.

3.1 Experimental Setup

Setup. ReSHQ allows for multiple parameter settings, and in this experiment, we adopted the following settings:

- Initial retrieval method: BM25
- Number of initial retrieval results: 100
- Hypothetical query generation model: Llama3.1 8b 4bit quantized model
- Number of hypothetical queries generated: 5
- Scoring method for queries and hypothetical queries: Contriever model

The retrieval experiments were conducted using the Pyserini toolkit [7].

Evaluation Datasets. As evaluation datasets, we used TREC DL19 and TREC DL20 (based on the MS-MARCO dataset), which are Web search datasets, and six datasets from BEIR, including various low-resource datasets. The BEIR datasets include TREC-COVID for biomedical information retrieval, FiQA focusing on open-domain opinion-based question answering, TREC-NEWS for background information retrieval of news articles, ArguAna for argument retrieval consisting of pairs of arguments and counterarguments from online discussion platforms, DBPedia for entity retrieval with diverse queries, and SciFact for fact-checking scientific claims, which is sometimes used for scientific paper citation prediction.

Evaluation Metrics. In this study, we evaluate retrieval accuracy using Mean Average Precision (map) and nDCG@k (k = 1, 3, 5, 10), which are evaluation metrics for information retrieval. map is a metric that measures the precision of retrieval results, particularly considering the balance between precision and recall. It is suitable for comprehensively evaluating the quality of retrieval results because it can evaluate the trade-off between precision and recall by considering the ranking of relevant documents. nDCG@k is a metric that evaluates the quality of the ranking of retrieval results, particularly targeting the top k rankings. It gives higher evaluations as more relevant documents are ranked higher. Its feature is that it emphasizes the quality of the top rankings and considers the ranking of relevant documents and the degree of relevance.

Table 1. Web Search Results on DL19/20. The highest score for each metric is signified in bold.

	DL19				
	map	nDCG@1	nDCG@3	nDCG@5	nDCG@10
BM25	30.1	54.3	52.3	52.8	50.6
Contriever	24.0	45.7	46.1	45.6	44.5
HyDE (Llama3.1 8b 4bit)	**38.2**	**63.2**	**59.6**	**58.8**	**56.5**
ReSHQ (Llama3.1 8b 4bit)	27.7	57.0	55.3	55.1	55.9
	DL20				
	map	nDCG@1	nDCG@3	nDCG@5	nDCG@10
BM25	28.6	57.7	50.2	50.7	48.0
Contriever	24.0	46.9	46.1	43.7	42.1
HyDE (Llama3.1 8b 4bit)	**37.5**	**64.2**	**61.9**	**61.2**	**57.2**
ReSHQ (Llama3.1 8b 4bit)	31.4	62.4	55.7	53.7	52.5

Comparison Methods. As comparison methods, we use the following methods that do not require supervised learning:

- BM25: A classical information retrieval method that evaluates the relevance between a query and a document based on term frequency (TF) and inverse document frequency (IDF).
- Contriever: A retrieval model using dense vectors trained by unsupervised contrastive learning. Unlike traditional vocabulary-based methods, it can detect highly relevant documents even when there is no lexical overlap by performing retrieval using semantic embeddings of documents.
- HyDE: A method that generates hypothetical documents from queries using instruction-following language models and performs retrieval with Contriever using these hypothetical documents as queries. The only difference from Contriever is the query construction method.

3.2 RQ1: Can the Proposed Method Improve Retrieval Accuracy Compared to Unsupervised Retrieval Methods Such as BM25 and HyDE?

To evaluate the retrieval accuracy of the proposed method in comparison to existing unsupervised retrieval methods, we utilize TREC DL19 and TREC DL20, which contain diverse queries from Web searches. This allows us to validate the effectiveness of the proposed method in real-world Web search scenarios. Furthermore, we investigate how the proposed method is affected by the number of retrieved documents in the initial retrieval stage. Additionally, we examine whether the proposed method can enhance retrieval accuracy in zero-shot

Table 2. Web Search Results on DL19/20 with Varying Numbers of Retrieved Documents in Initial Retrieval. The highest score for each metric is signified in bold.

	DL19				
	map	nDCG@1	nDCG@3	nDCG@5	nDCG@10
ReSHQ (top100)	27.7	57.0	**55.3**	**55.1**	**55.9**
ReSHQ (top300)	31.4	58.5	54.3	54.8	55.1
ReSHQ (top500)	**32.1**	**61.6**	54.6	54.7	54.6
	DL20				
	map	nDCG@1	nDCG@3	nDCG@5	nDCG@10
ReSHQ (top100)	31.4	62.4	55.7	53.7	52.5
ReSHQ (top300)	33.6	**65.1**	57.5	55.9	**55.1**
ReSHQ (top500)	**33.7**	**65.1**	**57.8**	**56.0**	55.0

retrieval scenarios. We select six datasets from the BEIR dataset and comparatively evaluate the retrieval accuracy of the proposed method against existing unsupervised retrieval methods.

Web Search. Table 1 presents the evaluation results for TREC DL19 and TREC DL20. Regarding the map, ReSHQ underperformed compared to BM25 in TREC DL19 but outperformed it in TREC DL20. On the other hand, in nDCG@k, ReSHQ outperformed BM25 in both datasets. These results suggest that ReSHQ may be superior to BM25's ability to rank highly relevant documents at the top. In other words, ReSHQ is considered effective in presenting information that users seek at the top of search results.

However, compared to HyDE, ReSHQ showed inferior results in all map and nDCG@k metrics for both datasets. Nevertheless, in nDCG@10 for TREC DL19 and nDCG@1 for TREC DL20, ReSHQ showed results comparable to HyDE. This indicates that while ReSHQ is inferior in overall performance compared to HyDE, it is competitive in some metrics.

These results are based on experiments with 100 documents that were retrieved during the initial retrieval. It is expected that increasing the number of documents retrieved during the initial retrieval could improve the performance of ReSHQ. Therefore, Table 2 shows the experimental results with varying numbers of retrieved documents. In both datasets, an increasing trend in ReSHQn's map was observed as the number of retrieved documents increased. This is likely because considering more documents increases the possibility of retrieving relevant documents. On the other hand, it was shown that increasing the number of retrieved documents does not necessarily improve accuracy in nDCG@k. However, in nDCG@1, it was shown that increasing the number of retrieved documents improves accuracy. Especially when the number of retrieved documents in the initial retrieval was set to 300 or 500, nDCG@1 for TREC DL20 outper-

Table 3. Low-Resource Tasks from BEIR. The best-performing system is indicated in bold. The proposed method, ReSHQ, is denoted with ↑ if its accuracy is improved compared to BM25, and ↓ if it is decreased.

	TREC-COVID	FiQA	TREC-NEWS	ArguAna	DBPedia	SciFact
nDCG@1						
BM25	**68.0**	**22.2**	**42.7**	**17.4**	36.4	**55.3**
Contriever	40.0	21.1	37.0	16.4	36.9	51.7
HyDE (Llama3.1 8b 4bit)	61.0	21.0	24.3	0.02	**46.4**	51.3
ReSHQ(Llama3.1 8b 4bit)	65.0 ↓	21.5 ↓	34.5 ↓	7.2 ↓	37.6 ↑	43.0 ↓
nDCG@3						
BM25	**64.6**	20.6	**42.9**	**29.6**	33.2	**64.3**
Contriever	34.8	21.0	36.6	28.4	31.6	60.3
HyDE (Llama3.1 8b 4bit)	62.3	**21.1**	24.9	16.9	**39.4**	60.0
ReSHQ(Llama3.1 8b 4bit)	61.2 ↓	20.3 ↓	37.8 ↓	20.3 ↓	33.1 ↓	50.2 ↓
nDCG@5						
BM25	**63.2**	21.5	**41.3**	**34.5**	32.4	**65.7**
Contriever	31.1	**22.5**	35.9	32.5	29.9	63.1
HyDE (Llama3.1 8b 4bit)	58.1	22.2	25.1	22.9	**37.3**	63.3
ReSHQ(Llama3.1 8b 4bit)	59.3 ↓	22.0 ↑	40.1 ↓	26.8 ↓	31.5 ↓	53.0 ↓
nDCG@10						
BM25	**59.5**	23.6	39.5	**39.7**	31.9	**67.9**
Contriever	27.3	**24.5**	34.8	37.9	29.2	64.9
HyDE (Llama3.1 8b 4bit)	56.8	**24.5**	24.1	30.0	**35.6**	66.4
ReSHQ(Llama3.1 8b 4bit)	57.0 ↓	24.1 ↑	**40.2** ↑	33.5 ↓	30.6 ↓	57.0 ↓

formed HyDE. This result suggests that ReSHQ can perform better than HyDE in top-1 accuracy by considering sufficient documents.

We consider the reason why ReSHQ significantly underperformed HyDE in TREC DL20 except for nDCG@1 but outperformed HyDE in nDCG@1. HyDE generates hypothetical documents from queries using language models. In this process, while general answers and related information to the query are included, specific information may be missing, or noise information not directly related to the query may be included. On the other hand, ReSHQ generates hypothetical queries directly from the documents to be retrieved. This approach enables the generation of hypothetical queries that precisely reflect the content of the documents. Since important information and specific content in the documents are condensed into the hypothetical queries, the comparison with the input query measures a stricter degree of match. Although there is a disadvantage of information being reduced, the top accuracy improves when the input query and the hypothetical query strictly match, as hypothetical queries that match the content of the document are generated. Especially in nDCG@1, this strict degree

Table 4. TREC DL19/20 results for ReSHQ and HyDE with Varying Parameter Sizes. The accuracy of ReSHQ compared to HyDE with the same parameter size is indicated ↑ if it is higher and ↓ if it is lower. For ReSHQ with parameter sizes of 3b and 1b, hypothetical queries were sometimes not generated properly, and in those cases, the score was set to 0.

	DL19				
	map	nDCG@1	nDCG@3	nDCG@5	nDCG@10
HyDE (Llama3.2 1b 4bit)	30.1	54.3	52.3	52.8	50.6
HyDE (Llama3.2 3b 4bit)	36.6	55.4	57.1	55.5	54.9
HyDE (Llama3.1 8b 4bit)	**38.2**	**63.2**	**59.6**	**58.8**	56.5
ReSHQ (Llama3.2 1b 4bit)	27.2↓	61.2↑	57.2↑	56.2↑	**56.7**↑
ReSHQ (Llama3.2 3b 4bit)	27.0↓	54.3↓	56.9↓	56.5↑	56.1↑
ReSHQ (Llama3.1 8b 4bit)	27.7↓	57.0↓	55.3↓	55.1↓	55.9↓
	DL20				
	map	nDCG@1	nDCG@3	nDCG@5	nDCG@10
HyDE (Llama3.2 1b 4bit)	32.2	58.6	52.9	51.2	49.8
HyDE (Llama3.2 3b 4bit)	36.4	63.9	58.6	58.0	55.4
HyDE (Llama3.1 8b 4bit)	**37.5**	**64.2**	**61.9**	**61.2**	**57.2**
ReSHQ (Llama3.2 1b 4bit)	30.5↓	56.2↓	53.2↑	51.4↑	51.0↑
ReSHQ (Llama3.2 3b 4bit)	30.4↓	58.3↓	57.4↓	55.0↓	53.9↓
ReSHQ (Llama3.1 8b 4bit)	31.4↓	62.4↓	55.7↓	53.7↓	52.5↓

of match is directly reflected in the evaluation, so ReSHQ is thought to have performed better than HyDE in TREC DL20.

Low-Resource Tasks from BEIR. The low-resource results from BEIR, shown in Table 3, revealed challenges for the proposed method, ReSHQ. While ReSHQ showed performance exceeding BM25 in some datasets and evaluation metrics, it generally underperformed compared to BM25. However, in nDCG@10 for TREC-NEWS, ReSHQ achieved the highest score among all methods.

A potential factor contributing to the performance degradation is the small number of generated hypothetical queries relative to the length of the documents. A relationship was observed between the average number of words in the document length and the performance degradation of ReSHQ. For example, in DBPedia, which has an average word count comparable to MS MARCO, the score decrease from BM25 is relatively minor. Similarly, the reduction in score from BM25 was relatively minor in FiQA. The results from FiQA suggest that ReSHQ is effective in open-domain question-answering tasks.

Considering these results comprehensively, ReSHQ is likely to function particularly effectively in short-document datasets and question-answering tasks. However, additional refinements are suggested to improve performance in long-document datasets and specialized search tasks.

3.3 RQ2: Can the Proposed Method Maintain Retrieval Accuracy with Smaller Language Models Without Significant Performance Degradation Compared to Larger Language Models?

To evaluate whether the proposed method, ReSHQ, can maintain retrieval accuracy with smaller language models without significant performance degradation compared to larger language models, we compare and evaluate the retrieval accuracy of ReSHQ and the existing method, HyDE, for each parameter size using TREC DL19 and TREC DL20, which contain diverse queries from Web searches.

Table 4 shows the results of ReSHQ and HyDE for each parameter size in TREC DL19 and TREC DL20. HyDE showed a tendency for retrieval accuracy to improve with increasing parameter size. This is likely because larger parameter sizes allow for learning more knowledge.

On the other hand, ReSHQ showed smaller performance variations due to parameter size, and particularly in nDCG@10 of TREC DL19, ReSHQ (Llama3.2 1b 4bit) achieved the highest accuracy. Furthermore, in TREC DL19, ReSHQ showed comparable or better performance than HyDE with models of parameter sizes 3b and 1b, and in TREC DL20, it showed competitive results with parameter size 1b. These results indicate that ReSHQ can maintain retrieval accuracy with smaller models without significant performance degradation compared to larger models. This characteristic is beneficial in environments with limited resources.

4 Conclusion

In this paper, we proposed a re-ranking method that does not require labeled datasets and reduces reliance on internal knowledge. Specifically, it is a method that generates hypothetical queries from documents using language models and re-ranks based on the similarity between the input query and the hypothetical queries. Regarding the research question of whether the proposed method can improve retrieval accuracy compared to unsupervised retrieval methods such as BM25 and HyDE, ReSHQ showed results surpassing BM25 in TREC DL19 and TREC DL20. On the other hand, compared to HyDE, ReSHQ generally underperformed but showed comparable or better accuracy in nDCG@1. However, in the low-resource tasks of BEIR, ReSHQ underperformed compared to BM25. Regarding the research question of whether the proposed method can maintain retrieval accuracy with smaller language models without significant performance degradation compared to larger language models, ReSHQ demonstrated that it can achieve retrieval performance comparable to or exceeding HyDE with smaller models. This suggests the proposed method is beneficial in environments with limited resources. Future challenges include improving the method of generating hypothetical queries and evaluating performance on various datasets.

Acknowledgements. A part of this work was supported by JSPS KAKENHI Grant Number 23K11342.

References

1. Bajaj, P., et al.: MS MARCO: a human generated machine reading comprehension dataset. arXiv preprint arXiv:1611.09268 (2016)
2. Gao, L., Callan, J.: Condenser: a pre-training architecture for dense retrieval. arXiv preprint arXiv:2104.08253 (2021)
3. Gao, L., Ma, X., Lin, J., Callan, J.: Precise zero-shot dense retrieval without relevance labels. In: Proceedings of the 61st Annual Meeting of the Association for Computational Linguistics (Volume 1: Long Papers), pp. 1762–1777 (2023)
4. Izacard, G., et al.: Unsupervised dense information retrieval with contrastive learning. arXiv preprint arXiv:2112.09118 (2021)
5. Karpukhin, V., et al.: Dense passage retrieval for open-domain question answering. In: Webber, B., Cohn, T., He, Y., Liu, Y. (eds.) Proceedings of the 2020 Conference on Empirical Methods in Natural Language Processing (EMNLP), pp. 6769–6781. Association for Computational Linguistics, Online (2020). https://doi.org/10.18653/v1/2020.emnlp-main.550. https://aclanthology.org/2020.emnlp-main.550/
6. Lee, K., Chang, M.W., Toutanova, K.: Latent retrieval for weakly supervised open domain question answering. In: Korhonen, A., Traum, D., Màrquez, L. (eds.) Proceedings of the 57th Annual Meeting of the Association for Computational Linguistics, Florence, Italy, pp. 6086–6096. Association for Computational Linguistics (2019). https://doi.org/10.18653/v1/P19-1612. https://aclanthology.org/P19-1612/
7. Lin, J., Ma, X., Lin, S.C., Yang, J.H., Pradeep, R., Nogueira, R.: Pyserini: an easy-to-use python toolkit to support replicable IR research with sparse and dense representations. arXiv preprint arXiv:2102.10073 (2021)
8. Mass, Y., Carmeli, B., Roitman, H., Konopnicki, D.: Unsupervised FAQ retrieval with question generation and BERT. In: Jurafsky, D., Chai, J., Schluter, N., Tetreault, J. (eds.) Proceedings of the 58th Annual Meeting of the Association for Computational Linguistics, pp. 807–812. Association for Computational Linguistics, Online (2020). https://doi.org/10.18653/v1/2020.acl-main.74. https://aclanthology.org/2020.acl-main.74/
9. Nogueira, R., Yang, W., Lin, J., Cho, K.: Document expansion by query prediction. arXiv preprint arXiv:1904.08375 (2019)
10. Sakata, W., Shibata, T., Tanaka, R., Kurohashi, S.: FAQ retrieval using query-question similarity and bert-based query-answer relevance. In: Proceedings of the 42nd International ACM SIGIR Conference on Research and Development in Information Retrieval, pp. 1113–1116 (2019)
11. Thakur, N., Reimers, N., Rücklé, A., Srivastava, A., Gurevych, I.: Beir: a heterogenous benchmark for zero-shot evaluation of information retrieval models. arXiv preprint arXiv:2104.08663 (2021)
12. Wang, K., Thakur, N., Reimers, N., Gurevych, I.: GPL: generative pseudo labeling for unsupervised domain adaptation of dense retrieval. In: Carpuat, M., de Marneffe, M.C., Meza Ruiz, I.V. (eds.) Proceedings of the 2022 Conference of the North American Chapter of the Association for Computational Linguistics: Human Language Technologies, Seattle, United States, pp. 2345–2360. Association for Computational Linguistics (2022). https://doi.org/10.18653/v1/2022.naacl-main.168. https://aclanthology.org/2022.naacl-main.168/

13. Xiong, L., et al.: Approximate nearest neighbor negative contrastive learning for dense text retrieval. arXiv preprint arXiv:2007.00808 (2020)
14. Yu, Y., Xiong, C., Sun, S., Zhang, C., Overwijk, A.: COCO-DR: combating distribution shifts in zero-shot dense retrieval with contrastive and distributionally robust learning. arXiv preprint arXiv:2210.15212 (2022)

Multi-hop Question Answering in SlideVQA Based on Beam Retrieval

Mizuki Yamano(✉) and Hisashi Miyamori

Faculty of information Science and Engineering, Kyoto Sangyo University, Kyoto, Japan
{i2586263,miya}@cc.kyoto-su.ac.jp

Abstract. This paper addresses the SlideVQA task, which involves answering visual multi-hop questions on presentation slides. SlideVQA requires complex reasoning abilities, such as understanding relationships between multiple document images and numerical reasoning. Conventional methods have demonstrated significantly lower performance in multi-hop question answering than simple single-hop. Specifically, one instance has shown a performance drop of over 10 points in the F1 score, indicating insufficient performance. Furthermore, while conventional studies have demonstrated that accurate evidence selection improves overall task performance, there remains room for improvement. This paper focuses on improving the performance of multi-hop question answering and evidence selection in the SlideVQA task, thereby enhancing the overall performance of the question-answering task. To this end, we propose Multimodal Beam Retrieval (MMBR), a multimodal extension of Beam Retrieval, a retriever for answering multi-hop questions on text documents. Through experiments using the SlideVQA dataset, we aim to clarify whether the proposed method improves the performance of evidence selection and contributes to the overall performance enhancement of the question-answering task.

Keywords: SlideVQA · Multi-hop Question Answering · Beam Retrieval

1 Introduction

Realizing a technology that can perform inference based on given natural language inputs and return appropriate answers is a crucial challenge in AI. In recent years, simple question-answering tasks that can return answers in a single inference step from a given document have surpassed human performance by developing deep learning technologies and datasets such as SQuAD 2.0 [8,16]. Therefore, a more complex form of multi-hop question answering has been gaining attention. Multi-hop question answering is a question-answering task that returns an answer by undergoing multiple inference steps, utilizing various clues present within the documents. Questions used in real-world settings often require numerous pieces of information and step-by-step reasoning to derive answers (called

R. Ichise (Ed.): NLDB 2025, LNCS 15836, pp. 484–499, 2026.
https://doi.org/10.1007/978-3-031-97141-9_33

multi-hop questions). In contrast to single-hop questions, where answers can be derived through a single inference step, multi-hop questions necessitate not only straightforward information extraction but also the extraction of multiple pieces of information and the establishment of associations between information. For instance, diagnosing a patient in medical settings often necessitates multiple inference steps to correlate information across various documents, such as medical history and test results, and infer causal relationships. Realizing a technology that can accurately answer given multi-hop questions holds the promise of expanding the scope with which human decision-making can be more appropriately supported.

SlideVQA is a question-answering task that returns answers when given a slide deck composed of multiple slide images and a corresponding question [12]. SlideVQA requires complex reasoning abilities such as multi-hop reasoning and numerical reasoning in addition to single-hop reasoning. It is said to improve AI's reading comprehension ability because it requires reasoning on not only single images or documents but also multiple images or documents and understanding the content of visual information expressions such as infographics.

Conventional models that have tackled SlideVQA have shown relatively high performance in single-hop question answering. However, in multi-hop question answering, a more complex task, the performance is more than 10 points lower in F1 score compared to single-hop question answering. Conventional studies have also shown that accurate evidence selection improves overall task performance.

Therefore, this paper focuses on improving the performance of multi-hop question-answering in the SlideVQA task. We also aim to improve the performance of evidence selection, which selects appropriately relevant slides from the slide deck for the question, and the overall performance of the question-answering task.

To this end, we propose Multimodal Beam Retrieval (MMBR), an extension of Beam Retrieval [15], a retriever with high performance in multi-hop question answering on text documents, to accommodate multimodal information. Beam Retrieval specifically focuses on evidence selection and demonstrates superior performance on multiple datasets for multi-hop question answering. However, this method performs evidence selection based solely on text information and thus has not been able to consider multimodal information such as visual information. In this paper, we aim to improve the selection of correct evidence for multi-hop questions in SlideVQA by extending Beam Retrieval to process multimodal information, such as visual information, thereby enhancing the overall performance of the task.

The experiments will verify to what extent the proposed method improves the performance of evidence selection and answer generation. Using the SlideVQA dataset, we compared the performance of the baseline method and that of the proposed method. As evaluation metrics, we use Exact-Match (EM) and F1 score, following conventional methods.

The contributions of this paper are as follows:

- We propose a multimodal question-answering method that extends the conventional Beam Retrieval to handle text and visual information.

- In the multi-hop question-answering task of SlideVQA, we verified to what extent the proposed method can improve the performance of evidence selection compared to the baseline method.
- We verified whether using the evidence selection results of the proposed method contributes to improving the performance of question answering.

2 Related Work

2.1 Multi-hop Question Answering on Text Information

In previous studies, the process of multi-hop question answering for text information is often divided into two steps: a Retriever and a Reader [6]. The Retriever extracts relevant contexts from a given set of information. The Reader reads the contexts from the Retriever and identifies the final answer. In answering multi-hop questions, the importance of the Retriever is generally considered high. This is because if a Retriever fails to obtain appropriate context, it is almost impossible for the subsequent Reader to arrive at the correct answer.

Existing Retrievers can be divided into Preliminary Retrieval, which broadly searches for relevant contexts in a large corpus using a fast and high-recall method [7], and Final Retrieval, which further removes noisy contexts from the set of contexts obtained in Preliminary Retrieval or from a pre-determined set of contexts related to the question, and selects contexts relevant to the question.

Final Retrieval is considered to significantly influence the performance of the Retriever as it selects only the information necessary to answer the question. Final Retrieval is performed by concatenating all contexts without filtering and passing them directly to the reading step, known as context concatenation [13], or by re-ranking the input contexts based on specific criteria in unsupervised re-ranking, and by scoring and ranking the input contexts in supervised re-ranking.

Among these, supervised re-ranking involves concatenating the context with the given question, generating scores using BERT [3], and retaining a predetermined number of paragraphs with the highest scores [4], or applying the beam search method to retain the beam width, known as Beam Retrieval [15]. Beam Retrieval has achieved high performance on datasets for multi-hop question answering for textual documents.

In this paper, we extend Beam Retrieval, which has achieved high performance as a Final Retrieval for textual documents, to explore multimodal information.

2.2 Multi-hop Question Answering on Multimodal Information

In real-world applications, information is represented in various formats, including natural language, images, and charts. Therefore, to perform appropriate reasoning across different representation formats, multi-hop question answering for multimodal information has gained attention. Representative datasets include the MultimodalQA [10], which uses text, tables, and images as inputs, and WebQA [1], which uses images and text from the Web. In these multimodal QA tasks, many methods employ the Retrieve-and-Reader framework. In the Retriever, datasets for multimodal multi-hop question answering, such as MultimodalQA and WebQA, have clearly separated modalities like images and text. Therefore, different modalities are individually encoded, and information is retrieved based on similarity calculations [2] or classification [1]. In contrast, the SlideVQA task addressed in this paper requires the model to read text and tables from slide images and obtain answers from multiple slide images. Therefore, rather than processing each modality separately as in conventional methods that address multimodal multi-hop question answering, this paper understands and encodes each piece of information in each slide image in parallel and outputs answers for multiple slide images.

2.3 SlideVQA

SlideVQA [12] is a question-answering task for slide decks. It includes questions that require answering by integrating text information, visual information such as tables and graphs, and their integrated information within document images. Previous models that have tackled the SlideVQA task include M3D [12] and InstructDoc [11]. InstructDoc is a model that can adapt to unknown visual-document understanding tasks based on natural language instructions. It processes multimodal information and performs multi-task learning uniformly for all tasks as instruction-based sequence transformation. M3D considers multimodal information within slides, simultaneously understands multiple document images, and performs multi-task learning of answer rationale selection and question answering within a sequence transformation framework. However, these methods have faced challenges in improving the performance of evidence selection and enhancing performance in multi-hop reasoning.

In this study, we extend Beam Retrieval, which has achieved high performance in the Retriever for multi-hop question answering over text documents. In the Retriever, we select an appropriate beam size and use the rationale for the required number of hops for question answering. This broadens the search range and is expected to improve the performance of evidence selection. Therefore, we expect the proposed method to improve the overall performance of the question-answering task.

3 Preliminaries

In this section, as a preparation for explaining the proposed method in this paper, we describe Beam Retrieval, which has achieved high performance in the Retriever of multi-hop question answering for text information.

3.1 Beam Search

Beam search is a type of breadth-first search that efficiently finds the optimal solution by fixing the candidates to be considered during the search, which is called the beam width. As an advantage, compared to an exhaustive search, which searches for all possible solutions, it is possible to reduce computational costs and proceed with the search while keeping only a certain number of potential candidates.

3.2 Beam Retrieval

Beam Retrieval [15] is a method that performs evidence selection using beam search to retain multiple relevant contexts. This method has achieved state-of-the-art performance on various datasets for multi-hop question-answering tasks composed of text information. It is said to demonstrate performance even for questions with two or more hops, and its flexibility is improved compared to conventional methods.

The processing procedure is as follows: First, an encoder converts the "question" and the "paragraph of interest" into internal representations. Then, paragraph candidates are scored using two classification heads, one for the first hop and the other for subsequent hops. The classification heads score multiple candidates at each step and select the paragraph with the highest score. By introducing beam search, multiple contexts are maintained, reducing inaccurate paragraph selection.

4 Proposed Method

4.1 Problem Formulation

This paper addresses the SlideVQA task, which includes single-hop and multi-hop questions. In the SlideVQA task, the context is defined as a single slide image. One context is the overall information of a single slide image, which includes all the elements within that slide, such as text, images, and layout.

Based on the above, we define the SlideVQA task as follows:

Let $\mathbb{C}$ be the set of all contexts, Q be the set of all questions, and $\mathcal{A}$ be the set of all answers.

Given a question $q \in Q$ and a related context set (slide deck) $C \subseteq \mathbb{C}$, $C=\{ p_1, p_2, p_3, ..., p_n \}$ (where p_i represents a single context), this task aims to approximate the function $f : Q \times C^n \to \mathcal{A} \cup \{\Phi\}$.

$$f(q, C) = \begin{cases} a \in \mathcal{A} & \exists P_q = \{p_1, \ldots, p_k\} \subseteq C, \\ & \quad k \geq 1, \\ & \quad P_q \models (a \text{ answers } q), \\ \Phi & \text{otherwise.} \end{cases} \tag{1}$$

Here $\models$ denates implication and Φ represents the output when question q cannot be answered using the context set (slide deck) C. When a question q and a context set (slide deck) C are given, the function f returns an answer a. The answer a is the output for q using the contexts (support contexts) P_q, which is determined to have an answer basis for question q from the context set C.

In SlideVQA, since single-hop and multi-hop questions are included, the number of support contexts k is greater than or equal to 1. This definition reflects the common approach of dividing the task into two steps: a Retriever and a Reader. The function f can be decomposed into two components: the Retriever, defined as the function $g : Q \times \mathcal{C}^n \rightarrow \mathcal{C}^k$, and the Reader, defined as the function $h : Q \times \mathcal{C}^k \rightarrow \mathcal{A} \cup \{\Phi\}$. In this paper, we aim to approximate the function g of the Retriever, thereby achieving a more accurate approximation of the function f.

4.2 Processing Procedure

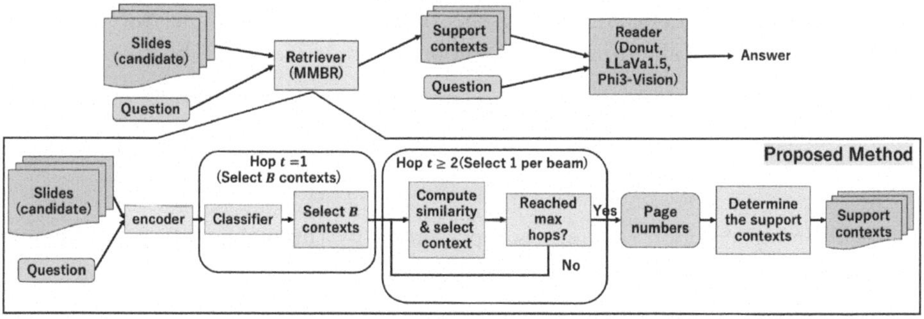

Fig. 1. Overall Process Overview and Processing Procedure of the Proposed Method

We propose **Multimodal Beam Retrieval** (MMBR), a Retriever that extends Beam Retrieval, which originally supports only text information, to support multimodal information. MMBR enables evidence selection from visual and layout information, an important information source for slides, by considering information other than text.

In MMBR, we introduce contrastive learning as a selection method for the second and subsequent hops. The conventional method, Beam Retrieval, which only handles text information, uses paragraph-level text as context and performs classification while cumulatively concatenating the contexts selected at each hop. However, this method has an issue of excessive information accumulation as the number of hops increases. Therefore, cumulatively concatenating them as in the conventional method can lead to redundancy in the overall information.

To address this, we introduce contrastive learning to select similar contexts based on the context specified in the previous hop. As positive pairs for contrastive learning, we define arbitrary pairs from the set of contexts that constitute a ground truth for a multi-hop question. Specifically, for each question, we perform learning to maximize the similarity between contexts that serve as the ground truth answer, treating these as semantically highly related positive pairs and bringing them closer in the embedding space. On the other hand, negative pairs are defined as pairs consisting of a context that belongs to the ground truth set and a context that does not, both existing within the same context set, and the learning objective is to minimize their similarity.

During training, we obtain the internal representations of each context and calculate the contrastive learning loss based on cosine similarity. We optimize the model to increase the similarity for positive pairs and decrease the similarity for negative pairs. This facilitates the efficient selection of appropriate information based on the chosen contexts, while mitigating information redundancy.

Figure 1 shows the overall process overview and the processing procedure of the proposed method.

A slide (context) $p_i \in C$ contained within a slide deck (context set) $C = \{\ p_1, p_2, p_3, ..., p_n\ \}$ is represented as a pair of a sequence of semantic regions r_{p_i} and the overall image of the slide v_{p_i}. Here, a semantic region represents a semantic content element composing the slide, such as "title" or "table". If the semantic regions contained in p_i are $\text{region}_{i,j}$ $(j = 1, 2, ..., m)$, then:

$$p_i = (r_{p_i}, v_{p_i}), \tag{2}$$

$$r_{p_i} = (\text{region}_{i,1}, ..., \text{region}_{i,j}, ...\text{region}_{i,m}). \tag{3}$$

Each semantic region $\text{region}_{i,j}$ is represented by three elements: text, layout, and segment.

$$\text{region}_{i,j} = (\text{text}_{\text{region}_{i,j}}, \text{lay}_{\text{region}_{i,j}}, \text{seg}_{\text{region}_{i,j}}), \tag{4}$$

where the text $\text{text}_{\text{region}_{i,j}}$ refers to the string extracted from the semantic region via OCR, and the layout $\text{lay}_{\text{region}_{i,j}}$ represents the bounding box coordinates indicating the position of the semantic region within the slide. The segment $\text{seg}_{\text{region}_{i,j}}$ is a label indicating the name of that region. The input sequence x_i $(i = 1, ...n)$ for the Retriever is represented as:

$$x_i = (q; p_i), \tag{5}$$

where ';' denotes concatenation.

The embedding z_q for a question q is given by:

$$z_q = z^q_{\text{text}} + z_{\text{lay}}([0, 0, 0, 0]) + z^q_{\text{seg}} \in \mathbb{R}^{l_q \times d}, \tag{6}$$

where z^q_{text} is the text embedding of the question, $z_{\text{lay}}([0, 0, 0, 0])$ is a fixed layout embedding, and z^q_{seg} is the segment embedding of the question. The layout embedding $z_{\text{lay}}([0, 0, 0, 0])$ is a fixed value and does not influence the positional information of the question. Furthermore, l_q represents the sequence length of the question.

The embedding z_{p_i} for p_i is obtained through the following procedure. First, for each region $\text{region}_{i,j}$, an embedding $z_{r_{i,j}}$ is acquired from the three features belonging to that region:

$$z_{r_{i,j}} = \text{z}_{\text{text}_{i,j}} + \text{z}_{\text{lay}_{i,j}} + \text{z}_{\text{seg}_{i,j}}, \tag{7}$$

where $z_{\text{text}_{i,j}}$ is the word embedding of the text information, $z_{\text{lay}_{i,j}}$ is the layout embedding of the layout information, and $z_{\text{seg}_{i,j}}$ is the embedding of the segment information. Additionally, for the image information v_{p_i}, a visual feature embedding z_{vis_i} is obtained. The embedding z_{p_i} of p_i is obtained by integrating these as follows:

$$z_{p_i} = LN(\Sigma_j z_{r_{i,j}} + z_{vis_i}) \in \mathbb{R}^{L \times d}, \tag{8}$$

where $LN()$ denotes layer normalization, L is the sequence length of the context, and d is the hidden layer dimension.

The embedding of the input sequence x_i can be expressed as:

$$z_{x_i} = (z_q; z_{p_i}) \in \mathbb{R}^{(l_q+L)\times d}. \tag{9}$$

We use LayoutLMv3 [5] as the multimodal encoder. The embedding of the input sequence x_i is passed through the Transformer layers of LayoutLMv3 to derive the internal representation H. We obtain the embedding of the CLS token, $h_{CLS}^{(i)}$, which encapsulates the compressed information of the entire slide image serving as the context. By concatenating $h_{CLS}^{(i)}$ obtained for n contexts, we get:

$$H_{CLS} = (h_{CLS}^{(1)}, h_{CLS}^{(2)}, \ldots, h_{CLS}^{(n)}) \in \mathbb{R}^{n\times d}. \tag{10}$$

From this point, we describe the multi-hop inference procedure. Let the beam size be B. In the first hop, H_{CLS}, which concatenates the internal representations of the n contexts and the question, is scored through a classification head (Classifier). The classification head projects the input internal representations of the n contexts into a 2-dimensional space, representing 'relevant' and 'irrelevant'. The score of the 'relevant' side is then taken as the score for that context. The top B contexts $\{p_1, p_2, ..., p_B\}$ with the highest scores are selected as the contexts for the first hop. For subsequent hops t ($t \geq 2$), the next candidate contexts are selected using the B partial hypotheses chosen so far. In beam b, the context P_{t-1}^b selected up to hop $t-1$ is represented using the context (partial hypothesis) $\hat{p}_i^b$ selected at hop i in beam b as follows:

$$P_{t-1}^b = (\hat{p}_1^b, \hat{p}_2^b, \ldots, \hat{p}_{t-1}^b), \quad b = 1, \ldots, B. \tag{11}$$

Furthermore, the set of unselected contexts at hop $t-1$ is:

$$P_{\text{unselected}}^{(t-1),b} = \{\hat{p}_i^b\} \quad (i = 1 \ldots t-1). \tag{12}$$

Here, we compute the similarity between the embedding $h_{CLS}^{(p_k)}$ of an unselected context $p_k \in P_{\text{unselected}}^{(t-1),b}$ and the embedding $h_{CLS}^{(t-1),b}$ of the context $\hat{p}_{t-1}^b$ selected at the previous hop $t-1$, and select the most similar context. Similarity here refers to the closeness of the semantic feature vectors of each context. The selected context is then added to the partial hypothesis. The contexts selected up to the t-th hop are represented as follows:

$$P_t^b = (\hat{p}_1^b, \hat{p}_2^b, \ldots, \hat{p}_t^b), \quad b = 1, \ldots, B. \tag{13}$$

This process is repeated for a predetermined number of hops. Finally, the page numbers of the one or more contexts with the highest score at the last hop, deemed relevant to the question q, are output. The contexts corresponding to the outputted page numbers are defined as the support context P_q.

4.3 Reader

In Reader, the answer a is output based on the support context P_q selected by evidence selection and the question q. This paper adopts three models for the Reader and compares their performance. Models capable of question answering on document images in a zero-shot manner are mainly used.

1. **Donut** naver-clova-ix/donut-base-finetuned-docvqa[1]
2. **LLaVa1.5** llava-hf/llava-1.5-7b-hf[2]
3. **Phi3-Vision** microsoft/Phi-3-vision-128k-instruct[3]

Donut is a model for document images, which extracts text from images and performs question answering while considering the structure and layout within the document image. LLaVa1.5 can understand the interaction between text and images and is a model that has achieved high performance in TextVQA [9], which requires inference using text information in images. Phi3-Vision is a model that integrates vision and language and is compatible with a wide range of visual information such as general real images, chart images, structured data such as tables, and document images.

5 Experimental Setup

5.1 Experimental Objectives

In this experiment, we aim to clarify whether the proposed MMBR, which considers multimodal information and enables search, contributes to the performance improvement of evidence selection, which is the Retriever in the SlideVQA task. Furthermore, we aim to clarify whether using the evidence selected by MMBR contributes to the overall performance improvement of the question-answering task. Specifically, we aim to clarify the following three research questions:

RQ.1 Does the proposed method contribute to improving the performance of the Retriever?

RQ.2 What is the optimal beam size for the Retriever?

RQ.3 Does the proposed method improve the performance of question answering?

[1] https://huggingface.co/naver-clova-ix/donut-base-finetuned-docvqa.
[2] https://huggingface.co/llava-hf/llava-1.5-7b-hf.
[3] https://huggingface.co/microsoft/Phi-3-vision-128k-instruct.

5.2 Experimental Settings

We describe the semantic region extraction method applied to the proposed method, MMBR. We extract text, layouts, and segments, which are elements of the semantic region, from the slides. First, we acquire the semantic region as a layout from the slide, cut out the image within the obtained bounding box, and extract the text using OCR. As OCR, we used surya[4], which supports various document images such as PDFs, Word images, and slide images. For layouts and segments, we used the data included in SlideVQA so that it does not depend on the acquisition method.

We used LayoutLMv3 [5] as the encoder for MMBR. The learning was set to 10 epochs, the batch size to 1, and the learning rate to 1e−5.

We evaluate the respective results obtained from evidence selection and question answering. Following HotpotQA [14] and SlideVQA [12], which are working on multi-hop question answering, we evaluate using the F1 score and EM (Exact Match). At that time, we evaluate the processing results of each of the Retriever (evidence selection) and the Reader (question answering) using three methods: the entire test data, single-hop questions only, and multi-hop questions only.

5.3 Dataset

We use SlideVQA [12] as the dataset. SlideVQA contains 14,484 QA pairs for 2,619 slide decks and has the largest number of semantic domains and the largest average number of OCR words that the model should consider among existing datasets for document image question-answering tasks. It is also characterized by including complex questions involving multi-hop reasoning and numerical reasoning. Table 1 shows the total number of questions in the dataset.

Table 1. Total number of questions in SlideVQA

	train	dev	test
Single-hop questions	9,381	1,437	1,648
Multi-hop questions	1,236	215	567
Total	10,617	1,652	2,215

The types of questions include single-hop questions, which can be inferred by referring only to information within a single slide, and multi-hop questions, which require multi-stage inference using multiple pieces of information in two or more slides. Multi-hop questions include two types: 2-hop and 3-hop.

[4] https://github.com/VikParuchuri/surya.

5.4 Experimental Method

RQ.1 To clarify whether the proposed method contributes to improving the performance of the Retriever, we compare the proposed method with M3D and H-LayoutLMv2 [12], which tackled the evidence selection of the SlideVQA task, as comparative methods.

RQ.2 To clarify the optimal beam size, we change the beam size and investigate the adequate beam size for the Retriever. The range of change was from 1 to 3.

RQ.3 To clarify whether the proposed method improves the performance of question answering, we compare the proposed method with M3D and Instruct-Doc, which tackled the SlideVQA task, including the Reader. As the Reader, which is the subsequent processing of the proposed method, we compare the proposed method in combination with three types of question-answering models: Donut, LLaVA1.5, and Phi3-Vision, which are described in Sect. 4.3. At that time, to clarify the performance of each model, we also compared the combinations in the case of using the correct answer evidence (GT) and the case of using the answer evidence obtained by the proposed method (MMBR).

6 Experimental Results

6.1 Comparison with Conventional Methods (Retriever)

Table 2 compares the proposed method and the conventional method in the Retriever (evidence selection). The results for MMBR, the proposed method, are for the case where the best-performing beam size of 2 was applied. In terms of the F1 score, the result was about 3 points lower than H-LayoutLMv2. On the other hand, it showed the highest value in the EM score.

In addition, compared to the conventional methods, the proposed method reduced the difference between the F1 and EM scores. This is likely due to the improvement in performance for multi-hop questions that can consider partial matches and the increase in results with an F1 score of 1.0 and an EM score of 1.0. In other words, it is suggested that the proposed method is likely to have improved the partially matched results to perfect matches.

Table 2. Comparison with Conventional Methods (Retriever)

Method	DEV		TEST	
	F1	EM	F1	EM
H-LayoutLMv2 [12]	**89.5**	81.1	**85.6**	69.8
M3D [12]	87.7	83.1	83.8	75.0
MMBR	86.7	**84.9**	82.4	**77.5**
Human			98.0	97.7

6.2 Experimental Results for Each Beam Size (Retriever)

Table 3 shows the results when varying the beam size of MMBR. For all question types, the highest values were observed at a beam size of 2.

Furthermore, to verify the usefulness of changing the beam size, Fig. 2 show the distribution of F1 scores for each beam size and question type. For all question types, a beam size of 2 resulted in the highest number of scores of 1.0. Additionally, there is no significant difference in the number of scores of 1.0 between beam sizes 2 and 3 for all question types. On the other hand, a beam size of 1 shows a significant difference compared to the other two types. This suggests that setting the beam size to 2 or 3 is effective in the Retriever of SlideVQA.

Table 3. Results for Each Beam Size of MMBR (S: Single-hop Questions, M: Multi-hop Questions)

Beam Size	F1			EM		
	S+M	S	M	S+M	S	M
1	81.1	82.7	76.4	75.9	82.7	56.0
2	**82.4**	**83.9**	**78.0**	**77.5**	**83.9**	**58.7**
3	82.1	83.7	77.4	77.2	83.7	58.0

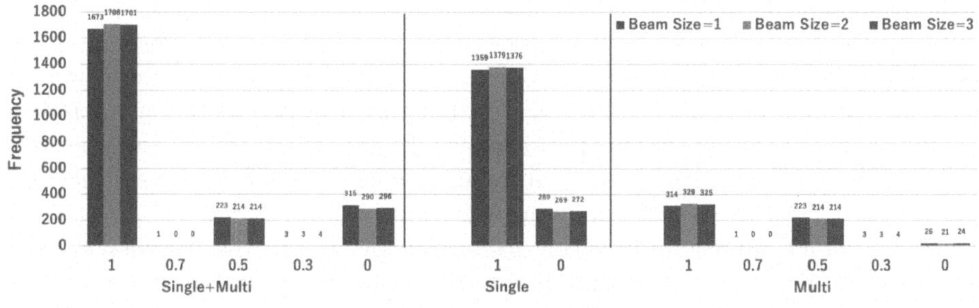

Fig. 2. Distribution of F1 Scores (S: Single-hop Questions, M: Multi-hop Questions)

6.3 Ablation Evaluation (Retriever)

Table 4 shows the results of the ablation evaluation. Performance degradation is observed when each piece of element is excluded. Particularly, significant performance degradation is observed when layout information and text information are excluded. This indicates that the coordinate information and text of each element of the slide are particularly important in evidence selection.

In the Retriever, regardless of the beam size, there is a tendency to make errors when answering questions about the number of elements, shapes, arrows, and company logos that make up the slides, as well as the overall composition of the slides. This indicates that visual information does not contribute to performance in the Retriever and that correct selections are not being made.

Table 4. Ablation Evaluation (test data, beam size 2)

Model	F1			EM		
	S+M	S	M	S+M	S	M
MMBR	**82.4**	**83.9**	**78.0**	**77.5**	**83.9**	**58.7**
w/o visual	81.8	83.6	76.5	76.5	83.6	55.6
w/o contrastive learning	81.1	82.8	76.1	75.8	82.8	55.1
w/o segment	80.3	81.9	75.6	74.9	81.9	54.2
w/o layout	37.8	36.3	42.1	31.0	36.3	15.6
w/o text	11.8	10.2	16.8	8.1	10.2	2.1

6.4 Question Answering Results (Reader)

Table 5 shows the results of question answering, which is the Reader. In the table, MMBR represents the case with beam size 2, which showed the best performance in the proposed method.

Using the evidence selection results of the proposed method, answering the question with Phi3-Vision achieved approximately 20 points higher performance than conventional methods. This indicates that the proposed method contributes to improving question-answering performance. In particular, unlike the other two models, Phi3-Vision can read and comprehend visual elements such as charts and tables, which may have led to more accurate reasoning.

In any model, question answering using the correct answer evidence showed higher performance than question answering using the proposed method's evidence selection. Therefore, it is understood that improving the Retriever's performance (evidence selection) remains crucial, as with previous approaches addressing SlideVQA.

Furthermore, when we performed question answering using the evidence selection results of MMBR, the performance improved compared to the results of question answering using the entire context without evidence selection. This also shows the importance of the Retriever (evidence selection) in SlideVQA. It also shows the importance of using specialized models for each step rather than a single model for multi-task learning of the Retriever and Reader and the importance of a two-step approach to the task.

Table 5. Question Answering Results (Reader) (S: Single-hop questions, M: Multi-hop questions)

Method	F1			EM		
	S+M	S	M	S+M	S	M
M3D [12]	41.7			33.5		
InstructDoc [11]	40.2			31.9		
Donut	2.9	3.6	0.9	1.7	2.2	0.2
Donut+MMBR	15.2	18.8	4.4	10.7	13.3	3.0
Donut+GT	16.9	21.0	4.9	11.6	14.4	3.5
LLaVA1.5	18.3	17.5	20.8	14.6	13.7	17.3
LLaVA1.5+MMBR	26.9	27.8	24.4	20.6	20.7	20.4
LLaVA1.5+GT	29.1	30.8	24.0	22.0	22.9	19.4
Phi3-Vision	32.8	33.9	29.6	25.0	25.5	23.5
Phi3-Vison+MMBR	**60.5**	**66.0**	**44.2**	**51.4**	**55.8**	**38.3**
Phi3-Vision+GT	68.3	73.6	52.9	57.9	62.4	44.8
Human	89.8			93.0		

Note: In the table, **MMBR** represents the results with MMBR (beam size 2), which showed the best performance in the proposed method, and **GT** represents the results using the correct answer grounds.

7 Conclusion

This paper addresses the task of answering visual multi-hop questions for presentation slides. We propose MMBR, an extension of Beam Retrieval to handle multimodal information, focusing on improving the Retriever's performance (evidence selection), which has been a challenge in previous SlideVQA methods.

Experiments have demonstrated that the proposed method improves the Retriever's performance. Furthermore, we confirmed the effectiveness of increasing the beam size in SlideVQA's Retriever and revealed that the proposed method improves the question-answering task.

Future directions include applying MMBR to evidence selection at the semantic region level within slides and validating the effectiveness of MMBR on other multimodal multi-hop question-answering datasets.

Acknowledgements. A part of this work was supported by JSPS KAKENHI Grant Number 23K11342.

References

1. Chang, Y., et al.: WebQA: multihop and multimodal QA. In: Proceedings of the 2022 IEEE/CVF Conference on Computer Vision and Pattern recognition, pp. 16495–16504 (2022)
2. Chen, W., Hu, H., Chen, X., Verga, P., Cohen, W.: MuRAG: multimodal retrieval-augmented generator for open question answering over images and text. In: Proceedings of the 2022 Conference on Empirical Methods in Natural Language Processing, pp. 5558–5570 (2022). https://doi.org/10.18653/v1/2022.emnlp-main.375
3. Devlin, J., Chang, M.W., Lee, K., Toutanova, K.: BERT: pre-training of deep bidirectional transformers for language understanding. In: Proceedings of the 2019 Conference of the North American Chapter of the Association for Computational Linguistics: Human Language Technologies, pp. 4171–4186 (2019). https://doi.org/10.18653/v1/N19-1423
4. Huang, Y., Yang, M.: Breadth first reasoning graph for multi-hop question answering. In: Proceedings of the 2021 Conference of the North American Chapter of the Association for Computational Linguistics: Human Language Technologies, pp. 5810–5821 (2021)
5. Huang, Y., Lv, T., Cui, L., Lu, Y., Wei, F.: LayoutLMv3: pre-training for document AI with unified text and image masking. In: Proceedings of the 30th ACM International Conference on Multimedia, pp. 4083–4091 (2022)
6. Mavi, V., Jangra, A., Jatowt, A., et al.: Multi-hop question answering. Found. Trends® Inf. Retrieval **17**(5), 457–586 (2024)
7. Qi, P., Lin, X., Mehr, L., Wang, Z., Manning, C.D.: Answering complex open-domain questions through iterative query generation. In: Proceedings of the 2019 Conference on Empirical Methods in Natural Language Processing and the 9th International Joint Conference on Natural Language Processing (EMNLP-IJCNLP), pp. 2590–2602 (2019). https://doi.org/10.18653/v1/D19-1261
8. Rajpurkar, P., Jia, R., Liang, P.: Know what you don't know: unanswerable questions for SQuAD. In: Proceedings of the 2018 Conference of the Association for Computational Linguistics (Volume 2: Short Papers), pp. 784–789 (2018). https://doi.org/10.18653/v1/P18-2124
9. Singh, A., et al.: Towards VQA models that can read. In: 2019 IEEE/CVF Conference on Computer Vision and Pattern Recognition, pp. 8309–8318 (2019)
10. Talmor, A., et al.: MultimodalQA: complex question answering over text, tables and images. In: International Conference on Learning Representations (2021)
11. Tanaka, R., Iki, T., Nishida, K., Saito, K., Suzuki, J.: InstructDoc: a dataset for zero-shot generalization of visual document understanding with instructions. In: Proceedings of the AAAI Conference on Artificial Intelligence, vol. 38, pp. 19071–19079 (2024)
12. Tanaka, R., et al.: SlideVQA: a dataset for document visual question answering on multiple images. In: Proceedings of the AAAI Conference on Artificial Intelligence, vol. 37, pp. 13636–13645 (2023)
13. Yadav, V., Bethard, S., Surdeanu, M.: Unsupervised alignment-based iterative evidence retrieval for multi-hop question answering (2020)
14. Yang, Z., et al.: HotpotQA: a dataset for diverse, explainable multi-hop question answering. In: Proceedings of the 2018 Conference on Empirical Methods in Natural Language Processing, pp. 2369–2380 (2018). https://doi.org/10.18653/v1/D18-1259

15. Zhang, J., Zhang, H., Zhang, D., Yong, L., Huang, S.: End-to-end beam retrieval for multi-hop question answering. In: Proceedings of the 2024 Conference of the North American Chapter of the Association for Computational Linguistics: Human Language Technologies, pp. 1718–1731 (2024). https://doi.org/10.18653/v1/2024.naacl-long.96
16. Zhang, Z., Yang, J., Zhao, H.: Retrospective reader for machine reading comprehension. In: Proceedings of the AAAI Conference on Artificial Intelligence, vol. 35, no. 16, pp. 14506–14514 (2021). https://doi.org/10.1609/aaai.v35i16.17705

Author Index

R. Ichise (Ed.): NLDB 2025, LNCS 15836, pp. 501–503, 2026.
https://doi.org/10.1007/978-3-031-97141-9

The manufacturer's authorised representative in the EU is Springer Nature Customer Service Centre GmbH, Europaplatz 3, 69115 Heidelberg, Germany. If you have any concerns regarding our products, please contact ProductSafety@springernature.com

Printed and bound by CPI Group (UK) Ltd, Croydon, CR0 4YY
30/09/2026
02225585-0018